The Rise and Fall of Communism in Russia

Robert V. Daniels

Yale University Press   NEW HAVEN & LONDON

Published with assistance from the foundation established in memory of Philip Hamilton McMillan of the Class of 1894, Yale College.

Set in Ehrhardt Roman by IBT Global.

Printed in the United States of America by IBT Global.

Library of Congress Cataloging-in-Publication Data
Daniels, Robert Vincent.
 The rise and fall of Communism in Russia / Robert V. Daniels.
  p. cm.
Includes bibliographical references and index.

 ISBN: 978-0-300-10649-7 (cloth : alk. paper)
 1. Communism—Soviet Union—History. I. Title.

HX311.5D38 2007
947.084—dc22   2006022011

A catalogue record for this book is available from the British Library.

The paper in this book meets the guidelines for permanence and durability of the Committee on Production Guidelines for Book Longevity of the Council on Library Resources.

10 9 8 7 6 5 4 3 2 1

THE RISE AND FALL OF COMMUNISM IN RUSSIA

Contents

PART III. The Left Opposition between Lenin and Stalin

PART IV. Stalinism

PART V. Reform versus Bureaucracy, from Khrushchev to Brezhnev

Preface

In the late 1940s, when I began studying the history of Communism in Russia, it was already a thirty-year phenomenon of extraordinary complexity and moral ambiguity. By then, its most tumultuous, tragic, and ironic years lay in the past. The task I set myself was twofold: to explain how the realities of governing had shaped the early revolutionary regime and to analyze the ongoing character of the Soviet system in my own time. My dual subject proved to be one of deep paradox and contradiction—the formation and ultimate exhaustion of a postrevolutionary regime that steadfastly refused to admit its deviation from its own revolutionary ideals. Very early in my studies I observed that the development of Soviet society was not toward socialism but to quite another social order, rationalized with the obligatory socialist terminology. Attempts at reform from Nikita Khrushchev to Mikhail Gorbachev only underscored the difficulty, perhaps the futility, of correcting this inherently false basis of the system.

My quest to understand the evolution of the Soviet phenomenon resulted in *The Conscience of the Revolution: Communist Opposition in Soviet Russia* (1960), expanding on my doctoral dissertation, and subsequent books, including *A Documentary History of Communism* (1960; 3rd ed. 1993), *The Nature of Communism* (1962), *Red October: The Bolshevik Revolution of 1917* (1967; repr. 1984), *Russia—The Roots of Confrontation* (1985), and finally *The End of the Communist Revolution* (1993). Along with these works, over the years, I have written a series of articles and conference papers amplifying or extending my inquiry. The present work is designed to make these studies more broadly available and to highlight their significance by combining them in book form according to their logical and chronological connections, not necessarily in the order of their composition. This is, in fact, the nearest thing to a general narrative of the Soviet saga that I have attempted.

After the introductory essay on the main themes of Soviet history, part I of this book addresses the ideological background of the Bolshevik Revolution and the Soviet experience. Part II analyzes the revolutionary process in Russia, including Leon Trotsky's latter-day assessment of it, and part III treats the struggle of the Left Opposition against Lenin and then Stalin. Part IV examines Stalinism, central to the Soviet experience, and parts V and VI investigate the sequence of efforts to reform the system that Stalin bequeathed to his heirs. Finally, part VII presents some post-Soviet perspectives on the Soviet experience as a whole.

The particular publications and papers on which the respective chapters of the book are based are identified in the endnotes. I have edited the original texts to eliminate overlap, improve readability, and highlight the logical flow from one item to the next. However, I have not felt a need to redo their substance or revise my judgments, except to correct tenses as necessary from the present to the past. If I have had second thoughts, they would temper the optimism about Russia that I expressed in the late 1980s and again in the late 1990s.

Hopefully this collection can be read as a whole, as an analytical history of the Soviet experience from the Revolution of 1917 to the collapse of 1991. The work does not claim comprehensiveness and touches but little on social life, the national minorities, or foreign relations. This is not to minimize the significance of those spheres of Soviet history; it simply reflects the focus of my own interest in Russian national politics and political thought, the realm that I happen to feel was most crucial in shaping the destiny of the Soviet peoples. I hope that my studies in this area, as I have attempted to rework them into a coherent whole, make a worthwhile contribution to understanding the multifarious Russian past that still weighs upon everyone who has emerged from it.

Countless friends and colleagues helped me with their thoughts and comments as I formulated the original studies underlying the present collection. My research and writing were facilitated at various times by the generosity of a number of institutions, including the Harvard Russian Research Center (now the Davis Center for Russian Studies), the Project on the History of the CPSU at Columbia University, the Rockefeller Foundation, the National Endowment for the Humanities, the John Simon Guggenheim Foundation, the Kennan Institute of the Woodrow Wilson Center for Scholars, and the International Research and Exchange Board (IREX), together with periodic sabbaticals afforded me by the University of Vermont. In the work of organizing and revising my articles I have had helpful comments from Professor David Macey, Professor Mark Von Hagen, and my son, Professor Thomas L. Daniels. My wife, Alice M. Daniels, has backed me up throughout my years of struggle to produce the elements of this work. I am indebted to Jonathan Brent, Kate Shepard, and Sarah Miller of the Yale University Press for their editorial guidance in producing the present volume, to Debra Smail of the University of Vermont for the arduous work of putting my revisions into readable form, and to Robin DuBlanc for meticulous copyediting of the end product.

In transliterating Russian names I have employed a modified Library of Congress system, using more familiar forms such as the -sky ending in personal names (for example, Trotsky, not Trotskii). Place names accord with the usage of the moment (for example, Petrograd from 1914 to 1924 but Leningrad from 1924 to 1992). Dates are Old Style (thirteen days behind the West) until the reform of 1/14 January 1918. In style, my preference is to capitalize *Communist, Communism, Left, Right,* and so on when they refer to actual people and movements and to lowercase them when they refer to theoretical concepts and abstract political positions (like the American usage of *Republican* and *republican* and the like). *Soviet* is capitalized when it refers to the country or the system, lowercased when it refers to the governmental councils.

Introduction

Revolution, Modernization, Socialism—Baselines of Modern Russian History

Since 1991, historians have been monumentally challenged to explain the collapse of the Soviet Union and Communist rule in Russia. But a deeper problem, less often addressed, is the real nature of the Soviet system that was finally swept away. Understanding the convulsions of the recent past in Russia is impossible without an answer to this question, which in turn demands reconsideration of a century of tumultuous history.

The astonishing events of 1991 implanted an almost universal stereotype about the fallen regime. It is considered, in Russia as well as abroad, to have been a seventy-four-year experiment that failed, or some variation on that theme. This judgment flows from a literal, simplistic reading of Communist ideology as the main determinant of the Soviet experience. It differs from official Stalinist and neo-Stalinist propaganda only in putting a negative sign on that record. The entire Soviet era is thus presumed to have had a simple historical unity as the direct, undeviating pursuit of a disastrous revolutionary "utopia."

Today's common but deeply unhistorical understanding of the Soviet experience revolves around three basic problems. First is the nature of the Russian Revolution as a long-term process and its significance as the framework for the overall development of Russian society. Second is the challenge of modernization that Russia faced all during its revolutionary experience along with the ambiguous relationship between Russia and the West in this respect. A related question is the character of postrevolutionary society in Russia and its connection to modern social trends around the globe. The problem of modernization and social change leads in turn to the third focus of misunderstanding, the relation between ideology and reality and the confusion that Communist doctrine has created about the nature of the Soviet system. Out of an investigation of these foundations of Soviet reality some conclusions can perhaps be derived about the alleged successes and failures of the revolution and about the assumptions that have shaped understanding of the post-Soviet regime.

Revolution, obviously, is the central fact in the history of Russia in the twentieth century as well as a cardinal theme of global history in this era. Russians do not need to be reminded that revolution is a tragic experience. It is tragic not only in the human suffering it entails but in the hopes for a better world that it feeds on and then betrays. But it would be misguided just to blame those hopes, and the ideologies that convey them, for the crimes that may have been committed in their name. This is the approach of ideological reductionism, a familiar error in the understanding of revolutions and their consequences and a nearly universal mistake in the post-Communist atmosphere. All the misery of revolution is attributed to the wrongheaded ideas of revolutionaries, whose thinking supposedly traces back to the Enlightenment and the hubris of rational intervention in the affairs of society. In reality, revolutions are far more complex and multidimensional, far more deeply embedded in the historical evolution of a given society than the simple explanations of dangerous ideas or nefarious plots imply. Ironically, as a revolution unfolds, little survives either of utopian idealism or of rational intervention.

The ordinary conception of revolution, which is also the most antirevolutionary, is easy to understand: A revolution is the work of fanatical plotters who seize power in order to impose a utopian program on an unwilling society and persist with increasing ferocity until that society finally rebels and throws them off. This picture, while superficially plausible, fails to reckon with the real nature, causes, and consequences of a revolution. A revolution is not just a deliberate seizure of power, although such actions do figure in its unfolding. As an objective process, it breaks out and proceeds by stages that are basically independent of the will of individual revolutionaries, even though the latter may entertain the illusion that they are completely in command.

Typically, a revolution begins as a movement for moderate reform, even if it is marked by violence: thus the constitutional monarchy in France in 1789–91 and the Provisional Government in Russia in 1917.[1] There may not be any deliberate action or even expectation that revolution is imminent; Vladimir Lenin's famous statement of January 1917, "We, the oldsters, may not live to see the decisive battles of this coming revolution," is an ironic illustration of the point.[2] Certainly, the first-stage revolutionaries have little sense of the intensity the process will later exhibit, when society reaches a point of insoluble crisis.

Moderate experiments yield step-by-step to extremist takeovers and new, fanatical leadership: the Jacobin dictatorship of 1792–94 in France and in Russia the October Revolution, followed by the rigors of "War Communism" during the civil war. Inevitably, the extremists overreach, and they are either cut down or forced to retreat: the fall of Maximilien Robespierre in the original "thermidorean" reaction of 1794, the New Economic Policy in Russia in 1921. All these regularities testify to the deep social forces and needs that are evoked by a revolution, far beyond the particular actions of revolutionaries.

The next stage of the process, after the thermidorean reaction, is not so well integrated into mainstream thinking about revolution, but upon reflection it is more than obvious. This is the displacement or overriding of the thermidorean regime by a postrevolutionary dictatorship, led by an aggressive egomaniac of whatever ideological persuasion who commands the effective instruments of power. Exemplified by Napoleon Bonaparte with his army and Joseph Stalin with his party apparatus, the postrevolutionary dictatorship synthesizes the worst of the revolution and the Old Regime. It may end overtly in a monarchical restoration, as in France, or there may be a more subtle shift to conservative and nationalist guideposts, as in Stalinism after the mid-1930s.[3] This outcome, not any sort of revolutionary utopianism, was the kind of system that prevailed in Russia from the later 1930s until the 1980s and then, finally, broke down.

Whether it takes the openly restorationist form or not, the postrevolutionary dictatorship may endure for years, even decades, but it eventually wears thin. In an attenuated replica of the original revolutionary situation, the dictatorship is overwhelmed by the social forces and demands that have continued to mature under its aegis and even with its active encouragement. At some point of crisis, usually war or a leadership succession, the regime crumbles and gives way to a movement back in the direction of the original reformist spirit of the revolution. This is the end stage of the process. It is not a new revolution but a cleansing of the original one, a moderate revolutionary revival, so to speak, exemplified by the Revolution of 1830 in France and in Russia initiated by Mikhail Gorbachev's perestroika—his "restructuring" in the later 1980s.[4]

This scheme of revolutionary stages might appear to reduce the role of leaders, parties, and ideologies to that of puppets strung to the cosmic forces of history, eliminating the question of individual motivation, choice, and responsibility. As the pioneer Russian Marxist Georgi Plekhanov said, when History needs the man, she will find him.[5] That is to say, each stage of the revolutionary process offers an opportunity to a certain kind of individual, and someone is usually available to seize the moment.

Until an impasse between changing society and rigid government has reached the breaking point, revolutionaries have little chance of taking power. Without the requisite preconditions, revolutionary activity may even have the opposite effect of inflaming political reaction. When the crisis actually comes, it is the moderates with some standing in the old order who have the first opportunity to rule. They fail precisely because they are moderate, as the explosion of accumulated social tensions invites the fanatics to take over. Thermidoreans and postrevolutionary dictators, in turn, can only respond to the role that the respective stage offers.

An individual revolutionary can nevertheless be held responsible for two things. One is the kind of moment that he decides to exploit: whether he will be a moderate or an extremist or a pragmatist or a monster—though if he does not choose the role appropriate to the current stage of the process, he will fail, and someone else who is psychically more in tune with the times will come forth to grasp the same opportunity. The second point of responsibility is how a successful leader steers or pushes the course of events within the limitations of the given stage of the revolution and the scope of his own power. Individual leaders cannot set the process in motion if the time is not ripe nor hold back the tide once it has begun to flow, but they can obviously influence the form, the timing, the details of the revolutionary stage that they dominate.

Indeterminacies that depend on the decisions of leadership appear at critical points in the revolutionary process. Sometimes a moderate revolution can be snuffed out or at least delayed by the forces of the Old Regime if they act firmly enough: Compare their weakness in France in 1789–91 and their resilience in Russia in 1905–7. Movement from the moderate to the extremist stage is harder to stop. In France in 1792, in Russia in October 1917, the moderates were incapable of handling the explosive social forces—peasants and workers—that the revolution had released. Determined leadership has much to do with the staying power of an extremist regime, more so than with the initial extremist takeover, which is more a question of who than whether. The Bolsheviks, for instance, were much less single-minded in accomplishing the October Revolution than they were in prosecuting the civil war. In October, despite Lenin's demand for an armed uprising, his lieutenants (including Trotsky) hoped for a peaceful takeover by the Congress of Soviets; it was only the feeble countermeasures attempted by the government of Alexander Kerensky that precipitated the Bolshevik action and presented Lenin with the forcible seizure of power that he had been agitating for.[6]

Putting a premium on organization and violence, especially in civil war, the extremist stage of a revolution offers an opportunity for competing forms of radical dictatorship, operating under opposite ideological banners of Left and Right, to struggle for hegemony.[7] If critical military engagements had turned out differently in August 1918 or in October 1919, Russia could have found itself under a White dictatorship rather than Red, as Spain did after the civil war of 1936–39. Obviously, Lenin's personal leadership was important, as was Trotsky's, in fighting off the counterrevolutionary contenders for power in 1918–20, but his most decisive act governed the form of the Russian Thermidor. By declaring an end to War Communism and introducing the New Economic Policy (NEP), Lenin avoided the fate of Robespierre. Thermidor in this case proceeded as a retreat rather than a coup, and the revolutionary organization managed to hold onto power with its ideology intact, even though the rulers had to accommodate the ebb tide in the revolution. This circumstance later became crucially important in shaping the nature of the Russian postrevolutionary dictatorship and the nearly universal misunderstanding of it.

Imagine the contrary possibility, more like the French scenario. Lenin is unyielding in the face of peasant uprisings and the Kronstadt Revolt. A coalition of dissident Communists with Mensheviks and Socialist Revolutionaries who come out of the underground overthrows him and institutes a NEP-like regime, but it is not tough enough to resolve competing social interests and achieve political and economic stability. All eyes turn to the military, in the person of Marshal Mikhail Tukhachevsky. When Tukhachevsky seizes power there is no difficulty in recognizing his postrevolutionary dictatorship as a new instance of Bonapartism. In the actual event, as Stalin appropriated the party organization and ideological labels that had survived from the revolution, his form of Bonapartist postrevolutionary dictatorship was almost everywhere misperceived.

The postrevolutionary dictatorship is the point in the revolutionary process where personality has its freest play. By its nature, this stage puts extraordinary decision-making power in the hands of one individual. Stalin's personal impact was incalculable, as he drove Russia through a "revolution from above" guided as much by his own whims and animosities (hatred of the peasants, hatred of intellectuals, hatred of his Communist rivals) as by any rational judgment of national interest, let alone social experimentation. Nevertheless, the basic framework for what Stalin could do was established by the stage the country had reached in the revolutionary process. Furthermore, the needs Stalin had to meet, if not his methods for addressing them, were posed quite objectively by another fundamental process, namely the global challenge of modernization.

If the dynamics of the stage-by-stage process determined the overall form of the revolutionary experience in Russia, the challenge of modernization determined

its basic content. Modernization underlies the outbreak of revolution, the clash-
ing social forces that drive it along, and the tasks that a revolutionary society
must address one way or another. Whatever its failures and betrayals, the revolution forced Russia to become modern.

What makes conditions ripe for the outbreak of revolution is a matter that
goes deeply into the nature of modern social evolution. Essentially, it is a matter
of a changing society with its new interests, needs, class forces colliding with a
tradition-bound political system, where everyone, even the officialdom, ceases
to believe in the Old Regime. The system becomes vulnerable to any momentary crisis—perhaps economic, as in France, perhaps military, as in Russia—to
trigger a political breakdown.

Modernization encompasses all the forms of social change that set up the
conditions for a revolution. It may be defined as the emergence of a pattern of
life based on science, literacy, industrialization, urbanization, and seculariza-
tion, common to the whole world, though with different timing and tempos.
Cyril Black characterized it as "one of the great revolutionary transformations of mankind, . . . the process by which historically evolved institutions
are adapted to the rapidly changing functions that reflect the unprecedented
increase in man's knowledge . . . that accompanied the scientific revolution."[8]
Modernization is often identified with Westernization, but that is only because
the modern way of life originated in the Atlantic West; it has posed as much of a
revolutionary challenge within the West as it has in other societies where it has
taken the form of an outside challenge and model.

The natural course of modernization in the West proceeded through a series of distinct stages. Each of these was expressed by a distinct ideology and
offered a distinct model to any other society attempting to replicate the results
of the process.

In its first stage, roughly from the sixteenth century to the eighteenth,
modernization was more often than not a top-down effort, an elite and governmental matter rather than a mass transformation. Pursuant to the philosophies
of mercantilism and enlightened despotism, governments assumed responsibility to promote their respective nations' trade, industry, and technology, often
through monopoly privileges extended to the ancestors of the modern corporation. This form of modernization—Modernization I—was what Peter the Great
encountered on his western travels and attempted to appropriate for Russia.

The second stage of modernization, proceeding in the liberal political atmosphere of England, Atlantic Europe, and North America in the eighteenth
and early nineteenth centuries, was distinguished by individualist capitalism
and the laissez-faire doctrine identified with John Locke and Adam Smith.

This form of modernization—Modernization II—was but little assimilated in Russia before it was overwhelmed, in the manner of Trotsky's "law of combined development," by the third stage.

This most recent era—Modernization III—has seen the concentration of social life in large bureaucratic organizations: corporate industry and financial conglomerates as well as governments, universities, political parties, labor organizations, and so on. Even before the Russian Revolution, Nikolai Bukharin recognized this trend as "organized capitalism," potentially "a new Leviathan."[9] Strangely enough, the effect of Modernization III on social classes and class relations was never anticipated either in liberal theory or in the Marxian frame of analysis: The individualist bourgeoisie was gradually being supplanted as the dominant class by the "meritocracy" or "New Class" of managers and specialists. In sum, the world was developing more according to Max Weber than to Karl Marx.[10]

Ideologies have rarely reflected the realities of Modernization III. In the English-speaking world, above all in the United States, the free-market ideology of Modernization II has persisted almost without challenge, despite its disconnect with the new socioeconomic order. Indeed, nonsocialist democratic theory has never come to terms with the realities of corporate economic power under Modernization III and the new social hierarchies necessitated by it. Other ideological alternatives, emerging between the late nineteenth century and the mid-twentieth in response to these developments, were equally wide of the mark, though they appealed successfully to social elements abused or marginalized by the trend to centralized power. Socialism, whether in its reformist Social Democratic variant or in its revolutionary Marxist-Leninist variant, based itself on the myth of the proletariat as the future ruling class. This was the utopia that Lenin so fervently enunciated in his *State and Revolution* but quickly abandoned after October (even before the book was published). Fascism, for its part, offered a backward-looking utopia to the petty-bourgeois and lumpen proletarians who had been bypassed by the new forms of modernization, even while it was fashioning its own version of the Leviathan State. St. Simonianism, the early-nineteenth-century doctrine of technocracy, would have been a more fitting ideology to express the new organizational trend, but its antidemocratic tone was too frank for any modern political movement.

None of these ideological ventures has survived to offer meaningful guidance to post-Soviet Russia. Fascism, of course, was crushed militarily; its epigones are a ludicrous fringe element. Socialism in its extreme, militarized Soviet form was discredited by its association with the crimes of Stalinism. The "third way" of reformist Social Democracy or liberalism in the American New Deal sense has been beclouded, illogically, by rejection of the Soviet model; in most places it has been diluted into little more than Capitalism with a Human Face. When the moment came, therefore, for Russia to look for Western guidance after the collapse of the Stalinist dictatorship, the only visible alternative was the free-market ideology, 150 years out of date but professed more confidently than ever by Western leaders and economists.

The global process of modernization naturally raises questions about the Russian Revolution and its ultimate social nature. Contrary to ideological assertions by its leadership about the mission of the proletariat and the goal of a workers' state, the Russian Revolution was a powerful accelerator of the trend toward bureaucratic society and rule by the managerial meritocracy. Weber recognized this at the very outset of the revolution. [11]

Beginning with controversies over the employment of "bourgeois specialists" under War Communism and extending all the way to Stalin's legitimation of the "toiling intelligentsia," Russian experience showed that the New Class was the key both to effective government and to national survival. Lenin himself made it clear soon after the revolution: "Without the guidance of specialists, the transition to socialism is impossible."[12] The hegemony of the New Class was both facilitated and necessitated by the destructive impact of the revolution on the nascent bourgeoisie in Russia; the vacuum in organizational functioning had to be filled. Modernization III thus constituted the social foundation of the postrevolutionary dictatorship in Russia.

At the same time, there were peculiar Russian distortions of the trend to managerial society. Driven by the revolutionary process and by the age-old determination on the part of the country's rulers to maintain a standard of national power beyond what their resources could readily sustain, Russia jumped ahead of the West to the most extreme form of bureaucratic organization, namely totalitarianism.[13] The leap was reinforced by Russia's background of premodern statism, long since recognized by Marx and Engels as "semi-Asiatic," a form of "oriental despotism."[14]

Totalitarianism is the characteristic form of postrevolutionary dictatorship under modern conditions, though its manifestations have differed in degree in different instances. Whatever reservations may be raised as to how "total" Russian totalitarianism was, in its time it represented more nearly total political control over society than any other case of the phenomenon, Nazi, Fascist, or whatever.[15] The reasons were simple—despotic traditions, the prerevolutionary immaturity of Russian society, and the impact of the revolution in sweeping away weak preexisting economic structures. Here was the social essence of Stalinism: subjecting the precapitalist sectors of agriculture, trade, and ser-vices—the "petty-bourgeois" realm of the economy that encompassed the vast majority of the population—to artificial and often violent bureaucratization. Throughout the Stalinist and neo-Stalinist era, these sectors never fully re-covered from that treatment, whereas in the West the corresponding activities have been more gradually incorporated into centralized enterprises by the less disruptive operation of market forces.

The managerial revolution in Russia was further complicated by overt po-litical hostility to the social elements most important to this development. The technical intelligentsia was never allowed to become a "ruling class," though it was clearly the "dominant class" (according to the distinction drawn by Svetozar Stojanović)[16] that made the system function. The Communist Party controllers never rested easy with their dependence on the experts, even while they were cultivating and exploiting them. The consequent climate of purges and control had a constantly negative effect on Soviet society, especially in the qualitative respect, except where special compensating efforts and concessions were made by the state, as in military-related science. Thus, the drag on the progress of Soviet society up to 1985, obvious in the "era of stagnation," was inherent in the excesses and distortions of Russia's revolutionary leap to mana-gerial society.

Reflection on the historical pattern of the revolutionary process and on the social forces that underlie these upheavals indicates that revolutions are not primarily driven by a priori ideologies toward unwavering goals. Nevertheless, ideologies are so prominent in revolutions that it has been easy to fall into the error of supposing that they are decisive. This assumption continues to govern most retrospective thinking about the Russian Revolution.

What is an ideology, then, if it is not a master plan for revolutionary ac-tion? While the verbal form of an ideology may spring from the brain of a par-ticular thinker or from a particular intellectual tradition—which is quite true of Marxism—ideologies, like religions, do not draw their mass following and their emotional force from their literal programs and rational arguments. They express and justify much deeper drives and interests that attach themselves to available surface beliefs. Vilfredo Pareto expressed this paradox in his scheme of "residues" and "derivations," the latter offering historically variable expres-sion to the basic cultural needs designated by the former.[17] Accordingly, though a particular ideology may be linked firmly to a given revolution, the passage of that revolution through a series of very different stages will cause its ideology to be given radically different meanings in each stage.

Literal ideology and actual practice inevitably diverge. As the revolution turns from the utopian and militant to the pragmatic and institutional, its ideology becomes less inspirational and more instrumental, less a guide for the exercise of power and more its tool. Karl Mannheim saw this as a natural progression in all political movements, as the original set of evocative beliefs—a "utopia"—turned into justification—an "ideology"—of whatever kind of system the movement eventually resulted in.[18] In the Russian case, this transformation of the function of ideology and its relation to reality was facilitated by the instruments of totalitarian control that the revolution had bequeathed to its heirs.

Ideology never had quite the function at any stage of the Soviet regime that ideologically based propaganda claimed for it. The Communists' incessant assertion of the "unity of theory and practice" was never anything but a masquerade. Lenin's seizure of power was the work of an adroit revolutionary tactician who had, in the words of Alfred Meyer, "a strong aversion to theory when the party could *act*."[19] When his drive for violent revolution was resisted by serious Marxists of every persuasion, Bolshevik as well as Menshevik, as a gamble with civil war and disaster, Lenin answered by quoting Goethe: "Theory, my friend, is gray, but green is the eternal tree of life."[20] Marxism permitted Lenin to expect the global overthrow of capitalism, and thereby gave him the excuse to defy Russia's developmental immaturity and strike the first blow for the anticipated world revolution. But Marxism offered the Communists little guidance for actually governing; they simply had to improvise, especially in response to civil war. The truer adherents to an ideological vision among them were the oppositionists who repeatedly took issue with Lenin and with the regime's actual evolution under him.

Totalitarian imposition of ideological discipline and the injection of ideology into all aspects of life and culture were made both necessary and difficult by the discrepancy between theory and practice that widened with each successive stage of the Soviet Union's postrevolutionary development. In part, this high-pressure quandary goes back to Lenin's unique revolutionary role, not in his leadership of the extremist revolution, which was fairly typical of the revolutionary process, but to the Soviet Thermidor of 1921, when he saved the nominal power of the Communist Party by his strategic retreat with the NEP. All subsequent stages of the revolutionary and postrevolutionary experience up to 1985 were saddled with the formal continuity of the Communist Party organization as the ruling authority, and with the verbal continuity of Marxist-Leninist doctrine as its legitimizing ideology. These circumstances made it both necessary and possible to bridge the widening gap between theory and practice by means of the totalitarian manipulation of ideology.

Stalin's decisive initiative in ideological revision was the "theory of Social-ism in One Country," first enunciated in 1924.[21] The significance of this argu-ment is not whether or not it truly revealed Russia's political prospects in the absence of world revolution, but the purpose of the theory and the manner in which Stalin advanced it. Initially, it was a purely tactical move to embarrass the Trotskyist opposition, accomplished by nothing less than falsifying Lenin and the whole previous Communist worldview. Consequently, the theory could be sustained only by censorship and political coercion. The "Socialism in One Country" episode thus put in place the methods of ideological manipulation and control—strictest of all in matters concerning Marxist theory—that pre-vailed until the very end of the Soviet regime. After his success with "Socialism in One Country," it was relatively easy for Stalin to assert any new ideological formulation in the name of Marxism, as he did all through the 1930s.

Subject to such authoritative reinterpretation from above, the verbal ideol-ogy of Stalinism created pervasive and enduring misunderstanding of the nature of the Soviet system, among its friends, enemies, and subjects alike. For people who grew up under Stalinism and neo-Stalinism and had the official ideology constantly drilled into them, it was natural to assume that Marxist theory di-rectly depicted and guided the regime. It was just as natural for people abroad who were not sophisticated about Soviet history to make the same assumption. Hence the temptation in the post-Communist era to see the entire sequence Marx-Lenin-Stalin as the logical working out of a single guiding idea.

To the question why "Communism" or "the Russian Revolution" or "the sev-enty-four-year Soviet experiment" failed, there is no simple answer. The sys-tem that collapsed in 1991 was vastly different from the one that the Bolsheviks attempted to put in place in 1917. It had gone through all the stages of the revo-lutionary process and had been shaped both by the Russian historical legacy and by the challenges of modernization. What changed least was the framework of ideological legitimation to which successive Communist leaders clung, giv-ing the illusion of continuity to a history of deep flux.

In a sense, the Russian Revolution was failing even as it started. By mid-1918, the premises of workers' control and of democracy under the soviets were withering in the hot blasts of civil war. For the sake of survival, the Communist regime found itself reviving bureaucratic instruments of power in government and the economy, a trend documented by vain protests from the series of Left Opposition groups—Left Communists, "Democratic Centralists," Workers' Opposition—who split off from the Communist mainstream between 1918 and 1921.[22] The NEP ended hopes of a spontaneous transition to socialism in the context of world revolution, leaving only an array of interesting but politically marginal experiments in cultural and social policy (modernism in the arts, unstructured education, society's responsibility in criminology, and so on). These initiatives were all rudely liquidated by Stalin as he moved to supplant the revolutionary ideal with a form of barracks socialism and the priorities of militarized industrialism. By the late 1930s, after the cultural counterrevolution that he carried out under the revolutionary banner, Stalin had left nothing of the original revolutionary experiment.

Marxists of an independent mind—Mensheviks and Trotskyists—had their explanation or excuse for this: The Russian Revolution was premature, triggered by World War I in a country that lacked the full material prerequisites for the socialist program that it had embraced. This is true as far as it goes, but the issue is broader. Breaking out in countries where the process of modernization is rapid but incomplete, all revolutions are to one degree or another premature, and they are all destined to disappoint the hopes of their original supporters.

Nevertheless, in relation to the real tasks that history imposed on it, the Soviet "experiment" was far from a complete failure. The key jobs were to carry through the process of modernization that had been interrupted by the revolution and to mobilize the resources of national power that would enable Russia to survive and compete in a world of advanced military technology. This the Stalinist postrevolutionary dictatorship did accomplish, cruelly, inefficiently, no faster than the United States or Japan in other time frames, but nonetheless successfully, as witness the strength it showed against heavy odds both in World War II and in the Cold War. By totalitarian methods of coercion and state allocation of resources—the "command-administrative system," as the Gorbachev reformers termed it—Stalinism transformed a mainly peasant society into a nation that was largely urban, educated, and technologically sophisticated—in a word, modern. Soviet Russia was no longer precapitalist, as theories of post-Communist "transition" often assumed, nor was it postcapitalist, as Marxist-Leninist theory held, but an alternative to capitalism, a parallel form of modernization by wholly different methods. The result, to be sure, was a modern society of a peculiar form, skewed toward military power and biased against mundane consumer needs (except for the elite, to be satisfied in secret). It was straitjacketed by the bureaucratic centralism that had been encouraged by all the main influences in twentieth-century Russian history—the Russian bureaucratic tradition, the needs of modern society, and the totalitarianism engendered by the revolutionary process. It was the Second World, neither the Third nor yet the First.

A new dialectic was at work in this complex and paradoxical system. The totalitarian state, by bringing Russian society into the modern world, sowed the seeds of its own destruction. Communist postrevolutionary rule generated needs and expectations, both material and mental, that it could not respond to without consuming its own basis. That was the dilemma inherited by the architects of perestroika, when the events of a troubled succession opened the way for change in the direction of the moderate revolutionary revival. The longer the old system was perpetuated, the weaker were its sources of support and the more likely it became that the least crack could progress to total collapse.

PART I

Marxism and Leninism

CHAPTER I

Marx and the Movement of History

Marxism was one of the most remarkable systems of social thought to emerge in the nineteenth century, not least because it incorporated the most outstanding historical and philosophical premises of its day. It was an attempt to analyze and explain the whole of history—or the whole of Western history—scientifically. It incorporated the new economic and technological interests of the century, emphasizing the conditions of ordinary life. It was optimistically evolutionary, a cyclical variant of the faith in progress, complete with an eighteenth-century heaven-on-earth at the end of the line. Finally, it was an attempt to use the scientific analysis of history as a political weapon in a struggle for the revolutionary reconstruction of society.

Marx's system of thought was not the cast-iron structure that both disciples and critics have typically made it out to be. Indeed, its many points of vagueness, incompleteness, and even self-contradiction have permitted diverse interpretations and emphases respecting the master's meaning. Not surprisingly, Marx's thought had its own historical development, with changing directions of emphasis and considerable evolution in the meaning of his basic concepts.

The years from Marx's graduation from the University of Berlin in 1841 to the publication of *The Poverty of Philosophy* in 1847 were a time of philosophical preparation. This was when he worked his way from Hegelianism into the now-familiar problem of "alienation" and thence (with help from Friedrich Engels) into his distinctive emphasis on economic conditions, the class struggle, the liberating role of the proletariat, and the ideal society of communism. *The Poverty of Philosophy* represents the first fully developed model of his philosophical system.[1]

Marx's second period, from 1847 to 1852, was ardently political. Practically all his writing in this period was occasioned by his activity in the revolutionary movement preceding and during the upheaval of 1848 and by his interest in the aftermath of the revolutions in France and Germany. His philosophy was still implicitly activist, with major attention to the problems of leadership, organization, and political action for both the revolutionary and conservative forces.

After 1852, Marx settled down in the British Museum to study the economic development of capitalism, with the intention of demonstrating the inevitability of its collapse. By 1865, he had done practically all his work on *Das Kapital*. Volume 1 was published in 1867, while volumes 2 and 3 remained incomplete and unpublished until after his death. It was during this third period, with his effort to establish the natural laws of capitalism and the proletarian revolution, that Marx's work came nearest to the deterministic image of his thought that posterity has inherited.

Marx's fourth period, slightly overlapping the third, commenced in 1864 with his renewed interest in active politics within the context of the International Workingmen's Association, the "First International." This and other currents in the European labor movement, plus the revolutionary crisis of 1870–71 in France, absorbed most of his attention until 1872. During those years he emphasized the possibilities of gaining and holding proletarian state power through democratic procedures.

From 1872 on, Marx's creative work lapsed almost completely, a striking fact that most of his biographers have glossed over. It was in this later period that Engels produced most of his own independent work—*Anti-Dühring, The Origin of the Family, The Dialectics of Nature,* and much more. It has usually been assumed that Engels was working in close concert with Marx, and that all this material represented Marx's own point of view and was approved by him, but in view of the evidence of Marx's illness, depression, and inactivity, there is good reason to doubt that he really exercised such influence over Engels. On the contrary, Engels was developing his own more deterministic version of the doctrine, considerably at variance with Marx's more activist outlook.[2] Engels and those who followed him more clearly reflected the atmosphere of mechanistic scientism and the evolutionary faith in progress that prevailed in late-nineteenth-century European thought. Nevertheless, in his last years, long after Marx's death, Engels undertook to correct the overly deterministic impression of Marxism that had taken hold in Social Democratic circles.

In the forty years following Engels's death in 1895, Marxism was subject to the most diverse interpretations and profound metamorphoses, so much so that we can regard Marx's most committed Communist disciples as real Marxists only by defining as Marxism any profession of belief in ideas *called* "Marxist." The main theoretical interests offered by latter-day Marxism are the problem of historical law and individual action and the relationship between countries at different stages of economic development. This latter issue encompassed the neo-Marxist theory of imperialism; attempts to clarify problems of nationality, national minorities, and international class loyalty; and, above all, application of the Marxian schema to Russia in its state of early capitalist development. The Bolshevik Revolution was carried out under the theoretical rationale that Russia was the "weakest link" in the "chain of imperialism" and that a workers' uprising there would precipitate the long-awaited international revolution.

The accession of Marxists to power in a manner and setting scarcely envisioned by the prophets entailed a fundamental transformation in the meaning and function of Marxist theory as the Russians comprehended it. Starting as an intellectual creation by individuals, Marxism became an official rationale of governmental policy and virtually a state religion. Thanks to the enforced manipulation of theory, the pronouncements of Soviet Marxism after Stalin achieved supremacy in 1928 cannot be taken seriously as genuine philosophical efforts.

The core of Marx's theory of history, a point of view to which he adhered with but slight shifts of emphasis from the mid-1840s to the end of his life, is the doctrine of "historical materialism." Marx and Engels had clearly established this approach when they wrote in *The German Ideology* in 1845–46, "The social structure and the state are continually evolving out of the life process of definite individuals, but of individuals not as they may appear in their own or other people's imagination, but as they really are, i.e., as they are effective, produce materially, and are active under definite material limits, presuppositions, and conditions independent of their will." Against the prevailing philosophical idealism of their epoch, Marx and Engels exclaimed, "Life is not determined by consciousness, but consciousness by life."[3]

Economic conditions and economically oriented actions, therefore, constituted the base of the social structure and as such profoundly influenced all other aspects of human existence and activity. Marx succinctly expressed this model of the social system in the preface to his *Contribution to the Critique of Political Economy*, published in 1859: "In the social production which men carry on they enter into definite relations that are indispensable and independent of their will; these relations of production correspond to a definite stage of development of their material powers of production. The sum total of these relations of production constitutes the economic structure of society—the real foundation, on which rise legal and political superstructures and to which correspond definite forms of social consciousness. The mode of production in material life determines the general character of the social, political, and spiritual processes of life."[4]

The hierarchical model of the levels and interrelationships of social phenomena that Marx presents is impressive and still useful. However, the question of the preponderant direction of influence between the levels, upward or downward, is much more debatable. Marx's own meaning has been disputed. Some writers have reduced his historical scheme to a purely technological determinism where all significant social changes are traceable ultimately to changes in the techniques of production. But clearly, Marx did not mean that human behavior was exclusively determined by economic motives and interests; his point was to stress the overriding necessities and limits that economic conditions imposed on all human activities.

A second cardinal principle in Marx's social theory, along with his stress on the economic base, was his doctrine of classes and the class struggle. "The history of all hitherto existing society is the history of class struggles," he and Engels declared at the opening of *The Communist Manifesto*.[5] Classes were the fundamental social units, each generated by economic conditions and defined by a particular relationship to the resources and forces of production, that is, by whether the members of a class owned property, what kind of property, or how they worked for the owners of property. Every form of society would tend to crystallize into two sharply opposed classes—the haves and the have-nots. These classes and their antagonisms—slave owners versus slaves, nobility versus serfs, capitalists versus proletarians—Marx regarded as the main dynamic forces in history. The history of any society was driven by the struggles between its classes, the increasing self-consciousness and determination of the subordinate class, and the ultimate revolutionary battle between the classes.

The class struggle created by the conditions of production and property ownership governed in turn the basic characteristics of a society's political and economic life. The state itself was explained as a product of the class struggle. "The state arose from the need to hold class antagonisms in check," Engels wrote in *The Origin of the Family* of 1884, "but as it arose, at the same time, in the midst of the conflict of these classes, it is, as a rule, the state of the most powerful, economically dominant class, which, through the medium of the state, becomes also the politically dominant class, and thus acquires new means of holding down and exploiting the oppressed class."[6] Thanks to the use of political power by the ruling class to maintain its dominance, the class struggle must take a political form, and victory for any rising class necessarily depends on political revolution, which under most circumstances will be violent.

Ideas no less than political power were for Marx and Engels weapons in the class struggle, selected and publicized on the basis of class interest: "The ideas of the ruling class are, in every age, the ruling ideas. . . . The dominant ideas are nothing more than the ideal expression of the dominant material relationships, . . . and thus of the relationships which make one class the ruling one."[7] This use of ideas to serve the class is not considered cynical; the ruling class actually persuades itself that the ideas corresponding to its interests are timelessly and absolutely valid. Here is the essence of Marx's theory of "ideology" as a system of "illusions" making the dominance of any ruling group seem eternally necessary and proper. It was the fate of Marxism in Communist states to become, in a more literal way than its founders ever imagined, the ideology of a new totalitarian and bureaucratic social system.

Marx's notion of the levels of social life and their interaction describes the structure of society at any given moment—that is, the nature of the particular "socioeconomic formation" characterized by a given mode of production and the corresponding class and property relationships, government, and ideas. Over the span of historical time Marx distinguished a series of different socioeconomic formations, each with its characteristic economic, social, political, and ideological makeup. The beginning of the process was presumed to be the primitive communal economy of tribal society, which with the rise of private property and class differentiation yielded to a series of class societies. "In broad outline," Marx wrote in the preface to the *Critique of Political Economy*, "we can designate the Asiatic, the ancient (slave-owning), the feudal, and the modern bourgeois methods of production as so many epochs in the progress of the economic formation of society."[8] After the bourgeois or capitalist phase of history, analysis became prediction, as Marx looked forward to an inevitable revolution by the proletariat and the appearance of an altogether new socialist society based on the economics of large-scale industrial production.

This scheme of the succession of social systems presents a number of difficulties. For one thing, Marx vastly oversimplified the transition from "feudalism" to "capitalism," and he did not comprehend Europe's complex political and social development between the thirteenth and eighteenth centuries. A more general weakness of the scheme is that social systems of presumably great diversity—the Asiatic, the ancient, and the feudal—were all based on the same conditions of production, that is, ox-and-plow agriculture. Marx did not note that great differences in social organization could arise—for military reasons, for example—independently of economic conditions.

Historical development from one social stage to another Marx explained as the operation of the forces that he analyzed in his model of the social structure. The prime mover was change in the techniques or resources of production, which generated new social forces and interests pressing for a change in the institutional structure. This point, too, is formulated in that remarkable epitome of Marx's whole philosophy, the preface to *Critique of Political Economy:* "At a certain stage of their development, the material forces of production in society come into conflict with the existing relations of production or . . . with the property relations within which they had been at work before. From forms of development of the forces of production these relations turn into their fetters. Then comes the period of social revolution. With the change of the economic foundation the entire immense superstructure is more or less rapidly transformed."[9]

Revolution is thus the characteristic political form of the transition from one socioeconomic formation to another. Marx took the French instance as his model for revolution, and here the bourgeois class factor is obvious. However, the farther afield one proceeds from that model, back or forward in time, the less Marx's class analysis of revolution holds up. In any case, he attributed no suprahistorical power to revolutions, and no new class could rise to the top until conditions were ripe for it: "No social order ever disappears before all the productive forces for which there is room . . . have been developed, and new, higher relations of production never appear before the material conditions of their existence have matured in the womb of the old society."[10]

The major part of Marx's life work, which consumed most of his energy in the 1850s and 1860s and left him too exhausted to make any significant contribution after that time, was the application of his system of social analysis to European capitalism. Starting with the premise that capitalist society was destined to be overthrown by the rising forces of the proletariat, Marx threw himself into the effort to establish historically and empirically "a process of natural history" with its "natural laws of capitalist production, . . . tendencies working with iron necessity towards inevitable results."[11] Herein lay the purpose of his voluminous economic studies on the labor theory of value, the theories of surplus value and capitalist exploitation, and the trends of capitalist accumulation and profit.

In the historical development of capitalism, Marx had an empirical foundation for his theory of social stages. Capitalism took shape, he found, in the interstices of the feudal system, but its critical development occurred in the process of "primary capitalist accumulation." This, according to Marx, was based on the dispossession of individual peasants and craftsmen by capitalistic landlords and merchant-employers who took over the resources and markets of the old "petty-bourgeois element." The latter, reduced to the status of a propertyless proletariat, were compelled to work for wages at the minimum subsistence level and thus provided the necessary labor force for capitalist industry.

For all its horrors of greed and exploitation, on which Marx so graphically expanded, capitalism performed for him the indispensable progressive function of developing the powerful new productive forces of scientific technology and large-scale enterprise. Thanks to his self-imprisonment in the labor theory of value, Marx did not clearly appreciate the possibilities of multiplying the productivity of labor through capital reinvestment (with correspondingly enhanced bargaining power and welfare potential), but he saw in the large-scale factory organization of production a source both of efficiency and of the social cohesion that was an essential condition for progress toward the goal of socialism.[12]

In the most crucial—and most questionable—part of his analysis, Marx maintained that the inner laws of capitalist development would lead the system into a state of deepening crisis, and the inability of a system of private ownership to realize the productive potential of a system of large-scale social production would become increasingly apparent. Two of the considerations making for such a crisis were unconvincing even in his own presentation and soon disproven by events—the "law" of the increasing immiseration of the proletariat, and the "law" of the declining rate of profit, both of which depended on the dubious support of the labor theory of value and the expectation that wages would rise hardly, if ever, above the subsistence level. Marx conceded that absolute immiseration might not take place, and his predictions then rested on the notion of "relative" immiseration, as the proletariat failed to advance in wealth as fast as the bourgeoisie, so that the gulf between them widened.[13] A third point that Marx stressed proved to be a much more serious threat to capitalism. This was the business cycle and its tendency to ever more serious recurrences of depression.

The great irony in Marx's critique of capitalism is that the economic theory in which he invested most of his effort is dubious in the extreme, while the sociological comments that he made briefly and in passing have lasting merit. Apart from his economic analysis, Marx observed the revolutionary social effect of capitalism in its steady concentration of the proletariat into larger and more self-conscious groups, while capitalist enterprise itself was amalgamating in the direction of trusts and monopolies. The workers would combine into unions and increasingly acquire political class-consciousness: "This mass unites, it is constituted as a class for itself. The interests which it defends are the interests of its class. But the struggle between class and class is a political struggle."[14] In the *Manifesto* Marx and Engels declared, "The development of modern industry therefore cuts from under its feet the very foundation on which the bourgeoisie produces and appropriates products. What the bourgeoisie, therefore, produces, above all, is its own gravediggers."[15]

Marx remained convinced that the natural outcome of capitalism was the proletarian revolution and the creation of the classless society of communism. In the closing pages of volume 1 of *Capital* he wrote, "Centralization of the means of production and socialization of labor at last reach a point where they become incompatible with their capitalist integument. This integument is burst asunder. The death knell of capitalist private property sounds. The expropriators are expropriated."[16] To be sure, the revolution might take a nonviolent form, and might even come by gradual stages. Marx hailed any meliorative measure, such as Parliament's limitation of the working day in England, as a victory for the socialist principle, but he looked for the day when the proletariat would take power through a democratic republic, destroy the remains of capitalist property, and begin to realize the presumably unlimited potential of socialized industry.

After some educating by Engels, Marx deliberately based his discussion of capitalism and its fate on England as the "classic" case and readily admitted differences of detail between countries.[17] In effect, he was using England as a Weberian "ideal type." He made no attempt to apply his analysis as a universal law outside of Western Europe and America. When his Russian sympathizers appealed to him in the 1870s for his opinion on their country, he rejected the attempt to "metamorphose my historical sketch into a historico-philosophic theory of the general path every people is fated to tread."[18] While the dynamics and fate of capitalism were inexorable wherever the system might take hold, its rise was not generally inevitable, and Russia might still preserve the peasant commune as the basis for a direct transition to socialism. Otherwise, "If Russia continues to pursue the path she has followed since 1861 [toward capitalism], she will lose the finest chance ever offered by history to a people and undergo all the fatal vicissitudes of the capitalist regime."[19]

Marx's view of history does not present, as so often thought, a unilinear path of obligatory stages. He offered a distinct alternative to the sequence ancient-feudal-bourgeois in his notion of "Asiatic society," where the political state and urban civilization developed upon the economic base of communal village agriculture. Marx's German American disciple K. A. Wittfogel elaborated the

Asiatic concept into a theory of "agromanagerial" society, whose most recent manifestation was none other than the Communist regime in Soviet Russia.[20] This is Wittfogel's view; Marxism proper is strictly a theory about capitalism and its fate, leaving the question of why capitalism emerges in a particular time and place indeterminate.

The approach to history that Marx employed throughout his economic and social analysis was the philosophy of dialectics that he had borrowed from Hegel. For Hegel, the dialectic process of "thesis," "antithesis," and "synthesis" represented the logical development of the Absolute Idea, of which human history was merely the material manifestation. Marx, like most of his student contemporaries at the German universities, was steeped in Hegelianism, but he rejected Hegel's philosophical idealism and instead took dialectics as a way of looking at the realities of human history. "In direct contrast to German philosophy, which descends from heaven to earth, here we ascend from earth to heaven," Marx and Engels wrote in "The German Ideology." [21] An oft-repeated remark by Marx was that he found Hegel standing on his head and turned him right side up.

In Marx's hands, the meaning of dialectics was that all human existence is in flux, without eternal truths or institutions; that the significance of the part depends on the whole; that change, development, and progress take place by way of contradiction and conflict; and that the resulting change leads to a higher unity. In particular, Marx viewed the class struggle and the transition from one social system to another as a dialectical process, in which the ruling class, viewed as the "thesis," evoked its own "negation" in the challenger class. This was supposed to lead to a synthesis through revolutionary transformation, resulting in a higher organization of elements from the old order.[22]

The dialectical approach to history was at best a stage on the road to social science. In its suggestion of a historical demiurge shaping the universal course of events, it was hardly conducive to the truly scientific frame of mind that Marx professed. It did convey a sense of the dynamic interaction of all the complex phenomena in the social system, if only in metaphysical terms.[23] The dialectical method imposes sharply defined stages and forces upon the continuity and gradations in the social process, and then explains the process as dialectical conflict among these stages and forces. This view makes violent conflict and abrupt, revolutionary change appear to be the normal thing, and it encourages misleading oversimplifications about the course of history and the structure of society. It was the dialectical approach that compelled Marx to concentrate so heavily on the internal workings of capitalism, to try to demonstrate the "inevitable" emergence of the proletarian negation that the dialectic called for.

One difficulty in Marx's theory of history is the question why the dialectic would stop after the proletarian revolution. Presumably the proletariat embodies qualities, such as alienation from all property interest, that would enable it to put an end for all time to the dialectical antagonisms on which social change had heretofore depended. This vision rests on Marx's faith in the proletariat. It leaves unanswered the question whether and how social progress could continue after the proletarian revolution.

Marx never got around to the systematic elaboration of the dialectical philosophy that he hoped to write, and it was left to Engels, after Marx's creative period was over, to generalize and defend the dialectic method. In Engels's treatment, the dialectic process became more nearly automatic and implicitly universal, not only with regard to human history but to the world of nature and natural evolution as well. At the same time, Engels transformed the dialectical struggle of forces within a system into a plainly mechanistic cause-and-effect interaction, consistent with late-nineteenth-century scientific evolutionism and the faith in automatic progress. The mechanistic emphasis prevailed thereafter among most Marxists, including the Bolsheviks, until well after the Russian Revolution.

Interpretation of the dialectic process became a subject of acute philosophical and political controversy in Soviet Russia in the late 1920s, when the mechanistic viewpoint associated with Nikolai Bukharin and the Communist right wing came under attack by a new school of "dialecticians." Through two successive phases of controversy, each settled by the intervention of the party leadership, the official Soviet view of dialectics was revised to stress the dialectical "jumps" or discontinuities between successive phases in the history of society. The Soviet regime thenceforth considered itself released from the laws of value that prevailed under capitalist economics, and free to direct the course of economic development by deliberate planning.[24]

A preconceived conclusion lay behind Marx's whole dialectical conception of history and revolution. At the very outset of his career as a philosopher, he had committed himself to the need for radical social change—initially, it seems, in reaction to religion and the conditions of social oppression that made the "illusory happiness" of religion necessary. "The immediate *task of philosophy*," Marx wrote in 1842, "once the *saintly form* of human self-alienation has been unmasked, is to unmask self-alienation in its *unholy forms*."[25] Thus the great moral necessity for mankind was its "emancipation" from illusion and alienation.

To accomplish this total liberation, Marx looked for a real social force with no stake in the existing order and its illusions, and this force he found in the new industrial working class, the proletariat.[26] Under the influence of the French utopian socialists, he committed himself to the abolition of private property in the means of production, and he devoted one of his major early works, the *Economic and Philosophical Manuscripts* of 1844, to a critique of the dehumanizing effect of the "alienation" imposed on employers and employees alike by the capitalist system of production.[27] Even with his elaboration of a more thoroughly dialectical and deterministic analysis of capitalism, Marx remained at heart the impassioned moralist, railing against the evil of capitalist exploitation: "In its blind, unrestrainable passion, its werewolf hunger for surplus labor, capital oversteps not only the moral, but even the merely physical maximum bounds of the working day, . . . shortening the extent of the laborer's life as a greedy farmer snatches increased produce from the soil by robbing it of its fertility."[28] In short, the capitalist world was evil, the proletariat would have to destroy it, and history and economics must be made to yield up the scientific "laws" that would show how this would "inevitably" come to pass.

Through his dialectical analysis of capitalism, Marx satisfied himself that the proletariat as the "negation" of the bourgeoisie would grow in numbers, organization, and self-consciousness. With the guidance of philosophers like himself, the proletariat would prepare itself to seize political power when the growing contradictions in the capitalist system, expressed in increasing concentration and deepening crisis, would set the stage for revolution. The task he proclaimed for the Communist League in 1848 was to educate and unite working-class parties everywhere, to prepare them "to raise the proletariat to the position of the ruling class, to establish democracy." When this stage was reached, "[t]he proletariat will use its political supremacy to wrest, by degrees, all capital from the bourgeoisie," so that finally, "after class differences have been eliminated the public power will lose its political character." There would then no longer be any property rights or class exploitation to enforce.[29]

On the actual manner of the proletarian seizure of power, not to mention the subsequent "dictatorship of the proletariat," Marx was never very explicit, though he did give increasing attention as time went on to possibilities for revolution by democratic means. "We do not deny," he declared in Amsterdam in 1872, "that there are countries, such as America, England, and—if I understand your institutions correctly—Holland, where the workers can attain their goals by peaceful means."[30] When the Paris Commune rebelled in the spring of 1871 and set up a short-lived revolutionary regime, Marx hailed it as the actual model of a workers' government. As he saw the Commune, it had eliminated all the repressive functions of the old state and created a new administration with its officials made directly responsible to the democratic electorate and held to the level of "workmen's wages."[31] Engels was ultimately very firm about democratic methods: "History has shown us to have been wrong. The mode of struggle of 1848 is today obsolete in every respect." Street fighting was largely out, and universal suffrage had proved to be the workers' most effective weapon. "The irony of world history turns everything upside down. We, the 'revolutionists,' the 'overthrowers'—we are thriving far better on legal methods than on illegal methods and overthrow."[32]

With the consummation of the revolution, according to Marx, the mission of the proletariat as such would come to an end. After abolishing private property and the class differences that rested on it, the proletariat itself would cease to exist as a class, and the proletarian negation of capitalist society would be dialectically superseded by the classless society of communism. This did not mean mere collective ownership and forcible equalization, which Marx denounced as "general private property" and "envy and leveling [that] in fact constitute the essence of competition," where "the role of worker is not abolished, but is extended to all men." Soviet Russia with all its emphasis on "state property" seems to have fallen into Marx's category of "crude communism," which he called "only a phenomenal form of the infamy of private property." True "communism," he maintained, is "the positive abolition of private property, of human self-alienation, and then the real appropriation of human nature through and for man."[33]

Marx was not so utopian as to expect all social problems to end immediately after the revolution. He noted in his "Critique of the Gotha Program" of 1875 that the "bourgeois right" (that is, law) of payment according to the individual's labor would still be necessary "in the first phase of communist society as it is when it has just emerged after prolonged birth pangs from capitalist society." Only in the "higher phase of communist society," when labor had become natural, its internal differentiations diminished, and its product more abundant, "only then can the narrow horizon of bourgeois right be left behind and society inscribe on its banners: 'From each according to his ability, to each according to his needs.'"[34] Lenin and his followers in the Communist movement after 1917 sharpened this distinction between the two postrevolutionary phases, and applied the terms "socialism" and "communism" to designate the earlier and later phases respectively.[35] "Socialism" in this special sense was extended by the Soviet authorities to denote a long "transitional period," and only under Nikita Khrushchev was the program of effecting the "transition to communism" officially initiated. Of course, this phraseology, like most official Marxian theory under actual Communist society, became an arid scholastic exercise.

Marx's theory of the proletarian revolution raises a number of questions suggesting that his certainty about the victory of the proletariat was a preconceived act of faith rather than a scientific conclusion. One problem is the suspension of the dialectical process, presumably governed by the higher social nature of the proletariat as the only class capable of ending the class struggle. Lying behind this was Marx's original attachment of his moral hopes to the victory of the proletariat. But by the logic of his own conception of history, there was no reason to expect the proletariat to follow the bourgeoisie as the new dominant class. Feudalism had presumably been overthrown not by the peasants whom the nobles exploited but by a new minority group based on new conditions of production and new forms of property—the capitalists. To follow the parallelism, one should look for still another dominant minority, basing its power on the conditions of large-scale production, to supplant the capitalists step-by-step, with the proletariat (or whoever succeeded them under the conditions of modern technology) kept under firm control by the new ruling class. This is the direction that some neo-Marxist thinkers later took in analyzing postcapitalist society in both Communist and non-Communist countries.[36]

From its very beginning in the early 1840s, Marxism rested on faith in the mission and victory of the proletariat, or whatever was called the proletariat. Lacking this faith, no one could call him- or herself a Marxist; with it, almost anyone could. It is this enduring proletarian emotionalism that gave continuity to the professedly Marxist movement of the Communists, even though the proletarian quality of the movement ultimately became an elaborate fraud. The social systems ruled by the Communists were far from constituting Marx's ideal society and were not likely to lead on to such a society.

Perhaps the most difficult problem in understanding Marx is his conception of the economic laws of history and their determining effect on other aspects of life. Controversy over this issue has gone on chronically among non-Soviet writers on Marxism, while the Soviet regime under Stalin reversed its interpretation, from the most extreme determinism to a highly activist emphasis on the role of political organization and leadership.

Marx's writings of the 1840s were, for all their economic slant, decidedly activist. Economic life to him was a form of action—the most important—and the economic conditions that shaped people were at the same time the product of human action. The old materialism, Marx complained, "forgets that it is men that change circumstances, and that the educator himself needs educating."[37] Activism was Marx's metaphysical justification for stressing the economic factor, on the ground that people were "the authors and actors of their own history,"[38] and that they had to be understood as concrete economic and social experience had shaped them. In the *Manifesto,* Marx and Engels constantly speak of the conscious activism of the proletariat, which, armed with the weapon of philosophy, must struggle for its own revolutionary emancipation.

In the later stages of Marx's economic work, the dialectical interaction of conscious action and social conditions that he tried to express assumed an increasingly deterministic tone, at least as regards the formation of the proletariat and the breakdown of capitalism. Marx became more and more deeply ensnared in the logical inconsistency of the activist revolutionary effort on the one hand and, on the other, the "scientific" laws of history that made the revolution appear inevitable and independent of the actions or ideas of any particular individual. Neither Marx nor any of his followers made clear what they meant by "laws" of history. They failed—and the Communists continued to fail—to distinguish between the conditional "if—then" laws in which the propositions of natural science are usually couched and the absolute "law" of a foreordained course of events. While Marx probably meant the former, he allowed his directives to sound more like binding predictions. Engels and the Social Democrats clearly understood the proletarian revolution as a historical inevitability, subject only to the uncertainties of timing and possible bloodshed. For the ensuing Marxist orthodoxy, the conscious action of the proletariat was itself the product of social conditions, as Engels himself suggested in *Anti-Dühring:* "Conflict between productive forces and modes of production exists . . . in fact, objectively, outside us, independently of the will and actions even of the men who have brought it on. Modern socialism is nothing but the reflex, in thought, of this conflict in fact; its ideal reflection in the minds . . . of . . . the working class."[39]

Despite his deterministic language, Marx himself acknowledged in many contexts the role of noneconomic powers, particularly political action. His idea of "primitive capitalist accumulation," in which individual producers were dispossessed in order to get capitalist enterprises going, presumes deliberate intervention by force. "Force," he wrote, "is the midwife of every old society pregnant with a new one. It is itself an economic power."[40]

Of more contemporary import, Marx developed in his journalistic comments on the politics of France between 1848 and 1851 a concept of "Bonapartism" as the independent state machine standing over and above the strife of more or less evenly balanced social classes.[41] In their reflections on the Paris Commune, Marx and Engels laid great stress on the proper political steps by the proletariat in order to "safeguard itself against its own deputies and officials" and prevent even the revolutionary state from transforming itself "from the servant of society into the master of society."[42] Such remarks implied that there was a fork in the historical road *after* the proletarian revolution, and that political action alone would decide whether the revolutionary society took the true path or was diverted into a bureaucratic perversion. Bukharin, writing in 1916, depicted the alternatives as "militaristic state capitalism" or diversion of the course of history by the proletarian revolution and the destruction of the bourgeois state.[43]

In this light, Soviet society was the proletarian revolution gone wrong, where the revolutionaries failed to prevent the state from becoming the master of society, the "new Leviathan." Thus, as Sidney Hook put it, "In the very interests of the socialist society which Karl Marx anticipated, . . . it is not the mode of economic production but the mode of political decision which is of decisive importance."[44] Just as a variety of social and political systems could arise as the institutional superstructure over ancient agriculture, so is it possible to choose among a variety of political and economic forms, democratic or totalitarian, that all rest on the economic base of modern industry.

Marx never resolved the ambiguity in his philosophy between determinism and voluntarism, and his writings offered ample basis for his followers to stress either the one or the other. In the 1880s and 1890s, the trend was heavily deterministic, and Engels found it necessary to state certain reservations regarding historical materialism. He made it clear, for one thing, that economic laws did not mean exclusively economic determination of the actions of individuals. However, the individual might have entirely free will but be powerless to affect the social process. Here Engels was groping toward something like the modern notion of statistical laws of causation, valid in the case of large numbers though not necessarily for the particular instance.

More significant for the Marxian system was Engels's concession regarding the role of the social superstructure. He denied that economics was the only determining factor and noted that the political and intellectual forces of the superstructure "also exercise their influence upon the course of the historical struggles and in many cases preponderate in determining their *form*. There is an interaction of all these elements in which, amidst all the endless host of accidents, . . . the economic movement finally asserts itself as necessary." Governmental force, as Marx had long before noted, could decisively accelerate or impede economic and social development: "Why do we fight for the political dictatorship of the proletariat, if political power is economically impotent?"[45]

By the time of Engels's death in 1895, the deterministic version of classical Marxism had taken firm hold as the official theory of the Social Democratic parties, especially in Germany. Karl Kautsky, the chief Social Democratic theoretician, expounded the rigorous laws of inevitable proletarian victory. He still spoke of the revolution as an abrupt and decisive overturn, though he hoped to achieve it without violence. Kautsky was convinced that the best that proletarian leaders could do to facilitate the final outcome was to use and improve the instruments of political democracy.[46]

This "orthodox" fusion of Marxian revolutionary prognosis and peaceful political practice evoked sharp criticism. On the right, Eduard Bernstein broke with Marx's dialectical identification of the desirable and the inevitable. His "revisionism," influenced by neo-Kantian ethics, posited socialism as an ethical goal, not necessarily guaranteed by any laws of history but only an aim to be realized through persistent democratic gradualism.[47] Bernstein's evolutionary socialism prevailed, first in their practice and then in their theory, in all the West European Socialist parties, and they thereby ceased to be dogmatically Marxist.

Before 1917, the Marxist left wing was much less influential, but it foreshadowed the later activist reinterpretation of Marxism in Russia. Rosa Luxemburg in Germany and a number of Dutch Marxists (Anton Pannekoek, Herman Gorter), reflecting the anarcho-syndicalism that was then in vogue in many parts of Europe, laid increasing stress on direct "mass action" and the general strike to effect the proletarian revolution.[48]

The Russian interpretation of Marxism represented by Georgi Plekhanov was ultradeterminist. Plekhanov played down Marx's qualifications about the role of noneconomic factors in history and ignored his suggestions that world history need not be unilinear. To Plekhanov, Marxism was a watertight dogma of the coming of capitalism and the emergence of proletarian socialism after capitalism had completed its work.[49] Lenin followed Plekhanov in his theoretical position, although in his stress on the role of the disciplined revolutionary party there was a new, implicit activism echoing Marx's early pronouncements and drawing also on the voluntaristic philosophy of the nineteenth-century Russian revolutionary movement.[50] To justify the "vanguard" function of the party, Lenin belittled the "spontaneity" of the working class and maintained, in direct though unwitting contradiction to Marx, that "political class consciousness can be brought to the workers *only from without*, that is, only from outside of the economic struggle, from outside the sphere of relations between workers and employers."[51] In 1917 he was to rest all his hopes on the "art" of insurrection.[52]

If Marx is viewed not as a prophet or an Antichrist but only as a complex figure in the history of thought, it is possible to recognize his epochal though time-bound achievement as a social philosopher and a social critic, without subscribing to any of his particular theories, predictions, or political programs.

His most substantial contribution to social science was his model of the various levels of phenomena in the social system—economic base, class structure, political and ideological superstructure—and his conception of the interaction among these levels. In this framework each aspect of life can be viewed in relation to every other, and none need be neglected. The British historian Herbert Butterfield wrote, "The chief contribution of the Marxists has been that they, more than anybody else, have taught us to make our history a structural piece of analysis."[53] Marx's theory of ideology, in particular, opens the way to the whole area of the sociology of knowledge.[54]

The other major element in Marx's sociology, his conception of the sequence of class-dominated societies, is far less useful, except where it belabors the obvious regarding the transition from feudalism to capitalism. His concept of class is ill defined and arbitrary, and the dialectical approach to history cuts a complex development up into stages of artificial simplicity. Dogmatic Marxists became prisoners of Marx's particular class and period concepts and could not comprehend new developments outside the Marxian frame of reference. Ironically, Marx himself readily suspended his scheme in writing about matters as diverse as French politics and the Russian peasant commune. He has enduring significance not in the literal terms of his system but in the awareness of economic pressures and social antagonisms which, more than any other thinker, he impressed upon all Western social science since his day.

CHAPTER 2

Fate and Will in the Marxian Vision

M arxism is shot through with dualism, notwithstanding the assertions of both its exponents and its critics that it is a "monistic" philosophy. To begin with, there is the dichotomy of theory and practice, of scientific (or pseudo-scientific) analysis and revolutionary action. Until well after the Russian Revolution, Marxists everywhere were convinced that they had scientific proof of the objective inevitability of the proletarian revolution, while at the same time they worked with energy and dedication in their Marxist parties to bring this event about. The logical contradiction between a determinist philosophy of history and the vigorous conduct of political action is obvious, but in psychological terms it makes a great deal of sense. This might be termed the "predestination paradox," which Marxism shared with much Christian theology: People who are convinced of the inevitability of their cause strive all the more vigorously to make sure it succeeds. This is a puzzle only if the unwarranted assumption is made that the action is motivated by the doctrine. According to the Marxian approach, or from any sociological point of view, revolutionaries are so oriented not by virtue of any theory but because of the effect that their social situation has had upon them. Individuals thus inclined to revolution embrace Marxian determinism as an appealing rationalization for their own impulses, which continue to impel them to action. Philosophy does not create the will to action but only reinforces it. People are Marxists because they are revolutionary, not vice versa.

Extreme determinism is not hard to understand: Emphasis on the economic factor was the distinctive feature of the Marxian interpretation of history, so much so that it was easy for both its friends and enemies to conclude that the theory ended simply with that. "Marx and I," conceded Engels, "are ourselves partly to blame for the fact that younger writers sometimes lay more stress on the economic side than is due to it. We had to emphasize this main principle in opposition to our adversaries, who denied it, and we had not always the time, the place or the opportunity to allow the other elements involved in the interaction to come into their rights."[1]

Voluntarist conclusions about Marxism could equally be entertained, and in Russia, they would be much more in accord with revolutionary actuality. Lenin's doctrine of the party, in particular, turned on the assumption that without deliberate, organized action by correctly inspired leaders—that is, Bolsheviks—the proletarian revolution would never come to pass. The Bolshevik Revolution itself was the triumph of one man's overriding will.

There is a second Marxist dualism in the objective interpretation of the historical process, quite apart from the subjective question of taking action to affect that process. Is the course of history shaped or influenced more by "material conditions" that operate through natural laws independent of the will of any given individual, or more by the ideas, decisions, and impulses of certain individuals? Are human events a matter of collective fate or individual will? Does history make the person or do personalities make history?

Marx's answer was not a one-sided one: Man makes history *and* history makes man, as he put it in so many words. It was therefore possible, depending on personal preferences, political requirements, and the changing intellectual fashions of succeeding generations, for Marxists to find in the scriptures whichever emphasis they wished to make, and they did so. A person who is interested in theoretical understanding more than in revolutionary action can readily stress the deterministic reading of the theory. Someone of contrary bent, the revolutionary activist, will naturally seek out and emphasize that aspect of the theory that accords a decisive role to willful action. This sums up the doctrinal development of the Bolsheviks. Activist Marxists, they molded their beliefs into an activist Marxism.

Among the Mensheviks in Russia, and among most Marxists elsewhere, determinism was adhered to much more strictly, but here again temperamental considerations are involved. Around the turn of the century, the psychological referents of the determinist belief changed. Previously it had been an inspiration to revolutionaries; subsequently it became more and more the resort of people who temperamentally were not very revolutionary at all. The fatalistic connotations of historical materialism, as Bolshevik polemics pointed out, served to justify the evasion of deliberate revolutionary action at a time when the socialist tradition still made it politically difficult for socialist leaders to forswear their radical terminology. Kautsky in Germany and Plekhanov in Russia were the outstanding examples of this state of mind.

Initially challenging the exclusively idealist conception of history that prevailed in their time, Marx and Engels became identified with the opposite extreme. Some of their oversimplified statements, particularly Marx's introduction to the *Critique of Political Economy*, give the impression of pure economic determinism, but in other writings there are important qualifications to this extreme view. The explicit statement of these reservations was primarily the work of Engels after the senior partner died in 1883. They can be subsumed under three major points, which taken together make clear the subtle complexity of the Marxian philosophy.

One qualification to Marxian determinism concerns the relationship between the economic forces of society's "base" and the political and intellectual forces of the social "superstructure." As Engels explained in a late letter, the relationship is one of "reciprocal interaction," in which each sphere affects the other, though he attributed the stronger and in the long run more independent causative influence to the economic base.[2] But if the political and intellectual superstructure could sometimes be decisive, how did Marxists see the role of these factors in the success of their own movement? Was the proletarian revolution not blindly inevitable but subject to acceleration, shaping, retardation, or deflection to another line of development? To what extent was it the undetermined product of willful action?

Marx always stressed that historical necessity operated through the agency of conscious action. He did not deny the efficacy of will and political power but claimed to have explained their nature and direction on the basis of economic forces and the class struggle. Freedom of the will is an illusion—individuals are unconsciously made to want what they do by the social and economic circumstances that shape their mentality.

When Lenin undertook to justify revolutionary action, he departed sharply from Marx's identification of necessity and will, though he had Marx's stress on the latter as his authority. Lenin assumed that consciousness and willful action were not only independent of social circumstances but decisive in acting upon them. Consciousness, embodied in specially endowed individuals, would be injected into the historical process from the outside and would dictate the ultimate success of the revolution. Lenin stated this in so many words when he asserted that only outsiders could give the workers class consciousness: "Give us an organization of revolutionaries, and we shall overturn Russia."[3]

Remarks of this sort Lenin made not with any intent of challenging the philosophical presuppositions of Marxism but only in immediate justification of the organizational and tactical measures that he insisted the revolutionaries take. Nevertheless, the implications of his thinking were immediately apparent to orthodox Marxists like Plekhanov, who seized upon them for purposes of rebuttal. "The disputed question consists in this," wrote Plekhanov. "Does there exist an economic necessity which calls forth in the proletariat a demand for socialism, makes it instinctively socialistic, and impels it—even if left to its own resources—on the road to social revolution, notwithstanding the stubborn and continual effort of the bourgeoisie to subject it to its own ideological influence? Lenin denies this, in face of the clearly expressed opinions of all the theorists of scientific socialism. And in that consists his enormous mistake, his theoretical fall into sin."[4] Thanks to Lenin, by the time the party took power the Bolsheviks' Marxism had become highly inconsistent. Most party leaders, like Lenin himself, thought themselves to be out-and-out determinists, however much their political practice contradicted this belief. But the materials were present for a thorough reinterpretation when the course of Soviet politics pressed upon Lenin's successor the need for a correction in his doctrinal justifications.

Another refinement of Marxian determinism is the notion of historical causation as a matter of probabilities. This aspect of the doctrine has been almost completely neglected, which is unfortunate, since its implications are extremely interesting. The essence of this notion of probabilities is to concede to individual actions and historical accidents a broad play but to insist that the net resultant of the constellation of events—after the probabilities are added up and opposite quantities cancel each other out—is governed by economic forces and the basic social structure. As Engels expressed it in 1890, "History makes itself in such a way that the final result always arises from conflicts between many individual wills, of which each again has been made what it is by a host of particular conditions of life. Thus there are innumerable intersecting forces, an infinite series of parallelograms of forces which give rise to one resultant—the historical event. This again may itself be viewed as the product of a power which, taken as a whole, works *unconsciously* and without volition. For what each individual wills is obstructed by everyone else, and what emerges is something that no one willed. Thus past history proceeds in the manner of a natural process."[5]

The clarity of Engel's formulation could easily be improved upon with the use of more modern terminology, though his meaning does not seem to be in doubt. What he is trying to express is the statistical nature of the laws of social causation. Causative forces do not operate with rigor in any individual case, where either accident or free will can indeed operate. The basic economic and social factors have their effect as probabilities, which become decisive as large numbers of individual cases are reached. We might take suicides or traffic deaths as understandable, if morbid, examples: The rate of such mishaps for a whole country over a year's time can be predicted with fair accuracy on the basis of past experience. Beyond certain relatively narrow limits of variability, the rate of these fatalities is the inevitable consequence of the sum total of social circumstances. On the other hand, barring exceptional cases of obvious pathology, no one can anticipate the fate of any particular individual. Statistical law, acting only as a probability, leaves undetermined the individual instance, but it may become a practical certainty for the society as a whole. The analogy with the physical concepts of indeterminacy and the merely statistical lawfulness in the behavior of atomic particles is very close.

Further sense can be made of Engel's proposition by calling upon the modern psychological concept of unconscious motivation. While Engels can hardly be called a forerunner of Freud—his catalogue of the basic human motives reads far differently—the idea that in general people can be governed by forces of which they are not consciously aware answers neatly to Engels's aim of "investigating the driving powers which—consciously or unconsciously, and indeed very often unconsciously—lie behind the motives of men who act in history."[6] What people will, according to this approach, is conditioned by their social circumstances and in the preponderance of cases will be governed by these circumstances. Combining the concepts of unconscious motivation and statistical causation explains how historical determinism can operate despite the ubiquity of accident and the appearance of individual will.

This formulation still does not extend to Stalinist voluntarism. What becomes of determinism in those instances where the course of events is not the resultant of many individual wills but is dictated by a few or even one particular will, as in the case of an authoritarian political leader? To be sure, the possibility of such a concentration of decision-making power may perhaps be attributed back to the social structure, as Plekhanov insisted: "Individuals can influence the fate of society. Sometimes this influence is very considerable; but the possibility of exercising this influence, and its extent, are determined by the form of organization of society, by the relation of forces within it."[7] This only means, however, that a given set of circumstances may determine a condition of indeterminacy for a particular society at a particular time.

Taken together with the indeterminacy of individual action, the concept of reciprocal interaction of base and superstructure permits any kind of social structure to be described in these terms. The superstructure can influence the base; the action of the superstructure may under certain circumstances be governed by one or a few individuals; and the action of these individuals is indeterminate. Here is an avenue for recognizing possibly far-reaching indeterminacy in a society's historical development, depending on the position and power of individuals within the political superstructure. Thus it is possible to deduce from Marxian premises a theory of the decisiveness of political forms.

The third important qualification of Marxian determinism underscored by Engels is the notion of the revolution as a "leap to freedom." One feature of the classless socialist society that the proletarian revolution would establish was the escape of humanity from the determining influence of economic forces. According to Engels, "Man's own social organization, hitherto confronting him as a necessity imposed by nature and history, now becomes the result of his own free action. . . . Only from that time will man himself, with full consciousness, make his own history—only from that time will the social causes set in movement by him have . . . the results intended by him. It is the ascent of man from the kingdom of necessity to the kingdom of freedom."[8]

Underlying this glowing hope is the conviction that human control over the objective forces of history can be established by nothing more than understanding and will: "Active social forces work exactly like natural forces: blindly, forcibly, destructively, so long as we do not understand and reckon with them. But when once we understand them, when once we grasp their action, their direction, their effects, it depends only upon ourselves to subject them more and more to our own will, and by means of them to reach our own ends."[9]

The human decisions that thus prevail over objective social forces are not predetermined. This makes possible a completely indeterminate future, if the conditions that limit the efficacy of the human will are corrected. Knowledge and a socialist economic organization are presumably enough. If people understand the laws of historical cause and effect, they can foresee the results of their action and secure results that actually correspond to their intentions (thus escaping from the blindness of presocialist history making). If the wills of a multitude of contending individuals are replaced with one enlightened social will pursuing the interest of the collectivity, the canceling and averaging effect in atomistic society will be overcome, and the laws of deterministic probability will lose their effect.

It would seem, on the surface, that the new social order would scarcely be short of an Elysium of untrammeled free humanity, shackled neither by nature nor by social authority. However, the Marxian vision omits a crucial question about the decisiveness of political power and institutions. Who understands, who plans, whose will is realized? The Russian Revolution gave birth to political institutions that decided this question in a very definite way—the dictatorship of the planner, who is not effectively answerable to society at large and who subjects the entire population to his personal will on every matter he desires.

Freedom, in Engels's sense of freedom for the social organism to violate economic necessity or alter its direction, was achieved in the USSR to a high degree. Guided by dictatorial planning, Soviet economic development was relatively free from the forces that act with statistical determinacy through the decisions of a multitude of individuals. The preferences of the multitude had little if any direct effect on decisions taken by top authority, and at that level determinism did indeed give way to free will. Freedom of choice for the leaders means necessity—political compulsion—for the citizenry. Thus, surmounting the forces of economic necessity implies totalitarianism.

In like measure, a society without totalitarian controls, where decisions are made independently by a multitude of individuals, will remain more or less at the mercy of impersonal historical forces, which determine with statistical regularity the aggregate behavior of the population. Each individual is free, but all individuals are subject to the pressure of social and economic conditions that establish the probabilities of their response en masse. Once an opinion poll has carefully sampled a few thousand people, it can predict with high accuracy the national response on any question whatsoever. Freedom for individuals means that the society will be shaped by impersonal forces beyond the control of any individual.

There exists, of course, a middle ground, though the prophets of Marxism never explored it. A democratic society need not drift in leaderless anarchy. It can—and does, in some measure—have an authority representing the collective will that takes action in definite directions, that assumes responsibility, provides leadership, and shapes events. For such action to be effective without totalitarian power, however, the leadership must have reliable knowledge of the objective forces operating in society, so that it can intervene in ways that will procure the desired results.

The ultimate paradox is that the opposing totalitarian and democratic societies of East and West were each wedded to historical conceptions that made sense only for the other. The dictatorial Soviet Union clung to the formula of a deterministic philosophy while all its political experience revolved around the most exaggerated voluntarism. Western democracy treasures the illusions of free will while the central virtue of its system guarantees that impersonal forces will have a preponderant influence on society's future course.

Partisans of individual liberty who railed against historical determinism as a denial of human freedom were as illogical as were Soviet spokesmen who denounced "bourgeois idealism" as a menace to the rule of the Communist Party. Neither side seriously faced history's real challenge—to devise ways for society intelligently to plan the future and still preserve freedom for its individual members.

CHAPTER 3

Lenin as a Russian Revolutionary

To what extent did Lenin, the Bolshevik movement, and the Soviet regime embody the philosophy of Marxism? Or to what degree were they instead products of Russian history? It can be argued that Lenin radically transformed his Marxian heritage, both in substance and spirit, in the direction of the ideas espoused by the Russian revolutionaries who preceded him. Notwithstanding the Bolsheviks' Marxist language, the Russian Revolution was shaped by Russian beliefs, and it yielded an intrinsically Russian result—all deceptions of terminology to the contrary. It was not Marx's revolution, but Lenin's.

Lenin was of course a Marxist—a fervent believer, an adept disciple. He assimilated intimately the entire literal body of Marxian doctrine as his base of intellectual operations and the arsenal from which he habitually drew his weapons for revolutionary discourse. Yet it is far easier to point out where Lenin differed from Marx than to indicate comprehensively where he stayed faithful in spirit.

For a comfortable distance there was no opposition between Marx and the Russian revolutionary mentality—Marx, after all, was eagerly received by the revolutionary intelligentsia. For both Marx and Lenin, the revolution meant socialism (however defined), and it was inspired by radical antipathy toward the bourgeois world. Both expected the revolution to be international, violent, and total. Finally, the revolution necessarily had to occur—though here, turning on different meanings of "necessity," a profound difference emerges. For the Russians, the revolution was a moral necessity—necessary if the good life were to be achieved. For Marx, it was this too, but primarily something else: a scientific necessity, the inevitable outcome of the inexorable operation of laws of nature.

Sometimes Lenin followed Marx against other Russian revolutionaries. He loudly rejected certain ideas of the Russian tradition—in particular, individual terrorism and the theory of the peasant commune as the anteroom to socialism. And his internationalism, at least until World War I, was not of the Russian messianic sort: The "Dark People" hardly constituted the refined clay that the molding of socialism was presumed to demand. Nevertheless, at every critical turn in the examination of Lenin's thought the impact of Russian circumstances shows itself. This is only natural, but while it may explain Lenin's divergence from the program laid down by Marx, it does not exculpate him. Not for nothing did Marx predicate his socialism on the achievements of bourgeois civilization.

Herein lay the doctrinal impasse for the Russian Marxists, who were in this respect more Marxist than Marx. Feudalism, capitalism, socialism—the sequence, for them, was rigidly established: *inferno, purgatorio, paradiso,* as it were, and no escaping the divine ordination of things. How, then, to take one's stand for the proletarian revolution when the future for the next lifetime lay with the capitalists? How to be both a revolutionary and a Marxist in Russia?

Lenin's solution, like that of Trotsky and the radical Marxists in general, was based on doctrinal subterfuge, to justify and at the same time obscure an intention to avoid the bourgeois stage of history altogether. For Trotsky it was "permanent revolution," with the *deus* "world revolution" appearing *ex machina* to save the day for the proletarians of Muscovy. Lenin was less consistent in his escape from the dilemma. In 1917 he was to adopt in every respect but name Trotsky's thesis, with all its encouragement of ambitious action in the assurance that the workers of Europe would come to rescue the Russian revolution. Earlier, and after the revolution as well, it was to the peasants that Lenin looked as support for his revolutionary thrust. Contrary to the orthodox strictures of Plekhanovite Marxism, these arguments rested on a twofold faith in Russia—in the peasant as a natural revolutionary, if properly led, and in the mysterious power of Russia to summon from abroad that new regenerative outburst that the foreigners would not achieve without Slavic inspiration. The Bolsheviks' faith in their own power to evoke the saving response abroad is incredible by any standard of rationality, let alone historical materialism. At the extreme, among the Left Communists of 1918, there was more of Dostoevsky than of Marx.

Nevertheless, for Lenin, the support of the peasants and of the Europeans was subsidiary. The central force was the revolutionary movement itself, the conscious organization of the proletariat. In default of an effective middle-class revolutionary movement, this body would conduct the revolution: the bourgeois revolution executed by the proletariat, a socialist government without socialism or even its presumed material prerequisites. Take power, and then—the implication was revealed in the gray postrevolutionary dawn—start "building socialism" by governmental decree. Tsar Peter, self-styled the Great, would have been at home here.

Bolshevik thought is repulsive in its dogmatism, at least to the unconverted. Lenin expressed his intolerance very frankly: "The only choice is: either the bourgeois or the socialist ideology. There is no middle course. . . . Hence, to belittle the socialist ideology *in any way, to turn away from it in the slightest degree,* means to strengthen bourgeois ideology."[1] The Truth is comprehended intuitively, and revolutionaries persuade themselves that they enjoy its exclusive possession. They are anxious about preserving its purity, but nonetheless derive vast confidence from it. To question this faith then becomes criminal. "Lack of faith in the strength and capabilities of our revolution," argued Stalin in 1924, "is what lies at the root of . . . Trotsky's . . . theory of 'permanent revolution,' . . . a variety of Menshevism."[2]

Lenin's intolerance was reinforced by his understanding of the function of doctrine. This was crucial—on correct ideology depended the entire future of the revolution. In default of the successful propagation of uncorrupted socialist doctrine, the working class would fall under the spiritual sway of the bourgeois order, and the cause of revolution would be lost. The decidedly un-Marxian implication is that ideas determine the course of history. No wonder, then, that Lenin was so concerned to maintain what he considered orthodox Marxism: "From this Marxian philosophy, which is cast from a single piece of steel, you cannot eliminate one basic premise, one essential part, without departing from objective truth, without falling prey to a bourgeois-reactionary falsehood."[3]

An echo rings back from the past—how Russian it was to embrace some faith from the West more literally, even, than its author had espoused it! Marx himself opined that young Russian aristocrats "always run after the most extreme that the West can offer. This does not prevent the same Russians, once they enter State service, from becoming rascals."[4] An eloquent example of this radical Russian Westernism comes from N. V. Butashevich-Petrashevsky (memorable for the 1848 arrest of his "circle," which included the young Dostoevsky): "The social science of the West said its last word, gave us the forms in which must be molded the final development of mankind. . . . The genius of

Fourier freed us from the great work of invention, gave us the true doctrine."[5] Yet in the very effort to follow so faithfully, distortion was facilitated and the spirit betrayed. Lenin in all sincerity believed none to be a better Marxist than himself, an assurance that made it all the easier for him to redrape the cloak of doctrine over underlying premises that were entirely foreign to it.

For most Russian revolutionaries, the revolution was an end in itself. It was not a mere instrument but an absolute value, a kind of social purgation, gratifying to contemplate. To consider any solution other than total upheaval was immoral. Here is the root of Bolshevik disgust with "opportunism." Alexander Herzen once said of "reformers," before he became one himself, "On the whole, they do nothing but lay down the pontoons so that the peoples whom they have themselves led onward can cross from one bank to the other. For themselves there is no place beyond a shadowy and constitutional 'neither the one nor the other.'"[6]

To the Russian mind, revolution was not simply a commandment by the goddess of historical materialism—there was, in fact, no genuine faith in historical materialism. Lenin found it perfectly natural to argue in "What Is to Be Done?" in that famous passage about trade union consciousness, that the workings of historical materialism—the "spontaneity" that he found so odious—would, if left alone, *prevent* the revolution, not bring it about.[7] He was taking a leaf from the nihilist Pyotr Tkachev, who had written, "We cannot wait. . . . We assert that the revolution in Russia is urgently essential, and essential at this very time. . . . It is now or very remote, perhaps never!" In another context Tkachev warned, "A revolutionary doesn't prepare a revolution, he 'makes' it. Do this! Do it quickly! Any irresolution, any delay, is criminal."[8] What was Lenin saying in October 1917? "The Bolsheviks must *take power immediately*. . . . To hesitate is a crime. . . . It is my deepest conviction that if we 'await' the Congress of Soviets and let the present moment pass, we *ruin* the revolution."[9]

The emotional power of the idea "revolution" is one of the overwhelming facts of the Russian tradition. This primeval anarchism would be content with nothing save the total destruction of all authority—Lenin's *State and Revolution* reads in places like a Bakuninist tract—and the price is of no concern, though it be a power worse than the one destroyed. "My God is negation," exclaimed the radical literateur Vissarion Belinsky.[10] Everything hung on the act of rebellion, an eschatological leap to the City of God. All Good, all values paled before this: No human activity could have independent significance apart from its contribution to this political drama of salvation. Here is the premise of the "civic art" philosophy. No possible contribution to the goal, not even from the arts, could be left neglected and not enlisted in the cause, for the outcome remained in doubt; it was now or never. A political act would decide all else. This is a contingent determinism of a type wholly alien to Marx.

Lenin, it need hardly be said, was preeminently a practitioner of revolution. Theory was but a device, bent to the requirements of the goal bequeathed to him by the Russian tradition. It was natural, therefore, that his thinking about revolution dealt mainly with tactics, the *how* rather than the *why* of revolution. The *how* he expressed above all in his idea of the party.

The party was the core of Bolshevism, the indispensable instrument of revolution. This meant, for Lenin, military discipline in an elite corps of professional revolutionaries. There was, indeed, something neither Russian nor Marxist, but oddly Prussian, about this disciplinarian admirer of Clausewitz. (Perhaps it was the Volga-German influence in Lenin's upbringing.) Absent the party, Lenin discounted almost as much among the intelligentsia as among the workers any natural ability to become real revolutionaries—the workers would become trade unionists, and the intellectuals would lose themselves in the empty wrangling of the "circles."

But where Lenin's party was un-Russian, it was tailored to cover a very Russian deficiency in respect to organizational facility and self-discipline. Here, no doubt, is the secret of some of the Bolshevik appeal and a key to the party's success in ruling as well. The party would give both the intellectuals and the masses what they needed for successful revolution—unity, efficiency, will, and the infallible guide of correct doctrine. The party would provide the essential means to secure the objective that it alone could guarantee—the success of the revolution. "In its struggle for power the proletariat has no other weapon but organization," Lenin wrote. "The proletariat can become, and inevitably will become, an invincible force only when its ideological unification by the principles of Marxism is consolidated by the material unity of an organization which will weld millions of toilers into an army of the working class."[11]

Underlying the doctrine of the party were certain presumptions that make up the real foundation of Lenin's philosophy. There could be no revolution without the party, without the right leader, and without the correct doctrine. The masses, left to themselves, would never become a revolutionary force. Western Marxists and most Russian Social Democratic leaders recoiled in horror from the dictatorial "Blanquism" that they sensed in Lenin's phrases. For the European, the factory generated revolution; in the eyes of the Russian, the factory threatened to smother it. Revolution, as Lenin had it, must be brought to the masses by a body of dedicated and inspired intellectuals. The *narodniki* could have said as much. And no class basis could be adduced to account for the rebellion of the guilty aristocrats: Commitment to the revolution came from an act of sheer moral dedication.

The trend of emendation in Lenin's reading of Marx is consistent and clear. The general, the natural, the economic, the mass are supplanted by the individual, the moral, the political, the willful. Economic conditions and mass movements cease to be decisive. The revolution, in sum, is the resultant of ethics, will, and power. This is the stuff of the Russian philosophy of history.

The view of history shared by most nineteenth-century Russian revolutionaries, though not often systematically expressed, was in its essence firmly consistent. Basic to the thinking of this school of "Russian subjectivism" were certain propositions concerning the nature of society that were first articulated by the lonely philosopher Pyotr Chaadaev. Chaadaev postulated a tie between hierarchy and process: "The masses are subject to certain forces located at the summit of society. They do not think themselves; there are among them a certain number of thinkers who think for them, who give impetus to the collective intelligence of the nation and make it go forward. Just as this small number think, the rest feel, and the general movement takes place."[12] Russia's peculiar weakness, inherited from its uncivilized past, lay in the near absence of such creative thinkers—all initiative was concentrated in the state: "The deepest trait of our historical physiognomy is the absence of spontaneity in our social development."[13] Herzen, despite his revolutionary fervor, also found the masses essentially passive, depending on "revelation, . . . apostles, men whose faith, will, convictions, and force coincide perfectly with their own."[14] The radical publicist Nikolai Chernyshevsky voiced a like view, speaking of the rare men of genuine intellect: "They are the primal sources of energy. . . . Knowledge is the essential energy to which politics, industry, and all else in human life are subordinated."[15] The masses were characteristically a tabula rasa, inert but receptive to whatever a driving leadership might inscribe.

Given these assumptions, the state and the exercise of political power acquired decisive responsibility for Russia's historical development. Pleaded Chaadaev, "If only a sovereign will would speak out among us, it would suffice to efface every opinion, make every belief bend, make every spirit open itself to the new thought that is offered to it."[16] The apotheosis of Peter the Great was inevitable, and in this Chaadaev initiated that curious but enduring fashion in Russian political thought, the dream of the tsar-revolutionary.

From the conception of society—especially Russian society—as a milling herd given direction only when inspired shepherds took command, it was natural to proceed to a doctrine of elitism when prospects of actual revolutionary activity opened up. Said Herzen, "The masses want a social government that will govern *for them,* and not against them, as at present. To govern themselves—this idea never occurs to them."[17] For Pyotr Lavrov it was the "critically thinking individual," without whose dedicated efforts no progress could be made out of the morass of social injustice. "The time for unconscious suffering and dreaming has gone by," he wrote in his *Historical Letters.* "The time has come for calm, conscious practitioners." Linking the latter with the masses was the party: "Its core is a small number of experienced, thoughtful, energetic people for whom critical thought is inseparable from action."[18] Lenin could have asked for no more.

To be sure, Lenin strove to cast the aura of scientific necessity about his patently Russian postulates on revolutionary strategy. But in this he was no more successful than some of his predecessors. Chernyshevsky tried similarly to conform to the materialist fashion of his time but could not dispense with the ultimate decisiveness of individual leaders—"strong personalities, who by the character of their action give this or that character to the unchangeable direction of events, accelerate or retard their movement, and who by their superior force *impart a right direction* to that chaotic tumult of forces that animate the mass of the people."[19] Here, as with Lenin, predestination had the paradoxical effect of stimulating the sense of individual responsibility and action.

Plekhanov, in what is perhaps the most sophisticated defense of historical materialism that does not abandon its own postulates, had to concede a good deal to appease the voluntaristic bent of the Russians. His best answer was his suggestion that the scope of possible individual influence, such as Madame Pompadour's in the era of King Louis XV, was itself determined by the character of the social system, and could vary accordingly.[20] Perhaps one can say that the historical development of Russian society, as the Russians saw it, was determined to be undetermined.

Where a small minority of enlightened individuals held the future in its hands, motives for its hoped-for action had to be established. Not even here, however, did the Russians really accept determinism. It was ethical commitment on the revolutionary lines dictated by knowledge and conscience that alone could impel the decisive minority to assume its historical role. To the Populist Nikolai Mikhailovsky, free moral dedication was so vital that it demanded a struggle against "objective" necessity, if need be.[21] The motif "against the stream" is prominent throughout the history of Bolshevism. Proclaimed Stalin, "There are no fortresses which Bolsheviks cannot capture."[22] The *Narodnaya Volya* (the People's Will) was able to demand of its members, "Promise to dedicate all your spiritual strength to the revolution. . . . Give all of yourself to the secret society."[23] To become a revolutionary was, for those who enjoyed the requisite consciousness, a moral obligation. This axiom, as expounded by Chernyshevsky, appears to have made an indelible impression on the young Lenin.[24]

The revolution attracted its devotees as an ethical objective, as a good per se. The old order is diseased and dying, as Herzen so dramatically depicted it. Revolution, and only revolution, will bring freshness, rejuvenation, new life.[25] For Bakunin, the destructive urge is a creative urge—the slate is to be wiped clean, the foul excrescences of the past must be purged. A primordial radicalism gripped the Russian revolutionary movement: The system had to go. To temporize with less than total solutions was to betray the revolution. "Every political revolution that does not have economic equality as its *immediate* and *direct* aim," wrote Bakunin, "is, from the point of view of popular interests and rights, only a hypocritical and disguised reaction."[26]

It is remarkable how seldom utilitarian considerations figured in the calculations of these people, who were, after all, professed socialists. For some, economic progress was welcome as a preliminary to the establishment of the new moral order. This was true for people like Chernyshevsky and the more orthodox Marxists, who tried to make their thinking materialist. For other individuals, economic progress was highly suspect—thus Tkachev, Lenin, and the Populists, all fearing that Russia's revolutionary potential would be dissipated by reform or industrialization. Russia's virtue, in the legend going back to Chaadaev and Herzen, lay in its very backwardness, its freedom from the bondage of past successes. Russia had nothing to lose but its chains.

The nature of the anticipated Russian revolution followed logically from the emotions with which the revolutionary idea was invested. Europe's footsteps were to be avoided; the bourgeois order was an abyss of corruption that Russia must escape—and could escape, if guided by its Slavic instincts—in the ascent to social perfection. Parliaments, constitutions, the whole range of liberal political ideals had to contend in Russia with the stubborn prejudice against everything that appeared to represent bourgeois society. How, then, could Marxism, forecasting that very success of capitalism that so repelled them, have had such an appeal among the Russian intelligentsia? It was the fascination of the stage beyond: Russia could transcend its fear of capitalism and accept the bourgeois order in the assurance that the moneyed class could be exploited and then tossed on the trash heap of history. Nevertheless, the less tether allowed the capitalist beast the better, and the revolutionaries had best get themselves quickly installed in the decisive position, the possession of governmental power. Here was Lenin's solution.

Lenin was a Russian revolutionary in heart and soul, though Marxism was on the tip of his tongue. The basic assumptions of the revolutionaries before him were Lenin's as well. They can be summarized, with fair accuracy, thus: History is made by ideas, moral ideas. Ideas are effective as they enlist in their service the willful action of enlightened individuals. The moral decision and the commitment to struggle are crucial. The goal is the historical Armageddon, the revolution, when the forces of Good marshal their ranks against the forces of Evil in the decisive battle, the fight for control of governmental power. Afterward will reign the blissful peace of socialism.

The religious influence in this revolutionary schema is obvious. Any apocalyptic radicalism, including Marxism, shares it. Complementing such doctrine is the quasi-religious psychology of the Russian revolutionaries, so often described with its manifestations of guilt, atonement, martyrdom, fanaticism, even asceticism. Lenin's standards for a Social Democratic party member have many times before, in different garb, been the basis for selecting a priesthood.

It remains to seek out the reasons for the historical premises of the Russian revolutionaries, to attempt, as it were, a determinist explanation of the popularity of the indeterminist philosophy. The task is not hard. Russian thinkers of the nineteenth century were obviously indulging in generalization about their own society. In Russia, ideas, leaders, will, force, power were indeed decisive, or far more so relative to the constellation of social forces than in the complex societies of Western Europe. Hypertrophy of the state and the efficacy of power and violence figure prominently in almost any interpretation of the Russian past.

One could fruitfully apply here the notion that determinacy and indeterminacy in historical events are themselves functions of the structure of society. The more complex, decentralized, or individualistic is the social system, then the more the development of the whole is independent of individual wills and discrete powers. Conversely, the less complex or the more autocratic the society, the more that political power engulfs organized social life, then the more may certain individual wills and decisions affect the course of events. The conclusion is a paradoxical one: Self-descriptions by both sides to the contrary, democracy is where determinism works and totalitarianism is the sphere where the voluntaristic philosophy applies.

It follows that the philosophy of Russian subjectivism was an accurate rendering of the way things happened and were going to happen in Russia. The doctrine of critically thinking individuals taking it upon themselves to push the revolution along was literally a description of the behavior of the Russian intelligentsia. The masses were in fact passive and backward; though capable of violent outbursts, they were quite lacking in organizational capacity or staying power. It was perfectly natural to conclude that revolution was the only way to surmount the obstacle of a medieval monarchy trying to hang on in defiance of modernity, and that the only way to succeed was to counterpose superior force, superior leadership, and superior organization. Lenin, when he twisted his Marxism to fit the Russian scene, was correct—or at least a good case could be made for his doctrines, though he was not intellectually honest with himself. It was no doubt true that the working class, left to itself, would fail to become revolutionary. We have the evidence of Western Europe and America. Marx, with respect to this prediction, was wrong, and Lenin was right—right in proportion as he ceased to be Marxist.

Can a given set of thought patterns, such as the voluntarism of the Russian revolutionaries, have a reciprocal influence on society? More autocratic societies such as prerevolutionary Russia are particularly susceptible to the influence of ideas if they are embodied in decisively placed individuals. In the Russian case, at least, the autocratic political situation repeatedly prompted historical theories putting a premium on individual will, power, and ideas. Lenin's organizational doctrine was merely the most highly developed product of this milieu. In turn, the voluntarist philosophy pointed directly to the seizure of power and the erection of a new autocracy. Mutual reinforcement between autocratic society and voluntaristic philosophy actually took place: The Soviet government was as potent as its predecessor, or more so, and the Marxian verbiage lost most of its determinist meaning through the process of reinterpretation.

The end point in this development came with the doctrinal freewheeling of the Stalin era. The strictures of Marxism, which Lenin strove to assimilate into his Russian nature, were now dissolved and flushed away. The state was frankly hailed as the driving force in social change; properly inspired leaders, at each critical juncture, took command and turned the course of history to its appointed destination. "Never before in history," declared Stalin's staff theologian, "has any party or state ever played . . . so great and decisive a role in the development of the productive forces as that being played by our party and our Soviet Socialist state."[27] All this is quite correct. Soviet history was indeed made by leaders and political power. The record fully accords with the statist background of Russian society and with the voluntarist philosophy of the Russian revolutionaries.

CHAPTER 4

The Bolsheviks and the Intelligentsia

There is a well-established historical consensus on the nature of the Russian intelligentsia and the distinctive part it played in bringing on the revolution. Typically, the nineteenth-century Russian intellectual was detached from practical affairs, committed to some sort of abstract doctrine, and morally alienated by the autocracy and class privilege. This reaction reflected the cultural precociousness of Russia's Westernized upper class, contrasting with the frustrating backwardness of the government and the economy. Educated and sensitive Russians had nowhere to turn except to theory.

The cultural cleavage between this theorizing elite and the toiling masses left enduring traces—for example, in the long-standing classification of the Soviet population into workers, peasants, and "toiling intelligentsia" and in the remarkable prestige enjoyed by academic pursuits in Russia. There was a saying going around Moscow in the 1950s that neatly expresses the survival of these distinctions: "Trudiashchiesya mnogo rabotayut a malo dumayut; intelligentsiya mnogo dumaet a malo rabotaet" (The toilers work a lot but don't think much; the intelligentsia thinks a lot but doesn't work much).

While some of the nineteenth-century flavor obviously survived, the simple distinction of intellectuals and masses is not adequate in dealing with revolutionary and postrevolutionary Russia. Only backward, static, and hierarchical societies have a more or less homogenous intelligentsia, as in Russia up to the middle of the nineteenth century. After that, under the impact of modernization and industrialization, important differences emerged among various groups that still had the intellectual label. One can distinguish the "literary intelligentsia," the "technical intelligentsia," and the "quasi-intelligentsia."

The nineteenth-century Russian intelligentsia was largely made up of literary intellectuals. That group included not only writers but anyone interested in the creation and transmission of ideas, who pursued artistic, literary, political, scientific, philosophical, or religious matters as ends in themselves—in other words, the audience as well as the performers, more concerned with ideas than with everyday pursuits. This describes the gentry intelligentsia in nineteenth-century Russia, in Western Europe up to the eighteenth century, and in the static civilizations of the East before the impact of Westernization.

The literary intelligentsia was the seedbed of the revolutionary movement. Until the emancipation of the serfs in 1861, critical thought and organized revolutionary action were almost exclusively the work of wellborn devotees of abstract theory. With the expansion of education after the middle of the nineteenth century, the social sources of the intelligentsia broadened, and the so-called *raznochintsy,* or "men of various ranks," made their appearance. The political importance of the intelligentsia grew steadily during the second half of the nineteenth century. Intellectuals—whatever their background—supplied the principal leadership for the three great class parties that developed in the early 1900s: the Social Democrats for the workers, the Socialist Revolutionaries for the peasants, and the Constitutional Democrats for the middle class.

As the base of the intelligentsia broadened and its numbers multiplied, it acquired a new flavor and differently motivated elements. The broad, fuzzy, passionate, humane thinking of the older intellectuals like Herzen had to share ground with the doctrinaire pseudoscientific narrowness of the Nihilists and their intellectual descendants. Here is Ivan Turgenev's classic distinction between the "fathers" and the "sons," as devotion to principles gave way more and more to commitment to a cause or to an organization.

The quasi-intelligentsia is a characteristic development in backward societies that have come under Western influence and the pressure to modernize. It is made up of people who are not really intellectuals with a genuine interest in ideas, but who are merely seeking status by taking on the appearances of education and intellectuality. This occurs when culture change shakes up a country's traditions and makes large numbers of people aware of the possibility of advancing themselves. Many lower-class persons with some ability note the prestige that intellect shares with wealth. Since they lack wealth, they try to assume an intellect. But real intellectuals must either be very good themselves or have other income from property or profession. Rising quasi-intellectuals have no wealth but disdain practical work. They are not good enough to earn a living as creative intellectuals. If there is no other opening for them, they become frustrated and resentful members of the intellectual proletariat, ready recruits for a revolutionary movement. (This picture is supported by biographical data on the People's Will organization, the assassins of Tsar Alexander II, which show a disproportionately large number of nongentry intellectuals from the Ukraine and other border regions—where Western influences were stronger and society as a whole was more in flux.[1])

The rebellious quasi-intelligentsia is a familiar force in many parts of the world today, particularly in South Asia and the Moslem world. It became an important political factor in late-nineteenth-century Russia when the ranks of the intelligentsia were swelled by people of this new type. It is of course true that many nongentry intellectuals became first-rate, self-supporting thinkers—Belinsky, Chernyshevsky, and Trotsky, to mention a few—and there was no sharp line between the real intellectuals and the status seekers. On the other hand, the half-insane egoism of such lowborn revolutionary students as Pyotr Zaichnevsky and Sergei Nechaev marked the appearance of the true quasi-intellectual. The growing dogmatism of the revolutionary parties by the early 1900s testifies to the increasing role of the quasi-intellectual element in their ranks. And by that time, political interest was beginning to decline among the real literary intelligentsia, as illustrated by the new religious bent of the Vekhi group and the nonpolitical modernist currents in the arts.

The event that brought the quasi-intelligentsia into its own as a political force was the formation of the Bolshevik Party. To be sure, Lenin did not exclude real intellectuals from the party—he could easily qualify as a literary intellectual himself—but the ideas on which he based the organization were extraordinarily well adapted to the thinking and ambitions of the quasi-intelligentsia. In his conception of the revolutionary party, Lenin followed Russian tradition, rather than Marxism, by discounting spontaneous mass action. It is often presumed that Lenin relied instead on the intellectuals to provide the revolutionary impetus, but this is not strictly true. He did not rely on the real intellectuals, the literary intelligentsia.

Lenin's writings are replete with violent anti-intellectualism. For example, when he was organizing his separate Bolshevik faction after the Social Democrats split in 1903, he attacked his opponents with such barbs as "the unstable mentality of the intellectual," "bourgeois intellectuals who fight shy of proletarian discipline and organization," "the flabbiness and instability of the intellectual," "bourgeois-intellectual individualism," "spineless whining of intellectuals," "[a] Girondist who yearns for professors and high-school students, who is afraid of the dictatorship of the proletariat," "aristocratic anarchism . . . characteristic of the Russian nihilist."[2] A decade later Lenin had not changed a bit. In 1914, attacking Trotsky and the Mensheviks, he railed against "the arrogantly conceited leaders of coteries of intellectuals." [3] During the party crisis on the eve of the October Revolution, when he called for Zinoviev and Kamenev to be expelled from the party, he wrote, "Only in this way is it possible to make the workers' party healthy, to cleanse ourselves of a dozen spineless intellectuals, and . . . march with the revolutionary workers."[4]

Lenin distrusted the workers for their lack of consciousness, and he despised the intellectuals for their lack of discipline. Then to what social group did he turn? This was never stated in so many words, but implicitly Lenin was appealing to the quasi-intelligentsia. His pronouncements enabled them to feel different from the workers and superior to the literary intellectuals. He gave them hard-and-fast statements of simple doctrine to which they could adhere without question. He gave them a cause to work for and full sanction for their feelings of dogmatic intolerance and hostility. In other underdeveloped countries, the quasi-intellectuals have often turned to the army as the vehicle of their would-be historical mission. In Russia they found it in the Bolshevik Party. The essence of Communism could be described as the rebellion of the quasi-intelligentsia.

During and immediately after the Russian Revolution, the political lines between the different types of intelligentsia were by no means clear. The Bolshevik Party contained a strong contingent of genuine intellectuals, and the revolution evoked much sympathy among the literary intellectuals outside its ranks. However, the Bolsheviks' involvement with the real intelligentsia proved to be a chronic source of discord. The antagonism between the literary intellectuals adhering to Communist principles and the quasi-intellectuals attracted to the Communist organization was a major factor in the factional controversies that rocked the party between 1918 and 1929.

The outcome of these struggles in the party was the complete victory of the quasi-intelligentsia. It found leadership in one of its own number, Joseph Vissarionovich Stalin. Stalin, the half-educated divinity student, made his standards clear when in 1927 he called the Trotsky opposition "a group of petty-bourgeois intellectuals, divorced from life, divorced from the revolution, divorced from the party, from the working class."[5]

In 1929, politically triumphant under Stalin's leadership, the quasi-intelligentsia commenced the wholesale destruction of the literary intelligentsia. Up to this time, genuine intellectual activity was still flourishing in Soviet Russia, despite the political constraints introduced by the revolution. Russian intellectuals were abreast or even in the lead of modern trends in almost every cultural field. All this came to an end after 1929, as absolute party standards and totalitarian controls were imposed on one area of intellectual activity after another. The Communist Party condemned every idea of more recent vintage than 1890 as "formalism" or "bourgeois idealism." As the quasi-intellectuals of the party apparatus found their great opportunity, the genuine intellectual interests of the literary intelligentsia were completely eradicated from Russian public life. A symbol of this victory of the quasi-intelligentsia was the obscene adulation of Stalin as history's greatest genius in every conceivable field of thought.

As Stalin's pose indicates, the triumph of the quasi-intelligentsia did not mean the explicit repudiation of intellectuality. Intellectual discourse was captured and watered down to what the quasi-intellectuals of the party understood, liked, or found useful. To paraphrase the official definition of Socialist Realism, culture became intellectual in form, quasi-intellectual in content. The quasi-intellectual clings to the appearances of intellectuality, for this is what confers a sense of achievement—hence the Communist passion for "theory." However, the quasi-intellectual is secure only when theory becomes unchallengeable dogma and when the competition of genuine intellectuals has been eliminated. This is accomplished by political control: Literary intellectuals, if not liquidated, are impressed into an entirely different function. They become paid propagandists, members of the vast new class of specialized experts to which the Russians conveniently gave the name "technical intelligentsia."

The technical intelligentsia, like the quasi-intelligentsia, is a product of particular social conditions, in this case the rise of modern industrial and technological society. The technical intelligentsia is the class of trained experts and professional people, whose status and income is based on their specialized education and skills. Where the technical intelligentsia is well developed, as in the countries of the West that were earlier to industrialize, the quasi-intelligentsia is not a significant force. Here the status of intellect is not so exclusively attractive, and many other avenues of advancement are open. People with ambition and modest ability can get training and employment in thousands of specialized occupations and thus become members of the technical intelligentsia instead of the quasi-intelligentsia. In an advanced country with a good educational system and ample job opportunities in the technical intelligentsia, the problem of the revolutionary quasi-intelligentsia is ruled out.

A technical intelligentsia began to appear on a modest scale in Russia in the later nineteenth century. Job opportunities for trained expertise began to expand after the reforms of the 1860s, at first mainly in the professions and government service, but by the turn of the century in industry as well. Politically, this growing technical intelligentsia was inclined to the liberalism of the Constitutional Democrats, although it never became a very effective force.

The Bolsheviks gave little heed to the technical intelligentsia or its functions until they were on the verge of taking power. Lenin's writings on this problem in 1917 were highly ambivalent, but once in power, he turned sharply toward the technical intelligentsia, or the "bourgeois specialists," as they were termed immediately after the revolution. There was no practical alternative, even though ideological purists in the Communist Party at first objected loudly to what they regarded as betrayal of the proletarian ideal. The so-called proletarian revolution in Russia had occurred in a country where capitalist industrial development had just got under way, and one of the main tasks facing the Communists was to continue this development. To do so, they were compelled to use the small technical intelligentsia that already existed in Russia while trying to train proletarians to take over the work. But the result was simply to add new people to the technical intelligentsia. The hierarchy of education, income, and success became a permanent Soviet institution. Some sociological data has suggested that individual members or descendants of the old privileged classes actually had a better chance than workers and peasants to move into the Soviet intelligentsia.[6]

By the postwar years, the technical intelligentsia was as elaborately developed in the Soviet Union as in any country in the world. It stood out even more sharply because it did not share its status with the nonintellectual business class that figures prominently in capitalist countries. The only way to get ahead in Russia was to get a specialized education and a government job. There was no longer any reason for a quasi-intelligentsia to exist.

Nevertheless, Soviet society still bore traces of its quasi-intellectual heritage in the mentality of the Communist Party. There was chronic friction between the party apparatus and the technical people of all sorts whom it controlled, undoubtedly intensified by the intellectual disparity between the quasi-intelligentsia and the technical intelligentsia. By Khrushchev's time, however, this distinction appeared to be on the wane, especially with his effort to make the party apparatus acquire technical competence and provide direct supervision for technical work. The party officialdom was becoming simply a managerial branch of the technical intelligentsia.

The place of the intellectual in Russia is ironic. The revolutionary movement was a creature of the old literary intelligentsia, yet ultimately the revolution destroyed its initiator. Power was seized and held by representatives of the quasi-intelligentsia, who tried violently to stamp their way of thinking upon all aspects of Russia intellectual life. But the real victor was the group who had taken the least initiative of all. The technical intelligentsia was indispensable as the key class in modern industrialism, and Soviet ways of living and thinking were adapted step-by-step to fit its interests at the expense of the quasi-intellectual standards of the Stalinists. Any government—or corporate enterprise—that does not effectively recruit, train, employ, and reward experts will fail. Whatever the different histories that various industrial societies have experienced, the results with respect to the technical intelligentsia are remarkably alike. This, on a worldwide scale, is the rise of the "meritocracy."

CHAPTER 5

Lenin's Vision
The State and Revolution

I n virtually all quarters, Lenin's *State and Revolution* is accepted as the core of his doctrine of revolution and the proletarian dictatorship. It was even used as evidence in the 1948 trial of the leaders of the American Communist Party for conspiring to overthrow the government. And to Soviet commentators no less than to their most bitter adversaries, *State and Revolution* set up the premises from which Soviet reality was considered to be the logical conclusion.

Yet in fact, *State and Revolution* is a work conforming neither to Lenin's previous thought nor to his subsequent practice. It stands as a monument to its author's intellectual deviation during the year of revolution, 1917. Nevertheless, the ideas of *State and Revolution,* permeated with an idealistic, almost utopian spirit, were made to serve as the reference point for rationalizing the subsequent evolution of the Soviet state in an entirely different direction.

In *State and Revolution* Lenin developed for the first time a political program for the proletarian dictatorship that was to come after the expected revolutionary victory. The plan was not complicated in its outlines, comprising three main provisions for the ordering of the new body politic: (1) the destruction of the repressive machinery of the bourgeois state; (2) the establishment of a real democracy of the working class, with political representatives strictly subordinate to the will of the masses; (3) transfer of the tasks of administration directly into the hands of the masses. Lenin summarized the future regime thus: "The workers, having conquered political power, will break up the old bureaucratic apparatus, they will shatter it to its very foundations, until not one stone is left

upon another; and they will replace it with a new one consisting of these same
workers and employees, *against* whose transformation into bureaucrats measures will at once be undertaken, as pointed out in detail by Marx and Engels:
1) not only electiveness, but also instant recall; 2) payment no higher than that
of ordinary workers; 3) immediate transition to a state of things when *all* fulfill
the functions of control and superintendence, so that *all* become bureaucrats
for a time, and *no one,* therefore, can become a 'bureaucrat.'"[1] Such would be
the constitution of the regime intended to liquidate the remnants of the bourgeois order, superintend the socialist reorganization of the economy, and pave
the way for the transition to the stateless society of communism.

In this vision, Lenin mentioned the party, as an element in his theory of
the revolution, exactly *once,* and then only obliquely.[2] The central position that
the party otherwise held in his thought hardly needs to be stressed. In "What
Is to Be Done?" he declared, "The spontaneous struggle of the proletariat will
not become a genuine 'class struggle' until it is led by a strong organization of
revolutionaries," that is, the party.[3] For Lenin, the party was the key element
in the revolution. Inside the party, "[a]s regards the ideological and practical
direction of the movement and the revolutionary struggle of the proletariat,
the greatest possible centralization is necessary. To lead the movement we must
have the smallest possible number of the most single-minded groups, of professional revolutionaries tested by experience."[4] This is far removed from the faith
in the masses that Lenin proclaimed in 1917 and more in line with his reliance
after the revolution on "iron discipline," "obedience of labor," "centralization
of economic administration" where "[t]he elective principle must be replaced
by the principle of *selection.*"[5] In 1921 he summed up his postrevolutionary
philosophy in a single sentence: "The dictatorship of the proletariat is impossible except through the Communist Party."[6]

Lenin cannot be understood within the usual conception of Bolshevik history as a straight line of unfolding Leninist strategy, flanked by deviations that
split off in either direction. In reality, two distinct lines of thought and policy
ran through the Bolshevik movement almost from its inception to the political
destruction of the Left Opposition in 1927.[7] Of these currents, the dominant
one was the Leninist—the familiar doctrine and organization that the party's
founder expounded up until 1917 and from 1918 on. Stalin eventually inherited
the leadership of this stream. The other tendency was represented by various
self-styled Left Opposition groups. Not that the Leninist element was particularly "rightist"; it was distinguished, rather, by its organizational "hardness."
The Leninist and leftist streams of thought originated in separate prerevolutionary splits from the prevailing Social Democratic orthodoxy, in two different

dimensions reflecting their organizational hardness or programmatic leftness. For a time, many followers of these two tendencies believed themselves to be in the same camp, until disagreements arose after the Revolution of 1905. However, a number of future Left Oppositionists, from Trotsky on down, remained outside the Bolshevik ranks as late as 1917.

Between the two wings of the Bolshevik-Communist Party there were clear-cut and consistent differences of outlook. The leftists emphasized the egalitarian and anarchistic social goals of the revolution and pressed for the rapid realization of them; the Leninists stressed the means of struggle and the organization of power to attain their goals. The leftists were revolutionary idealists, the Leninists revolutionary pragmatists. In their backgrounds, the leftists tended to be middle-class intellectuals, the Leninists proletarian or peasant and nonintellectual and less likely, as well, to have had experience as emigrés in the West. Understandably, then, the leftists tended toward a theoretical and international outlook, the Leninists toward a practical and national approach.

Over the years the leftist tendency was expressed fairly consistently by a succession of oppositionist groups—the Otzovists, Ultimatists, and Vperyodists during the period 1907–1912, the "Left Bolsheviks" during the war years, the Left Communists in 1918, the Democratic Centralists and the Workers' Opposition during the period of War Communism, the Trotskyists in 1921 and again from 1923 to 1927. The year 1917 was different, thanks in part to the revolutionary situation and the influx of non-Bolshevik leftists into the party. But the decisive factor was Lenin himself, as his goal of a second revolution led him to shift from his own Leninist wing to the leftist wing of the party. This is why Lenin's April Theses were such a shock to most of the people from the underground Bolshevik organization. Gaining momentum, the leftist upsurge carried the party through 1917 and, overriding objections on the part of some of Lenin's formerly closest disciples, consummated the victory of October. *State and Revolution,* placed in this context as the most complete formulation of the leftist program, begins to make some sense.

Up until 1916, in company with most of his Social Democratic contemporaries, Lenin had given little or no attention to the problems treated in *State and Revolution* or to the works of Marx and Engels in which these questions were originally discussed. Quite suddenly, late in 1916 and early in 1917, he developed an avid interest in these matters and commenced the study and writing that eventually took published form in *State and Revolution.* This sudden focus on the theory of the revolutionary state was apparently instrumental in precipitating his shift over to the leftist stream of Bolshevik thought.

Primary credit for inspiring Lenin's new thinking belongs to Nikolai Bukharin, at that moment the most prominent leader of the left-wing Bolsheviks. Bukharin's influence on Lenin was noted by the editor of the collection of Lenin's notes and miscellaneous writings, *Leninskii Sbornik*, published in 1924: "Under the pseudonym of 'Nota Bene,' N. I. Bukharin placed in no. 6 of the journal *Jugendinternationale* an article on the question of the state, in which he subjected to criticism the commonly held but in fact Kautskian interpretation of the teaching of Marx on the state. It was precisely this article that induced Vladimir Ilyich to occupy himself more closely with the corresponding question. From the article prepared by Vladimir Ilyich arose his work *State and Revolution*."[8] In a letter to Alexandra Kollontai of 17 February 1917, Lenin wrote, "I am preparing an article on the question of the relation of Marxism to the state. I have already come to conclusions more sharply against Kautsky than against Bukharin."[9]

The article that attracted Lenin's attention was "Der imperialistische Raubstaat" (The Imperialist Robber-State), one of a series in which Bukharin argued that a fundamental task of the proletarian revolution was the literal destruction of the existing bourgeois state. The rationale of this program Bukharin set forth most profoundly in another article, where he revealed what in retrospect can be seen as amazing prophetic insight. This was "Teoriya imperialisticheskogo gosudarstva" (The Theory of the Imperialist State), an essay so apt as an analysis of a major social trend of the twentieth century that its virtual oblivion imperatively should be remedied.[10]

Bukharin's thesis in this article was that in the era of imperialism a new form of political and social organization was evolving out of bourgeois society. This was militaristic state capitalism, under which, he wrote, "[t]he state power sucks in almost all areas of production; it not only embraces the general conditions of the exploitative process; the state becomes more and more a direct exploiter, which organizes and directs production, as a collective capitalist."[11] The ultimate result of this tendency would be "a new Leviathan, in comparison with which the fantasy of Thomas Hobbes seems like child's play."[12]

Socialism, to Bukharin's mind, had nothing in common with the totalitarian bureaucratic state whose possible evolution he foresaw: "Socialism is the regulation of production directed by *society*, not by the state. It is the abolition of class contradictions, not their intensification."[13] The proletarian revolution would not simply be the midwife of the new socialist society that was bound to come forth from the shell of the capitalist society. Rather, there were two alternative successors to capitalism—militaristic state capitalism, under which the whole force of social organization bore down on the proletariat to exploit it, where "the worker is transformed into a slave"—*or* socialism. "Theoretically, there can be two possibilities here: Either the workers' organizations, like all the organizations of the bourgeoisie, will merge into the statewide organization and be transformed into a simple appendage of the state apparatus, or they will outgrow the framework of the state and burst it from within, as they organize their own state power (the dictatorship [of the proletariat])."[14] To the proletarian revolution Bukharin assigned the crucial task of forcing the development of society out of the course toward state capitalism and into the course toward socialism. (To his personal misfortune, Bukharin did not realize, until too late, the possibility that a successful proletarian revolution might fail to divert the course of history and, under certain conditions, actually accelerate the evolution of the Leviathan that he so feared.)

The tactical conclusion that Bukharin derived from his theory of contemporary social evolution was ultraradical: "A general attack on the ruling bandits. In the developing revolutionary struggle the proletariat destroys the state organization of the bourgeoisie."[15] Lenin echoed this dictum in *State and Revolution:* "A revolution must not consist in a new class ruling, governing with the help of the *old* state machinery, but in this class *smashing* this machinery and ruling, governing by means of *new* machinery."[16]

In this approach toward the old political order, Bukharin and Lenin were following in the footsteps of certain left-wing European Marxists, notably the Dutch Social Democrat Anton Pannekoek, an astronomer by profession but by avocation a revolutionary theorist. Pannekoek had asserted, "The state power is not a simple neutral object in the class struggle; it is a weapon and a fortress of the bourgeoisie, the strongest support, without which the bourgeoisie could never retain its place."[17] Accordingly, Pannekoek contended, "The struggle of the proletariat is not simply a struggle against the bourgeoisie *over* the state power as an object, but a struggle *against* the state power. The content of this revolution is the destruction and dissolution of the state's means of force by the proletariat's means of force."[18]

Underlying the emphasis placed by Pannekoek, Bukharin, and (following them) Lenin on revolution as an act of smashing the state was an aspect of Marxian political theory that was subject to a great deal of misunderstanding. This was the question of the relation of the state machinery to the class struggle. As popularly understood, Marxism is simple; the state is nothing more than the organ of the ruling class to suppress the masses and maintain the conditions of exploitation.[19] Wrote Bukharin, "From the point of view of Marxism, the state is nothing other than the greatest general organization of the ruling classes, the basic function of which consists of the preservation and extension of the exploitation of the oppressed classes."[20] In *State and Revolution,* Lenin is quite clear on this point: no class conflict, no state.[21]

Reference to the original sources of the Marxian theory of the state reveals a different implication. According to Engels, "The state . . . is by no means a power forced on society from the outside. It is simply a product of society, . . . the confession that this society has become hopelessly divided against itself. . . . In order that . . . classes with conflicting economic interests may not annihilate themselves and society in a useless struggle, a power becomes necessary that stands apparently above society and has the function of keeping down the conflicts and maintaining order. And this power, the outgrowth of society, but assuming supremacy over it and becoming more and more divorced from it, is the state."[22] Here Engels made a point that most of his successors never really grasped: The class struggle explains the origin of the state but not necessarily its continued existence. Once established, the state organization tends to become its own raison d'être and can exist more and more independently of the conditions that originally produced it. To be sure, the state continues to play a role in the class struggle: "This public power of coercion . . . increases in the same ratio in which the class antagonisms become more pronounced, and in which neighboring states become larger and more populous. A conspicuous example is modern Europe, where the class struggles and wars of conquest have nursed the public power to such a size that it threatens to swallow the whole society."[23] Thus Engels took account of a particularly important aspect of the modern state, as a unit in an anarchistic international society, with the consequent pressures of defense and/or aggrandizement. This international role was ignored almost totally in most Marxist thought on the state, though it came to play a key part in Soviet political rationalizations after the revolution.

Marx agreed that the state could become an independent evil in society, apart from any given ruling class. He saw this in France, whose government until 1848 had been "a mere tool in the hands of the dominant class. Not until the second Bonaparte rose to power, does the state seem to have become completely independent. As against bourgeois society, the state machine has fortified itself so thoroughly that the chief of the Society of December the Tenth [Louis Napoleon Bonaparte's brownshirts] can function as its director."[24] Later on, Marx described the Bonapartist dictatorship of the Second Empire as an instance of the state power becoming independent at a time when the contending social classes, in this case bourgeoisie and proletariat, were almost evenly balanced in strength: "It was the only form of government possible at a time when the bourgeoisie had already lost, and the working class had not yet acquired, the faculty of ruling the nation."[25]

The interesting point here lies in Marx's reference to "ruling the nation" as a social function that needs to be carried on entirely apart from the class struggle. This suggests that the class struggle theory of the state was all along supposed to be understood in a limited sense, as referring only to the means by which one class repressed another. Recognizing that the state power could become dangerously independent, Marx drew upon the experience of the Paris Commune to prescribe a course of action to ensure a successful proletarian revolution. In *The Civil War in France,* he outlined measures to end permanently the threat to the proletariat posed by the old state institutions and to "restore to the social body all the forces hitherto absorbed by the state parasite feeding upon, and clogging the free movement of, society."[26] Complete democratic control over all political functions was to be assured by election of all officials, the right of immediate recall of elected officials, limitation of the salaries of all government officials to the level of workmen's wages, local and municipal autonomy as far as practicable, and above all the replacement of all police and military formations by the national guard, that is, the collectivity of the population, the "armed people."[27] The Paris Commune, Marx thought, was "essentially a working-class government, the product of the struggle of the producing against the appropriating class, the political form at last discovered under which to work out the economic emancipation of Labor."[28]

Engels, in his 1891 introduction to *The Civil War in France,* went even further: "The Commune was compelled to recognize from the outset that the working class, once come to power, could not carry on business with the old state machine; that, in order not to lose again its own position of power which it had but just conquered, this working class must, on the one hand, set aside all the old repressive machinery previously used against itself, and on the other, *safeguard itself against its own deputies and officials* by declaring them all, without any exception, subject to recall at any moment." The old governmental organs "had in the course of time, in pursuance of their own special interests, transformed themselves from the servants of society into the masters of society."[29] Since the state was not ultimately a derivative of the class struggle but was (in Engels's Rousseauian phraseology) "created" by "society" "to look after its common interests," there was no reason to conclude that with the termination of the class struggle by a proletarian revolution the state would necessarily wither away. It would simply cease to be an organ of class repression, because there would no longer be classes to be repressed by each other. The state would still exist and would continue to threaten the successful establishment of a socialist society because of the possibility of "transforming itself into the master of society." Therefore the proletariat needed to take the measures of democratic control that Marx had outlined and that the Paris Commune presumably exemplified.[30]

No sooner had Lenin acquainted himself with the program of smashing the bourgeois state than he incorporated it wholeheartedly into his scheme of the revolutionary process. However, he failed to grasp the basic rationale of the smashing dictum—protection of society against the dangerous independence of the state machinery—and as a result, he allowed the entire program of popular control over the exercise of political power to be vitiated after his party came to power. Lenin did not go beyond the narrow class-determined conception of the state. This simple view, justifying all the rigorous measures actually taken later in the name of the dictatorship of the proletariat while promising the ultimate withering away of the state, became binding doctrine for the Communist Party. The subtleties of Marx and Engels about the broader, dangerous aspects of political institutions remained in convenient oblivion as far as Communist theoreticians were concerned.

In *State and Revolution,* Lenin followed Engels on the eventual withering away of the narrowly conceived state: "Once the majority of the people *itself* suppresses its oppressors, a 'special force' for suppression is *no longer necessary.* In this sense the state *begins to wither away.* Instead of a privileged minority, the majority can itself directly fulfill all these functions; and the more the discharge of the functions of state power devolves upon the people generally, the less need is there for the existence of this power."[31] It was, however, only to the state in the narrow sense, as an instrument for class repression, that Lenin applied the dicta of smashing and democratic controls (measures that Marx and Engels had urged to prevent the state in the broader sense from becoming the "master of society").

Lenin's shift after the October Revolution, back to his characteristic emphasis on pragmatic power considerations, was foreshadowed even in *State and Revolution* as he revealed his readiness to maintain a strong institutional authority and to retain the old bureaucratic and managerial personnel. The anarchistic ideal, he reasoned, was rendered utopian in economic affairs by the actual development of the conditions of production under industrialism: "Take a factory, a railway, a vessel on the high seas. Is it not clear that not one of these complex technical units, based on the use of machines and the ordered cooperation of many people, could function without a certain amount of subordination and, consequently, without some authority or power?"[32] This need clearly led to preferment for the trained technical and managerial personnel inherited from the Old Regime: "We need good organizers in banking, and in the work of combining enterprises (in these matters the capitalists have more experience, and work is done more easily with experienced people); we need more and more engineers, agronomists, technicians, scientific experts of every kind. Probably, we shall only gradually bring in equality for all work, leaving a temporary higher rate of pay for such specialists during the transition period, but we shall put them under an all-embracing workers' control. As for the organizational form of the work, we do not invent it, we take it ready-made from capitalism."[33]

Notwithstanding his revolutionary victory, Lenin continued to try to reconcile the narrow, strictly class conception of the state with the patent necessity of organization and authority to direct the growingly complex affairs of modern society. He told a congress of local economic councils in May 1918, "There is no doubt that the further the conquests of the October Revolution advance, the greater and higher will become the role of the economic councils, which alone among all state institutions will preserve for themselves a lasting place. The nearer we come to the establishment of a socialist system, the less we need a purely administrative apparatus, an apparatus engaged only in government, strictly speaking. This apparatus is doomed, after the resistance of the exploiters has definitely been smashed, after the toilers have learned to organize socialist production—this apparatus of administration in the proper, narrow, restricted sense of the world, this apparatus of the old state is doomed to die; but an apparatus of the type of our Supreme Economic Council is destined to grow, develop, and become strong, fulfilling all principal active functions of an organized society."[34] The "state" might wither away, to be sure, but the meaning of "state" and "withering" were being progressively constricted to remove all theoretical constraints on the new revolutionary regime.

After the October Revolution, the party as an institution once again took first place in Bolshevik thinking, and under the pressure of civil war, most party members ceased to take the program of *State and Revolution* seriously. Local councils—the "soviets," literally speaking—supposedly embodied the control measures of the 1917 Bolshevik program, but they fell into abeyance as the locus of real political power shifted to the party and its higher organs. Independent of any popular control or class dominance, the Soviet state did in fact become the "master of society."

PART II

The Bolshevik Revolution

CHAPTER 6

Russia and Revolution

R evolutionaries are often denounced for believing that the end justi-
fies their violent means. But great revolutions are not usually begun deliberately. "A revolution can be neither made nor stopped,"
remarked Napoleon in his St. Helena exile.[1] Revolutions stem from
complex causal patterns of situational proclivities and triggering mechanisms, a
confluence of ultimate and immediate causes. Intentional action by revolutionaries does not usually succeed at all, but only leads to abortive coups and futile
acts of terrorism. In the rare instances where a major revolution is actually initiated by a deliberate coup (for instance, in China in 1911), the revolution may
run a course that far outdistances the intentions and expectations of its initiators. The famous statement by Friedrich Engels comes to mind: "People who
boasted that they had made a revolution have always seen the next day that they
had no idea what they were doing. That the revolution *made* did not in the least
resemble the one they would have liked to make."[2]

A revolution is not an event, it is a process. It develops over a period of years,
through discernible stages. Naturally, different revolutions are not identical, but in
one form or another they all display the same characteristic phases. Schematically
these phases are: the breakdown of the Old Regime; the rule of the moderates; the
dissolution in whole or in part of the old institutional fabric; the emotional mobilization and polarization of the population; and the struggle for power between
left-wing extremists and right-wing counterrevolutionaries. This, of course, is
the model made familiar by the late Crane Brinton in his *Anatomy of Revolution*,
drawing in turn on the less well known but pioneering work by the American
church historian Lyford P. Edwards, *The Natural History of Revolution*.[3]

Up to a point, the Edwards-Brinton model works very well for a multitude of diverse revolutions. But for the later phases of revolution, after the moment of crisis when revolutionary extremism peaks, the model needs to be extended. The breakdown of authority and the emotional mobilization of the populace during a revolution sooner or later bring the country to a crisis whose outcome is historically indeterminate. At that point, a nation's course may lead to left-wing dictatorship, to right-wing dictatorship, or to a precarious moderate balance, and there is substantial scope for individual action and accidental events in deciding the outcome. This is when deliberate choices by revolutionaries can become decisive, when moral judgments can indeed be applied, and when responsibility for the outcome really can be fixed on individual revolutionaries or counterrevolutionaries.

The victory of revolutionary extremism in Russia was the result of just such an indeterminate crisis situation. Bolshevik success was the outcome of personal and unpredictable circumstances, including vigorous leadership, bungling by the counterrevolutionaries, and default by the wrangling parties of the Provisional Government, plus sheer accident and good fortune in the events of October 1917. To say this is not to deny the role of vast social forces among the emotionally aroused populace—the Petrograd workers, the armed forces, and above all the peasantry. Obviously, it was only the process of revolution involving these forces that created even a possibility for the extremist seizure of power. Similarly, the fact that Russia was a relatively undeveloped and unreformed country contributed heavily to the extremists' chances for success. Underdevelopment assured a wider response of unsatisfied social elements, of workers without established organizations, of soldiers without the right to be treated as humans, and above all of peasants without land (or without enough of it). Modern history shows, by and large, that revolutions in less-developed countries where there is a great gap between expectations and satisfaction tend to work out to the advantage of the Left. In more-developed countries, the bulk of the population has something to lose, and if it does succumb to revolution, it will usually swing to the right at the moment of crisis.

There is one aspect of the Russian Revolution that deviates altogether from earlier cases. This was the ability of the regime created by the revolutionary extremists to keep itself in power for decades and avoid an overt thermidorean countercoup or restoration. Of course, it was touch and go for many months in the Russian Civil War, but the Bolsheviks adapted quickly enough in the direction of bureaucratic organization and military methods to avoid the decisive defeat that past revolutionary dictatorships had sooner or later suffered. On the other hand, the Bolsheviks did not institutionalize "permanent revolution" at this point. They managed to maintain the continuity of their regime only by a series of flexible responses to events—the party dictatorship in the civil war, the retreat to state capitalism after the crisis of 1921, the Stalin revolution of collectivization and five-year plans resolving the contradictions of the New Economic Policy. Thanks to this series of responses to concrete social and economic challenges, the Soviet regime all along reflected the continued unfolding of the revolutionary process, even though in muted form, without further explicit overturns in the political system.

The NEP involved suppression of the idealist Ultra Left as well as conceding a partially free economy to the general population. In substance, if not in form, it clearly represented the Thermidor of the Russian Revolution. Following the characteristically extremist regime of War Communism, it was a timely retreat executed by the Communist leadership itself to avert its own overthrow. Seven or eight years later, Russia shifted gears again without any abrupt break in the government, when the NEP yielded to the Stalin revolution. Stalin's enemies were on firm ground when they called the new phase "Bonapartism." To put it a bit more impersonally, the Stalin revolution ushered in the phase of postrevolutionary dictatorship, in which revolutionary slogans were melded with traditional methods to mobilize new national energy in the pursuit of a dictator's grand ambition.

Russia obviously had no restoration comparable to the return of the Stuarts or the Bourbons to their respective thrones. However, if Hitler had been more adroit in World War II and Stalin's government had been toppled, a restoration in some sense might well have been accomplished. But even without this eventuality, developments took place in the era of the Great Purge that in some respects could indeed be regarded as the functional equivalent of a restoration. These changes included the recrystallization of a permanently hierarchical and authoritarian society with conservative and nationalistic norms in its social and cultural policies as well as the wholesale liquidation of old revolutionaries in the climactic episode of the purges, the Yezhovshchina (as it was known from the then commissar of Internal Affairs [the NKVD] Nikolai Yezhov).

While it may be easy to track Russian developments with the classical model of revolution, the Soviet experience was still distinctive. There were, of course, abrupt changes in policies and personnel, and a great discrepancy between the original intentions of the revolutionaries and the outcome that their efforts led to. Nevertheless, the continuity of the Communist regime allowed certain aspects of the early extremist dictatorship to be perpetuated, notably its Marxist-Leninist ideology and its habit of rationalizing everything it did in those terms.

Thanks to its political continuity, the Russian Revolution bequeathed a sort of fabricated legitimacy to its heirs. This compelled the Communists to justify the outcome of the revolutionary process by referring to the original intent, despite the divergence between the two. Hence the Soviet government's compulsion to maintain total control over public communication and the self-defeating cruelties that this commitment entailed.

Many writers have distinguished two basic kinds of revolution. One, up to the French Revolution, or in some versions up to the Russian, is the political revolution: creative, liberating, good. The other, starting with the French Revolution for some authors, with the Russian for others, is the social revolution: destructive, repressive, bad.[4] This simplistic typology does recognize that different revolutions represent different demands, different programs, and different motive forces. It recognizes also that there is a certain temporal sequence from one revolution to the next in the development of new aims, as the achievements of one revolution become the starting point for the next.

Revolutions up through the French were primarily religious and political, aiming at freedom of conscience and rights of political participation. In Marxist terminology, this was the "bourgeois" revolution, though neither in France nor anywhere else was it the exclusive accomplishment of that class. In mid-nineteenth-century Europe, revolutionary activity began to take on a new dimension of social and economic demands, challenging the economic dominance of the property-owning classes. This, of course, was the movement that Marxism articulated as the "proletarian" revolution, even though its actual accomplishments were no more than in the bourgeois revolutions the achievement of a single class.

The working-class pressures and socialist ideas involved in a potential revolution against capitalist private property were by no means uniquely Russian, even though Russia was the first place where they succeeded. They were bound to constitute the main thrust of any revolution that might have broken out after the development of capitalist industry and its socialist antithesis in the nineteenth century. However, socialist thought in prerevolutionary Russia was accentuated by the utopianism and extremism of the Russian intelligentsia, some of whom hated the old native petty bourgeoisie and kulaks as much as they hated the new Western-style bourgeoisie. Liberal capitalism had practically no native defenders.

Russia was unique as the scene of the first great successful revolution with a socialist inspiration. It is quite true, as the Soviets used to say, that the Russian Revolution opened a new epoch in history, as the prototype of an economic revolution against the power of private property. That was one kind of power that the revolution clearly did destroy in Russia, no matter what abuses of other kinds of power it might have condoned. Thanks to its total elimination of capitalists, the Russian revolutionary experience came to represent for the world at large the natural form of the economic revolution that had been brewing for a couple of generations in Europe. Socialism and Russia were identified in many minds, both sympathetic and hostile. Socialism made Russia look good, or Russia made socialism look bad, depending on the proclivities of the viewer.

The Bolsheviks deeply assimilated the anticapitalist principle. Anticapitalism was reinforced not only by their Marxist heritage but also by the long-standing biases of both the intelligentsia and the populace in Russia against the *meshchanstvo,* the trader class. The anticapitalist principle was upheld right down to the Soviet collapse, and upheld with striking fidelity, considering the changeability of almost everything else in Soviet thinking. From Stalin's time on, private property in the means of production was nonexistent in the Soviet Union. Private employment of one individual by another was "exploitation," an economic crime. Private trade—even so much as purchase and resale of a shirt or a pair of shoes—was "speculation," an equally heinous offense. In this respect, Soviet practice contrasted even with the East European Communist countries, where varying degrees of compromise with small-scale individual enterprise were observed. In Soviet Russia, anticapitalism was a moral absolute. It was a fundamental commitment that was stubbornly maintained, not because it was practical for political or developmental reasons or whatever, but in the face of great impracticalities and great sacrifices that persistently arose from extreme application of the principle. In pursuit of the anticapitalist absolute, the Communists committed great cruelties and jettisoned the heritage of earlier revolutions in human liberation. Anticapitalism was the one distinctive quality of Russian revolutionary extremism that survived undiminished with the perpetuation of the revolutionary government, and it naturally contributed its share toward the compulsive enforcement of revolutionary ideology.

Internationally, anticapitalism was the cardinal appeal of the Russian Revolution during its early days. In both hemispheres, beneficiaries of the status quo were shocked and panicked over the possible effect of Russian propaganda and example on their own laboring classes. Some governments yielded and allowed nonrevolutionary reformers to inoculate their respective bodies politic with small doses of welfare-state socialism. Others, in their anxiety to curb the Communist challenge, went the route of coercive counterrevolution—in other words, fascism. But one way or another, the main focus of political debate in the Western world during the third and fourth decades of the twentieth century was the basic economic question posed by the Russian Revolution, namely, the question of curtailing or destroying the power exercised by the owners of property over nonowners.

Some aspects of the Russian Revolution in its early days that were equally shocking to the bourgeois world proved to be more ephemeral. There were great hopes for a new era in social relations—equality of the sexes, equality of the skilled and unskilled, and liberation of the individual from all the constraints of traditional authority, ranging from the family to the school to the jail. But these dreams of utopian anarchism were soon dashed in practice, much to the chagrin of protesting groups of idealistic ultrarevolutionaries. The purists were up against the realities of the workaday world, complicated by Russia's underdevelopment, the disruptions of war and revolution, and the overriding ideological commitment of the Communists to root out capitalist enterprise. These constraints made social liberation a liability rather than an attraction, and not only for the authorities. What value, after all, does liberated education have for the illiterate, or the postcard divorce for the peasant wife? In short, the Communists clung to the economic revolution and forsook the social revolution. Social revolution was left as a lingering ideal to be revived two generations later by the Western New Left and—briefly—by the Cultural Revolution in Communist China.

Rejection of the social revolution by the Russian Communists was more than a pragmatic maneuver. One of the signal aspects of the Stalin revolution— of Soviet Bonapartism—was the systematic repudiation of the social ideals of the liberation and equalization of individuals, given up in practice and very often in words as well. Stalin signaled the new orientation in his famous remark dismissing *uravnilovka*—leveling—as un-Marxist, and in his reaffirmation of social controls through school, family, and law.[5] His social conservatism, in fact, was so profound, and so firmly accepted by his surviving lieutenants and heirs, that one is compelled to seek deep psychological and cultural factors. This leads naturally to the broader question of whether Russia as a whole was culturally and economically mature enough for the kind of revolution that the Communists attempted.

Up to 1917, Marxists of all stripes concurred in the founder's prophecy of proletarian revolution in the most mature capitalist countries, based on his dictum that "No social order ever disappears before all the productive forces for which there is room in it have been developed."[6] Mature capitalism would, on the one hand, provide the technological and organizational basis to produce the material abundance required for the reorientation of human attitudes on socialist lines. On the other hand, capitalism would simultaneously assure its own demise, thanks to its advanced internal contradictions. But in Russia a supposedly proletarian revolution took place and held out in a country where everyone had acknowledged that the preconditions for rule by the workers were lacking. From this anomaly, according to the determinist argument of anti-Communist Social Democrats, there followed all the distortions and injustices of a postrevolutionary society where material resources were insufficient to sustain the humanistic aspirations of the socialist revolution.

Actually, at the time they took power, not even the Bolsheviks professed to be attempting to establish socialism in Russia alone, or right away, under the existing circumstances. Before 1917, both Lenin and Trotsky had tried to rationalize their hopes for an immediate revolutionary role for the Russian working class, as against the Mensheviks' reliance on historical evolution. But Lenin's expectation was only that the workers could somehow lead the bourgeois revolution (according to his theory of the "democratic dictatorship of the proletariat and peasantry"), while Trotsky thought they could take temporary advantage of it (according to his theory of permanent revolution). The workers' regime would then have to wait for the subsequent internal maturation of industrialism (according to Lenin) or foreign revolutionary aid (according to Trotsky) to support a truly socialist program in Russia.

When the revolutionary opportunity came in 1917, Lenin and Trotsky could both explain it as the result of the war then still going on. They could also agree (until Russia signed a separate peace with the Germans at Brest-Litovsk) that the war's greatest significance was the chance it gave them to inspire international revolution in the West. In their stress on the war the Bolshevik leaders were of one mind with those who thought that the Russia of the semiconstitutional Duma years from 1906 to 1917 was on the track of liberal capitalist evolution. In either view, only the war intervened to cause the revolutionary crisis. At that moment, Lenin called for the armed seizure of power on the ground that the war offered a unique chance, never to be repeated, for Russia to strike the first blow for international revolution. Banking on foreign revolutionary support, the Bolsheviks bid successfully for power, and then found themselves stranded on their barren and isolated island of proletarian revolution when the anticipated rescue from abroad failed to materialize.

If the October uprising was indeed a premature proletarian revolution, the fact that it could succeed under the circumstances then prevailing in Russia immediately calls into question the Marxian premise that revolution does not take place until after the full flowering of the old society and the exhaustion of its developmental possibilities. But a broader look at the major revolutions of history, such as the English and the French, suggests that Russia was not alone in its prematurity.

Revolution does *not* typically come after the complete maturation of a given social system, and certainly not of capitalism. The Marxian premise that the old system had to exhaust its potential was not only wrong for the Russian case; it was wrong altogether. Revolution is a natural accompaniment of modernization, yet it typically occurs not at the end of the process but at an early middle point, that is, at the time of the most rapid change and the greatest accumulation of tension between a changing society and rigid institutions. Marx notwithstanding, revolution is not a clear-cut battle between a rising class and an obsolete class but a structural crisis in the development process that always involves a mixture of dissatisfied social elements, with the particular mix depending on the times and the circumstances.

Societies that have successfully negotiated the passage to mature industrial capitalism without a revolutionary upheaval seem to develop an immunity to violent revolution. Revolutions occur most naturally in any society when they are "premature," both in the incompleteness of the social change that bring them on and in the unbounded aspirations that such change arouses. The point when a society is most vulnerable to revolution is when rising expectations run farthest ahead of the development of resources to meet those expectations. When a revolutionary breakdown occurs at this point, illusions run riot about the possibility of achieving everyone's aspirations immediately. This is the mood that elevates the revolutionary extremists to power. Unfortunately, reality will not sustain the revolution in this spirit. The new rulers must resort to expediency and coercion or go down fighting. Engels saw the problem: "The worst thing that can befall a leader of an extreme party is to be compelled to take over a government in an epoch when the movement is not yet ripe for the domination of the class which he represents. . . . He is compelled to represent not his party or his class, but the class for whose domination the movement is then ripe. In the interests of the movement he is compelled to advance the interests of an alien class, and to feed his own class with phrases and promises, with the assertion that the interests of that alien class are their own interests."[7] Faced with such choices, the extremists typically split between the power-oriented and the ideal-oriented elements. Inevitably the idealists fail; only the people who are both ruthless and flexible enough have a chance to keep the idea of revolution going.

Engels seems not to have realized that the extremists' accession to power before conditions are "ripe" is a natural law of revolution. Hence, frustration and deception of the revolution's followers are inevitable. The conditions that create the opportunity for revolutionary action preclude the realization of revolutionary aspirations. Conversely, where conditions are sufficient to realize these aspirations, there need be no revolution. Lenin was correct in warning that, contrary to Marx's expectations, peaceful progress and economic gains would deaden the revolutionary consciousness of the workers and leave the proletarian revolution as he conceived it forever unachieved.

As things actually turned out, revolution interrupted Russia's development at an early stage of industrialization, when the country's economic base was still woefully inadequate to support the distributive justice that socialism was supposed to represent. Instead of sharing the country's meager wealth, the more compelling challenge faced by the revolutionaries was to pick up where capitalism had left off and apply the political and economic institutions of socialism toward the objective of renewed economic growth. This was the case de facto from 1918 on, and it garnered Stalin's theoretical blessing as "Socialism in One Country" in 1924.

The question then naturally arose in Marxist minds as to whether the postrevolutionary government surviving in Russia could still remain truly a workers' state when the socioeconomic base for such an advanced superstructure was inadequate. Consequently, was the Soviet government subtly evolving, despite its rhetoric, into something different in terms of its class essence? The potential social degeneration of the Communist dictatorship was the main theoretical issue in the polemics between the Left Opposition and the ruling party leadership in the mid-1920s, though the oppositionists hesitated to push the argument to a firm conclusion. In part, their problem was the lack of a clear theoretical alternative. If the Soviet Union was not a workers' state, what in fact was it, when it was obviously not capitalist? Following the logic of historical materialism, the revolution would install a new ruling minority of leaders basing themselves on the newest means of production in large-scale industrial and technical organizations. They would obviously be the organizers, managers, and technologists. Such, indeed, were the beneficiaries or creatures of the Russian Revolution. The type was not unique to Russia, but because of the revolutionary crisis in Russia they were thrust to power much more abruptly and nakedly than in countries developing more gradually, where the appearances of private capitalism continued to hold.[8]

The rule of this "New Class" in Soviet Russia evolved in the course of the revolutionary process, emerging fully formed under Stalin in the phase of postrevolutionary dictatorship, when the heirs of revolutionary extremism sought to address the problems of incomplete industrialization. The New Class subscribed without too much question to the dictatorial methods and the anti-capitalist commitment forged in the revolution, and found its raison d'être in the distinctive Soviet approach to development through bureaucratic socialism. Judged by its results, the method was no more efficacious than capitalism in its periods of most rapid development. But the Soviet method of totalitarian socialism was not chosen for the sake of optimum development—it was the product of revolution, a given, originally institutionalized in the Communist Party and then applied to problems of economic development that had previously been unrecognized or avoided. Soviet totalitarianism was a means, created by Lenin, to achieve the goal of revolution. Stalin's contribution, after the flush of revolutionary idealism had faded, was to bring together the old means of dictatorship and the new goal of industrial and military power.

The New Class became the social base of the Russian postrevolutionary dictatorship, and Marxism became the ideological "false consciousness" legitimizing these arrangements. Culturally, some of the most deeply rooted and primitive habits of the Old Regime emerged to be integrated with the system of bureaucratic socialism. Notable among these were the autocratic principle according to which the dominant class served rather than ruled; the hypercentralized police state; and an obsession with rank and hierarchy in the one exclusive structure of power.

Like other countries in their prerevolutionary times, the trouble that Russia encountered in the early years of the twentieth century was a structural crisis in the development process, caused by an impasse between changing society and rigid government. This standoff was intensified by Russia's unusual cultural bifurcation, resulting from two centuries of Westernization that mainly affected the upper and middle classes, the privileged, educated, and property-owning elements. These were the same people against whom the main force of the revolution was directed when it finally broke out. Thus, in Russia the political and economic conflict of diverse class elements that characterizes the revolutionary process also became a cultural conflict of the less Westernized masses against the more Westernized landowning and bourgeois strata—the *burzhui,* as they were popularly termed. However, the bulk of the revolutionary leadership, even in the extremist stage of the process, was made up of Westernized intellectuals—whose political success, ironically, struck at the cultural sources of their own identity.

Because of the peculiar cultural stratification of Russian society on the eve of the revolution, and the particularly bitter character of the civil war following the extremist takeover, the net effect of the Russian Revolution was to deprive the country of much of its internal cultural resources of a Westernized type. Emigration of much of the old landowning and bourgeois elements, if not their physical liquidation, and elimination of the remainder from positions of influence (unless they were revolutionaries themselves) decimated the Westernized culture-bearing class. The surviving Westernized contingent of Old Bolshevik intellectuals soon found itself under a cloud in the Communist Party, and in the Great Purge this element was virtually annihilated. The purges, opening the path of advancement to thousands of young officials newly risen from the ranks of the workers and peasants, represented for the time being the complete triumph of the Old Russian cultural substratum over the veneer of Westernization that had superficially marked Russian society since the eighteenth century.[9]

What all this implies is that the Russian Revolution was as much a struggle of cultures as it was of classes. Combining the two concepts, Michal Reiman (a historian at the Institute for the History of Socialism in Prague until he was forced to emigrate after 1968) described the Russian upheaval as a "plebeian revolution," through which attitudes and values of the uneducated masses came to prevail in the new society.[10] The concept of a plebeian revolution, marked by the resurgence of a narrow, nativist mentality at the expense of patrician cosmopolitanism, goes far toward explaining the postrevolutionary and particularly the postpurge regime in Russia, when a youthful new leadership was rapidly promoted from humble origins by way of night schools and correspondence courses, and then proceeded to grow old in office.

The postpurge plebeian elite, if that self-contradictory characterization may be permitted, was anti-intellectual, xenophobic, anti-Semitic, and in large measure Great Russian chauvinist. Trained in the narrowly technical side of the Western tradition, the members of this elite were simultaneously pragmatic and dogmatic. They manifested the habits and prejudices of the tsarist ideology of official Orthodoxy, though in a different language. They had no taste for the free play of ideas or for art for art's sake; they mouthed the philosophy of the Enlightenment and the scientific revolution but rejected the spirit of independent critical inquiry that underlay these fundamental achievements of Western culture. They clung to a reincarnated tradition of autocratic authority, claiming omnipotence and omniscience for the party-state, and they practiced an elaborate game of bureaucratic rank and precedence according to their own unwritten laws. Still, their unpresuming tastes and directness of style made them personally congenial to many Americans, who sensed in them a kinship of cultural democracy. Implicitly but systematically, they evaded the social revolution of personal equality among men and women, old and young, expert and nonexpert, social success and social victim. In the 1960s they recoiled in horror from the egalitarian experiments of their ideological kindred in China. With few exceptions, they excluded their wives from public life, treated their private lives as state secrets, and appeared at the opera like a bunch of the boys stopping at a pub. Their revolutionary spirit, insofar as it lingered, was mainly the revolution against foreign influence and the sense of foreign superiority. This, perhaps, is what explains the moralistic intensity of the Soviet regime's repudiation of any practices of private capitalism; it was a fundamentally alien mode of life.

Though Russia tracked one way or another with the successive phases of the revolutionary process, this was the first instance where the organization and ideology installed in power by the revolutionary extremists persisted for generations afterward. The phase of postrevolutionary dictatorship was thereby intensified and perpetuated in a form benefiting from contemporary technology—in other words, totalitarianism. The revolutionary extremists were anticapitalist and antiforeign, two emotions that were mutually reinforcing in Russia, and they implanted these attitudes in the new regime while shattering Russia's Westernized social veneer to the advantage of ruder elements from below. The latter then took their places in a New Class of stratified bureaucrats, mobilized to address the problems of a premature revolution. They had to continue economic development by means other than the repudiated system of capitalism, and they had to justify this effort and their own privileged existence in terms of a utopia that could never be realized under the conditions that brought the revolution about. Finally, the catalyst to effect this combination of political instruments and social forces was furnished by the ambition and political acumen of one individual, Joseph Stalin, whose legacy lived on for decades in the structure and values of the postrevolutionary society over which he once presided.

CHAPTER 7

Revolution from the Inside
Trotsky's Conception of the Process

L eon Trotsky was unique among revolutionaries in articulating a broad theory of the nature of revolution, pari passu with his own political career. Much of what he had to say, especially after the Soviet regime was established, was polemical or self-justifying. Nevertheless, he was making a serious effort to understand the events in which he was involved and by which he was ultimately destroyed. Coming to terms with the peculiarities of revolution in Russia, Trotsky transcended the limitations of his Marxist faith and step-by-step approached the conception of revolution as a long but interconnected process of political and social struggle.

The understanding of revolution as a process was widely developed by Western writers after the upheaval in Russia impressed upon them its parallels with the French Revolution. Robert Lansing, American secretary of state under President Woodrow Wilson, foresaw for Russia, "first, moderation; second, terrorism; third, revolt against the new tyranny, and restoration of order by arbitrary military power."[1] Crane Brinton proposed a medical image: "We shall regard revolutions . . . as a kind of fever. . . . This works up, not regularly but with advances and retreats, to a crisis, frequently accompanied by delirium. . . . Finally the fever is over, and the patient is himself again, perhaps in some respects actually strengthened by the experience, immunized at least for a while from a similar attack, but certainly not wholly made over into a new man."[2]

By the test of the process model, the Marxian theory of revolution is entirely inadequate. Marxism makes much of revolution as the transfer of power from one class to another but devotes little theoretical attention to the way revolutions actually unfold.[3] Revolution as the simple displacement of classes is belied by the mix of social elements, interests, and ideas in every actual revolution. More important, classical Marxism misses the nature of revolution as a complex and extended process and lacks any conception of the natural sequence of stages. Further, Marxism misstates the causal conditions for revolution, seeing them as the full development of the old social system. Thus, the flowering of capitalism is believed to be the precondition for the next revolution, which is assumed without proof to be "proletarian."

Actually, history shows revolution to be most likely at an intermediate point in the experience of modernization as it affects a given country: that is, when the tempo of change is at its maximum and popular expectations have risen beyond the particular country's capacity to satisfy them. It is not true, as Marx believed, that "mankind always takes up only such problems as it can solve."[4] Revolutions invariably overreach, beyond what the material conditions and psychological development of the given society will support, and hence must sooner or later go into retreat.

It is a familiar paradox that Russian radicals were attracted to Marxism at the turn of the century by its quasi-scientific laws of progress toward utopia, despite the difficulty in applying the doctrine to a country deemed unready for proletarian revolution and socialism. The attraction of Marxism was not logical but psychological, and psychology governed as well the ways in which different Russian Marxists addressed the problem of the waiting period between the still unachieved bourgeois revolution and the ultimate proletarian revolution. The Mensheviks, including most of the older leaders of the Social Democratic movement, were prepared to play the loyal opposition while Russia accomplished the requisite capitalist development—a position of correct Marxism but of fatal politics, as matters turned out. Lenin and his Bolsheviks, determined to lead the workers to power without delay, bent their Marxism to fit their own psychic requirements by asserting that the proletariat would have an immediate role in taking over the bourgeois revolution from its weak middle-class sponsors and then in presiding over the country while economic development caught up with the political sphere.

Lenin was never one to acknowledge his revisions of Marx. But as early as 1905 he envisioned the workers taking the lead in the bourgeois-democratic revolution "when the bourgeoisie recoils from it and when the masses of the peasantry come out as active revolutionaries side by side with the proletariat" to create the "revolutionary-democratic dictatorship of the proletariat and the peasantry."[5] In this formulation, Lenin was beginning to recognize revolution as a complex, multistage process—a process, moreover, which might carry the political regime to a point beyond what the socioeconomic development of the country could be expected to sustain.

It fell to Trotsky to carry this modification of the Marxian concept of revolution to a bold new statement of the complex revolutionary process in Russia. This was his famous "theory of permanent revolution," or "uninterrupted revolution," as he himself originally styled it. He worked the idea out, first as a participant-observer in the Revolution of 1905, and then during the leisure of imprisonment following those events.[6] Prompted by his friend of that era, the German Social Democrat Alexander Helphand, alias "Parvus," Trotsky undertook to assess the social forces that had manifested themselves in Russia in the abortive upheaval of 1905 and to justify an immediate radical role for the workers.[7]

In brief, "permanent revolution" held that in Russia, because of the "law of uneven development" or "combined development," the workers had become a revolutionary force while the middle class still vacillated and the peasant mass waited for leadership. Consequently, a bourgeois revolution would lead in an uninterrupted development to intervention by the workers to secure their socialist demands. Thus, "[w]ithin the limits of a revolution at the beginning of the twentieth century, which is also a bourgeois revolution in its immediate objective aims, there looms up a prospect of an inevitable, or at least possible, supremacy of the working class in the near future."[8] Inadvertently, in a compound class theory designed for Russia alone, Trotsky had grasped the nature of revolution as an unfolding process leading through various stages. His bourgeois revolution corresponded to the moderate phase in the Brintonian model, and the proletarian takeover corresponded to the extremist phase. "Above all," wrote John Molyneux, "he perceived that the revolution was an historical process which, once unleashed, could not be stopped half way."[9]

Trotsky furthermore sensed, in the Russian case at least, that the process would temporarily carry extremist politics to a point more advanced than the nation would indefinitely support. This was not, of course, a peculiarly Russian problem but a phenomenon of any revolution; all societies caught up in a revolutionary crisis have manifested "uneven development." Therefore, barring external factors, the revolution would inevitably be set back in a step Trotsky was later to equate with the thermidorean reaction. However, he hoped that defeat for the workers in Russia would be averted by a deus ex machina, the international proletarian revolution that he believed would be triggered in the mature industrial countries by the Russian example. This prognosis gave the uninterrupted or permanent revolution an international dimension as well:

"The political emancipation of Russia led by the working class will raise that class to a height as yet unknown in history, . . . will make it the initiator of the liquidation of world capitalism."[10]

This argument was not Marxism but Russian messianism. Nevertheless, it eventually gave the Bolsheviks of 1917 their theoretical rationale for seizing power. When the forecast proved wrong, they were left in the sensitive position where their proletarian class legitimacy depended on unrealized revolutionary hopes abroad. According to Trotsky's theory, the failure to win revolutionary support in the West portended the inevitable decay of the workers' regime in Russia. Coming to terms with this implication was the central problem in Trotsky's later thinking about revolution.

Trotsky's theory of permanent or uninterrupted revolution in its internal, Russian sense was borne out precisely by the sequence of revolutionary events in 1917. This was one of the rare instances in history where theory was validated by reality and where reality was in turn steered by the adherents of the theory. A moderate revolution ascribed to the bourgeoisie unleashed a revolutionary mobilization of the worker and peasant masses and ended in an extremist takeover that its beneficiaries chose to style a proletarian revolution. In line with his theory, Trotsky was able to predict in March 1917, "The Russian Revolution will not stop. . . . The revolution will make a clean sweep of the bourgeois liberals blocking its way, as it is now making a clean sweep of tsarist reaction."[11]

The October Revolution was accomplished by a party implicitly sharing the premises of permanent revolution. Lenin's embrace of this viewpoint was what shocked his followers when he returned to Russia in April 1917: "The present situation in Russia . . . represents a *transition* from the first stage of the revolution—which . . . placed the power in the hands of the bourgeoisie—*to the second* stage, which must place the power in the hands of the proletariat and the poorest strata of the peasantry."[12] Bukharin told the clandestine Bolshevik congress in August 1917, "We are going to have a great new upsurge of the revolutionary wave, . . . the declaration of a revolutionary war. . . . By such a revolutionary war we will light the fire of world socialist revolution."[13] Disbelief in such Russian messianism was what lay behind the opposition of Zinoviev and Kamenev to the armed seizure of power in the October Revolution.[14]

No modesty inhibited Trotsky from announcing his prescience when he wrote shortly after the Bolshevik victory, "The standpoint he [Trotsky himself, in 1906] then supported can be outlined as follows: The Revolution, having begun as a bourgeois revolution as regards its first tasks, will soon call forth powerful class conflicts and will gain final victory only by transferring power to the only class capable of standing at the head of the oppressed masses, namely, to the proletariat."[15] As the mechanism of this shift he saw a suddenly accelerated process of social psychology, going beyond the classic Marxist framework: "The significance of the revolution lies in the rapid changing of the judgment of the masses, in the fact that . . . ever new strata of the population acquire experience, verify [i.e., test] their views of the day before, sweep them aside, work out new ones, desert old leaders and follow new ones in the forward march."[16] He now recognized the same process of a grand "sweep" or "ascending line" at work in the French Revolution, manifested through the politics of "dual power": "By the steps of the dual power the French Revolution rises in the course of four years to its culmination."[17] In the Russian case, Trotsky affirmed the crucial role of the Bolshevik Party and its leadership (including himself) in consummating the extremist victory, but he conceded later on, "The most favorable conditions for an insurrection exist, obviously, when the maximum shift in our favor has occurred in the relation of forces . . . in the domain of consciousness." The party had to seize the crucial moment, because "during revolution all these processes take place with lightning speed."[18]

Throughout the violent period of civil war, terror, and utopian experiment from 1918 to 1921 known appropriately as War Communism, Trotsky continued to view the struggle as a validation of his theory and the theory as a justification for the revolutionary dictatorship. "The events in which we are now participating," he wrote in 1919, "and even our methods of participating in them, were foreseen in their fundamental lines some fifteen years ago."[19] As far as he was concerned, critics of Bolshevik extremism—notably the Mensheviks and Western Social Democrats like Karl Kautsky—were traitors to the working class. In his theoretical scheme of revolution he made no distinction between the sequence of class stages—from bourgeois to proletarian—and the sequence of revolutionary methods—from moderate to extremist: "The question as to who is to rule the country, i.e., of the life or death of the bourgeoisie, will be decided on either side, not by references to the paragraphs of the constitution, but by the employment of all forms of violence."[20] Trotsky was convinced that everything the Bolshevik regime did was necessitated by the circumstance of a workers' government in Russia struggling to hold out against all the forces of bourgeois reaction until the world revolution would itself be touched off by that struggle.

Despite the high hopes of 1919, world revolution failed to materialize. In Russia powerful opposition crystallized, especially among the peasants, against the system of War Communism. The Bolshevik leaders had to reconsider not only their tactics but the whole theoretical rationale of their regime. Up to this point, messianic notions about the international impact of their revolutionary example had spared them from hard thinking about the later course of the revolution. But Trotsky had given a clear warning back in 1906 of what would happen to the workers' government if the world revolution should somehow fail them. As he recognized in retrospect, "War Communism had exhausted itself. Agriculture and with it everything else had arrived in a blind alley. . . . It was a crisis of the whole system of War Communism."[21] The outcome, of course, was the New Economic Policy, instituted by Lenin in 1921 with the concurrence of the entire party leadership including Trotsky.

The introduction of the NEP made immediate the question of where the revolutionary process would lead in Russia after its phase of Jacobin-Bolshevik extremism. To certain outside observers the trend was clear: "With the New Economic Policy of 1921 began Russia's Thermidor," Brinton wrote.[22] There was, of course, an anomaly in this "strategic retreat" from the pinnacle of revolutionary zeal: self-executed, not imposed by a coup d'état. The Mensheviks, including Yuly Martov, immediately recognized the thermidorean parallel.[23] Kautsky, whose writings as a publicist seem more insightful than his theorizing, even predicted such a self-initiated shift. He wrote as early as 1919, "Lenin's government is threatened by another Ninth Thermidor . . . in some other way. . . . It is not impossible that the collapse of the communist experiment in Russia may equally transform the Bolsheviks, and save them as a governing party. . . . The Bolsheviks have developed the art of adaptation to circumstances in the course of their rule to a remarkable degree."[24]

The most peculiar aspect of the Soviet Thermidor was the inability of the Communist leadership to recognize the real meaning of its own move, despite—or perhaps because of—its self-identification with the Jacobins. Trotsky did admit at the time that the party had made concessions to "the Thermidor moods and tendencies of the petty-bourgeois," though he could not imagine a real Thermidor except as the violent overthrow of the radical party by outright counterrevolutionaries, with the restoration of capitalism.[25] He insisted, "Historical analogies with the Great French Revolution (the fall of the Jacobins) made by liberalism and Menshevism for their own nourishment and consolation, are superficial and inconsistent."[26]

Only when Trotsky found himself slipping out of the inner circle as the succession struggle began in 1923 did he awaken, and then not to a Thermidor already a reality but only to the possibility of "thermidorean influences."[27] In his slashing attack on the party leadership in late 1923, particularly in his "New Course" articles, he called for a campaign to preserve the revolutionary spirit

against the encroachments of "bureaucratism" and warned, "The internal social contradictions of the revolution, which were automatically compressed under War Communism, . . . under the NEP unfold unfailingly and seek to find
political expression." Replying to Menshevik predictions of an anti-Bolshevik
coup comparable to the overthrow of Robespierre, Trotsky insisted that the
Russian Revolution still had its strong proletarian base with peasant support
and would be sustained by an "inevitable extension of the revolution" throughout Europe. Nevertheless, he warned that a recrudescence of capitalistic elements under the NEP could lead to "either the direct overthrow of the workers'
party or its progressive degeneration."[28]

Trotsky's hints of a possible thermidorean tendency within the Communist regime were particularly galling to his colleagues in the party leadership,
who sought some way of countering him in the arena of doctrine as well as by
direct political pressure. One result was Stalin's theory of Socialism in One
Country, designed to argue with appropriately culled quotations from Lenin
that the Soviet regime was in no danger of losing its proletarian purity, because
it did not after all need the world revolution in order to hold out in Russia as
a genuine workers' state.[29] Another tactic was to turn the French revolutionary
analogy against Trotsky by accusing him, as commissar of war, of representing
a threat of Bonapartism. This charge served to justify his removal from that
strategic post in 1925.

In 1926 and 1927, after he had allied himself with Zinoviev and Kamenev
for a last-ditch fight against Stalin and Bukharin, Trotsky responded to the
growing repression of the opposition with more and more shrill charges against
the party leadership. At the same time, he expressed a new pessimism about
the revolutionary process. In November 1926 he noted, "Revolutions have always in history been followed by counterrevolutions. Counterrevolutions have
always thrown society back, but never as far back as the starting point of the
revolution." Accordingly, "in a sense the hopes engendered by the revolution
are always exaggerated. This is due to the mechanics of class society. . . .
The conquests gained in the struggle do not correspond, and in the nature of
things cannot *directly* correspond, with the expectations of the broad backward
masses." Here was the extraordinary admission by Trotsky, like Engels's a half
century earlier but going further, that all revolutions are naturally premature
in relation to the availability of resources to carry out their promises. Thanks
to temporary political momentum, a revolution could outrun its base: "The
awakening of the broad backward masses upsets the ruling classes from their
accustomed equilibrium, deprives them of direct support as well as confidence,
and thus enables the revolution to seize a great deal more than it is later able to

hold." The backswing, sooner or later, would be hard to escape: "The disillusionment of these masses, their return to routine and futility is . . . an integral part of the postrevolutionary period."[30]

This new, fatalistic sense of the revolutionary process Trotsky tried to throw in the teeth of the party leadership during his last stand before expulsion from the party and exile from the Soviet Union. Defending himself before the pro-Stalin Central Control Commission in the summer of 1927, he invoked the full cycle of the French revolutionary model: "In the Great French Revolution there were two great chapters, of which one went like this [points upward] and the other like that [points downward]. . . . When the chapter headed like this—upwards—the French Jacobins, the Bolsheviks of that time, guillotined the Royalists and the Girondists. We, too, have had a similar great chapter when we . . . shot the White Guards and exiled the Girondists [i.e., the Mensheviks and Socialist Revolutionaries]. And then there began another chapter in France, when the French Ustrialovs[31] and semi-Ustrialovs—the Thermidoreans and Bonapartists from among the Right-wing Jacobins—began exiling and shooting the Left Jacobins—the Bolsheviks of the time." Reshaping his notion of Thermidor as a mere retreat, not a rout, Trotsky observed, "It is thought that the Thermidoreans were arrant counter-revolutionaries, conscious supporters of the monarchic rule, and so on. Nothing of the kind: The Thermidoreans were Jacobins, with this difference, that they had moved to the right."[32] In Marxist terms, for Trotsky, the situation in Russia was simple: "Thermidor . . . is a departure from the rails of the proletarian revolution to the petty-bourgeois rails," opportunistically condoned by the revolutionary leadership themselves.[33]

As a theorist, Trotsky did his most creative work under the immediate impact of events around him. When he first formulated "permanent revolution," and on through his initial perception of the revolution in decline, he made no effort to extend his theory to countries other than Russia. It was the abortive Communist bid for power in China in 1927, first in alliance with Chiang Kai-shek's Nationalists and then against them, that prompted him to universalize his concept of the revolutionary process. In April 1927, just before Chiang turned against the Chinese Communists, Trotsky wrote of "an alliance of workers and peasants, under the leadership of the proletariat" and foresaw a "possibility of the democratic revolution growing over into the socialist revolution," while the Soviet Union would play the role of outside ally envisaged for the Western proletariat in the original, Russian version of permanent revolution.[34] By extension, this situation made permanent revolution the general model for underdeveloped and colonial countries.[35] The Italian scholar Pier Paolo Poggio commented, "For Trotsky, in Russia and in general in backward countries, the seizure of power by the consciously organized proletariat . . . will be easier and quicker than in the advanced capitalist countries."[36] In 1928, incorporating this perspective into his polemical reformulation of permanent revolution, Trotsky expressed what Les Evans and Russell Block termed "the theory of permanent revolution as we know it today—as a general theory of the necessity of socialist revolution in the colonial world."[37]

The radically new departures undertaken by Stalin after he defeated Trotsky, including his break with the Communist right wing and his initiation of intensive industrialization and collectivization, threw his critics into a new theoretical quandary. At first Trotsky was inclined to describe the Stalin Revolution as a "prolonged zigzag to the left," driven somehow by pressure from the workers and the Left Opposition but still under the pull of the "thermidorean" bureaucracy.[38] "Stalinism is inverted Kerenskyism on the road to Thermidor," he suggested, "the *last* form of the rule of the proletariat."[39] By now the trend of the NEP years was clear to him: "A period of reaction can occur not only after a bourgeois revolution but after a proletarian one as well. For six years we have been living in the USSR under conditions of mounting reaction against October, paving the way for Thermidor."[40] To his supporters in Italy Trotsky wrote, "When we speak of Thermidor, we have in mind the creeping counterrevolution which is being prepared in a masked way and which is being accomplished in several stages."[41]

With the perspective of an additional half decade, Trotsky was more certain about the retrograde course of the Russian Revolution: "Stalin . . . is the living embodiment of a bureaucratic Thermidor."[42] Looking back from the year 1935, he concluded, "Today it is impossible to overlook [the fact] that in the Soviet revolution also a shift to the right took place a long time ago, a shift entirely analogous to Thermidor, although much slower in tempo, and more masked in form. . . . The year 1924—that was the beginning of the Soviet Thermidor."[43] Thus Trotsky finally recognized that a Thermidor had in fact occurred, not as an overt bourgeois coup but as a more subtle political shift within the ruling party. His only trouble was that he persisted, for reasons of his own self-justification, in placing the shift after Lenin's death and three years after the real turning point of 1921.

Simultaneously with his recognition of the Russian Thermidor, Trotsky was compelled to admit the possibility of a further postrevolutionary phase, distinct from Thermidor, that was still not clearly a counterrevolution. In the

French model, this was the era of Bonapartism. Thermidor, in this context, was "a transitory phase between Jacobinism and Bonapartism."[44] Stalin naturally represented the last, Bonapartist stage of the revolutionary process. According to Trotsky, Russia was thereby observing the laws demonstrated in "the consecutive stages of the great French Revolution, during its rise and fall alike," though he still tried to describe these stages as a sequence of distinct class elements: "In the successive supremacy of Mirabeau, Brissot, Robespierre, Barras, and Bonaparte, there is an obedience to objective law incomparably more effective than the special traits of the historic protagonists themselves."[45]

For a Marxist, Trotsky had an unusually supple understanding of history in general and of revolution in particular. While wedded to the usual class categories for explaining political events, he was able to grasp the complexities of a phenomenon such as revolution that in fact transcended the Marxian mode of analysis. He attempted a running explanation of unfolding developments in Russia by applying a process conception and extending it as new stages appeared: "There are certain features common to all revolutions. . . . The *tendency* toward Thermidor, Bonapartism, and Restoration [is] to be found in every victorious revolution worthy of the name."[46] This was more than a mere analogy, though Trotsky expressed it in French revolutionary terminology; it was "an obedience to objective law."[47]

Constantly attempting to use his understanding of the revolutionary process as a political weapon, Trotsky did not always react at once to a new stage. He was slow to recognize Thermidor and the rise of postrevolutionary dictatorship in Russia. In time, however, he was able to set these phenomena into the framework of his model. "Revolution itself is neither a single nor a harmonious process," he wrote in 1931. "Revolution is full of contradictions. It unfolds only by taking one step back after taking two steps forward. Revolution in its own turn sweeps into power a new ruling stratum which strives to secure its privileged position." Here was a hint of the New Class theory. Finally, Trotsky called the whole Marxian logic into question: "The epochs of ideological reaction which, more than once in history, have run parallel with economic successes, engender the need for revising revolutionary ideas and methods; and create their own conventional lie."[48]

CHAPTER 8

The Bolshevik Gamble

The Bolsheviks' accession to power in Russia was neither entirely deliberate nor strictly speaking a seizure. It was a step-by-step ascent in the partial political vacuum that was revolutionary Russia. The so-called insurrection of 25 October/7 November was really just an incident in this process, and it transpired under circumstances of very confused intention.

Like the other great revolutions of history in their early phases, the Russian Revolution that began with the fall of the tsar in February 1917 led to a nearly complete breakdown in national authority. As the political scientist C. W. Cassinelli observed, the normal exercise of political power under practically any kind of regime is based on the population's readiness to obey, whether out of fear, conviction, or lethargy.[1] In the truly revolutionary situation, this normal state of popular acquiescence is replaced by a normal state of popular disobedience.

Every dissatisfied group in Russia in 1917—and their dissatisfactions were many and profound—sought the remedy for its grievances in defying all remaining shreds of discipline and legal force. The peasants tired of talk about land reform and in their time-honored way commenced seizing the properties still in landlord hands, with no small degree of personal violence to the dispossessed owners. Factory workers, balked in their pursuit of realistic gains by the nation's economic crisis, rebelled against the minimum essentials of industrial discipline, went on strike regularly, elected factory committees to dispute the authority of the owners, and sometimes physically expelled managerial personnel from the plants. The repudiation of authority was most damaging of all

93

in the army, where, beginning with the famous "Order Number One" issued by the Petrograd Soviet, the authority of the officer corps was undermined from above and defied from below to the point that a disciplined military force almost ceased to exist. Even those groups of the population with a stake in maintaining discipline—the officer corps in particular and property owners in general—had no choice but to join in repudiating the shaky authority of the Provisional Government.

From the outset, power was divided between the Provisional Government and the soviets, which had no less legal foundation than the informal committee of Duma members who organized the government of Prime Minister Prince Georgi Lvov. In actual influence over the rebellious populace the soviets soon got the upper hand. This did not cause serious conflict as long as the soviets were led by Menshevik and Socialist Revolutionary (SR) moderates who were content to let the provisional cabinet point the way, but the potential existed for open conflict if extremists should assume the leadership.

In fact, Bolshevik extremists soon did win a dominant place in the soviets, thanks to Lenin's alignment with the revolutionary emotions of the most embittered groups among the soviets' constituents. Together with the Left SRs, the Bolsheviks were the only party to endorse unequivocally the revolutionary behavior of workers, peasants, and soldiers, and to renounce the prosecution of the war under existing auspices. Other old revolutionaries were stunned by the feelings that welled up after the fall of the tsar, and even most Bolsheviks, prior to Lenin's return to Russia in April 1917, were slow to appreciate the possibilities for further revolutionary success. At this juncture, Lenin's personality was decisive—his drive and vision coupled with the leadership ability to pull his followers along despite their doubts. He was responsible for the party's positions—unqualified opposition to the war and endorsement of direct action in the social conflicts of city and countryside—that marked the Bolsheviks (with their Left SR allies) as the only group that truly represented the popular spirit of defiance.

When a society falls into a state of revolutionary chaos, it is unlikely that any order can be built up again save by dictatorial violence. The moderate representatives of political decency are ineffective precisely because they are moderate, as the more objective Russian moderates later recognized. The Menshevik Vladimir Voytinsky, depicting the internal paralysis of the Provisional Government, suggested that the moderate soviet leaders could have forestalled the Bolshevik demand for "all power to the soviets" only by taking full power themselves.[2] Michael Florinsky put the possibilities bluntly: "If . . . Kerensky . . . had made immediate peace and given all land to the peasants, it is possible that Lenin would never have come to the Kremlin. Such a program, of course, *was* Bolshevism in 1917. . . . Its rejection by the moderate elements assured the triumph of their opponents."[3]

The circumstances of revolution and Lenin's genius in identifying himself with the strongest forces of dissatisfaction made Bolshevik accumulation of power a logical, almost inevitable process. By June, they already enjoyed the support of a majority of workers in the major cities. From the start, they dominated the factory committee movement, which was the basis for organizing the "Red Guards" on whom the Bolsheviks relied so heavily in October. Month by month and sometimes day by day, Bolshevik influence grew in the soviets and in the army committees, as the factories and military units used their right of recall to repudiate deputies who proved too moderate and sent extremists to represent them instead.

In most revolutions the crisis of extremism has been resolved by the forces of the Right. In Russia this alternative was represented by property-owning and military elements who were convinced that the Provisional Government would have to yield to a force more resolutely prepared to reckon with the Bolsheviks and the soviets. Kerensky afterward wrote bitterly of the tacit cooperation between the conspirators on the right and on the left, equally determined to get rid of him.[4] The upshot was the abortive coup by chief of staff General Lavr Kornilov in August, a misadventure that only accelerated the Bolshevik upsurge. Early in September the party won majority control of the heart of the revolution, the Petrograd Soviet, and elected Trotsky its chairman.

Although control of the soviets did not mean majority support in the country as a whole, it clearly reflected the pro-Bolshevik mood of urban Russia in the fall of 1917, and urban Russia was the force that counted. This revolutionary power was rapidly being backed up in the countryside by the mushrooming appeal of the Left SRs, who endorsed the peasants' violent land seizures and lent their strength to the Bolshevik goal of soviet power. With Left SR support, the Bolsheviks were gaining ground so rapidly that it is hard to see what could have stopped the scheduled Second Congress of Soviets from voting itself governmental power.

Given this groundswell of political success, it is difficult to understand why the Bolsheviks would decide on an armed uprising that involved more risk than advantage. In point of fact, the decision was Lenin's alone, and the rest of the party leaders held back as much as they could, just as they had in April when Lenin first called upon the soviets to take power. They failed to understand that Lenin was insisting on violent insurrection as an end in itself.

This "adventurism," as Alfred Meyer styled it, characterized Lenin's whole career.[5] To maintain an aura of exclusive revolutionary correctness, he would take stands so extreme that no one save his own unquestioning followers would go along with him. This urge to be radically alone impelled Lenin time and again to break with the majority of his Marxist associates—over the party organization in 1903, over cooperating with the liberals in 1905, over war and peace in 1914, and over the Provisional Government and the soviets in April 1917. He acted the same way in opposing a coalition government in November 1917 and in insisting on the peace of Brest-Litovsk in 1918. He had to accord himself a monopoly of political virtue even at the risk of complete defeat.

In September 1917, when Lenin found the Bolsheviks taking over leadership of the soviets, his instincts told him to press nonetheless for a violent uprising. When he spoke of compromise with the Mensheviks and SRs, it was always as a lost chance. Probably he meant to undercut other Bolsheviks' hopes for just such a coalition. Throughout the month and a half before the actual coup, Lenin went out of his way to insist on avoiding the legality that the impending Soviet Congress could confer on a Bolshevik takeover. He demanded that the party seize power before the congress met, no matter what. It seems that he was bent on tainting the revolution with blood, just so that no one else of independent stature would venture to share power with him.

But the Bolshevik Party in those days was hardly the monolithic instrument transmitting Lenin's will to the masses and making his intentions reality. In fact, the Bolshevik Party is probably the most overrated factor in the entire history of 1917. The party had burgeoned almost overnight from a sect into a mass movement; its membership rose nearly tenfold between February and August. The Secretariat consisted of Yakov Sverdlov and half a dozen women; it was all they could do to maintain their correspondence with provincial party organizations, let alone discipline anyone. It even took Lenin a couple of months to disabuse some of the provincial Bolsheviks of the notion of reuniting with the Mensheviks. The party maintained a large press but was chronically short of funds; the documents published by Z. A. B. Zeman show no evidence of German money reaching the Bolsheviks after the July Days.[6]

Dissension over tactics in the top Bolshevik leadership is of course well known, especially the resistance of Zinoviev and Kamenev to the whole idea of an armed insurrection. What is less widely realized is the tacit opposition among many more Bolshevik leaders, persuaded that an insurrection prior to the Congress of Soviets was a reckless gamble when victory was almost within the party's grasp anyway. Lenin twice pressed the Central Committee to resolve in favor of an uprising (on 10 [23] October and 16 [29] October), but no firm date was set and no definite action was taken, even though the Congress of Soviets that Lenin wanted to anticipate was scheduled to convene on the 20th.

On the 18th, the All-Russian Central Executive Committee of the Soviets, still under moderate leadership, postponed the Congress of Soviets five days, until the 25th, because of delays in delegates' arrival in Petrograd. Were it not for this fortuitous extra time, there could have been no Bolshevik seizure of power prior to the congress.

Preparations for any uprising were last-minute improvisations. The Military-Revolutionary Committee, usually dated 9 or 12 October (Old Style) when the Petrograd Soviet adopted the idea, did not meet and begin work until the 20th. Its ostensible task was to direct the Petrograd garrison in defense against a possible right-wing coup. On the 21st, the committee gained recognition by the garrison as the de facto military command, a step that the Menshevik observer Nikolai Sukhanov regarded as the real Bolshevik seizure of power.[7] At the very least, it amounted to the independent exercise of sovereignty by the Petrograd Soviet, paralleling and rivaling the Provisional Government. Subsequent events were really maneuvers in a civil war between these two authorities. In no real sense was there any "overthrow" from below.

Some sources contain vague references to military plans made by Vladimir Antonov-Ovseyenko and the Bolshevik Military Organization, but no details are available on when these plans were made or when they were supposed to go into effect, and whether they really involved anything more than defense of the de facto authority of the soviet. Members of the Military Organization, aware of the cowardice and unreliability of the reservists in the Petrograd garrison, were among the most emphatic *opponents* of an attempt to seize power before the Congress of Soviets opened, as Lenin demanded. John Reed's hearsay report that on 21 October Lenin set the uprising to coincide with the congress is clearly in error.[8] When the Bolshevik Central Committee met on 21 October—without Lenin—nothing was said about an uprising; the members talked exclusively about using the Soviet Congress as the vehicle for assuming power.[9] In the absence of evidence to the contrary, it appears that the Central Committee was ignoring Lenin's demand to strike prior to the congress.

The crisis was finally precipitated by Kerensky's decision on the night of 23–24 October to try to suppress the Bolsheviks and the Petrograd Soviet by force. Attempts early on the 24th to close the Bolshevik newspapers and open the Neva drawbridges appeared to the Bolsheviks as the first blow in a plan to suppress the Congress of Soviets, and they called out their few reliable men for what they thought was a desperate holding action. To the surprise of both sides, the government found that it could command no effective force, and Petrograd fell by default. Nevertheless, when the soviet met at 7:00 p.m. on the 24th, Trotsky merely warned that the government would meet overwhelming counterforce if it tried to move further before the Soviet Congress met the next day.[10] Up to this point, there was no clearly documented Bolshevik intention to seize power. However, some time before midnight on the 24th, the soviet defense was transformed into offensive action, and Bolshevik forces were moving to take over the city of Petrograd altogether.

How the Central Committee's course of waiting for the Soviet Congress was transformed into Lenin's line of seizing power before the congress remains unclear—though much of the terroristic nature of the ensuing Soviet regime hinged on what happened during those few confused hours in the evening of 24 October. One known fact is that Lenin, who was still in hiding in the Vyborg district of Petrograd and had received no news during the day, sent a violently worded letter to Bolshevik headquarters in the Smolny Institute to warn that all would be lost if an uprising were not launched immediately instead of waiting for the Soviet Congress the next day. But in official histories prior to the 1960s there was frequent garbling of the fine chronology to make the party's stance more logical. Lenin's note, warning that "delay is death," was often introduced into discussions of the Bolsheviks' dispositions of the morning of the 24th to suggest that his directive actually set the revolutionary machinery in motion. In fact, he wrote the note around 7:00 in the *evening* and in ignorance of the troop movements with which the Military-Revolutionary Committee had already begun to counter Kerensky's forces—and some Soviet specialists even doubted that the note ever reached or influenced anyone at all.[11] There was supposedly a session of the Petrograd City Committee of the Bolshevik Party on 24 October that passed a resolution on overthrowing the government; the only source for this event, a memoir written years afterward, placed the meeting at 6:00 a.m. and thus made its decision both prior to and clearer than that of the Central Committee, which met later in the morning. But this report on the Petrograd Committee is either spurious or wrongly dated, though it was brought into Soviet accounts because it was the only document attributed to 24 October that seemed to support in so many words the Communist contention that the party had by this time finally decided on the armed insurrection.

The question whether the Bolsheviks had set any date for action, and if so what date, is one of the most intriguing historiographical problems of the entire revolution. In the 1960s Soviet scholars began to raise the question of precisely when the Bolshevik action of 24 October, beginning as a riposte to the government's seizure of the party press, actually became an insurrection.

This leaves open the hypothesis that one day before the Congress of Soviets was to meet, the party had not yet set a time for the insurrection, even though Lenin had demanded that it come before the congress. In other words, it appears that the party was following the course that much party history attributed to Trotsky—to wait for the congress with revolutionary troops readied to defend it and to seize the excuse to destroy the Provisional Government should it forcibly resist being voted out of existence.

Here, for once, the Soviet line on Trotsky was on firm ground, citing his wait-and-see statement to the Petrograd Soviet in the evening of 24 October, which undoubtedly represented his position at the time. Trotsky later wrote that he had been dissimulating, but his lying more probably came after the event. What the official history always ignored was that the whole Central Committee followed Trotsky and left Lenin isolated. Hence the "delay is death" note by Lenin when he heard about the clash of the 24th, and his unauthorized trek to the Smolny Institute to take command.

Lenin was clearly obsessed with the chance for an independent Bolshevik Party takeover. Perhaps his words were enough—if they were actually received—to make the harried leaders at Smolny decide that nothing but an immediate offensive could save the soviets. By midnight of 24 October a wire had gone to Helsingfors to summon the Baltic sailors, and by 2:00 a.m. on the 25th Red Guards were systematically occupying most of the strategic points in Petrograd. As Sukhanov suggests and Trotsky concedes, the operation had been hastily improvised, and Sukhanov notes that Bolshevik spirits were still not sufficiently offensive to entertain an attack on the Provisional Government in the Winter Palace when it could still have been taken with ease.[12]

If the Bolshevik leaders actually made a definite decision on their own to undertake more aggressive action, Lenin was not notified. It was late in the evening of the 24th before he received even an incidental account of the crisis. From this he concluded that the uprising must have been launched after all, and he set off for Smolny by streetcar to take command.[13] That was when the affair took on the appearance of a planned insurrection.

From all the available evidence, it appears that at the point when the so-called insurrection began, the overthrow of the Provisional Government was neither planned nor expected. The Kadet leader Pavel Miliukov sensed this when he wrote, "The power fell into [Trotsky's] hands of its own accord before the Congress [of Soviets] had time to assemble and express itself."[14] If the armed takeover had not been triggered before the Soviet Congress, the likelihood was for a broad coalition government, which even after the insurrection was strongly urged by Right Bolsheviks, Left Mensheviks, and Left SRs. The chances for an eventual one-party Bolshevik regime would have been correspondingly reduced, though Lenin would still have tried to create such a dictatorship. His demand for a Bolshevik seizure of power was realized by accident, though he probably never understood this, and his followers were glad to forget it. So there has been little or no questioning of the Communist myth that the October uprising was "the most carefully planned revolution in history."

According to some historians, especially Marxists, the October Revolution was the product of the deepest historical trends in the Russian past, though Soviet historians always contended at the price of a certain inconsistency that Lenin's personal genius had to be present to make the inevitable revolution happen. Most non-Communist historiography has represented the Bolshevik coup as a deliberate and untoward interruption of what is presumed to have been Russia's natural evolution toward constitutional democracy. The Bolshevik success, in this view, has to be explained by the singular qualities of monolithic organization, brilliant chicanery, and unabashed will to power that presumably characterized Lenin and his "instrument," the Bolshevik Party. But neither this personal will theory nor the inevitability theory is particularly convincing if evaluated critically in the light of the historical record. An alternative explanation lies in the often-neglected realm of contingency and default.

The Marxist theory of the proletarian revolution to which the Bolshevik victors dogmatically subscribed held that the development of the productive forces and class structure of a society inevitably propelled it, sooner or later, from the feudal social system into capitalism, and then (when the latter had come into contradiction with the maturing forces of large-scale industry) into proletarian socialism and the classless society. Applied to Russia, the scheme immediately ran into difficulties that the Communists resolved only by fiat. One is the obvious paradox that the so-called proletarian revolution came not in the most advanced countries, as even Lenin expected as late as 1916, but in Russia. The other, associated problem is the ridiculously short duration—eight months—assigned to a "bourgeois" regime in Russia. The Russian Revolution was premature and telescoped. From the theoretical standpoint, these are serious aberrations, which call into question either the truth of Marxism or the Marxist legitimacy of Communist power.

There were various Marxist attempts to resolve this problem. The simplest was the view of the Mensheviks that Russia was in fact only ripe for a bourgeois regime in which the Social Democrats would become the loyal opposition. In a vain attempt to make this theory stand up in 1917, the Mensheviks threw away their chance to lead a truly popular revolution.

A more sophisticated adjustment of Marxism to Russia was Trotsky's "theory of permanent revolution," his proposition of 1905 that the "uneven development" of Russia would cause the bourgeois revolution to swing directly into a workers' takeover. This, in turn, would inspire international proletarian revolution and assure the foreign support required for the survival of the Russian Revolution. This messianic hope was practically official Bolshevik doctrine in 1917, and it predicted events in Russia remarkably well, though on the international side it fell through.

In the chaotic circumstances of 1917, it is not surprising that the Bolsheviks, as the most radical force in the country, could capitalize on the hopes and fears of the masses and strike for power while their rivals were divided. The uniqueness of Lenin's movement, however, was its ability to hang onto power after the takeover against the forces of a prospective military dictatorship. No one on the entire political spectrum, from the Far Right to the Zinoviev-Kamenev faction of Bolsheviks, expected Lenin's party to be able to hold out alone.

It may be argued that Bolshevik success was historically necessary in a sense different from the Marxian, as a national requirement to deal with just those problems of backwardness that made the dictatorship of the proletariat so anomalous from the Marxian standpoint. Modernization, as Cyril Black pointed out, has confronted practically every country in the world with the hurdle of violent change.[15] The Bolsheviks had the qualities of discipline and determination to hold power under the difficult circumstances of a country in transition, and eventually they undertook the systematic modernization of Russia by dictatorial measures of state socialism. But this is not to say that theirs was the only alternative. A military dictatorship with a paternalistic state-promoted capitalism—perhaps something like Japan before World War II—could have done as well. In any case, the modernizing role had nothing to do with the Bolsheviks' victory in 1917 and little to do with their successful tenure of power in the early years of the Soviet regime. In their doctrine and program, the Bolsheviks were completely unprepared for the modernizing role. They were counting on the world revolution to bail them out. The industrializing function of the socialist dictatorship had to be worked out blindly and painfully in the course of the succession struggles in the Communist Party in the 1920s.

A final necessitarian theory is cultural, suggesting that thanks to Russian tradition and the Russian psychocultural heritage, nothing but a dictatorship could successfully keep power in the country. Russia's unfortunate experiment with every sort of democracy in 1917—political, industrial, even military— supports the notion that Russians tend to swing from passive submission to an altogether unworkable anarchism. The history of the Russian revolutionary movement is full of examples of impatience with democratic procedures and the conviction that the masses need the tutelage of their leaders to reshape them into the Good Society. It can well be argued, given the circumstances of 1917—the weak foundation for democracy, the heat of the revolutionary fever, the facts of class conflict, the challenge of modernization—that no democratic regime could have held out in Russia against a resolute dictatorial movement. On the other hand, the Communists were not the only alternative for that role. A military dictatorship would have answered to the situation much more directly and quickly.

While circumstances made victory possible for the Bolsheviks, it was neither inevitable nor, except on a temporary basis, likely. Their success in taking power by armed insurrection and holding it as a one-party dictatorship is inconceivable without Lenin's personal force, his truly Nietzschean will to power. From the moment he returned to Russia in April 1917, he sensed the chance to take power and rule alone, and from then on he did not seriously contemplate any alternative. He was determined to seize power by force and violence, *even if they were not necessary*, to baptize his revolution in blood and to drive encumbering and equivocal allies into an opposition stance where he could destroy them. Without Lenin, the Bolsheviks would have been just another radical debating society, if they kept any identity separate from the left-wing Mensheviks.

Lenin was a brilliant propagandist and sloganeer, even if Trotsky and Anatol Lunacharsky were more enthralling speakers. He was able to sense the mood of the masses and play upon it adroitly with promises of bread, land, peace, and power to the soviets. He knew how to exploit momentary issues and misunderstandings to great effect—for example, the rumors early in October 1917 that there was a right-wing plot afoot to surrender Petrograd to the Germans and thus stifle the revolution. This is not to say that Lenin's line was a cynical deception: There was no reason for him to disbelieve such rumors. The point is the adroit use he made of his opportunities.

It is plausible that Lenin, with his will to power, his sense of timing and slogans, a few steadfast lieutenants (Sverdlov, Felix Dzerzhinsky, Ivan Smilga in Finland), and the Bolshevik Military Organization with its toehold in the Petrograd garrison, could have engineered a deliberate conspiracy in the tradition of the nineteenth French revolutionist Auguste Blanqui. (Lenin's denials of Blanquism protested too much.) It is sometimes held that Lenin attempted a conspiratorial coup in the July Days. But in fact there is very little evidence of a careful conspiracy either in July or in October. Two regiments, some sailors, and a couple thousand untrained Red Guards were the only troops that the Bolsheviks could count on when the crisis came, and if the rest of the Russian army had not been neutral or paralyzed, Lenin would never have had a chance.

From any rational contemporary standpoint, the Bolshevik Revolution was a desperate gamble, unlikely to succeed and still less likely to hold out. This is what everyone believed, from the rightists who hoped the Bolsheviks would get rid of Kerensky, through moderates like the Menshevik leaders Fyodor Dan and Irakly Tseretelli who feared the same thing, to those Bolsheviks who worried with Zinoviev and Kamenev that recourse to arms might mean the destruction of the Bolshevik Party. Everyone in this whole range of opinion judged—with good reason—that if Russia's tenuous democratic equilibrium were disrupted, a military dictatorship was the most likely outcome.

Why, then, did Lenin take the chance he did? Because, for him, this slim opportunity at the peak of the revolutionary wave was the *only* possibility for the personal dictatorship to which he aspired. Lenin had his own theory of the willful reversal of the trends of history: "The fate of the Russian and world revolutions depends on two or three days of fighting. To delay is death."[16] In other words, Marxism or no, history gave Lenin this one opportunity, which might never be repeated.

This explains why Lenin tried, but not how his long-shot gamble actually succeeded. It was, as it turned out, a victory partly by default, partly through a series of lucky developments that no one could have counted on. Most of the popular grievances that Lenin capitalized on were the consequences of default, particularly the failure of the Provisional Government to do anything meaningful about the war or the land. Lenin captured the emotional appeal of the soviets because the Mensheviks and Socialist Revolutionaries, nominal socialists, were unwilling to lead a revolution against the interests of property. Finally, Lenin made telling use of fear of the Right, a fear made real and acute by General Kornilov's attempted putsch. In October 1917, Russia was in a state of panic over invasion and counterrevolution resembling France in August 1792. In both cases, it was this fear that galvanized the insurrectionists into action and paralyzed the moderates.

The circumstances of the moment, though not of the long term, did give Lenin a plausible chance. But his control over the party was weak, and his own followers, including Trotsky, were about to let the moment slip by. They were really waiting for the Congress of Soviets to be convened, just the course that Lenin condemned as a "constitutional illusion," fatal to the sort of revolution he wanted. Indeed, there would have been no one-party armed insurrection at all but for another stroke of historical accident: Kerensky's ill-conceived effort to silence the Bolshevik press on the morning of 24 October.

Chance put Lenin in power, and chance kept him there during the dizzying days that followed. No one could have counted on the Cossacks' refusing to defend the Provisional Government. No one could have anticipated that General A. V. Cheremisov, commander of the northern front, would stop the orders to the troops who were to relieve the Winter Palace. No one could have foreseen the collapse of General Pyotr Krasnov's march on Petrograd nor the premature rising and defeat of the officer cadets in the city. No one could have bet with assurance on Bolshevik victory in the civil war. The accession and survival of the Soviet regime in its early days was little short of a historical miracle.

Human reason rebels at the thought that any great development, good or bad, could depend on the random play of contingency. Yet there are critical points in the history of nations where two or more divergent alternatives lie open and where the accidents of politics, the words of a negotiator, the path of a few shots, can decide the fate of generations. It was a series of such unpredictable events that diverted Russia from the customary course of modern revolutions and paved the way for the unique phenomenon of twentieth-century Communism.

CHAPTER 9

Left Communism in the Revolutionary Era

I t is not often appreciated that in the early revolutionary years Communist doctrines, ideals, and oratory were honestly and intensely believed by many in the movement. Revolution, of course, devours its children, and none were consumed more completely than the people most devoted to the revolution's original aims. Memory of these true believers is dim, but a backward glance at their efforts and aspirations helps to put the subsequent evolution of Soviet Communism in a more accurate perspective.

"Left Communism," to extend generically the factional label used in 1918, was a more or less continuous tendency throughout the formative years of Communism, almost always as an opposition to the official leadership. This kind of resistance was possible thanks to the political pluralism that persisted within the victorious Communist Party, even during the most violent and uncertain period of revolutionary struggle, the era of War Communism between 1918 and 1921. Though opposition outside the party was suppressed step-by-step in the first half of 1918, internal Communist opposition to Lenin's policies continued active and vocal until after the end of the civil war. However futile, protests by this opposition were important in documenting the changing methods and direction of the nascent Soviet regime. The more famous struggle for the succession to Lenin in the 1920s was not as free or as profound in the issues it raised as the controversies of the War Communism era. Not until General Secretary Mikhail Gorbachev opened the way for political reform late in the day, in the 1980s, was a comparable debate possible over the fundamental principles of the Soviet system.

At the psychological core of Left Communism was a dogmatic commitment to Marxian theory and an idealistic belief in the struggle for the perfect society. In prerevolutionary times, there were people of this mind among both the Bolshevik and Menshevik factions of Russian Social Democracy. In the Bolshevik movement, the left-wingers were distinguished by their romantic attachment to utopia through insurrection, expressed in the long controversy over participation in the tsarist Duma. The Menshevik Left—Fyodor Dan, Yuli Martov, and others—thought in terms of international revolution and long rejected Bolshevism as a projection of Lenin's polemical style and disciplinarian methods. Prior to 1917 both currents of thought were centered in Russian emigré circles abroad and strongly reflected the influence of left-wing Marxism in Western Europe, with its democratic and even anarcho-syndicalist emphasis on international mass action.

Three short years after the inception of the Bolshevik movement in the Social Democratic split of 1903, the distinctive signs of the Left Communist tendency were making their appearance in the form of opposition to Lenin's leadership. In what way was Lenin not "left" enough to satisfy the revolutionary appetites of the romantic hotheads whom he had attracted into his Bolshevik organization? Initially, it was because he disappointed their hopes for a renewed armed uprising on the model of Moscow in 1905. Lenin's decision in 1906 to put up Bolshevik deputies for the Duma in order to take advantage of its modest propaganda value evoked outrage on the part of two left groups. The Otzovists (Recallists) wanted to recall the deputies, and the Ultimatists demanded that they behave in a more revolutionary manner. Both groups stood up to challenge the Leninists in bitter controversy, not only in Russia but also in the emigration.

The incipient Left Communism of the Otzovists and Ultimatists was no mere flare-up of an insignificant fringe. Heading the opposition was Lenin's own second in command, the extraordinary physician-philosopher Aleksandr Bogdanov (real name Malinovsky, but no relation to Lenin's later favorite, the agent provocateur Roman Malinovsky). Bogdanov was supported by another early Lenin lieutenant, Leonid Krasin, an engineer turned bomb maker who ended his career as Soviet commissar of foreign trade; also by the leading Bolshevik intellectuals—the writer Maxim Gorky, the historian Mikhail Pokrovsky, the litterateur Anatoli Lunacharsky; and by a host of up-and-coming young Bolsheviks, including such future luminaries as Lev Kamenev and Nikolai Bukharin.

From their tactical disagreements, the leftists moved on to theoretical speculations of a sort Lenin found intolerable—Gorky's "god-building," which represented socialism as a religion, and Bogdanov's sophisticated philosophy of knowledge, called "empirio-monism." The latter was the target of Lenin's heavy-handed polemic, *Materialism and Empirio-Criticism,* one of the more obnoxious items in his collected works. But theoretical refutation was not enough for Lenin; in the summer of 1909 he called a meeting of the Bolshevik leadership and formally expelled the "left fools" from what was not yet officially a party. This move was a landmark in developing the practice of totalitarian political control, and it would not be the last time Left Communism was made to serve as the anvil on which Lenin hammered out this formidable Russian contribution to twentieth-century culture.

During the war years, a new "Left Bolshevik" opposition, aiming to make the anticipated revolution total and international, made its appearance under the leadership of the great idealist of Communism, Bukharin. But the issue of the war itself served to bring Lenin, the old and new Left Bolsheviks, and the Left Mensheviks back together on the common ground of internationalism and the defeatism that hoped to see tsarism discredited. Cemented by absorption of Trotsky and most of the Menshevik Left into the Bolshevik ranks in the summer of 1917, this alliance provided the bulk of the leadership that carried the Bolsheviks to a victory discounted and feared by many of Lenin's closest lieutenants.

In 1917 the Bolshevik Party was repeatedly shaken by controversies between the traditional Leninists and the rising tide of utopian enthusiasm. The left-leaning Bolshevik leadership that first surfaced in Petrograd in February was deposed by Stalin and Kamenev in March, but Lenin's return to Russia in April and his startling espousal of the overthrow of the Provisional Government threw the scales heavily toward the Left. By October, only an overcautious remnant led by Zinoviev and Kamenev ventured to oppose armed insurrection openly, though few even of the romantic hotheads went as far as Lenin in espousing the tactics of a military coup and the establishment of a one-party dictatorship. In the end, the dream of proletarian revolution came to pass more by accident than by design.

Both the left and right wings of Bolshevism were uneasy about the implications of absolute one-party rule. When, just after the Bolshevik coup, Lenin rejected the idea of sharing power with other socialist parties, five figures of the Bolshevik Right—including Zinoviev, Kamenev, and the future prime minister Aleksei Rykov—temporarily resigned from the party Central Committee in protest, and several newly appointed people's commissars also turned in their government portfolios. Labor commissar Aleksandr Shliapnikov, a member of the Bolshevik Left, sided with the dissenters, while Bukharin, another left-wing stalwart, hoped for a compromise that would salvage the forthcoming Constituent Assembly. The only achievement of these protests was to create vacancies allowing temporary inclusion of the Left SRs in the Council of People's Commissars.

If the left wing of the Bolshevik Party shared the misgivings of the Right in regard to one-party dictatorship, it was much more vigorous in its opposition to the new regime's actions in foreign affairs. A week after he dispersed the Constituent Assembly in January 1918, Lenin shocked his entire party by calling for peace with Germany and the temporary abandonment of revolutionary war. His critics in the right wing now joined him in this counsel of caution, while the purists on the left were aghast. This realignment set up the ongoing confrontation between Lenin and the Left Opposition that continued in one form after another until 1921 and echoed throughout the 1920s.

Bukharin and the opponents of peace in 1918 contended that the agreement with Germany would hamstring revolutionary Russia's mission to spread the socialist revolution internationally, and would thereby sacrifice the opportunity to win the foreign support that they deemed essential for the survival of the proletarian revolution in Russia itself. Argued Bukharin at the Seventh Party Congress in March 1918, "The conditions of the peace . . . reduce to nothing the international significance of the Russian Revolution. . . . The way out . . . is revolutionary war against German imperialism."[1] He and his supporters were prepared to fall back to Siberia and wage guerrilla war against the enemy while appealing to the European workers to overthrow their respective governments and come to the aid of revolutionary Russia. If the Russian Revolution were thrown back upon itself, they feared, it would be obliged to compromise with bourgeois elements and turn into a system of state capitalism. "If the Russian Revolution were overthrown by violence on the part of the bourgeois counterrevolution," declared the internationalist Karl Radek, "it would rise again like a phoenix; if, however, it lost its socialist character and by this disappointed the working masses, this blow would have ten times more terrible consequences for the future of the Russian and international revolutions."[2]

Denoting themselves the "Left Communists," the Bukharin group mustered four votes against Lenin's five in the crucial decision by the Bolshevik Central Committee on 28 February 1918 to accept Germany's peace terms, while four other Central Committee members, following Trotsky's formula of "No war, no peace," abstained. The narrow victory for Lenin made possible by this split in the Left established the survival of the revolutionary Russian state as the first priority of Soviet foreign policy and relegated international revolution to the secondary, instrumental role that it continued to play throughout the life of the Soviet regime.

In their outrage at the peace, the Left Communists held talks with the Left SRs, who were equally opposed to the treaty, with the object (legitimate in a democratic state) of removing Lenin as head of the government, forming a new ruling coalition, and resuming the war. Though the Left Communists quickly backed out of the scheme, it was recalled and used against Bukharin when he was on trial for his life in 1938, with the new allegation that the opposition had planned to kill Lenin.

Rebuffed when the Seventh Party Congress endorsed the Treaty of Brest-Litovsk, the Left Communists (now led by the economist Valerian Osinsky-Obolensky) turned to issues of internal policy. They were utterly outraged by Lenin's new steps to create a bureaucratic chain of command in government and industry at the expense of the revolutionary philosophy of soviets and workers' control touted by the Bolshevik leader himself in *State and Revolution.* In their short-lived journal *Kommunist,* they warned of "the deviation of the Soviet power and the majority of the party on the ruinous path of petty-bourgeois policies" and threatened that "the left wing of the party will have to stand in the position of an effective and responsible proletarian opposition."[3]

Upon the outbreak of civil war in May 1918, the Communist revolution took a sharp turn to the left, with the suppression of all remaining non-Communist parties, the sweeping nationalization of private enterprise, and the forcible requisitioning of food from the peasantry. Viewing the civil war as a fight for the immediate implementation of the utopian communist goal, the Left Communists temporarily closed ranks with the party majority in a life-and-death struggle for survival. The program adopted by the Communist Party at its Eighth Congress in March 1919 fully embodied the spirit of the Left in affirming "proletarian democracy," "suppression of the resistance of the exploiters," and "eventually the abolition of state authority."[4]

Meanwhile, after Germany's collapse in November 1918 eased pressure on the Soviet regime, new disagreements broke out between the leadership of the party and its left-wing elements. A distinct fissure now appeared within Left Communism between the most idealistic tendency and the proponents of a more pragmatic and authoritarian approach to the future society. Trotsky and most of the Left Menshevik recruits to Bolshevism fell into this latter category and filled high positions in the party leadership during War Communism. At the same time, the purists again went into opposition.

At the core of these new controversies was the degree of centralized power and autocratic methods being exercised by Lenin's government. One focus of contention was the new Red Army as Trotsky had set it up, with conventional military command and discipline and the employment of former tsarist officers—the "military specialists" or *spetsy*. This trend was resisted by Communists still enamored of the democratized army of 1917 and informal guerrilla tactics. Led by the Left Communist Vladimir Smirnov and initially with Stalin's encouragement, this "Military Opposition" challenged Lenin and Trotsky at the Eighth Party Congress in March 1919, particularly over the abolition of elected party committees in the army. At a secret session of the congress they won more than a third of the delegates for their alternative.

Soon afterward, led by Smirnov, Osinsky, and Timofei Sapronov, the leftists formed the Group of Democratic Centralists (more accurately, democratic anticentralists) to challenge the whole direction of the Communist regime. They questioned Moscow's growing supremacy over the provinces, the primacy of executive organs over the soviets, and the dominance of party institutions over the government and other institutions at all levels. Defending the egalitarian ideal and the "collegial principle" of administration by committees, the Democratic Centralists highlighted the excesses of military methods and the trend to hierarchies of individual authority throughout the political and economic system.

A particularly strong center of decentralist sentiment, capitalizing on the issue of autonomy for an ethnic minority, was the Ukraine. The issue of the minorities in the Russian Empire had divided Left and Right Bolsheviks before the revolution, with the former (notably Grigory Piatakov) calling for "proletarian internationalism" and the latter (including Lenin) endorsing national self-determination. In practice, when the leftists led by Piatakov and the Democratic Centralist Andrei Bubnov gained control of the Communist Party in the Ukraine during the civil war, the positions were reversed, the Left advocating decentralization and the Right insisting on centralism. In April 1920, Moscow ordered a thorough purge of the elected Ukrainian leadership and put an end to this base of opposition.

Toward the middle of 1920, as a Communist victory in the civil war appeared assured, the Left Opposition was again invigorated, both in the form of the Democratic Centralists and in a new group based on the trade unions that took the name Workers' Opposition. Led by Shliapnikov, Alexandra Kollontai (the Bolshevik feminist, first commissar of social welfare, and a Left Communist in 1918), and the metalworkers' chief S. P. Medvedev, the Workers' Opposition harked back to the workers' control movement of 1917 and called for the trade unions to run industry independently of the party.[5] Kollontai denounced both bourgeois experts and Communist bureaucrats and protested, "The working class, *as a class,* . . . is becoming an ever less important factor in the affairs of the Soviet republic."[6] The Workers' Opposition wanted to expel all nonproletarians from the party and require officials to work at least three months a year in manual labor.

A high point of left opposition sentiment came at the Ninth Party Conference in September 1920, as support for both the Democratic Centralists and the Workers' Opposition peaked. Almost half the party members in Moscow supported one or the other. The Ninth Conference adopted a remarkable resolution affirming the norms of democracy and free criticism within the party and calling for steps to curb bureaucracy and eliminate economic inequality.

All these developments set the stage for the most divisive controversy yet in the history of the Soviet republic, specifically over the future role of the trade unions in the Communist system, but by implication over the prospects and methods for constructing the new society as a whole. The struggle was resolved at the Tenth Party Congress in March 1921, with a decisive downturn in the fortunes of Left Communism. Divided between the anarchists and the authoritarians, and embarrassed by the Kronstadt Revolt, the leftists were powerless to stop Lenin's moves to terminate the revolution by introducing the New Economic Policy and abolishing factional freedom within the party. Thenceforth, any serious effort by the Left to protest discrepancies between doctrine and practice was held to be a breach of the essence of Leninism that subjected critics to the irresistible power of the party Secretariat and Central Control Commission.

Nevertheless, echoes of the opposition of the War Communism era continued to be heard. In March 1922, the Workers' Opposition vainly appealed to the Communist International against the suppression of "workers' democracy" in Russia. In 1923, one of their number, Gabriel Miasnikov, organized a new antibureaucratic movement, the Workers' Group, only to see it quickly suppressed. The Democratic Centralists made common cause with the Trotskyists in the "New Course" controversy over party democracy in December 1923— January 1924, the first in the series of fruitless efforts by the Left Opposition of the 1920s to reverse the trend toward totalitarianism. In 1927, the Democratic Centralists again appeared as a separate group to plead for the restoration of democracy in the party, only to be expelled along with the Trotskyists at the Fifteenth Party Congress in December of that year. Most of the leaders of the opposition movements of 1918–21 were liquidated in the purges of 1936–38, without benefit of trial. An exception was Alexandra Kollontai, who survived to serve as a Soviet diplomat until her death in 1952.

Perhaps the most exotic and certainly the longest-lived contribution of Left Communist thinking was the doctrine of revolutionary culture, the roots of which went back to Aleksandr Bogdanov in the early 1900s. Bogdanov and his followers proceeded from the exaggerated Marxian notions that all culture is class-bound, that truth and values for one class have no meaning for another, and that therefore the proletariat had to create its own new culture and destroy the old bourgeois traditions. Though no longer a Bolshevik in 1917, Bogdanov was allowed shortly after the revolution to establish the *Proletkult* (proletarian culture) movement, an attempt to evoke proletarian art and writing from actual proletarians.

Disbanded by the party in 1921, Proletkult nevertheless had an echo in the antibureaucratic Workers' Truth organization that surfaced in 1923 to call for a new Workers' Party. Like Miasnikov's Workers' Group, the Workers' Truth was quickly broken up by the police. Bogdanov's intellectual heirs, notably the historian Pokrovsky and the former Democratic Centralist Bubnov (as commissar of education), achieved their heyday when Stalin ended the intellectual tolerance of the NEP period and put the leftists briefly to work to impose tight controls on most fields of thought and culture in the name of the proletariat. This rule by the Left proved to be short-lived, however; by the mid-1930s, Stalin was purging them everywhere and replacing them with people who would enforce his new, conservative cultural standards.[7]

Hand in hand with their belief in proletarian class culture, the Left Communists affirmed that the new culture would be attained through the elimination of all traditional institutions of constraint over the individual. Thus, along with the "withering-away" of the state, Kollontai preached the withering-away of the family; P. I. Stuchka and Ye. B. Pashukanis argued for the withering-away of law; and V. N. Shulgin anticipated the withering-away of the school. Utopia was just around the corner, but the NEP put it off, and then Stalin took a different turn.

The principles of Left Communism were the principles of the October Revolution. The makers of the revolution and the new regime were adherents of this leftism or, like Lenin, had swung over to ride its crest to power. Left Communism *made* the revolution, expressed the feelings that made the revolution possible, and gained its only substance through the revolution. The ultimate failure of Left Communism meant the failure of the revolution.

In terms of personal background, the left opposition leaders were disproportionately connected with experience in the prerevolutionary emigration. Lenin, an emigré himself, used these people in 1917 to press his own radical agenda, but subsequently he always managed to overcome them by appealing to members from the prerevolutionary Russian underground, usually workers, who had risen into the lower and middle levels of the postrevolutionary party bureaucracy. Typically impatient with theoretical disputations and democratic challenges to their own status, these apparatchiki provided the authoritarian nucleus for Stalin's rise to dominance in the party and the destruction of all opposition groups.

A consistent set of ideas, grounded in the emigré experience, ran from one manifestation of Left Communism to the next. They were semianarchist utopians, with an unbounded faith in the workers. They were anti-intellectual intellectuals or semi-intellectuals, particularly when it came to the employment of the technical intelligentsia in positions of authority over the workers. (This theme was temporarily revived by Stalin with his antiexpert show trials during the upheaval of 1928–32.) The Left were internationalist, with messianic assumptions about the impact of the Russian Revolution on the rest of the world; this was the conviction that mobilized them behind Lenin's drive for power in 1917 and just as emphatically turned them against him in 1918. In social and cultural life, they meant to liberate the individual entirely from the grip of bourgeois tradition and mores.

The Left Communists believed ardently in the processes of democracy and political pluralism, but only for the working class and (after mid-1918) only within the framework of the single "proletarian" party—a fatal limitation, as it turned out. They recognized from an early moment the drift of the new Communist system away from the direct democracy and egalitarianism of 1917 and toward bureaucratic authoritarianism. Again and again, the Left returned to the principle of the direct participation of the masses in administering their own destiny in government, in the military, and in industrial relations. They disliked the money economy as a survival of capitalism and looked forward to an egalitarian "natural economy" under communism. At bottom, Left Communism took seriously the violent road to the utopia of free and equal individuals. On the other hand, the Left had little interest in the peasantry and made little of the potential issue of rural suffering. In failing, they nevertheless created a record of protest documenting the evolution of the Soviet system away from the utopianism of 1917.

In almost every substantive respect, the Soviet regime sooner or later repudiated the principles of Left Communism that had embodied the revolutionary spirit of 1917. Internationalism—the real internationalism that could view

Communist power in Russia as something expendable—was sacrificed by 1918. Participatory democracy in the government, army, and economy was on the way out just as soon, though its defenders were able to keep up a rearguard action for a few years more. Proletarian culture died in agony after it helped perfect Stalin's dictatorship. The goal of a classless society of free and equal citizens survived in Russia only as one of the more ironical pieties of party programs.

Many factors contributed to the failure of the Left between 1918 and 1921. The small Russian working class on which the opposition intended to rely was dissipated by the conditions of War Communism. The opposition's antibureaucratic and antiexpert philosophy ran directly counter to the technology-based requirements of modern life and moreover defied the centralist habits of the Russian political tradition. Outside of Moscow and a few provincial centers, the opposition had no significant social base. The Left was usually divided, as it was between the Trotsky and Bukharin factions in the Brest-Litovsk controversy and between the Democratic Centralists, the Workers' Opposition, and the Trotskyists in 1920–21. It lacked strong leaders able to stand effectively up to Lenin; Trotsky had the necessary charisma, but he was inclined to authoritarianism himself and vacillated at key moments. Bewitched by the mythology of the dictatorship of the proletariat, the Left failed (with few exceptions) to challenge the Communist monopoly of power or to question the terror tactics used against non-Communists, until they fell victim themselves when the one-party system was tightened into a one-faction system and then into a one-man system.

With the later expansion of Communism outside the USSR, certain intriguing developments occurred that bore at least a superficial connection with the old principles of Left Communism. The first was the Yugoslav Communists' attempt after 1948 to decide where the evolution of socialism in Stalinist Russia had gone astray and their consequent rediscovery and pro forma application of workers' control in the form of workers' councils in industry. In most other respects, however, the Yugoslav experiment drew more from the cautious and gradualist Communism of the Russian NEP than from the ideas of Left Communism. Tito acted more like the later Bukharin of the Right Opposition than the early Bukharin of the Left.

A much more striking parallel with Left Communism can be found in the Maoism of Communist China. After some years of cautious consolidation, reminiscent of the Soviet NEP, China launched into a series of convulsive "revolutions from above" that resembled the worst of Stalinism curiously combined with the most extreme ideals of Left Communism. Among the dreams of 1918–21 that came to life in China were rural communes (never more than isolated experiments in Russia); espousal of revolutionary war; and finally the "cultural revolution," recalling Left Communist precepts of proletarian culture, participatory democracy, and egalitarianism (even applying another unused Russian idea, the subjection of officials and intellectuals to extended terms of obligatory manual labor). In fact, the Maoists attempted far more seriously to implement the spirit of 1917 than was ever accomplished in Soviet Russia. Needless to say, China's official Stalinism precluded any acknowledgment of the ideological debt that the Red Guards owed to Stalin's old enemies of the Left Opposition.

The spirit of left-wing utopianism was also conspicuous in revolutionary Cuba in the 1960s. There and among the Latin American adherents of Castroism, it was particularly the international aspect of leftism—revolutionary war—and the guerrilla approach to military operations (complete with militia committees) that attracted the most ardent revolutionaries. Again, there was no acknowledgment of the forerunners of these ideas, but the likeness underscored the difference in spirit between the Chinese and Cubans on the one hand and the Soviet leadership on the other.

It is tempting to wonder what the course of events might have been if the Left Communists had prevailed in the early Soviet political struggles. Reasonable speculation is difficult because different conditions have to be imagined to make the success of the Left a realistic possibility. For one thing, as Communists, they necessarily accepted the one-party dictatorship, though they worked against its implications. They thus made themselves a vulnerable target for the Leninist professionals who were less circumspect about the adjustments necessary to assure their own tenure of power. Second, the various groups of the Left were unable to unite when it counted. At each stage of intraparty struggle, much of the potential opposition stood with the party leadership for political reasons—as, for example, the authoritarian Left in 1919–20 and the Zinovievists in 1923–24. Finally, the isolated and backward circumstances of the Soviet state made a meaningful triumph of the Left unlikely. The Left Communists themselves saw little hope for the kind of regime they wanted in the absence of international revolution. For a revolution confined to Russia, the domestic conditions of economic and cultural development were far short of what Marxists thought necessary to make the utopian hopes of the Left feasible, and there is every reason to believe that a Left Communist leadership would have been worn down sooner or later. Equality would not turn the machines, proletarian culture would not cure illiteracy, revolutionary threats would not promote trade with the capitalists. On the other hand, if Communist revolution had spread quickly to one or more major powers—say Germany—this would have had incalculable consequences for the nature of the entire movement.

Lacking the potential for a new revolution, the Russian Left probably could not have sustained its ideals for long. The one-party dictatorship and the realities of political survival in a society wracked by revolution and civil war reduced the anarchistic aspirations of the Left to a misty dream. Left Communist leadership could not have survived without postponing and effectively abandoning its distinctive character. Such a fall from virtue was shown early on by the authoritarian branch of the Left when it made common cause with Lenin during War Communism. But for what it counts, the leaders of the Russian Left were personally honest and dedicated individuals, even though tarnished by the excesses of the party dictatorship. At the very least, they could hardly have been as cruel and mendacious as the people who came to power with Stalin.

CHAPTER 10

Russian Revolutionary Extremism

Every great revolution has ended in some sort of dictatorship. Why, though, should the revolutionary process develop in this manner, and how may the features of the earlier stages of a revolution con-tribute to the dictatorial outcome? In the Russian case, this problem is central in understanding the connection between 1917 and 1928, why the thermidorean NEP failed, and how the character of the Russian Revolution paved the way for Stalinism.

Once a revolution has undergone an extremist phase, it is difficult to avoid some form of postrevolutionary dictatorship. The experience of extremist dicta-torship and terror becomes part of a country's stock of political precedent and methods. The revolutionary experience upsets society's reliance on legitimacy, not only the specific legitimacy of the Old Regime but any possibility of rule resting on habitual acceptance; coercion to one degree or another becomes the main recourse of governing, whoever inherits the revolution. Finally, the disrup-tions of revolution put a premium on the restoration of stability. Overt ideologi-cal continuity is less important; revolutionary doctrine, if not explicitly repudi-ated as in the rightist regimes, will be selectively reinterpreted and manipulated to suit the very different purposes of the postrevolutionary regime. All of these considerations play into the reestablishment of coercive authority and the op-portunity for a megalomaniac despot to take charge. The postrevolutionary dic-tatorship maximizes the role of individuals in history, putting at their disposal political machinery that can magnify and impose their every whim.

Under such leadership, potent but capricious, the postrevolutionary dicta-torship may do new damage to society even as it tries to repair previous injuries.

It may exhaust society in new ventures of pseudo-revolutionary expansion, or wage war against its own people in the name of some higher national virtue, or a combination of these. The ultimate in the postrevolutionary dictatorship was not reached, however, until the twentieth century, when the availability of modern techniques of administration, surveillance, and propaganda, combined with age-old methods of terror and murder, made possible the phenomenon of totalitarianism in its various guises and degrees. Totalitarianism can indeed be defined as the characteristic form of postrevolutionary dictatorship in the twentieth century.

For revolutionary Russia, like other analogous cases in history, it was natural if not inevitable to end up under some form of postrevolutionary dictatorship of the totalitarian variety. However, it is wrong to regard totalitarianism as an absolute category that explains everything, as some sort of Aristotelian essence, sharply distinguished from "authoritarianism," for instance. The label "totalitarianism" actually covers a range of cases, from the less to the more nearly total, from Franco's Spain and Mussolini's Italy—and Tito's Yugoslavia—to Nazism and on to Stalinism. What requires more circumstantial explanation is Stalinism per se, the embodiment of the postrevolutionary dictatorship in Russia that was not only totalitarian but with respect to its own population the most extreme and vicious example of the genre ever known, with the possible exception of some of its Far Eastern offshoots. In particular, how did the specific Russian experience in the extremist phase of revolution contribute to the unprecedented rigors of the postrevolutionary dictatorship?

The record of all revolutions suggests that there is an element of latent extremism present in every society, waiting to be activated and released when the breakdown of the Old Regime opens the possibility of radical popular mobilization. Extremism in Russia was distinctive because it had already been active for decades beforehand, in a self-consciously revolutionary tradition of inflammatory rhetoric and terrorist action. This background was not originally Marxist, but lay rather in the tradition of Russian Jacobinism that extended from the Decembrist Revolt of 1825 through the Nihilists, the Populists, and the *Narodnaya Volya* to the Socialist Revolutionary Maximalists. All of these movements were based on belief in the conspiratorial seizure of power to remake the nation from above. Russian Jacobinism influenced Lenin and the Bolsheviks at least as much as Marxism did, and it generated the main distinction between the Bolsheviks and the Mensheviks.[1] Nor was it confined to the Bolsheviks in 1917, showing itself in other, less successful candidates for the extremist role in the revolution, such as the Left SRs and the Anarchists.

Once the revolutionary process got under way, starting in 1905, a movement ideologically and psychologically prepared beforehand for the extremist role was ready to exploit the opportunity to play it, unlike earlier revolutions where self-conscious extremism emerged only reactively, in the course of events. When their respective revolutions began, neither Cromwell nor Robespierre themselves knew that they were destined for the role of extremist leader; Lenin did.

Russian Jacobinism did not rest comfortably with the emigré international-ists of a Left Bolshevik or Left Menshevik persuasion, including such figures as Bogdanov and Trotsky, but it was automatically assimilated by the Bolshe-vik undergrounders in Russia. The undergrounders, representing Michal Rei-man's "plebeian revolution," went on to dominate the postrevolutionary party apparatus until the time of Stalin's purges, while the emigrés supplied the core of the successive Left Opposition movements, vainly protesting the progressive bureaucratization of Soviet political life.[2]

With Lenin we have to acknowledge the unique role of the individual in histo-ry, in his case extraordinary fanaticism, charisma, and tenacity, coupled with a tactical adroitness and freedom from scruple that allowed him not to be a slave to doctrine. He was able to organize a movement that, if not ideally disciplined in 1917, was more so than any of its rivals. He could take risks and seize oppor-tunities, as when he announced at the First Congress of Soviets in June 1917, "There is such a party" willing to try to rule on its own—not to mention his bid for power in October. Once he had seized power, Lenin was prepared to use any means of terror and coercion to hold it, as recent documentary revelations have only underscored.[3] Thanks to his leadership, revolutionary extremism came on much more abruptly and intensely than might otherwise have been the case. Later on, Lenin proved flexible enough to suspend this same revolution-ary extremism when that sacrifice became necessary to save the revolutionary regime for another day.

To be sure, the onset of extremism in the October Revolution occurred through a convoluted chain of circumstances, some of them quite accidental, that reinforced Lenin's propensity for dictatorship. When Lenin glimpsed the chance to seize power by force in the fall of 1917, amid waves of revolutionary agitation in the working class, the peasantry, and the army, his urgings to armed action were judged by most of his own Bolshevik associates to be an unneces-sary as well as unacceptable risk. Even Trotsky held out for a peaceful assump-tion of power by the Congress of Soviets, with armed action coming into play only if the Provisional Government should attempt to resist by force. It was

Kerensky's feeble attempt to put down the forces of the Petrograd Soviet that triggered the Bolshevik uprising which, as contemporary documentation shows, was initially intended in just that defensive sense.[4] But the uprising looked to all the world—and still does—as if it were the military coup that Lenin had been demanding. The Bolsheviks themselves so asserted immediately. The consequence was to draw an indelible line between them and all other revolutionary elements in the soviets (except, temporarily, the Left SRs), who rejected what they construed as Lenin's resort to force and his rupture of the alignment of all socialist parties.

Judging by earlier historical precedents, and considering Lenin's own uncompromising character, a peaceful assumption of power by the soviets, with a coalition government of some sort—which was the expectation of most Bolsheviks before the crisis of 24–25 October—would have eventually broken down. The point, however, is that the unanticipated events of the October Revolution forced a break between the extremists and the moderates more quickly and more sharply than would otherwise have been the case. The Bolsheviks were essentially left to rule on their own if they were to rule at all, a circumstance that put a premium on Leninist discipline and the use of force.

Force became the arbiter of events immediately after the Bolshevik takeover, as anti-Bolshevik elements—primarily the officer cadet schools in Petrograd and frontline army units rallied by Kerensky—attempted to reverse the decision of 25 October. In these clashes, followed by the bitterly fought Moscow uprising of 28 October–2 November, the revolution was baptized in blood far deeper than any shed in the so-called storming of the Winter Palace. Thus, a situation of civil war set in almost immediately after the extremists' assumption of power, polarizing the political scene with a spirit of life-or-death struggle well before the outbreak of nationwide fighting between Communists and anti-Communists in May 1918.

Even so, Lenin did not immediately undertake a very radical program, apart from ratifying peasant land seizures and the workers' control movement. His hand was forced by circumstances—the food crisis inherited from the tsarist and Provisional governments and the outbreak of general civil war in the spring of 1918.[5] It was thus in a moment of desperation that the Communists launched the ill-fated programs of "War Communism"—"requisitioning" of food from the peasantry and the wholesale nationalization of business enterprise.[6]

Civil war has marked most revolutions. It usually breaks out at an earlier stage than it did in Russia, whether as a counterrevolutionary rising against the initial moderate revolutionary regime (as in England and Spain) or as the extremists' campaign to take power (as in China). Russia was unusual as a case where the extremists faced a nationwide civil struggle after they had come to power, a struggle that aligned almost all other political elements, from moderate revolutionaries all the way over to monarchists and protofascists, against the newly ruling party. For the Communists, at that point, the choice was literally victory at any cost or death.

The Russian Civil War scarred the entire subsequent history of the Communist regime, and it did so in a totally unanticipated way. The fears expressed by Zinoviev and Kamenev on the eve of the October Revolution were only that civil war could end in the overthrow of the Bolsheviks. The civil war made Soviet Communism more Leninist than Lenin, so to speak, and paved the way for such an exaggerated pupil of Leninism as Stalin.

To begin with, the civil war drove home the polarization between the extremists and all others that the accidental events of the October takeover had set up. Prior to the October Revolution and the onset of civil war, Lenin had stated no explicit doctrine of one-party dictatorship as a mode of rule after the revolution. Once that kind of authoritarian government became a reality, he tried to claim it as an eternal Marxian verity. To be sure, the opposing sides in the civil war were not sharply aligned. The Mensheviks tried to remain neutral as late as 1920, when they were finally suppressed, and the anti-Communist movement suffered from a deep internal division between the moderate Socialist Revolutionaries, who predominated at first, and the rightist authoritarians, who prevailed on the White side from early 1919 until their defeat in 1920. Yet events had convinced the Communists that everyone who was not with them was against them—precisely Lenin's premise from prerevolutionary times. The theory and practice of one-party dictatorship were thereby solidified. "The Bolsheviks," Sheila Fitzpatrick has argued, "had the formative experience they were looking for in the civil war. It was the formative experience for which their past and thoughts had prepared them."[7]

The direct physical effect of the civil war was indeed grave, in terms of material destruction and lives lost or broken, though it was hardly worse in this respect than Russia's costly involvement in the First World War. Economic collapse accompanying the civil war brought privation to the entire country that was more painful than anything experienced in the war with Germany. But what was even more serious was the psychological effect of civil war, with its internecine viciousness. The Bolshevik goal of socialism was hardened as it raised the stakes, intensified the commitments of both revolutionaries and counterrevolutionaries, and transformed the radical ideal into a system of coercion rather than liberation. The victorious Communists emerged with the sense, documented in innumerable statements by Lenin and Trotsky, that there were no limits on what the regime might properly do to ward off actual or perceived threats to its power and program.

As a struggle for survival waged by a party that already exhibited the psychology of either-or extremism, the civil war had a profound effect on the Communists' system of rule. The party found itself cast primarily in the role of military organizer and disciplinarian. Political processes within the party, relatively decentralized and democratic in 1917, were steadily tightened up, as the elective committee system gave way to the top-down chain of command through appointed party secretaries. At the same time, given the reality of one-party rule, power shifted from the nominal government structure of the soviets, local and central, to the corresponding party organs, with the Politburo and the Secretariat at the top. All other entities in society—the trade unions, the youth organizations, cultural and professional associations, along with the bodies of civil government—were reduced to the role of "transmission belts" to convey the will of the party leadership. None of these developments were anticipated in prerevolutionary theorizing by Lenin or anyone else, except by remote implication. Lenin's doctrine of the party had envisaged it as an instrument for accomplishing a revolution; the civil war converted the Bolshevik organization into a system for ruling the state. "Without this," asserted Lenin in 1921, "the dictatorship of the proletariat is impossible."[8]

Along with organizational militarization, the civil war left an indelible psychological imprint on the Communist Party, Robert Tucker's "culture of War Communism."[9] While such an immediate impact of events may not be a matter of "culture," strictly speaking, it was nevertheless a permanently distorting effect, conditioning the Communists to see all political life as a struggle for survival justifying resort to any measures of discipline and combat that a particular situation seemed to call for. The unity and infallibility of the exclusive ruling party, as the Tenth Party Congress confirmed, became obsessive absolutes—and a recipe for the totalitarianism that Stalin afterward effectuated. In particular, the culture of War Communism made it impossible for any Communist dissident thenceforth to seek political recourse outside the framework of the monolithic and exclusive Leninist party.

For a time, the civil war and the culture of War Communism were accompanied by an impassioned outburst of revolutionary utopianism, aiming to construct the New Jerusalem of socialism overnight.[10] This was expressed in the radical egalitarianism and antimarket, even antimonetary policies of War Communism, for the moment replacing the material incentives of the mercantile or capitalist economy with a combination of ideological exhortation, military command, and physical coercion, not to say terror. Between 1918 and 1920, practically all legal economic activity in the urban sector of the economy was nationalized, and economic relations with the peasantry shifted from the customary monetary basis to a combination of barter and plunder.

From the orthodox Marxist standpoint, these efforts at total and immediate socialization were hopelessly premature in a country such as Russia with its underdeveloped industrial base and overwhelmingly peasant population. A less doctrinaire approach to socialism, perhaps within the framework of Russian Populism, might have led the revolutionary extremists to seek a social coalition of workers and peasants as the basis of their regime, as they belatedly and inconsistently tried to do during the NEP. For a non-Marxist, there is no reason in principle—practical considerations of efficiency and capital investment aside—why a revolutionary government cannot develop state enterprise without waiting for a capitalist industrial base to mature beforehand. In the mid-twentieth century many Third World regimes tried to do just this. But for the Communist regime in Russia, Marxist ideology combined with the struggle for food during the civil war to bequeath a powerful antipeasant bias, a bias especially strong against any agricultural activity carried on outside the bureaucratic chain of command.

The peasantry was not the only class problem that the revolutionary extremists created for themselves. They were faced with the compelling logic of modern organizational life that points to some form of ruling (or at least dominant) class of bureaucrats and experts—the meritocracy—instead of the proletariat favored by Marxist eschatology. Yet the Communists' ideological commitments, and the plebeian instincts of the rank and file, set them deeply at odds with the so-called bourgeois specialists who had to be called upon to serve in Russia. The result was a protracted era of tense ambivalence toward the specialists, at times persecuted, at times cultivated, at times both simultaneously. During the civil war, the party was divided between Lenin's pragmatic willingness to employ the specialists and the utopian Left's condemnation of them. After the reprieve of the NEP, the spirit of class struggle against the specialists returned with a vengeance, to be exploited by Stalin in the first phase of his revolution from above.

Revolution often revolves around wars of national independence from colonial rule. This kind of struggle cut across the Russian Revolution on account of the multinational character of the Russian Empire and the aspirations of various of its minorities for self-determination when the revolutionary collapse of the monarchy invited them to demand autonomy or outright independence.

Generally speaking, the minority movements in Russia were politically close to the moderate parties of the Provisional Government and unsympathetic to the Bolsheviks.

This is typical; autonomist movements within a revolutionary country are likely to be caught between the centralizing urges of both the extremist revolutionaries and the counterrevolutionaries. In this position, minorities are doomed to fail unless the forces of foreign intervention are able to protect them, as the British did for the Baltic republics in 1919–20.

Internal divisions within a nation in rebellion against rule from outside usually break out along class lines, where one side sees its advantage in independence and the other feels more secure with the colonial power. In the Russian Revolution, class and ideological affiliations cut across the lines of nationality everywhere, as radical leaders and propertyless followers supported the centralism of the Soviet regime against local independence movements made up primarily of so-called bourgeois nationalists. But it was the power of the Red Army that ultimately secured Communist rule in the Ukraine, Byelorussia, and Transcaucasia, as well as in Central Asia, and laid the basis for the USSR.

National minority separatism combined with foreign intervention to make the Russian Civil War particularly arduous. Key revolutionary centers, especially in the south (Tsaritsyn and Baku, for example), had to be defended against a succession of different enemies—ethnically Russian counterrevolutionary forces, direct intervention first by the Central Powers and then by troops of the Western Entente, and secessionist movements that defied all of these forces as well as the Russian Communist center. At the same time, the blockade maintained by the Entente after the Armistice of November 1918 effectively isolated the Soviet republic both politically and economically at a time when internal conditions within Soviet-controlled territory were verging on the catastrophic.

The civil war was the overwhelming preoccupation of the new Soviet government. Military considerations were paramount in driving the Communist Party toward centralism, bureaucratic hierarchy, and top-down administrative methods, contrary to all its ideals and promises of 1917. Practically every Bolshevik leader served at some point as an army commander or commissar. Military service was a significant channel of social mobility for ambitious sons of the working class and peasantry, who rose in the Red Army and then entered the Soviet officialdom. Unfortunately, they knew no other political culture than the Old Regime and the military.[11]

Along with class war against the peasantry and the specialists, and colonial war against minority separatists, Russian revolutionary extremism embraced cultural war, to wipe out the "bourgeois" heritage and create a new, "proletarian" style of life and thought. This urge reflected the prerevolutionary ultraradicalism of Bogdanov and the Left Bolsheviks. During the civil war the Communists gave it institutional form, appropriately under Bogdanov's leadership, in the Proletkult movement.[12] In the run-up to the NEP, Lenin liquidated Proletkult as a threat to the party's organizational monopoly, but Bogdanov's disciples continued to flourish in various intellectual fields. Under Stalin, they offered their services to root out all manifestations of allegedly bourgeois influence.[13] To be sure, their ascendancy proved to be short-lived in the face of Stalin's conservative shift in the second phase of the postrevolutionary dictatorship, and many of them fell victim to the purges. By then, in the practical realm—including such matters as party and university admission preference—the proletarian ideal was abandoned, and the cleansed bureaucracy and a new "toiling intelligentsia" took over the country's direction.

Cultural excrescences aside, the most unusual aspect of revolutionary extremism in Russia was the way it was halted. Here Lenin's leadership was decisive. Unlike Robespierre, who had to be liquidated to make way for the original thermidorean reaction, Lenin was politically astute and flexible enough in the general crisis following the civil war to order the revolution into retreat and thereby execute his own Thermidor. The analogy was unacknowledged—even Trotsky, when he raised the point, dated it only from Lenin's death, and then against a torrent of orthodox denunciations for slandering the purity of the soi-disant proletarian regime.[14] Nevertheless, the events of 1921 clearly align Russia with the precedents of Cromwell's repudiation of the Puritan utopians in 1653 and Robespierre's downfall in 1794. In each case, the revolution was reaching beyond what society could sustain, and the rule of the revolutionaries was threatened. Lenin's uniqueness—more distinctive even than his quest for power in 1917—was to suspend revolutionary extremism while keeping intact the machinery of revolutionary power represented by the party as well as its exclusive ideological legitimation represented by Marxist doctrine. Having won the military conflict with the Whites, he called off the social war against Russia's two key class components, the peasants (numerically preponderant) and the specialists (functionally essential). At the same time he tightened the lines of political control and targeted both the utopians within the party (the Workers' Opposition and kindred groups) and surviving socialist critics outside (especially the SRs, put on trial and jailed or exiled).

Thanks to the way Lenin resolved the crisis of 1921, the revolutionary mechanisms of power, steeled during the civil war, remained available for new leaders and new purposes pointing toward the postrevolutionary dictatorship. Stalin's significance was to be the individual who personified this transition in his role as general secretary, working during the NEP to perfect the party as an instrument of control while top-level struggle went on to succeed Lenin and define the nature of the postrevolutionary society. In successive stages, Stalin implemented the "culture of War Communism" to a degree never actually attained in its formative years: first organizationally; then ideologically, with the manipulation of enforced unanimity; then in the militarization of all sides of economic life that marked the first phase of his revolution from above. Thus he perfected the Russian version of totalitarianism, T. H. Rigby's "mono-organizational society," as an application of revolutionary methods and military organization to the task of building a modern society.[15]

The Militarization of
Socialism in Russia

W as the Soviet Union "socialist," as the revolution shaped it? And if so, was socialism exclusively defined by its Soviet form? The great French sociologist Emile Durkheim had a broader conception: "We denote as socialism every doctrine which demands the connection of all economic functions, or of certain among them, . . . to the directing and conscious centers of society."[1] It is thus more fruitful to ask what type and degree of socialism developed in the course of the Soviet experience and what philosophical background and historical circumstances might be invoked to explain its form.

If indeed the Soviet Union represented a form of socialism, it was a version governed by Russia's particular historical traditions, its revolutionary experience, and the international trend toward managerial society. It is hard to explain the actual nature of Soviet socialism by the ideology of Marxism with which it was officially associated. On the contrary, the real character of Soviet socialism was not rule by the working class but a new form of military society, both in the structure of the regime and in its spirit and purposes. To review the distinctive features of Soviet totalitarianism—its centralized command structure, its ranks and hierarchies, the manner in which it mobilized its resources, the discipline in thought and action enforced by the police and censorship apparatus, and the solidarity demanded of the nation in the face of its external enemies—is to recite the standard features of a military organization. Soviet Russia became a garrison state, where everyone, in effect, was in the army. The late Cornelius Castoriadis termed it a "stratocracy," that is, a system ruled by military interests.[2] It came close to what the Marquis de Mirabeau (and perhaps Voltaire before him) said of Frederick the Great's Prussia: "not a country that has an army" but "an army that has a country."[3] This was a strange outcome for a system dedicated to socialism, considering that socialism until 1914 was identified everywhere with antimilitarist, anti-imperialist, antinationalist, and antiauthoritarian views. In the Soviet experience, socialism was turned from the antithesis of militarism into its instrument, where the resources of society were maximally geared to the needs and priorities of the military interest.

The militarization of socialism in Russia began, clearly, with Lenin and his ideal of the revolutionary party. A military model of political organization and action was the core of Bolshevism as he formulated it in his early writings and in the course of his split with the Mensheviks. The party, in Lenin's view, should be "a regular army of tested fighters," stressing "organized preparation for battle."[4]

Marx and Engels, to be sure, bequeathed a certain psychological climate of combat inherent in the philosophy of class struggle. Engels went so far as to call Social Democratic voters "the international proletarian army."[5] But for both Marx and Engels, the military model did not carry over into the organization of the future socialist society. Indeed, pointing to the outcome of the French Revolution of 1848 in a military dictatorship, they were at pains to warn the working class against the danger of creating a bureaucratic power beyond its control.[6] They rarely if ever went so far as to use the expression "class war," a Soviet term that does not appear to have come into general use until the Russian Civil War made it more than a metaphor.

Lenin's entrancement with military modes of thinking comes through not only in his conception of revolutionary political organization but in his dicta about the methods required for political success, both internally and internationally. The experience of the 1905 revolution brought him close to Bismarck in the belief that "major questions in the life of nations are settled only by force."[7] Hoping to follow up that first abortive assault on tsarism, he wrote, "We would be deceiving both ourselves and the people if we concealed from them the fact that the impending revolutionary action must take the form of a desperate, bloody war of extermination."[8] When international conflict broke out in 1914, it was not enough for Lenin to oppose the war effort as did left-wing socialists all over Europe. He denounced "priestly-sentimental and stupid sighing" about "peace no matter what" and called instead for "the transformation of the present imperialist war into a civil war."[9]

Habitually excited by new ideas, Lenin immediately wove them into his Marxist worldview without stopping to think that Marxism had thereby become less immutable. Thus his infatuation with the classic Prussian strategist Carl von Clausewitz, whom he discovered and read in Switzerland in 1915. What he extracted from Clausewitz was little more than the familiar maxim "War is the pursuit of politics by other means," which he thereafter quoted at every opportunity.[10] This formula seemed to support his implicit conviction that politics had to be pursued by the most warlike means.

The thinness of Lenin's military study did not prevent latter-day Soviet theorists from describing him as the fountainhead of Soviet military thought. According to a treatise of 1972 by A. S. Milovidov and V. G. Kozlov, "The brilliant theorist and architect of the new socialist world, V. I. Lenin, was also the most profound theorist in philosophical problems of modern war, armed forces and military science. . . . V. I. Lenin was the founder of Soviet military science."[11] Naturally, it would have been too much at that late date to expect Trotsky, who had learned something of military matters from his experience as a correspondent during the Balkan Wars, to receive credit as the organizer of the Red Army. As for Trotsky's own view of Marxist military thought, he cautioned in a lecture of 1922 when he was still commissar of war, "Even if one grants that 'military science' is a *science,* it is nevertheless impossible to grant that it can be built with the methods of Marxism; because historical materialism isn't at all a universal method for all sciences. . . . It is the greatest misconception to try to build in the special field of military matters by means of the method of Marxism."[12] This is probably the best commentary ever made on the scientific level of official Soviet military philosophizing.

In 1917, when most of the Bolshevik leadership preferred to avoid a violent test of strength against the Provisional Government and to wait for the anticipated Second Congress of Soviets to vote them into power, Lenin remained obsessed with the opportunity for a military coup against Kerensky's government. In the directives he sent to party headquarters from his hiding places, he fulminated against any delay. "History has made the *military* question now the fundamental *political* question."[13] A simple military action would decide the day. "We can launch a *sudden* attack. . . . We have thousands of armed workers and soldiers in Petrograd who can seize *at once* the Winter Palace, the General Staff building, the telephone exchange, and all the largest printing establishments. . . . Kerensky will be compelled to *surrender*."[14] Lenin was not bothered by the logical contradiction between the decisiveness of military action and the philosophy of historical materialism. As it must be with any military thinker, his implicit philosophy was not determinist but voluntarist. He was a believer in will and decision. The party, he thought, had a unique chance for victory by armed action that might never return if allowed to slip away. "To wait is a crime against the Revolution. . . . Delay truly means death."[15]

The actual course of the October Revolution was compounded of accidents and ironies.[16] Confronted in the event itself with just the sort of armed fait accompli that Lenin had urged, the Congress of Soviet split bitterly. Moderate Mensheviks and Socialist Revolutionaries walked out to protest the forcible deposing of the Kerensky government, and the stage was thus set for civil war and one-party dictatorship. This is not to assert with any certainty that such an outcome could have been avoided, but the events of 24–25 October and the abortive but bloody uprising of anti-Bolshevik military units in Petrograd and Moscow that followed, in fact committed both sides to an armed resolution of the revolutionary situation. Thus, by a chain of accidents, the new Soviet regime immediately found itself in the violently polarized circumstances of a civil war, a struggle shortly to be extended nationwide.

This vicious two-and-a-half-year struggle has rightly been credited with the militarization of the Soviet Communist Party, with inuring the new regime to terror and cruelty, and with the formation of a new culture of revolutionary violence.[17] However, there is no reason to suppose that Lenin anticipated civil war as it developed in Russia. His call to "turn the imperialist war into a civil war" was a rhetorical flourish against nonrevolutionary pacifism, and at most meant using international feeling against World War I to support the revolutionary struggle. The actual conquest of power came much more easily than anyone, including Lenin, could have expected, though his dissident lieutenants Zinoviev and Kamenev warned of the risk of provoking civil war when they opposed the idea of an armed uprising. Once in power, confronted with armed resistance by elements of the old army, Lenin was ready for the worst: "Every great revolution, and socialist revolution in particular, even if there were no external war, is inconceivable without internal war, i.e., civil war, which is even more devastating than external war."[18]

For the first six months of Soviet rule, Lenin's policies in the economic realm (in contrast to the political) were relatively moderate, in line with the old Marxist assumption that Russia was unready for ambitious schemes of socialization. Agriculture, unfortunately, was already in a state of anarchy with the culmination of the land seizure movement of 1917. This led to a food supply crisis and to forcible "requisitioning" of grain from the peasants. Early acts of nationalization were confined mainly to the financial system, though private ownership of many enterprises was being rendered fictional by the spread of workers' control on the one hand and by the government's ban on dividend payments on the other. Calling his policy "one foot in socialism," Lenin argued against excesses of "democratization" in industry, defended the retention of bourgeois experts and managerial authority, and made clear his attachment to the principle of top-down authority. "The revolution has only just smashed the oldest, strongest and heaviest fetters to which the masses submitted under duress. That was yesterday. But today the same revolution demands—precisely in the interests of its development and consolidation, precisely in the interests of socialism—that the masses *unquestioningly obey the single will* of the leaders of the labor process."[19]

Civil war on a broad scale did not actually break out until the uprising of the Czech Legion in May 1918 and the Allied intervention that immediately followed. These crises abruptly radicalized the Soviet regime, both in its politics and in its economics. In June and July, with a few provincial exceptions, all non-Communist political activity was outlawed, and the one-party system became a reality. At the same time, on the pretext of saving Russian property from German claims, a program of sweeping nationalization was launched that by the end of the year extended to every craft and trade establishment larger than a family shop.

These quick steps of mid-1918, prompted if not required by military exigencies, contributed to the ultimate form of Soviet socialism more than the entire year of 1917 and all the decades of ideological preparation that preceded it. As he did on other occasions, Lenin seized on the most readily applicable theoretical rationale. ("Truth is not in systems," he wrote in his notes on Clausewitz.[20]) In this case, his model happened to be the "war socialism" of Germany's World War I economy, an example of bureaucratic economic mobilization that had begun to intrigue him during his exile in Zurich.[21] In 1918, he made it obligatory doctrine for the Communist Party, even though the Left Communists protested the trend. Conceding that Russia so far enjoyed only "state capitalism," Lenin rhetorically asked the Central Executive Committee of the soviets in April 1918, "What is state capitalism under Soviet power? . . . We have the example of state capitalism in Germany. . . . State capitalism *is our salvation*."[22] The following month he wrote, "Germany. Here we have the 'last word' in contemporary large-scale capitalist technology and planned organization, *subordinate to junker-bourgeois imperialism*. Strike out the italicized words, put in place of the military, junker, bourgeois, imperialist state, a state, but a state of the socialist type, of class content, a soviet state, i.e., proletarian, and you realize the *total* sum of conditions which yield socialism."[23] In other words, put leaders in charge who enjoyed the requisite state of ideological grace, and the German bureaucratic model would do as the framework of Russian socialism.

Meanwhile, in a life-or-death struggle around Russia's entire periphery, the Communist leaders turned themselves into a military staff, with military expediency and effectiveness as their primary criteria of policy. Trotsky began to build the new Red Army on traditional lines of command and discipline, much to the disgust of the purists—the "Military Opposition"—who advocated self-governing guerrilla units in the spirit of 1917. After the attempt on Lenin's life in August 1918, the Cheka was unleashed to pursue Red Terror in earnest. Newly nationalized industries were placed under the direction of the Supreme Economic Council and its various "chief administrations" (*glavki*) in Moscow, in order to redirect what was left of the economy in the service of the war effort. Finally, the Communist Party itself underwent a major transformation, as its organization and membership were enlisted to further the cause of victory.

In 1917, with its burgeoning numbers and the eclipse of discipline by enthusiasm, the party approximated the democratic model represented by its rules and jargon more closely than at any other point in its history. In the early months of the Soviet regime, as Lenin and his colleagues settled into their government posts, it was not clear that the party as an institution would become anything other than an opinion-mobilizing and propagandizing body, even if an exclusive one. But with the onset of serious civil war, the party was quickly forged into the country's main institution of power and administration, even more authoritative than the nominal government.

In its new mission of mobilizing Red-ruled Russia for victory in the civil war, the party turned back to the organizational vision that Lenin had articulated in *What Is to Be Done?* Power shifted from the institutions of government—the central and local soviets—to the party. Within the party, power gravitated from the membership to the apparatus, from the local level to the center, and from committees to appointed bureaucrats at all levels. These trends were codified into official doctrine at the Eighth Party Congress in March 1919. That congress formally created the Politburo and the Secretariat as the organs of policy and organizational command, and proclaimed, "The party finds itself in a position where the strictest centralism and the most rigorous discipline are absolutely necessary. All decision of higher jurisdictions are absolutely binding for lower ones. . . . Outright military discipline is essential for the party at the present time."[24]

Pursuant to the party's new military forms and responsibilities, the leadership assigned and transferred personnel as needed, broke up nodules of democratic opposition, and converted nominally elected local party officials into the appointed agents of the center. The apparatus of full-time party officials, euphemistically known as "secretaries," became the decisive element in the party, in distinction to ordinary members who held other jobs but took orders from party officials. In effect, the apparatus turned into a new government, standing within and behind the nominal government of the soviets. This development, capped by Stalin's designation as general secretary in 1922, remained the foundation of the Soviet political structure until the end.

The militarizing spirit of War Communism was carried to its extreme by none other than Trotsky, not only during the course of the civil war but even after the Communists had won. "The problem of revolution, as of war," he wrote in his apology for terrorism, "consists in breaking the will of the foe, forcing him to capitulate."[25] In 1920, with the enemy collapsing and the economy in ruins, Trotsky wanted to turn the Red Army and its principles of organization to the task of reconstructing transportation and industry. He openly called for "militarization of labor," "compulsory labor service," and "labor armies." "We can have no way to socialism," he went on, "except by the authoritative regulation of the economic forces and resources of the country, and the centralized distribution of labor-power in harmony with the general state plan."[26] As a prophet of the command economy, Trotsky was truly the first Stalinist.

Lenin's New Economic Policy of 1921 was a major deviation from the trend toward militarization in the Soviet economy. Whether the NEP model might have persisted under sympathetic leadership, or whether it suffered from an inherent incompatibility with the new Communist principles of government, is a question that is still unsettled. In some respects, militarization not only persisted under the NEP but even advanced. Industry, though less subject to orders from the center, settled into more conventionally bureaucratic patterns of administration within enterprises, in accordance with the principle of individual authority (*edinonachalie*). Under the influence of the flamboyant civil war leader Mikhail Tukhachevsky, the Red Army moved away from the territorial militia idea toward strict professionalism. But the key development of these years was the emergence of the Communist Party apparatus as the dominant political force in the Soviet Union. Restaffed and manipulated by Stalin in the course of the succession struggle that began in 1923, the apparatus became a near-perfect embodiment of Lenin's original idea of the party as a corps of disciplined professional revolutionaries operating through a military-style chain of command.

Undertaking his first theoretical pronouncement about the party shortly after Lenin died, Stalin echoed the founder's military metaphors. The party, he said, was "the vanguard detachment of the working class," the "General Staff" leading the proletariat to seize and hold power through its "solidarity and iron discipline" and its "unity of will."[27] As it battled Trotsky's Left Opposition and then Bukharin's Right Opposition, Stalin's party apparatus put these principles into practice, perfecting the monolithic organization capable of conducting what was billed as a new phase of class struggle.

During the years of collectivization, industrialization, and purges that followed his takeover, Stalin deliberately cultivated a military spirit, appealing to the traditions of War Communism as he embarked on his campaign to transform the country. He revived all the themes of that era, of class war and political and cultural struggle against the alleged remnants of the bourgeois order. In the countryside, there was often literal class war to compel the peasants to accept collectivization. Those who resisted too vigorously were resettled or liquidated—in effect, rendered prisoners or casualties of war. Military terminology was introduced everywhere: "shock workers" in industry, "brigades" in agriculture, and "class war on the historical front" as bourgeois culture came under assault.

In the political realm, the military mode was rounded out when Stalin emerged as the supreme "chief" (*vozhd'*) and became the subject of shameless adulation, even though he held no formal government post until 1941. Collectivization of agriculture in the form it took was protested by the Bukharin group as a system of "military-feudal exploitation of the peasantry," harking back to the days of serfdom.[28] In the urban-industrial sector, the practices of centralization familiar from the civil war period came back, as the plan supplanted the market, small business was renationalized, and the trade unions were consigned to the function once envisaged by Trotsky of enforcing labor discipline and rewarding productivity. Direction of labor culminated in the State Labor Reserves set up shortly before World War II, amounting to labor conscription. A parallel feature of militarized socialism was the Soviet state's outright consumption of human capital in the nefarious enterprises of the Gulag.

Even the planned economy under Stalin became less scientific, less balanced, and more the object of essentially military commands.[29] The First Five-Year Plan was drastically though unavowedly revised when shortages of everything made its targets unrealizable. When sacrifices had to be made, it was light industry and consumer needs that had to give way, while heavy industry and the energy infrastructure were helped to make spectacular gains. Later, priority for the heavy industrial sector was openly and steadfastly acknowledged, not only by Stalin but by his successors. (Violation of this principle was one of the reasons Nikita Khrushchev gave for sidelining his rival Georgi Malenkov in 1955.) "Building socialism," as the Soviet regime described its mission for over half a century, lost all real content of progress in social values. "Absolute power," observed the Yugoslav economist Branko Horvat, "turned out to be just as counterrevolutionary as successful bourgeois counterrevolutions."[30] Official Soviet history, as *Washington Post* correspondent Dusko Doder has said, "reads like the annual reports of a construction company."[31]

As the industrialization and collectivization drive got under way, Stalin began to justify it in terms that would have sounded familiar to the tsar he most admired, Peter the Great. In 1928 he called for putting an end to "the age-old backwardness of our country,"[32] and in 1931 he delivered his famous speech on how Russia had been beaten by one foreign power after another "because of her backwardness." "To slacken the tempo," Stalin warned, "would mean falling behind. And those who fall behind get beaten. But we do not want to be beaten." With a nod to Marxist orthodoxy, he went on to say, "In the past we had no fatherland, nor could we have one. But now that we have overthrown capitalism and power is in our hands, in the hands of the people, we have a fatherland, and we will defend its independence."[33] This was even before the Manchurian incident of September 1931 first raised the specter of aggression against the Soviet Union by right-wing imperialist enemies.

By the mid-1930s (not merely during World War II), the virtue of patriotism and the rehabilitation of the military glories of prerevolutionary regimes became priority themes for Soviet domestic propaganda, as illustrated, for example, by the famous Eisenstein film epic *Alexander Nevsky*. "The defense of the fatherland is the supreme law of life," a *Pravda* editorial proclaimed in 1934 on the occasion of the reinstitution of the death penalty and collective family guilt for treason or defection.[34] The restoration of formal ranks, insignia, and medals in the armed forces (even medals named after tsarist generals) completed the symbolic synthesis of the traditional and the revolutionary in the military realm.

The militarization of socialism in Russia did not take place in a vacuum. It was deeply and permanently influenced by the international environment of hostile powers in which the Soviet regime found itself from its beginning—a hostility, to be sure, to which the Communists themselves contributed significantly. Outside studies of the development of the Soviet system have usually stressed historical, ideological, or personal factors and tend to depict militarization as largely internally determined. But one cannot fully understand how and why the Soviet model of socialism took such a form without considering the traumas and threats—real or imagined—that the Soviet state experienced from 1917 on.

For the nature of socialism in Russia to be conditioned by a hostile international environment was impossible, according to the Marxist premises that underlay the Bolshevik seizure of power, since the Russian revolution was supposed to inspire world revolution. The failure of this millenarian expectation to materialize created a great quandary about "Socialism in One Country." How could one nation, still relatively backward in terms of capitalist industrialization, simultaneously institute socialism, develop its economic resources, and hold off capitalist powers that had already shown how they were inclined to respond to the challenge of revolutionary socialism when they intervened against the Soviet state shortly after its birth?

The resolution of this problem was intimately bound up with Stalin's political triumph and his drive for rapid industrialization. He used "Socialism in One Country" as the test case in imposing political control over the discussion of Marxist philosophy and simply affirmed that backwardness was no bar to the establishment and survival of a socialist system. Industrialization, rather than a prerequisite for socialism, became a postrequisite, so to speak, a program to be pursued by means of the socialist organization of national resources toward the goal of building the country's economic and military capacity to defy the "capitalist encirclement."

The deep impact of Western intervention and the Russian Civil War in the early militarization of the Soviet system is widely acknowledged. The years of the NEP offered a respite from outside pressures, as the Soviet government sought security through diplomatic normalization and alliances with such diverse and temporary partners as Weimar Germany and the Chinese Nationalists. And contrary to retrospective belief, no great change in the international environment was behind Stalin's rejection of the NEP or his decisive "revolution from above." These steps were in part a response to Russia's internal economic problems and in part reflected the politics of Stalin's succession struggle with Bukharin. With the object of discrediting Bukharin and his more moderate sympathizers within the foreign Communist parties, Stalin rhetorically conjured up a new world revolutionary crisis, expressed in the so-called Third Period line that he actually enunciated before the Great Depression set in to validate it.

In the same way, Stalin's call in 1931 for a massive industrial effort to forestall foreign invasion came before the shadow of Japanese militarism arose to justify it. Despite Moscow's class war propaganda, trade relations with the outside world during the First Five-Year Plan became more important than ever. In short, the most fundamental steps toward militarized socialism were undertaken independently of specific foreign threats and indeed in defiance of elementary considerations of national morale, especially as regards collectivization. Stalin's revolution must be explained instead as the confluence of diverse factors—postrevolutionary politics, economic hurdles, traditions of centralism, and personal ambitions.

Once Stalin had his revolution in place, with the command economy enlisting every last peasant and storekeeper as a private in the army of socialism, the foreign threats that could make it seem necessary indeed materialized. In the purge era, the imperialist menace became inextricably woven into Stalin's system of political legitimation, as his pretext for liquidating his political opponents and as the theoretical excuse for the failure of the state to wither away. The challenge of the Axis powers and the actual life-and-death struggle of the Great Patriotic War did not substantially alter the new Stalinist model of socialism but only reaffirmed it, justified it, and cast it in concrete for the indefinite future. This was exactly the conclusion that Stalin drew in his famous election campaign speech of February 1946: "Our victory means . . . that the Soviet social order has successfully passed the ordeal in the fire of war and has proved its unquestionable vitality." Specifically, Stalin cited his collectivization policy and the priority given to heavy industry over light industry as the keys to victory and to the future economic growth he projected. "Only under such conditions can we consider that our homeland will be guaranteed against all possible accidents."[35]

To such an extent did Stalin rely on militant confrontation with outside enemies that one wonders whether his system could ever have managed without international conflict. Would Stalin have had to create the menace of the infidels if it did not already exist? As it happened, the menace did not need to be invented. For Stalin, the new capitalist threat was unveiled by Winston Churchill in his "Iron Curtain" address of March 1946, scarcely a month after the election speech. In a quick rejoinder, Stalin denounced Churchill's "racial theory" of Anglo-Saxon cooperation and asserted, "There is no doubt that the set-up of Mr. Churchill is a set-up for war, a call to war with the Soviet Union."[36] Thus Stalin sounded the keynote for the entire Cold War era of Soviet-Western relations. The constant alarm of "imperialist" threats all validated the institutions and priorities of militarized socialism.

In its congealed form, persisting from World War II to the 1980s, Soviet socialism represented, both in its organizational structure and in its operational values and priorities, a militarized system of societal and economic relations. "Owing to the advantages of its economic and political system," asserted the 1968 textbook *Marxism-Leninism on War and the Army*, "the socialist community can use the resources needed to satisfy its defense needs according to a plan, that is, much more efficiently than the capitalist states."[37] In fact, the system confronted its own population as much as the outside world with a siege mentality, where all personal interests and relationships were supposed to fit the dictates of military-style social discipline. As the Soviet theorists Milovidov and Kozlov maintained, "The economic relations of socialism to a substantial degree enhance the military-economic capabilities of the socialist state above those of the capitalist state, which is based on private ownership. The advantages of socialism, as Lenin emphasized, derive from the unity of the people's goals to strengthen the nation's defensive capability, goals that express the interests of all of society, all its groups."[38]

Militarized socialism went beyond mere "totalitarianism," a category embracing all of the most notorious twentieth-century dictatorships. In the economic and social spheres, particularly, Soviet totalitarianism went to further excess than any other instance of the genus. It was more militarized than any other Communist state with a modicum of independence and more socialist than any totalitarian regime on the right.

Stalin's militarized socialism did not involve an inordinate influence on policy by the professional military, as "militarism" would imply. The political leadership controlled the military so well, on the one hand, and on the other shared its attitudes so fully, that no room was left for differences other than those of a very practical nature. In the tangible matter of representation in the party leadership, the uniformed services displaced the trade unions after World War II as the third largest category.[39] According to Milovidov and Kozlov, "The principle of the party approach means that the very method of organizing the defense of a socialist state must coincide with the nature of socialism, that it must be directed at maximum utilization of the capabilities and superiority of the socialist system. It is indeed here that the essence of the Leninist concept of the inseparable bond between military and socialist power lies."[40]

Militarized socialism was not an end in itself but rather a political instrument. It was a mode of social organization functioning analogously to the old society of serfs and nobles, as the most dependable means of sustaining military power and national success against more aggressive or more advanced neighbors. The model even served as an instrument for the extension of the Russian military base, when it was imposed as a system of imperial control and exploitation on the satellite states of Eastern Europe, much as it had earlier been imposed on the Soviet peasantry. Militarized socialism was Stalinist Russia's answer to life without real allies in a hostile world. For its own maintenance and legitimization, the Soviet system required the perpetuation of an intense sense of the foreign menace. This meant not only unending isolation and internal stress but even provoking or prolonging foreigners' hostility, all of which perfectly served the regime's political needs.

As Stalin was so well aware, militarized socialism was an effective system (though certainly not the only one) for channeling the resources of a semideveloped country to enhance its military power and maintain what amounted to a permanent state of mobilization in order to guard against the allegedly unrelenting menace of imperialism. To quote the 1968 textbook, "The socialist mode of production makes it possible to create and develop a qualitatively higher, more efficient type of modern military organization, to mobilize the greatest amount of resources necessary for the conduct of war, to secure the highest combat efficiency and morale in the armed forces and inimitable staunchness and endurance in the popular masses, at the front and in the rear throughout the war."[41] However, by the 1960s and 1970s, when the Soviet Union had achieved a high degree of industrialization, technological complexity, and educational opportunities in its pursuit of superpower status, the advantages of militarized socialism were played out. Hence the growing chorus among Soviet experts about economic reform, incentives, decentralization, marketizing, and the potential attraction of the models being worked out in those years in Eastern Europe and China. These initiatives reflected the economic mix of the NEP in Russia before Stalin made his total commitment to military forms and methods in civilian society. A surprising dialectic emerged, as the success of militarized socialism undercut its own effectiveness. The revolution was over, and the time for evolution was at hand.

The Stalinist system against which the reformers of the 1980s were reacting was certainly a form of socialism within the limits defied by Durkheim, but it was a peculiar and unanticipated form. Furthermore, it had been dressed up with a version of socialist theory that departed radically from the old tradition, though inside the Soviet Union prior to the Gorbachev era such divergence could never be acknowledged. What if that system could have been operated without the secrecy, mendacity, and terror associated politically with Stalin? It might have thrown a bridge between Old Russian political culture and the Weberian bureaucratic trend of modern industrial society, both of which looked to organized hierarchies to manage society's public functions. But no faction in the early Soviet years understood the alternatives this way. The Left Opposition up to 1927, and the Right Opposition in 1928–29, condemned the bureaucratic monster wherever they saw it, as the enemy of any independent thinking or democratic procedure. Stalin, for his part, embracing the bureaucratic trend without fully acknowledging it, could not tolerate any such honesty about his system. He gladly accepted the burden of thought control to square everything he did with Marxism.

CHAPTER 12

Bureaucratic Advance and Social Lag in the Revolution

Thanks to the peculiar nature of the Russian Revolution, Russia leaped ahead of the capitalist world toward bureaucratic forms in its political and economic institutions, while society at large lagged behind the capitalists or even regressed. Neither anomaly can be accounted for in the usual theoretical perspectives. Soviet society cannot be classified either with the First World of industrial capitalism or with the Third World trying to rise out of precapitalist, traditional ways; it was distinctly the Second World, overdeveloped in some ways and crudely underdeveloped in others. This contradiction has left an intractable legacy for post-Communist reformers, whose task is far more daunting than a simple "transition to market democracy."

Western capitalism is a natural baseline for measuring the character and development of the Soviet system, as long as it is not assumed to be a foreordained channel for every modern society. But this measure has not stood still: Dynamic change has always been the essence of capitalism, even though the classical and neoclassical economics adduced in the West to explain the system have usually analyzed it with unreal, static assumptions.[1] The history of capitalism has been virtually synonymous with the process of modernization and the transformation this has brought about in the life of society. Now a new kind of revolution has been running its course in the countries of advanced capitalism, without a violent political break. This is the process described by many writers from Max Weber on as the transition from bourgeois society to managerial society, from individualism in economics and politics to the dominance of hierarchical organizations and the "preeminence of the professional and technical class," in Daniel Bell's formulation.[2]

Some terminological clarification is in order at this point. "Bureaucratic" and "managerial," though often used synonymously, are more accurately distinguished in the same manner as "capitalist" and "bourgeois," the one concept referring to the structure of the social system and the second to the corresponding dominant class together with its ethos. The bureaucracy and the managers are commonly referred to as the "New Class," although Milovan Djilas when he popularized the term had in mind only the ruling elite under Communism.[3] A more workable term for the ruling class under Communism is the *nomenklatura,* the pyramid of officials (mostly governmental and industrial) subject to party approval for their jobs.[4] The American economic historian Harold Perkin called the whole modern trend "professionalism."[5]

Sometimes, especially in earlier writings, the "New Class" is identified with the intelligentsia, but the meaning of this term varies, and the facts are at issue. The Soviet usage of "intelligentsia" was much broader than the Western, extending to the entire class of technically trained and white-collar workers, a large, diverse, and internally stratified segment of society. Potential class rule by the intelligentsia, understood more narrowly as the educated professional and culture-creating segment of society, has been attacked in works ranging from the prerevolutionary Polish anarchist Jan Machajski (who warned of a "dictatorship of the intellectuals") to the Hungarian dissidents George Konrad and Ivan Szelenyi (who saw the intelligentsia accommodating Stalinism to advance its class interests).[6] But politically the intelligentsia in this stricter sense was more victim than victor in the Russian revolutionary process, yielding to the distinctly anti-intellectual controllers in the nomenklatura. Weber distinguished under capitalism "the propertyless intelligentsia and specialists" and "the classes privileged through property and education"; it was the latter, more or less, that the Soviet system replaced with the party officialdom, merely giving the nascent meritocracy a new master.[7]

Understanding of the contemporary revolutionary transformation has been obscured both by Marxist assumptions about the nature of historical change and by free-market ideological images of the contemporary world. Major shifts from one socioeconomic formation to another, from the dominance of one class to that of another, are not usually abrupt but gradual and mixed. In fact, the notions of clear-cut socioeconomic formations and the corresponding rule of successive classes is an oversimplified imposition upon history. It follows that violent political revolution is not inevitable in this process of change.

Marxists have found it harder to conceptualize the managerial-bureaucratic transformation than have non–Marxist critics of capitalism. To be sure, the proposition that the proletariat is the class destined to supplant the bourgeoisie as the ruling class quickly proved in the course of the Russian Revolution to be one of the more mythical aspects of Marxism. This left the problem of defining the ruling class under Communism as well as the ongoing development of capitalist society. Probably the first person to suggest the emergence of the bureaucracy as a new ruling class was the exiled Trotskyist Khristian Rakovsky.[8] Trotsky himself would concede only a "bureaucratic deformation" in what to him remained a "workers' state": "From the Marxist point of view, it is clear that the Soviet bureaucracy cannot change itself into a new ruling class."[9] Other analysts in the Marxist tradition have struggled to reconcile the facts with Marxist class theory by looking to "collective property" or "bureaucratic collectivism" as the basis of bureaucratic class rule.[10]

It remained for certain former Trotskyists, notably the Italian Bruno Rizzi and the American James Burnham, to combine the separate insights about capitalist and Soviet society into a general theory of contemporary social evolution toward bureaucratic class rule, whether it proceeded under the aegis of Communism, fascism, or democratic reformism (Social Democracy or the American "New Deal").[11] They posited the emerging dominance of a new elite that was coming to power in some form of the "managerial revolution," to rule not on the basis of private property but through its expertise and its control of organizational hierarchies, public or private. Russia, in this perspective, was only the most advanced instance, "in some ways the first professional society," as Harold Perkin has described it, "if that society is defined as the rise to dominance of the professional elites and the displacing of their landed and capitalist rivals," even though the Soviets represented only "one extreme, admittedly pathological, species of professional society."[12]

Ideology never caught up with this novel class reality, either under capitalism or under Communism, even though there were earlier sources for the managerial concept. Saint-Simon anticipated it with his faith in the "industrials" to consolidate the liberal revolution,[13] while Marx himself opened a different avenue to the idea of bureaucratic rule in his references to the "Asiatic mode of production" (a notion suppressed under Stalin because of its embarrassing implications). To the end, the Soviet regime represented itself as the workers' state anticipated by Marx, while contemporary globalized corporate capitalism, for its part, continues to represent itself as the system of individual private property and free markets heralded by Adam Smith. Labels aside, the Soviet system of state socialism was not the polar opposite of capitalism, as both its apologists and its enemies always claimed, but only an extreme instance of the common managerial trend.

Viewed in the perspective of the general managerial transformation of modern society, the Russian Revolution was at odds with itself. The Bolsheviks initially saw the trend toward bureaucratic structures and New Class rule exclusively as a phenomenon of late capitalism, leading to the new Leviathan state that Bukharin saw looming. The socialist revolution was supposed to cut off this line of development in favor of the participatory rule of the workers, but that hope proved to be chimerical, under the constraints both of Russia's backwardness and of the direction that modernization was taking everywhere.

It has always been difficult to reconcile the Russian Revolution with the principles of classical Marxism. Russia at the point of the revolution was not the most advanced capitalist country with the most mature proletariat, but an underdeveloped, largely peasant society with a prebourgeois, autocratic government that was destabilized by the rapid development of capitalism in the late nineteenth and early twentieth centuries. To describe the contrast of capitalist industrial islands with a precapitalist, peasant sea, Trotsky offered his "law of uneven development" or "combined development," an observation that could apply to any developing country.[14] Lenin's description of Russia as "the weakest link in the chain of imperialism" suggested both the greater likelihood of an anticapitalist revolution in Russia and its destabilizing impact on the more advanced capitalist countries (a deduction from his mechanical metaphor that proved to be greatly exaggerated).

Lenin's and Trotsky's theories help explain why an overt anticapitalist revolution should have taken place in Russia, but they do not address the Marxist proposition, subscribed to even by the Communists until the mid-1920s, that Russia by itself was unready for socialism. Russia's uneven development, along with the strain of war, could explain the outbreak of anticapitalist revolution, but the revolution was nonetheless premature, even in the terms of its own ideology. Indeed, all revolutions, as they intensify from their moderate beginnings to their peaks of utopian violence, develop radical aspirations that are premature in relation to the readiness of society at large to sustain them.

The consequence for Russia of the inevitable discrepancy between revolutionary aims and social reality was a series of deep contradictions in the behavior of the victorious Bolsheviks. It was easy to liquidate the new institutions of a nascent capitalism but more difficult to replace their functions, particularly for a party entranced by the presumed revolutionary mission of a social group—the proletariat—that was too weak to start with and ill-equipped for the role of managing a modern society. Once in power, Lenin quickly forgot the utopianism of his *State and Revolution,* and with Trotsky's support, came to terms with the need for bureaucratic hierarchy and technical expertise.

At the same time, the Communist regime had to deal with the precapitalist sectors of Russian society that had not yet been concentrated into large units by capitalism. In the heat of civil strife, under War Communism, the revolutionary government virtually declared war on these elements by way of its policies of confiscating food from the peasants and attempting to nationalize all trade, manufacturing, and services, however small the scale of the enterprise. With these steps, the Communists were attempting to impose exaggerated principles of noneconomic direction from above before the natural process of capitalist concentration could take place and render the "petty-bourgeois" sectors ripe for socialization.

With the introduction of the NEP, the Communist regime relented in its hostility both toward the precapitalist peasantry and traders and toward the postcapitalist technical intelligentsia. This was a compromise line of policy that might have given Soviet Russia a very different face had it not been for the events of the late 1920s that ushered in a postrevolutionary dictatorship with its own radical agenda. At that point Stalin, aiming to consolidate his personal control over the party and defeat his political rivals of the moderate Bukharin group, mobilized the residual class-war sentiments of the early revolutionary years and ended the thermidorean period with his revolution from above, extending the bureaucratic principles of the party to the whole of society.

Bukharin, like Trotsky earlier, awoke to the dangers of the bureaucratic trend when Stalin turned against him. In 1928–29 he published a series of oblique warnings about the overgrowth of the state machinery: "We are *much too* centralized. We must ask ourselves whether we cannot take a few steps in the direction of Lenin's Commune state," that is, the ideological mirage of *State and Revolution.*[15] Citing the Weberian sociologist Hermann Bente on the worldwide trend toward "organized capitalism," Bukharin appealed for "mass participation" as "the basic guarantee against a bureaucratic transformation of the cadre group."[16] But Stalin's version of the managerial revolution could not be stopped; it was the essence of the postrevolutionary dictatorship that lasted until the 1980s.

Built into the Stalinist system was continuing tension between the controllers in the party apparatus and the experts—the technical intelligentsia—in other sectors of government and society.[17] It is hard to say who was the "ruling class," unless, following Pareto, one distinguishes between "governing elites" and "nongoverning elites," or in Svetozar Stojanović's terms, the "ruling class" and the "dominant class."[18] Though Marxist ideology officially remained in force, the movement for the workers' paradise turned into its diametric opposite. "Thus," Weber had predicted in 1917, "the abolition of private capital would simply mean that the *top management* of the nationalized or socialized enterprises would also become bureaucratized. . . . State bureaucracy would rule *alone*."[19]

The revolutionary creation of a bureaucratic social system did not take place all at once but only by stages, governed by the unfolding revolutionary process, and it involved bitter conflicts among the revolutionaries themselves. There was plenty to build on in the Russian governmental and military tradition, reinforced as it had been by administrative borrowings from the West from the time of Peter the Great on. (Bakunin called the tsarist regime a "Germanic empire with the knout.")[20] At the same time, the Communist leap to managerial bureaucracy lacked a firm basis of organic development in civil society, though there were new resources for it in the large-scale corporate form of Russia's nascent capitalism, nourished in the immediate prerevolutionary years by the influx of foreign capital and by expanded technical training for Russians.

As befits the author of "What Is to Be Done?" Lenin was not blindly enamored of the spontaneous revolutionary forces that swept him into power. Along with the utopian dream of *State and Revolution,* where any cook could learn to manage the state, he reminded his followers of the need for authority and organization; socialism, he argued, was "nothing but state capitalist monopoly *made to benefit the whole people.*"[21] For political reasons, he had to endorse the burgeoning movement for workers' control in industry, but only as a check on the private owners, not as a form of nationalization: "By confiscation alone you will do nothing, for in that there is no element of organization."[22]

Some five months after coming to power, endeavoring to resolve the growing controversy in the party between the utopians and the pragmatists over how to organize the economy, Lenin made a statement to the Communist Central Committee that foretold the whole future metamorphosis of the revolutionary society into a managerial bureaucracy.[23] He had been proceeding cautiously with nationalizations, and while leftist sentiment was building up for a wholesale takeover by the workers, he stressed only the need to restore managerial authority and labor discipline in both corporate and public enterprise, including "dictatorial authority" on the railroads.[24] Now, still gesturing to the "independent creative work" of the masses, Lenin reminded the party leadership of the need for "an extremely intricate and delicate system of new organizational relations," supported by "self-sacrifice and perseverance" and "the strictest and universal accounting and control of the production and distribution of goods."

To this admonition he added an acknowledgment of the role of the meritocracy and appropriate compensation for its members: "Without the guidance of
specialists in the various fields of knowledge, technology, and experience, the
transition to socialism will be impossible."[25] Nor could this transition be accomplished "without coercion and without dictatorship. . . . The revolution
has only just smashed the oldest, strongest and heaviest fetters to which the
masses submitted under duress. That was yesterday. But today the same revolution demands—precisely in the interests of its development and consolidation,
precisely in the interests of socialism—that the masses *unquestioningly obey the
single will* of the leaders of the labor process."[26]

Lenin's new stance was bitterly attacked by the revolutionary purists, the
Left Communists, warning of what they could only conceive of as "a petty-
bourgeois policy of a new form" opening the way to "the full domination of
finance capital."[27] This was just the first clash in a ten-year series of futile opposition protests reflecting the tension between the revolutionary ideal and the
bureaucratic requirements of modern society and documenting the step-by-
step accommodation of the party leadership to the latter.

War Communism, ushered in by the outbreak of general civil war and
the sweeping nationalizations with which the Soviet government responded
in May–June 1918, combined leftist appearances and an intensification of the
underlying bureaucratic trend. Once the competition of other socialist parties
had been suppressed in mid-1918, the Communist Party apparatus displaced
the nominal government as the commanding authority, reverting from its loose
practices of 1917 back to Lenin's prerevolutionary conspiratorial model, infused with what Rosa Luxemburg had called "the sterile spirit of the night-
watchman."[28] Almost overnight, the party apparatus emerged as the totalitarian
society in microcosm.

Bureaucratic arrangements were quickly restored in the military and in
industrial organization. Trotsky promised to dispose of objections to traditional
military command with "complete ruthlessness."[29] This authoritarian philosophy, and especially its corollary of employing ex-tsarist officers, was bitterly
resisted by the "Military Opposition" at the Eighth Party Congress in March
1919. These critics were immediately denounced as "petty-bourgeois"—"To
preach guerrilla warfare as a military program is the same as to recommend
turning back from large-scale industry to handicraft trades"—though controversy over revolutionary versus conventional principles of military organization continued to the end of the 1920s.[30]

Parallel objections to the employment of spetsy in industry and the suppression of workers' control were voiced by the Democratic Centralists and the

Workers' Opposition, as they tried vainly to sustain the antimanagerial critique initiated by the Left Communists in 1918. Instead, the economy was brought under completely top-down direction through the *glavki*. Trotsky wanted to carry this principle to its logical conclusion by forming "labor armies," merging the trade unions into the government structure, and applying "measures of compulsion" to effectuate "a single economic plan,"[31] though this vision evaporated upon the introduction of the NEP.

The Communists' transition to the NEP in 1921 was an admission that their drive toward a totally bureaucratic economic system, relying on compulsion rather than incentives, had gone too far and too fast. Thanks to the conditions of civil war, the disruption of transport, and the regime's own policies, industrial production had ground virtually to a halt, and the peasants were in revolt. A retreat to market socialism and "bourgeois" law codes could not be avoided. However, these concessions did not reverse the trend toward managerialism in state-owned enterprises, trusts, and conglomerates; the last vestiges of the revolutionary experiment in industrial democracy were liquidated.

Corresponding tendencies toward "bureaucratism" in the government machinery were now lamented by the Communist leadership. Noting in one of his last articles that "the political and social overturn has proved to be a predecessor of the cultural overturn," Lenin underscored "the task of overhauling our apparatus, which is simply good for nothing and which we have taken over in toto from an earlier era."[32] Bukharin warned, "The whole economic apparatus of the proletarian state does not facilitate, but only *hinders the development of the forces of production*. . . . Iron necessity compels the proletariat to destroy such an apparatus"—something, of course, that was easier said than done.[33]

Despite these worries about bureaucracy, nothing effective was undertaken to curb it. On the contrary: Lenin cast the die for unstoppable bureaucratic authority in the party organization with the measures that he proposed to the Tenth Party Congress in 1921 to tighten discipline and outlaw factional dissent. That was followed by his nomination of Stalin in 1922 as general secretary in command of the party apparatus. Lenin seemed to think that a bureaucratic party riding herd on the bureaucratic government could cure the evils of "bureaucratism." Trotsky, transformed by the power struggle into a critic of authoritarianism, documented with his complaints the takeover of the party as well as the government and the economy by the appointed nomenklatura.

Stalin's revolution from above of the late 1920s and early 1930s was a triumph of the bureaucratic principle. It imposed bureaucratic organization in agriculture, reimposed it in the trade and service sectors of the economy, and subjected

cultural life to a corresponding regimentation, to the great detriment of production and performance in all these areas, none of them organically prepared
for advanced forms of managerial administration. As the bureaucratic principle
was extended downward and outward, organizational advancedness was offset
by social and cultural backwardness, manifested in the corruption, self-serv-
ing, slothfulness, and indifference to adversity among the populace that have
distinguished Russian bureaucratic life before and after Communism as well as
in the Soviet era.

The revolution from above was an uneven experience among different sectors of society and from one time period to the next. While it rested politically on
the General Secretary's ever-tighter bureaucratic control of the party apparatus,
in economics it initially seemed to revert to the most radical sentiments of the
War Communism era, with show trials of alleged industrial saboteurs, mobilization of workers to collectivize the peasants, and campaigns against "bourgeois"
intellectuals in all fields. Genuine economic planning was suppressed in favor
of what the Gorbachevians later termed "command-administrative methods," in
other words, a simplistic military approach to the economy, in a military spirit
and with military priorities.

In 1931–32, in the face of critical difficulties with the Five-Year Plan, industrial policy changed again. Managerial authority and labor discipline were
restored, and the experts were rehabilitated.[34] "A 'status revolution' took place,"
writes Moshe Lewin, "that switched the orientation of the regime from workers to officials as carriers of the state principle."[35] It was in the midst of this
turnabout that Stalin saw fit to proclaim the victory of "socialism" and the abolition of class exploitation, an acute irony to anyone who took the classical understanding of socialism seriously. Condemning egalitarianism as "reactionary
petty-bourgeois absurdity,"[36] he anointed the meritocracy as the "toiling intelligentsia," abolished the "party maximum" that had limited members' salaries,
and terminated such symbolic gestures toward real workers as preference in university admissions and party membership. The purges were a gruesome shock,
entailing the sudden restaffing of the whole bureaucratic system. This allowed
more upward mobility for newer elements of the meritocracy, but it did not alter the accomplished fact of a hierarchical and authoritarian social structure,
dressed up in the language of Marxian socialism. In Karl Mannheim's terms,
the utopia of inspiration had turned into the ideology of legitimation.[37]

This was the circumstance that prompted the more farsighted Trotskyists
to try to define an entirely new socioeconomic formation, neither capitalist nor
socialist in the traditional understanding of the terms. Stalin in his own way
agreed. In 1939, in the aftermath of the Great Purge, he still found it necessary

to condemn "views hostile to the Soviet intelligentsia and incompatible with the party position," that is, antiexpert attitudes that he had cultivated himself during the first phase of his revolution from above. His explanation was pure managerialism: "The remnants of the old intelligentsia were dissolved in the new, Soviet intelligentsia. . . . The old theory about the intelligentsia, which taught that it should be distrusted and combated, fully applied to the old pre-revolutionary intelligentsia, which served the landlords and capitalists. That theory is now out of date. . . . A new theory is needed for our new intelligentsia, one teaching the necessity for a cordial attitude toward it, solicitude and respect for it, and cooperation with it in the interests of the working class and the peasantry."[38]

It has not been easy to define and classify the social system that prevailed in the Soviet Union after the revolution from above was consolidated. If ideological formulas are set aside, it is easier to say what the Stalinist system was not: It was not capitalism, and it had no entrepreneurial class, at least not legally, but it was not a workers' state in any real sense except insofar as many former workers had joined the nomenklatura. As a form of government and society, it was far removed from the expectations of prerevolutionary socialists, whatever their factional orientation. As Rudolf Hilferding wrote, "We never imagined that the political form of that 'managed economy' which was to replace capitalist production for a free market could be unrestricted absolutism."[39]

Nevertheless, if socialism is strictly defined as any system of public control over economic enterprise, Stalinism fits its essential terms, even though it dispensed with the egalitarian and communitarian characteristics that were initially uppermost in the minds of the revolutionaries. It was a form of militarized, barracks socialism, embodying Russia's leap to managerial society, based on bureaucratic hierarchy and functional rather than economic stratification. In a highly idiosyncratic way, Stalinism combined elements of Old Russian tradition and the most advanced elements of modern industrial society in a postrevolutionary framework of state socialism legitimized and distorted by a revolutionary ideology. This was the essence of Soviet totalitarianism.

Socialism and totalitarianism are not coterminous, though the categories obviously overlap. While totalitarianism had its seeds in Lenin's political philosophy and its beginnings under his revolutionary rule, it did not come to full flower in Russia until Stalin collectivized the peasants, shackled the workers, and disciplined the intellectuals, thereby extending the hierarchical principles of the party to the whole of society. By contrast, aside from their corporate-state vocabulary, fascism and Nazism did not institute direct and comprehensive socialist administration of the private economy. Thus the Stalinist model turned out in practice to be far more totalitarian than its counterparts on the right, bringing the development of bureaucratic society to its ultimate, and perhaps unsustainable, extreme.

The picture of the Soviet system as an extension of the managerial-bureaucratic trends already at work under capitalism naturally suggests the theory of convergence, the notion that capitalist and Communist societies were approaching a common form, even if they came from different starting points and by different routes. As early as 1926, John Maynard Keynes wrote of a "natural line of evolution" from bureaucratized capitalism to state socialism.[40] Convergence was a popular idea in the 1960s and 1970s, consistent with East-West détente, although it was indignantly rejected by the ideologists of both systems. Daniel Bell defined it as "common problems" but not "like responses."[41] Convergence did not necessarily mean that the two systems were equally virtuous to begin with, or that their convergent end would incorporate the best of both worlds—it could be the worst, depending on one's point of view.

Convergence anticipated that capitalist systems would continue their evolution in the bureaucratic direction, bringing together such trends as oligopolistic concentration of enterprise, the separation of nominal property ownership and actual managerial control, the regulatory role of the state, and centralization of the formerly precapitalist sectors of the economy into chain operations. In politics and communications, convergence has expressed itself in the West in the growing dominance of highly centralized mass media, making possible the manipulation of opinion and the electoral process by financial wealth—in other words, the capitalist version of the propaganda state. Convergence toward managerialism has obviously been going on for a long time, accomplishing in the capitalist West the de facto socialization of economic activity within the shell of private property relations.

A more recent development is the extension of capitalist concentration to previously individual enterprise in agriculture, retail trade, and services, the areas that in Russia were precapitalist before the revolution and rudely yanked by the Communist regime into the postcapitalist era. For Russia, convergence entailed the social modernization of the population through urbanization, education, and industrial employment, and the achievement of high-tech industrial and scientific operations, albeit primarily for interests of state in the military-industrial complex. Until the end of the Communist era, convergence was impeded by intractable distortions in the Soviet system, including administrative overcentralization, tension between the controllers and the people who tried to get things done, paranoid information controls, and stupidly military standards and methods in planning and decision making—all of which contributed disastrously to the crisis of the Communist system in the 1980s. The capitalist experience shows that the dominance of the bureaucratic elite and the manipulation of public opinion do not have to be totalitarian, and are actually more effective, as well as more accommodating to the requirements of technological innovation, if they allow a little looseness. Unacceptable critics can easily be drowned out or marginalized.

In the aftermath of the collapse of Communist rule in the Soviet Union in 1991 and the simultaneous resurgence of free-market ideology throughout the West, it might appear that convergence in the bureaucratic direction has been broken off, and that the whole historical model of postcapitalist evolution has been nullified. The notion of Russia's "transition to market democracy" implies that a different kind of convergence has set in, as Russia shifts direction in order to emulate free-market capitalism and catch up with its achievements. But such conclusions fail to consider deeply enough the ongoing underlying evolution of Western society as opposed to its formal ideology. Such an awareness might have ameliorated the crisis brought about in Russia for the second time in its history by theory-driven attempts to reverse the course of its natural development.

Russia entered the post-Communist era still suffering from bureaucratic overdevelopment and overcontrol along with lingering underdevelopment of the formerly precapitalist sectors—in other words, falling short both above and below in its progress toward convergence with Western society. The country's distorted, militarized development had endowed it on the one hand with an overgrown heavy industrial plant and a modernized, educated population and on the other hand a chronic deficiency in meeting demand for consumer goods and services, even for food. Yet post-Communist Russia chose in a doctrinaire way to ignore both the managerial trend in Western social evolution and Russia's convergence with it in favor of an illusory model of early capitalism that attempted to repudiate the country's postcapitalist features.

Until the years of perestroika and glasnost, Russian economic thinkers, experienced solely in the hyperbureaucratic Soviet system, had only the dimmest notions of Western economics. Then, beginning with the abortive "Five Hundred Days Plan" of 1990, they abruptly opted for the neoclassical free-market model as a cure-all for the late-term crisis of the militarized planned economy. Taken into the councils of state under the Yeltsin regime, the theorists of reform launched a concerted attack on Russia's postcapitalist institutions, including central planning, state ownership of enterprise, control of foreign trade and financial transactions, and collectivized agriculture. This artificial, state-commanded attempt to re-create the economic arrangements of pure capitalism did succeed, to be sure, in liquidating the hyperbureaucratic controls and military priorities that had governed the Soviet economy following the dismantling of totalitarian rule in the political sphere between 1985 and 1991. But the reforms destroyed more than they repaired, breaking up the managerial institutions of coordination and priority setting on which, the wisdom of hindsight shows, the Soviet economy depended. No heed was paid to the legal, financial, and cultural underpinnings of a market economy, which were lacking in the bureaucratic Soviet environment. Just as the Communists had decapitated the market economy and supplanted it with hyperbureaucracy, so the post-Communist reformers answered the defects of hyperbureaucracy by decapitating it in turn, hoping that market magic would take the place of the dirigiste mechanisms holding together a complex but vulnerable monster.

Deprecating the Communist legacy of industrial plant and managerial-technical expertise, the reformers of the Yeltsin era ran into the precapitalist, Third World outlook toward the market still embedded in Russian culture. To the average Russian, commercialism meant speculation rather than production. Meanwhile, surprisingly, the reformers took no cognizance of the long organic evolution of capitalism in the West and its history of political struggles to achieve a balance between the market and social justice. Writes Harold Perkin, "The unregulated free market recommended by naive Western advisors, who seem to have no conception of how their own system works and how it depends on a self-regulating culture which they do not recognize, still less understand, is only intensifying the chaos in a country which has never known a free-enterprise system."[42]

Post-Communist reform was a frontal assault on the most advanced, managerial features of the Russian economy, with consequences more disruptive than anything experienced since the Russian Civil War. Former prime minister Yegor Gaidar implied this parallel when he justified the post-1991 collapse in class-struggle terms, much as Bukharin had in his time—for Bukharin to destroy the bourgeoisie, for Gaidar to restore it.[43] In practice, much of the old administrative nomenklatura succeeded in transforming themselves into a new kind of parasitic class of speculators and robber barons, who simply shifted from command of the socialist bureaucracy to exploitation of postsocialist chaos. "Former top Communist leaders who take on a new role are sometimes really skillful at transforming themselves," wrote an *Izvestia* staffer in 1996.[44] Lower members of the nomenklatura have simply sat in place and watched their bureaucratic ranks grow larger than ever.

The formerly precapitalist sectors have not fared well in the dismantling of the militarized planned economy. To be sure, trade and services catering to the affluent minority have flourished in a few urban centers, giving the surface illusion of prosperity, though the goods in question are mainly imports paid for by energy and raw material exports. Commercial agriculture and native consumer goods manufacturing, far from making up the deficiencies of the Soviet era, declined precipitously in the face of inflation and the flood of imports made possible by untimely liberalization of the economy. All in all, the post-Communist economy is the chaotic outcome of political decisions encouraged by ideology—or in this case, an anti-ideology—but with little or no analytical understanding of the circumstances or the consequences of these so-called reforms.

Russia's self-inflicted retrogression has been represented in most Western appraisals as an expression of a universal process, natural and virtually inevitable, the "transition to market democracy." From what kind of system this transition is presumably occurring is not so clearly analyzed; often it is pigeonholed with the development of precapitalist societies toward the supposed Western model. "The East has become the South," asserts Adam Przeworski.[45] The actual Soviet heritage is not the Third World but the Second World of distorted bureaucratic industrialism. This, and the evolving Western social structure toward which the Soviet system had been converging, are both implicitly denied. This thinking has become a self-fulfilling prophecy, as Russia watches its most advanced social and economic structures disintegrate and does indeed sink down to the level of a Third World land.

PART III

The Left Opposition between Lenin and Stalin

CHAPTER 13

Socialist Alternatives in the Crisis of 1921

Socialism, broadly considered, was the heart of the revolutions of 1917. It was a faith or a goal all across the center and left of the 1917 political spectrum. But this socialism was more a spirit than a structure. Russian revolutionaries of whatever party affiliation embraced socialism not as a projected set of institutions but rather as a utopian antithesis to present reality, as an ideal way of life toward which their society could be led or pushed.

Marxism did not help to clarify the meaning of socialism. Subscribing to the doctrine of the natural march of events from capitalism through socialism to "communism," Marxists gave relatively little thought to the details of the future society. In Russia, before, during, and immediately after the revolution, the Bolsheviks' attention was absorbed by questions of tactics and even of political survival, while the ultimate arrangements of socialism and communism were expected to be taken care of by the dialectic of history. "No blueprint guided the Bolshevik leaders in devising the new system," wrote Thomas Remington. "The ideas they followed consisted either of generalized images of an ideal system or of improvised responses to particular dilemmas."[1] Until nearly the end of the period of War Communism, the character of the socialist institutions and policies established by the Communists was governed more by ad hoc political and economic necessities than by any deliberate, long-run legislative program.

It was only after victory in the civil war, when the Communist leaders began to view their new system in a longer time perspective, that definite conceptions began to be formulated for the road ahead. The occasion evoking this consideration of future alternatives was the so-called Trade Union Controversy that agitated the ranks of the Russian Communist Party in 1920–21. Three principal platforms were represented in the discussion, the Leninists, the Trotskyists, and the Workers' Opposition, reflecting three fundamentally different conceptions of socialism and of the path to the ultimate goal of communism.

The various positions in the Trade Union Controversy can readily be placed on the left-right political scale according to the degree of romantic adventurism or of cautious pragmatism that they exhibited. Thus, on the left stood the Workers' Opposition, espousing the 1917 ideal of workers' control and confident of a rapid and direct transition to communism. On the right, contrary to the conventional historiography,[2] the Leninists should be located. They were the people persuaded by the crisis of War Communism that the Soviet government would have to retreat to a state capitalist system and only then resume a very long and careful journey to socialism and communism. The center, then, was occupied by the Trotskyists (and by the slightly more leftist adherents of Bukharin's platform, who merged with the Trotskyists in the course of the controversy). The Trotskyist position was to pursue socialism rapidly but with instruments of centralized power and coercion—in other words, the model of barracks socialism.

Each faction in the trade union debate represented a different source in the revolutionary tradition and a different psychological orientation toward the prospects of the transition to socialism. The Workers' Opposition expressed the utopian current of thought that went back to the prerevolutionary Ultra Left (among both Bolsheviks and Mensheviks) and to the anarcho-syndicalist movement.[3] They were close to the Left Communists of 1918, who rebelled not only against the Treaty of Brest-Litovsk but also against Lenin's efforts to curtail workers' control in industry and restore the managerial hierarchy. Like their forerunners, the Workers' Opposition were confident that socialism could be reached quickly and easily by giving free rein to the masses through the institutions they had created in the course of the revolution, the factory committees (or the trade unions, which had absorbed these bodies) and the local soviets. The faith in the masses expressed by the Workers' Opposition paralleled the premises underlying Bogdanov's Proletkult. The Ultra Left rejected the centralist and coercive policies of War Communism as a violation of their democratic-communitarian ideal, which according to their thinking could and should be directly implemented and not postponed.

The Leninists of 1920–21, identified in the Trade Union Controversy as the adherents of the "Platform of the Ten," included those Bolshevik leaders who were consistently skeptical of the maturity of the masses and cautious about the difficulties to be encountered in the revolutionary transition to socialism. Zinoviev, Kamenev, and Rykov had backed Lenin against the Left Bolsheviks before 1917; they held back on the eve of the October Revolution; and then they supported the pragmatic Brest Treaty and Lenin's polemics against the Left Communists. For them, socialism under Russian conditions could only be the end result of a long and difficult evolution while the workers' state endeavored to consolidate its gains. Like the Workers' Opposition, the Leninists also turned against the policies of War Communism, but for the opposite reason—they simply found this system to be ineffective at Russia's current stage of development.

The Trotskyists and Bukharinists, taking the middle position in the Trade Union Controversy, combined the direct push toward socialism embraced by the Workers' Opposition on the left with the more realistic sense of the difficulties lying ahead stressed by the Leninists on the right. Their position can be traced back both to the impatience of the prerevolutionary Ultra Left and to the hardening experience that War Communism represented for the entire party. Interestingly enough, their forces included the three men who had served as party secretaries in 1919 and 1920—Nikolai Krestinsky, Yevgeny Preobrazhensky, and Leonid Serebriakov. Following the most uncompromising theories of War Communism as expressed by Trotsky, Bukharin, Yury Larin, and Lev Kritsman,[4] the adherents of the center position rejected what they considered the romantic optimism of the Left as well as the unnecessary caution of the Right. Making a virtue of necessity, they proposed to retain the War Communism methods of centralization, compulsion, and militarization as they pushed ahead toward the quick achievement of socialism.

The first clear position on the trade unions was that of the centrists, beginning with Trotsky's proposal early in 1920 for the militarization of labor. "If we seriously speak of planned economy," he told the Ninth Party Congress, "the working masses cannot be wandering all over Russia. They must be thrown here and there, appointed, commanded, just like soldiers."[5] This objective dictated the function of the trade unions: "not for a struggle for better conditions of labor, . . . but to organize the working class for the ends of production, to educate, to discipline."[6] Bukharin, in his own platform on the unions, picked up a phrase first used at the Second Trade Union Congress in 1919, "governmentalizing" (*ogosudarstvlenie*) of the unions; he called this "the state form of workers' socialism" and expected it to prevail until the state withered away according to the Marxian prophecy.[7]

Both the Left and Right positions—Workers' Opposition and Lenin-ist—took shape in reaction to Trotsky's hard-line philosophy. The precipitating event was Trotsky's initiative in the summer of 1920 to merge the Commissariat of Transport with the railroad workers' union, plus a new, military-style political administration of the railroads, to form the Central Committee for Transport (*Tsektran*). (Lenin cited this idea in his "Testament" as an example of Trotsky's arbitrariness.) At the Fifth Trade Union Conference in November 1920, Trotsky proposed to extend the Tsektran system to the entire state sector of the economy, converting the unions from "trade" (*professional'nyi*) to "production" (*proizvodstvennyi*) unions. He dismissed objections to this model as "Kautskian-Menshevik-SR prejudices."[8]

The first concerted criticism of Trotsky's model for the unions and socialism came from the Ultra Left, banking on the still-surviving 1917 tradition of workers' control and committee administration in industry. Even the Party Program of 1919 had endorsed this approach: "The trade unions must proceed to the actual concentration in their own hands of all the administration of the whole economy."[9] Almost word for word, the Workers' Opposition took this position in its theses of January 1921: "The organization of the administration of the economy belongs to the All-Russian Congress of Producers, united in trade-production unions, who elect the central organs that administer the whole economy of the republic."[10] Both Aleksandr Shliapnikov for the Workers' Opposition and Valerian Osinsky-Obolensky for the Democratic Centralist group proposed the concept of a "separation of powers" among the party, the soviets, and the trade unions or, as Osinsky put it, among the "military-soviet culture," the "civil-soviet culture," and the "trade union . . . sphere of culture."[11] Among these, pride of place as the voice of the workers in shaping the new society went to the unions. "Through the creative powers of the rising class in the form of industrial unions," wrote Alexandra Kollontai, "we shall go toward the reconstruction and development of the creative forces of the country; toward purification of the party itself from the elements foreign to it; toward correction of the activity of the party by means of going back to democracy, freedom of opinion, and criticism inside the party."[12]

The position of the Ultra Left disturbed both Lenin and Trotsky as a threat to the political monopoly of the party apparatus. At the Ninth Party Congress, party secretary Krestinsky flatly called the Ultra Left "counterrevolutionary," and their goal of political autonomy for the unions was duly repudiated.[13] Nevertheless, under the leadership of Shliapnikov and Kollontai, the Ultras gained strength during the following twelve months, particularly in the metal workers' union and in industrial centers of the south, and they organized themselves formally as the Workers' Opposition.

The high point of the Ultra Left challenge was the Ninth Party Conference, held in September 1920, when all immediate military threats to the Soviet regime had finally been surmounted. The conference seethed with rank-and-file protests against the bureaucratic trend in the party, and the leadership of Leninists and Trotskyists temporarily yielded to allow passage of the remarkable resolution "On the Coming Tasks of Building the Party." Targeting "bureaucratism," this document directed "the attention of the whole party again and again toward putting more equality into practice" and called for "publications which are capable of realizing broader and more systematic criticism of the mistakes of the party and general criticism within the party." Above all, the resolution demanded "fully effective practical measures to eliminate inequality (in conditions of life, the wage scale, etc.) between the 'spetsy' and the responsible functionaries on the one hand and the toiling masses on the other. . . . This inequality violates democratism and is the source of disruption in the party and of reduction in the authority of Communists."[14] While Shliapnikov and Kollontai never ceased to reject the charge of syndicalism, the Workers' Opposition clearly had some of that flavor, enough to justify Mikhail Tomsky in calling its ideology "industrialism and syndicalism."[15] That was after Tomsky switched from the union cause to Lenin's group. "Syndicalist deviation," reflecting the alleged "petty-bourgeois element," was the main charge against the Workers' Opposition when the Tenth Party Congress condemned their factional activity.[16]

Lenin's own faction in the Trade Union Controversy took shape only gradually during the year 1920, as the top party leadership divided over Trotsky's stern approach to the national crisis bequeathed by the civil war. As early as the Ninth Party Congress, consistently cautious Communists such as Rykov, V. P. Miliutin, and V. P. Nogin objected to economic militarization, even though Lenin at this point stood with Trotsky to use the unions as an instrument of labor discipline.[17] A different emphasis quickly developed, however, around the potential educational and propaganda function of the unions. Still fighting resistance to the restoration of one-man management and bourgeois specialists in industry, Lenin persuaded the Ninth Party Congress to resolve: "The unions must take upon themselves the task of explaining to the broad circles of the working class all the necessities of reconstructing the apparatus of industrial administration, . . . the maximum curtailment of administrative collegia, and the gradual introduction of individual management."[18]

Lenin kept his options open for a time, while anti-Trotsky sentiment grew in the Central Committee. He allowed Trotsky to personify the methods of War

Communism while preparing his own reversal of course and encouraging Zinoviev (a consistent enemy of Trotsky ever since 1917) to develop the anti-Trotsky argument. Trotsky later recalled, "Stalin and Zinoviev were given what one might call their legal opportunity to bring their struggle against me out into the open."[19] The actual break between Lenin and Trotsky came at a meeting of the Central Committee early in November 1920, when Lenin cast the deciding vote to reject Trotsky's theses on the trade unions, eight to seven.[20]

By the time the debate reached a public forum at the Eighth Congress of Soviets in December 1920, Lenin was moving rapidly away from any administrative role for the unions in favor of their educational and political function coupled with the presocialist notion of protecting the interests of the workers: "We must use these workers' organizations for the defense of the workers from their state and for the defense of our state by the workers."[21] Shortly afterward, Lenin's position was endorsed in the Platform of the Ten, emphasizing the unions' functions of "a school of communism," "production propaganda," and "the setting of rates of pay," all of course under the direction of the party. However, the document still spoke of the unions' "direct participation" in "working out and implementing the comprehensive economic plan" and called on them to "undertake the closest participation in the business of organizing and administering industry."[22]

The struggle during the precongress debate early in 1921 was the most serious controversy the Communist Party had experienced since Brest-Litovsk. At the outset, Lenin's victory was by no means assured. The Leninists felt compelled to call for the election of delegates to the Tenth Congress on the basis of factional platforms, presumably so that Lenin's personal prestige could decide the outcome; they pushed this rule through the Central Committee by another narrow margin of eight to seven against the Trotskyists.[23] Their strategy was successful, even without the aid of the Orgburo and the Party Secretariat, which were still controlled by the Trotskyists. In one local party meeting after another, regularly reported by *Pravda*, the Leninists overwhelmed both oppositions. Calling for unity of the party and the suppression of syndicalism, Lenin dominated the Tenth Congress and secured adoption of the famous resolutions embodying these two themes. On these fundamental political questions the Trotskyists went with Lenin; nevertheless, on War Communism and the unions, Lenin implacably rejected their line. The Tenth Congress essentially adopted the Platform of the Ten, denouncing governmentalizing of the unions and Trotsky's ventures in militarization. In the following months, as the NEP was implemented step-by-step and the Communists acknowledged their retreat to state capitalism, the traditional role assigned to the unions became clear. As the Politburo resolved in January 1922, "One of the most pressing tasks of the trade unions is to defend in every aspect and by every means the class interests of the proletariat and its struggle with capitalism."[24]

The two most systematic rationales for War Communism were composed by Trotsky and Bukharin—respectively, *Terrorism and Communism* and *The Economics of the Transformation Period.* (How these men managed to find time to write theoretical treatises along with their heavy official responsibilities and the incessant crises of the civil war is still a mystery.) Trotsky was blunt about persevering with War Communism as the road to socialism: "We can have no way to socialism except by the authoritative regulation of the economic forces and resources of the country, and the centralized distribution of labor-power in harmony with the general state plan."[25] He reaffirmed the militarization of labor, compulsory labor service, and the absorption of the unions into the state: "The road to socialism lies through a period of the highest possible intensification of the principle of the state."[26] Bukharin expressed a cloudy optimism, somewhat closer to the Workers' Opposition until the realignment on the eve of the Tenth Congress. He saw "a new network of human systems," while the proletariat "builds its own apparatus." But he came down closer to Trotsky on specifics: "Militarization . . . is a method of self-organization of the working class."[27] With the talent for theoretical rationalizations that made him popular as the party's number-one ideologue, Bukharin accepted the use of bourgeois experts and claimed that the growingly bureaucratic administration of industry was "a contracted, condensed *form* of workers' control of industry."[28] For both men, the system of War Communism would remain the norm for an indefinite period of time, though they still looked to the ultimate attainment of socialism, when "there will be no need for the harsh military style of management" (Bukharin), and "there will not exist the apparatus of compulsion itself, namely, the State: for it will have melted away entirely into a producing and consuming commune" (Trotsky).[29]

For the Workers' Opposition, by contrast, socialism had to be the direct achievement of the working class if it was to be realized at all. "Who shall build the communist economy?" asked Kollontai. "Who is right—the leaders, or the working masses endowed with the healthy class instinct?" This was closer to Rosa Luxemburg's thinking than to Leninism. Kollontai continued, "Through the creative powers of the rising class in the form of industrial unions we shall go towards reconstruction of the creative forces of the country; towards purification of the party itself from the elements foreign to it; towards correction of the activity of the party by way of going back to democracy, freedom of opinion, and criticism within the party."[30] Alone of the contending factions, the Workers' Opposition sensed that the proletariat's revolutionary victory could be snatched away just as the bourgeoisie had snatched it away from the sans-culottes in revolutionary France.

For the Leninists, it was enough to assert that the Soviet regime was a work-ers' state, guaranteeing the transition to socialism however long the process might take. Lenin's consistent priorities for the economy from 1918 on were the supremacy of party control and restoration of the conventional managerial au-thority and engineering expertise that the Workers' Opposition found so repug-nant. By 1921, he and his supporters were abandoning their assumptions both about the country's readiness for socialism (contrary to the Workers' Opposi-tion) and about the allegedly socialist character of the methods they had resorted to under War Communism (contrary to the Trotskyists). Beneath the level of the dictatorial state, the Leninists were ready to accept a new sort of pluralism, with relatively independent functions for the industrial leadership, the trade unions, and any other social organization or interest, including the intelligentsia. In ef-fect, the Leninists were retreating to Lenin's old image of the "democratic dic-tatorship of the proletariat and peasantry," in which the vanguard party would hold power while the country continued to mature to the point where real social-ism would be feasible.[31] This was the basic ideology of the NEP.

Diversity of revolutionary factions and their competing notions about the fu-ture road was by no means unique to the Russian Revolution and the Com-munists. Every great revolution has generated differences, not only for and against the basic aims of the revolution but about the definition of those aims and the tempo of their realization. As the revolution gathers momentum and the moderate parties fall by the wayside, power goes to those who are most determined to realize the goals of the revolution by any means, including dic-tatorship and civil war. But disagreements soon emerge among these commit-ted revolutionaries, representing basic differences in human psychology. The most idealistic and utopian people—the Enragés and the Hébertistes in the French Revolution, the Workers' Opposition and the Democratic Centralists in Russia—persuade themselves that the masses need only to be freed and encouraged so they can realize the revolutionary ideal. The center position is taken by those of the Robespierrist persuasion, who are emboldened by com-bat and the feel of authority and believe they can overcome all obstacles by force: "There are no fortresses that Bolsheviks cannot capture," to cite Stalin's famous statement of a later date.[32] Meanwhile, the more cautious elements conclude that the revolution risks destruction unless it falls back and tries to resume the advance more gradually—the sentiment of the right-wing Jacobins who overthrew Robespierre. Here, of course, the Russian and French revolutions differ in important detail. In France, the leader of the militant center was overthrown and guillotined on the Ninth of Thermidor; in Russia, the prime leader sided with the right wing of the revolution and carried out his own Thermidor, so to speak, while letting the Robespierrist Trotsky take the onus for the excesses of War Communism and the Terror.

In neither the French nor the Russian case, of course, did the thermidorean reaction represent a repudiation of the aims of the revolution, but only of its violent excesses. Lenin must be credited with unusual political perspicacity and skill as a leader of the radical revolution who could see that the time had come for revolutionary retrenchment and was able to lead the retreat and maintain the rule of his own party instead of suffering Robespierre's fate. This strategic maneuver, even more than the victory of October, was arguably the most decisive instance of the impact of Lenin's personality on the otherwise impersonal process of revolution in Russia. He had the flexibility that Trotsky, the purer ideologue, lacked.

The models of socialism expressed or implied by the three factions in the Trade Union Controversy were all paralleled at one point or another by subsequent developments in the Soviet Union or the international Communist movement. In Yugoslavia in the 1950s, the semisyndicalist ideal of the Workers' Opposition was reincarnated in the doctrine of "workers' self-management," though this ancestry was not directly acknowledged. Milovan Djilas says the idea of self-management came to him when he was rereading Marx to find arguments against Stalinism after the Soviet-Yugoslav break in 1948; Edvard Kardelj, one of the most enthusiastic backers of the self-management concept, studied in Moscow in the 1930s and may conceivably have become acquainted with the history of the Russian Ultra Left at that time.[33]

Lenin's position in the trade union debate—the nondoctrinaire recognition of the time-consuming difficulties along the path of fundamental social change in an incompletely developed country—was later reiterated everywhere by pragmatic Communist reformers, not least in the Soviet Union under Gorbachev. Interestingly enough, Soviet students of radical Third World regimes observed in the 1970s and early 1980s that Lenin's NEP model of market socialism and limited state intervention was more appropriate under conditions of "superbackwardness" than Stalin's totally centralized system.[34]

What of the proposition that Stalin's "command-administrative system" was a direct revival of the War Communism model and of Trotsky's concept of militarized socialism? In 1928–29 the Bukharinists were charging explicitly that Stalin was breaking with the NEP and resorting to the methods of War Communism. The renewed spirit of class struggle and the mood of hysteria directed against bourgeois specialists, beginning with the Shakhty Trial (when a number of mining engineers in the Donets Basin were accused of "sabotage"), recall the views of the Ultra Left during War Communism. Robert Tucker believes that the "culture of War Communism" lived on among the new Stalinist apparatchiki of the 1920s and then emerged to dominate the political scene of the 1930s.[35] (Perhaps this explains why the former leaders of the Workers' Opposition supported Stalin against the Trotsky-Zinoviev Opposition, though it does not account for the fate that most of them subsequently suffered.) Stalin's measures of centralized mobilization and compulsion obviously recall the center, Trotskyist position in the trade union debate. By this time, however, Trotsky had rejected compulsion in favor of fiscal methods of planning and constantly criticized the manner in which Stalinist industrialization and collectivization were implemented.[36]

Trotsky is perhaps the most difficult figure to explain among the major Communist leaders. In his prerevolutionary career and in his years as an oppositionist after 1923, he resisted the unqualified centralism and discipline usually associated with Leninism, yet from the time of the October Revolution until the Kronstadt Revolt he was the most ruthless and authoritarian of revolutionaries. To be sure, he claimed to have anticipated the NEP by proposing to the Central Committee in February 1920 an end to the uncompensated requisitioning of food products from the peasantry. Failing this, so he says in his autobiography, he insisted that military methods be applied even more systematically.[37] Trotsky's psychological orientation toward power changed according to whether he held it or not. His tragedy was that he was too big a man to subordinate himself to Lenin or any other individual or party or doctrine and yet too small a man to do without the political legitimacy that loyalty to such an individual or party or doctrine provided for him. This contradiction lay at the root of his failure in the fateful political struggles of 1923–27.

CHAPTER 14

The Left Opposition and the Evolution of the Communist Regime

T he hallmark event of the mid-1920s in the Soviet Union was the running controversy between the leadership of the Communist Party and the movements of protest collectively known as the Left Opposition—the "struggle for power," as the standard accounts label it. These opposition movements during the era of the NEP reflected step-by-step Stalin's rise to power, and they are a key to understanding the evolution of Stalinist Communism together with the issues that still arise in discussions about the history of the Soviet system. With the destruction of the Left Opposition, basic alternatives were closed, and the peculiar Stalinist form of rule combining the Communist Party bureaucracy and Marxist-Leninist ideology became entrenched for the long haul.

The record of the Left Opposition is the record of a desperate struggle to hold the evolution of the Communist system as nearly as possible in the original direction of the revolution. This struggle failed, as it was perhaps doomed to fail, because of historical circumstances and laws of social development of which the oppositionists had only a dim understanding. But in going down to defeat, the oppositionists left a remarkable record of theoretical analysis and practical protest that documents the transformation in Soviet Russia from a revolutionary dictatorship to a bureaucratic despotism. The oppositionists had little idea of why this was happening and less of how to combat it, but they did recognize the outlines of the dismal totalitarianism that was falling heir to the revolution. It is the lasting significance of the Left Opposition's saga and of its eloquent statements of protest and analysis, to have recorded for posterity the world over the nature of the Stalinist transformation and the perversion of the spirit of 1917 that it represented.

Marxism, naturally, was the language of the Left Opposition. Its logic and perceptions were wholly suffused with Marxian presuppositions. It is ironic that the oppositionists were eventually condemned as an anti-Marxist deviation, considering that one of the reasons for their failure was their literal devotion to the premises of Marxism. They were unable to work their way out of the contradictions inherent in a Marxist movement attempting to hold power in an underdeveloped country such as Russia.

As good Marxists, the oppositionists viewed themselves as mere agents of the laws of history, which naturally were believed to be working inevitably toward those goals that Marxists desired. They did not begin to resolve the contradiction between determinism and voluntarism in Marxism but struggled heroically to establish the dictatorship of the proletariat that they believed at the same time to be inevitable. They had no theoretical equipment to deal with the possibility that the laws of history might be working the wrong way. As the neo-Kantian Revisionists had warned before the revolution, moral goal and objective social development might not coincide. Postrevolution, objective social development was confounding the goal of workers' democracy.

Even in the Marxian perspective, it is difficult to find sustenance for the hopes entertained by the Left Opposition. As Marxists of all hues acknowledged up until 1917, Russia was unready for socialism as they understood it, even though special circumstances might temporarily thrust the proletariat into power. This quandary set the scene for the controversy over Socialism in One Country when Stalin asserted, on the basis of some quotation-lifting from Lenin, that Russia's backwardness and isolation were no impediment to the immediate construction of socialism. The oppositionists were compelling in their logic but futile politically, as they tried to demonstrate the inconsistency between Stalin's proposition and the understanding of Marxism that had been expounded by all its leading lights in Russia up to that time. Groping and hesitant, the oppositionists were nevertheless beginning to show that the party leadership under Stalin was converting Marxism into an ideological rationale not for the proletarian society but instead for the kind of society that Russian conditions invited, that is, some sort of despotic managerialism. So the opposition had to be silenced for telling the truth.

Rooted in the prerevolutionary factional splits in the Russian Social Democratic movement and in the recurring controversies of the civil war years, the Left Opposition recrystallized amid the tangled interrelationships of the leading Communist personalities in the uncertain months of Lenin's illness, extending from May 1922 to his death in January 1924. Though the Politburo nominally constituted a collective leadership, Zinoviev openly aspired to fill Lenin's shoes. To achieve this objective, he had to neutralize Trotsky, the obvious heir in terms of his revolutionary and civil war record and his public prestige. "We were strongly of the opinion that one man, and one man only, had a right to that position, because he was head and shoulders superior to his fellow-claimants and could depend upon our unswerving loyalty," a party member recalled. "That one was Trotsky."[1] Much has been written about the personal enmity of Trotsky and Stalin, but this is in part an ex post facto projection. More compelling was the recurring personal clash between Trotsky, the flamboyant individualist, and Zinoviev, the constant shadow of Lenin, a rivalry that began before the revolution and escalated when Trotsky upstaged Zinoviev as the number-two Bolshevik in 1917.

To isolate Trotsky within the Politburo, Zinoviev arranged the so-called troika, of himself, his alter ego Kamenev, and General Secretary Stalin, backed by the remaining members Rykov and Tomsky, plus Bukharin as a candidate member. During the intrigue-ridden winter of 1922–23, issues of industrial development, foreign trade, grain prices, the national minorities, and above all Lenin's personal break with Stalin presented Trotsky with good opportunities for a comeback, but he did not see the right political opening to move against the troika. He held aloof even when, at the Twelfth Party Congress in April 1923, his friends were openly criticizing Stalin for his role in coercing the Communists in Soviet Georgia. Possibly Trotsky contemplated an alliance with Stalin against Zinoviev—hence his failure to develop the anti-Stalin campaign that Lenin entrusted to him, even though he had a sharp personal clash with Stalin on the eve of the congress over the handling of Lenin's criticisms of the party leadership.[2]

Meanwhile, both economic and political issues were bringing the Ultra Left and the moderate Left together, as former members of the old Democratic Centralist group and some of the Workers' Oppositionists joined forces with the now-eclipsed Trotskyists to challenge the policies of the interim leadership. Trotsky opened the attack in October 1923 with a letter to the Central Committee attacking the bureaucratization of the party.[3] This jab was quickly seconded by the Declaration of the Forty-Six, one of the most cogent warnings against shortsighted error and repressive cover-up to be produced in the whole history of the opposition.[4] Its signatories, including Trotskyists such as Preobrazhensky and Piatakov and Democratic Centralists such as Osinsky and Sapronov, were obviously inspired by Trotsky if not actually guided by him.

These protests prompted a heavy-handed though behind-the-scenes rejoinder from the leadership denouncing the criticism as factionalism that potentially violated the rule of the Tenth Party Congress.[5] Historical precedent from other countries gave the anti-Trotsky combination some grounds to fear that he might use his control over the Red Army to attempt a coup.[6] To forestall this contingency, they removed Trotsky's supporters from the military-political administration (including the hero of October, Vladimir Antonov-Ovseyenko) and turned it into an instrument to hamstring oppositionist influence in the armed forces.

For the public, the party leadership professed to endorse a sweeping reform effort, embodied in the Politburo's "New Course" resolution of 5 December.[7] This action gave Trotsky his opportunity to try to bind the leadership to its reform promises, which he undertook to do in his open letter "The New Course" of 8 December.[8] By this time Trotsky had fallen ill of the undiagnosed fever that kept him out of Moscow at the time of Lenin's death, but Preobrazhensky endeavored to follow up the letter by leading a campaign for democratization in the Moscow party organization.

This challenge provoked the party leadership to launch a campaign of open vilification of the opposition, lasting up to the convening of the Thirteenth Party Conference early in January 1924. This was the first party conclave where Stalin's apparatus systematically excluded the opposition, and it pronounced the verdict that was to echo in every subsequent condemnation: the opposition was a faction, violating the Tenth Congress rule against such groupings, and as such it necessarily represented interests hostile to the working class, since (as it was claimed) only the Communist Party, by definition, could speak for the proletariat.

Following their defeat in January 1924, the Trotskyists made no serious attempt for several months to resist the official chorus extolling unity and denouncing opposition heresy. Then, in October 1924, Trotsky reopened the controversy with the publication of his essay "Lessons of October," linking the Communist failure in Germany in 1923 to the faintheartedness of Zinoviev and Kamenev in 1917.[9] This sally drove those two temporarily back into the arms of Stalin and Bukharin, who joined them in a frenetic denunciation of the evils of Trotskyism and permanent revolution, now established as archheresy. Trotsky ended by being shorn of his last influential office, that of commissar of defense, in January 1925.

In the light of this experience, it was no surprise that Trotsky would choose to bide his time when the tension between Stalin-Bukharin and Zinoviev-Kamanev resumed openly in mid-1925. Recognizing that Stalin had outmaneuvered them in the course of consolidating his own control over the party apparatus, Zinoviev and Kamenev now appropriated some of the arguments of the Left Opposition and directed them against Stalin—the charges of conciliating the peasants too much and neglecting the workers, the matter of party democracy, and the theoretical issues of state capitalism and Socialism in One Country. It is difficult not to regard this phase of the controversy as a purely opportunistic political maneuver. Zinoviev and Kamenev had heretofore never been associated with the Left Opposition, and their main base for resisting Stalin was their control of the party organization in the Leningrad province through bureaucratic manipulation just as systematic as Stalin's was in the rest of the country. In any case, this "Leningrad Opposition" went down to ignominious defeat in December 1925 at the Fourteenth Party Congress—the last until the 1980s when any open opposition was heard. The Trotskyists, despite the fact that many of their own arguments were being invoked, made no effort at this point to speak up to support the Zinovievists.

After the Fourteenth Congress, it was not hard for the party leadership to remove the Zinovievists from their fiefdom in Leningrad. Zinoviev was so shaken by this debacle that he decided to attempt an alliance with his old enemy Trotsky, whom he had so effectively helped to defeat in 1923 and 1924. After some hesitation, in the spring of 1926, the Trotskyists accepted Zinoviev's overtures after he admitted that the whole campaign against "Trotskyism" had been a political concoction and that the Left had correctly warned about the bureaucratization of the party. Trotsky, for his part, toned down the theory of permanent revolution. "A mutual amnesty," Stalin called the agreement.[10]

For the moment, the United Opposition bloc appeared to be a formidable political combination, including as it did most of Lenin's leading associates of the revolutionary period, of every faction, Right, Left, and Ultra Left, and even his widow, Nadezhda Krupskaya. Over the next year and a half, the bloc kept up a vehement campaign against the party leadership, making this the most intense period of factional controversy in the entire history of the Communist movement. By late 1927, Stalin's critics were close to accusing him of betraying the dictatorship of the proletariat and were about to create what amounted to a new party to fight him in the name of the workers and international socialism.

An early crisis came in the summer of 1926, when the opposition presented its first systematic statement of principles since 1923, the so-called Declaration of the Thirteen, denouncing the trend to bureaucratism and attributing it to the neglect of the proletariat and poor peasants.[11] In response, Zinoviev was ousted from the Politburo, and Kamenev was removed from his Commissariat

of Trade. Pointedly, the leadership refrained from penalizing Trotsky, suggesting a hope of dividing the new-formed opposition bloc. When the oppositionists nonetheless resumed vigorous criticism they were condemned for factional
splitting, and Trotsky and Kamenev were removed from the Politburo, leaving it entirely in the hands of the leadership. At the same time Zinoviev was
forced to yield the chairmanship of the Comintern to Bukharin. An attempt by
the opposition in December to take its case to the Comintern was unavailing;
Trotsky's foreign supporters were all isolated. Under all this pressure, the old
Workers' Oppositionists, as well as Krupskaya, abjured dissent and made their
peace with Stalin.

In the spring of 1927 the fortunes of the revolutionary process in China
took center stage in the factional controversy in Russia. When the Chinese Nationalist Party, with Communist support, succeeded in reviving the revolutionary movement of 1911, the country had become as exciting to the Russians
as Germany had been from 1918 to 1923, as the potential site of an international breakthrough against imperialism. Then, when Chiang Kai-shek turned
against his Communist allies with a bloody purge in April 1927, the Russian oppositionists hastened to blame the setback on the "opportunism" of Socialism
in One Country.[12] Soon afterward, when the opposition cited the war scare with
Great Britain as reason for a change in leadership, Stalin and Bukharin charged
them with a treasonable threat to party unity and national security. Meanwhile,
the opposition lost another contingent from its left wing, the former members
of the Democratic Centralist group still led by Sapronov, who rejected the party leadership in even more uncompromising terms and, despite their miniscule
numbers, undertook to go their own way as a separate party.[13]

When the party leadership belatedly scheduled the Fifteenth Party Congress, the United Opposition drew up yet another platform, destined to be
its last, a book-length indictment detailing again the failure of the leadership
to pursue workers' democracy and international socialism.[14] The document
was suppressed, as were opposition meetings and demonstrations. Stalin had
Trotsky and Zinoviev expelled both from the Central Committee and from the
party and eliminated the last of their associates from the Central Committee
and the Central Control Commission.

At this point, the bonds of expediency that had held the Trotskyist and
Zinovievist wings of the opposition together finally broke. With Kamenev as
their spokesman, the Zinovievists abjured opposition as tantamount to a second
party and threw themselves on the mercy of the leadership, while the Trotskyists refused to give in. For the moment, the congress treated all opposition elements equally, by expelling them from the party, but harsher measures awaited

the Trotskyists in the form of deportation and forced domicile in Siberia or Central Asia. With these measures, the last legal opportunity for political self-expression in Soviet Russia came to an end.

The history of the opposition's struggle against the Stalin-Bukharin leadership richly documents the evolution of the Soviet regime and the alternatives facing it. Sounded throughout the period was the opposition's theme of party democracy, countered by repeated charges from the leadership of factionalism and violation of party unity. Intermittently, fundamental questions arose about the nature of the Soviet system as it was seen from the Marxist standpoint, including the issues of Thermidor, state capitalism, and Socialism in One Country. Virtually every significant question that has subsequently arisen in evaluating the Soviet system was anticipated in these final years of open factional struggle.

In economic policy, the basic question was where the NEP was to lead, as a long-term "evolution" or as a short-term, transitional "tactic." Further development of the NEP implied more concessions to the peasantry and to small-scale private enterprise regarding taxes, prices, and legal scope for their activity. This, the opposition alleged, threatened the economic interests of the proletariat as the true social foundation of the regime. Instead, the oppositionists took up the cause of state-planned industrial development to draw more people into the proletarian foundation of the state.

There is a double irony in this idea. First, it was logically incongruous for Marxists, believing that the social-economic base determined the shape of the political superstructure, to suppose (1) that their government could be a workers' state without the existence of a sufficient working-class base; and (2) that political action by the soi-disant workers' state could build up that base beneath itself. Second, the self-imposed task of noncapitalist industrialization had never been dealt with either in the Marxian scriptures or in the early policy pronouncements of the Soviet regime. It was only for the political and sociological reasons advanced by the opposition that discussion of this momentous effort got under way.

The great industrialization controversy dominated the economic side of the intraparty struggle in its last years. Represented especially by Preobrazhensky, the opposition pushed a vigorous, centrally planned industrialization drive, financed by forced savings through the tax system ("primary socialist accumulation") in lieu of capitalist savings or foreign investment. For the party leadership, Bukharin was the chief spokesman; he had made a virtue of necessity by shifting from the left to the right in response to the NEP and succeeded to Lenin's Politburo seat. Bukharin exemplified the method of "market social-ism," as Trotsky later termed it.[15] This meant more gradual and less stressful development through the accumulation of profits by state-owned enterprises, as they served the consuming public and indirectly stimulated heavy industry by spending these funds to expand their plants. The obvious parallel of this ap-proach with conventional capitalistic expansion invited opposition complaints against "state capitalism," a development they associated with Thermidor as a long-term abandonment of the cause of the workers.

In this vein, the opposition hinted broadly that the Soviet regime under the Stalin-Bukharin leadership was in danger of losing its quality as a workers' state. This insinuation led directly to the most acute ideological controversy in the entire factional struggle, the debate over Socialism in One Country. "So-cialism in One Country" was not, as is often assumed, a dispute between the advocates of a world revolutionary offensive and those who would retreat be-hind the walls of Fortress Russia. Both the leadership and the opposition held to the doctrine of world revolution in theory, while after the final collapse of Communist revolutionary hopes in Germany in October 1923, they all sup-ported expedient efforts to normalize Soviet foreign relations and find allies and trade partners. Arguments swirled repeatedly around alleged leadership blunders in the pursuit of this line, notably the alliance with the British Labour Party from 1924 to 1926 and the alliance with the Kuomintang in China from 1922 to 1927. But the fundamental question was the doctrinal dilemma of the proletarian state isolated in a backward society. What did the long prospective delay in the world revolution imply for the survival and purity of the dictator-ship of the proletariat in Russia?

At this juncture, the premises of Trotsky's theory of permanent revolution came into play as a contentious political issue. Accepted tacitly or explicitly by most of the Bolshevik Party as their guiding belief in 1917, permanent revo-lution left the victorious Bolsheviks in a state of acute uncertainty as long as the international revolution did not materialize to bring them support from the outside. The Treaty of Brest-Litovsk, resisted by the more theory-con-scious Bolsheviks as the abandonment of a crucial opportunity to stimulate international revolution, implied a basic priority—observed in practice ever after—for the survival of the Soviet state in Russia. In the practical sense, So-cialism in One Country had been a fact of life ever since 1918. Survival in iso-lation then posed the theoretical question, in terms of permanent revolution, whether the Soviet government could really maintain its character as a workers' state, or whether it might have to transform itself subtly into another form of regime as the price of survival in a country with an overwhelming peasant and petty-bourgeois majority. The Left Opposition could not resist the temptation to insinuate just this sort of degeneration as an actual or potential threat under the pro-NEP, pro-peasant, and potentially thermidorean leadership of Stalin and Bukharin. It was to defend himself and the party leadership against such an ideological attack by his cornered factional adversaries that in November 1924 Stalin broached his doctrinal alternative of Socialism in One Country.[16]

The essence of this proposition was that neither backwardness nor the forces of capitalist encirclement could prevent the construction of socialism in Russia alone. As his authority Stalin cited a passage by Lenin written in 1915 to the effect that "the victory of socialism is possible first in several or even in one capitalist country, taken singly."[17] Trotsky's theory of permanent revolution, according to Stalin, reflected an "underestimation of the peasantry" and a "lack of faith" in Russia's potential for revolution—in other words, a Menshevik heresy. However, as Kamenev pointed out in open party forum in 1926, Lenin had in mind not Russia but one of the more advanced capitalist countries that might be prepared to lead the way.[18] Stalin had in fact snatched the Lenin statement out of context to make it serve his own purposes by alleging that it proved the feasibility of Russia's building socialism alone.

This seemingly scholastic dispute over permanent revolution and Socialism in One Country proved to be highly significant as an indicator of Stalin's method—to be followed for the rest of his life—of seeking political justification by doctrinal manipulation, and his inclination, "scholastic" in the most literal sense, to seek such justification in textual authority rather than in empirical data.[19] But for steps of this sort to serve their purpose, Stalin had to completely ban any independent discussion of the texts and concepts of Marxism. The measures he took to ward off criticism made him more vulnerable to further criticism and required him to take still more stringent measures to suppress oppositionist views. Ever after, it was the possibility of criticism from within the movement and from a Marxist standpoint that was most intolerable to the Soviet regime.

Once the system of doctrinal authority and control implied by Socialism in One Country was established, the possibility of critical reference to the original meaning of Marx or even of Lenin was ruled out. It became easy for Stalin to modify his policies at will, while reinterpreting Marxist doctrine to make it appear to justify each new policy as the only correct application of the true faith. This Stalin commenced to do across the board—in economics, in law, in cultural policy, in foreign policy, in the liquidation of his enemies—once he had made himself the unquestioned master of the party in 1928–29. As these revisions proceeded, it became impossible within the Stalinist system to judge policy in relation to any theoretical guidelines, since the interpretation of theory was constantly subject to change at the whim of political authority in order to square it with changes of policy and circumstances. It consequently became impossible to speak of an ideological motivation of Soviet policy, domestic or foreign; ideology was made to conform to policy instead of governing it. The Stalinist frame of mind, begun with Socialism in One Country and maintained to the end of the Brezhnev era, was not the doctrinal motivation of policy but the policy motivation of doctrine.

While Stalin's manipulation of Communist theory, colored by a mixture of cynicism and self-justification, was breaking free of all logical and political restrictions, the Left Opposition was not above the political use of ideological arguments to score doctrinal points against the Stalinists. The oppositionists always averred their Leninist orthodoxy, never challenging the one-party system nor even the antifactional rule, but only protested that their own critical efforts, allegedly based on a true appreciation of the interests of the workers, could not possibly be factional. They endeavored to make political capital out of the leadership's foreign policy embarrassments while denying that they meant to undermine the tactical success of these policies. Above all, they were profoundly inconsistent about the economic potential of the isolated Russian state. On the one hand, they vehemently attacked the theory of Socialism in One Country and the possibility of building socialism in Russia alone as an artificial, un-Marxist, and impossible concept. On the other, they called for a far more vigorous and rapid effort by the Soviet government to expand the industrial foundations of socialism in Russia. In other words, their answer to the shortage of resources for the effort to build socialism was to attempt the building even faster, before the shortage might become socially and politically too debilitating.

This contradiction in the Left Opposition's economics, the "Preobrazhensky dilemma," as the economist Alexander Erlich termed it, was "a choice between mortal sickness and virtually certain death on the operating table."[20] The impasse underscored the proposition that socialism as understood up to 1917 would not work in an underdeveloped country such as Russia, at least not in isolation. Preobrazhensky himself could only hark back to the premises of permanent revolution and "leaning for support in the future on the material resources of other socialist countries."[21]

Under pressure of all this controversy, Stalin and Bukharin adjusted their economic line in the direction of a synthesis of the market and planning approaches. The same Fifteenth Congress that saw the Left Opposition expelled from the party voted for the principle of a five-year plan of industrial development. But Stalin and Bukharin soon parted company, each clinging to one horn of the Preobrazhensky dilemma. While Bukharin held out for a gradualist and nonviolent approach within the outlines of the plan, Stalin opted for a crash program of industrialization. In his startling "left turn" of 1928, he adopted every argument advanced by the Left Opposition in industrialization policy, peasant policy, and foreign policy—though not in the question of party democracy or the ideology of Socialism in One Country—and put them into practice in extreme form. Such was the ironic policy contribution of the Left after its political demise.

The last act in the struggle to hold back Stalin's Bonapartist transformation of Soviet politics was played out behind the official façade of party unity, as Stalin parted company with his ideological comrades of the NEP, Bukharin, Rykov, and Tomsky, and let them take their turn at futile resistance. The Left Opposition, crushed and scattered, was thrown into utter disarray by Stalin's left turn and his contest with the Right Opposition. Some of Trotsky's followers, led by Piatakov and Krestinsky, saw Stalin's hard line on the peasants and industrialization as a vindication of the arguments of the Left Opposition, and "capitulated" one after another to return to the party and the government in various administrative capacities. Radek and Preobrazhensky took this step in 1929, just before Trotsky, still condemning Stalin's personal rule, was physically expelled from the Soviet Union in the most unusual move yet taken against the Left Opposition. Meanwhile, Bukharin approached the Zinovievists, mainly for the purpose of commiseration, it seems, since no action resulted from their discussions save additional embarrassment for the Right when these contacts were revealed a few months later.

With respect to economic policy, the Right Opposition may well have represented a more realistic alternative to Stalinism than the Left, embracing as it did the NEP and a gradualist approach to socialism, industrialization, and cultural modernization. It did not have to rely intellectually on illusions about the international revolution. On the other hand, as regards the political issues of party democracy and bureaucratization, the leaders of the Right erred fatally in backing Stalin's apparatus against the Left until all chance of defending any form of criticism, including their own, had been obliterated. Bukharin was as fanatic as any in his diatribes against the Left's alleged factional menace to the Communist regime, until he belatedly realized the danger posed by Stalin. He confided to Kamenev, "The differences between us and Stalin are many times more serious than all our former differences with you."[22] A year later, Bukharin and his associates were being removed one by one from all their leading political positions, and the Stalin Revolution was under way. Everything that happened afterward to both Left and Right Oppositionists was anticlimactic: denunciation, expulsion, arrest, trial, liquidation, oblivion.

The demise of all the Communist oppositions, Right, Left, and Ultra Left, can readily be explained in simple political terms: disunity, indecision, tactical errors, confusion of purpose. In particular, their record of attack and retreat, of capitulations to party discipline followed by renewed assaults on the leadership, was disconcerting and demoralizing to potential followers. These mistakes stemmed from one essential faulty premise, namely, acceptance of the Leninist myth of the single united party exercising the dictatorship of the proletariat. None of the oppositions were prepared to follow the logic of their position qua opposition and to question the one-party monopoly, however much they might try to stretch the opportunities for factional struggle within the party. To set up an independent organization and argue for multiparty democracy would be a Menshevik heresy from which they all recoiled, though they were nonetheless accused repeatedly of this very sin. In fact, the virtue of the Left Opposition was that it was really so close to the Mensheviks in this regard. In the end, it would have had nothing to lose and perhaps a good deal to gain by frankly avowing that position. It would have been in character with the basic political orientation of the Left Opposition since prerevolutionary days. As events turned out, the opposition was defeated as much by its own acceptance of the one-party concept as it was by the bureaucracy of that one party, which it rightly rejected.

Beyond that, could the programs represented by the various oppositions have succeeded under any conceivable conjuncture of political circumstances? The hopes of the Left to curb the peasant proprietary economy and push industrialization while simultaneously reviving the 1917 spirit of workers' democracy were impossible to reconcile, as the Preobrazhensky dilemma demonstrated. In any revolution it is difficult to sustain the original spirit of self-sacrificing idealism. In Russia, particularly after the militarizing effect of the civil war on all the country's political institutions, the notion of workers' democracy was altogether chimerical. The proletariat in whose name the dictatorship was being exercised was in large measure a raw new working class recruited from the peasantry after the revolutionary proletariat of 1917 had been killed off or promoted into the bureaucracy or dissipated during the economic collapse of War Communism. For all the opposition's appeals, the industrial workers of the 1920s remained firmly in the grip of the party apparatus; the

"Lenin enrollment," diluting the party with hundreds of thousands of new worker-members in 1924, actually spelled the end of any opposition chance to win over a significant segment of the rank and file.

The Left Opposition's crusade for socialism based on an industrializing workers' democracy was altogether quixotic under Russian conditions. Socialism, in the old sense of the just distribution of abundant goods, was impossible without more economic development, but economic development was impossible without a ruling class—bureaucrats, if not capitalists—that could put the necessary pressure on the masses and direct the energies of the nation into the enhancement of production. It was the merit of the Right Opposition to scale down its ambitions both for socialism and for production in order to avoid the totalitarian bureaucracy toward which this combination of goals pointed. It was the genius of Stalin, by contrast, to recognize that the problem of production might be successfully attacked by means of socialism in the sense of central state planning and control, while abandoning (except as to Engels's "phases and promises") the old ideal of just distribution.[23]

As the Stalinists proceeded to redefine the goals of Soviet socialism, the existence and even the memory of the opposition became an intolerable threat to the regime's ideological self-justification. In the last months of its struggle against the United Opposition, the leadership undertook to recast the entire history of the party in order to represent opposition spokesmen as diabolical agents of counterrevolution. By deporting Trotsky, Stalin set up an external target for hatred and denunciation that could help discredit all questioning of the regime in power. (The analogous deportation of Alexander Solzhenitsyn in more recent times served a similar purpose.) In its extreme twisting of fact about the record of the opposition, culminating in the preposterous treason charges at the show trials of 1936, 1937, and 1938, Stalin's regime inculcated a veritable national neurosis. Like a neurotic individual, the Stalinized Communist Party created obsessive myths about its own past in order to explain away the contradictions of its present and reacted with the most violent anxiety toward any attempt from within or without to get back to the historical truth. Khrushchev's de-Stalinization and rehabilitation campaign of 1956, restoring to history the Stalinists and the military men who had perished in the purges, stopped short of reconsidering the role of the opposition and its critique of Stalin (though Khrushchev did concede that the death penalties of 1936–38 were excessive). Everything Stalin accomplished up to 1934, including his suppression of the opposition, his industrialization and collectivization program, and the whole system of ideological manipulation, was reaffirmed by Khrushchev and maintained by Brezhnev.

CHAPTER 15

Trotsky on Democracy and Bureaucracy

Trotsky was a man of baffling paradoxes—staunch prerevolutionary enemy of Leninism, its most ardent champion in the revolution and in the civil war, ultimately the devil figure in the political theology of the postrevolutionary regime. Yet to many minds, he has appeared only as the revolutionary master of ceremonies, the civil war commander, the firebrand of international revolution, the Stalinist before Stalin, perhaps deserving of his fate. These images miss a major part of the real Trotsky, as much as, say, impressions of Lenin or Bukharin based only on their records during the War Communism era would neglect how they evolved afterward. Trotsky's political outlook changed profoundly during the succession struggle that broke out in 1923, though not enough to enable him to break out of the doctrinal loyalties that bound him to Stalin's sacrificial altar. Trapped between the rigidity of his theoretical commitments to Marxism and Leninism and the bitter political adversity that afflicted him in midcareer, Trotsky was truly the protagonist of a Greek tragedy played on the Soviet stage.

The Trotsky of the 1920s and 1930s cannot be properly understood without reference to his thinking before the revolution. His disputes with Lenin are well known. It was Trotsky who wrote as early as 1904 of Lenin's model for the party, "These methods lead, as we shall yet see, to this: The party organization is substituted for the party, the Central Committee is substituted for the party organization, and finally a 'dictator' is substituted for the Central Committee."[1]

This warning about Lenin's centralism did not mean that the author of the theory of permanent revolution was any less committed in his revolutionary fervor. Between the revolutions of 1905 and 1917, Trotsky was part of a radical Social Democratic tendency that included both Left Mensheviks and Left Bolsheviks. At the time he joined the Bolshevik ranks in the summer of 1917 with such other left-wing Mensheviks as Radek and Rakovsky, Lenin's growing party was at its nadir of organizational rigor, and the radical democrats could well find it a logical and comfortable vehicle for their revolutionary enthusiasm.

Six years later, the Communist Party had gone through the steeling experience of civil war and had converted itself from a mass revolutionary movement to a disciplined administrative organ exercising a monopoly of power in the new revolutionary state. Trotsky changed along with most of the party, as circumstances brought him to the command of a revolutionary army and put a premium on the most desperate methods in a life-or-death struggle with the counterrevolution. After 1921, history took another turn, and Trotsky found himself all but excluded from the collective leadership formed by the old Leninists when their revolutionary chief was stricken with terminal illness. In the fall of 1923, it was not the Trotsky of the civil war but the Trotsky of the old radical democracy who decided to speak out against that leadership and its violation of the workers' democracy that was supposed to be the Communist norm.

The qualified democratic agenda that Trotsky set forth in the fall of 1923 guided his political activity for the rest of his life. His first and most extensive public statement in this critical vein was his "New Course" letter, with accompanying articles, published in December 1923, first in *Pravda* and then in pamphlet form.[2] Even earlier, as his feud with his Politburo colleagues commenced behind the scenes, Trotsky had fully formulated a critique of the bureaucratization of the party and the violation of workers' democracy already being perpetrated under Stalin. He never really improved upon the charges he made in his letter of 8 October 1923 to the Central Committee: "This present regime . . . is much farther from workers' democracy than the regime of the fiercest period of War Communism. The bureaucratization of the party apparatus has developed to unheard-of proportions by means of the method of secretarial selection."[3]

While these unsettling charges were being echoed in the "Declaration of the Forty-Six," Trotsky's enemies maneuvered for time and position and allowed him to compose his reformist manifesto. This was actually endorsed by the Politburo in its resolution of 5 December 1923 to target "a whole series of negative tendencies" and to warn of "losing the perspective of socialist construction as a whole and of the world revolution" along with "bureaucratization of the party apparatuses and the rise everywhere of a threat of cleavage between the party and the masses."[4]

Having won this concession, Trotsky overplayed his hand by publishing the "New Course" letter to warn against unnamed "conservative-minded comrades" motivated by "a profound bureaucratic distrust of the party" who might try to evade the 5 December resolution. Claiming victory, he asserted, "The party must subordinate to itself its own apparatus without for a moment ceasing to be a centralized organization." This was the proverbial attempt to square the circle. "Democracy and centralism are two faces of party organization," Trotsky tried to explain. "The question is to harmonize them in the most correct manner." Unabashedly, he attacked his colleagues for acting in bad faith: "Now the bureaucrats are ready formally to 'take note' of the 'new course,' that is, *to nullify it bureaucratically*"—not a surprising stance when Trotsky was calling for a purge of the apparatus.[5] That abruptly provoked the torrent of invective against Trotsky's alleged factional disloyalty that culminated in his denunciation by the Thirteenth Party Conference the following month. Thus ended the most serious opposition challenge to the bureaucratic trend in the Soviet system. And there was no further deepening of the Left Opposition's case for democracy. Until they were finally suppressed in 1927, Trotsky and his friends did no more than echo the lines they had spoken and written in 1923, while they were going down to a pitiful defeat.

The Thirteenth Party Congress in May 1924, the first after Lenin's death, was the occasion of Trotsky's celebrated confession, "Comrades, none of us wants to be or can be right against the party. In the last analysis the party is always right, because the party is the sole historical instrument that the working class possesses for the solution of its fundamental tasks." But these words, spoken in the peroration of a long address to the congress stressing again the danger of bureaucracy and the need to boost the working class as a social force, were clearly intended to be sarcastic. And Trotsky qualified his recantation immediately: "I for my part believe that I am only fulfilling my duty as a party member who warns his party about what he considers to be a danger. . . . Not only an individual party member but even the party itself can make occasional mistakes."[6]

As Trotsky sharpened his critique of the bureaucratic trend, his view of the trouble broadened and his understanding of it deepened. Before he went into open opposition, bureaucracy seemed to him largely a problem of the governmental machinery, stemming mainly from the holdover of tsarist personnel and habits. He spoke out in the spring of 1923 to underscore Lenin's last articles about bureaucratic malfunctions and cultural backwardness, and complained of "a state machine of which it has been said that it is . . . little different from the old tsarist machine." This was "bureaucratism," the red tape, petty squabbles, avoidance of responsibility, and public-be-damned attitude popularly attributed to the old officialdom, the *chinovniki*. But Trotsky was still confident that the party, as a healthy new organization of alert workers, would eventually overcome these survivals from prerevolutionary days.[7]

What drove Trotsky into opposition in 1923, or at least coincided with that move, was his perception that bureaucracy had seriously invaded the party as well. In an addendum to his "New Course" articles, he warned of the deleterious influence of bureaucratic habits upon party members serving in the government and attributed "bureaucratism" to "the heterogeneity of society, the difference between the daily and fundamental interests of various groups of the population, . . . the lack of culture of the broad masses." These conditions "could place the revolution in peril." But salvation still lay with the party, despite its own increasingly bureaucratic habits of appointment from the top down: "As the voluntary [*sic*] organization of the vanguard, of the best, the most active, and the most conscious elements of the working class, it is able to preserve itself much better than can the state apparatus from the tendencies of bureaucratism."[8] It never occurred to Trotsky that a society with a high level of culture might incline as much or even more to bureaucratic forms of organization, as all of modern sociology, following Max Weber, is well aware. Trotsky's only theoretical source was Marx, mainly the notion that the bureaucracy could achieve temporary autonomy as the mediator between contending classes.[9] Of Engels's warning about the bureaucratic state organs becoming "the masters of society," Trotsky seems to make no mention.[10]

When the turn of Zinoviev and Kamenev came in 1925 to fall under the relentless wheels of Stalin's apparatus, Trotsky called a plague on both of the bureaucratic houses, in Moscow and in Leningrad. The Leningrad Opposition was to him at best a "bureaucratically distorted expression of the political anxiety felt by the most advanced section of the proletariat."[11] After he formed the United Opposition bloc with Zinoviev and Kamenev in 1926, Trotsky returned to the theme of the Communists' failure to develop industry and expand the working class fast enough: "The bureaucratization of the party . . . is an expression of the disrupted social equilibrium, which has been and is being tipped to the disadvantage of the proletariat. . . . It is absolutely clear that a change of regime in the direction of workers' democracy is inseparable from a change in economic policy in the direction of genuine industrialization and a rectification of the line of the party leadership toward genuine internationalism."[12]

To the end of his Soviet career, Trotsky refused to say that the regime had lost its essential Marxist virtue. "Our state is a proletarian state, though with bureaucratic deformations," he still maintained in November 1926, after he, Zinoviev, and Kamenev had been ousted from the Politburo.[13] The September 1927 opposition platform linked the growth of bureaucracy with the pro-kulak, antiworker line that the Left attributed to the party leadership. The country was becoming dominated by "an innumerable caste of genuine bureaucrats," contributing to a Soviet Thermidor.[14] Workers newly recruited into the bureaucracy, Trotsky observed, were fusing with the class enemy: "The proletarian part of the state apparatus, which was earlier sharply divided from the cadres of the old bourgeois intellectuals and did not trust them, in the last few years has separated itself more and more from the working class and, in its style of life, has drawn closer to the bourgeois and petty-bourgeois intellectuals, and has become more susceptible to hostile class influences."[15]

Stalin's break with Bukharin's right wing of the party in 1928 had little immediate effect on Trotsky's thinking, even when many of his supporters capitulated. Trotsky was now more direct about the danger of a "Bonapartist" coup in the interest of the petty bourgeoisie: "The further the Stalin regime goes, the more it appears as a dress rehearsal for Bonapartism. . . . On its back the power is sliding over from the proletariat to the bourgeoisie. . . . Stalinism is Kerenskyism moving from left to right."[16] But he still dreamed that his group could "mobilize the proletarian core of the party" to save the workers' state from the "monarchist-Bonapartist principle" of the bureaucratic and petty-bourgeois Thermidoreans.[17]

During the weeks just before his expulsion from the USSR, Trotsky contemplated a more systematic treatise on the problem of bureaucracy, but he actually left only fragments.[18] "The bureaucracy," he insisted still, "was never an independent class," even if it "towers over and above society, including the class which it serves."[19] Trotsky was hanging on to the traditional Marxian class formulation by a very thin thread, a thread that his friend Rakovsky was just then breaking altogether.

Rakovsky, the Bulgarian from Romania who had joined the Bolsheviks and served as prime minister of the Soviet Ukraine, was sent to Astrakhan at the same time that Trotsky was exiled to Alma Ata. Together with a handful of co-exiles, he endeavored to work out his own explanation of the social nature of Stalinism: "When a class seizes power, a certain part of this class is transformed into agents of the power itself. In this way the bureaucracy arises. In the proletarian state, where capitalist accumulation is not permitted for members of the ruling party, this differentiation is at first functional, but then it becomes social. I do not say class, but social. I mean that the social position of the Communist who has an automobile at his disposal, a good apartment, regular leaves, and earns the party maximum, is distinct from the position of that same Communist if he works in the coal mines where he gets fifty to sixty rubles a month."[20]

Up to this point, Rakovsky did not go in principle beyond Trotsky, but with the passage of time he and his group made the leap to a distinctly new position: "Before our eyes a great *class of rulers* has been *taking shape* and is continuing to develop."[21] Here, in embryo, was the "New Class" theory later embraced and amplified by other Marxists or ex-Marxists—Bruno Rizzi, James Burnham, Milovan Djilas, Rudolf Bahro, Michael Voslensky.[22] Rakovsky still tried to make his insight fit the terms of Marxian sociology by means of some forced redefinitions: "The unifying factor of this unique class is that unique form of private property, governmental power."[23] The Left Opposition was finally vindicated by this theoretical breakthrough, if not by political victory: "The opposition of 1923–1924 foresaw the vast harm to the proletarian dictatorship that stems from the perversion of the party regime. Events have fully justified its prognosis: The enemy crept in through the bureaucratic window."[24]

Exile abroad did not immediately alter Trotsky's own perception of the Stalinist regime, still in some mysterious sense a "workers' state," however much it was perverted by "bureaucratic deformation" and threatened by outright bourgeois counterrevolution. He recognized now that postrevolutionary fatigue had led to "an unquestionable reduction in the level of direct mass intervention," while "the party has been artificially diluted with a mass of half-raw recruits." These weaknesses allowed the bureaucracy to assume more and more power and independence: "The government official is increasingly filled with the conviction that the October Revolution was made precisely in order to concentrate power in his hands and assure him a privileged position." In turn, the bureaucrats "seek a peaceful thermidorean switching back on to the track leading to bourgeois society."[25] Trotsky still could not conceive of any sociopolitical alternative besides the proletariat and the bourgeoisie: "Soviet power . . . is falling increasingly under the influence of bourgeois interests. . . . Not just the state apparatus, but the party apparatus as well, is becoming, if not the conscious agent, then at least the effective agent of bourgeois conceptions and expectations."[26]

As year followed year in exile, Trotsky became progressively more absorbed in the factional infighting and doctrinal hairsplitting among Communists outside the Soviet Union. Despite the tragic unfolding of Stalin's experiment with revolution from above, Trotsky would not bend the rigid Marxian framework of his own views. To be sure, he wrote in the spring of 1930, "The bureaucracy has restored many characteristics of a ruling class and that is very much how the working masses consider it," but he hastened to add, "From the Marxist point of view, it is clear that the Soviet bureaucracy cannot change itself into a new ruling class."[27] This conclusion permitted him to hope that his supporters could still somehow rouse "the proletarian nucleus of the party to reform the regime in a struggle against the plebiscitary Bonapartist bureaucracy."[28] Meanwhile this same bureaucracy, hoping to wind down the revolution, "feels it has been double-crossed by its leader since 1928," leaving Stalin to depend on "the open and cynical establishment of the plebiscitary-personal regime" against the "tens of thousands of old Bolsheviks and hundreds of thousands of young potential Bolsheviks [who] will rise up at the moment of danger."[29]

By 1933, despite all his past protestations against splitting the Communist parties, Trotsky decided that the time had come to repudiate the whole Communist International and to organize his followers everywhere into a new movement. Nevertheless, the new International would make "the defense of the workers' state from imperialism and counterrevolution" one of its cardinal principles.[30] Trotsky would not yield on the proposition that Moscow still represented the dictatorship of the proletariat, albeit "a sick dictatorship."[31] "The bureaucracy," he now asserted, could not be a class, because it "has no independent position in the process of production and distribution. It has no independent property roots"—the point of Marxian dogma that still blinded him about the emerging Stalinist reality. "The biggest apartments, the juiciest steaks and even Rolls Royces are not enough to transform the bureaucracy into an independent ruling class." In short, "We have to deal not with class exploitation in the scientific sense of the word, but with social parasitism,"[32] a fine distinction that did not alter the outcome: "In the last analysis, the stifling of workers' democracy is the result of the pressure of class enemies' through the medium of the workers' bureaucracy."[33] In consequence, "The bureaucracy can be compelled to yield power into the hands of the proletarian vanguard only by force." Even so, for Trotsky, the greater danger of civil war was posed by the lurking forces of bourgeois counterrevolution.[34]

Trotsky summed up his analysis of Soviet society in his book *The Revolution Betrayed: What Is the Soviet Union and Where Is It Going?* written in Norway in 1936 and published in 1937 in English, French, and Spanish.[35] He reiterated his argument that the Soviet regime was not yet socialist but only "a preparatory regime transitional from capitalism to socialism"; but it was still a workers' state in its metaphysical essence.[36] Though the bureaucracy, which "has neither stocks nor bonds," still fell short of the definition of a ruling class, Trotsky finally went so far as to term it "an uncontrolled caste alien to socialism." He now conceded that the bureaucracy had already consummated the Soviet Thermidor.[37] Stalin's regime was "a variety of Bonapartism—a Bonapartism of a new type not before seen in history," ruling in a manner that Trotsky himself called "totalitarian."[38] Only a new proletarian revolution could restore the Soviet Union to the socialist path: "There is no peaceful outcome for this crisis."[39]

Now at last Trotsky gave up the Leninist proposition that the working class could legitimately have only one political party to represent it. He claimed that the Bolshevik suppression of other parties soon after the October Revolution had only been intended as "a temporary evil," which unfortunately gave rise to "the monopoly of an uncontrolled bureaucracy." Then his crucial new realization: "Classes are heterogeneous. . . . One and the same class may create several parties."[40] As to the CPSU, "The ruling party which enjoys a monopoly in the Soviet Union is the political machine of the bureaucracy."[41] A few months later Trotsky reaffirmed these conclusions, ending his Odyssey of theory in terms prophetic of the East European revolutions of 1989: "It is necessary to prepare the arena for two parties, . . . maybe three or four. It is necessary to smash away the dictatorship of Stalin. . . . If this new political upheaval is successful, the masses, with these experiences, will never permit the dictatorship of one party, of one bureaucracy."[42]

In the last year of his life, shaken by Stalin's purges on the one hand and the "New Class" heresies of some of his followers on the other, Trotsky toyed with the possibility that democratic proletarian socialism might not be the natural outcome of the revolution as per Marx. If it turned out that the proletariat suffered a "congenital incapacity to become a ruling class," one would have to acknowledge that "in its fundamental traits the present USSR was the precursor of a new exploiting regime on an international scale."[43] But Trotsky could not accept this alternative prospect, certainly not as one excluding his lifetime ideals. Baruch Knei-Paz commented, "He, at least, would remain a socialist, out of moral conviction if not out of 'scientific' certainty."[44]

Most of what Trotsky was able to publish or otherwise disseminate during the succession struggle fell on deaf ears or was turned back against him as material for still more charges of heretical thinking. Could Trotsky not have known that his tiresome diatribes, however well documented by references to the collected works of Lenin, would have little or no impact on the enemies who were politically determined to destroy him? Indeed, many spokesmen for the party leadership relished in baiting Trotsky, as the extant records of debate between them vividly show.[45] An alternative explanation is that Trotsky was really speaking and writing not in the vain hope of persuading his enemies but simply to establish a record vindicating himself, for his own self-satisfaction and for posterity.

To this end, Trotsky struggled obsessively to prove that despite his pre-revolutionary differences with Lenin, he had become a loyal Bolshevik in 1917 and had unswervingly followed Lenin ever since. His fatal mistake was to accept the 1921 ban on factions within the party as a nondebatable premise, thereby putting himself in a position where he had to prove that he was not what he really was. He could only try to deny that his oppositional efforts constituted factional activity within the terms of the ban while suggesting at the same time, "It is absolutely inevitable for an apparatus regime to breed factions from its own midst."[46] Nevertheless, the oppositionists declared, "We will struggle with all our force against the formation of two parties, for the dictatorship of the proletariat demands as its very core a united proletarian party."[47] Thus Trotsky and his followers rejected precisely what the country needed. They would not accept and defend the real logic of their own position, which was to say that bureaucratism in the party showed the faults of Lenin's centralist conception of organization and that factional freedom—or better yet, multiparty freedom—had to be allowed in order to fight effectively against the bureaucratic trend. At no time did Trotsky or his followers propose any concrete democratic procedures to record the voice of the rank and file of the party, let alone of the nonparty masses, in considering policy alternatives and in the choice of leaders.

Trotsky failed to see that the proletariat was not the new revolutionary vanguard being generated by industrial society. Nor could he see that the bourgeoisie as commonly understood was not the real alternative for postrevolutionary social dominance. This role was being steadily assumed, as some of Trotsky's followers ultimately realized, by the bureaucracy itself, state and party in the Soviet Union, governmental and corporate in capitalist countries. Thus the tide of social evolution was on the side of those who accommodated themselves to the bureaucratic reality, whatever slogans they might toss off to appease other elements who thought the revolution belonged to them. The only true options, as the world has seen in so many recent instances, are whether to let that bureaucratic reality rule by fiat, in the name of some disproven revolutionary dogma, or to subject it to the democratic mechanisms of restraint and control that theorists too sure of themselves used to dismiss as "bourgeois."

CHAPTER 16

The Left Opposition as an Alternative to Stalinism

Western historians, like Soviet writers during the first years of glasnost, have often looked on Trotsky and Trotskyism not as an alternative to Stalinism but as its forerunner. In that view, Stalin won in a purely personal struggle for the leadership role. This interpretation overlooks the distinctive sources and premises of the Left Opposition, as compared with both the Leninist and Stalinist leadership of the Communist Party, and neglects the development of this movement during the first decade after the revolution.

Between 1923 and 1927, the Left Opposition strove to alter the direction of national policy, which it thought ruinous to the goals of the Bolshevik Revolution. Whether these goals could have been realized under the conditions then obtaining in Soviet Russia is, in retrospect, certainly questionable, but one thing is clear—the failure of the Left Opposition meant the elimination of any political force genuinely attempting to realize the aims of the revolution in the near term. From the demise of the Left Opposition in 1927 until the repudiation of neo-Stalinism in the later 1980s, the revolutionary mystique served only as a fulcrum of self-justification for regimes and policies that veered widely away from the original mark.

What distinguished Left Bolshevism, before and after the revolution, from the line represented by Lenin? It was, to begin with, more exclusively a movement of emigré intellectuals, who were more influenced by Western democratic ideas than were the undergrounders in Russia. Intellectuals who had been in emigration constituted the core of the Left Opposition of the 1920s.[1] Molotov pointedly used this fact against the Left at the time they were being expelled from the party in 1927: "Writing articles and making speeches is by no means sufficient to make one a consistent and enduring revolutionary."[2]

Ever since Bogdanov's eminence before the revolution, the Left had embraced an almost mystical faith in the proletariat and its international solidarity. At the same time, the leftists were less willing than Lenin to resort to methods of command and discipline, either in leading the Bolshevik Party before the revolution or in leading the Russian state afterward. The Left was strategically more idealistic and tactically more rash—even "adventurist"—than those people (usually from the underground in Russia) whose more practical interest in organization and greater sense of tactical prudence led them to rally around Lenin most of the time. These characteristics explain why it was the Left that differed most with Lenin before the revolution, supported him most ardently in 1917, and criticized him most sharply in the months that followed. In short, two different psychologies competed in the party—one more utopian, the other more authoritarian.

Ideologically, the Left Opposition was marked by its genuine, even dogmatic, belief in the virtue and mission of the working class. Lenin's dictum in *Chto delat'?* that "the working class, exclusively by its own effort, is able to develop only trade union consciousness," was never accepted by the leftist strand in Bolshevism. They were convinced that the October Revolution had created a workers' state, despite the acknowledged weakness of the industrial proletariat in Russia and its virtual disintegration during the period of War Communism.[3] The NEP, with its concessions to the petty-bourgeois instincts of the peasantry and the Nepmen, was to these people at best a necessary evil, a "tactic" that they hoped and expected to be short-lived.

Commitment to the ideal of the working class, coupled with recognition of the dire straits in which the proletarian ideal actually found itself in postrevolutionary Russia, underlay every other facet of the Left Opposition's beliefs and programs. Given the premises, the conclusions were logical. Fear of the social weight of the peasant masses was realistic, whether or not it was meaningful to call them petty-bourgeois. It was equally realistic to fear concessions by the party leadership that would prolong and deepen the NEP at the expense of the urban workers. It was perhaps more fanciful, though still logical, to look to the international revolution for salvation and to hang future hopes for a socialist Russia on the success of Communist movements abroad, in keeping with Trotsky's theory of permanent revolution.

A more questionable line of reasoning underlay the Left's advocacy of accelerated industrialization to strengthen the social base of the self-styled workers' state by turning more peasants into workers. "In the last analysis," Trotsky wrote in 1923, "the working class can maintain and strengthen its guiding position not through the apparatus of government, not through the army, but through industry, which reproduces the proletariat itself."[4] This sociological argument called for the Communist state to create its own class undergirding, even though in classical Marxism that achievement was supposed to result from economic development, with the workers' state following naturally. All the while, according to the Left, bureaucratic trends in the party and the state had to be fought in order to maximize the role of "workers' democracy" and keep the ship of state headed in the socialist direction.

Ironically, there was no effective worker support for the Left Opposition. The party apparatus had better control over worker-Communists than it did over any other element of the party. After 1923, even the utopians of the Workers' Opposition preferred to support the party leadership. Active support for the Left came primarily from intellectuals and students, naturally concentrated in Moscow.

Of the issues raised by the Left Opposition, industrialization was the earliest to crystallize and the one debated most bitterly throughout the NEP years. The social goals of the Left required quick industrialization, faster than could be accomplished through market forces. Almost all the defects in the social and political order of NEP Russia were attributed to "the lag of industry behind the economic development of the country as a whole" and the consequent "lowering of the specific gravity of the proletariat in the society" and "lowering of the political and cultural self-esteem of the proletariat as the ruling class."[5]

Trotsky launched the idea of systematic, planned economic development as early as 1923 in his "Theses on Industry" prepared for the Twelfth Party Congress: "Only the development of industry creates an unshakable foundation for the proletarian dictatorship. . . . All state activity in general must give primary concern to the planned development of state industry." This document is as interesting for Trotsky's admonitions as it is for his emphasis on planning. Industry and agriculture would have to develop in balance; industry depended on agriculture, but state industry could not lag behind, lest "private industry . . . swallow up state industry or suck it dry." He continued with qualifications still pertinent to subsidized and debt-burdened state industry even in the Brezhnev era: "Only such industry can be victorious that gives more than it swallows up." Planning should be comprehensive but careful in its methods: "Arbitrary administration by bureaucratic agencies is replaced by economic maneuvering."[6] In 1924, Trotsky wrote prophetically of "objective limitations" to the pace of industrialization—"the level of peasant economy, the actual equipment of industry, the availability of working capital, the cultural level of the country." Therefore, he concluded, "any attempt to leap over these limitations would surely take its own bitter revenge, striking the proletariat at one end and the peasantry at the other."[7]

Industrial development continued to be a major source of polemics between the Left and the party leadership until the final silencing of the Trotskyists. Preobrazhensky argued for the Left that industry could not wait for the market mechanisms of consumer demand to stimulate its growth but needed direct injections of capital accumulated from the agricultural sector through the taxing power of the state—"primary socialist accumulation," he termed it, paraphrasing Marx's notion of "primary capitalist accumulation." Assuming that agriculture would remain in private hands, Preobrazhensky frankly proposed that it be exploited until the socialist system developed all its natural advantages over capitalism.[8]

When the United Opposition of the Trotskyists and Zinovievists was formed in 1926, they sounded the alarm again about the lag in the development of state industry and complained (vainly, in the Declaration of the Thirteen, because the statement could not be published) that the industrialization resolution of the Fourteenth Party Congress—the document hailed in Stalinist historiography as the beginning of the great industrialization drive—was not being implemented. Nevertheless, the party leadership, represented by Bukharin and Rykov, was moving toward the kind of systematic planning insisted on by the Left. Ironically, the resolution on the First Five-Year Plan, which Rykov introduced at the Fifteenth Party Congress, was adopted simultaneously with the expulsion of the Left from the party.

The issue of industrialization was inseparable from the question of agriculture and the peasantry. To Left and Right equally, the peasantry was both a problem and a resource for progress toward socialism; they disagreed over how to manage the problem and how to exploit the resource. Both sides in the debate assumed that the peasantry was petty-bourgeois in its instincts and a threat to the workers' state, but they perceived the threat differently. The Right feared a peasant uprising and advocated concessions to let agriculture prosper while a long, gradual cultural revolution prepared the peasants for socialism; Lenin had advocated much the same approach in his last articles. "The proletariat after its victory," Bukharin declared in 1924, "must *get along* with the peasantry *no matter what*," and by extension, with peasants who lived under colonialism elsewhere in the world. "Therefore, we must ideologically liquidate Trotskyism, . . . for the question of the worker-peasant bloc is the central question."[9]

In contrast, the Left feared concessions to kulak capitalism and the influence of petty-bourgeois attitudes *within* the workers' state. The Zinovievist P.

A. Zalutsky warned in 1925 that these tendencies could, if not combated, lead to a Soviet Thermidor.[10] (All factions failed to realize that the real Soviet Thermidor had already taken place with the introduction of the NEP, distinguished in the Russian case by the ability of the revolutionary party to retain power while retreating from the utopian, extremist program of War Communism.) According to the Left, thermidorean and petty-bourgeois tendencies had to be combated by a pro-worker orientation that would make the peasantry pay. Preobrazhensky wrote, "The state economy cannot do without taking away part of the surplus product of the village and of craft production, without deductions from capitalist accumulation for the benefit of socialist accumulation."[11]

After the formation of the United Opposition in 1926, Trotsky took up the anti-Stalin theme himself. He charged that "the further development of the bureaucratic regime leads fatally to individual rule" and referred explicitly to the warning about Stalin in Lenin's "Testament." By mid-1927, Trotsky, Zinoviev, and Kamenev were alleging "the most extreme usurpation of the supreme rights of the party," and Trotsky himself pointed to "a vast discrepancy between Stalin's intellectual resources and the power which the party and state apparatus has concentrated in his hands."[12] Facing expulsion from the Central Committee in October 1927, Trotsky again recalled Lenin's "Testament" and asserted that "the rudeness and disloyalty of which Lenin wrote are no longer mere personal characteristics. They have become the character of the ruling faction, . . . its belief in the omnipotence of methods of violence—even in dealing with its own party."[13]

The party leadership reacted frantically: "Unity," "iron discipline," and "ideological purity" were touted as the cardinal political virtues, and the Left Opposition was accused of anti-Leninist heresy. "We Leninists," Bukharin said, "have always imagined that the proletarian dictatorship can only be secure in our country if our party plays its role properly and when this party is in the first place the *sole* party in our country, that is, when the legal existence of other parties is made impossible, and in the second place the party is *unitary* in its structure, that is, represents a structure excluding any independent and autonomous groups, factions, organized currents, etc."[14] Stalin, living up to his reputation for rudeness, spoke contemptuously of "the opposition, hobbling behind the party like a decrepit old man with rheumatism in his legs, pains in the side, and pains in the head, the opposition sowing pessimism and poisoning the atmosphere with its whining to the effect that nothing will come of our efforts to construct socialism in the USSR." At the Fifteenth Party Congress he pronounced final judgment: "The opposition utterly breaks away from the Leninist principle of organization and takes the path of organizing a second party, the path of organizing a new International. . . . The opposition has slipped into Menshevism."[15]

In their psychology of authoritarian intolerance, the Stalin-Bukharin leadership encouraged the most primitive and abusive attacks on dissenters in the party and effectively stamped out all free opinion and political independence outside the bureaucratic chain of command. Political differences, it was asserted, were the expression of class differences and, since the party and its general line by definition represented the proletariat, any deviation was automatically antiproletarian, pro-bourgeois, and hence taboo. No one, not even in the opposition, asked why the proletariat, like the bourgeoisie in a parliamentary system, could not be represented by two or more parties. On the contrary, allowing anyone to question the leadership's proletarian rectitude, Bukharin warned, was "bound to lead sooner or later to the idea of the overthrow of the Soviet power—it can lead nowhere else."[16] For all his post-1985 popularity as a new Soviet cult figure, Bukharin cannot be exonerated of his role in perfecting the principle and practice of the monolithic party, of which he was shortly to become a victim himself.

Would Trotsky and the Left Opposition necessarily have acted the same way as the Stalinists did if they had prevailed in the struggle for power? The case for Trotsky as a proto-Stalinist rests mainly on his record during War Communism, including his advocacy of the militarization of labor. But the Left Opposition of the 1920s cannot be judged on the basis of Trotsky's position during War Communism, any more than Lenin or Bukharin should be understood only from their positions in that period. All three leaders changed, in different ways, in response to the failure of War Communism and the new conditions of the NEP. Trotsky and his supporters reverted to the more genuinely democratic views they had held before 1917. To suggest that Stalin's victory over Trotsky made no difference is to deny the former's unique personal influence and his arbitrary and perhaps paranoid decisions that put his stamp on the character of the Soviet regime.[17]

Many of the most distinctive features of Stalin's rule—his campaigns against bourgeois experts beginning with the Shakhty trials, his contemptuous anti-intellectualism and the dogmatization of Marxism, the purges—run totally counter to Trotsky's thought. Trotsky condemned wholesale collectivization and "planomania" and coined the now-familiar term "market socialism" as a mechanism to make the economic plan self-correcting.[18] Despite the affinity of some of Stalin's methods with the idea of militarizing the economy during War

Communism, Trotsky later rejected such policies as a concession to backwardness in the isolated socialist state.[19]

An initial similarity between Stalin's economic program and that of the opposition was clearly apparent to many of the Trotskyists, who accordingly agreed to "capitulate" and to collaborate with the general secretary. Preobrazhensky, for instance, declared in April 1929, "The policy of the party did not deviate to the right after the Fifteenth Congress, as the opposition described it, . . . but on the contrary in certain substantive points, it has seriously moved ahead on the correct path," which constituted in his mind "a great moral victory for the views of the opposition."[20]

In any case, speculation about how Trotsky and his supporters might have acted if they had stepped into the shoes of the Stalinists is not very fruitful. A review of the actual stands that the Left took as a critical alternative to the Stalin-Bukharin line until 1927 is more important. To be sure, the Left gave industrialization a much higher priority than did the Bukharinists, though they never contemplated the crash methods of planning or the violent uprooting of the peasantry undertaken by Stalin. On the international plane, the practical differences between the camps have been exaggerated. No matter how Trotsky felt about the difficulties for Russian socialism in the absence of world revolution, he was in reality no more prepared than Stalin or Bukharin to risk war or the loss of foreign trade opportunities.

The Left Opposition contrasted most sharply with Stalinism in the matter of party democratization and bureaucratization. On this issue, the Left Opposition anticipated the most serious evils of the Stalin era. They recognized Stalin's character as an unprincipled power grabber and saw the danger inherent in the concentration of power in his party apparatus. They protested the new doctrine of unanimity in political opinion, before finally falling victim to it.

The record of the Left Opposition is still important in any effort to understand the political and social circumstances that made Stalinism possible. Even if the opposition's criticisms were futile, they document the totalitarian trend in Soviet politics. The warnings of the Left, although usually unpublished, show that by the mid-1920s, Stalin's dictatorship and the dangerous consequences of his rule could be foreseen. While the oppositionists may not have fully comprehended the social forces contributing to Stalinism, they clearly recognized the bureaucratic trend in Soviet political life that Stalin exploited. For all these reasons, the Left's critique of the party leadership during the 1920s still deserves study and credit as a major benchmark in understanding Stalinism.

PART IV

Stalinism

CHAPTER 17

Foundations of Stalinism

The word "Stalinism" was not used under Stalin, though "Stalin-ist" (*stalinskii*) appeared frequently in connection with his pro-claimed triumphs. He always insisted, as did his successors, that the system he built was the realization of the socialist society pre-dicted by Marx and Engels. This assertion went uncontested not only by the Stalinist Left but by most commentators on the right, who gladly cited the horrors of Stalinism as proof of the perniciousness of Marxist doctrine or even of socialism in general.

Rejection of Stalinism by the Left outside of Russia was long impeded by ideological commitment to Marxism. As long as they believed that Stalin's re-gime in Russia represented the realization of scientific socialism, it was natural for those in the camp of social justice and class equality to overlook the defor-mations attributable to unfortunate Russian circumstances and stand together in solidarity with the first socialist country on the face of the globe. Thus the ideological façade of Marxism was vital to Stalin in his efforts to rally foreign sympathizers to defend the interests of the Soviet Union.

Stalinism's obvious divergence from the expectations of Marxism, above all in its bureaucratic hierarchy and the totalitarian state, points to major limitations in the Marxian theory of history. In its original form, Marxism failed to account for the possibility of socialist revolution in a relatively backward country such as Russia. It failed to consider the impact of unmet developmental and defense needs on a premature socialist regime. It rested on a questionable faith in the self-governing potential of the proletariat. Apart from certain warnings about the influence of the old state bureaucracy, it failed to recognize the modern postcapitalist trend everywhere toward the exercise of power independently of property ownership by government and corporate bureaucrats.

There remains another theory of Marxism's evil ideological influence that has come into vogue in recent years. This is the argument advanced by the American Catholic political philosopher Eric Voegelin, among others, that the commitment of Marxists to a political belief at one and the same time both deterministic and utopian was a form of "gnosticism," a heresy of hubris, leading them inexorably to the monumental crimes of Stalinism.[1] In this view, the Marxian vision dictated the Stalinist outcome not because the communist utopia was inevitable but because it was impossible.

The problem with this reasoning is that it substitutes for Marx's economic determinism a sort of philosophical determinism, asserted after the fact, holding that the Marxist ideas championed by the Russian revolutionaries, though wrong, were wholly or mainly responsible for the Stalinist outcome. In the extreme view advanced by some conservative thinkers—J. L. Talmon for one—the Stalinist horror, that is, "totalitarian democracy," is inherent in the whole tradition of rationalistic social change ever since the Enlightenment.[2] But philosophical determinism is unrealistic in presuming that people are driven more by the logic of their beliefs than by their underlying values or by the facts of their situation. It fails to account for those Marxists, the Social Democrats, who rejected the use of revolutionary force. It neglects the powerful historical circumstances that conditioned the efforts of Marxist revolutionaries, starting with Russia. It underestimates the individual psychological proclivities that may draw fanatical adherents of a given doctrine (one could cite Christianity as well as Marxism) into forms of behavior highly antithetical to the original spirit of their belief.

When the full record is considered, it makes little sense to try to understand Stalinism either as the victorious implementation of Marxism or as the pure fury of fanatics who cannot achieve their imagined goal. Stalinism meant the substantive abandonment of the Marxian program and the pragmatic acceptance of postrevolutionary Russian reality, while the power of the dictatorship was used to reinterpret and enforce Marxist doctrine as a tool of propaganda and legitimation. No genuine ideological imperative remained. Marxism could be made to appear to justify Stalinism, but it was no longer allowed to serve either as a policy directive or an explanation of reality.

Stalinism was not generated by ideology but by actual historical events. Apart from the experience of revolution, Stalinism could not have existed. Neither the nature nor the achievements of Stalinism can be understood without placing the phenomenon properly within its historical context in revolutionary Russia.

The political structure of Stalinism had its origins in the early era of revolutionary extremism, in the course of the Russian Civil War and War Communism. Under the influence of Lenin's philosophy of democratic centralism,
one-party power, and the struggle for survival against the armies of the counterrevolution and Allied intervention, the Communist Party acquired a form
and a spirit essentially military in nature. This was the "culture of War Communism," as Robert C. Tucker has termed it—the psychological source of the
militancy and authoritarianism that attracted the party bureaucracy to Stalin
in the 1920s.[3] While the revolution was in a period of remission during the
years of the NEP, Stalin developed his own power base in the party apparatus,
perfecting the nomenklatura system of appointments and ranks and eventually
establishing personal control over the Central Committee and the Politburo.
By the late 1920s, dominating the only effective organ of power, Stalin was in a
position comparable to that enjoyed by Napoleon Bonaparte with his command
of the army to realize the potential for personal despotism offered by the postrevolutionary condition of his country.

In the perspective of the revolutionary process, the debate about Marx's
responsibility for Lenin and Lenin's responsibility for Stalin loses much of its
meaning. As the terminal phase of revolution in Russia, Stalinism quite naturally contradicted Marx's predictions and violated his prescriptions. Thanks to
the nominal perpetuation of the Communist Party and Marxist dogma, Stalin
was able to accomplish a counterrevolution while dressing it up in revolutionary garb.

Although he adapted himself adroitly to the waning phases of the revolution, Stalin was not free of personal responsibility for Russia's ultimate
postrevolutionary shape. A postrevolutionary dictator, taking advantage of a
battered nation's need for authority, enjoys great scope to impose personal idiosyncrasies. Like other upstart leaders at this point in the process, Stalin was
an egomaniac opportunist. He was evidently driven to compensate for his own
inadequacies and perceived humiliations by murdering all his past rivals, rewriting history, identifying himself with the power and prestige of the Russian
nation ("the truly Russian tendency [of] the Russified non-Russian," as Lenin
termed it[4]), glorifying himself as the coryphaeus of all knowledge, and turning
the country's intellectual life into a pathetic parody.

Stalinism's most indisputable achievement, the success that compelled Khrushchev to accept the cost of the excesses committed by Stalin up to 1934, was to
set in motion the machinery of state-planned industrialization. Armed with the
powers of the totalitarian state and the command economy, Stalin was able to

channel Russia's resources into the extraordinary tempo of industrial construction that the country pursued during the first two Five-Year Plans. He thus laid the economic base to withstand the German onslaught of World War II and then to challenge the United States in military competition in the era of the Cold War.

These successes were bought at tremendous cost, not only in economic terms and in immediate human suffering but also in an enduring institutional deformation of Soviet society. The underpinning of Stalin's approach to modernization was anything but modern—it was, in essence, the reintroduction of serfdom. In this, Stalin resembled Peter the Great, whose reforms in the name of Westernization rested on more coercion and unfreedom, not less. Soviet industry as reorganized by Stalin was militarized both in the command relationship between the center and the enterprise and in the discipline imposed on the workers. The trade unions were converted into another agency of pressure from above, while the State Labor Reserves, operating from the late 1930s until Stalin's death, amounted to a system of labor conscription. In the rural sector, through the mechanism of the forcibly established collective farms and legal restrictions on freedom of movement, the Soviet peasantry was subjected to what Bukharin called "military-feudal exploitation," so that the state could appropriate the grain needed to feed the cities and the army and to pay for importing the equipment required by the industrialization drive.[5] So relentless was the collective farm system that delivery quotas could be enforced even upon drought-stricken Ukrainian villagers, causing the artificial, unacknowledged famine of 1932–33 and its casualties running into the millions. This was the low point, but Stalinism's impact on agriculture and on the consumer goods and service sectors of the Soviet economy remained retrogressive to the end.

The Stalinist method of industrialization was indeed one effective way of pursuing the goal of modernization and competitive national power, though it was not the only alternative—one may cite Japan, whose economic growth rate in the same era was comparable, or the program of development by means of the market socialism of the New Economic Policy, vainly defended by Bukharin. Indeed, long-term growth would probably have been greater if the Soviet Union had followed Bukharin's gradualist program rather than Stalin's crash methods.

Stalin's choice of a method of industrialization was not based on rational economic calculation or forethought. It was a political decision that he arrived at during 1928 and 1929, when he was fighting the Right Opposition and looking for issues that would enable him to condemn Bukharin and his friends as deviators from the general line of the party. In fact, the Right Opposition was only defending the cautious method of planning developed during the NEP. Stalin simply raised his targets for the tempo of industrialization and collectivization until the impossibility of the pace forced the Right Opposition to speak out, whereupon it was condemned and politically destroyed. Thanks to this episode, Stalin became committed to the methods of command in both industry and agriculture. By an accident of politics, he had stumbled upon a logical new alternative for Russia's development, though it was neither the most humane nor the most economical.

The approach to modernization that Stalin formulated for narrowly political reasons appeared to justify itself up to a point in its impressive record of industrial growth and technological achievement, not only in the 1930s but from World War II down to the early 1970s. In economic terms, the crisis of Stalinism did not come until the later Brezhnev years, when the growth rate fell to a crawl, the technology gap vis-à-vis the capitalist powers widened, and the frustrated expectations of Soviet consumers contributed to rising social pathology and ebbing national morale. Stalinist economics was a workable alternative for the early and middle phases of industrialization; it became counterproductive in addressing the new economic challenges of more recent decades.

In most critical commentary, particularly in the English-speaking countries, Stalinism is still subsumed in the concept of totalitarianism. There is some confusion in academic ranks over the term, with a tendency to restrict the "totalitarian model" to the period prior to the repudiation of Stalin's personal excesses. This is an error. If totalitarianism has any generic meaning at all, it still applied to the post-Stalin system, despite the functional divisions and putative "interest groups" that existed within the command context.

In the great volume of literature on totalitarianism, the phenomenon has been accurately described but poorly explained. For example, Carl J. Friedrich and Zbigniew Brzezinski analyzed all the features common to Fascist, Nazi, and Communist regimes but could only explain their origins on the basis of simple ideological fanaticism.[6] The totalitarian model generally lacks a sense of the historical situations and forces that make totalitarian regimes possible, above all the context of revolution.

Totalitarianism of the left—Stalinism—is a direct and natural product of revolution. Totalitarianism of the right is the outcome of a successful counter-revolutionary struggle against an actual or possible revolution. In either case, every available means of coercion, amplified by modern technology in weapons, surveillance, and record keeping, is employed to preserve power and control society. Totalitarianism is the characteristic twentieth-century form of the postrevolutionary dictatorship, whether it has been arrived at from the right or from the left.

There is much truth in the notion that in totalitarianism "the extremes meet." As the Right becomes more revolutionary and the Left becomes more traditionalist, differences between the two totalitarianisms shrink to matters of degree and rhetoric. Only the leftist language of Stalinism obscured how it psychologically approached the more openly acknowledged authoritarian principles of the Right. The party, conceived by Lenin as an instrument of revolution, was transformed during the 1920s into a permanent means of autocratic rule. This worked through the bureaucratic structure of the party apparatus, charged with surveillance and control over every aspect of society. Ever since the factional struggle against the Left Opposition, the mentality of the apparatchiki was distinguished by a fierce insistence on unity, unanimity, and conformity to the will of the leader. Stalinism evinced the same authoritarian personality traits that have been described by Erich Fromm and Theodor Adorno in the Nazi regime.[7] Through the Communist Party's elaborate system of cadre selection and training these traits were perpetuated in the Soviet power structure. In his later years, Stalin openly embraced rightist elements of ideology, particularly Great Russian nationalism and anti-Semitism, and these became the main sources of any lingering political enthusiasm under his rule.

In its thoroughness of control, above all in economic life, Stalinist totalitarianism went well beyond its counterparts on the right. Russian traditions of centralism and subservience helped make this extreme possible, while the needs of industrialization and defense gave it a purpose. Totalitarianism was not fully realized in Russia until Stalin applied the power of the party to collectivize the peasants, militarize the urban economy, and tyrannize all sectors of cultural and intellectual life. The terror that followed far transcended any violence inflicted by the totalitarians of the right upon their own nationals and equaled in scope and irrationality Hitler's campaigns of international genocide.

Stalinist terror was made possible by totalitarianism. The terror was not, however, essential to the system. The post-Stalin reforms still left intact the totalitarian structure of Soviet politics and society.

Throughout the worst of the terror and privation inflicted by his regime, Stalin was able to soften or deflect the judgment of reality by claiming to have achieved the goal of socialism. In many minds, Stalinism gained indisputable legitimation by its attachment to the sentiments of social justice that the term *socialism* implied for the Left, the labor movement, and anti-imperialists in most countries.

In the official Stalinist view, Soviet Russia was the first socialist society in the world, the beacon light that all other nations were expected to follow.

What merit was there in the Soviet claim to represent not only a form of socialism but its highest attainment? The contention that Soviet Russia had to be socialist because it was the embodiment of the proletarian revolution was a myth vigorously disputed by the non-Communist or anti-Stalinist Left. After Khrushchev began his de-Stalinization campaign in 1956, no one beyond the reach of Moscow's discipline defended the claim that Russia had laid down the one true road to socialism. Many anti-Stalinists went on to maintain that the Soviet Union was not socialist at all but rather a form of "étatism," as Titoist Yugoslavs said, or "bureaucratic state capitalism," or "totalitarian state economy," as Rudolf Hilferding once described it.[8]

These formulations are understandable as efforts to deny the Soviets the political legitimacy that the label "socialist" might convey, but they depend on semantic hairsplitting. If socialism is to be given any simple and workable definition, it is the principle of social control over economic activity, however organized and under whatever political system. The Soviet system might have been repugnant on political or ethical grounds, but it was nonetheless a system of socialism based on social control—in fact, extreme and uncompromising social control—over economic activity. The perfection of a nearly total system of socialized economy was a distinct accomplishment of Stalinism. Legislation promulgated when the NEP was liquidated remained in force until perestroika, to suppress all private enterprise (save the private farm plots and family operations) and to impose criminal sanctions against any private trade as "speculation" and against any private employment as "exploitation."

Stalin's traumatic modernization program of the 1930s was always officially described as "building socialism." In effect, the attainment of the Marxian state of grace was equated with the expansion of industrial production. According to Stalin, the stage of "socialism," or what Marx termed the "first stage of communism," had been reached when he promulgated the 1936 constitution, on the grounds that the exploiter classes had been liquidated. Subsequently, Soviet theorists devised various ritualistic categories to describe the country's progress—"perfecting socialism" or "preparing the foundations for the transition to communism," and toward the end, "developed socialism" or "real existing socialism." All of these formulations served to put off the question of Marx's higher stage of "communism"—a utopia that neither Stalin nor his successors had any intention of implementing.

Granted, Stalinism succeeded in implanting an extreme form of socialism, though not in transforming human nature according to the collectivist ideal of the "New Soviet Man." In the rapid advance of heavy industry and military potential Stalinist socialism was a distinct success, though it eventually reached a time of diminishing returns. In other respects, in agriculture and in the small-scale economy of trade, crafts, and consumer services, Stalinist socialism came near to disaster, and its retrogressive effect has still not been overcome. By collectivizing agriculture and nationalizing small business, Stalin chose not to wait for capitalism or even market socialism to accomplish the process of "primary capital accumulation" in what could have been an economically more progressive way. In respect to both industrial construction and the socialization of small enterprise, Stalinist socialism was not the sequel to capitalism but an alternative to it, supplanting the capitalist mode of concentrating a country's resources for development and using the coercive powers of the state to this end. Stalinist socialism involved a fundamental reorientation in goals as well as methods, abandoning the traditional socialist pursuit of justice in the distribution of economic values in favor of economic mobilization to maximize production, primarily in the interest of the state and its military power.

The Russian experience shows that there is no historical inevitability to the perfect socialism that idealists long envisaged. Betraying even Russia's own spirit of absolute democratization that had erupted in 1917, Stalinism fashioned a system of bureaucratic state socialism paralleling the latest capitalist trends of organizational concentration, enforced by the political mechanisms of totalitarianism, and guided by the imperatives of modernization and national power. Perhaps all this was hard to avoid, given the burden of Russia's historical legacy and the requirements of successful competition and even survival in the modern world. But for the cause of social justice around the globe, it was a tragedy that Russia, of all places, should be the locale of the world's first great socialist undertaking.

While trumpeting the revolutionary language of proletarian internationalism, Stalinism actually turned away from the outside world, though the shift was temporarily masked by Stalin's pursuit of conventional diplomacy and alliances from the beginning of the Popular Front era to the end of World War II. He rehabilitated Russian nationalism, cultivated an espionage mania to excuse his purges, and denounced every sort of foreign influence. Building formidable foundations for Russian imperial power, Stalinism set Russia against the world, not only against the capitalist world but against the revolutionary world insofar as it was not Soviet-controlled. Soviet Russia reverted to the xenophobia rooted in the oldest layers of Russian political culture that had come to the surface with the Stalinist leadership.

The core of Stalinist foreign policy was to maximize the security and influence of the Soviet state. Marxist doctrine, though dogmatically asserted as the legitimation of each step taken by the Soviet Union in its foreign relations, lost all guiding force, just as it had in the country's internal affairs. Through his agencies of indoctrination internally and through the Comintern externally, Stalin was able to redefine Marxist goals and categories so flexibly that entire social systems could be reclassified from reactionary to progressive or vice versa depending on whether their governments happened to be allies or adversaries of the Soviet Union. Even a Communist country—Yugoslavia—could be transformed from socialism into fascism by a stroke of Stalin's pen. For Stalin, in foreign relations as well as in internal politics, anyone beyond the reach of his army and police was a potential enemy. Foreign Communist purge victims, even the Hungarian revolutionary leader Bela Kun, learned this to their sorrow in the late 1930s, as did a long series of "National Communist" leaders shortly after they had been installed in power in Eastern Europe following World War II.

If Stalin had one positive principle in his foreign policy, it was Russian nationalism, buttressed as occasion demanded with Marxist-Leninist language. During the test that Stalinism underwent in World War II, Russian nationalism was the main propaganda theme. Marxism-Leninism, revived after the war, was fused with Russian nationalism to become an ideology of superpower confrontation between the "socialist" and "imperialist" camps. This was the atmosphere in which Stalin sealed his country off from foreign contacts of every sort—strangely so for a regime that claimed to be the world model for the future. Far from any international revolutionary confidence, it was fear of contamination and exposure that governed Stalin's view of the outside world.

One of the most remarkable achievements of Stalinism was its transformation of an international revolutionary movement into an instrument to serve the interests of the Soviet Union. This was made possible only by the imposition of Stalinist-type control by Moscow over the affairs of the foreign Communist parties, including leadership selection, political tactics, and ideological acknowledgment of Soviet guidance. The demand for such conformity originated with Lenin's "Twenty-One Conditions" of 1920, but it did not become a reality until the "Bolshevization" of the Comintern in the middle and later 1920s. Attacking first the supporters of the Russian Ultra Left, then the supporters of Trotsky, then the supporters of Bukharin, Stalin succeeded by 1930 in expelling from the movement practically all the original founders of the various Communist parties. Thereafter, with the notable exception of China, the Comintern parties proved by and large to be dependable defenders both of Soviet ideological claims and of the zigzag line of Soviet foreign policy from the United Front and the eclectic search for allies in the 1920s, to the Third Period of renewed revolutionary rhetoric from 1928 to 1934, to the Popular Front and Collective Security, and on to the period of the pact with Hitler and the Great Patriotic War. It is ironic that this was the same period in which Stalin was transforming the Soviet Union internally into a conservative totalitarianism and burying the last embers of true revolutionary feeling in his counterrevolutionary purges.

From the standpoint of Russian national aspirations, international Stalinism was extraordinarily successful during the years immediately following the end of the war. Russian power filled the vacuum left in Eastern Europe by the collapse of Nazi Germany and thereby absorbed into the Soviet sphere practically all the lands that had been eyed by the Pan-Slavists of the nineteenth century as targets for Russian domination. Not only this; Stalin was able to impose on his new East European satellites the model of totalitarian socialism that had taken shape in Russia under his aegis. This was an unnatural achievement, not only because it represented a coercive, foreign imposition on the national life of Eastern Europe, but also because the Stalinist model reflected the specifically Russian legacy of autocracy, backwardness, and revolution. Once the grip of Stalinism was relaxed by Khrushchev, it was natural if not inevitable that the reaction against it would be much sharper in Eastern Europe, particularly in those more developed and more sophisticated countries better described as Central European.

Stalin's program in Eastern Europe was just one facet of the mission that he took on to counterbalance the United States in the postwar confrontation between the two superpowers. His success in this context was considerable but not unqualified. Stalin signally failed in his effort to use Western Communists to prevent the solidification of the NATO alliance that he had provoked against him, and he was unable to keep the major part of Germany out of the Western alignment. Because of his guiding Cold War premise of the inherent hostility of the outside world, he could not see that his own counterproductive tactics of political and military pressure were responsible for much of the actual animosity he encountered. The same premise explains his shortsighted failure to exploit the nationalism of colonial or newly independent nations, as his successors did more successfully. As a Russian development intimately tied to Russian national interests, Stalinism proved to be inapplicable anywhere else in the world except by the exertion of Russian power. Other countries and parties in the Communist movement were kept loyal to the USSR only by various combinations of deception and force. When Khrushchev broke the magic spell with his de-Stalinization campaign in 1956, these allies were ready to challenge the Stalinist model and reject Soviet dictation of their respective destinies.

In its most extreme form, Stalinism proved too severe even for the country that had engendered it. The excrescences of terror, cultural repression, and xenophobia that had stemmed primarily from Stalin's personal idiosyncrasies—not to say madness—did not survive his death. On the other hand, the structural aspects of Stalinism, reflecting the historical experiences and needs of post-revolutionary Russia, proved impervious to serious reform for another generation. These lasting features included, obviously, the entire economic setup of planned industry and collectivized agriculture, the apparatus of political control, and the social system of bureaucratic hierarchy with its cadres advancing through the ranks of the nomenklatura to share at one level or another in the exercise of power.

Khrushchev's reforms were hailed all over the world as de-Stalinization. But within the Soviet Union, by ameliorating the most destructive and demoralizing excesses of Stalinism, reform actually made the basic Stalinist system more tolerable and more durable. Outside the Soviet Union, the effects of de-Stalinization were far more serious. Upon the signal of Khrushchev's "Secret Speech," the mental hold of Stalinism both in East European governments and in Western Communist parties gave way, with spectacular consequences. Without the rigor of Stalin's own Stalinism, both in its ideological claims and in its readiness to resort to coercion, Moscow could no longer maintain the political dominance over the international movement that it had enjoyed for a generation. The year 1956 was not only the year of the crisis of Stalinism but the year of its end as a meaningful political phenomenon beyond the tips of the Soviet Army's bayonets.

CHAPTER 18

Stalinism as Postrevolutionary Dictatorship

As François Furet observed about the French Revolution, the revolutionary experience is replete with ironies and surprises—"a very great event that took a bad turn."[1] Nothing really happens according to the intentions of the people who thought they were leading the process at each stage, and even less according to their announced self-justification. As Hegel said, we make history blindly and realize the meaning of our actions only when it is too late to alter the consequences. This is true even for Marxists, who thought they were implementing the scientific laws of history.

Postrevolutionary dictatorship has been recognized by a host of writers, from Trotsky on, as "Bonapartism." It combines elements of the revolution and the Old Regime, usually more systematic, despotic, and "modern," after the chaos and fanaticism of the earlier revolutionary phases. In Weber's terms, this development is the *Veralltäglichung des charisma*, the "routinization of charisma," responding to modern economic needs and inevitably leading to "bureaucratization."[2] In the twentieth century, with modern means of surveillance and coercion, postrevolutionary dictatorship took the institutional form of totalitarianism. The "totalitarian model" does not have to be rejected completely; instead, it needs to be understood as a historical conception limited to the postrevolutionary context. In this restricted sense, the totalitarian model is appropriate and illuminating.

Naturally, postrevolutionary dictatorship varies in detail among different times and places. It may appear under the banner of the revolution and the Left or under the banner of counterrevolution and the Right. In either case, ideology masks the actual integrating function of the postrevolutionary regime as it combines both revolutionary and prerevolutionary symbols, forms of authority, and dominant social elements in the totalitarian sociopolitical structure. Those who prefer the Hegelian language will see here the "synthesis" of the Old Regime "thesis" and the revolutionary "antithesis," but it is a synthesis coming much quicker and much more to the disadvantage of revolutionary values than the theorists of Marxism have usually recognized.

Postrevolutionary dictatorship takes hold when utopian enthusiasm has spent its force in terror or civil strife or war, leaving society exhausted and cynical, and when the popular longing for a return to order and authority outweighs attachment to the values of the revolution. This thermidorean cast of mind sets up the opportunity for an individual strongman, controlling whatever is the most effective organization of power bequeathed by the revolution, to become a personal dictator. For Cromwell and Bonaparte, it was the revolutionary army. For Stalin, it was the apparatus of the revolutionary party. In any case, the power base of the dictatorship, set against the disruption of old loyalties and values, traditional and revolutionary alike, gives the postrevolutionary dictatorship extraordinary scope for personal leadership and influence. Thus the exact character of any given postrevolutionary dictatorship becomes unique and indeterminate.

What was distinctive to postrevolutionary dictatorship in Russia, replicated in subsequent Communist revolutions, was the organizational and ideological continuity that Stalin maintained between the revolutionary era and his own regime. He himself came out of the apparatus of the party of revolutionary extremism and made this apparatus the foundation of his postrevolutionary rule. At the same time, he insisted on the formal observance of revolutionary ideology, now designated "Marxism-Leninism." This was crucial to legitimate his rule internally and to propagandize for it externally. It was possible for Stalin to use the doctrine for these purposes because he commanded the power to reinterpret its meaning as he chose and thus make it serve the new social structure over which he presided. In other words, he turned Marxism into a system of ideological "false consciousness" in the original Marxian sense of the term.[3]

Distinctive in Stalin's postrevolutionary dictatorship were its bureaucratic social base and its cultural conservatism. In any revolution, the social segment that emerges from the revolutionary process as the dominant element is not the same as those who contributed the most fire to the extremist stage. In the Russian Revolution, workers and peasants were instrumental in boosting the extremist party to power and saw many of their sons rise to high rank under the new regime, but they never exercised class power as such. Instead, the successor to the dispossessed landlords and bourgeoisie as the nation's dominant social force was the new party and governmental bureaucracy—in other words, the New Class. It was the New Class, expanded and elaborated, that became the basis, the instrument, and the beneficiary of the postrevolutionary dictatorship. Its position was reflected in Stalin's repudiation of the goal of egalitarianism and in his doctrine of the three "strata"—workers, collective farmers, and the "toiling intelligentsia"—within the nominally "classless" society of socialism.

Along with the ascendancy of the New Class, Stalin's postrevolutionary dictatorship rejected revolutionary experiment in everything from education and labor relations to criminology and family law.[4] All this was replaced (in the name of Marxism) by highly traditionalist policy norms attempting to put the burden on individual discipline and responsibility in addressing every kind of social and economic problem. The much-touted "New Soviet Man" was but the image of an artificially imposed Protestant ethic restated in Marxist language. In cultural life, the imposition of absolute party authority was accompanied by corresponding reversions from revolutionary to traditionalist norms—though still in Marxist language—with the suppression of modernism in all the arts as "degenerate bourgeois formalism." Modern theories were even condemned in such scientific fields as physics and biology. Most remarkable of all in Stalin's return to conservative models was his embrace of Russian nationalism. In the spirit of the new nationalism, antinationalist Marxist history was rejected, compromise was reached with the Russian Orthodox Church, and foreign policy was freed from ideological constraints.

Like any postrevolutionary dictator, Stalin imprinted his own style and personality on the policies of the state. He was guided by no higher vision than his own personal glory, as well as vindictiveness toward past rivals and suspected enemies, though psychohistorians might fathom deeper roots of his conduct in the recesses of his psyche. What does strike the ordinary historian was his concern for immediate, short-term political success, in both internal and international matters, and his skill and shrewdness in maneuvering to achieve one limited goal after another. Contrary to the image Trotsky promoted, Stalin was not ignorant in matters theoretical; he was adroit in the manipulation of ideological arguments and precedents to embarrass his opponents and justify his own positions, as he first demonstrated during the Socialism in One Country controversy. His personal predilections of cultural conservatism and Russophilia come through distinctly in his policy choices, along with his unusual passion for doctrinal legitimacy, a deep resentment or contempt for genuine intellectual commitment, and an elemental anti-Semitism.

Was Stalin insane? If so, as Russian critics from Khrushchev on have hinted, he was far from the only instance of a megalomaniac despot. His was a type of personality that the postrevolutionary situation invites to take power. Mad or not, Stalin was clearly unrestrained by normal ethical standards, though the Bolshevik tradition had already reasoned such considerations out of the way as an impediment to the class struggle. As one expedient and amoral action led to another, he wove a web of criminality and mendacity of an extent without precedent in modern times. By all accounts, he developed a paranoid suspiciousness about potential plots and enemies on every hand, although it is in the nature of any despotism to generate opposition that can only take the form of conspiracy. If Stalin's fear was unfounded, then it is the lack of effective opposition to his capricious rule that is the surprising thing, not the fear. The autocrat's suspicion of enemies tends to become a self-fulfilling prophecy.

Stalin's historic role was a great one, even greater than the one that his sycophants attributed to him. As a devotee of short-run maneuver and problem solving, dressed up at each point in casuistical ideological legitimacy, he managed a regime that was maximally responsive to the deeper forces in Soviet society. In this manner, he adapted to Russia's postrevolutionary need for stability and authority; the challenges of modernization and military self-sufficiency; the universal trend toward the bureaucratic organization of modern political and economic life; and the resources of the Russian tradition of "orthodoxy, autocracy, nationality" as a form of reconciling all these needs. These challenges and Stalin's responses to them were all essential constituents of the postrevolutionary synthesis in Russia.

But this synthesis was accomplished in a form uniquely governed by Stalin's personal actions and decisions. One especially oppressive feature was his attachment to the letter of Marxist-Leninist orthodoxy and his imposition of pervasive and stultifying controls in intellectual life in order to sustain his own ideological authority. This was but one facet of his mania for total control, building on but far exceeding the tsarist tradition of autocratic centralism and contributing to the most extreme form of totalitarianism to emerge anywhere in the revolutionary twentieth century. Finally, Stalin personally inspired an atmosphere of terror and violence that caused his country untold damage and suffering.

It is a distraction from some of the worst aspects of Stalinism to suggest that any other Communist leader—Trotsky, for example—would necessarily have behaved the same way. To argue that someone else would have had to take the same path Stalin did is to say that Stalin's personality, his lust for power and legitimacy, his pathological criminality, did not make any difference. This is the opposite extreme from the Khrushchev fallacy of blaming the evils associated with the Stalin era solely on the leader's personality. In the case of postrevolutionary Russia, one must not underestimate the role of the individual in power, any more than one should hold an impersonal system or abstract law of history exclusively responsible.

Stalin's postrevolutionary dictatorship did not take final form all at once. As in other revolutions, it unfolded by stages, as the leader responded to the challenges confronting him and then to the new problems created by his own responses. Under cover of doctrinal continuity, Stalin adjusted to the realities of a country coming out of revolution that were addressed in other instances by more avowedly counterrevolutionary regimes or monarchical restorations.

Often Stalin's personal impact is described as a "revolution from above," when the all-powerful leader imposed violent and disruptive change upon the country he commanded.[5] The Russian precedents usually cited are Peter the Great, ordering the nation into the Western cultural orbit in order to restore its military competitiveness, or Ivan the Terrible, crushing the independence of the nobility in order to give the nation the strength of an absolute autocracy. Recognizing their parallels with himself, Stalin had his official historians restore both these tsar-revolutionaries to the pantheon of national heroes.

Strictly speaking, a "revolution from above" is a misnomer, if "revolution" means the violent overthrow of a political system. However, it has an acceptable metaphorical sense as a radical and coercive change of policy imposed by the governmental leadership. Stalin's early years in full authority, the era of the First Five-Year Plan from 1929 to 1932, were clearly a time of revolution in this sense.[6] This was the form of his postrevolutionary dictatorship in its first phase.

The features of Stalin's revolution from above are familiar. Economically it instituted total socialization and militarization through collectivization of the peasants, the elimination of the private commercial enterprise of the Nepmen, the institution of comprehensive central planning in lieu of the market socialism of the NEP, and the subordination of the rights of industrial labor and the trade unions to the needs of the state for greater production and surplus value. In turn, the new economic institutions required more bureaucratic control and a hierarchical distribution of power from the leader down through the party apparatus. At the same time, control from above was extended to all other organized social institutions and activities, including cultural and intellectual life.

This is why one can justifiably say that the Soviet system became totalitarian in the early 1930s.

A number of writers consider these years a period of "cultural revolution," sometimes with the upheaval in China of the 1960s in mind.[7] It is true that Stalin was able to tap a certain residue of ideological fervor and class struggle feeling among younger intellectuals and workers and perhaps poor peasants and to mobilize this sentiment in campaigns against kulaks, saboteurs, and bourgeois culture in general. But in Stalin's case, cultural revolution was not the work of a new social force from below that the leader merely unleashed as Mao Tse-tung did. Rather, it was a matter of manipulating culture as an instrument of propaganda and control to reinforce the totalitarian aims of the postrevolutionary dictatorship.

The underlying national need addressed by all these steps was, of course, modernization. To be sure, Stalin's effort did not begin with an entirely undeveloped society but rather from the midpoint at which industrial progress under tsarism had been broken off by World War I and the revolution. This is not to say that Stalin's methods of modernization were the most effective or that they were rationally arrived at. There is much evidence that he made his key decisions of 1928 initiating the Stalin Revolution without any broad conception of a new era of policy but only as a series of short-run political maneuvers to secure victory over the Bukharin faction of party moderates. Ironically, the foreign threats of fascist imperialism commonly cited in justification of Stalin's totalitarian path of accelerated modernization did not materialize until the program had already been under way for two or three years. Furthermore, there is serious question whether Stalin's methods put the country in the best position to resist outside aggression when it finally struck in 1941.

Struggle, it seems, is in the nature of the postrevolutionary dictatorship. If the regime is not strong enough to engage in revolutionary imperialism against the outside world, as Bonaparte and Hitler did, then it turns against its own people or vulnerable minorities among them. Stalin declared war on the peasantry, forcing it, under cover of socialist slogans and the class struggle against all those defined as kulaks, back into a form of serfdom. Nevertheless, collectivization had a rational, if inhumane, goal—namely, to exploit agriculture in order to finance rapid industrial construction. It was Stalin's methods, making struggle an end in itself and annihilating suspected enemies by the millions, that were irrational and ultimately counterproductive. Reconstructions of the economic record have shown that the violent implementation of collectivization weakened Soviet agriculture so badly that the rural sector became a net consumer of resources, not a source for profitable exploitation.[8]

The second phase of Stalin's postrevolutionary dictatorship is not widely recognized as a period distinct from the first. Beginning in 1931, Stalin took advantage of his now unlimited power in matters of policy and doctrine to order the sweeping changes in social, cultural, and intellectual policies that rejected ultraradical experiments and substituted traditionalist values and norms in one area after another. The entire operation was camouflaged by preserving the vocabulary of Marxist-Leninist orthodoxy and designating the new, conservative line "Marxist" while old ideas advanced in the name of Marxism were denounced as bourgeois and counterrevolutionary. In sum, following the revolution from above of 1929–31, the period 1932–36 was a time of counterrevolution from above, changing the mix in the postrevolutionary synthesis from a preponderance of revolutionary elements to a preponderance of the traditional.

There were pragmatic reasons for much of Stalin's shift in the conservative direction, and these again reflected the underlying needs of a postrevolutionary society still facing the challenge of modernization. With his slogan "Cadres decide everything," he accepted the necessity of bureaucratic organization and elite authority in modern industrial life as well as the convergence of this need with the Russian tradition of bureaucratic centralism. He boldly confronted the ideological heritage of egalitarianism when he asserted in 1934, "Equalization, . . . leveling the requirements and the individual lives of the members of society . . . has nothing in common with Marxism, with Leninism."[9] It was sufficient for his sense of doctrinal rectitude that he could proclaim the abolition of classes while extending as permanent policy the wide differentiation in wage and salary levels that had first been reluctantly accepted during the NEP to reward responsibility and encourage productivity. Educational policy abruptly felt the new winds, when radical libertarian experimentation was condemned in 1931–32 and replaced by a combination of revived academic traditionalism for the elite and practical literacy and vocational training for the masses. The party "maximum" on money incomes was abandoned, and proletarian preference in education and party life gave way to de facto preference for the children of the elite. All of these steps reflected Stalin's postrevolutionary accommodation to the social reality of the New Class, to the emergent *egemonia* of the bureaucratic stratum.

Accepting the requirements of a stratified industrial society, Stalin swept away practically everything in the realm of social experiment and cultural innovation that had been attempted in the name of the revolution for the previous fifteen years. The guiding spirit in pre-Stalin social thought was "withering-away"—the withering-away of any and all coercive social institutions in a spirit of Rousseauian utopianism. Not only was the state supposed to wither away, but along with it law, the school and, in the minds of some, the family. Now, in the 1930s, all of these institutions were rehabilitated as pillars of socialist society. The traditional leftist approach to individual deviance and failure as the consequences of adverse social conditions and class deprivation was rejected in favor of the philosophy of individual responsibility and the practice of coercive discipline. The nation was restored both as a historical category and as a focus of loyalty. All these steps embodied the essence of conservative social control as it would have been advocated by Edmund Burke, for example, horrified though he might have been at the despotic Russian manner of restoring such authority.

At the same time, artistic experimentation in the modernist vein, in which Russia had been an international leader both before and after the revolution, was cast aside and replaced by the most conventional norms—a sort of Soviet Victorianism, one might say. Perhaps, as some writers suggest, this reversal in cultural standards reflected the tastes of the sons of workers and peasants newly arrived in the bureaucracy as well as of Stalin and his entourage personally.[10]

The international environment was not a decisive factor in the first phase of Stalin's postrevolutionary dictatorship. In the so-called Third Period of the Comintern, Stalin had to go out of his way to set Communists against everyone else for the short-run purpose of undermining the influence of his rivals in the Bukharin camp. In practical matters, Soviet trade with the capitalist world actually increased during the First Five-Year Plan, at the same time that Stalin was beating the nationalist drum about catching up or being beaten as had so often happened to Russia in the past. In the second phase of Stalinism, the international threat was clearly more serious, as the menace of Japanese and then German expansionism became a reality. This new circumstance obviously contributed to Stalin's ideological volte-face in regard to Russian nationalism as a source of popular loyalty and to his shift from revolutionary rhetoric to conventional alliance diplomacy in 1933–35 (diplomatic relations with the United States, membership in the League of Nations, the doctrine of Collective Security, and the Popular Front line for the Comintern).

In historical perspective, Stalin's counterrevolution from above is not in the least surprising. The essence of postrevolutionary dictatorship is to synthesize the new and the old, the revolutionary and the traditional, selecting from each source in the immediate interest of political expediency but in a manner cumulatively reflecting the requirements of a society that has been overstretched and torn by the revolutionary experience. Again, it needs to be reiterated that the most unusual thing about Stalin's fulfillment of the postrevolutionary role was his success in covering the vast transformation in the nature and policies of his regime with the language of revolutionary orthodoxy.

In some instances, postrevolutionary consolidation went so far as monarchical restoration, when military defeat (Bonaparte) or the death of the leader (Cromwell) opened up the opportunity for avowed counterrevolutionaries to take control of the state. They could not undo the revolution's most basic changes in institutions, social values, and the mix of class elements enjoying egemonia in society. However, they did effect great changes in leading personnel and in the overt symbols of authority and belief, carrying the trends of the postrevolutionary synthesis even further in the conservative direction.

Though Russia experienced no overt restoration, one can imagine something like it had Hitler waged political warfare more intelligently in 1941 and accomplished the outright overthrow of Stalin's regime. Yet in terms of personnel and symbols, Stalin went almost as far as any monarchists might have. The Great Purge, marking the third period of his postrevolutionary dictatorship, decimated the cadres of Old Bolsheviks. Practically everyone of stature over the age of thirty-five in the party, the government, or the military—in other words, anyone old enough to remember the revolution, save the members of the Politburo and a few ideological acolytes—was liquidated or sent to a lingering death in the camps. (Significantly, similar fates befell most refugee foreign Communists who had sought asylum in the USSR from fascist dictators at home.) Below the leadership level, however, the New Class was simply restaffed—to be sure, with sons of peasants who gave it a less intellectual and more nativist cast than before—and its bureaucratic mentality and its pursuit of rank and privilege became even more pronounced. A compulsive sense of status reminiscent of unreformed tsarism set in within the party's own leadership, evidenced in the unwritten but consistent rules by which, from Stalin's time to Gorbachev's, membership in the Politburo and Central Committee was awarded on the basis of bureaucratic rank and function.[11]

Simultaneously with the purges, Stalin became the object of official adulation and glorification as the omniscient and omnicompetent ruler, beyond anything seen before in the history of monarchy in Russia or almost anywhere else. Rank and hierarchy were restored in the most visible ways, from military titles and diplomatic uniforms to official limousines and Kremlin Hospital privileges. The State Labor Reserves and the forced labor of the Gulag amounted to a restoration of serfdom in the industrial sector as well as the agricultural, recalling the approach of Peter the Great to modernization. The national minorities, prime victims of the collectivization era and the purges, had to yield, as they did for centuries before the revolution, to the primacy of the Great Russians and the Russification of their own histories and cultures. Implicit and later overt anti-Semitism became a hallmark of the new regime as it had been of the Old.

Other symbolic steps toward national tradition came during or immediately after World War II, the "Great Patriotic War of the Soviet Union." The Comintern was abolished and with it underwriting of foreign revolution for its own sake; the "Internationale" was supplanted as the national anthem by the "Hymn of the Soviet Union"; and compromise was reached with the Orthodox Church, though not a full embrace, since Stalin had his own orthodoxy in the form of Marxism-Leninism as a state religion. Tellingly, the revolutionary title of "people's commissar" yielded to the reactionary "minister." Celebrating the surrender of Japan, Stalin hailed the rectification of Russia's territorial losses of 1905—in a war in which he himself, as a good Bolshevik at the time, had advocated the defeat of the tsarist government. All that was unusual, if Stalin were compared with his imperial forebears, was the use of an international revolutionary doctrine and an international movement loyal to Moscow because of that doctrine as instruments to protect or advance the interests of the Russian Empire.

The process of revolution, as history shows, has never ended with the postrevolutionary dictatorship or counterrevolution or even with a restored monarchy. There remains one more distinctive step, when the nation throws off the burden of postrevolutionary conservatism and finally comes to terms in a nonfanatic way with its original revolutionary inspiration. This is the "moderate revolutionary revival," representing the final achievement of national stability around the principles and practices of the first, moderate phase of the revolutionary process, but without the passions and polarization that almost always destabilize moderate politics at that point and open the way to violent dictatorship either of the Left or of the Right.[12]

In this perspective, Mikhail Gorbachev represented just such a final turn in the sequence of events set in motion by the Russian Revolution. Reform under Nikita Khrushchev could be considered an early, abortive attempt at introducing the moderate revolutionary revival. The "era of stagnation," in between Khrushchev and Gorbachev, then can be understood as an artificial prolongation of the postrevolutionary dictatorship, with all its ensuing consequences of frustration and demoralization in Soviet society.

Khrushchev never attacked the postrevolutionary dictatorship in its institutional or doctrinal fundamentals; he seems to have been that rara avis, a true believer. Clearly he rejected the third phase of Stalinism with the purges and the personal cult, and he did moderate Stalin's second postrevolutionary phase by taking steps toward a more egalitarian ideal, for example in his educational ideas (an immediate failure) and in his labor and wage policies (to the ultimate detriment of the Soviet economy). Evidently Khrushchev took seriously a foreseeable transition to pure communism, even though the actual authors of his party program did not.[13] Gorbachev, by contrast, challenged every phase of Stalinism.

Neither Khrushchev nor Gorbachev altered the reality of New Class egemonia. What finally seemed to be taking place with Gorbachev's moderate revolutionary revival was a distinctive shift of influence among the elements of the dominant stratum, with the partial eclipse of the party bureaucracy and the sons of peasants, and the liberation of the creative intelligentsia. Whereas postrevolutionary dictatorship responded to national needs for stability and authority in the pursuit of economic development and modernization, the moderate revolutionary revival was a response to a mature society that demanded the release of its creative forces. Khrushchev's attempt at reform was ill conceived and perhaps for Russia premature; Gorbachev's was long overdue.

CHAPTER 19

From Distributive Socialism to Production Socialism

What distinguished Marxian socialism from all other forms was a theory of how socialism was to come about: as the natural consequence of the historical laws of class struggle and revolution that Marx thought he had discovered. As to the specific characteristics of the future socialism, Marx was always advisedly vague; he added little to the hopes and plans of the Utopian Socialists of the generation preceding him. Marx's socialism was utopianism with a difference: The earlier ideal of a stateless collectivism with complete distributive justice was reinforced with a sophisticated theory of social and economic development. Marx was the first philosopher in history to incorporate in his thought the full importance of economic development through technical progress and industrialization, which by multiplying society's capacity to produce would finally give some realistic substance to the old dream of abolishing human misery. The stark facts—largely overlooked by Marx's Utopian predecessors—were that given the limits on productivity in preindustrial society, no redistribution of the wealth of the small privileged class could make much of a dent, on the average, in the poverty of the vast majority. Redistribution would only undermine the culture-bearing class, and it could be evaded by any group with the drive and the power to spare itself from reduction to the average level of misery.

The crucial function of economic development was, according to Marxism, to furnish the material prerequisites for the effective socialist redistribution of wealth in the name of justice. This developmental function was not the responsibility of socialism but was supposed to be the distinctive work of capitalism. The Marxian law here is rigorous: Socialism was bound to follow capitalism, but by the same token capitalism must precede socialism. Where capitalism has not entered the picture to play its "progressive" role, the productive capacity and the propertyless working class would not exist to provide the indispensable foundation for socialism. To be sure, Marx deviated from his own scheme when he conceded that Russia might be able to skip capitalism and develop directly into socialism on the basis of the country's traditional communal agriculture, if the simultaneous international success of socialism provided a favorable setting. His Russian followers—both Menshevik and Bolshevik—were more orthodox than the prophet and insisted on the preparatory function of capitalism.[1]

The great paradox of Marxism is that the proletarian socialist revolution envisioned by Marx never came to pass in the more advanced industrial countries where he expected it but instead proclaimed itself in Russia, where the economic transformation under capitalism was still at an early stage. In 1917—as all schools of Russian Marxism conceded—Russia was still dismally lacking in the industrial maturity and proletarian majority required for socialism. It was for this reason that the Mensheviks and even right-wing Bolsheviks opposed the attempt at a "socialist" revolution going beyond the "bourgeois democracy" of the Provisional Government. The Bolsheviks drew their rationale for the seizure of power from Trotsky's theory of permanent revolution—the contention that a working-class uprising in Russia would inspire general socialist revolution in the riper countries of the West. When the great world-revolutionary hopes of 1917–19 faded away in the early 1920s, the supposedly proletarian socialist regime of the Russian Communists was left hanging in midair, as it were, without much of the industrial and proletarian base that was presumably the prerequisite for it.

The history of the theoretical gyrations performed by the Soviet leaders to square their power and their practices with the Marxian perspective leads naturally to a fundamental question: Could Soviet Communism in any real sense be regarded as the proletarian socialism predicted by Marx? Or was it not a quite different phenomenon, entirely outside the Marxian framework, which only made claim to the Marxian label, in effect using Marxism as "ideology" or "false consciousness" in the service of a distinctly new movement?

The Russian Revolution and most Communist successes were products not of a great proletariat and industrial maturity but of the stresses of early industrialization and the alienation of the intelligentsia. This is particularly the case in countries outside Western Europe and North America, where the Communist movement was typically a response to the challenge of Westernization.

Its ambitions were those of anti-Western Westernizing nationalists, for whom the anticapitalist and anti-imperialist phraseology of Marxian socialism provided an irresistible theoretical vehicle. It makes no difference that the country concerned was not ripe for the Marxist revolution and might not yet have entered its bourgeois phase; the Marxist revolutionary appeal is psychological rather than logical. Marxism typically reached its greatest strength—in late-nineteenth-century Germany, in early-twentieth-century Russia, in Asia in the second quarter of the twentieth century—when a country was just beginning its most rapid transformation.[2] The Marxist revolution—or rather, the revolution of the Westernizing intelligentsia with a Marxist "ideology"—really rested on the possibility of the *diversion* of a society's development away from capitalism and into revolutionary socialism. This socialism was not the successor to capitalism but an alternative, which was likely to be ruled out if capitalism were allowed to develop too far. Such diversion was made more likely by various circumstances—by the lack of a liberal democratic development prior to the onset of industrialization; by overly rapid industrialization (such as foreign capital permits); and above all, by difficult anticolonial struggles or the military defeat of the traditional government, as in the cases of Russia and China.

Once such a revolutionary regime was in power, it had to contend with the problems of economic development that would have been handled by capitalism had it not been overthrown. Since the new regime was socialist in principle, it began to apply its socialist forms of economic organization and control to the task of economic development. An utterly new kind of socialist ideal then emerged—not the socialism of redistributive justice but what might best be termed "production socialism." Production socialism tried to do capitalism's job of accumulating capital and developing the productive forces of society. This fundamentally different economic content of socialism in the USSR underlay the sad history of the Communists' betrayal of democratic and egalitarian ideals and their creation of what can well be called bureaucratic state capitalism.

What happened in Soviet Russia became the model for the whole international Communist movement. Lenin fought with the left-wing Communists as early as 1918 over the restoration of hierarchical authority in industry and the army. In 1920 Trotsky proposed the militarization of labor and the trade unions in order to create a machine that could mobilize the effort required by Russia's dire economic straits. In the early 1920s Trotsky and Preobrazhensky borrowed the industrial planning model of German wartime socialism and for the first time anywhere laid down the principle of planned industrial development by the socialist state. The novelty of the idea is attested by the resistance it encountered on the part of Trotsky's political opponents, inspired by Bukharin, who insisted that development could only proceed in the capitalistic fashion of stimulus (even of state-owned industry) by market demand. Preobrazhensky frankly added the principle of "primary socialist accumulation"—deliberate exploitation of the people (especially the peasants) by the socialist state in order to squeeze out the surplus required for industrial capital formation.[3]

The theory of the new production socialism worked out by the Trotskyists awaited only its adoption by the dominant political force in the country. This was precisely what happened in 1928 when Stalin, having crushed the Trotsky Opposition, plagiarized its ideas and turned against the cautious Bukharinists. The intensive industrialization that followed under the Five-Year plans provided the foundation for the Communist economy, both dynamically and structurally, that lasted through the Brezhnev era. Soviet economic development was based on the use of the dictatorial state to accumulate capital—by taxes, obligatory farm deliveries, wage control, and monopoly state trading profits—and to channel this capital through the central planning system into the construction and equipment of heavy industry. Ownership and basic production decisions as represented in the plan were, of course, in the hands of the state, individual enterprise being tabooed altogether regardless of considerations of efficiency and incentive. Below the level of ownership and the plan, however, the requirements of industrial effectiveness led the Soviet regime at an early date to revert to almost all the familiar capitalist forms—or rather, to the bureaucratic forms that corporate capitalism and state-owned industry can display in common: the managerial hierarchy and individual responsibility in preference to the workers' control and committee administration that was the Communists' initial ideal; salary differentials, bonuses, and piece wages; strict industrial discipline; and a fully monetary, profit-and-loss accounting system. The Soviet enterprise differed little from the capitalistic corporation except that the profit motive was replaced by plan fulfillment, and there was no significant labor-management bargaining.

The Stalinist system was undeniably a form of socialism, in the broad sense of the term as social control over economic activity. The particular kind of social control that distinguished this system was the all-embracing bureaucratic hierarchy embodied in the totalitarian state. As its purpose, this socialism set for itself not distributive justice but the development of industrial production and national power. It can well be visualized as the capitalist corporation on the scale of the national state, where the whole country is a company town (with insurance and pension plans, to be sure), and the citizen-stockholders are manipulated by the managers in rigged meetings.[4] Add to this, of course, the oriental political habits of Russian despotism and the quasi-religious requirements of theoretical indoctrination that the system inherited from its Marxist background, and there are all the essentials of Stalinist society.

This description of Soviet socialism would not be complete without reference to a particular school of early socialist thought, remarkably paralleled by Soviet developments. This was the doctrine of the French Utopian Henri de Saint-Simon, whose writings in the first quarter of the nineteenth century sketched out a model of the new industrial society as organic, hierarchical, enlightened by science and technology, and infused with moral concern for the welfare of the workers.[5] Saint-Simon's socialism was frankly elitist, with careers open to the technically talented—a form of "meritocracy," if you will—and its emphasis on natural obedience and the propagandizing of virtue had strongly totalitarian implications. The irony is that the socialism of Marx's Russian followers conformed in practice much more closely to this precursor whom the Marxists meant to reject. Saint-Simon's insights about the coming forms of industrial society were so accurate that his ideas would have made a much more realistic "ideology" for the industrializing totalitarianism established by the Russians in the name of Marx.

Some neo-Trotskyist analysts tried to combine the Marxian conception of the class struggle with a sort of Saint-Simonian view about the bureaucratic industrial society. People like James Burnham and Milovan Djilas represented Soviet socialism as a new type of class society—the "managerial revolution" or the "new class"—succeeding the bourgeoisie.[6] This was a dubious effort as far as salvaging the Marxian class analysis is concerned, but it did appropriately emphasize the nonproletarian nature of the Stalinist system. It was a form of society that in function paralleled early capitalism and to this end borrowed and exaggerated the bureaucratic institutions of mature capitalism.

As such, Soviet socialism was an outstanding success in the task it set itself, of rapid industrialization and the achievement of a self-sufficient military potential. This is not to say that the same results could not have been accomplished in a capitalist-mercantilist manner, as in Japan and Imperial Germany. The Soviet system was not the only developmental alternative, even though it worked. What Soviet socialism could not offer was any substantial progress toward the freedom and the egalitarian justice of the nineteenth-century socialist ideal.

It might seem that when the industrial transformation of the USSR had largely been accomplished, a liberalization could follow with more scope for democratic procedures and egalitarian ideals. This was the fond hope of neo-Marxists who felt that industrialism meant democracy and that the economic success of Soviet totalitarianism was, so to speak, sowing the seeds of its own destruction. In point of fact, stable democracy is a product of the preindustrial commercial societies of Western Europe of the seventeenth and eighteenth centuries. Wherever industrialization has commenced without a prior liberal political base—that is, outside of the North Atlantic community—democracy has not been able to achieve a secure existence. Far from laying the groundwork for democracy, Soviet economic development entailed a profound bureaucratization of political and economic life.

Even when the original justification for "primary socialist accumulation" by dictatorial means had passed, the bureaucratic structure of the Communist Party and the Soviet state had an ongoing life of its own, and for decades after Stalin's death no force appeared that could effectively challenge it. Systems of organized power can—Marx to the contrary notwithstanding—perpetuate themselves for long periods of time after the conditions that brought them into being have disappeared. European feudalism endured almost a thousand years after it performed its function of restoring order out of Dark Age anarchy. Until its sudden collapse, the bureaucratic hierarchy of Stalinist socialism proved equally hard to undo.

CHAPTER 20

Stalin's Cultural Counterrevolution

The Russian enigma was largely a product of the preconceptions into which the outside world customarily forced the observed facts of Soviet life. Not the least serious among such a priori distortions was the assumption that the affairs of the Soviet government were guided by a fixed system of ideology. Both the fixity and the guidance are in fact highly questionable.

Nowhere was change as sharp in Soviet Russia as in the field of ideological pronouncements and intellectual work. Changes of this order in the various fields of mental activity have all been noted abroad, but usually such awareness has been confined to specialists' understanding of particular subjects.[1] There were, however, striking correspondences between developments in different cultural fields that form a pattern suggesting how and why these changes came about and what they reveal about the emergent nature of Soviet society.

Under Stalin, Soviet society became a stable though very tense structure, requiring the disciplined, authoritarian personalities who make the best cogs in a military-industrial machine. Since this new order continued to describe itself as the true executor of the Marxian scheme, a sweeping revision of ideology had to be imposed to justify this reality and to explain away older expectations about the revolution.[2]

From the time of Stalin's accession to power the Soviet system developed largely outside the compass of Marxian sociology. Rather than determining the basic form and development of society, economic forces depended on the state as the prime mover of history. The role of leading personalities—above all, the dictator himself—became decisive: Society was to develop henceforth through command from above. Ideology was duly revised to reflect this new reality. Old revolutionary leaders who had supported Stalin but perhaps lacked the cynical flexibility required by these maneuvers were liquidated. Nevertheless, the regime insisted that its new ideology was the only correct interpretation of Marxism and that all other versions represented counterrevolutionary treachery.

Up to 1929, intellectual life in Soviet Russia enjoyed a remarkable degree of freedom. Many prerevolutionary cultural figures continued their work. The party recognized limitations to its competence in areas outside of politics, although it encouraged Marxist thinkers. "I favor . . . a general leadership and the maximum of competition," declared Bukharin when he was still the party's main theoretical voice.[3] Much contact was maintained with the outside world. Soviet arts and sciences were generally abreast of the rest of the world; modernistic developments similar to those abroad, amid a variety of schools of thought, animated the Russian scene. Party doctrine, dominant though not rigorous in the social sciences, was characterized by thoroughgoing Marxian economic and environmental determinism and by mechanistic views of nature, history, and personality—ideas not greatly at variance with intellectual fashion abroad.

In social policy under the NEP, the party continued to affirm the ideals of the revolution, even if they were toned down in practice. Social reform was limited by an acute awareness of Russian cultural backwardness and by the consolidation of the state and industrial administration on more or less conventionally bureaucratic lines. Particularly in industry, practical considerations militated against revolutionary ideals; workers' control of factories was condemned by 1921, and income inequality grew. Notable efforts continued to be made to realize certain revolutionary ideals—progressive education, the equality of women, the antireligious campaign, and the party "maximum," a ceiling on monetary income for party members.

Stalin's dictatorship set the context for the coming transformation in Soviet cultural and intellectual life. All opposition in the party was crushed, and party doctrine was elevated to the level of an absolute, compulsory, and exclusive creed. *Partiinost'*—"partyness" or party spirit—and service to the party were imposed on intellectual activity as the supreme criteria of value and truth. A sweeping offensive was directed against nonparty people and nonconforming party members, especially people imbued with the traditional Marxian deterministic and mechanistic outlook, who were now identified with the Bukharin opposition. Their works were suppressed; they lost their jobs; and frequently they were arrested as counterrevolutionaries. This crackdown was directed by party strongmen in the various cultural fields who put power ahead of intellectual integrity and who, invested with the party's authority, proceeded to suppress all dissenting thought. Such were Mikhail Pokrovsky in history, A. B. Zalkind in psychology, and L. L. Averbakh in literature (and later on, T. D. Lysenko in biology). All this action was described as the pursuit of the class war "on the ideological front," "on the historical front," and so on. In the name of class war, Soviet cultural life was thoroughly militarized.

After the system of party control and supremacy in intellectual activity was established, and as crises developed in each field, the control system was used to compel drastic changes in the substance of ideas and policies. The imposition of extreme Marxism had devastated one field after another. In literature and the arts, little or no worthwhile work was produced; in history, students failed to learn the chronology of events; psychology failed to make the most out of the available human material; no one was taking law schools seriously. As the regime became aware that the "proletarian" thought and policies it was imposing were not the most expedient for its purposes, the extreme Marxism of the First Five-Year Plan period was successively repudiated in one field after another. The people who had espoused these views and imposed them in the name of the party were denounced as anti-Marxist wreckers and in many cases liquidated. Revolutionary intellectual fashions were then replaced by a surprisingly obvious traditionalism, which was declared to be the sole true application of Marxist principles. The controls put in place during the process of imposing extreme Marxism were turned around to operate in the opposite direction. Traditionalism, under the labels of "Socialist Realism," "Soviet humanism," or "dialectical materialism," as opposed to "vulgar economic materialism" or whatnot, was imposed with all the compulsions at the party's command. Moreover, where extreme Marxism had broken down in 1929–32, traditionalism in intellectual life, under strict controls, satisfied the practical needs of the regime.

This transformation took place with surprising consistency in a wide variety of fields. It occurred in literature and in the arts between 1932 and 1934, with the liquidation of RAPP (the Russian Association of Proletarian Writers) and the analogous organizations in other artistic areas, and the instituting of the norm of "Socialist Realism." In history, the shift was accomplished in 1934 with the restoration of the traditional kings-and-battles pedagogy and the rehabilitation of the Russian past, followed by the posthumous repudiation of Pokrovsky as an anti-Marxist in 1936. Law came next, with the downfall of Ye. B. Pashukanis and the repudiation of his theory of the withering-away of law in 1936–37. In psychology, there was a gradual reaction away from the doctrine of environmental conditioning and toward emphasis on individual will and responsibility, culminating in 1936. Political theory awaited Stalin's pronunciamentos, the clearest of which came in 1939—the state would be the chief instrument for the building of "communist society" as well as for protection against the capitalist encirclement, and it would not wither away as long as these needs existed.

Parallel developments took place in social policy. Finding inadequate for its needs the stimulus of proletarian enthusiasm supplemented by outright force, the regime turned progressively to the building blocks of the traditional social order—glorification of the state and of legality; encouragement of status distinctions; income differentiation as an incentive; traditional authoritarian family and educational policy—to cultivate the self-driving yet compliant qualities needed by the new bureaucratic industrial order. Patriotism was rehabilitated as a potent source of loyalty to the state; even a de facto accord with religion was reached as the Orthodox Church, in return for a measure of toleration, undertook to encourage political loyalty to the state.

The pattern of change in social and cultural policy was striking in its regularity. It had powerful implications about the real nature, interests, and motivations of the Stalinist state—the kind of state for which the intellectual and social policies adopted in the 1930s were most appropriate. But the transition left unclear what the party (above all, Stalin) really wanted—to eradicate the revolutionary tradition and replace it with a conservatism that would make the state and the economy easier to run. But this goal could not be stated explicitly, because the stability of the regime and its support abroad depended on continuity with the revolutionary tradition. So the party was compelled to continue professing its adherence to Marxism, while the objectionable features of Marxist thought were discarded and pronounced un-Marxist. This reversal of content under the old labels was highly confusing to Soviet intellectuals, steeped for years in all aspects of Marxism. They did not realize what was wanted; they could not be told this directly; and they were unlikely to come to an understanding of it on their own because the regime was to them axiomatically the pure embodiment of Marxism. Consequently, official condemnations of their work came as bolts from the blue, completely incomprehensible. Intellectuals could only try to learn by trial and error what work would be condemned and what would be approved.

In literary life, as in other cultural fields, there was wide latitude for creative work in the 1920s. Although direct party control of literature was advocated by some extremist literary groups, the party did not accord its official sanction to any one school. Lenin, Trotsky, and Bukharin all endorsed the position of the moderate Marxist critic Aleksandr Voronsky: "No literary current, school, or group must come forward in the name of the Party."[4] In 1929, however, the party gave a free hand to Averbakh's group of extreme Marxists, who proceeded to impose on all writers rigid utilitarian standards of propagandistic "proletarian" writing. Those who resisted in the name of artistic freedom, as well as the Marxist group led by V. F. Pereverzev that contended that only proletarians could write proletarian literature, were condemned. The attack on the Pereverzev people for "vulgar economic determinism"[5] illustrates the new voluntarist philosophy with its emphasis on subjective factors such as the enthusiasm of individuals. Political dedication could prevail over "objective conditions," including class status.

The spirit of the campaign for partiinost' and against any nonconformity or notion of art for art's sake was belligerently expressed by the playwright V. M. Kirshon at the Sixteenth Party Congress in 1930: "We must pass over to a decisive offensive, mercilessly liquidating bourgeois ideology." He went on, "Any liberalism, any respect for aesthetic language [that] may be directed against us, is direct aid to the class enemy. . . . The whole purpose of our activity and our work lies in the fight for the building of socialism."[6] Even the celebrated proletarian poet Vladimir Mayakovsky was attacked, a shock that apparently contributed to his suicide that year.[7]

Intense politicizing of literature under RAPP led to an early crisis. This was the beginning of the second phase of cultural revolution, to compel the restoration of traditional content disguised as Marxism. Realizing that under RAPP, literature was no good, the party leadership abolished the organization in 1932, and made its leaders scapegoats for the disastrous policy they had carried out in the party's name. Both Averbakh and Kirshon, among others, fell victim to the Great Purge. Thus were the extreme "proletarian" policies of 1929–32 repudiated as anti-Marxist, while the infallibility of the party was preserved.

The new official line for literature, Socialist Realism, was soon extended to the other arts. At first it had little definite meaning; only as various artists were criticized for failing to conform did the traditionalist desires of the regime become clear. One observer recognized this "paradoxical development" in spite of his political sympathy: "It is a fact that new revolutionary political ideas are faced with reactionary stylistic principles in art. The same government that is courageously piloting the ship of state through the uncharted seas of socialistic practice is enjoining its artists to stay behind in safe haven."[8]

Patterns of change in other fields of artistic work were much the same as in literature. All the arts went through the period of proletarian propaganda beginning in 1929. All then experienced a more or less abrupt change from revolutionary content to the traditionalism of Socialist Realism—the theater and film in 1932, music in 1932–33, architecture around 1935. Even the ballet toed the party line with precision.[9]

Socialist Realism was characterized by impassioned nationalism (corresponding to the revival of nationalist propaganda and historiography), by reverence for the classics (corresponding to the rehabilitation of the Russian past), by an emotional rather than analytic approach, and by catering to the public taste. "Socialist Realism," the literary historian Gleb Struve pointed out, was "a reaction against what was described, sweepingly and therefore meaninglessly, as 'bourgeois formalism.' This phrase was used to include all experiments with form and technique. . . . Those who were responsible for running the most 'advanced' state in the world," Struve concluded, "suddenly turned conservative and began to look askance at all revolutionary experiments in art."[10]

Such positive philosophy as Socialist Realism contained was initially expressed by Maxim Gorky: an optimistic individualism idealizing the "New Soviet Man."[11] A later formulation called for "monumental works wherein the man of our age, the man of the Stalin type, the creator of the Plans, will be revealed in his full stature; works in which will be shown how was forged the willpower of that man, how his soul was formed and how his consciousness was strengthened, enriched, and armed by the teaching of Marx, Engels, Lenin, and Stalin."[12] The parallelism of the new conception of personality in literature, psychology, and history was perfect.

Under the conditions of a totalitarian state, this new individualism was largely of and for the leaders, who patently did "make history." For the masses, it seems, Socialist Realism in the arts was designed to reconcile people to the regime, to satisfy vicariously their aspirations for power and control over their own fates, and to stimulate eager participation in the projects undertaken by the regime. For the arts, no new development was possible, but since the style to which they were now constrained was an artistically meaningful one with much vitality in its history, artistic production did manage to go on.

In the writing and teaching of history, party spirit and Marxist orthodoxy were imposed suddenly and violently. Pokrovsky, a professional historian but also a long-standing party member, head of the Communist Academy and the Institute of Red Professors and a member of the Central Control Commission of the party, set up a virtual dictatorship in the field of history, terminating the fairly broad tolerance that had been accorded to the activities of nonparty historians during the NEP. Between 1929 and 1931, non-Marxist historical science was eradicated, and all important positions were filled with newly trained party men.[13]

The kind of historical thought that Pokrovsky imposed in the name of the party was distinguished by absolute economic determinism, an acerbic antinationalist approach to the Russian past, and a highly abstract treatment of history in a rigid framework of class struggle and socioeconomic formations, where the individual was merely the agent of impersonal forces. According to the doctrine of partiinost', history was simply a weapon in the class struggle. There was no such thing as objectivity, all science being merely class science, so the scientist could not fail to take sides. Stalin himself set the tone, denouncing as "rotten liberalism" any failure to accept party principles as "axioms."[14]

Shortly after the change of course in literature and the arts, it became evident to the regime that the line in history left by Povrovsky at his death in 1932 required corrective action. In 1934 the Central Committee and the Council of People's Commissars decreed, "The teaching of history . . . is unsatisfactory. . . . Instead of the teaching of civic history in an animated and entertaining form with an exposition of the most important events and facts in their chronological sequence and with sketches of historical personages, the pupils are given abstract definitions of social and economic formations, which thus replace the consecutive exposition of history by abstract sociological schemes."[15] Another sweeping decision, in January 1936, attributed all these difficulties to the insidious influence of the Pokrovsky school of historians.[16] Like RAPP in literature, Pokrovsky's ghost was made a scapegoat for the nonsensical extremes and pedagogical failures of the party's recent policy in history. Describing his alleged deviation as "vulgar economic materialism," the leadership condemned Pokrovsky's extreme relativism: "Every theory in a class society has a class bias, and serves as a weapon for one class or another. But from this it does not follow that every theory is false, subjective. Today only Marxism defends absolute truth, i.e., fundamental science."[17]

Because they insisted on the old Marxist terminology, party officials had great difficulty in sifting the influence of the Pokrovsky school out of the work of Soviet historians. The textbook competition of 1936–37 yielded such unsatisfactory results that no first prize was awarded; only a "second prize" went to the work by A. V. Shestakov, which nevertheless stands as a milestone in the transition back to the traditional style of narrative, nationalistic political history.[18] Most striking was the new emphasis on the role of the great men who by their exceptional understanding of the laws of history supposedly provided the proletariat with the farsighted leadership essential for its victory—that is, Marx, Engels, Lenin, and Stalin. As early as 1934, Stalin disposed of the old

Marxian model by emphasizing the critical importance of the party and the Soviet state. "It is their work that now determines everything, or nearly everything," not "so-called objective conditions."[19]

Nowhere was the doctrinaire determinism of traditional Marxism carried to such extreme defiance of reality as in the field of legal theory. According to Pashukanis, who dominated Soviet jurisprudence until his fall in 1937, law was exclusively a phenomenon of the bourgeois social order. Like state power, it was to be used by the proletariat as a temporary measure in the struggle against vestiges of the old society, and then it would wither away. The most remarkable thing about this theory was that it was seriously applied: Civil law was neglected, and law schools indeed threatened to wither away from lack of interest.[20] The concepts of guilt and punishment were rejected as implying an un-Marxian notion of individual responsibility.[21]

In keeping with the philosophical shift from determinism to voluntarism in the First Five-Year Plan period, the dynamic conception of *plan* was formulated to contrast with law, and Pashukanis had to adapt by emphasizing the role of the state and the plan in building socialism.[22] Then, in 1936, with the introduction of the new constitution, the entire revolutionary conception of law was suddenly repudiated. Stalin demanded "stability of laws" and denounced the notion of the withering-away of law as wrecking. Pashukanis, vainly recanting, was disgraced early in 1937 and had to yield his place at the head of the Soviet legal profession to his erstwhile assistant Andrei Vyshinsky. Instead of the subordination of law to political expediency, "revolutionary legality" was redefined as strict observance of the law. Conventional law codes and prerevolutionary law professors were restored to their places.[23] "Crime," "punishment," and the concept of individual guilt were restored as legal principles. The standards for determining the responsibility of psychopaths and minors were drastically tightened.[24]

As long as the Soviet leadership was still interested in revolutionary change, it viewed law as an obstacle to the supreme authority of the party and its policies. When stability became the prime concern, law in its most traditional forms (under the "socialist" label, to be sure) was restored to buttress the authority of the state and help enforce a sense of individual responsibility. In this respect, there was a close correspondence of law with the new line in political theory, psychology, family policy, and education.

Changes in political theory closely paralleled the shift in law. From the original view of the proletarian state as a necessary evil destined to wither away after the revolutionary transformation, party doctrine shifted 180 degrees, to extol the state as the highest form of social organization and a great creative force.[25] Already, as early as 1924, Stalin had extended Lenin's doctrine of the leading role of the party, applying it not only to the preparation and execution of the revolution but to the organization of the postrevolutionary socialist order. For Stalin, even at this early date, it was not underlying economic development that should be relied upon for "preparing the conditions for the inauguration of socialist production" but rather the indoctrination of the masses by the party.[26]

During the First Five-Year Plan period Stalin made the positive functions of the Soviet state more explicit. Perhaps the irony of his "dialectical" twist escaped him when he told the Sixteenth Party Congress in June 1930, "We are in favor of the state dying out, and at the same time we stand for the strengthening of the dictatorship of the proletariat, which represents the most powerful and mighty authority of all forms of state which have existed up to the present day."[27] Similarly, in 1934 he called for "intensifying the class struggle" in order to "build" the classless society.[28] Thus did Stalin arrive at a fundamental revision of the Marxian theory of the state and the role of political factors in history, asserting their transcendence over "objective conditions." It is not mere coincidence that conventional history was rehabilitated at the expense of Pokrovsky's sociologizing in the same year.

With the promulgation of the Stalin Constitution in 1936, class exploitation was officially declared to be at an end,[29] but this did not mean diminishing the rigors of the dictatorship of the proletariat—in disregard of the most elementary Marxian notions about the responsibility of class antagonisms for social conflict. Beginning with the purges, political opposition was described and explained more in moralistic than in social terms—"dregs of humanity," "White Guard insects," "traitorous hirelings of foreign intelligence services," "Trotsky-Bukharin fiends"—rotten apples, in short, corrupted by something approaching original sin.[30]

In 1939 Stalin further addressed the need to bring official theory into accord with the obvious permanence of the Soviet state machinery, especially given its responsibility for national defense. Marx and Engels to the contrary, the state would not even wither away under the stage of "communism" if the "capitalist encirclement" continued. "Engels' general formula about the destiny of the socialist state in general cannot be extended to the particular and specific case of the victory of socialism in one separate country," Stalin explained.[31]

Sometimes Stalin actually found it opportune to criticize the masters directly, particularly where his theory of Socialism in One Country was involved. Back in 1926, in reply to attacks on this notion by the Left Opposition, he maintained, "Engels . . . would welcome our revolution, and say: To hell with all old formulas! Long live the victorious revolution in the Soviet Union."[32] In truth, it was not the capitalist encirclement that would necessitate retention of the state even under the phase of "communism" but the reverse: Ideologically speaking, the continued existence of the state required a continuing fear of the capitalist encirclement.

In Soviet educational thought, as in other fields, there was a great deal of diversity before 1931. Resources were short to meet the vast educational needs of the country; universal compulsory primary education was not achieved until around 1937.[33] Lenin nevertheless recognized education as an important weapon of the proletarian dictatorship in extending the influence of the working class and in preparing the population, particularly the backward peasantry, for socialism.[34] This political requirement distinguished Soviet education ever after, whatever the changes in the direction of the political line.

Though he embraced the goal of "self-motivation [*samodeyatel'nost'*] of children in the school," Lenin was relatively conservative in comparison with many Soviet educational specialists.[35] Anatol Lunacharsky, commissar of education until 1929, was a promoter of the progressive education methods then becoming popular in the West. The head of the Marx-Engels Institute for Pedagogy, V. N. Shulgin, was the chief exponent of the theory of "unorganized" or "spontaneous" education, according to which organized education was only a temporary measure to be supplanted by the "socialist environment" as the school withered away along with the state.[36] Though many Soviet educational leaders, including Krupskaya, found this doctrine too anarchistic, Soviet education during the NEP was generally guided by belief in the innate goodness of humanity and the spontaneous development of personality. "Learning by doing" was the ideal method; formal instruction and discipline were to be held to a minimum.[37]

Under the impact of the First Five-Year Plan and rejection of the mechanistic interpretation of Marxism, drastic change was bound to occur in educational doctrine. An alternative approach had already been formulated, positing the state as a "purposive organization" that deliberately utilized organized education to manipulate unorganized educational influences on the child.[38] Concerned with fitting education to the immediate needs of economic development, the party leadership issued a series of decrees in the fall of 1931 attacking "left opportunists" for the doctrine of the withering-away of the school; abolishing Shulgin's pedagogical institute; criticizing progressive methods; reestablishing the separate teaching of traditional subjects, at the

expense of craft and technical training; and restoring old-fashioned discipline and grading.[39] Progressive educational theory was rejected on the same
grounds as the mechanistic philosophy, for running counter to the regime's
demand for a purposeful effort to transform the nation.

The new attitude of the regime in education was closely related to the
changes officially encouraged in Soviet psychology, where again in 1930–31
the mechanistic and deterministic orientation was being replaced with a more
purposive and voluntaristic, less biological approach.[40] Together with emphasis on consciousness and will went the restoration of authority in educational
practice. As Stalin demanded, the state now relied on command from above to
accomplish its purposes in spite of inadequate material conditions. Practical
results in the inculcation of knowledge, as well as in the molding of personalities to make them more amenable to social discipline, became the norm for the
educational process.

The trend back to formal, disciplined education continued during 1932–34,
expanding to higher education, while the ideas of the "leftist deviation" continued to be attacked.[41] A decree of July 1936 abolished the science of "pedology"
(developmental child psychology) because it stressed "fatalistic conditioning"
by hereditary and environmental factors and neglected the allegedly vast potentialities of education in directly molding personalities.[42] The final measure, in
1937, was the abolition of polytechnical training in the schools and the return
of the entire formal educational effort to traditional subjects.[43] Overall, changes
in educational policy reflected the acceptance of sharpening social differentiation between the intelligentsia and the masses and marked the abandonment in
practice of an ideal still verbally adhered to, the elimination of the distinction
between mental and manual labor.

During the revolution, the Bolsheviks targeted the institution of the family, as
they did education, as part of the authoritarian legacy of the past. Among its
early acts, the Soviet government secularized marriage, affirmed the complete
equality of women, curtailed parental authority, legalized abortion, and made
divorces available automatically at the request of one party. There was much
explicit advocacy of free love (exemplified by Alexandra Kollontai), although
Lenin was critical of it. Ultimately, the family was expected to wither away,
except as an entirely informal association. In conformance with this theory, the
legal code of 1927 made de facto nonregistered marriages legally equal to reg-
istered ones.

The attack on traditional family ties was intensified during the First Five-
Year Plan. Compulsory labor assignments sometimes split families, with no

redress. Revolutionary repudiation of the bourgeois amenities sometimes gave rise to a sort of Communist asceticism, making virtues out of unkemptness and abstention from social pleasures.[44]

A change in official social values occurred very suddenly in 1935–36, as the regime moved from one extreme to the other.[45] One precipitating reason, no doubt, was the social pathology generated by intensive industrialization and collectivization, including a declining birthrate, a high divorce rate, and serious juvenile delinquency. But the regime used these problems, paralleling the damage done by extreme revolutionary notions in fields such as literature, history, and law, as the excuse to repudiate as a matter of principle the earlier libertarian family policy. Instead, the family was extolled as a pillar of socialist society: "So-called 'free love' and all disorderly sex life are bourgeois through and through."[46] The Victorian attitude toward female chastity was affirmed. A decisive step was the law of 27 June 1936, which prohibited nontherapeutic abortions, made divorce possible only through legal procedure and with the payment of a fee, and established special allowances for large families.

These switches were accompanied by a burst of official commentary justifying the new policies and denouncing earlier ideas about the informality of family relationships: "Assertions that socialism brings the withering-away of the family . . . play into the hands of bearers of the survivals of capitalism in people's consciousness, who are trying to conceal their exploitative behavior with empty-sounding 'leftist phrases.' The family under socialism does not wither away but is strengthened."[47] Some statements conveyed a hypertraditional conception of the family: "The state cannot exist without the family. Marriage is a positive value for the socialist Soviet state only if the partners see in it a lifelong union. So-called free love is a bourgeois invention and has nothing in common with the principles of conduct of a Soviet citizen. Moreover, marriage receives its full value for the state only if there is progeny, and the consorts experience the highest happiness of parenthood."[48] Also reversed was the attitude toward parental authority: "Young people should respect their elders, especially their parents."[49] From exile Trotsky reacted sharply: "Instead of openly saying, 'We have proven still too poor and ignorant for the creation of socialist relations among men, our children and grandchildren will realize this aim,' the leaders are forcing people to glue together again the shell of the broken family, and not only that, but to consider it, under threat of extreme penalties, the sacred nucleus of triumphant socialism. It is hard to measure with the eye the scope of this retreat."[50]

Changes in family policy were paralleled in approved standards for social conduct. All of the ordinary bourgeois amusements returned, even dancing and fashionable dress, to the evident gratification of the population.[51] These developments reflected the increasing social stratification facilitated by the repudiation of egalitarianism and the emergent material desires among the newly privileged bureaucratic strata.

In family policy, in the judgment of Nicholas Timasheff, the Soviet regime merely sacrificed an unpopular element of the revolution, "one of the most unpleasant, almost intolerable aspects of the Communist Experiment. . . . The government . . . conceded nothing and gained very much."[52] For Trotsky, this was thermidorean betrayal of revolutionary humanism. Rudolph Schlesinger saw the change as the natural result of postrevolutionary stabilization, and Alex Inkeles believed that "the development of Soviet policy on the family constitutes a striking affirmation of the importance of that institution as a central element in the effective functioning of the type of social system which is broadly characteristic of Western civilization."[53]

Regarding religion, Soviet policy changed neither as soon nor as much as in other areas. The persecution that commenced with the revolution was exacerbated during collectivization and the First Five-Year Plan by the Society of Militant Atheists and its antireligious propaganda. By 1936, however, there was a distinct relaxation, marked by certain symbolic concessions such as curtailment of antireligious demonstrations and the restoration of Sunday as the day of rest. Civil disabilities were lifted from the clergy by the Stalin Constitution.[54] A measure of the resiliency of religion was the official estimate of 1937 indicating that half the population were still believers.[55] Like traditionalist social policy, the regime came (notably during World War II) to see the potential of the Orthodox Church as an instrument for strengthening popular loyalty and discipline.

Like hostility to religion, the ideal of egalitarianism was firmly rooted in the Russian revolutionary tradition. It was not long after the Bolsheviks came to power, however, that they found they had to resort to preferential pay for experts and to the conventional bureaucratic system of individual authority. Nevertheless, by 1920 a nearly complete egalitarianism was reached, more by necessity than design, as inflation and shortages reduced the urban population to a common level of rationed consumption. The range in real factory wages from lowest to highest was negligible. Wage and salary differentiation returned during the NEP, reaching capitalistic proportions by 1928, though the personal income of party members remained limited by the "party maximum."[56] The ideal of equality was still an effective restraint on further income differentiation.

At the onset of intensive industrialization, the regime tried to rely on propaganda and revolutionary fervor for the "building of socialism," but monetary incentives soon had to be extended to replace flagging enthusiasm. In 1931 Stalin openly rejected "the 'Leftist' practice of wage equalization" and stressed monetary incentives to cultivate skills and improve productivity. He warned a meeting of industrial administrators, "Whoever draws up wage scales on the 'principle' of wage equalization, without taking into account the difference between skilled labor and unskilled labor, breaks with Marxism, breaks with Leninism."[57] In this spirit, the party maximum was relaxed in 1929 and subsequently allowed quietly to lapse.[58]

By 1934, Stalin made a virtue of necessity and disposed of the embarrassment of Marxian egalitarianism by redefinition. "Every Leninist knows," he said, "that is, if he is a real Leninist, that equality in the sphere of requirements and individual life is a piece of reactionary petty-bourgeois absurdity worthy of a primitive sect of ascetics, but not of a socialist society organized on Marxian lines." He made the slogan "To each according to his needs" require inequality because people's needs were different; no doubt those of the ordinary worker and the high official diverged considerably. With his slogan "Cadres decide everything," Stalin directed the emphasis of the government to well-trained and well-rewarded administrators.[59] Wage differentials and incentives were extended and enshrouded with a mystical halo by the Stakhanovite movement, begun in 1935. De-rationing and official sanction for the material amenities of life, commencing in 1934–35, lent added effect to income differentiation as an incentive for maximum effort and efficiency. Status differences and bureaucratic authority intensified; individual management with broad powers along with heavy responsibility became the rule in industry. Overt trappings of authority, often reminiscent of prerevolutionary Russia, began to return.

Developments in the army stood out. In 1935 conventional rank designations for officers (except generals) were restored, and the new title of marshal was created; generals came back later, in 1939. Discipline and subordination to higher authority were increasingly stressed as ends in themselves.[60] Pursuant to the revival of patriotism and national tradition after 1934, tsarist military figures became heroic models, and medals were even named after them. By the end of World War II, epaulets, the subordination of political officers to military commanders (after several false starts), the institution of guards units, and finally changing the name Red Army to Soviet Army completed the refurbishing of the military on traditionalist lines.

The trend toward income and status differentiation in the 1930s was accompanied by the end of social and political discrimination against the intelligentsia as such and a growing cleavage between the class of administrative and technical specialists on the one hand and the masses of workers and peasants on the other. Reconciliation with members of the old intelligentsia was, like so many other policy changes in this period, signaled by Stalin (in 1931) as the fervent class struggle of the First Five-Year Plan period gave way to more pragmatic considerations.[61] From that time on, ability and skills (together with political loyalty) displaced class considerations as the basis for the selection of responsible personnel. Educational preference on class grounds was ended in 1934.[62]

In 1936, as the new constitution was about to be promulgated, the attainment of "socialism," defined now as the elimination of class antagonisms, was officially proclaimed. Soviet society was thenceforth conceived of as comprising three "strata" or "non-antagonistic classes," the workers, the peasantry, and the "Soviet intelligentsia."[63] At the same time, the new constitution eliminated all political disabilities based on former membership in the old ruling classes. Thus, by 1936, the theoretical route was paved for the recovery of social leadership by the class of educated specialists, including both those remaining from the Old Regime and those trained under Soviet rule. "Bolsheviks without party cards," Stalin termed them.[64] Political recognition came shortly afterward: Negativism toward members of the intelligentsia was eliminated in the Komsomol in 1936 and in the party itself in 1939, with the end of the traditional membership preference for proletarians.[65] At the Eighteenth Party Conference in February 1941, Georgi Malenkov pointedly rejected considering social background at the expense of technical and personal qualifications in the appointment of party and state officials.[66]

While the educated class was coming into its own in political status and economic position, the lines between the intelligentsia and the masses became sharper and stiffer. By 1941 academic education had become the prime consideration for social advancement; for example, the technical school rather than experience as a skilled worker became the main avenue to work in industrial management.[67] The "unity of mental and physical labor" had long been a point in the Communist program, fitfully reflected in efforts to combine regular education with training in manual skills, but the ideal was virtually abandoned in practice. Industrial training was completely separated from academic education in 1937.[68]

Acceptance of social inequality, like other policy changes under Stalin, reflected the practical needs of industrialism that had never been sufficiently considered in socialist thought and, at least in Russia, made the old ideal inoperable. Thus, the Communist system became something very different, never spelled out verbally but only implied in practice, including a rigorously organized system of social inequality. The privileged stratum of qualified and reliable executives approached the status of a ruling class, to which the regime had to adapt in order to keep the group functioning satisfactorily.

After all its changes of the 1930s, in ideology as in policy, why did the regime persist in claiming to represent the revolution? Why did it continue to enforce a body of doctrine requiring comprehensive control of thought and expression, with the consequences of intellectual stagnation and widespread disaffection? There are several facets to the explanation.

1. The retention of orthodox Marxist belief among the top leadership is a question impossible to decide. It is unimportant from the standpoint of analyzing Soviet policy, for invariably practical considerations prevailed and ideology was reinterpreted as much as was necessary to justify any policy. Perhaps the Soviet leaders really believed that they were leading humanity on the road to the great goal of communism, though ultimate faith was not allowed to interfere with the regime's short-term interests in power and stability. Even if faith had failed, it would be inconceivable for the leadership to admit that for a long time it had been either wrong or cynical.

2. Some political support accrued to the regime on the basis of the revolutionary ideology. Ideology gave it a sense of moral justification for the stern exercise of power, supporting the conviction that what the government was doing must be correct. At times, much backing was derived from ideologically motivated enthusiasm.[69] By contradicting unpleasant realities, ideology disoriented potential opponents of the regime.[70] Finally, ideology seems to have played a part in the driving motivation of the fanatic personality that figured importantly in the party control apparatus.[71]

3. Ideology was useful in controlling the educational impact of cultural activity. The Stalinist system required a rigid and authoritative form for stating the purposes of the state, to guide the molding of citizens' minds. The official ideology, as amended and reinterpreted, served as such a guide and standard.

4. The foreign support enjoyed by the Stalinist state came largely from people who identified the Soviet regime with their own revolutionary aspirations. Soviet reality therefore had to be concealed above all from Soviet sympathizers, by keeping contact between the Soviet Union and the outside world to a minimum. Changes in ideology or policy, if introduced too suddenly, could cause embarrassment abroad, since foreign Communist parties not in power were not insulated from divergent points of view. This vulnerability contributed to the high rates of defection and turnover among the membership of some foreign Communist parties.

5. Stalinism needed an external enemy to justify the privation and controls that it imposed in the interest of building national power. It stimulated patriotic feeling in support of the regime and explained internal deviants as agents of foreign powers. International hostility helped minimize foreign contacts, which in turn was necessary to curb disaffection and to prevent the free circulation of untoward ideas.

Finally, conflict fit well the military state of mind in Stalinist politics. The Stalinist regime—and it was far from alone in this—could not conceive of politics except as a struggle against an enemy. Marxist-Leninist ideology served to define the enemy and enhance enmity on both sides. Without ideology, there would have been little material basis for East-West conflict. Thus the paradox of an ideology far removed from Soviet reality being asserted with great effort to create the artificial sense of conflict and foreign danger that the Stalinist regime required for its internal stability.

Developments in official Soviet thought during the 1930s demonstrate that the regime had changed in its *essence* since the revolution. The pattern of transformation within the core of party ideology, the official purpose-system, cannot convincingly be written off as a series of mere tactical ruses or strategic zigzags. The Stalinist regime could express no higher articulation of social purpose than its Marxist-Leninist ideology, but that ideology had been reduced to rationalization after the fact. There was no fixed star for the Stalinists to steer by; they had no ultimate principles that were not subject to reshaping over the years. Regardless of its labels, the Stalinist regime no longer represented the same movement that took power in 1917. This fact should be a guide for anyone who undertakes to establish just what kind of regime it actually was.

CHAPTER 21

Stalinism and Russian Political Culture

I
n the 1970s "political culture" emerged as one of the most widely invoked concepts in the interpretation of Soviet affairs. Acknowledging how depths of the past pull on the surface of the present, the notion makes a salutary contribution to balanced understanding of the character of the Soviet system and its behavior.

But generalities about Russian tradition and national character are not enough to demonstrate how the cultural legacy of the remote past may continue to affect the politics of the present. One of the best efforts yet to identify concretely the substance of Russian political culture, as well as to explain how it influenced the postrevolutionary Soviet Union, is the work of Edward Keenan.[1] Keenan has brought to light some extraordinary parallels between old, pre-Petrine Russian patterns of political behavior and the Soviet modus operandi. Indeed, the correspondence is so close that one finds it hard to believe that Keenan did not have the Soviet regime in mind when he constructed his image of Muscovite politics. In any case, the resemblance between the two epochs implies a powerful carryover of ancient ways into the postrevolutionary mentality.

To a student of culture in its proper anthropological sense, the sort of continuity that Keenan depicts in Russian politics is not in the least surprising. Culture, to cite the definition offered by Edward Tyler over a century ago and never improved upon, is "that complex whole which includes knowledge, belief, art, morals, law, custom, and any other capabilities and habits acquired by man as a member of society."[2] Passed from one generation to another by learning or osmosis, the cultural heritage is not easily altered except in the most superficial respects.

The notion of political culture first achieved currency in the 1960s through the work of such political scientists as Gabriel Almond and Lucian W. Pye, primarily with reference to the problems of political modernization in the Third World.[3] Its application to Russia and to Soviet studies in the 1970s was undertaken mainly by British political scientists, including Archie Brown and Stephen White.[4] For the most part, these studies embraced a narrow or "subjectivist" sense of political culture, confining it to expressed political sentiments, as against the broad or behavioral understanding of culture preferred by anthropologists.[5] The latter have distinguished "overt" and "covert" or "explicit" and "implicit" culture, thereby taking cognizance of those aspects of culture that lie buried in the implications of people's actions and folkways, as well as what they say about them.[6] One might invoke here Vilfredo Pareto's contrast of "residues" and "derivations"—on the one hand, the underlying modes of behavior embodying implicit culture and on the other, the more variable forms of their overt expression at the self-conscious, verbal level.[7]

Russia represents an extreme case in the governance of society by unacknowledged political folkways. Writes Keenan, "The abiding deep structures of that culture have not found systematic expression either in legislative or in descriptive codifications."[8] Consequently, the narrow approach to political culture simply will not do, even if this means that political culture and its influence are rendered even less tractable than they might be as objects of scientific testing.

While political scientists have inappropriately restricted the meaning of political culture in one direction, they have embraced a questionable extension of it in another, to include formal ideologies or "official political culture."[9] Official doctrine may or may not represent a significant policy guide for a revolutionary government, but the culture concept is abused if it is stretched to cover formal ideology. There was, of course, a culture (or subculture) of the Communist leadership and bureaucracy, just as there was a court culture in the old days, but the important thing in getting at the reality of this level of culture is to distinguish it from formal ideology, not to identify the two. For example, the "dictatorship of the proletariat" is ideology, not culture; but the authoritarianism and reliance on coercion that it meshes with are indeed aspects of culture. Similarly with "socialism," as distinguished from its Russian cultural underlay of antipathy to individual enterprise and reliance on state responsibility.

A common error in the Soviet instance is to assume that ideology represented a set, unchanging cultural force. Early applications of the notion of political culture to the Soviet scene cast it as an effort by the Communist regime to inculcate the presumably new and fixed official culture into the populace in place of its old culture.[10] The reality was more nearly the opposite. The key to understanding the role of Russian political culture under Stalinism and after is to recognize that the operative meaning of ideology was in many respects changed radically by pragmatic responses to events and by high-level reinterpretation (for example, regarding Russian nationalism or socioeconomic stratification). The reinterpreted ideology itself came to reflect the old political culture in a new guise. Mary McAuley tellingly quoted the dissident literary scholar Lev Kopelev to this effect: "The actual ideology of the Stalinists, which still lives today, . . . is an ideology of authoritarian bureaucratic party discipline, of superstate chauvinism, of unprincipled pragmatism. . . . In its true essence the Stalinist ideology is significantly further both from the old Bolshevism and even more from all varieties of Marxism, old and new, than from certain contemporary conservative nationalist and religious ideologies."[11]

The broader conception of culture, including its implicit behavioral manifestations, is not without pitfalls in its application. One of them is to treat culture as a given, outside of time, exempt from historical change; the other is to view a particular national culture as a unique entity without comparative associations. For Keenan, Russian political culture appears quite abruptly in the second half of the fifteenth century and then works its unique way without fundamental change (apart from the "aberration" of 1890–1930) right down to Brezhnev. It is hard to accept the implication that changing circumstances before and after the time of Ivan III had so much less influence. Nor was Russian political culture as unique as Keenan suggests. Much of what he finds, if one stops to think about it, is only the Russian variant of traditional society in general, such as the political centrality of family relationships, hereditary class status, and the need to believe in a personal embodiment of authority.

To correct these limitations, one needs a more historically oriented conception of political culture as well as of culture in general. Political culture is both continuous and changeable, steadily absorbing new infusions from a society's historical experiences and contacts, while older elements are eroded, metamorphosed, or washed away like a series of geological deposits. Describing a given country's particular political culture is therefore a very complicated proposition. For one thing, it is not always the oldest and deepest elements of a culture that are most likely to disappear in the face of new experiences. As Keenan notes, it was the newer, Western-derived elements in

Russian political culture that were most seriously weakened by the upheaval of the revolution.[12]

In a wide range of political features, the Soviet regime fit like a glove over the old anatomy of Russian government. In its centralism, in its passion for top-down control, in the distribution of political power at the top and in the style of its use, and in the role of ideological legitimation of the whole, the congruence of the new Moscow with the old one leaps out at the perceptive observer. Many are the visitors, diplomats, and journalists who have commented on the eerie similarity of Soviet practices—secrecy and isolation of foreigners, for example—with old tsarist custom.[13] Stephen White, an exception to the political science mainstream in his sense for the past, says quite bluntly, "Soviet political culture is rooted in the historical experience of centuries of autocracy."[14] Where Keenan stands out is in taking the past rather than the present as his point of departure. Instead of projecting a political schema back from the Soviet scene to find past roots or analogues, he goes directly to the past and lets the evident continuities from then on speak for themselves. He avoids some of the distortion inherent in present-mindedness, while his own sixteenth-century-mindedness turns out to be highly persuasive.

Muscovy always stood out among early modern states in its degree of centralism and the lack of legal or customary restraints on the despotic power of the tsar. Keenan notes the Russian fear of self-destruction if power were left in local hands and the importance of the "idea" of someone at the center who is absolutely in charge.[15] The leap to neo-Stalinism and the yearning for a *krepkii khoziain*—a tough boss—is not great. "Russia needs a strong autocrat," wrote the emigré Yuri Glazov. "De facto Stalin did not differ from any strong monarch of pre-Petrine Russia."[16] Keenan is undoubtedly correct in seeing in the fusion of the court and peasant subcultures the paranoiac basis for Russians' continuing need to control and to be controlled, so as to forestall the horror of "chaos."[17] One recalls here the revealing pleas to avoid "panic" broadcast at the time of Stalin's death and again when Brezhnev departed the scene.

The extraordinary Russian interaction of regime and populace, ancient and modern, has been well described by Piero Ostellino, a longtime Moscow correspondent of *Corriere della sera:* "The Power anticipates the upsurge of complaints, acting so that the people accept their role in the existing order of things, do not dare to imagine an alternative to such an order, and end by considering it natural and unchangeable. . . . The overall coercive power of the system . . . comes to be considered inevitable and therefore acceptable by getting used to it."[18]

Some of the most intriguing continuities and parallels between Muscovy and the Soviet Union are to be found in what was not said about the system. Both regimes were wedded to secretiveness, not only about policy decisions but about the whole policy-making process as well as the personal actors in that process: *Iz izby soru ne vynesi*—"Don't take your dirt outside your house," that is, Don't wash your dirty linen in public.[19] For the audience, domestic as well as foreign, decisions always had to be made to appear unanimous, masking the actual debate and infighting that went on within the oligarchy.[20] Shades of "democratic centralism"! Most provocative of all is Keenan's description of the oligarchic politics of contending clans or clientele groups, covered up then as in Soviet times by the myth of a political monolith.[21] The Muscovite picture bears an uncanny resemblance to the image that speculative Kremlinology worked out, of bureaucratic competition among high party chieftains and their followers (*Seilschaften*, "climbing teams," from the analogy of a team of mountain climbers who all depend on the same rope).[22] Power resided in concentric circles around the Kremlin, institutionalized in the Soviet Union as the Politburo, the Central Committee, and the lesser nomenklatura. "Interest group" or "conflict model" interpretations of Soviet politics, or "participatory bureaucracy," reflect the perpetuation of Old Russian habits of struggling for power through proximity to the court, under the guise of loyal unity and subordination.[23]

One of the highest priorities of both Muscovite and Soviet political culture was to keep the principles of that culture—the real rules of the game—from being divulged at all. "Those who needed to know such rules knew them, and those who had no need to know were kept in ignorance," explains Keenan.[24] Under Stalin, a set of remarkably strict but unwritten rules (Graeme Gill calls them "conventions") took shape to govern the assignment of Central Committee rank to bureaucratic positions. These rules illustrate the perpetuation of the obsession with rank and precedence that characterized the old court culture.[25] Unacknowledged but fundamental practices of this nature highlight the true role of ideology for both eras—not a statement of operating principles or goals but a thick smoke screen to divert attention from the way things were actually done, "to decorate and to conceal the system's essential features."[26] To be sure, neither Russia nor Communism were alone in this ideological hide-and-seek; it was only the degree that distinguished them. So, while formal ideologies should be considered distinct from political culture, the manner of their use is fundamental to political culture.

Along with the Muscovite-Soviet parallel in the political process, there was an equally strong continuity in the relationship between the political realm and society in general. This characteristic revolved around the hypertrophy of the state and society's submission to that fact, stressed by generations of prerevolutionary Russian historians. As Alain Besançon has observed, "Development through coercion—and the substitution of the State for civil society—constituted the historical originality of Russia."[27] Such underlying assumptions entailed religious (or quasi-religious) ideology in justification of authority; the political insistence on one correct mode of philosophical belief, served as well by Marxism as by Orthodoxy; and a liturgical, formula-ridden mode of public discourse, whatever its philosophical substance. Many other peculiar habits of the Soviet government, ranging from the lack of a concept of honorable retirement to the seclusion of the wives of the leaders, could be traced to Muscovite origins, certainly more readily than to Karl Marx.

Another salient continuity in Russian political culture is the xenophobic attitude toward neighboring ethnic groups and toward foreign nations—specifically, the urge to dominate where it is possible, and fear and suspicion where it is not. Edward Allworth has noted how ethnic Russians have regarded border minorities as a cushion against foreign countries, and how from behind this buffer they have viewed the rest of the world with "suspiciousness of outsiders, envy, parochialism, intolerance, and above all, unthinking, blind patriotism."[28] The common lament of emigrés that Communism was fundamentally un-Russian misses the point.[29] Russia russified Communism more than Communism communized Russia.

However compelling all the apparent associations of ancient and recent political culture in Russia, the question remains of explaining how these folkways could persist through the revolutionary cataclysm of the twentieth century. This task is not as difficult as it might seem if the nature of the revolutionary process is fully appreciated.

Great revolutions typically represent themselves as crusades to uproot all the evils inherited from the nation's past and open the path to a future utopia. However, they come to pass not as simple conspiracies to impose a new and alien ideology (the conservative view shared by Russians like Alexander Solzhenitsyn) but as extended crises in the nation's social development, in the Russian case brought on by the late-nineteenth-century surge of industrialization. While the Old Regime may be brought down by a fortuitous combination of triggering circumstances, the sequence of upheavals released by the demise of traditional authority is an almost inexorable law of history: the attempt at governance by ineffective moderates; the usurpation of power by radical fanatics, resisted by equally fanatical counterrevolutionaries; the quandary of utopianism and the search for forms of compromise and reconstituted authority; finally, the postrevolutionary dictatorship of the opportunistic strongman who synthesizes the new rhetoric and the old methods. In this context, the resuscitation of Old Russian political folkways under Stalin is not only understandable but entirely natural.

Revolution can change culture, especially on the overt level, but not necessarily in ways intended by the revolutionaries. The revolution releases forces for change that have been generated beforehand by the nation's social evolution, and it can rapidly shift what are recognized to be the prevailing political and cultural norms. It can shift them too far, in fact, for the implicit cultural system to sustain them, which accounts for the strength typically observed in postrevolutionary reactions and the revival of old cultural forms (acknowledged or not) that accompanies them. There is a sort of "return of the repressed" operating here. At the time when Central Europe was in a revolutionary shambles after World War I, the Austrian psychoanalyst Karl Federn wrote a book called *The Fatherless Society,* in which he warned of the irrational quest for a substitute authority that would animate people suddenly deprived of the old object of their allegiance.[30] It is perhaps not so paradoxical, then, that a European observer of the Soviet regime could call it a "nonhereditary monarchy."[31]

The "aberration," as Keenan terms it, in Russia's political life in the first quarter of the twentieth century is no mystery if the circumstances of the revolutionary crisis are taken into account. Prior to the revolution, Russia was undergoing an extraordinarily rapid change toward Western models in economy, society, modes of thought, and political practices. Culturally, these changes were absorbed from the top down, affecting the worker and peasant masses least. At the same time, the revolutionary movement that launched the Communist dictatorship had incorporated many Old Russian forms under new labels—conspiratorial tactics, ideological totalism (including a religion of antireligion), and anticapitalism. So socialism had no trouble fitting in with Old Russian biases, provided it was socialism organized around the despotic state.

In other respects, the revolution and its sequelae dealt a devastating blow politically and demographically to the most Westernized, culture-bearing social strata. This was the effect of the "plebian revolution," according to Michal Reiman's thesis.[32] Old, unverbalized political folkways were physically brought up into the realm of political life by the new postrevolutionary recruits to the ruling apparatus—the "sons of peasants," as Theodore Shanin has described them, first represented by the former Bolshevik undergrounders who rallied around Stalin in the 1920s and then by the *vydvizhentsy* (promotees) who moved up to fill the shoes of the purge victims in the 1930s.[33] "At each successive crisis," Jack Gray has observed, "there was a choice, and in each case the preferred solution was that which more nearly approximated to Tsarist practices. . . . The Russian political culture provided no effective barriers to the re-creation of an autocracy prepared to control the thought of citizens, maintain power through a system of secret police, and brook no rival power in society."[34] The process is documented in the Communist Party's official decisions, notably the resolution "On the Organizational Question" of the Eighth Party Congress and the resolution "On Unity" of the Tenth Party Congress. With Stalin's rise and the defeat of the more Western-influenced Left Opposition, the Communist Party became, in its tribal-unity mentality, its leader worship, and its sadistic persecution of deviance, a latter-day embodiment of the political primitivism still latent in modern societies (as other varieties of totalitarianism attest). In sum, the Russian revolutionary experience testifies to the negative effects of an attempt to change a country too far and too fast in ways that run counter to its deep political folkways.

In the cultural perspective, Stalinism represented the triumph of Old Russian forms of latent political culture, dampened down by the Westernism of the late-nineteenth–early-twentieth-century era but revived with a vengeance once the movement of the revolutionary cycle reopened the path to the past. Under Stalin's rule, Russia experienced the synthesis of new institutions and new language with old methods and old values that is characteristic of the postrevolutionary phase, to yield the paradoxical reincarnation of Old Russia that Kopelev described so well. Stalinism entailed a reversion from the optimistic revolutionary view of human nature, requiring only liberation from all those coercive institutions that would "wither away," to the pessimistic view of humanity embedded in the Russian tradition, requiring the intense discipline, stimuli, and coercion that only the all-powerful state could enforce. Such was the direction adopted under Stalin, in every area of social theory and policy practice from education through labor relations to criminal justice. The purges, elevating the sons of peasants to the vacancies left by dead Westernizers, undergirded this cultural counterrevolution with the new bureaucratic recruits whom they put in place.

The comeback of Old Russian political folkways in the later phases of the revolutionary process accords with Keenan's view of the years when the revolution brewed and erupted as a Westernizing aberration. One might go even further, though this is more controversial, to argue that Soviet totalitarianism was not only compatible with Russian political culture but drew powerfully upon it.

The intensity and persistence of Soviet totalitarianism invite a cultural explanation as the congruence of the revolutionary occasion and the underlying bent of Russian political folkways. Elements of these folkways in the minds of both rulers and ruled that helped push postrevolutionary Russia toward the totalitarian extreme included the compelling tradition of centralism and the lack of a sense of individual, local, or group rights as against the central power; the fear of chaos and the abhorrence of publicly expressed dissent; caution or resignation in the face of questions that the central authority was expected to decide; and xenophobic supersensitivity. The paradox of Stalinism, explicable only in these cultural terms, is its combination of an ideology of Enlightenment optimism, internationalism, and technological omnipotence with a deeply misanthropic and even paranoid view of its own human material.

If the postrevolutionary regime known as Stalinism was so deeply embedded in the underlying proclivities of Russia political culture, what prospect was there for democratization of the system? Specifically, could the reformist leadership around Gorbachev have succeeded in pushing through changes that went radically against old folkways? Keenan's account of traditional Russian political premises sounded an ominous counterpoint to the catchwords of the Gorbachev administration. Decentralization versus centralism, glasnost versus *neglasnost'*, radical restructuring versus conservative caution, appeals to initiative versus evasion of responsibility, rejection of the party's infallibility versus the reassurances of orthodoxy—perestroika could not have been couched in terms more antithetical to Russian habits and expectations. It is not hard to understand why Gorbachev's appeal for a new revolution met with widespread unease and foot dragging, not only among the bureaucratic special interests but at all levels of Soviet society.

Two opposite potentialities were exerting their pull in the 1980s. One was the old political culture of the autocratic tradition, reincarnated in Stalinism and perpetuated in Brezhnevism. The other was the cultural infusion of the period of the aberration, climaxed by the spirit of 1917 and selectively endorsed on the verbal level by the same Stalinist regime that came to embody the conservative authoritarianism of Old Russia. Gorbachev tried to shift the balance significantly, if not totally, back to the direction of the aberration. But if political culture could subvert the essence of the revolution, what hope was there for an individual reformer, however powerful, to change the foundations of the system?

Not only did Gorbachev's reform efforts appear inauspicious in the light of the cultural heritage that still seemed to operate in Russia, the oft-voiced hope that world tensions could be resolved if only the Soviet Union would change—that is, abjure its Marxist ideology—seemed hopelessly fatuous. Russia was what it was politically, in its international as well as domestic behavior, for reasons that went far deeper than its ideological language. A switch in languages, if we are to credit Keenan, would only be—perhaps has already become—a different kind of protective cover for the profound hostilities toward themselves and toward others that seem to govern the Russians' political nature.

CHAPTER 22

Stalinist Ideology as False Consciousness

Belief in Marxism as the inspiration and plan that guided the development of Soviet-style socialism ever since the revolution of 1917: This is the central myth of Stalinism. With the abandonment of old orthodoxies in the Soviet Union and Eastern Europe in the late 1980s, Marxism was accordingly adjudged a failure, by many Russian intellectuals as well as by outsiders.

This conclusion suffers from the fallacy in its major premise. It was not Marxism that failed under Brezhnev, since Marxism had not really guided the Soviet Union for more than half a century before. It was not Gorbachev but Stalin who put an end to its sway, by revising the meaning of theory and by physically liquidating anyone of stature who took the theory seriously. Only the rigid shell of obligatory public dogma remained, a new state religion using the language of Marxism to confer legitimacy upon a reincarnation of Old Russian despotism and to exploit the loyalties of any within the country or outside who remained faithful to the forms of the doctrine. What Gorbachev and the promoters of perestroika represented, in ideological terms, was not the rejection of Marxism but the shedding of the withered skin of Stalinist dogma.

Despite its attractiveness before and after the revolution, Marxian theory was never appropriate to Russia's circumstances; Russian Populism would have fit the revolutionary movement much better, with its premise of the direct transition of a peasant society to socialism under the guidance of a dedicated intellectual elite. Yet Marxism had manifested an extraordinary intellectual pull in Russia because its aura of scientific inevitability leading to a utopian future answered the emotional needs of *déraciné* elements at all levels of a society in transition, alienated both from their traditional culture and from the power centers of Western capitalism.

Marxism in its inevitabilistic reading, carried to power by its Russian devotees, thus became the legitimizing belief of an extremist revolutionary regime lacking most of the conditions that would have made the propositions of the doctrine minimally realistic. It did not provide a program for the conscious legislative enactment of socialism and therefore cannot be judged by any empirical test of success or failure. At every step, Lenin and his lieutenants and successors improvised their concrete policies, with the criteria of political survival or factional victory uppermost in their minds. All that Marxism did was to cast a veil of sanctity and self-justification around these pragmatic steps. Official representations of the theory became more defensively dogmatic as expedient practice carried the Soviet regime ever further from the prerevolutionary spirit of its faith.

In consolidating his personal power, Stalin proved adept at manipulating ideological verities for factional advantage, above all in the Socialism in One Country controversy of 1924–25. That episode established the ability of the party leadership to advance reinterpretations or even patent misrepresentations of Marxist theory and to impose these new versions of the truth in all public discourse. What is more, the new versions of theory were said to be what Marxism had always meant from the beginning. Ultimately, all this was codified in the *Short Course,* which became the obligatory textbook for Communists all over the world. "Any independent research was considered out of place," observed the Italian Eurocommunist Giuseppe Boffa. "The essential task of the scholar was in practice the exegesis and correct commentary on Stalin's works."[1]

Such dogmatic claims obviated any public acknowledgment of the distance between original Marxist propositions and current interpretations thereof and any possibility of correcting the latter by reference to the former. And because interpretation was the province of political authority, original Marxist propositions lost all force for that authority even as ultimate guides to action. There was no way to call the leadership to account ideologically. Marxism, in short, became whatever Stalin said it was at the moment. As such, Marxist ideology became the most sensitive and most tightly guarded area of discussion in all of Soviet life.

Paradoxically, the function of Marxist ideology as a vehicle of political control and intellectual discipline grew all the more prominent as the substantive meaning and guiding role of the doctrine were being suppressed. This was a source of profound confusion for outside observers. Until perestroika, the

Soviet Union was permeated verbally with Marxist ideology in every aspect of life, yet the system embodied institutional forms and social values that had nothing in common with Marxism except in the most superficial sense.

After he defeated the Left and Right oppositions, Stalin took two more significant steps to tighten political control over the meaning of ideology. The first was a conference in April 1929 of "Marxist-Leninist Scientific Research Institutions" that called for a heightened effort "in instilling the methodology of Marx, Engels, and Lenin in the various fields of specialized knowledge." The document went on to warn against "ideological tendencies openly inimical to Marxism-Leninism, as well as various revisionist deviations" that "sometimes array themselves in Marxist dress and come forth under the flag of specialized knowledge, or . . . distort Marx, Engels, and Lenin, and conceal themselves with incorrectly explained citations from their works."[2] In other words, the authority of the political leadership to define doctrinal truth was now to be extended to all fields of intellectual and cultural life.

Stalin's second step was a letter to the journal *Proletarskaya revoliutsiya* in 1931, addressing a controversy over Lenin's prerevolutionary consistency. Stalin put received doctrine ahead of historical inquiry: "The question as to whether Lenin was or was not a real Bolshevik cannot be made the subject of discussion."[3] The ideological line might change, as it often did, but the principle was firmly established that ex cathedra pronouncements by the leader in the name of the party would be the last word in any field of thought or endeavor.

The most salient emendations of Marxism subsequently introduced by Stalin are familiar enough: antiegalitarianism, exalting the role of the state instead of anticipating its withering away, revival of nationalism, and repudiation of modernistic culture and social experiment. To justify his purges, Stalin proposed the infamous doctrine that the class struggle intensifies as the bourgeoisie approaches annihilation. Simultaneously, he abandoned policies in education and party recruitment that until the mid-1930s had still favored the proletariat as a class. On the other hand, he clearly did retain a form of socialism in the sense of publicly owned enterprise, carried to the extreme of bureaucratic statism in the Russian tradition.

If Stalinism did not really embody the dictatorship of the proletariat, what kind of social system did it in fact represent? Social advancement in the 1930s for sons of the proletariat and peasantry did not make the proletariat as such the ruling class—it only enabled selected individuals to rise out of the proletariat (or the peasantry) and enter the bureaucratic hierarchy. This was a classic example of Pareto's "circulation of the elites," where circulation may renovate and alter the ruling class but does not put an end to the fact that a ruling class still rules.[4] At the same time, the concept of the bureaucracy or the "New Class" as a ruling elite presents a number of difficulties. The most immediate one, to a Marxist, is that this top group is not based on private property but rather on public function. This discrepancy gave rise to numerous contrived efforts by critics of Stalinism to argue that the Soviet bureaucracy really controlled state property in its private interest and exploited the masses for its personal benefit.[5]

A more serious problem is that the New Class cannot be reduced to one homogeneous social group. Was it the intelligentsia? The bureaucracy in general? The nomenklatura of the party? Or all educated nonmanual workers, *sluzhashchie,* the "Soviet intelligentsia"? In fact these were all elements of a complex social system, where, just as under modern capitalism, it is impossible to draw sharp lines between classes and analyze society into two clearly opposed camps of exploiters and exploited. There is a long-standing historical distinction, particularly in Russia, between the creative intelligentsia and the technical intelligentsia, along with the "quasi-intelligentsia" characteristic of developing countries.[6]

In Russia the quasi-intelligentsia was the main source of the Bolshevik mentality that combined a futuristic faith in modernity with a primitive dogmatism. This spirit became the reigning ethos of the Communist nomenklatura. The creative intelligentsia was ambivalent about the revolution and was the prime basis for such critical sentiments as the circumstances of the party dictatorship permitted to emerge. Influential in the early years of Soviet rule, it was heavily victimized by the purges and revived only after the death of Stalin, ultimately to become the most enthusiastic source of support for reform under Khrushchev and Gorbachev. The technical intelligentsia, indifferent or hostile to the revolution, was its most favored beneficiary in class terms. Vastly expanded by postrevolutionary programs of education, shading down into the millions of vocationally trained technicians and white-collar workers, and offering until the end of the Stalin era a wide avenue of social mobility to ambitious individuals from the masses, the technical intelligentsia became the backbone of modern Soviet society.

But where, in this hierarchical maze of social elements, is the ruling class? Here it is useful to invoke the distinction made by Svetozar Stojanović (and hinted at previously by Antonio Gramsci) between the "ruling class" and the "dominant class."[7] The dominant class is that sector of society whose function, interests, and outlook contribute most to the general character of the system; the ruling class is the sector where power actually resides, even though its effective exercise must respect the integrity of the dominant class. In this analysis, the dominant class in the Soviet Union was the intelligentsia, creative and technical taken together, and the ruling class was obviously the nomenklatura, in its precise sense as the party apparatus plus party members holding responsible positions in civil government, the military, and all other organized social institutions.

The great paradox of the Stalinist system was the persistence of the ideology of the classless society at the same time that a complex new social hierarchy was settling into place. There is ample historical precedent for revolution yielding to thermidorean reaction, as the class brought to dominance by the upheaval consolidates its gains, but prior to the Russian Revolution, there was no precedent for the continuity of the revolutionary party and the revolutionary ideology into the postrevolutionary stages of Thermidor and Bonapartism. This was Lenin's unique achievement, to adapt the party to the circumstances of an ebbing revolutionary wave and to hold power in the name of the revolution after the revolution was over. This maneuver gave his successors an indispensable stake in clinging to the verbal forms of the ideology as well as to the dictatorship of the party. Thus, the fact that the state of the New Class was saddled with the doctrine of Marxism as its point of reference for ideological legitimation was essentially a historical accident.

Nevertheless, Stalin had no choice among ideologies to legitimize his dictatorship: Marxism was a given that he was obliged to use as his point of departure even though it was much more at variance with the actual Soviet situation than were either fascist or liberal ideologies in relation to their respective societies. To be sure, Stalin and his entourage made very clever use of Marxian doctrine, without in the least permitting it to circumscribe what they adjudged to be their real interests. Certainly, after Stalin tightened his grip on the country, no one in a position of influence in the Soviet Union, neither the dominant intelligentsia nor the ruling nomenklatura, had any interest in the classless society. After the 1920s the classless society was no longer an operational goal of the regime. Assertions that it was in fact achieved only served to smother any concern about actually pursuing it.

If this position represented the interests of the ruling and dominant classes, how was the revolutionary ideology, so far at variance with reality, actually sustained? Here the Marxian model of society does become relevant, specifically in Marx's theory of the ideological superstructure. While ideological systems of law, philosophy, and religion, according to Marx, reflect and justify the class structure of society and the interests of the ruling class, they are not necessarily direct and accurate expressions of social reality. On the contrary, ideological systems may lag behind reality or may even be imposed by political authority in terms that contradict reality. In either case they are functional in the given socioeconomic formation as a whole, as sources of legitimation and self-satisfaction for the ruling and dominant orders of the social structure.

Who among all the diverse elements of the Soviet New Class actually benefitted from the imposition of Marxist ideology as a false public consciousness? Certainly not the creative intelligentsia, which was the most injured victim of the system of ideological control. Quite obviously the nomenklatura, exercising its power and enjoying its privileges in the name of the dictatorship of the proletariat. In a secondary and less direct way, the technical intelligentsia and white-collar class broadly speaking, at least to the extent that membership in these categories meant education, social status, and urban residence, if not always better pay than industrial workers. In general, the beneficiaries were the elements that had risen to fill the social vacuum created by the revolution. Marxism as false consciousness thus served until the end of the Stalin era and beyond to support the position and interests of the ruling class and a portion of the dominant class, leaving the creative intelligentsia in a state of demoralized but potentially dynamic opposition. The strength of the creative intelligentsia and the durability of its traditions of independence and devotion to true "consciousness" were attested by the leading role that it quickly assumed in the reforms of the era of perestroika.

In the Soviet instance, the concept of ideology as false consciousness is frequently cited though infrequently explored or applied. Karl Mannheim traced the history of the idea back to classical antiquity and ancient theology.[8] The emperor Napoleon popularized "ideology" in its pejorative sense and dismissed the liberal French thinkers, Antoine Destutt de Tracy and his school of *idéologues*—really psychological philosophers—as impractical dreamers.[9] Hegel felt that human consciousness was fated to remain "false" or "imperfect" because people cannot understand their actual role in history until they can look back at it retrospectively.[10]

Marx made the concept of ideology an important element in his social model of historical materialism when he asserted, as early as *The German Ideology* of 1846, that the social reality of classes and the class struggle governs the formulation of ideas and the influence they may have: "The ideas of the ruling class are in every epoch the ruling ideas. . . . Each new class which puts itself in the place of one ruling before it, is compelled, merely in order to carry through its aim, to represent its interest as the common interest of all the members of society, put in an ideal form; it will give its ideas the form of universality, and represent them as the only rationally, universally valid ones."[11] However, Marx never quite formulated his approach to ideology in the crisp term "false consciousness." That was the contribution of Engels, and only in a late letter. "Ideology is a process accomplished by the so-called thinker, consciously, indeed, but with a false consciousness," Engels wrote to the German Social Democratic scholar Franz Mehring. "The real motives impelling him remain unknown to him, otherwise it would not be an ideological process at all"—an intriguing anticipation of the Freudian unconscious. Engels then focused this insight on "the bourgeois illusion of the eternity and the finality of capitalist production"; the great error was to regard the laissez-faire philosophy of the eighteenth-century physiocrats and Adam Smith "not as the reflection in thought of changed economic facts but as the finally achieved correct understanding of actual conditions subsisting always and everywhere."[12] No one yet imagined that socialism, in its turn, could convert its own ideology into a false consciousness that would express the momentary interests of the ruling elite as if they were eternal truths.

Marxists made little effort until well after the Russian Revolution to work out the implications of false consciousness. Plekhanov, addressing the frequent discrepancy between conscious understanding and the state of the forces of production, did allude to the triumph of capitalist inequality in the French Revolution under the banner of universal principles of freedom and equality.[13] Eduard Bernstein noted how the Social Democrats often acted contrary to their theory, though he underestimated the staying power of verbal formulas: "A theory or declaration of principle which does not allow attention being paid at every stage of development to the actual interests of the working classes, will always be set aside."[14] Aleksandr Bogdanov, without doubt the most original of Russian Marxists, took an extreme relativist position that foreshadowed what Gramsci was to say about Marxist ideology a quarter of a century later: "Any given ideological form," positive though its role might be, "can have only a historically transitory meaning, not an objectively suprahistorical meaning. . . . Marxism includes the denial of the unconditional objectivity of any truth whatsoever," no exception being made for Marxism itself.[15] But no one before 1917 grasped the possibility of a systematic attachment to a false or deceptive image of reality to justify a postbourgeois social order.

As early as 1919 Karl Kautsky argued that the Bolshevik experiment was headed toward Caesarism and de facto counterrevolution, thanks to the one-party dictatorship and the immaturity of the Russian proletariat.[16] The Austrian left socialist Otto Bauer anticipated the same tendency almost as early; he wrote in 1921 of "a sort of technocracy, the hegemony of the engineers, of the economic managers and the state bureaucracy."[17] By 1930, when Stalin's new revolution was in full swing, Kautsky adjudged the Soviet system to be a new sort of feudal hierarchy, headed by the Communist Party bureaucracy as a "new class"—the first application of that term to the Soviet system—that ruled through its control of state property.[18] But the Stalinist system was still not linked to the "ideological" use of Marxism.

György Lukács used the term "false consciousness," but only to describe the limited outlook of the individual worker who could not rise to a clear view of the whole social situation.[19] His highly voluntarist reading of Marxism-Leninism, with its emphasis on the role of force and the instrumental function of historical materialism in the class struggle, came close to anticipating how Stalin would actually operate—and perhaps that explains why the Soviets condemned his *Geschichte und Klassenbewusstsein* so sharply: It was not a sufficiently false version of the ideology to serve their purposes. Meanwhile, Lukács had a direct influence on Karl Mannheim's formulation of the more general theory of ideology. As their connection has been described by Morris Watnick, "It was Lukács' highly instrumental Marxism . . . which suggested to Mannheim that all social and political doctrines which pass for knowledge might better be regarded as 'existentially determined' doctrines, i.e., as elaborate rationalisations of group interests—mainly the interests of classes—which must 'distort' the actualities of social life if they are to serve those interests effectively."[20]

For the first direct application of the theory of ideology to the Soviet system we have to turn to Gramsci. In his critical comments on Bukharin's *Historical Materialism* that appear early in the *Prison Notebooks,* Gramsci observed, "The meaning which the term 'ideology' has assumed in Marxist philosophy implicitly contains a negative value judgment," reaching in its extreme form "the assertion that every ideology is 'pure' appearance, useless, stupid, etc."[21] (This understanding of ideology, incidentally, approaches the prevailing view of ideology in the United States, which prides itself on being a very unideological society, though in fact an ideological false consciousness—in this case the myth of competitive capitalism according to Adam Smith—is deeply embedded in the national mentality. Far from arriving at the "end of ideology," the United States is so ideological that it is not even aware of the fact.)

Gramsci went on to distinguish the two different meanings that "ideology" had for him: It could be either "the necessary superstructure of a particular structure" or "the arbitrary lucubrations of particular individuals." Then he made a comment that is extraordinary for that date: "If the philosophy of praxis [Marxism] affirms theoretically that every 'truth' believed to be eternal and absolute has had practical origins and has represented a 'provisional' value, . . .

it is still very difficult to make people grasp 'practically' that such an interpretation is valid also for the philosophy of praxis itself." Gramsci was addressing Bukharinism, but unknowingly he was anticipating Stalinism: "As a result, even the philosophy of praxis tends to become an ideology in the worst sense of the word, that is to say a dogmatic system of eternal and absolute truths."[22]

Trotsky's postexile critique of Stalinism was more trenchant than Gramsci's in concrete social terms, though less so in the theoretical respect. "Stalinist Bonapartism" was "a contradictory society halfway between capitalism and socialism," in which "under a socialist banner . . . the bureaucracy . . . painstakingly conceals the real relations both in town and country with abstractions from the socialist dictionary."[23] Bruno Rizzi took Trotsky's critique further toward its logical conclusion, holding that the Soviet Union was "neither bourgeois nor proletarian" but had fallen under the domination of the bureaucracy as a class, which exploited the masses through the collectivized property that it controlled.[24] James Burnham broke with the Marxist schema altogether to assert that the USSR represented "a new structure of society—managerial society, a new order of power and privilege which is not capitalist and not socialist." It was only one case in an international trend legitimized by various ideologies—"Leninism-Stalinism; fascism-nazism; and at a more primitive level, by New Dealism." Here Burnham clearly grasped the notion of false consciousness: "Leninism-Stalinism ('Bolshevism') is not a scientific hypothesis but a great social ideology rationalizing the social interests of the new rulers and making them acceptable to the minds of the masses."[25]

Milovan Djilas made the function of ideology even clearer: "So-called socialist ownership is a disguise for the real ownership by the political bureaucracy. . . . The promise of an ideal world increased the faith in the ranks of the new class and sowed illusions among the masses." False consciousness, Djilas suggested, was a weakness of human nature—"Every ideology, every opinion, tries to represent itself as the only true and complete one."[26] György Konrad and Ivan Szelenyi went so far as to direct "false consciousness" against the intellectuals as a class: "The intellectuals of every age have described themselves ideologically in accordance with their particular interests, . . . to represent their particular interests in each context as the general interests of mankind" and thus "to maintain their monopoly of their role."[27]

The most coherent development of the concept of Stalinist false consciousness was the work of the Yugoslav social theorists in and around the "Praxis" group, following implicitly in the wake of Trotsky and Djilas. Veljko Korać, proceeding from the Yugoslav critique of Soviet bureaucratism and "étatism," wrote in 1964 of Stalinism and the "ascendancy of the technobureaucracy" as the outcome of attempting socialism in a backward country. "This led to an absolutizing of politics and to its conversion into a specific mythology and theology. . . . In the name of Marxism, Stalin distorted Marx's ideas into a closed system of dogmas, making of himself the sole and absolute interpreter of those dogmas."[28] The more official theorist Najdan Pašić called Stalinist ideology "a pragmatic-bureaucratic revision and dogmatization of Marxism carried to the extreme."[29] Stojanović elaborated the point: "In the degeneration of the October Revolution there developed a new class system—étatism—which is still being successfully legitimized ideologically as socialism. True Marxists have the duty of breaking through that curtain of myth to the statist reality."[30] In another connection Stojanović wrote, "The world is governed ideologically by those who possess the power to assign names to social phenomena."[31] Branko Horvat referred to a "theological socialism . . . masquerading as science," again the consequence of attempting to achieve socialism in a backward country. "Scientific ideology provides a justification for, and so an efficient defense of, established interests," that is, the counterrevolution of étatism.[32] Zagorka Golubović concluded even more directly, "A special place and role belong to Stalinist ideology, which is a necessary, integral part of the Stalinist order, because it preserves its legitimacy through ideology as a justification of the position of the ruling class."[33]

Italian Eurocommunist thinking closely paralleled the Yugoslav view. Boffa concluded in his history, "Ideological orthodoxy . . . actually represented the consciousness—or if you prefer, the 'false consciousness'—of the whole directing stratum of Soviet society."[34] This means, he contended in a later work, that "Marxist theory was in practice for Stalin . . . an instrument of power, manipulated by him casually at the moment of any changeable demand of policy. Theoretical concerns were manifested by Stalin only to the extent that they served to justify practice."[35]

Soviet critics in the Marxist tradition were inclined like the Yugoslavs to explain Stalinist ideology in religious terms. Roy Medvedev, recognizing how Stalin had been "masking his power in ultrarevolutionary phrases," suggested that with "the deification of Stalin . . . the social consciousness of the people took on elements of religious psychology. Perceptions of reality were distorted." The petty bourgeoisie and the degenerated bureaucracy "prefer dogmatism, which frees them from the need to think."[36] In a later context Medvedev lamented the "dogmatization of Marxism" and asserted, "The USSR is the last great religious state on earth."[37] Under perestroika, the religious analogy was even expressed publicly in the Soviet Union and Eastern Europe. A Soviet author, V. Chubinsky, introducing the first publication in the USSR of Arthur

Koestler's *Darkness at Noon,* referred to the "idolatrous mode of thought" of
Stalinism, and a Polish writer, Zbigniew Safjan, remarked on its "magic, liturgical language. . . . In Stalinist times, there was a magic code for reality that had
nothing in common with reality. It was spoken, and therefore it must be."[38]

The description of Stalinism as ideological false consciousness invites some
refinement. Mannheim distinguished two senses of ideology, the "particular"
and the "total." Ideology in the total sense denotes "the characteristics and
composition of the total structure of the mind of this epoch or this group."
In the particular sense it refers to ideas "regarded as more or less conscious
disguises of a situation, . . . all the way from conscious lies to half-conscious
and unwitting disguises; from calculated attempts to dupe others to self-deception."[39] Gramsci's distinction between the "necessary superstructure" and "arbitrary lucubrations" was elaborated by Martin Seliger as a contrast between
the "restrictive conception" of ideology (including the Marxist view), denoting
"specific, . . . extremist belief systems and parties," and the "inclusive conception" that extends it to "all political belief systems."[40] In the broader sense,
ideology thus extends far enough to embrace the familiar notions of culture in
anthropology and frame of reference in psychology, insofar as either concept
impinges on the political realm.[41]

Both senses of ideology apply to Soviet thinking under Stalin. On the one
hand, as the manipulative contrivance of an individual or clique, Stalinist ideology corresponded to the "particular" or "arbitrary" or "restrictive" meaning of
ideology, formed with a degree of self-deception and providing political cover
and self-satisfaction for the regime. On the other hand, when Stalinized Marxism was imposed on society as a whole to the exclusion of any independent
forms of political thought, even Marxist, it took on the "inclusive" role of "total ideology" or "necessary superstructure," even if it was ersatz. Thus, Stalinism extended the arbitrary false consciousness of ideology from the sphere of
individual thinking to the mental life of the whole society. As Rudolf Bahro
noted in his treatise on bureaucratic Communism, "The party organization of
today is a structure that *actively produces false consciousness on a massive scale.*"[42]

Lukács finally awoke to the real nature of Stalinist ideology after the Twentieth Party Congress. He wrote, "In the conditions of intellectual centralization
which he created it was impossible for any theory to be firmly established unless
it was at least authorized by him. . . . Stalin's unscrupulousness in this matter
reached the point of altering the theory itself if necessary." Lukács was among
the first to grasp the instrumental character of ideology in Stalinist behavior:
"Principles were simplified and vulgarized according to the exigencies (often

purely notional) of practice. . . . Because Stalin wanted to maintain at any cost a continuity 'in quotation marks' with Lenin's work, not only facts but Leninist texts were distorted. . . . For him, in the name of *partiinost,* agitation is primary. Its needs determine . . . what science must say and how it must say it."[43]

This situation did not escape the attention of Soviet observers who were set free by perestroika to draw the ultimate conclusions. Tatiana Zaslavskaya spoke of "a false public consciousness" that "continued to reflect the revolution's lofty aims and fed the masses' enthusiasm," while "the forms" of "a complex tangle of social relations" were "more often than not . . . at variance with their content," that is, "indirect exploitation by the *nomenklatura* stratum of the remaining mass of the population."[44]

Thanks to a lifetime of indoctrination, the arbitrary ideological assertions of Stalinism, faute de mieux, were genuinely absorbed by large numbers of the Soviet political class as their worldview, to the exclusion of any overt exercise of their own critical faculties. This Stalinist false consciousness was not the spontaneous product of the class structure, as the Marxian classics suggested, but rather a forcible imposition by the party-state that was accepted by the officialdom with a varying mixture of cynicism and self-deception. Its real implantation in the minds of that group was testified to by the strength of conservative resistance to the "new thinking" of perestroika.

Historically speaking, the ideological superstructure of a society is not entirely and automatically a matter of false consciousness. The reality is far more complex. Theorists up to Stalin's time, when they addressed false consciousness at all, always saw it as a more or less natural development within a given socioeconomic formation. This is often true, but the gap between ideology and reality can vary widely. Under Stalin, as a counterrevolutionary leader committed to a revolutionary ideology and armed with the power to command any form of belief he chose, the relationship was different. In this case the state imposed false consciousness—in other words, official lies—and inculcated it so effectively that to the end it remained part of the mental equipment of a large part of articulate Soviet society.

CHAPTER 23

Was Stalin Really a Communist?

I n the light of his record, was Stalin really a Communist? The question may seem absurd. Was the Grand Inquisitor really a Christian? This is not just semantic hairsplitting over the degree of difference that may have distinguished Stalin from the progenitors of the Bolshevik movement. It is the question whether the evil of Stalin and Stalinism flowed inexorably out of the essence of that movement, or whether it was injected by a megalomanic personality who, abetted by intractable circumstances, usurped the movement and turned it in an essentially different direction, albeit still dressed out in its original language.

The problem of the man or the system has long lain at the heart of historiographical debates about Stalin and Stalinism. After the revolution against Stalinism that culminated in 1991, the question acquired direct practical significance. What was the real nature of the regime that the Russians and the other nations under Communist Party rule were actually rebelling against? And what options and guidelines did the answer to this question leave the new successor governments as they tried to work out an alternative destiny?

Anti-Communists of the left, and like them the proponents of perestroika in the Soviet Union, always saw Stalinism as a criminal betrayal of the revolution and of Marxist ideals, already compromised by the excesses of Leninism. In this view, Stalin was able to seize the levers of power that had been set up by the Bolshevik Revolution and use them to alter the whole natural course of history in his own cruel and mendacious image. His attachment to Marxism and even to socialism, then, only served to camouflage the establishment of a new oriental despotism.

A contrary argument asserts that Stalinism was inherent in the evils of Leninism, or Marxism, or the Enlightenment—stop where you will. This is philosophical determinism, contending that Stalin and Stalinism stemmed logically from utopian theories that urged the conscious reconstruction of the world. Said the Russian political scientist Aleksandr Tsipko, "Socialism is precisely that historically unique society that is consciously built, on the basis of a theoretical plan. The defects in the structure are not just due to Stalin's departure from the original blueprint for socialism, . . . they also represent departures of theoretical thinking from life."[1] The lesson is that any attempt to tinker with the status quo, any heretical notion of social engineering, will inevitably lead down a slippery slope to totalitarianism.

Less subjectivist is the view that Stalinism emerged naturally out of the process of revolution, against the background of Russian backwardness, independently of the conscious intentions of the people who labored to set the process in motion. Stalin was thus a sort of Bonaparte or Hitler *à la russe,* a despot ready, willing, and able to exploit the possibilities that the waning of real revolutionary spirit offered him.

A full assessment of Stalin's place in history demands a combination of these diverse approaches. The revolutionary process, leading from the collapse of the Old Regime through ineffective liberalism to radical fanaticism and then to retrenchment and the despotic synthesis of the new with the old, has a certain objective character. It represents the pressure of probability in social dynamics, beyond the control of any individual and usually beyond the ken of those who think they are steering the process. But individual leaders, their passions and ideas, their tactical judgments, can have a great impact on the actual shape of the revolutionary process in a given country. Lenin and Leninism powerfully contributed to the harshness of the revolution in Russia. Even more, they contributed to the ability of the Communist Party organization and Communist ideology, steeled in the extremist phase of the revolution, to hold sway through the succeeding phases of thermidorean reaction and postrevolutionary dictatorship.

Stalin entered this picture as a decisive personality after Lenin's demise by taking command of the key instrument of power, the Communist Party apparatus, and hoisting himself to the position of a postrevolutionary dictator. In that role he had the characteristic opportunity to impose his will and his whims while working out a synthesis of revolutionary spirit and old-fashioned methods of rule. He inherited a totalistic concept of state socialism from the Russian revolutionary movement, but everything he did in practice moved it closer to traditional tsarist forms of bureaucratic centralism, militarized ethics, and office-holding elitism (the New Class), all Marxist-Leninist mythology about "communism" and the "withering-away of the state" notwithstanding. With its emphasis on production over justice, Stalin's socialism was not the successor to capitalism but an alternative to it, an alternative found wanting when competition with capitalism brought the Soviet Union face-to-face with the more sophisticated requirements of the postindustrial age.

Stalin's answers to the ebbing phase of the revolutionary process and to Russia's particular challenges of modernization and development were not the only ones. Here his personality entered in, first of all in his Machiavellian drive to amass power and destroy his old associates in the party leadership. These aims were central in his break with the Bukharin group and his embrace of a radical economic line in 1928–29. This approach was by no means the only answer to Russia's problems, but it was one that worked if pursued with the necessary single-mindedness. Once committed, Stalin showed himself capable of inhuman harshness in driving his program through.

Was Stalin a fanatic or, as George Kennan has written, "a man of incredible criminality,"[2] or does it not make any difference at the extremes? Stalin was certainly adroit in manipulating Marxist-Leninist doctrine to justify his exploits. To his contemporaries, he seemed to be little more than an opportunistic slogan-mongerer, as Bukharin discovered in 1928 ("He changes his theory according to whom he needs to get rid of") or as György Lukács commented, "Stalin's unscrupulousness . . . reached the point of altering the theory itself if necessary."[3] However, there is good reason to conclude that Stalin had to believe—and compel everyone else to believe—even as he proceeded with his diverse ideological maneuvers. Evidently he needed a sense of unconditional ideological legitimacy (conceivably rooted in his Orthodox religious training), regardless of how far he might actually depart from the earlier spirit of the movement. This need for a bridge between rigid theory and widely evolving practice, reversing the presumed dependence of practice on theory, led Stalin step-by-step to the totalitarian control of all realms of thought, culture, and public expression. But this was not enough for his warped personality, which carried him inexorably to the paranoiac nightmare of the purges as well as to eliciting obscene adulation of himself as history's greatest genius in every field of human endeavor.

The "Stalin Revolution" was the product both of the circumstances and the individual, of the process and the personality. Direct responsibility of Stalin's predecessors in the Bolshevik movement is less clear, if we bear in mind the manipulative approach he took to their ideological legacy. To be sure, the tidal wave of fanaticism, violence, and moral devastation in the Bolshevik Revolution and the civil war clearly helped to set the stage for Stalin's methods and provided him with his essential instrument, the party apparatus. However, the further he progressed into his new revolution from above, the less can he be linked to the Bolshevik heritage apart from his use of the Marxist-Leninist vocabulary, and the more the Russian element in his synthesis stands out.

Much of the confusion that still prevails about Stalin's historical role can be dispelled if the two phases of the Stalin Revolution are recognized, a revolution from above followed by what was in substance a counterrevolution from above. The first phase, running from 1928 to about 1932, was the time of Stalin's "cultural revolution," as some have called it, with a nod to Mao Tse-tung. It was the time of Stalin's forcible reconstruction of the Soviet economic order and his imposition of totalitarian controls in all walks of life, in an atmosphere of dogmatic Marxism and recharged class struggle against alleged enemies among the intelligentsia and the kulaks.

The counterrevolutionary phase of Stalin's violent reordering of Soviet life is less clearly recognized, when he systematically rejected most of the basic propositions of Marxism and most currents of revolutionary culture and social policy while clinging to the revolutionary language. This vast reversal proved relatively easy, thanks to the monopoly of public communication and the principle of party authority on every conceivable question that he had established in the first phase of his revolution from above. Thus Stalin could still claim exclusive Marxist-Leninist rectitude and condemn all who defended earlier versions of the truth as counterrevolutionaries and enemies of the people. Behind this smoke screen, he abandoned the egalitarian ideal, policy preferences for the proletariat, the primacy of economics over politics, the social explanation of individual deviancy, and the experimental spirit in culture and education. He turned to the principle of discipline in every realm, from the factory to the family. He embraced Russian nationalism, nationalistic history, and Russification of the Soviet minorities.

At the same time Stalin prepared and launched a campaign against the old leadership of the Communist Party that is still hard to comprehend. It was war against the old Bolsheviks, distinguished by the show trials and forced confessions by his old rivals of the various Communist opposition groups. This purge was supplemented by the sweeping though unannounced elimination of most of the people who had actually supported him in his bid for power in the 1920s and even during his revolution from above in the early 1930s. Khrushchev underscored this purge of the Stalinists in his Secret Speech of 1956, citing statistics on the majority of Central Committee members and Seventeenth Congress delegates who disappeared in the years of the Terror. What Khrushchev did not note was the clear age cutoff in the purge of the party apparatus—everybody of importance over the age of thirty-five (that is, born before 1902 and over fifteen at the time of the revolution), with the exception of a few Stalin cronies and the Politburo itself.

The import of the Great Purge, like Stalin's reversals in social and cultural policy, was obscured for the great majority of observers by his assiduous maintenance of ideological continuity. Labels aside, it was almost as much a revolution in the national leadership as 1917 was. Stalin killed more Communists than all the world's fascist dictators combined. In terms of the classic revolutionary process, Stalin went beyond Bonapartism. The ultimate effect of his counterrevolution was to bring the country in practical terms to an imperial restoration.

This perspective reopens the old question whether there was any essential difference between Communism and fascism, between Stalin and Hitler. Fascism, like Stalinism, came to power only after revolutions (in Germany and Spain) or near-revolutionary situations (in Italy). Fascism, like Stalinism, functioned as a postrevolutionary (or antirevolutionary) dictatorship, with the totalitarian methods characteristic of any postrevolutionary regime in the twentieth century. The differences between Communism and fascism lie in their overt ideologies and the routes by which they came to power as well as their approximation to the totalitarian "ideal type." Stalinism emerged from a revolution of the left and adhered mendaciously to a left ideology; fascism was avowedly antirevolutionary and operated much more openly with its antidemocratic, nationalist ideology. Thanks both to its ideological needs and to its practice of Russian-style bureaucratic socialism, Stalinism became more truly totalitarian than any of its rivals of the right. Yet in the substance of their social policies and cultural norms, even extending to anti-Semitism, there was progressively less to distinguish the two systems after Soviet Russia entered the counterrevolutionary phase of Stalinism. In this perspective, the Nazi-Soviet pact of 1939 was not such an affront to the principles of each side as it appeared to be at the time.

The great anomaly of the Russian Revolution, embodied in Stalinism, was the continuity of the Communist Party as an institution and the official attachment to Marxist-Leninist ideology through all the ups and downs of the revolutionary process. It is this continuity that has so confused and distracted all too many students of the Communist phenomenon. Even post-Communist reformers in Russia proved unable to distinguish clearly between the evolving Soviet reality and the continuous ideological illusion. To be sure, institutional and ideological continuity was itself a product of Lenin's unusual merit as a revolutionary organizer, to be able to put a political organization in power where it could withstand seventy years of crisis, policy reversals, and leadership upheavals. The crucial point, in the perspective of the revolutionary process, was not Lenin's seizure of power in 1917—any fanatic could do that—but his ability to hang on through the civil war and then to carry out his own thermidorean reaction in 1921 instead of getting himself liquidated by the pragmatists as Robespierre was. From then on, the revolutionary qualities of the party were available to serve Stalin's postrevolutionary dictatorship and in fact to perpetuate totalitarian rule for another three decades after his death. This is how Soviet Russia came to experience the abnormal and dysfunctional prolongation of postrevolutionary dictatorship.

How and why did all this finally come to an end? No revolution, or more precisely, no postrevolutionary dictatorship or restoration regime goes on forever. Sooner or later some shock to the dictatorship allows the nation to return to its revolutionary origins. This "moderate revolutionary revival" embraces revolutionary ideals—in the Russian case, democracy, self-determination, and democratic socialism—without extremist terror and violence. Such was the direction that Soviet Russia started to take during the Thaw of the Khrushchev era, though unfortunately Khrushchev did not give it consistent leadership and the party apparatus was still too strong. The moderate revolutionary revival when it should have taken place was thus aborted. Consequently, the country had to endure another generation of anachronistic authoritarianism with its cynical, pseudo-Marxist legitimation, while economic advance was matched by moral decay.

It was late in the day when the impasse in economic growth and generational change in the party leadership finally opened the way for the moderate revolutionary revival in the form of perestroika, as Gorbachev sought political and economic cures further and further back in Soviet history, all the way to the morning after the October Revolution. However, this attempt to turn back released forces, particularly national self-determination, ultimately swept Gorbachev away and with him the last vestiges of the regime's attachment to the "socialist choice" of October. This left his successors with the task of finding new guideposts amid the rubble of Soviet history.

Here the historical depiction of the Communist experience had direct policy consequences. If Stalinism and Brezhnevism were seen as the logical implementation of the October Revolution and its "socialist choice," a seventy-year "experiment," then any institution or policy associated with the label of "socialism" was to be rejected as the legacy of an era of criminal madness. If the system dismantled between 1985 and 1991 were seen to be the product of Stalin's postrevolutionary dictatorship and his disguised counterrevolution, then the Soviet experience before Stalin was left open as a source of policy guidance, such as the Gorbachevians tried to find in the NEP.

Since Gorbachev's fall, the successor leadership has not viewed Stalinism and its alternatives this way. Short of a return to monarchism and Prime Minister Piotr Stolypin (no one mentions Kerensky!), the new regime has been unable to find any native inspiration at all. This self-imposed intellectual blackout helps explain Russia's infatuation with the Western utopia of nineteenth-century liberalism. Unfortunately, this infatuation has not averted the revenge of Russian political culture, the steady drift back toward the Russian habits and expectations of authoritarianism in which Stalin himself was nourished.

PART V

Reform versus Bureaucracy, from Khrushchev to Brezhnev

CHAPTER 24

Khrushchev and the Party Apparatus

I n the power vacuum created by Stalin's death, there was a certain parallel with the succession to Lenin. As with Lenin, much of Stalin's authority passed away with him—the authority of the man who relentlessly piloted the Soviet state through the "second revolution" of collectivization and intensive industrialization and on to the relative stability of the totalitarian order, the authority of the man who liquidated every other political leader not fully dependent on him, the authority of the man who was increasingly glorified over two decades as a new prophet of the Marxist faith and the greatest intellect in the history of all humanity. Fully succeeding to Stalin's power would have required rebuilding that personal dictatorship. However, there was no opportunity to repeat Stalin's work of building up the machinery of party unity and discipline, liquidating the Old Bolshevik oppositionists, and steering the regime to its final postrevolutionary stabilization.

In Stalin's last few years, two substantial changes were made in the organization of the party and state leadership, only to be reversed immediately after his death. The first, in 1949, was the removal of prominent Politburo members from direct ministerial responsibilities, which took them one step away from what were potentially personal political machines. The police powers, significantly, had already been divided between the Ministry of the Interior (MVD) and the Ministry of State Security (MGB). The second change was announced at the Nineteenth Party Congress in October 1952: The Politburo of eleven men was abolished and replaced with a "Presidium of the Central Committee" consisting of twenty-five men. This change was manifestly designed to dilute and thus weaken the top organ of collective leadership in the party. At the same

275

time, Malenkov was virtually declared Stalin's heir apparent by being selected to give the political report to the congress, a function that Stalin had exercised ever since 1925. It appeared that Stalin was endeavoring to guarantee the clear-cut transfer of power to an individual successor by designating the man and by weakening the ability of his associates to assert de facto collective rule.

If this was Stalin's intent, he was not entirely successful. Malenkov could not prevent his colleagues from resuming direct control of their personal spheres of influence in the Soviet administrative machinery—Beria, Molotov, Nikolai Bulganin, and Anastas Mikoyan resumed respectively their ministries of Internal Affairs, Foreign Affairs, War, and Trade, and the two police branches were again combined under Beria. Moreover, Malenkov could not depend on the party organization; there was another man high in the party's councils who was the only member of the new Presidium engaged in full-time party work and (besides Malenkov) the only one also a member of the Secretariat—Nikita Khrushchev. It would prove of some significance that Khrushchev was the man whose position corresponded most clearly with that of Stalin in 1924.

Ultimately, the key to any Soviet succession was the "circular flow of power." With his powers of appointment and the apparatus of the central Secretariat, a Soviet leader controlled the selection of party secretaries at the provincial and district levels. Through them he could manipulate the nominally democratic committee and conference structure of the party at the local level. From this power base, he stage-managed the national party congresses and secured the automatic and unanimous approval of the Central Committee slate he had chosen. The configuration of this slate of prospective members was carefully arranged according to what Gorbachev called the "schedule of allocations"—a set of secret rules according to which Central Committee seats were allotted to the various functional components of the country's bureaucracy in accordance with their importance.[1] Thus, in time, a general secretary could control the whole circuit of power within the system and dictate the composition of the Central Committee, which in turn would confirm him in office as general secretary. This was the system created by Stalin in the course of his rise to power in the 1920s and reapplied each time the succession to the top Soviet post opened up.

Khrushchev's path to supreme power through his control of the Secretariat of the Communist Party was practically the same as that laid out by Stalin in the 1920s when he made the office of general secretary the jumping-off point for dictatorship. When Khrushchev relinquished his post as first secretary of Moscow Province on 13 March 1953 to replace Georgi Malenkov as first secretary of the entire CPSU, he inherited a central and local apparatus of secretaries that was largely the creature of Stalin and Malenkov. No doubt the central Secretariat was entrusted to Khrushchev because he was the man least feared by his colleagues in the party Presidium. To achieve personal control over the party, he faced the daunting task of rebuilding the entire apparatus with new men loyal to him.

The first step Khrushchev had to take toward this end was to get a firm grip on the central Secretariat, through which appointments to the provinces were made. He had to contend with a Secretariat of four members apart from himself: Mikhail Suslov, Pyotr Pospelov, Semyon Ignatiev, and Nikolai Shatalin, a group emerging from a behind-the-scenes reshuffle that eliminated all of Stalin's nine cosecretaries except Suslov and Khrushchev himself. Suslov was often credited by outside observers with substantial influence, perhaps even as the leader of a neo-Stalinist faction. His actual career, however, suggests that he was either a close supporter of Khrushchev or a relatively powerless agitprop specialist who survived in high office because he served his function well and constituted no threat. The same could be said of Pospelov, also an ideological specialist. Of the other two, perhaps more potent colleagues of Khrushchev, Ignatiev as former minister of internal affairs was implicated in the "Doctors' Plot" hoax and transferred to the provinces, as was Shatalin two years later.

By 1955, Khrushchev had dismantled the Secretariat as a top-level party collegium. He kept its lower professional staff, under his close personal control, as the instrument he needed to intervene in the provincial party organizations and reshuffle their personnel to guarantee his own ambitions. Then he could start reconstituting the collegium of top secretaries on his own terms, leaving all of the secretaries outside the party Presidium except himself and Suslov. This substantial separation of the two bodies no doubt helped Khrushchev assert his individual control over the party organization, while policy matters continued to be handled by the collective leadership. Here was the pattern of Stalin's rise all over again.

Khrushchev's first opportunity to establish personal power over the provinces came in the wake of Beria's fall in June 1953. That surprise was actually heralded by the ouster of the Ukrainian first secretary Leonid Melnikov earlier the same month. During the following eight months, the party leadership in Kazakhstan and the three republics of the Caucasus was completely overhauled. While Kazakhstan entered into a period of chronic instability, the new leadership in the Caucasus proved quite acceptable to Khrushchev, so much so in Georgia that the first secretary appointed in September 1953, V. P. Mzhavanadze, remained in office throughout the Khrushchev era. S. A.

Tovmasian, appointed Armenia's first secretary in December 1953, held the job to 1961, and the Azerbaidzanian I. D. Mustafaev held his first secretaryship from March 1954 until 1959. The Ukraine, under A. I. Kirichenko from June 1953 to December 1957, appears to have been made solid for Khrushchev, and neighboring Moldavia was brought into line early in 1954 under the new first secretary, Z. T. Serdiuk.

Late in 1953 Khrushchev made his first important move in the Russian Republic by ousting the first secretary of Leningrad Province, V. M. Andrianov. Andrianov's removal from Leningrad (followed by his utter disappearance and possible death) was regarded as a crucial early defeat for Malenkov that portended the direction of Soviet politics. The successor in Leningrad proved to be a key man in the Khrushchev era—he was Frol Kozlov, Andrianov's second secretary, who took over the province for the next four years until his move up into the central leadership.

Quickly following up his Leningrad victory, Khrushchev turned his attention to the other provinces of the Russian Republic. The task of winning control was a formidable one, as he faced fifty-one provincial and territorial secretaries (not counting Moscow and Leningrad), together with the twelve secretaries of the autonomous republics in the RSFSR. Khrushchev's approach was to deal with one large region at a time. He started with the provinces west and south of Moscow where his favorite issue, agriculture, was most relevant. Between December 1953 and February 1954, he cleaned out five secretaries from this region as well as a scattering of others. At the same time, to weaken other provincial secretaries in the central agricultural region, five new provinces (plus Magadan in the far east) were carved out of existing ones and put under Khrushchev appointees.

The efficacy of Khrushchev's demotions was attested by the fact that sixteen members of the Central Committee (besides the deceased Beria) failed to be nominated for the Supreme Soviet in March 1954. It could only be presumed that these people—mostly fallen secretaries—lost their voices in the Central Committee when they lost the jobs that entailed Central Committee rank.

Khrushchev's next step came in his own former territory, Moscow Province. When he became national first secretary, Moscow was given to the former Presidium and Secretariat member N. A. Mikhailov, presumably a Malenkov man. Khrushchev found a counterweight to Mikhailov in the Moscow City organization of the party, headed since 1952 by I. V. Kapitonov with Yekaterina Furtseva as his second secretary. In January 1954, Khrushchev moved Kapitonov over to be second secretary of the whole province, under Mikhailov, with Mme. Furtseva succeeding to the city leadership. Mikhailov was caught between the central Secretariat above and Khrushchev's man below, and in two months he was out—relegated, as was often the practice, to an ambassadorial post (in this instance, to Poland). Kapitonov took over the provincial first secretaryship and served to 1959.

The secretarial changes of early 1954 were evidently all that Khrushchev needed to tip the balance against Malenkov in the party organization. For the next year and a half, while he manipulated the industrialization issue to force Malenkov's resignation as prime minister and for some months thereafter, Khrushchev was quite circumspect with the party organizations. Most of his few changes of provincial secretaries in this period involved promotion of the incumbent to some more responsible position. But in the fall of 1955, with a remodeled Secretariat preparing for the Twentieth Party Congress, Khrushchev moved boldly on a broad front. In the space of five months (from October 1955 to February 1956), he summarily removed a dozen provincial secretaries, mostly in the north of European Russia but including the key positions of Gorky, Stalingrad, and Sverdlovsk. Ten other provinces were secured by new Khrushchev appointees in this period when the incumbent secretaries were transferred to other jobs. In either case, the replacements were typically the second secretaries of the respective provinces. However, five Russian provinces were put under men promoted from the Ukraine.

When the Twentieth Congress opened, Khrushchev's score in the provincial secretaryships filled by his appointees was impressive—thirty-eight out of the original fifty-three provinces and territories in the RSFSR, plus seven new provinces. The remaining fifteen were either in the periphery of the country or in areas of lesser importance whose secretaries held only candidate rank in the Central Committee. The provincial secretaries, of course, were the men who controlled the selection of provincial delegates to the congress and were first in line themselves for election to the new Central Committee afterward. They gave Khrushchev the power base from which to launch the issue of de-Stalinization against his rivals of the erstwhile collective leadership and finally to provoke them into a battle that they could not win.

The changes in the Central Committee voted at the Twentieth Congress testify to the extent Khrushchev had already transformed the Soviet leadership. Of the 125 members of Stalin's last Central Committee, only 80 were reelected (plus Marshal Georgi Zhukov, who had been a member since July 1953). Five members had died since 1952; 6 were demoted to candidate status or to the Central Auditing Commission. The balance—34 men—were dropped outright: 10 governmental figures and 24 from the party apparatus, reflecting the house-cleaning that Khrushchev had accomplished. Among the union republic 6 first secretaries were gone, as were 15 secretaries of Russian provinces along with 3 officials of the central apparatus.

In the new Central Committee of 1956 (expanded by 8 to a total of 133) there were 52 seats to be filled, with the lion's share going to the party apparatus to replace the gaps in its representation. Thirty-six members of the new Central Committee were altogether new to the top leadership—12 rising officials of the central and republic governments and 24 party secretaries. Of the 41 places on the Central Committee occupied by provincial secretaries from the RSFSR, 20 were filled by new men. Turnover between 1952 and 1956 was even heavier among the 110 old candidate members of the Central Committee, of whom 7 were demoted to the Central Auditing Commission and 45 dropped altogether. Sixty-eight new candidates were designated, heavily representing Khrushchev's appointments to provincial secretaryships and the union republics.

Despite the change he had brought about in the Central Committee at the Twentieth Congress, Khrushchev chose to leave his rivals in the party Presidium unchallenged for the time being. The Secretariat was expanded from six to eight, with the inclusion of Leonid Brezhnev and Moscow City boss Furtseva. At the same time, a new body was created to function as the party executive for the Russian Republic—the Bureau of the Central Committee for Affairs of the RSFSR. Khrushchev himself took the nominal chairmanship of this group, with Nikolai Beliaev in day-to-day charge as deputy chairman. Every member of the new Secretariat was either a member or candidate member of the Presidium or a member of the Bureau for the RSFSR.

After the Twentieth Congress, as his contest with Malenkov and Molotov was coming to a head, Khrushchev had a firm base among the provincial secretaries of the RSFSR. Now, for the first time since early 1954, he turned his attention back to the minority republics, with emphasis on replacement of second secretaries: Five of them (in the Baltic republics, Belorussia, and Georgia), along with First Secretary B. G. Gafurov of Tadzhikistan, were eased out into government posts between July and December of 1956. Next came the autonomous republics within the RSFSR, whose leaders Khrushchev had so far left untouched. During the first half of 1957 he transferred or ousted the first secretaries of seven out of these twelve jurisdictions, mainly in the middle Volga region.

The story of the crisis of the "Anti-Party Group" in 1957 needs no elaboration here. Khrushchev was challenged by a majority of the Presidium, but he crushed them in the nutcracker formed by the Secretariat and the Central Committee. The opposition's Presidium seats were given over to members of

Khrushchev's Secretariat. (Only one of the latter—Dmitri Shepilov—had involved himself in the plot; he lost his membership to the old theoretician Otto Kuusinen.) After June 1957, every one of the eight members of the Secretariat was also a member of the Presidium (except the propagandist Pospelov, who became a candidate member). The secretaries now constituted almost an absolute majority of the fifteen-member Presidium. Secretarial dominance of the party leadership was completed in December of the same year when Khrushchev appointed two of the remaining members of the Presidium (Kirichenko and N. G. Ignatov) to serve in the Secretariat as well and brought the Uzbek leader Dinmukhadin Mukhitdinov into both bodies. The Presidium, with ten of its fifteen members simultaneously constituting the Secretariat, became nothing but an enlarged sounding board. The Secretariat was Khrushchev's core executive body for all political affairs, and so it remained until the course of events began to turn against him in 1960.

From the summer of 1957 to the fall of 1959, the Communist Party structure was unusually stable. Khrushchev was evidently riding high, and his support seemed as assured as Stalin's was by the early 1930s. Cumulative changes in the apparatus, to be sure, were considerable: By the middle of 1959, twenty-eight out of the sixty-one RSFSR provincial secretaries in office at the time of the Twentieth Congress had been transferred or dropped (including eight of the fifteen holdovers from Stalin's time). Continuing shifts of late 1959 and early 1960 brought the total of secretarial changes since the Twentieth Congress to more than half the provinces.

The first sign of new friction in the party leadership came in the second half of 1959, after an accumulation of issues—including the China problem, the ill-conceived educational reform, and the failure of the Virgin Lands program—had opened Khrushchev to serious challenge. Khrushchev struck the first blow at his own foundation by making a scapegoat of Beliaev, who had been serving as Kazakhstan secretary as well as a member of the central Secretariat. But Beliaev's demotion to Stavropol Territory in November 1959 was closely followed in January 1960 by the transfer of Kirichenko from the central Secretariat to Rostov Province. (Both men were dropped altogether the following summer.) Meanwhile, between July 1959 and February 1960, two other republic first secretaries (I. D. Mustafaev, in Azerbaidzhan since 1954, and Ya. E. Kalnberzins, in Latvia ever since 1940) were eased out, and six second secretaries (Azerbaidzhan, Uzbekistan, Kirgizia, Latvia, and two Armenians in succession) were replaced. Evidently the neo-Stalinists—Brezhnev, Suslov, and Kozlov—had broken into the circular flow of power and taken control of appointments away from Khrushchev. From that time on, Khrushchev's enemies steadily tightened their control over the party apparatus, while leaving him to flounder at the policy level. This disruption of the "circular flow" perhaps explains some of the erratic behavior and "harebrained schemes" of Khrushchev's later years, as he tried to outmaneuver the neo-Stalinist opposition in a system over which he had lost ultimate control.

In May 1960, coincident with the U-2 spy plane incident, a number of cryptic changes were made in the top party leadership that can be read in retrospect very much in the way Robert Conquest speculated at the time, as a rising political tide against Khrushchev.[2] The central Secretariat was reduced by half, and the Bureau for the Russian Republic was completely divorced from it. Only five of the old Secretariat members continued—Khrushchev, Suslov, Brezhnev (soon to be eased out), Kuusinen, and Mukhitdinov—all members of the Presidium. Frol Kozlov, the rising star, was added to both the Secretariat and the Presidium. The secretaries now constituted altogether only five out of the fifteen members of the Presidium, which was thus restored as a distinct policy-making body in its own right. Of the seven ex-secretaries, five were relegated to government posts, and two (Kirichenko and Beliaev) were consigned to political oblivion.

　　With a new balance of forces at the top of the party, the most sweeping reshuffle of personnel since Stalin's time commenced in the winter of 1960–61. Between October and April no fewer than twenty Russian provinces and two autonomous republics got new secretaries, mostly through demotion of the incumbent. The first secretaries of Armenia, Tadzhikistan, Kirgizia, and Moldavia were replaced. Within the Ukraine, nearly half the provincial secretaries were changed. The losers both in the RSFSR and in the union republics were by and large Khrushchev's early appointees of the 1953–56 period. By the spring of 1961, all but four of the provincial secretaries whom Khrushchev had installed between 1953 and 1956 had been transferred or demoted. (Something of a landmark was passed when, just before the Twenty-second Congress, the last of Stalin's provincial secretaries, in Kaluga and Penza, were removed from their long-held jobs. Stalin appointees still held office in Estonia, Lithuania, and Daghestan.)

　　Khrushchev's emerging weakness was confirmed by the reshuffling of the Central Committee at the Twenty-second Party Congress in October 1961. The body was expanded by 42, to 175 full members. Fifty-five old members were ousted; 3 were demoted to candidate, and 7 had died. A total of 107 of the new committee members were new people or else promoted from candidate rank. Considering the 71 party officials in the old Central Committee, only 32 remained in party jobs at this rank, while 55 new party secretaries were brought into the new Central Committee. Twenty-eight of the 40 secretaries from the Russian Republic were new. The Ukrainian contingent was sharply increased, as 11 of Nikolai Podgorny's lieutenants in Kiev and the provinces were promoted to Central Committee rank. Another notable shift was the increase in military representation from 6 to 13. The ranks of the 122 former candidate members were even more drastically shuffled: 26 promoted to full member and only 31 retained in candidate status (plus 3 members demoted and 3 brought up from the Central Auditing Commission; 8 had died, and 57 were dropped). With an expansion to a total of 155, there was room for 114 brand-new candidate members.

Dramatic changes also occurred in the central Secretariat following the Twenty-second Congress. Khrushchev's appointee Mukhitdinov was dropped, and five new men were added: the former state security chief Alexander Shelepin, the agitprop man Leonid Ilyichev, Boris Ponomarev for international Communist affairs, and the Moscow City and Leningrad Province secretaries (P. N. Demichev and I. V. Spiridonov). It may be presumed that the forces opposing Khrushchev held their ground in the Secretariat and were only awaiting the opportunity to attack his power head-on.

If this were the case, the sweeping reorganization of the party structure announced by Khrushchev just a year later, in November 1962, makes sense politically even if it seems like madness administratively. The partition of most of the Russian provincial party organizations into urban and rural branches with separate secretaries seems to have provided Khrushchev with a device for breaking into the power structure again and building a new cadre of his own men. Conceivably the move staved off his eventual fall. Clearly it was disliked by his opponents. It was one of the first of his policies to be condemned and reversed after his overthrow, when most of the pre-1962 secretaries were restored to full control over their respective provinces.

Admittedly the propositions developed here about Khrushchev's political decline are inferential and tentative. Yet there are the hard facts of secretarial appointment and demotion, which were real manifestations of politics in the central structure of Soviet power. This information makes it hard to sustain an image of smooth monolithic routine. Much more consistent with this evidence is the "conflict model" of Soviet politics—and in particular, a pattern of conflict that extended far back into the years of Khrushchev's presumed dominance. Khrushchev, it appears, was defeated by the same tactics of secretarial appointment and demotion that brought him to the top leadership in the first place.

CHAPTER 25

Khrushchev and the Intelligentsia

U p to the 1980s, experience, institutions, and culture all conspired to lock the political life of the Soviet Union in a vise of postrevolutionary despotism. Yet major developments had transpired in Soviet society that by fits and starts activated contrary elements of the Russian tradition. These forces were embodied above all in the Russian intelligentsia, the representatives, if you will, of Edward Keenan's turn-of-the-century Westernizing "aberration."[1]

In Russia, prerevolutionary and postrevolutionary alike, the intelligentsia was the key to reform. It was the principal constituency for reform under Khrushchev, though neither the leader nor the class had the staying power to carry fundamental changes through successfully in that era. Later on, underlying the transition from Brezhnev to Gorbachev, the intelligentsia emerged more strongly as the decisive social force on the side of reform. In alliance with the country's political leadership it held the potential for effecting an epochal new turn in Russia's cultural and institutional foundations.

For more than two centuries, the intelligentsia and the Russian state coexisted in an uneasy relationship with one another. The state feared the intelligentsia and repressed it, but at the same time needed it and had to cultivate it. As the embodiment of the national conscience and national progress, the intelligentsia represented a commitment to ideas and cultural creation that perpetuated itself despite all kinds of national upheavals and disasters. "We have dedicated ourselves to a cause, but without hope," wrote Alexander Herzen. "The day of action may still be far off: The day of conscience, of thought, of speech has already dawned."[2] The intelligentsia defied the state, though its powers were sadly inferior; nevertheless, it was always the source of political change in Russia. "No single cause," said the emigré physicist and publisher Valery Chalidze, "can explain the tragic course of Russian history for the last two centuries, but the hostility, the lack of mutual understanding, between the state and the intelligentsia was surely a significant factor. Elimination of this conflict is absolutely necessary for Russia's health in the future."[3]

Historically, the intelligentsia came into being as the embodiment of Western influence—the scientific, literary, and political currents that shaped the mind of the educated class in Russia from the time of Peter the Great. Its members acquired distinctive prestige vis-à-vis both government and populace because until the late nineteenth century there was no commercial bourgeoisie to speak of to compete with them for influence—a condition to which Russia was returned after the revolution. In Russia the intelligentsia was the only source of articulate national leadership outside of the state power itself. "The intellectuals, the creative segment of the intelligentsia," according to the emigré sociologist Vladimir Shlapentokh, were "the principal group that resists the mythological activity of the political elite."[4] In Boris Shragin's words, "The Russian intellectual is a sighted person among the blind."[5]

The term *intelligentsia* requires some refinement. In prerevolutionary Russia, it connoted that distinctive social stratum that lived by ideas, whether as the creators or the audience. Soviet usage extended it to the entire white-collar class: "Those who earn their living without manual labor," in the words of the American literary observer Kathryn Feuer.[6] One May Day slogan counted the intelligentsia among the three constituent elements of Soviet society: "Hail to the indestructible alliance of the working class, the collective farm peasantry, and the people's intelligentsia."[7] In this diluted sense the intelligentsia or *sluzhashchie* ("employees," that is, white-collar workers) included many millions of families in the social pyramid (one-fourth of the entire labor force, Brezhnev reported in 1981[8]).

Conceived in these broad terms, the Soviet intelligentsia embraced a variety of disparate social elements, ranging from the privileged bureaucracy of nomenklatura rank through the various managerial and professional specialties of the technical intelligentsia to the vast army of clerical personnel serving all the branches of the administrative and economic apparatus. Up and down the hierarchy, the key to status and personal success was education.

Standing aside from this pyramid, much as it did in tsarist times, was the creative intelligentsia, embracing scientists, writers, artists, and those few people in the realm of history, philosophy, and social science who exhibited sufficient independence to warrant classification with this group rather than with the functionaries of the regime. To quote Feuer again, this was the class of "library habitués."[9]

Could the creative intelligentsia act as a social force? Certainly it always enjoyed special influence in Russia, whatever its deficiencies of strength or independence. The intelligentsia was like a church, wielding not the power of guns or money but the power of belief, truth, and argument. The Communist authorities clearly recognized this power in their efforts to control the thinkers and writers. As Solzhenitsyn put it, "The Soviet regime could certainly have been breached only by literature. The regime has been reinforced with concrete to such an extent that neither a military coup nor a political organization nor a picket line of strikers can knock it over or run it through. Only the solitary writer would be able to do this."[10]

When the opportunity for postrevolutionary reform finally came, it was the creative intelligentsia alone of all the elements of Soviet society that had the interest and the awareness to become the lead force in pressing for fundamental change. But it was a thin and delicate social stratum, hamstrung by political pressures and the lack of free access to its potential mass audience. The rigors of the decades of repression and official mendacity under Stalin had left the creative intelligentsia in a crippled and demoralized state, particularly so in history, social science, and speculative thought. Natural science, shielded by its own internal rigor, had suffered less, though the shadow of Lysenkoism in genetics loomed large. Under Soviet conditions, critical minds always found a safer haven in the natural sciences, and it is no accident that dissidents of the stature of Andrei Sakharov, Alexander Solzhenitsyn, and the Medvedev brothers should have emerged from the scientific or mathematical milieu. It was the field of literature, however, that by tradition and by its own irrepressible dynamism stood out as the source of reformist energy while reform was still a possibility, and of political dissent when a new freeze followed the years of the Thaw.

If the critical intelligentsia was the social embodiment of the push for postrevolutionary reform, its natural adversary was the bureaucracy of the party and state nomenklatura together with its careerist hangers-on in the intellectual professions. Presiding over the postrevolutionary social order, the party bureaucracy had a vested interest in the system of controls that both necessitated and sustained its own role in the system. There was a natural tension between this ruling class of political controllers and all those who attempted to contribute to society through their personal creativity or expertise. Just as naturally as the critical intelligentsia was the force behind post-Stalin reform, the party bureaucracy was the sustainer of the unreformed status quo.

The notion of a bureaucratic-managerial-intelligentsia ruling class has not satisfied those who note how the Soviet intelligentsia, or its greater part, labored under the oppressive external authority of the party apparatus. Clearly there were two branches of this class in the political respect, a smaller one with the power and a much larger one with its specialized functions. This division corresponds to Svetozar Stojanović's distinction between the "ruling class" and the "dominant class," with its application to capitalist as well as socialist societies.[11] In the Soviet instance, the ruling class was the party-controlled nomenklatura, while the dominant class, exercising a nonpolitical *egemonia* of values and work style, was the intelligentsia in its various ramifications.

There was cultural as well as functional tension between the classes: The ruling class that was carried over from Stalinism, the nomenklatura, with its typically worker-peasant origins, inherited the cultural veneer of the revolutionary quasi-intelligentsia but remained profoundly hostile to the dominant class of the trained and the creative. It embodied old, revived Russian political culture, set against the tradition of Westernization sustained in the dominant class of intelligentsia. At the same time, the ruling class was the repository of official ideology, the false consciousness legitimizing both the rule of the party and the social dominance of the intelligentsia.

The contest between ruling and dominant classes was not altogether unequal, though it was quite asymmetrical. Faced with the coercive power of the party-state, the police, and the censorship, the intelligentsia had the power of numbers and of indispensability. Through ordeals of war, revolution, and purge, the intelligentsia maintained and transmitted its traditions, both through the family and through formal education. The question for reformers was whether Soviet society had reached that stage in its development where the dominant class could shape or replace the ruling class to an extent that might give the country a regime more consonant with its own true needs and resources.

Under Stalin, beneath the cover of Marxist-Leninist language, the revolutionary intelligentsia was crushed and humiliated in the mid-1930s as much as the bourgeois intelligentsia had been in 1918–21 and 1929–32. Then came the physical decimation of much of the country's intellectual as well as political leadership in Stalin's purges. The creative intelligentsia as a group was crippled by the rigors that Stalinism required for its self-justification, even apart from the absurd personal glorification on which Stalin insisted more and more as the years went by. "We all have a dogmatist sitting inside," the Soviet novelist Chinghiz Aitmatov wrote. "We have all suffered a 'concussion' of the Stalinist epoch to a certain extent, weaned from thinking and acting without permission from above."[12]

The technical intelligentsia did not do badly under Stalin, with the in-fusion of hundreds of thousands of new Soviet-trained managers and engi-neers whose interests were legitimated by the rejection of egalitarianism and the abandonment of proletarian class preferences in political life and educa-tion. Meanwhile, the purged governing class, renovated with new recruits from the working class and peasantry, absorbed the Old Russian political culture of secretiveness, authoritarianism, nativism, and anti-intellectualism. Stalin had achieved what his tsarist predecessors had only wished for—a class of special-ists embodying Western technology, without the creative and hence threatening thought that Western contacts had always encouraged.

This state of affairs could not go on indefinitely, as modernization turned the Soviet Union into a more sophisticated and aspiring society and as the un-derground roots of the intelligentsia began to flow with life again. There was an unresolved contradiction in the abnormal disparity between Soviet ideology and reality, between the postrevolutionary regime and its revolutionary origins. By the time of Stalin's death, the progress of modernization had made the So-viet Union ripe for fundamental reform. Thereafter, the main social force natu-rally aligned with the cause of reform was the intelligentsia.

Reform remained unthinkable as long as Stalin lived, but his death immedi-ately opened the door to Russia's overdue return to the spirit of the democratic revolution. Yet, given the pervasiveness of the control apparatus inherited from Stalin and the practical weakness of the elements supporting change, the ques-tion of whether reform would be implemented or stifled still depended on the politics of high leadership and the whims and tactics of those who aspired to inherit Stalin's power.

The impetus to reform showed itself immediately upon Stalin's death, fol-lowing his successors' affirmation of collective leadership, curbs on terror tac-tics, and economic concessions to consumers and farmers. In intellectual life, with "a great burst of renewal," to quote the French scholar Isabelle Esmein, writers themselves quickly staked out their claims to creative freedom as the sine qua non of a cultural revival.[13] This was in fact the "Thaw," the dramatic unfreezing in the cultural climate so termed from Ilya Ehrenburg's mediocre but timely new novel by that title.[14]

At the outset, there was no particular association of the cultural Thaw with the personage of Khrushchev. If anyone stood out as an early supporter of cul-tural renovation, it was Malenkov, during the two years of his tenure as chair-man of the Council of Ministers. This was sensed by Soviet intellectuals, who even found support for the reform line in Malenkov's report at the last party congress under Stalin, when he had called upon literature and art to "burn away everything that is undesirable, rotten and moribund, everything that retards our progress."[15] Robert Conquest concluded, in his intensive study of the politics of the succession, "We can with great probability link Malenkov with a tentative patronage of the Thaw tendency."[16]

Initially, as he maneuvered for power against Malenkov, Khrushchev took the conservative position on all issues, in cultural matters as well as economics and foreign policy. One of the earliest signs of Malenkov's slippage was the August 1954 meeting of the presidium of the Writers' Union, where the liberal journal *Novyi mir* (New World) was censured for deficient ideological content and its editor Aleksandr Tvardovsky removed.[17] The long-heralded Second Congress of Soviet Writers in December 1954 (a full twenty years after the first) affirmed this temporary conservative reaction with a sharp attack on Ehrenburg's alleged political deficiencies (though, in a gesture of balance, Tvardovsky was elected to the presidium of the congress).[18]

By the beginning of 1955, Khrushchev was strong enough to challenge Malenkov directly and force him to relinquish the chairmanship of the Council of Ministers to Nikolai Bulganin. With this success behind him, Khrushchev co-opted the liberal position on all the issues, foreign and domestic, that he had used against Malenkov, and proceeded with the groundwork for the spectacular Twentieth Congress scheduled for February 1956. It would appear that Khrushchev was capable of adopting and discarding issues for reasons of simple political expedience, recalling what Bukharin said of Stalin many years before, "He changes his theory according to whom he needs to get rid of."[19] This trait was to appear again when Khrushchev came under political siege by the neo-Stalinist opposition in the early 1960s. But for the moment, it is significant that he found it expedient to embrace reform, whether for its long-run contribution to Russia's future development or simply as a device to provoke the rest of his old Stalinist rivals in the Politburo to show their hand and submit to a test of strength with him.

The intelligentsia did not figure prominently as an issue at the Twentieth Congress, marked as it was by the sensational political issues of peaceful coexistence, the cult of personality, and the rehabilitation of some of the victims of Stalin's purges. In his day-long public report to the congress, Khrushchev devoted only a very brief section to intellectual life, with the commonplace observation, "Our literature and art still lag far behind life, behind Soviet reality." Straddling the line between liberalism and conservatism, he warned, "The Party has fought and will continue to fight against untruthful representation of Soviet reality, against attempts to varnish it or, on the contrary, to scoff at and discredit what the Soviet people have achieved."[20] The dismal intellectual heritage of Stalinism was more directly addressed by Mikoyan in the speech that presaged Khrushchev's own Secret Speech, lamenting theories that were "lagging behind life," and "the atmosphere that surrounded scientific and ideological work."[21] Even Mikhail Sholokov, the one well-known writer to be tapped for an address to the congress and scarcely noted for his liberalism, attacked the secretary of the Writers' Union and supported the complaints of Khrushchev and Mikoyan: "Our prose has been in a disastrous state in recent years."[22]

While cultural issues remained marginal at the congress itself, the impact of the de-Stalinization campaign on intellectual life was electrifying. Ordinary Soviet citizens believed their country had taken a quantum leap toward freedom. In the literary world, Edith Frankel commented, "It was a period of extraordinary vitality. Great hopes had been inspired by the Twentieth Congress and were nurtured in the ensuing months by rehabilitations and other liberalizing measures. It was a time for pulling manuscripts out of the drawer and for sitting down and writing what might have been unthinkable only months before."[23] Wrote Solzhenitsyn, "We began to emerge from the black, bottomless waters and much sooner than I had expected, to emerge in our own lifetime."[24]

In the months immediately following the Twentieth Congress, the new mood of intellectual liberation had strong official encouragement. The journal *Voprosy filosofii* (Problems of Philosophy), to cite one striking example, harked back to the famous 1925 Central Committee resolution against party dictation of literary forms, denounced "the transformation of individuals' opinions into guiding ideas," and affirmed the principles of "free competition" and "self-government" in the arts.[25] Writers rushed to bring out a flood of new works, new journals, and new translations, including Vladimir Dudintsev's controversial novel *Not by Bread Alone,* which stirred both liberal and conservative passions with its realistic tale of a Soviet inventor's tribulations at the hands of the bureaucracy.[26]

Despite the excitement of de-Stalinization, neither Khrushchev's political leadership nor the spirit of liberalization in intellectual life were at all assured. The Stalinist hard-liners still resisted the trend, while Khrushchev compromised and maneuvered until the contest came to a head in the crisis of June 1957. After he prevailed against the Stalinists' attempt to unseat him and removed the "Anti-Party Group" of Molotov, Malenkov, and Kaganovich, and "Shepilov who joined them," from all their positions of power, the political climate surrounding Soviet intellectual life began to warm once again. From this point on, with minor ups and downs (notably the furor over Boris Pasternak's

Nobel Prize), conditions gradually improved as long as Khrushchev was in the political ascendancy.

One milestone was the reinstatement of Tvardovsky as editor of *Novyi mir* in July 1958. Then he was designated to speak at the Twenty-first Party Congress (late January and early February 1959). Tvardovsky's speech, condemning the sterility of much contemporary writing and extolling the individuality not only of the author but of the reader as well, was perhaps the supreme document of the era of the Thaw in Soviet intellectual life. He even chided the Komsomol boss (and later KGB chief) Vladimir Semichastny, a notorious Stalinoid: "Perhaps, upon hearing the partiality with which I speak of Soviet readers' private libraries, Comrade Semichastny, who delivered a fine speech here, will accuse me of advocating private property and will place the words 'my book,' 'my library,' in the same bracket as 'my car,' 'my country cottage.' But I am prepared to affirm that we can enter communism confidently and unafraid with this particular 'survival' form of property (laughter, applause.)"[27]

The years 1959 to 1962 were, relatively speaking, a golden age in Soviet intellectual life. Khrushchev himself appeared at the Third Writers' Congress in May 1959, to set the tone of intellectual détente and to oust the conservative Aleksei Surkov as secretary of the Writers' Union.[28] Tvardovsky's star continued to rise; at the Twenty-second Congress in 1961, he was not only selected again as a speaker but elected a candidate member of the Central Committee of the party. Meanwhile, remarkable works saw the light of day. Ehrenburg's memoirs, published in *Novyi mir* beginning in August 1960, were likened in the West to Khrushchev's Secret Speech as a revelation of the cultural crimes of Stalinism.[29] Evgeny Yevtushenko's memorable attack on anti-Semitism, "Babi Yar," appeared in the very official *Literaturnaya gazeta* shortly before the Twenty-second Congress.[30] A year later came the most sensational publishing event of the whole era of the Thaw, the appearance in *Novyi mir,* with Khrushchev's personal imprimatur, of Solzhenitsyn's exposé of prison camp life, *One Day in the Life of Ivan Denisovich.*

Perhaps Khrushchev intended this step as a blow against the neo-Stalinists in the party leadership.[31] Still, it was not enough to keep the political ground from shifting under his feet. The era of the Thaw and the whole opportunity for lasting reform in Soviet political and intellectual life were rapidly coming to a disappointing and dispiriting end.

The real question about the Khrushchev era is not why reform was attempted but why it failed. Of Khrushchev, the poet Andrei Voznesenky recalled, "I could not understand how one person could combine both the good hopes of the 1960s, the mighty sweep of transformations, with the impediments of old thinking."[32] From the time of his ascendancy in 1955, Khrushchev set himself against the historical anachronism of Stalinism as he endeavored to revive the early revolutionary spirit and repudiate Stalin's personal despotism. However, he was cautious and inconsistent in recognizing the intelligentsia as the key force for change, though it was responding to the Thaw with enthusiasm and renewed creativity.

For all his passion to attack Stalin and loosen old strictures on the intelligentsia, Khrushchev did not succeed or even attempt to bring about fundamental change in the Soviet power structure. The intelligentsia remained at the mercy of the political leadership and the shifting winds of factional struggle. The decisive social force continued to be the conservative bureaucracy.

Unfortunately for the immediate prospects of reform, the bureaucratic leadership was relatively youthful, having started to climb the ladder of power only after the purges of the 1930s had eliminated most of the older generation of Communists who stood in the way. Whereas de-Stalinization came from older top-level associates of Stalin—from Malenkov tentatively and more emphatically from Khrushchev and Mikoyan—their younger colleagues of the generation of Suslov, Kozlov, Kosygin, and Brezhnev, all born after 1900, were the immediate beneficiaries of Stalin and Stalinism. Their worker-peasant backgrounds and narrow education had made these neo-Stalinist representatives of Michal Reiman's "plebian revolution" a ready chorus for Stalin's anti-intellectualism.[33] They had little interest in changing the rules of the game while they looked forward to many more years growing old in office.

Once Khrushchev's reformist leadership faltered and the younger representatives of the Stalinist bureaucracy took over, the cause of reform was doomed for another generation. Against the nomenklatura and its physical arms, the police and the censorship, the intelligentsia was helpless to put up direct resistance. Its members could only turn—that is, the bolder and more alienated among them—to the equivalent of intellectual guerrilla warfare. This was the origin of the dissident movement, in all its varied currents, that marked the Soviet scene after Khrushchev's fall.

In retrospect, it is clear that Khrushchev never enjoyed the degree of personal dominance that outside observers credited him with after 1957. He always had to contend with conservatives in the party leadership, even including younger people whom he had initially promoted himself. His policies in cultural matters were always conditioned by these circumstances, though not in any consistent direction. At times, he took the liberal line to provoke or embarrass the conservatives, and at other points he tried to appease them with affirmations of the party's guiding role. He reportedly told the Central Committee in November 1962, "I favor greater freedom of expression, since the level we have achieved in the economy and technology demands this. But some of my colleagues in the Presidium think we must be cautious. Obviously we shall have to wait a while before going ahead any further."[34]

Pressure from the neo-Stalinists led by Suslov and Kozlov, as early as 1959–60, may well account for some of Khrushchev's "harebrained schemes" and his abrupt shift to a confrontational foreign policy after the U-2 Affair of May 1960. In cultural matters, however, he found it possible and expedient to hold the liberal course against his opponents, until the shattering events that commenced in December 1962.

The U-2 Affair of Soviet intellectual life was the exhibit of contemporary painting that opened in Moscow's Manezh gallery (the former imperial riding hall just off Red Square) on 1 December 1962. Khrushchev, still smarting from the embarrassment of the Cuban missile crisis, toured the show and launched into a vulgar tirade against the abstractionist paintings that had been included (for the first time since the rise of Stalin). "This is just a mess. . . . Judging by these experiments, I am entitled to think that you are pederasts, and for that you can get ten years. . . . Gentlemen, we are declaring war on you."[35] What followed, in the press and in top-level meetings of the leadership and the intellectuals, was a torrent of denunciation of liberal heresy in all the arts, including many of the works just recently published with official sanction. The chorus of neo-Stalinist orthodoxy hit a crescendo for the time being when Khrushchev addressed a major conference of intellectuals in March 1963. Now he ostentatiously called a halt to de-Stalinization and turned sharply against those writers, notably Ehrenburg and Yevtushenko, whom he had been supporting in their revelations of past evils. "The press, radio, literature, painting, music, the cinema, and the theater are a sharp ideological weapon of our party," Khrushchev affirmed in best Zhdanovite style. "The party will not allow anyone to blunt this weapon or weaken its effect."[36]

Despite these alarming signals, one more reprieve awaited the liberal intelligentsia. In mid-April 1963, Second Secretary Frol Kozlov suffered a heart attack that removed him from political life and ultimately proved fatal. Relieved of pressure from the conservatives for the moment, Khrushchev reversed himself once again in cultural policy as in foreign policy, and liberal views were allowed to compete with the orthodox for a few months more. Tvardovsky actually campaigned to get Solzhenitsyn the Lenin Prize, though this went beyond what Khrushchev was willing or able to carry through. When the party vetoed the award, Tvardovsky spoke to Solzhenitsyn in German to break the bad news: "Das ist alle. Ich sterbe." Solzhenitsyn took this as the beginning of the end for "The Man" Khrushchev.[37]

Thereafter, the neo-Stalinist conspiracy against Khrushchev rapidly took form for the denouement of October 1964. At first the intelligentsia did not recognize the dismal implications of this event as a fundamental rejection of the whole era of the Thaw in intellectual life. The moment of truth was the arrest on 8 September 1965 of two imaginative young writers, Andrei Sinyavsky and Yuli Daniel, on charges of publishing anti-Soviet literature in the West and "slandering the Soviet state." Their trial and sentencing were symbols internationally of the triumph of official neo-Stalinism over Soviet intellectual life for a generation to come. For the intelligentsia, the era of hope symbolized by the Twentieth Congress had closed; the pathetic era of subterranean dissidence had begun.

CHAPTER 26

The Fall of Khrushchev and the
Advent of Participatory Bureaucracy

The study of Soviet politics was always beset by peculiar problems. It was the study of a system based on a commitment to a dogmatic ideology that manipulated this ideology to conceal rather than advertise its fundamental political realities. Soviet practice was at variance with Soviet theory almost since the revolution itself—notably the ultrademocratic classless ideal versus the totalitarian bureaucratic actuality. Official Soviet statements and studies were no direct reflection of Soviet reality. Therefore, Soviet politics had to be studied indirectly, by inference and conjecture from the contrived statements and bits of information that reached the outside student. This art of educated guesswork was what went by the evocative term *Kremlinology*.

Kremlinology may be defined as the occult science of deducing what was going on in the Kremlin from whatever scraps of evidence might come to light. It had its margin of error in such modes of analysis as the order in which the Soviet dignitaries paraded themselves on top of Lenin's tomb, a distinctly unlaughable way of getting at the hierarchy of influence among them. When, on 7 November 1967, the new defense minister Marshal A. A. Grechko appeared alongside General Secretary Brezhnev and Premier Kosygin, it might have seemed that the military were rising in influence. But no—the military chief always had a place of prominence at the anniversary review—so nothing was proven. On the same occasion, one member of the Politburo, Piotr Shelest, was absent altogether. Had he fallen? No, he was reviewing the troops in Kiev; he happened to be the only representative of a non-Russian minority with full membership in the Politburo, and he went home to the Ukraine for the November celebration. But there was an earlier and memorable occasion when an absence proved to be of more significance—the evening in June 1953 when Lavrenty Beria failed to show up at the opera with his colleagues and gave the world the first hint that he had been purged.

Still, despite the inevitable percentage of miscalculations, the Soviets' profound rank-consciousness and passion for the proper precedence order among their officials was a constantly revealing source about relationships and attitudes inside the Kremlin. When a number of Soviet officials were named at some function, the practice was to list those at each rank in alphabetical order, starting with the members of the Politburo even if their membership in that body was not mentioned. Candidate members of the Politburo came next, then party secretaries who did not belong to the Politburo, then other officials. When *Pravda* on 8 November 1967 listed Yury Andropov at the beginning of the second alphabetical series, discerning readers were alerted to the fact that this party secretary, recently put in charge of the secret police, had now been accorded the status of candidate member of the Politburo, even though no such overt announcement was made.

At the cost of considerable labor in collecting data, significant inferences could be made about the status of lesser officials and about diverse political priorities. One odd Soviet custom was to list in detail, with full titles, every member of an official group that went to the airport to meet an incoming group of foreign leaders. The importance attributed to the foreign country could be deduced from the composition of the counterpart welcoming committee. Trips to the airport to meet the incoming Communist delegations on the eve of the November 1967 anniversary were particularly interesting because so many arrivals were crowded into one day's time. Eight such meetings were reported in *Pravda* on 2 November, each in a separate report in the style of the following (translated here verbatim and in its entirety):

> On 1 November, at the invitation of the CC of the CPSU, the Presidium of the Supreme Soviet of the USSR, and the Council of Ministers of the USSR, there arrived in Moscow for the celebration of the fiftieth anniversary of the Great October Socialist Revolution a party and governmental delegation from the Czechoslovak Socialist Republic headed by First Secretary of the Central Committee of the Communist Party of Czechoslovakia and President of the Czechoslovak Socialist Republic Comrade A. Novotný. The delegation included Member of the Presidium of the CC of the CPCz and Chairman of the Government of the CzSR Com. J. Lenart, Member of the Presidium of the CC of the CPCz and Chairman of the National Assembly of the CzSR Com. B. Lastovička, Member of the Presidium of the CC of the CPCz and

Chairman of the Slovak National Council Com. M. Chudik, and Secretary of the CC of the CPCz Com. V. Kouchý.

At the Vnukovo Airport the Czechoslovak comrades were met by: General Secretary of the CC of the CPSU Com. L. I. Brezhnev, Member of the Politburo of the CC of the CPSU and Chairman of the Council of Ministers of the USSR Com. A. N. Kosygin, Member of the Politburo of the CC of the CPSU and Chairman of the Presidium of the Supreme Soviet of the USSR Com. N. V. Podgorny, Member of the Politburo of the CC of the CPSU and First Deputy Chairman of the Council of Ministers of the USSR Com. K. T. Mazurov, Member of the CC of the CPSU and Deputy Chairman of the Council of Ministers of the USSR Com. L. V. Smirnov, Member of the CC of the CPSU and USSR Minister of Heavy, Power, and Transport Machine Construction Com. V. F. Zhigalin, Member of the CC of the CPSU and Chief Editor of the Newspaper *Pravda* Com. M. V. Zimianin, Member of the CC of the CPSU and USSR Deputy Minister of Defense Marshal of the Soviet Union Com. N. I. Krylov, Candidate Member of the CC of the CPSU and Head of a Department in the CC of the CPSU Com. P. K. Sizov, Member of the Central Auditing Commission of the CPSU and First Deputy Head of a Department in the CC of the CPSU Com. K. V. Rusakov, USSR Deputy Minister of Foreign Affairs Com. L. F. Ilyichev, and others. The delegation was also met by officials of the Embassy of the CzSR in the USSR.

The report on the Polish delegation followed on the same page and in the same form, together with this passage on the group meeting it:

At the Vnukovo airport the Polish Comrades were met by: General Secretary of the CC of the CPSU Com. L. I. Brezhev, Member of the Politburo of the CC of the CPSU and Chairman of the Council of Ministers of the USSR Com. A. N. Kosygin, Member of the Politburo of the CC of the CPSU and Chairman of the Presidium of the Supreme Soviet of the USSR Com. N. V. Podgorny, Member of the Politburo of the CC of the CPSU and First Deputy Chairman of the Council of Ministers of the USSR Com. D. S. Poliansky, Member of the CC of the CPSU and Deputy Chairman of the Council of Ministers of the USSR Com. I. T. Novikov, Member of the CC of the CPSU and USSR Minister of Transport Construction Com. E. F. Kozhevnikov, Member of the CC of the CPSU and First Deputy Minister of Defense Marshal of the Soviet Union Com. I. I. Yakubovsky, Candidate Member of the CC of the CPSU and USSR Minister of Civil Aviation Marshal of Aviation E. F. Loginov, Candidate Member of the CC of the CPSU and USSR Deputy Minister of Foreign Affairs Com. V. S. Semenov, Member of the Central Auditing Commission of the CPSU and First Deputy Head of a Department in the CC of the CPSU Com. K. V. Rusakov, First Deputy Head of a Department in the CC of the CPSU Com. I. P. Yastrebov, and others.

The delegation was also met by officials of the Embassy of the Polish People's Republic in the USSR.

The ritual went on and on, with similar reports on the arrivals of the Bulgarians, the Romanians, the Yugoslavs, the Mongolians, the North Koreans, and the Hungarians. (The North Vietnamese came the day before, the Albanians were not invited, the Chinese refused to come, and the Cubans failed to send a top-level delegation.) *Pravda's* odd practice of reporting each encounter with everyone's full name and title, without reference to the other reports involving the same Soviet personalities on the same page, made it apparent that the Soviet press was not concerned here with news so much as a sort of journalistic ceremony, to give each Soviet leader and each satellite government just the proper degree of prestige in print.

It was clear, of course, that all the satellite governments rated the presence of Brezhnev and Kosygin in the welcoming committee. (Whether Brezhnev and Kosygin trooped out to the airport for each separate arrival or sat out there to meet everyone as they came in was not revealed.) Each committee had military representation, though it was rotated so no marshal could claim the limelight. Each committee included a cabinet minister for some economic activity, carefully chosen to reflect that industry of the respective satellite that the Soviets judged most distinctive, such as the Romanians' oil and the North Koreans' fisheries. One theretofore obscure man, "First Deputy Head of a Department in the CC of the CPSU Com. K. V. Rusakov," turned up at every one of the meetings, conveying the significant unpublished information that he was one of the leading functionaries in the office for relations with bloc Communist parties.

There were always hazards, of course, in the inferences made from such reports. When Defense Minister Rodion Malinovsky failed to meet his counterparts from the satellites arriving for a conference in 1966, it appeared that he was going to be sacked; actually, the unfortunate man was sick and died a few months later. Whenever conjecture was used—as it had to be—it always needed to be labeled for what it was and discounted to the proper extent. Some overenthusiastic commentators wrote as if they had personally bugged the conference room of the Politburo and could report every word that passed among its members. This was irresponsible, but since conjecture, recognized as such, was under Soviet conditions of news control the nearest thing to knowledge, one could not help using it.

In these circumstances, it is not surprising that there was so much disagreement among the experts. There were two main schools of speculation, termed by Carl Linden the "totalitarian model" and the "conflict model."[1] The totalitarian model of Soviet politics assumed that power was stable and undivided once a new leader had firmly succeeded to the top position in the Communist Party. The conflict model presumed the continuance of factional infighting among liberal and conservative bureaucratic cliques behind the façade of Communist Party discipline.

Both interpretations had their merits, though each model is more convincing for a particular epoch: the totalitarian model under Stalin and the conflict model under Khrushchev. Thus, a fairly convincing case can be made for the existence of the anti-Khrushchev conservative faction led by party secretary Frol Kozlov from 1960 to 1963, subtly expressing its complaints in the wording of statements on such issues as steel versus chemicals or the degree of sin to be heaped on the Molotov-Malenkov opposition of 1957.

A more tangible clue of renewed seismic activity inside the Soviet political monolith was offered by the rise in the turnover rate among provincial secretaries in the period from late 1959 to mid-1961. In particular, the fall of Khrushchev's lieutenants Kirichenko and Beliaev was a sign that the opposition challenge was stiffening. In retrospect, it appears that Khrushchev's enemies had broken into the political circuit at the level of the Secretariat and were using the power of appointment against him in the same way he had used it himself earlier. Thanks to replacements and expansions, the Central Committee elected by the Twenty-second Party Congress in October 1961 consisted of over half new members, practically all of whom survived Khrushchev's fall in 1964 and were confirmed in their positions by the Twenty-third Congress in 1966. They were clearly supporters of the new group that wrested the appointment power away from Khrushchev in 1959 or 1960.

The shakeup in the Secretariat in May 1960, simultaneous with the U-2 incident, was the first open sign of the shift against Khrushchev. There followed a period of tense and unstable jockeying, when the opposition had enough influence to curb Khrushchev but not enough, presumably, to challenge his formal leadership. Khrushchev evidently retained prime influence in foreign policy and ideological matters and was perhaps manipulating the issues to keep the opposition politically off balance. This may help explain the seemingly impulsive vagaries of Khrushchev's foreign policy from 1960 to 1963, veering as it did from the Berlin ultimatum and the Cuban missile gambit to the Nuclear Test Ban Treaty and the open break with the Chinese. Khrushchev's ideological ventures in the 1961 Party Program and his bizarre experiments in party organization in 1962 may be similarly explained. The latter were undone forthwith by his successors in 1964.

The removal of Khrushchev, coming presumably as soon as the opposition had mobilized the strength and the determination to depose him, was a watershed in the history of Soviet politics. This was the first time in the entire history of Russia since the Viking prince Riurik that the established leader of the country was removed by the rules of representative procedure. Since the leader was removed, it follows naturally that he was and had been *removable,* and it follows equally that the successor leadership would be removable in the same way. A basic change had occurred in the circuit of power in the Soviet system: Real control did not pass to the top leader but flowed instead from the top collective bodies around through the party organization. The top leader was only a representative of the group, at most first among equals, and his tenure of leadership depended on the support of that group.

By making the succession to the leadership depend on the confidence of the Central Committee, Soviet political practice took a long step toward a sort of miniature parliamentary system at the top of the great bureaucratic pyramid of the party. The Central Committee could be likened to a parliament, the Politburo to the cabinet, and the general secretary to the prime minister (not to be confused with the actual governmental prime minister, who was only second in command in the party). There were of course vast differences as against a real parliamentary system: Issues and procedures were beclouded by the mask of public unanimity, and the "parliament," instead of being responsible to an electorate, was de facto appointed by the "prime minister" or the "cabinet." Nevertheless, as this system continued to operate, it seemed to permit change further down in the political system, as each participant in the parliamentarism of the Central Committee sought support further down among his "constituents" to enhance his own standing. Conceivably, the parliamentary practice could have spread to regional and local party committees, and the party might have become more and more a forum for the plurality of interests among the complex Soviet bureaucracy.

What appears to have been evolving in the Soviet Union, in the party framework, was a new kind of politics, a sort of participatory bureaucracy. This is familiar, actually, to anyone with experience in a Western government or corporation or university, though it is not recognized in political theory as a model for the political system as a whole. Conventionally, a bureaucratic structure is seen as a system where influence is transmitted only from the top down, whereas influence from the bottom up is presumed to operate only in the democratic party system. But in any bureaucratic organization, it is impossible to function purely from the top down: All manner of influences—information, advice, recommendations, problems, complaints—must flow upward, or else the top leadership cannot make the informed decisions on which the life of the entity depends. The problems of managing a complex economy based on modern technology made it abundantly clear to the Soviet leaders that they had to allow this reverse stream of influence to flow freely; their main concern was that the flow be kept within the organizational structure of the Communist Party.

The notion of participatory bureaucracy is based on recognition of the complex character of large organizations and the interplay of individual influences, upward as well as downward, that can take place within such entities. There is an extensive literature on the sociology of modern organizations underscoring the manifold constraints that complexity places on the leaders of the organization, the power enjoyed by experts and specialists by virtue of their expertise, and the ultimate requirements of autonomy for the branches of an organization if it is to meet the test of survival.[2] Along with this input come the inevitable complaints and conflicts among subordinates that the organization must respond to if it is to maintain reasonable efficiency and effectiveness.

The peculiar sclerosis of the Stalinist regime was its unwillingness to delegate responsibility and to accept accurate information, endeavoring instead to compensate for these deficiencies by force and terror. No truly modern organization can operate this way. If for reasons of economic success alone, it was clear that the USSR could not go back to these Stalinist methods. Participatory bureaucracy meant that the post-Stalin policy-making process had become complex and open-ended. It meant that experts and local officials had a substantial degree of security as well as influence. It meant that the ranks of the bureaucracy enjoyed a certain amount of power as against the top leadership, or at least that the vulnerability was mutual. It suggests that there were openings in the bureaucratic structure for the exercise of influence by all manner of individuals and interest groups.

Viewed according to the model of participatory bureaucracy, the Central Committee of the CPSU was the keystone of the entire Soviet system. In its makeup it represented all the constituent elements of the Soviet power structure, both functionally and geographically. Its sessions provided the country's only ongoing broad-based policy forum. Finally, it constituted the primary institutional counterweight to individual bureaucratic dictation in the Stalinist fashion. In short, it was the Central Committee that allowed the bureaucracy to be participatory.

The composition of the Central Committee had some rather obvious implications for its participatory functions. To begin with, membership in the Central Committee was enjoyed almost exclusively by individuals holding leading positions in one or another of the country's bureaucratic structures, primarily the party apparatus, then the civil government, the military, and miscellaneous institutions ranging from the trade unions to the Academy of Sciences. Every significant institution was represented, in close proportion to the importance accorded that institution in the Soviet scheme of things.

Evidence of congress after congress shows very clearly that Central Committee membership was not a matter of individual selection. The Central Committee was basically a collection of job slots—by the 1970s, the 200 or more most important jobs in the country, followed by the 150 or so next most important jobs carrying the rank of candidate member, and then the 70 or 80 lesser jobs carrying the rank of member of the Central Auditing Commission (which was in its makeup really an honorable mention category for jobholders who did not quite make the Central Committee). Membership in the Central Committee, at the appropriate rank, was automatically conferred on the holder of a job that carried Central Committee rank. This was a rule of Soviet politics that was invariably observed.

It followed from this unwritten but nonetheless stringent rule of Central Committee composition that a man who was secure in his job would be secure in his Central Committee membership, and that he could not be removed from the Central Committee without being removed from his Central Committee-level job. Correspondingly, a man who lost his job and did not move to another at the Central Committee level would almost always be dropped from the Central Committee at the next congress, unless an especially honorable retirement was intended for him. In general, the association of the job and Central Committee rank made it difficult for higher authority to reshuffle and pack the Central Committee at random without causing a commensurate disturbance in the agencies, party, government, or whatever, whose leadership was affected. While individuals could always be shifted by the authority of the central Secretariat, mass changes became increasingly difficult, and the tenure of any given Central Committee member therefore became reasonably secure.

The trend from one party congress to the next in terms of a Central Committee member's likelihood of reelection is marked: 63 percent and 50 percent under Khrushchev, 80 percent and 78 percent at Brezhnev's first two congresses. The stability of the post-Khrushchev leadership at the Politburo level was fully complemented by this evidence of continuity at the Central Committee level, contrasting vividly with the factional struggles and leadership shake-ups that followed the deaths of both Lenin and Stalin. Brezhnev did not impose himself on the Soviet leadership in the Stalin and Khrushchev manner; rather, he worked with the existing material, allowing himself—perhaps by force of necessity—to be the representative and the reflection of the existing bureaucratic hierarchy rather than the architect of a new political machine designed in his own image.

There was, of course, some opportunity for leadership influence in the expansion of the Central Committee membership carried out at each congress. However, the opportunity for personal manipulation was limited even in this respect, since the expansion was accomplished mainly by upgrading candidate-status jobs and their tenants with them. Among these people as well there was growing stability: The percentage of candidate members either promoted or held over fell from 53 percent in 1956 to 48 percent in 1961, but rose to 64 percent in 1966 and to 67 percent in 1971.

Was Brezhnev as removable as Khrushchev was, or did he find a more secure power base? There is no evidence that anything happened to change the balance of forces manifested in 1964. The Central Committee became more solidly entrenched than it ever was before. Brezhnev took no obvious steps to assert himself, presumably because he was not able to do so in the face of the established power of the Central Committee. It follows that the power of the top leader was narrowly circumscribed by the bureaucratic body of which he was merely the choice and the representative.

Individual members of the Central Committee were still vulnerable to the Secretariat's power of transfer or demotion from their Central Committee–rank jobs. On the other hand, the general secretary was highly vulnerable to any concerted opposition within the Central Committee. If he started to use his power of removal to threaten any substantial number of Central Committee members all at once, he would in all probability have provoked a general rebellion of the body, which could seriously endanger his own tenure of office. In other words, Central Committee member and general secretary were mutually vulnerable and mutually dependent.

Given the element of independent power enjoyed by the Central Committee, it follows that the discussion and decision of key issues among the members of that body must have involved a great deal more give-and-take and head counting than met the public eye. The reality of the Soviet policy-making process probably lay somewhere between the official claims of democratic centralism and the official appearances of monolithic conformity. Within the Central Committee, consequently, there must have been at least some opportunity for representation of the views and interests of all those constituencies whose chiefs held Central Committee rank.

This analysis suggests that the relation between the Central Committee member and his own regional or functional constituency may have borne some similarity to the relation of the top leadership and the Central Committee. The regional secretary or cabinet minister worked with committees and hierarchies of lesser functionaries, whose confidence and cooperation he needed in order to make a success of his job and thus minimize his vulnerability to intervention from the top. He would therefore be inclined to represent the views, interests, recommendations, and complaints of these subordinates in the deliberations of the Central Committee. These expressions of interest from below could include not only party views but the positions of all the diverse institutions—governmental, industrial, military, trade union, educational, and so on—that were represented in the provincial and local party committee structure. Conceivably, this participatory process may have been opening up well down in the party hierarchy, such that the party bureaucracy could come to serve as a fairly effective channel for the transmission of all manner of ideas and desires from below upward.

How far this participatory bureaucracy might actually have developed is, of course, only a matter of speculation. It was presumably a force felt at the top level and a factor for continuity that allowed gradual change in response to needs felt lower in the power structure, while a relatively stable leadership group maintained itself from congress to congress.

The power of the party and its monopoly position in the Soviet power structure remained the primary limitation on the free extension of bureaucratic representativeness within Soviet society. However they shared power among themselves, the party bureaucrats were clearly determined to perpetuate their power as an institution and, by extension, the power of the country they ruled. The power of the party apparatus did not really exist for any higher purpose: It was an end in itself. Even where and when it became economically or technologically dysfunctional, the control function of the party continued to be asserted as the first political absolute. The controllers had to maintain control in order to continue to be controllers.

As a body primarily oriented toward the maintenance of control for the controllers' sake, the party apparatus tended to attract a particular kind of person—energetic and ambitious, not the most intelligent, not too principled, willing to conform in order to share in the exercise of power. The apparatus of the 1960s was still dominated by men born between 1905 and the revolution who rose from humble beginnings and filled the top slots after Stalin's purges. Typically, they were anti-intellectual, nominally puritanical, and rigidly philistine in their views. They retained all the Stalinist habits of ideological manipulation to justify their own regime, imposing conformity on the rank and file and assuming the pose of official unanimity themselves. They pretended to represent the world's highest form of democracy; they gave the appearance of monolithic totalitarianism; their actual relationships within the leadership group were somewhere in the middle.

Between the party apparatus and certain segments of the Soviet populace, particularly the intelligentsia, there was growing tension. Like tsarist Russia, the Soviet regime had to contend with a profoundly disaffected opposition among the young educated class, as expressed mainly by the writers. But there was a newer type of recruit to the opposition, the young scientists, exemplified by Maxim Litvinov's physicist grandson Pavel. Thanks to the dead hand of party control in the humanities and social sciences, the most intelligent, creative, and sensitive people gravitated to the natural sciences. Almost invariably, foreign students studying in the Soviet Union, regardless of their own fields, found their most congenial friends among students of natural science, where the best Soviet minds found a haven of relative freedom and privilege.

Obviously the scientific and technical intelligentsia were of the utmost importance to the party leadership in its aspirations to build the international influence of the Soviet Union. Unlike the tsarist regime, the Soviet government depended heavily on the intelligentsia for the progress of sophisticated industry and science and had to treat the scientists and engineers with commensurate circumspection. The Soviet intelligentsia, in short, became the kind of social force singled out by J. K. Galbraith as the key power in modern society, the "technostructure," that is, the organized intelligence that has been replacing land and capital as the crucial factor in economic life everywhere.[3]

The party apparatus was psychologically as remote from the technostructure as the tsarist bureaucracy was from Turgenev's nihilists. Existing to maintain control for its own sake, the party bureaucracy was functionally an anachronism. It needed to cultivate and use the intelligentsia, but could not accord it freedom and power: It encouraged intellectuals and then frustrated them. This was the new Soviet class struggle; it was the stuff revolutions are made of.

Khrushchev's answer to this contradiction was to accentuate the role of the party organization. Consistently he promoted the authority of the party controllers over the governmental and industrial administrators as well as over the creative intelligentsia. This might be the practical significance of his reviving the doctrine of the "withering-away of the state" in 1961. The state might wither, but the party never would, and the only prospect Khrushchev offered was perpetual domination of Soviet life by the professional party secretaries. This was too much even for his successors in the party, who quickly repealed the economic functionalism Khrushchev had introduced into the party organization and silenced talk of the withering-away of the state.

The group of Communist leaders who unseated Khrushchev in 1964 managed to provide the country with remarkably stable leadership. Of the eleven men in the Politburo at the end of the Khrushchev era, seven were still in office in the early 1970s. One member died (Kozlov) and two retired with honors (Mikoyan and Shvernik); only Khrushchev himself had been summarily removed. In the Central Committee, as noted earlier, there was relatively little change; turnover at the Twenty-third Congress in 1966 was much lower (only 46 new members out of 195) than at the Twenty-second in 1961 or at the Twentieth in 1956. (The Twenty-first Congress in 1959 did not elect a new Central Committee.) In the party Secretariat, there were some changes of potential significance. When Brezhnev took over from Khrushchev as first secretary (retitled general secretary, as in Stalin's day), Podgorny was kicked upstairs to become chief of state. A little later, Shelepin was kicked downstairs to head the trade unions. The number-two man in the party organization appeared to be Aleksei Kirilenko, a close associate of Brezhnev in the Ukraine in the 1940s and early 1950s. All these points contributed to a picture of strengthened control in the hands of General Secretary Brezhnev, at least for the time being. The 1967 shake-up in the KGB, replacing Shelepin's protégé Semichastny with Party Secretary Andropov, reinforced the view that Brezhnev, through the party apparatus, was in a firm position of leadership.

The greater questions lay in the more distant future. Could the party bureaucracy hang on after outliving its usefulness, like the barons of medieval feudalism who perpetuated their control as a parasitic ruling class for centuries after their initial function of defense had lapsed? Or would the tendency toward participatory bureaucracy necessarily admit segments of the administrative and intellectual class into the decision-making and controlling process and thus permit a pluralistic evolution? Conflicts were inevitable, between aspirants for leadership who linked up with different elements in the technostructure and took different positions on the issues, and between the party structure as a whole and the aspirations of the entire technostructure for a freer and more effective voice in the destinies of the country. There were two main possibilities: The party bureaucracy could reaffirm its political monopoly and go back to Stalinist terror, at great cost in national progress and morale; or it could leave the door open to a sort of creeping constitutionalism that might gradually but profoundly transform the Soviet system.

CHAPTER 27

The Central Committee as a
Bureaucratic Elite

I n the 1960s and 1970s, a multitude of works reflecting the encroachments
of the behavioral revolution on the precincts of Kremlinology addressed
themselves to the analysis of the Central Committee of the CPSU as
an institutionally defined elite.[1] In good behavioral style and with much
statistical sophistication, these works explored the educational and career backgrounds of Central Committee members and probed the channels for "recruitment" or "co-optation" into that body.[2] They weighted the "representation"
of functional entities such as the party apparatus, government bureaucracy,
military, intelligentsia, and such, as well as various geographical regions and
social groups, in the makeup of the Central Committee membership.[3] Almost
never, however, and only by indirection if at all, did this school of investigation
actually inquire into the exact composition of the Central Committee and the
specific posts that were associated with Central Committee status.[4]

The membership of the Central Committee was arrived at, of course, neither
by free election nor by random appointment. The single list of proposed members, presented at each party congress and voted in unanimously as a matter of
routine, proves on close analysis to have been very carefully made up in accordance with a system of unwritten (or at least unannounced) rules. Except for a
few special cases, these rules (extending back to the early years of the Stalin era)
guaranteed Central Committee status to holders of elite-status bureaucratic offices—party, governmental, and military—with a sprinkling of the top figures
in the other sectors of society (trade union, academic, cultural, and so forth).[5]
In the party apparatus and government, it is fair to say that the true basis of

elite status was appointment to one of the leading jobs in the central and provincial administration. The automatic membership in the Central Committee that followed would then be more the visible badge of status than its source.

Since membership in the Central Committee was governed by previous appointment to a job carrying Central Committee status, it follows that the composition of the Central Committee was determined not at the time of the congress but over the entire period elapsing since the previous congress, as decisions were made to remove, install, or retain particular individuals in particular Central Committee–level slots. With a few possible exceptions, the makeup of the Central Committee was the reflection of a series of decisions about the composition of the elite that were merely revealed in the formal election of the body at the next congress.[6] How such decisions were actually arrived at, of course, was one of the best-kept secrets of the Soviet political process; one must assume that they were made at the level of the Politburo, with staff assistance or recommendations from the responsible heads of the party Secretariat.

Another type of decision may have been made more closely in conjunction with the congress itself—namely, the decision as to which additional jobs would be awarded Central Committee status or promoted thereto and how the representational balance of functional and geographical areas might be altered. Such decisions were evidently taken in a fairly restricted context, in a stable and long-term tradition, with change occurring in one direction only: upgrading of jobs, not downgrading (with rare exceptions), and steady expansion of the overall size of the Central Committee (see table 27.1).

TABLE 27.1. Expansion of the Central Committee

	19th Congress (1952)	20th Congress (1956)	22nd Congress (1961)	23rd Congress (1966)	24th Congress (1971)
Full members	125	133	175	195	241
(Increase)	—	(6.4%)	(31.6%)	(11.4%)	(24.6%)
Candidate members	110	122	156	165	155
(Increase)	—	(10.9%)	(27.9%)	(5.8%)	(–6.1%)
Central Auditing Commission	37	63	65	79	81
(Increase)	—	(70.3%)	(3.2%)	(21.5%)	(2.5%)

This trend meant a progressive lowering of the threshold for membership in the Central Committee or for candidate status or membership on the Central Auditing Commission (CAC), as jobs of marginally lower importance were accorded elite status at each successive congress. Thus, a sort of long-term inflation in the status value of Central Committee membership went on. This extension of status symbols was based, as far as any data indicate, on the significance imputed to the various job slots that were next in the line of intrinsic importance, and not on the identity of the individuals who happened to hold those jobs. Analysis of the increment to the Central Committee between 1966 and 1971 makes this job-status criterion quite clear. The only significant areas of discretion that the decision makers appear to have allowed themselves were (1) how much to expand the various ranks at any one congress; and (2) the apportionment of the resulting gains among the various functional areas represented in the Central Committee.

The widely entertained notion that the Central Committee was apportioned to "represent" various functional and geographical interests had a firm basis in actual Soviet practice. However, this apportionment of representation operated not in terms of individuals, fundamentally, but of job slots. The unwritten code allocated to each functional hierarchy and to each union republic (and often province) a proportion of the seats in the Central Committee corresponding to the imputed status and importance of the particular institution or region. These seats, in turn, were permanently attached to the highest-status job slots in the institution or region. The occupants of these job slots, whoever they might be, were then recognized by election to the Central Committee at the party congress.[7]

A fine sense of status differentials emerges in the assignment of Central Committee seats to the various constituencies. At the Twenty-fourth Party Congress in 1971, in the functional breakdown, the party apparatus naturally had the lion's share—99 out of 241 (41 percent), with the civil government somewhat behind—76 (32 percent) in the same year. Between them, these two hierarchies, party and governmental, consistently accounted for close to three-fourths of the Central Committee. Small delegations held the seats for the other institutional categories—the military (20, or 8 percent in 1971), the diplomats (16, or 7 percent, mainly ex-party secretaries in Communist capitals), the cultural and scientific sector (8, or 3 percent), the police agencies (2—KGB chairman Yuri Andropov and the head of the newly established Union Ministry of Internal Affairs, N. A. Shchelokov), and the trade unions (2—Chairman Alexander Shelepin and Chief Secretary V. I. Prokhorov). All this was in descending order

of magnitude and implicit status for each group. Geographical balance was observed within the party and governmental groups, with a careful assignment of
seats to central and regional job slots corresponding to the importance of both
the job and the region. Table 27.2 shows the allocation of seats to the various
functional areas in 1966 and in 1971.

In the party apparatus, apart from a block of seats (twenty in 1971) for
the central Secretariat and its staff, Central Committee membership was accorded to local party secretaryships on the basis of the importance of their jurisdictions. Full Central Committee rank was enjoyed by the first secretaries of
thirty-two of the fifty-five oblasts and *krais* in the RSFSR, including all of the
more populous and important ones, plus the first secretaries of the seven largest of the fifteen autonomous republics in the RSFSR. The list further included the first and second secretaries of the independent city of Moscow, the first
secretary of Leningrad City, and the second secretary of Leningrad Province,
reflecting the special importance of these two centers.[8] Also accorded Central
Committee status were the first secretaries of all of the fourteen other union
republics, plus subordinate secretaries and selected oblast secretaries in numbers commensurate with the importance of the republic. In 1971, in addition to
the first secretaries of the respective republics, there were twelve seats for the
Ukraine, five for Kazakhstan, two for Belorussia, one extra for Uzbekistan, and
one for Turkmenia (an evident anomaly).

In the civil government, the bulk of the Central Committee seats (fifty-
eight) were assigned to ministries and other cabinet-level agencies in the Union
government. Seven seats were allocated to the government of the RSFSR, including the Politburo-level seat of its prime minister. A few other seats were
reserved for the prime ministers of the more important union republics (the
Ukraine, Kazakhstan, Belorussia, Uzbekistan, and Georgia) and for the chair-
men of the presidia of the Supreme Soviet of the first four of this group, plus
Estonia for reasons that were unclear. One anomalous case completes the list—
a provincial government chief from the Ukraine.

The system of apportionment evidenced by the distribution of Central
Committee seats in the party apparatus and in the government strongly suggests the existence of a complex matrix of unacknowledged but strongly felt
status relationships in the Soviet political system. These relationships held
not just among individuals but also among job slots, ranked and represented
in highly stable and predictable ways, however much their individual tenants
might come and go. By the device of Central Committee rank, status differences were systematically and sensitively recognized among types of function and among geographical units as well as between obviously superior and

TABLE 27.2. Allocation of Central Committee seats, 1966 (in parentheses) and 1971

	Full members		Candidate members		Central Auditing Commission		Total	
Party apparatus	(86)	99	(69)	68	(30)	26	(185)	193
Central	(18)	20	(13)	11	(15)	14	(46)	45
Russian Republic	(38)	43	(36)	33	(8)	6	(82)	82
Other republics	(30)	36	(20)	24	(7)	6	(57)	66
Government	(87)	114	(75)	63	(35)	35	(197)	212
Central	(41)	58	(30)	22	(11)	19	(82)	99
Russian Republic	(7)	7	(9)	8	(4)	1	(20)	16
Other republics	(10)	11	(16)	16	(10)	7	(36)	34
Military	(14)	20	(17)	12	(4)	3	(35)	35
Police	(1)	2	(1)	—	—	1	(2)	5
Diplomatic	(14)	16	(2)	3	(6)	4	(22)	23
Other sectors	(11)	11	(7)	11	(8)	7	(26)	29
Trade unions	(3)	2	(4)	4	(3)	3	(10)	9
Scientific/intellectual	(8)	8	(2)	6	(5)	4	(15)	18
Miscellaneous	—	1	(1)	1	—	—	(1)	2
Mass representatives	(8)	16	(13)	12	(6)	9	(27)	37
Retired leaders	(3)	1	(1)	1	—	—	(4)	2
Position undetermined	—	—	—	—	—	4	—	4
Total	(195)	241	(165)	155	(79)	81	(439)	477

subordinate offices. The fine and enduring observance of these distinctions of rank is made even more apparent when the analysis takes account of the apportionment of candidate memberships in the Central Committee and of seats on the CAC.

There were two small categories in the Central Committee membership where the job-slot rule did not apply. One was the retired dignitaries, former leaders, usually of Politburo rank, who managed to avoid being bracketed with one "antiparty group" or another. (Only one man, Mikoyan, remained in this category at the Central Committee level in 1971.) The other group consisted of the "honored workers," industrial executives, milkmaids, and the like, who were presumably nominated to the Central Committee to give it the flavor of popular participation. Sixteen such individuals were elected in 1971 (a marked increase, incidentally, over the eight of 1966). Inclusion in this group depended neither on personal officeholding nor (so far as is discernible) on individual renown, but on the good fortune of selection to represent a social category. Within these terms, the rules of representation continued to apply, with apportionment of these "mass representatives" (to coin a term) among economic sectors and regions of the country roughly in relation to the importance imputed to each. All sixteen mass representatives in 1971 came from the Russian Republic, except for two Ukrainians. Four were directors of factories (including the Magnitogorsk Combine, regularly holding a seat); ten (including two women) were workers in industry or construction; while only two, a kolkhoz chairman and a kolkhoz brigade leader, represented the agricultural sector. It is difficult to regard the mass representatives as persons of influence, and in fact they tended to be replaced at each congress by comrades from the same constituency, at a much higher rate of turnover than the Central Committee as a whole.

The rules of job-slot apportionment applied as well to lesser levels of status, governing the selection both of candidate members of the Central Committee and of the members of the CAC. The latter institutional curiosity, whatever fiduciary functions it may have exercised, was not primarily what its name suggested. Its makeup showed it to be a sort of honorable mention category for jobholders whose slots fell just short of candidate status. With the inclusion of the CAC, there were thus three distinct ranks (plus the two superranks of Politburo and Politburo Candidate membership) in the institutionally defined Soviet elite. To give their tenants the appropriate status, job slots were classified among the various ranks of this elite with remarkable finesse. The status principle held throughout, among the various functional hierarchies and among the territorial divisions of the Union as well as between people of different formal rank in particular institutions. There is an intriguing analogy here with the tsarist *chin* system equating rank and bureaucratic job.

Tabulation of positions in the Central Committee demonstrates the consistency with which status and representational considerations were followed in determining the overall makeup of the institutionally defined elite group in Soviet society. Numbers of Central Committee seats at all three ranks were allocated to the functional bureaucracies in proportion to their imputed importance. Union republics and regions were represented, if at all, in numbers and at ranks proportionate to their importance, and in lesser numbers or at lower levels in bureaucracies that were less important. Where a given territorial entity qualified for a number of seats for its party or government officialdom, Central Committee ranks were always distributed in a manner consistent with the relative job status of the officials to be included—first secretary equal to or ahead of second secretary, prime minister ahead of or equal to chairman of the Presidium of the Supreme Soviet, and so on. At the same time, party precedence over the government was always maintained—first secretary of republic or oblast always equal to or ahead of the respective government chief. Tables 27.3 and 27.4 illustrate the operation of the status matrix in two particular cases, one simple (the cities with Central Committee representation) and the other fairly complex (the union republics). Note the consistent downward steps in rank proceeding both horizontally (left to right) through the job hierarchy and downward through the pecking order of cities or republics.

Where a few anomalies crop up in this close-knit matrix of status relationships they suggest a supplementary principle at work, of token representation of certain social categories. Evidently the "mass representatives" were not the only ones who accomplished this function. Most notable besides them were the five people (two of them women) who seem to have represented the lower party apparatus—and who were again distributed by importance of nationality (three to the Russian Republic, including one non-Russian individual; one to the Ukraine; and one to Kazakhstan).

TABLE 27.3. Status matrix: Cities with Central Committee representation, 1971

City	1st sec.	Chairman, Executive Committee	2nd sec.	3rd sec.	4th sec.
Moscow	PB	CC	CC	Cand.	Cand.
Leningrad	CC	Cand.	CAC	—	—
Kiev	Cand.	—	—	—	—
Novosibirsk	Cand.	—	—	—	—
Dneprodzerzhinsk (token)	Cand.	—	—	—	—

Note: PB = Politburo; CC = Central Committee; Cand. = CC Candidate; CAC = Central Auditing Commission.

TABLE 27.4. Status matrix: Union republics, 1971

	1st sec.	Prime minister	2nd sec.	Chairman, Presidium	1st deputy prime minister	3rd sec.
RSFSR	[none]	PB	[none]	CC	CC (2)	[none]
Ukraine	PB	Cand. PB	CC	CC	Cand.	CC
Kazakhstan	PB	CC	CC	CC	Cand.	CAC
Uzbekistan	Cand. PB	CC	CC	CC	CAC	—
Belorussia	Cand. PB	CC	CC	CC	—	—
Georgia	Cand. PB	CC	Cand.	CAC	—	—
Latvia	CC	Cand.	Cand.	Cand.	—	—
Moldavia	CC	Cand.	Cand.	Cand.	—	—
Tadzhikistan	CC	Cand.	Cand.	Cand.	—	—
Turkmenia	CC	Cand.	CC	CAC	—	—
Azerbaidzhan	CC	Cand.	Cand.	CAC	—	—
Kirgizia	CC	Cand.	Cand.	CAC	—	—
Estonia	CC	Cand.	CAC	CC	—	—
Lithuania	CC	Cand.	CAC	Cand.	—	—
Armenia	CC	Cand.	CAC	CAC	—	—
Tuva (autonomous oblast)	CC	—	—	—	—	—

For most members of the Central Committee, it would appear that any real personal influence they may have exercised was based on the jobs to which they were bureaucratically appointed rather than on their derivative status of Central Committee rank. It follows that the influence of particular individuals was more or less directly proportionate to the importance of their specific job. Numerous members of the Central Committee—the mass representatives, many nationality representatives, other token figures, and probably most of the incumbents of technical government ministries—could not be regarded as people of significant political weight. Consequently, the Central Committee taken as a whole cannot be considered to have been a collective leadership of basically equal individuals. If there was any significant collective leadership at work, it must have been a smaller group within the Central Committee holding inherently influential posts (and most likely people who had held such posts for some time). Expansions of the Central Committee, leaning to token jobholders and mass representatives of little influence, probably diluted the influence of the Central Committee as a whole and enhanced the importance of the putative leading group—perhaps twenty to thirty individuals in addition to the twenty-five making up the Politburo, its candidate members, and the Secretariat.

Whatever the political influence of the Central Committee as a whole, the job-slot basis of membership lent a measure of tenure to the individual member and of stability to the body as a whole. The weight of bureaucratic tradition, if nothing else, made it difficult to remove or demote a large number of individuals suddenly or capriciously, since the rules of the game would require that they be replaced in their specific jobs at the same time. Such removals would involve questions of relations with the local or functional constituency and the overall effectiveness of the system. Probably for reasons of convenience, if not salutary neglect, some Central Committee members in ministerial positions and minority republics had held their office and rank for extraordinarily long periods of time—the minister of railroads since 1948, the first secretary of Lithuania ever since the Soviet takeover in 1940 (both put on the Central Committee in 1952). To be sure, the top leadership had the power of discipline over the Central Committee by removing any jobholder from the position that conferred membership—but if this power were used too broadly and abruptly, threatening the entire membership at once, it is conceivable that the Central Committee could mobilize its statutory authority to depose the leadership as it was called on to depose Khrushchev in 1964, in line with the mutual vulnerability of the top leadership and the Central Committee elite.

In addition to these practical limits on its powers of removal, the discretionary authority of the top leadership over the membership of the Central Committee was further restricted, in the choice of replacement members and in picking those it might add by expanding the membership at the time of the party congress. The unwritten rules of the system called for replacing a fallen member of the Central Committee with the person who had assumed the predecessor's Central Committee–ranked job, and with minor exceptions at the lower ranks, this principle was followed closely. In effect, the decision about a Central Committee membership became a commitment at the time the aspiring functionary was appointed to a job carrying a Central Committee rank, possibly years before the next congress formalized the individual's status. While it might appear that expanding the Central Committee (substantial in 1961 and in 1971) would offer the party leaders an opportunity to pack it with individuals of their choice, the network of unwritten rules and expectations about Central Committee rank and job status very narrowly restricted the options of the leadership in opening up new membership slots. There was an overwhelming weight of practice and tradition governing the assignments of new memberships at all three levels to the jobs next in line, according to rank or territorial importance within each functional hierarchy. If the leadership made its decision to expand the Central Committee at the time of the party congress, it would largely be restricted in its choice of new members at each rank to the incumbents of the jobs that were most logically ready for promotion in status. Consequently, if the leadership wished to introduce or promote a particular group of new people, it would have to see that they were appointed well before the congress to jobs bearing the appropriate rank or to jobs that could plausibly be promoted. But here again, the leadership would have run into the political and practical problems of trying to make too many changes too fast in its vital bureaucratic hierarchies. Here, perhaps, is an institutional explanation of elite stability under Brezhnev's leadership.

The job-slot conception of Central Committee membership and the evident rules of apportionment, representation, and ticket balancing that governed the makeup of the body lend considerable substance to the "interest group" approach to Soviet politics. It must be borne in mind, of course, that Soviet "interest groups" were not the kind of independent private pressure groups familiar in pluralist societies but corresponded more to the competing functional interests discernible within a governmental bureaucracy. The difference is that the whole social system in the USSR was organized under such bureaucratic structures, all of which were subsumed and integrated through the central and local committees of the Communist Party.

All this being understood, it is nevertheless clear that special political interests were advanced by the various functional bureaucracies in the Soviet system, and that through the principle of representation in the Central Committee all these bureaucracies and the local branches of the major ones had a voice or at least an ear in the central councils of the decision-making process. Further, the representation of these functional and territorial groups, in proportion to their importance, was firmly established according to the unwritten code of Central Committee membership and was doubtless a matter of basic expectation within the various bureaucratic units. The level and amount of Central Committee representation defined the institutional weight accorded each functional and territorial interest group in Soviet society. Any attempt to tamper seriously with this representative principle would have serious consequences for the effective functioning of the system.

PART VI

Gorbachev and the End of the Communist System

CHAPTER 28

The Generational Revolution

T he Twenty-seventh Congress of the CPSU, held at the end of February and the beginning of March 1986, marked the end of an era. Not only had the Soviet Union gone through an unprecedented series of leadership changes, with the successive deaths of three national chiefs in less than two and a half years, the replacement of a whole generation in the bureaucratic elite was consummated as well. These experiences, however, did not yet constitute a crisis for the Soviet political system. Indeed, the continuity of the real mechanisms of power in the Communist Party was powerfully reaffirmed by events from 1982 to 1986.

The persistence of the power structure through years of great turmoil among the personalities who managed it prompts a series of questions about the nature of political power in the Soviet system. Where was real power located and on what basis did it rest? How was power mobilized and transferred? What of the gulf between formal and actual structures of power? What difference did the succession from one generation to another make as the experience of Stalinism receded into the past? It was easy to go to the opposite extreme from Soviet constitutional pretenses and embrace a simplistic totalitarian model wherein all power emanated from the man at the top. And it was almost as easy, as time eroded this image, to overcompensate for the overcompensation and to underrate the ongoing elements of totalitarianism in the system.

From 1953 on, the Soviet political system was more oligarchic than personalist. And contrary to the totalitarian model, a form of real politics did go on in the upper levels of the Soviet hierarchy.[1] However, politics in this realm was masked and insulated by the compulsion to suppress open controversy and

present the public appearance of monolithic unity. Soviet elite politics, involving bureaucratic infighting, special interest pressure, deals and coalitions, and
actual voting at the top level, was more akin to the politics within large organizations in Western society (government bureaucracies, corporations, universities, churches) than to the electoral politics that still constitutes the broadest,
integrating form of the political process in democratic countries. At the same
time, Old Russian political culture—popular assumptions and expectations,
nonverbal or at least nonpublic, about how government should be conducted—
still influenced the distinctive forms of bureaucratic life that lay behind the
published record.[2]

Compared with the political and social turmoil that extended with only short
periods of respite from World War I to the purges, the Soviet Union experienced after the late 1930s an extraordinary history of institutional stability and
continuity. Even the staggering challenges of World War II and its aftermath
disturbed the emergent structure of Stalinist government and society relatively
little. Reflecting this continuity and contributing to it was a remarkable generational phenomenon in the Soviet leadership—the perpetuation in power of
one distinctive age cohort, which inherited its position as the beneficiary of the
purges and as a group grew old in office until the laws of biology caught up
with it in the 1980s.[3]

A little-recognized fact about Stalin's purges, specifically the *yezhovshchina,* or secret mass purge of Stalinist officials, was its age-based cutoff. Apart
from the Politburo and a few other Stalin cronies,[4] virtually everyone in Soviet
public life who was over the age of thirty-seven in 1937 was eliminated from the
scene. This criterion is revealed in the otherwise inexplicable observation that
hardly anyone was available afterward to serve in the Soviet leadership at the
Central Committee level who had been born before 1900. (For the military, the
cutoff birth year was 1897.) Among the 125 full members of Stalin's last Central Committee in 1952, only 27 men, or 22 percent (mostly actual or former
Politburo members, military men, or theoreticians), had been born before 1900;
the median age was only forty-nine.[5] On the other hand, of all those members
whose birth year is known, there were only 7 born after 1912 and thus under
forty in 1952.

This extraordinary generational compression in the postwar leadership
underscores how, to fill the shoes of purge victims up and down the bureaucracy, Stalin had turned to his younger cadres. Their rise in the postpurge vacuum
was meteoric. To take one well-known example, Aleksei Kosygin, born in 1904,
ascended from factory manager to deputy prime minister in just two years.

Leonid Brezhnev, born in 1906, rose a little less dramatically from industrial engineer to deputy party boss of a province in the same length of time.

Once they had filled all the empty slots in the bureaucratic elite, normal life expectancy assured the youthful purge beneficiaries an extraordinary tenure of office. Furthermore, the leaders of this cohort made sure that replacements, when they had to be made, were nearly of the same age group. Naturally, age-mates more readily met the appointment criteria of familiarity and dependability, when there was no physical need to go to younger people. In consequence, one generation, marked by distinctive qualities in its selection and experience, dominated the Soviet political scene for nearly half a century.

The postpurge generation of the "class of '38" shared a distinct set of characteristics. They were defined, first of all, by the age cutoff of the purges. Typically, they were the fruit of Stalin's efforts in the early 1930s to recruit bright, tough young men as potential candidates for the party and state officialdom. In essence, they were the *vydvizhentsy* or "promotees" described by Sheila Fitzpatrick—sons or grandsons of peasants, who had been put through crash courses in engineering and agitprop to prepare them for higher responsibilities.[6] As a type, the vydvizhentsy seem to have been authoritarian, anti-intellectual, xenophobic, and anti-Semitic. They evidently embodied what Edward Keenan has termed the "fusion" of the self-protective political culture of the Russian village and the quasi-paranoid but pragmatic political culture of the Russian bureaucracy.[7] Finally, they were indelibly molded in their formative years by the successive traumas of the purges and the Second World War, so they were "survivors" in every sense of the word.

Thanks to selectivity based on youth, the postpurge leadership had the potential for extraordinary longevity in office as a generation. This demographic fact was the basis for the remarkable stability and slow turnover manifested in the Soviet leadership at the level of Central Committee membership, particularly after the disruptions of the immediate post-Stalin years had passed. Table 28.1 indicates the rate of holdovers in the successive intervals from one Central Committee to the next, from 1952–56 to 1981–86. These figures demonstrate the very high degree of continuity in the Soviet bureaucratic elite from 1961 to 1981, particularly when the count includes members who were previously at any one of the three prestige ranks.

Not surprisingly, low turnover allowed the leadership body as a whole to age steadily, as renovation failed to keep pace with the passage of time. Table 28.2 shows how the median age of the Central Committee rose during this era at the steady rate of one year of age for each two years of elapsed time. Renovation did not even occur as fast as the turnover rate might have allowed; age

TABLE 28.1. Turnover and retention in the Central Committee elite

	1956	1961	1966	1971	1976	1981	1986
CC members	133	175	195	241	287	319	307
Held over from previous CC	79 (59.4%)	66 (37.7%)	139 (71.3%)	149 (61.8%)	201 (70.0%)	230 (72.1%)	172 (56.0%)
Held over or promoted from Cand. or CAC	94 (70.8%)	97 (55.4%)	170 (87.2%)	195 (80.9%)	251 (87.5%)	278 (87.1%)	215 (70.0%)
Cand. members	122	155	165	155	139	151	170
CAC members	63	65	79	81	85	75	83
Total all ranks	318	395	439	477	511	545	560
Total all ranks held over	174 (54.7%)	158 (40.0%)	277 (63.1%)	313 (65.6%)	369 (72.2%)	392 (71.9%)	304 (54.3%)

was not a decisive criterion for retirement at each congress, and replacements tended to be made with people from the candidate ranks and the Central Auditing Commission who were not much younger than the aging holdovers. As a result, the median people of 1952 and 1981, over a span of nearly three decades, were born only fourteen years apart, in 1904 and 1918 respectively, biologically within the same generation as its leading and trailing edges, so to speak. This means that the median members of 1981 had still come out of the same basic experience as Stalin's last Central Committee of 1952—the purge of their elders as they themselves were moving from the Komsomol to the party; service in World War II; and promotion into the power-wielding class of the nomenklatura while Stalin was still living and tyrannizing the country.

The natural consequences of the leadership's aging have been widely recognized in the literature on Soviet politics. The postpurge officialdom was, by virtue of its origin, experience, and ossification in office, conservative and self-protective in its reflexes. It resisted or sabotaged innovation and clung to sterile bureaucratic methods and ideological formulas in the face of the new problems and potential of a modern society. To be sure, new blood was not entirely excluded from the leadership, and steady expansion in the membership of the

TABLE 28.2. Aging of the Central Committee

	1952	1956	1961	1966	1971	1976	1981	1986
All full members	125	133	175	195	241	287	319	307
Median birth year	1904	1906	1908	1909	1913	1915/16	1918	1924
Median age	48	50	53	56	58	60.5	63	62
Holdover members	—	79	66	139	149	201	230	172
Median birth year	—	1903	1906	1909	1911	1914	1916	1923
Median age	—	53	55	57	60	62	63	63
New and promoted members	—	54	109	56	92	86	89	136
Median birth year	—	1908	1910	1912	1918	1921	1923	1930
Median age	—	48	51	54	53	55	58	56
Members retained through 1981	12	19	51	82	150	231	—	—
Median birth year	1906/7	1905	1911	1911	1914	1917	—	—
Median age, 1981	74.5	76	70	70	67	65	—	—

Central Committee made it possible to bring in some younger and better-educated people without winnowing the older cohorts at the same rate. Nevertheless, as the age data show, most of the new blood was progressively older and more tired when it too reached the level of Central Committee membership. It was only a matter of time until illness, incapacity, and death would break the grip of the postpurge generation. This is precisely what occurred between Brezhnev's death and the Twenty-seventh Congress.

The study of Soviet elite politics and of the structures and practices that shaped that mysterious realm of human behavior is facilitated by the actual way in which the organization of the Communist Party defined its leadership elite. This was no more and no less than the Central Committee of the party, together with its candidate members and the members of the CAC.[8]

Ever since the late 1920s, membership in these groups was accorded almost exclusively on the basis of the tenure of high bureaucratic office in the party apparatus, the civil government, and the military, with small numbers allocated to the top people in the trade unions, diplomacy, and cultural and scientific work. Individuals were automatically elevated to the Central Committee at the next party congress after their appointment to a job carrying Central Committee rank (and they reportedly attended meetings from the time of the entitling appointment).[9] Conversely, individuals who were removed or retired from one of these elite positions and not assigned to another were almost always dropped from the Central Committee at the next congress (although they might still attend until that time as "dead souls," so called).

The fine lines of functional and regional status in the makeup of the Central Committee underscore a compulsion about rank and precedence that appears to have been deeply embedded in Russian political culture. These criteria reveal, if more evidence were needed, that the slate of Central Committee members voted in unanimously at each party congress must have been carefully prepared by the central authorities to reflect the appointments and removals effected since the previous congress and to maintain the required balance and rank of representation for all the functional hierarchies and geographical areas simultaneously.

The Central Committee elected at the Twenty-sixth Congress in 1981, the last under Brezhnev, reflected the long-standing order of precedence in the allocation of seats. Taking all three ranks together—full members, candidate members, and CAC, a total of 545 individuals—there were 211 (39 percent) from the full-time party apparatus, 179 (33 percent) from the civil government (central and union republics), 40 (7 percent) from the military, 6 from the police agencies, 21 ambassadors (usually former party officials), 11 trade union officials, 22 cultural and scientific officials, 4 heads of miscellaneous "social organizations," and 51 (9 percent) mass representatives. Geographically, the party and government categories broke down as shown in table 28.3, with a clear ranking in representation according to the importance of the republic and a definite precedence of party representation over governmental. Despite the abrupt surge in the rate of membership turnover, the new list established by the Twenty-seventh Congress in 1986 deviated hardly at all from the representative proportions observed in 1981. Table 28.4 demonstrates the degree of constancy from 1981 to 1986 in the allocation of full member seats, though there was a significant reduction in governmental jobs with Central Committee rank. In the category of "mass representatives" there was a distinct increase, practically all accounted for by adding women from the RSFSR. But in the main, the job-slot system of status and representation was faithfully observed by the new Gorbachev leadership, whatever its other commitments to reform. The status matrices shown in table 28.5 demonstrate how the unspoken rules

TABLE 28.3. Party and government representation in the Central Committee elite, by geographical area

Area	Party		Government	
	1981	1986	1981	1986
Central	63	49	123	124
RSFSR	80	87	26	18
Union republics	68	77	35	35
Ukraine	24	25	6	7
Kazakhstan	14	16	3	3
Uzbekistan	6	6	3	3
Belorussia	5	7	3	4
Georgia	2	2	2	1[a]
Azerbaidzhan	2	2	2	2
Latvia	2	2	2	2
Kirgizia	2	2	2	1[a]
Moldavia	2	2	2	2
Lithuania	2	2	2	2
Tadzhikistan	2	2	2	2
Armenia	2	2	2	2
Turkmenia	2	2	2	2
Estonia	2	2	2	2

Note: Figures include Central Committee members, candidate members, and members of the Central Auditing Commission.

[a]Figure does not include vacancy that was evidently filled after the congress.

still operated, with fine attention given at the party center to the prestige implications of all appointments.

In a more visible though less firmly established way, the job-slot principle of status was carried up into the Politburo itself. The pattern and its consistency are clear if the Politburo positions are arranged for each congress year according to the incumbents' functions. Table 28.6 shows the close relationship

TABLE 28.4. Allocation of full Central Committee seats, 1981 and 1986

	1981		1986		(Change in share)
Total	319 [8]	100%	307 [11]	100%	
Party apparatus	140 [1]	43.9%	135 [1]	44.0%	−5 (+0.2%)
Central	33	10.3%	33 [1]	10.7%	—
RSFSR	66 [1]	20.7%	63	20.5%	−3
Union republics	41	12.9%	39	12.7%	−2
Government	101 [2]	31.7%	84	27.4%	−17 (−13.6%)
Central	81	25.4%	69	22.5%	−12
RSFSR	10	3.1%	9	2.9%	−1
Union republics	10	3.1%	6	2.0%	−4
Other	78 [5]		88 [10]		+10
Military	23	7.2%	24	7.8%	+1 (+5.6%)
Police	5	1.6%	5	1.6%	—
Trade unions	5	1.6%	4	1.3%	−1
Diplomats	13	4.1%	11	3.6%	−2
Science & culture	11	3.4%	10	3.3%	−1
Social organizations	2 [2]	0.6%	3 [2]	1.0%	+1
Mass representatives	19 [2]	6.0%	27 [8]	8.8%	+8 (+46.7%)
RSFSR	15 [2]	4.7%	22 [8]	7.2%	+7
Union republics	4	1.3%	5	1.6%	+1
Retired dignitaries	0	0%	4	1.3%	+4

Note: Numbers of women are indicated in brackets.

TABLE 28.5. Status matrices: Central Committee representation of union republics, 1981 and 1986

Republic	1st sec.	2nd sec.	Prime minister	CPSS	1st deputy prime minister	Other
			1981			
Ukraine	PB	CC	CC	CC	CC	CC (14), Cands. (8)
Kazakhstan	PB	CC	CC	CC	CAC	CAC (4)
Belorussia	Cand. PB	CC	CC	CC	CAC	CC (6), Cands. (5)
Uzbekistan	Cand. PB	CC	CC	CC	CAC	CC, Cands. (2)
Georgia	Cand. PB	CC	Cand.	CAC		CC, Cands. (2), CAC
Azerbaidzhan	Cand. PB	Cand.	Cand.	CAC		
Latvia	CC	Cand.	Cand.	CAC		
Kirgizia	CC	Cand.	Cand.	CAC		
Moldavia	CC	Cand.	CAC	Cand.		
Lithuania	CC	Cand.	CAC	Cand.		
Tadzhikistan	CC	Cand.	CAC	Cand.		
Armenia	CC	Cand.	CAC	Cand.		
Estonia	CC	Cand.	Cand.	CC[a]		
Turkmenia	CC	Cand.	CAC	Cand.		
			1986			
Ukraine	PB	CC	CC	CC	CC	CC (13), Cands. (10)
Kazakhstan	PB	CC	CC	Cand.	CAC	CC (13), Cands. (7)
Belorussia	Cand. PB	CC	CC	CC	CC	CC (2), Cands. (3)

(continued)

TABLE 28.5. (*continued*)

Republic	1st sec.	2nd sec.	Prime minister	CPSS	1st deputy prime minister	Other
			1986			
Uzbekistan	CC	CC	Cand.	CC	CAC	Cands. (4)
Georgia	CC	CC	b	CAC		
Azerbaidzhan	CC	Cand.	Cand.	CAC		
Latvia	CC	Cand.	Cand.	CAC		
Kirgizia	CC	Cand.	b	CAC		
Moldavia	CC	Cand.	Cand.	CAC		
Lithuania	CC	Cand.	Cand.	CAC		
Tadzhikistan	CC	Cand.	Cand.	CAC		
Armenia	CC	Cand.	Cand.	CAC		
Estonia	CC	Cand.	Cand.	CAC		
Turkmenia	CC	Cand.	CAC	Cand.		

[a]In an anomaly, the former Estonian first secretary, Kebin, was allowed to keep his CC seat after being shunted to chairman of the Presidium of the Estonian Supreme Soviet.
[b]Table does not include vacancy that was evidently filled after the congress.

of Politburo membership with high party and government office as well as the striking stability in the positions represented, particularly when Politburo candidate status is considered along with full membership. The remarkable continuity of individual incumbents in jobs of Politburo rank during the Brezhnev era stands out as well. There are very few anomalies: the brief heyday of the chairmanship of the Central Council of Trade Unions, when that office was utilized to shunt Shelepin away from a bid for power, and the unusual status of the Ministry of Culture during the incumbency of ex–Secretariat member Pyotr Demichev. The precedence of the party apparatus over the government and the scaled representation of union republics, so clear in the apportionment of the Central Committee, are replicated in miniature in the Politburo.[10]

Comparison of the 1986 Politburo with earlier years shows that despite the sweeping change in leading personnel that took place during the transition after Brezhnev, Gorbachev continued to observe the established rules

TABLE 28.6. Functional representation in the Politburo, 1966–86

Position	1966	1971	1976	1981	1986
Party apparatus					
General secretary	Brezhnev	Brezhnev	Brezhnev	Brezhnev[a]	Gorbachev
Secretariat	Suslov	Suslov	Suslov	Suslov	Ligachev
	Kirilenko	Kirilenko	Kirilenko	Kirilenko	Zaikov
	Shelepin	Kulakov	Ustinov[b]	Chernenko	(Dolgikh)
	(Ustinov)	(Ustinov)	(Ponomarev)	Gorbachev	—
	(Demichev)	(Demichev)	—	(Ponomarev)	—
Chrm. party control	Pelshe	Pelshe	Pelshe	Pelshe	Solomentsev
1st sec. Ukraine	Shelest	Shelest	Shcherbitsky	Shcherbitsky	Shcherbitsky
1st sec. Kazakhstan	(Kunaev)	Kunaev	Kunaev	Kunaev	Kunaev
1st sec. Moscow City	—	Grishin	Grishin	Grishin	(Yeltsin)
1st sec. Leningrad .	—	—	Romanov	Romanov	(Soloviev)
1st sec. Belorussia	(Masherov)	(Masherov)	(Masherov)	(Kisilev)	(Slyunkov)
1st sec. Uzbekistan	(Rashidov)	(Rashidov)	(Rashidov)	(Rashidov)	—
1st sec. Georgia	(Mzhavanadze)	(Mzhavanadze)	—	(Shevardnadze)	—
1st sec. Azerbaidzhan	—	—	(Aliev)	(Aliev)	—

(continued)

TABLE 28.6. (*continued*)

Position	1966	1971	1976	1981	1986
Government					
Prime minister	Kosygin	Kosygin	Kosygin	Tikhonov	Ryzhkov
Chrm. Pres. Sup. Sov.	Podgorny	Podgorny	Podgorny	(Kuznetsov)[a]	Gromyko
1st dep. prime min.	Mazurov	Mazurov	Mazurov	–	Aliev
	Poliansky	Poliansky	–	–	–
Prime min. RSFSR	Voronov	Voronov	(Solomentsev)	(Solomentsev)	Vorotnikov
Prime min. Ukraine	(Shcherbitsky)	Shcherbitsky	–	–	–
Minister of defense	–	–	Grechko[b]	Ustinov	(Sokolov)
Minister of for. aff.	–	–	Gromyko	Gromyko	Shevardnadze
Chairman KGB	–	(Andropov)	Andropov	Andropov	Chebrikov
Chairman Gosplan	–	–	–	–	(Talyzin)
Minister of culture	–	–	(Demichev)	(Demichev)	(Demichev)[a]
Chrm. trade unions	(Grishin)	Shelepin	–	–	–
Total members	11 (6)	14 (5)	15 (5)	14 (7)	12 (7)

Note: Candidates are in parentheses.
[a]Kuznetsov was 1st deputy chairman of the Presidium of the Supreme Soviet when
Brezhnev held the title of chairman. Demichev was given this position shortly after the 27th Congress.
Demichev died just after the 25th Congress and was replaced by Ustinov.
[b]Grechko died just after the 25th Congress and was replaced by Ustinov.

in awarding rank in the Politburo as well as in the Central Committee. Nowhere did he deviate from precedent, except to downgrade the non-Slavic republics and to bring in the new head of Gosplan (a position not represented since the 1950s). Expectations of Politburo status for the country's top jobs were by this time so firm that the leader could do little more than marginally adjust ranks.

The tradition of making up the Politburo as well as the Central Committee on the basis of the status of particular individuals' jobs was a conservative and stabilizing element in Soviet politics. It was another circumstance contributing to the long political lives of the postpurge generation. Within the terms of the job-slot tradition, no change in the Central Committee or the Politburo was possible without removing the given individual from the bureaucratic command that conferred the corresponding rank. To accomplish a sudden overturn in the leadership bodies would require a corresponding sweep of the upper bureaucratic hierarchy. Short of a Stalin-style reign of terror, such a campaign would quickly arouse a defensive coalition among the apparatchiki and put the leader's power in jeopardy. The less risky alternative was simply to wait for targeted individuals to die or fall into decrepitude. However, the age composition of the postpurge generation made any wholesale housecleaning impossible until the passing of that cohort created unusual possibilities for personnel changes. Brezhnev's successors could seize the opportunity for new appointments in the party and governmental machinery and reshape the composition of the Central Committee as their new appointees were promoted to it. This opportunity was the key to a new foundation for personal leadership and policy.

It is ironic that the era dominated by the postpurge generation of Stalin's disciples proved to be the time of Soviet Russia's nearest approximation to the principle of collective leadership. Though Brezhnev's rule was based on a conservative reaction against the excesses of Khrushchevian reformism, it originated in the altogether un-Stalinist overthrow of the top leader. This in turn implied the removability of that leader's successors—scarcely a Stalinist idea.

Consistent with this fundamental change, Soviet politics after 1964 were governed by a sort of balance of power and consensus seeking among several political levels, including the general secretary, the upper oligarchy (that is, the Politburo), and the broad bureaucratic leadership at the level of the Central Committee. This did not mean a dismantling of central authority or a retreat from the principle of party control, as an exaggerated interest group interpretation might imply. What seems to have taken hold was a process of representation and balancing of functional bureaucratic interests going on under the broad umbrella of party authority and decision making. This is the system of "participatory bureaucracy."[11]

Continuity was the hallmark of the Brezhnev era. The circular flow of power slowed down, job-tenure membership in the elite was confirmed, and participatory bureaucracy brought the status quo interests of the upper official-dom strongly into the policy-making process. Moreover, there was only limited opportunity for natural leadership replacements, given the median age of the Central Committee in 1966 of only fifty-six. All the unwritten rules of Soviet politics—promotion tracks, representational entitlements, rights to status, and the balance of function and prestige—were deeply confirmed.

Under these conditions, there is little wonder that the Brezhnev era was distinguished by the stability of leadership documented so clearly in the high rate of retention of Central Committee members following the turmoil of the Khrushchev era (see table 28.1 and table 28.7). Yet stability did not mean that a fixed leadership group held office until death knocked at the door. After the un-usual continuity in 1966 that reflected consolidation of the 1961 cohort of new members, turnover went on in the Central Committee at a steady though mod-est rate. Thanks in part to the repeated expansions of the body (accomplished largely by upgrading candidate rank jobs to full membership), new members in 1971, 1976, and 1981 constituted 37 percent, 30 percent, and 28 percent of the respective central committees. As a result of expansion and replacements, the Central Committee always had a majority of members who were only in their first or second terms (even in 1981, when the "upperclassmen" were one seat short of a majority). However, well over half of the new members between 1966 and 1981 had served one or more terms as candidate members or members of the CAC, in contrast to the direct installation of the great majority of the new members in 1956, in 1961, and again in 1986.

Brezhnev's personnel choices did not entirely exclude younger people, contrary to the general impression. The median age for new members installed directly without service at candidate or CAC rank stayed in the range of forty-nine to fifty-three for each congress down to 1981 and only went up to the high of fifty-five in 1986. But these people were outweighed by those promoted from the lower ranks, who were closer in age to the holdovers in each Central Com-mittee. Overall, only a decade in median birth year separated the new entrants of 1961 and 1981, twenty years apart (see table 28.2). Drops were not numerous enough and new cohorts were not young enough on the average to prevent the median age of the Central Committee as a whole from creeping steadily upward until 1981. At the same time, a growing age spread was introduced between the old hands and the more youthful members of the new cohorts. The span in

TABLE 28.7. Survival in the Central Committee, by entry cohort

	1952	1956	1961	Survivors in CC 1966	1971	1976	1981	1986
Entry year								
1952	125[a]	79	40	36	23	15	12	3
1956	—	54	27	23	18	13	7	4
1961	—	—	108	85	69	57	38	13
1966	—	—	—	51	40	35	29	10
1971	—	—	—	—	91	81	67	32
1976	—	—	—	—	—	86	77	50
1981	—	—	—	—	—	—	89	60
1986	—	—	—	—	—	—	—	135
Total members	125	133	175	195	241	287	319	307

[a]Analysis does not extend back to 1939 or before; all members of 1952 are treated as if new.

median age between the oldest and youngest quartiles of the membership widened from fifty-seven to forty-nine in 1961 (eight years) to seventy to fifty-five in 1981 (fifteen years). It is also significant that ever since 1961, the contingent of Central Committee members from the party apparatus was kept consistently three to four years younger than the overall median,[12] while the governmental and military people regularly averaged older than the norm. Even so, the median age for party apparatus members crept up at the same rate as the whole body, from forty-nine and one-half in 1961 to fifty-nine in 1981.

Very little could be known, except by inference, about real politics at the top level of the Soviet structure. There was another unwritten law of Soviet politics (again rooted in Old Russian political culture, according to Keenan) that called for suppressing any public expression of individuality and disagreement among the leaders.[13] Nevertheless, there appears to have been a genuine political process of deals, threats, and coalitions going on in the upper reaches of the system, laterally as well as vertically, to arrive at decisions on both personnel and policy.[14]

Where preponderant and final power was located in this Byzantine system is another question that defies precise answer. Comparing Stalin's times with Brezhnev's, power had clearly spread from individuals to committees and from the top downward, though how far it is hard to say. Certainly the Central Committee had a potent role, through the local and specialized bureaucracies that its members directed as well as through its role as ultimate arbiter in any struggle for power at the top. One may presume that the same sharing of the decision-making power worked further down, as government ministers and provincial party secretaries accommodated their constituencies to avert dissension that might undermine their own positions in the eyes of the top leadership. Thus the mutual vulnerability of leader and oligarchy probably led to an inclusion of lower levels of officialdom in the real power process, as those above maneuvered for support below. This was not competitive electoral politics in the familiar Western sense but it bears analogy with the bureaucratic politics that go on in every hierarchically organized entity in modern society.

The death of Leonid Brezhnev in November 1982 signaled the passing of an entire dominant generation in the nation's top leadership bodies. Time finally caught up with the postpurge heirs of Stalinism, as death and debility opened the way for a generational revolution the like of which had not been seen since the time of the prewar purges. The crisis of biological limits was nowhere more evident than in the country's highest position, as the transfer of leadership first to one and then another representative of the old generation was foiled by death, leaving the field finally to a man two decades younger than his late predecessors.

Generational politics undoubtedly figured in the surprise turns of the political wheel during the triple succession to Brezhnev. To challenge Brezhnev's choice, Konstantin Chernenko, Yuri Andropov had to mobilize support in the Politburo and the Central Committee around the catalytic issues of discipline and reform.[15] By 1981, thanks to the modest but steady intake of younger members into the Central Committee, particularly in the contingent from the party apparatus, there was a substantial body of influential people who must have felt frustrated by the immobilism of policy under Brezhnev and repelled by the prospect of more of the same under Chernenko. Seweryn Bialer commented, "The new generation . . . are skeptical about the grander claims of Soviet propaganda concerning the system's merits. In private, they do not disguise their dislike of and lack of respect for the old generation."[16] This mood, together with the more obvious elements of military and police support, helps account for Andropov's dark horse victory following his surprising elevation to the Secretariat a few months before Brezhnev died. If this theory is accurate, Andropov's success was a major victory for participatory bureaucracy, of power resting on the consent, if not of the governed, then at least of some of the key governors.

Andropov's unpredictable selection, like that of both Chernenko and Gorbachev following him, is indicative of the real politics that must have been going on behind the scenes in the Kremlin during the era of the triple succession. While there was, contrary to common opinion, a clear mechanism for determining the succession to the post of general secretary—that is, selection by the Politburo and ratification by the Central Committee—the actual identity of the successor was not arrived at by any automatic formula. Rather, it was the outcome of political maneuver among powerful bureaucratic chieftains and their constituencies—again, participatory bureaucracy. To be sure, there was a constraint in yet another unwritten law, that the general secretary had to be chosen from among the three or four individuals who were simultaneously members of both the Politburo and the party Secretariat. Nevertheless, the possibilities of maneuver allowed ambitious members of the Politburo with their own constituencies to secure seats in the Secretariat, as Andropov did in 1982 and as Grigory Romanov did in 1983, to position themselves for a bid for power.

The chance sequence of three closely spaced vacancies in the office of general secretary underscored the significance of genuine, fluid politics at the pinnacle of the system as well as an opportunity for real input from below when aspirants for the leadership had to compete for bureaucratic support. Thus the ultimate locus of power would seem to be further diffused downward in a system that must be regarded as a complex oligarchy. It did not seem likely that this trend could quickly be reversed simply by the consolidation of a more stable leadership in the person of Gorbachev.

Once in the top office, Andropov set the circular flow of power in motion once again, forcing resignations and making new appointments in jobs of Central Committee rank. He did not do this in an all-or-nothing fashion that could have provoked a threatening bureaucratic rebellion to actualize the potential vulnerability of the general secretary but only proceeded step-by-step as vacancies arose. He did not disturb the Politburo at all except when death opened up the opportunity. Under the conservative Chernenko, for obvious reasons, renovation slowed down to a crawl, but a start had been made.

On the basis of Andropov's initiatives, Gorbachev was able to resume and accelerate the circular flow immediately upon assuming the general secretaryship in March 1985. He initiated a program of quick and sweeping changes in jobs of Central Committee rank both in the party apparatus and in the government. Between the Twenty-sixth and Twenty-seventh congresses, of the datable replacements of functionaries at Central Committee rank, twenty-seven were accomplished under Andropov, only ten during Chernenko's thirteen months in office, and fifty-seven in Gorbachev's first year. With this momentum,

Gorbachev was able to complete the circular flow by reaching into the Politbu-ro itself and ousting those members—Romanov, the Moscow City boss Viktor Grishin, and Prime Minister Nikolai Tikhonov—who had most conspicuously challenged him. The way was then open for him to carry through a renovation of the Central Committee at the forthcoming party congress to a degree that had not been seen in a quarter century.

The Twenty-seventh Party Congress clearly confirmed Gorbachev's leader-ship and his reform line as the outcome of the triple succession. In the Central Committee that it installed, the congress consummated the generational over-turn with the passing of the postpurge leaders at all levels. On the other hand, it also confirmed the continuity in the forms of political life that had marked the Soviet Union since the rise of Stalin.

A rich body of data in support of all these observations is the composi-tion of the 1986 Central Committee, elected unanimously, as was the custom, upon the nomination of a single slate on the last day of the congress. The prevailing job-slot basis of membership selection and the apportionment of seats according to the political importance of various bureaucratic functions and geographical areas continued to be observed. The operation of the circular flow of power, simultaneously effecting the generational transition and under-girding the leadership position of Gorbachev and the reformers, was compel-lingly manifested in the number of new Andropov and Gorbachev appointees who won membership on the committee—135 new people out of a total of 307 on the list of full members.

The 1986 Central Committee stands out in a number of ways from the trends of previous decades. For one thing, its numbers were reduced—from 319 to 307—for the first time ever in the history of the Soviet regime. Evi-dently the new leadership decided to call a halt to the progressive status infla-tion that had seen the Central Committee expand from 125 members in 1952 to its maximum of 319 in 1981, though the 1986 reduction was offset by an increase in the number of candidate members from 151 in 1981 to 170, the highest ever. Certain symbolic adjustments were made in the allocation of rep-resentation, notably a substantial increase in the number of mass representa-tives, the demotion of a number of central government ministries when their new incumbents were given only candidate rank, and an admonitory cut in the representation of the Central Asian republics. For the first time, a number of retired dignitaries—not just retired marshals and former chiefs of state—were allowed to keep their seats, so as to phase them out of office more gently than had been the custom. They included ex–prime minister Tikhonov, ex-Gosplan chairman N. K. Baibakov, and the retired party secretary and ideologist Boris Ponomarev. Another secretary (Ivan Kapitonov) was moved to the Central Auditing Commission to serve as its new chairman, with personal status more or less equivalent to Central Committee membership.

The increase in mass representatives while government representation was being cut was evidently a sign that the leadership wanted a more popular image. Moreover, it hoped to overcome the impression that it excluded women, who were increased from 8 out of 319 (2.5 percent) in 1981 to 12 out of 307 (4 percent) in 1986. However, the increase occurred largely in the mass representative category and did not extend to significant inclusion of women in positions of actual power. Among the nationalities, the Gorbachev message was even more firmly one of Russian and Slavic hegemony, as shown by that preference in the mass representative category and by the carefully graduated downgrading of Central Asian representation in both the party and governmental sectors.

More striking was the inclusion of people who were not only new but definitely younger. The 1986 Central Committee reflected the greatest percentage turnover of any since 1961 and was the first since 1952 to show an actual decrease in the median age of its members. The survivors of the postpurge generation were largely eliminated from the scene; of the 195 members of the first Brezhnev Central Committee, 86 of whom still held office in 1981, only 30 remained in 1986—barely one-tenth of the new membership. Only 3 individuals remained from Stalin's last Central Committee of 1952 (Party Secretary Mikhail Zimianin, retiree Baibakov, and the about-to-be-retired first deputy chairman of the Presidium of the Supreme Soviet, V. V. Kuznetsov) and only 4 from among those who entered the Central Committee in 1956 (Andrei Gromyko, Kazakhstan boss D. A. Kunaev, Ponomarev, and the chairman of the People's Control Committee, A. M. Shkolnikov) (see table 28.7).

Turnover and renovation in Central Committee slots were even more striking when broken down according to functional categories. Youth and freshness were most evident in the party apparatus contingent, where power was concentrated. New appointments moved the median birth year in this group seven years later, from 1922 to 1929, for a net reduction in age of two years while five years were elapsing. The central government ministers, subject to extensive restaffing, showed a striking drop in median age, from sixty-six in 1981 to sixty-one, but still remained on the average four years older than the party group. Other groups were held to roughly the same age, except for the cultural and educational leadership, which actually went up in age.

In and of itself, the Twenty-seventh Congress did nothing decisive. But it did register Gorbachev's personal triumph, for the time being, over any possible combination of older rivals. This was a victory reflecting a new generation of bureaucrats who scored their success by waiting for the demographic revolution that had to come. In turn, it opened the path to potential policy changes, presaged only by rhetoric at the congress but capable of altering the face of the country to a degree that at the time could only be conjectured.

Following the Twenty-seventh Congress, Gorbachev had the opportunity to press on with the circular flow of power through the appointment process and perhaps establish greater personal control over the Politburo. The issue of economic reform could well serve as the anvil on which these changes would be hammered out. Reform would in turn be advanced by the personnel changes made in its name. With new people and new issues, Gorbachev could indeed become a major figure in this epoch of the history of Russia.

But uncertainties remained. There was the haunting lesson of the overthrow of Khrushchev. The traditions of job-slot representation and participatory bureaucracy, though they limited how far and how fast the general secretary could move, had to be respected, on pain of provoking a bureaucratic rebellion that could endanger the leader's tenure altogether. Gorbachev's position was delicate—he needed to move the circular flow to make his personal dominance more meaningful than Brezhnev did yet could not drive these changes so vigorously as to stir up the sort of concerted counteroffensive of participatory bureaucracy that was Khrushchev's undoing. Soviet politics at the top seemed to depend still on the interplay of real politics among flesh-and-blood competitors for the sweet fruit of power.

CHAPTER 29

Reform and the Intelligentsia

T

wo decades after the debacle of reform under the aegis of Nikita Khrushchev, the Soviet Union reached another opening in its political life. This time the opportunity for change was presented not merely by the demise of a leader wedded to cultural orthodoxy and control but by the passing of an entire generation of leadership brought up in the school of Stalinist postrevolutionary self-justification. With Brezhnev, Andropov, Chernenko, and their age-mates, the party and government officialdom that as a group had been growing old in high office since World War II began rapidly to die off or invite removal for age and disability. Gorbachev won the general secretaryship in March 1985, not merely as a youthful symbol of renovation but as the physical representative of a new generation in charge of the Soviet ship of state. Supported by the spread of an alternative political culture and the unfulfilled legacy of the revolution itself, he tried his best to reverse the traditional Russian relationship between the holders of power and the intelligentsia. He appears to have recognized that the liberation of the intelligentsia from the constraints of state power was the key to reform and national progress, and that only a free intelligentsia could make his "restructuring" "irreversible."

The years of Brezhnev's leadership were actually a time of contradictory developments in the relationship between the Soviet bureaucracy and the intelligentsia. To be sure, neo-Stalinism prevailed politically for more than a quarter of a century after Stalin himself had left the scene. But, faced like the tsarist bureaucracy with the challenges of modernization and international power politics, the neo-Stalinist bureaucracy could not escape sowing the seeds of its own destruction.

339

The crack in the monolith most apparent to the outside world was the confrontation between the bureaucracy and the creative intelligentsia that marked the Brezhnev era and worsened toward its end. Typically, representatives of the bureaucratic outlook were installed in the nominal institutions of intellectual leadership, especially the unions of writers and other artistic categories. Repression of creative individuality, ranging from simple censorship or refusal to publish all the way to arrest, trial, and imprisonment or exile, put an end to the relative freedom of the Thaw of the 1950s and early 1960s and effectively drove the new surge of creative effort underground. In the best Stalinist style, Brezhnev told the Twenty-third Party Congress in March 1966, "We are unfailingly guided by the principle of party spirit in art and a class approach to the evaluation of everything that is done in the sphere of culture."[1] For the poet Andrei Voznesensky, the Brezhnev regime meant the "collapse of illusions."[2] The turning point was the arrest of Sinyavsky and Daniel in September 1965 and their trial and imprisonment in January–February 1966.

Renewed political repression did not suffice to sustain the constraints of Socialist Realism on artistic form. "In the past two decades," wrote the literary historian Deming Brown in 1978, "there have been so many inroads into this doctrine in actual practice as to render it virtually inoperative. . . . Socialist Realism . . . has largely been replaced by critical realism."[3] Writers who stayed within the official limits were often able to influence government policy, as in the movement to preserve historic buildings and the ultimately successful protest against the diversion of Siberian rivers to Central Asia.

By the end of the Brezhnev era, a variety of forces were working against the continued power of the neo-Stalinist bureaucracy. Modernization, the expansion of the intelligentsia, and the need to rely on its expertise all made constant and detailed political interference counterproductive if not impossible. Revolutionary language was losing all credibility, and the generation that sustained it was dying off. The old guard became mired in disbelief, corruption, and fear of change. The intelligentsia, for its part, saw its hopes and spirit fading and joined in the common pursuit of material success or mere survival. Nevertheless, potential for change remained in the enduring traditions of the intelligentsia, now being absorbed by the new, more sophisticated cadre of leaders rising through the bureaucracy. By the 1980s, there was reason to think that the long-standing dichotomy of bureaucracy and intelligentsia, cultural as well as political, might be overcome.

A running counterpoint to the expansion of the Soviet intelligentsia in the 1960s and 1970s was the "scientific-technical revolution." For the Soviets this meant a new appreciation of the intelligentsia, now hailed as a source of national power and progress. According to Suslov, speaking as the chief ideologist of the Brezhnev regime, "The contemporary scientific-technical revolution opens before society unseen possibilities in using science for mastering and protecting the forces of nature and solving social problems, . . . and at the same time it acts as material preparation for communist civilization."[4] Thus the "scientific-technical revolution" became an article of official faith, even though its full implications were never thoroughly defined. Cyril Black termed it "the most important development in Soviet ideology since 1917."[5]

Confidence in science and technological innovation as forces for progress and betterment of the human condition was axiomatic for the Soviet regime from the beginning, inherited from the nineteenth-century intelligentsia via the quasi-intelligentsia of the revolutionary era. In science, the outlooks of the bureaucracy and of the intelligentsia were substantially congruent.

Recognition of a "revolution" in science and technology came soon after Stalin died. In 1955, Prime Minister Bulganin, having in mind the promise of nuclear energy, spoke of "the threshold of a new scientific and technical revolution, the significance of which far surpasses the industrial revolutions associated with the appearance of steam and electricity."[6] Khrushchev included the scientific-technical revolution among his extravagant promises in the Party Program of 1961. Blatant imposition of party doctrine on scientific conclusions came to an end, even though Khrushchev patronized the quack biological doctrines of Trofim Lysenko right up to his downfall. "Step by step the Stalinist unity of science and ideology was dismantled," Alexander Vucinich observed.[7] As a result, scientists and other specialists won a growing degree of autonomy and influence, exemplified in the scope of their professional discussions and their voice in judging members and officials of scientific organizations.[8] Jerry Hough noted "the gradual broadening of open policy debates by those who are willing to work within the system."[9]

In the material respect, the post-Stalin decades saw "an enormous expansion of the Soviet research and development effort," in the words of Eugene Zaleski, as well as of the education base to support it.[10] The proliferation of new universities and institutes allowed a rapid numerical expansion in the technical intelligentsia and continuation of the social mobility that Soviet Russia had enjoyed since the 1920s, the opportunity of rising out of the masses and into the class of professional and white-collar workers through the avenue of education. Soviet statistics, whatever their accuracy, give a rough measure of the rate of growth: 37,000 engineers graduated in 1950, 170,000 in 1965.[11] The number of all specialists graduating with higher education, 177,000 in 1950, 343,000 in

1960, 631,000 in 1970 (for a cumulative total by then of almost 7,000,000).[12] According to Vucinich, the number of scientists doubled between 1947 and 1960 and doubled again between 1960 and 1966, at the cost of a considerable dilution in quality.[13] "A wholesale approach was taken in developing higher education," complained V. G. Afanasiev, subsequently editor of *Pravda*. "Many universities that were hastily established for official reasons of prestige . . . have found themselves in a particularly difficult situation."[14]

By the 1970s, this rapid growth in the training of specialists, spurred both by the state's aim for independence from foreign sources of knowledge and by the passion of Soviet youth to achieve intelligentsia status by way of education, resulted in an oversupply of experts in relation to what the Soviet economy could absorb. Zhores Medvedev referred to "hypertrophy" and "redundancy" in the scientific establishment.[15] Afanasiev protested "talk of a surplus of highly trained specialists" but conceded, "The desire far exceeds the need," thanks to "the higher prestige that attaches to the intellectual professions." In consequence, "[w]e have an overabudance (from the standpoint of present needs) of highly trained specialists, [but] a shortage of workers, and particularly skilled workers."[16] This was the circumstance giving rise to Khruschev's abortive education reform of 1958 and again to the education reform adopted under Chernenko, both endeavoring to restrict access to the intelligentsia and steer Soviet youth toward production at the bench. Competition for intelligentsia status may also have contributed to discrimination in admitting persons of Jewish nationality or even partial Jewish ancestry to intellectual jobs. Nevertheless, maintaining a century-long tradition of intellectual ambition, Jews continued to be represented in the research establishment well beyond their proportion in the population as a whole,[17] though the bureaucracy, according to one samizdat writer, disliked "smartness" and considered Jews "too smart altogether."[18]

Despite its growth and the vital character of its services, the intelligentsia as a whole did not achieve in the 1960s and 1970s either the material or political conditions of life that would satisfy it. While a few outstanding scientists and politically conforming performers were rewarded with spectacularly high incomes and accompanying privilege, the rank and file of professional personnel—engineers, physicians, teachers, and the like—earned scarcely more than industrial workers (and less than miners and drivers), despite their extensive training. Thanks to salary compression in the 1960s as manual workers' pay caught up, the remuneration of scientific researchers was only 50 percent above the average for industrial workers; for engineers, it was only 10 percent above.[19] Tatiana Zaslavskaya, a leading theoretician of perestroika, observed retrospectively, "The salaries of scientific and other creative personnel have not changed since the 1950s. . . . The shortsighted policy of wage control . . . ignores the fact that it is primarily the labor of scientists and engineers that forms the basis of scientific and technical progress."[20] As time went on, the lure of intelligentsia status failed more and more to compensate for inadequate income, and the conditions of life—cramped housing, waiting in line, scrounging for necessities—that most of the intelligentsia shared with more humble citizens manifestly contributed to the demoralization that grew steadily during the Brezhnev years. These conditions created a recruitment problem for the intelligentsia as a whole. Sometimes disaffected intellectuals chose to take manual jobs, the slight economic cost being more than offset by the gain in personal independence.

There were other limitations to the Soviet effort in science, technology, and education that reflected penetration of the bureaucratic culture into intellectual life. Soviet intellectual work was constrained by hierarchy and centralization, with a sharp pyramid of quality, prestige, and rewards. Geographically, the overwhelming focus was Moscow and secondarily Leningrad; with few exceptions, assignment to work outside the centers was felt by Soviet intellectuals as administrative exile.

To be sure, special research towns—many around Moscow, as well as the famous Akademgorodok, constructed for the Siberian branch of the Academy of Sciences near Novosibirsk—provided better living and working conditions for researchers. These settlements encouraged the geographical spread of high-level research, while at the same time they isolated the scientific intellectuals from the unsophisticated provincials.

The official mania for secrecy still balked the exchange of ideas, not only with the outside world but even among Soviet scientists themselves. Contact between institutes and disciplines, between researchers and teachers, and between pure research activity and the applied needs of industry was artificially restricted by organizational rigidity and traditions of specialization. The organization of Soviet intellectual life suggests a honeycomb, where communication between one cell and another depended on bureaucratic channels up and down. Such contact was inordinately difficult, and this encouraged inbreeding as institutions employed their own graduates. Soviet scholars in the same fields in the same city but in different institutions more often than not simply did not know one another.

Theory and the theoretical disciplines, above all mathematics and physics, have traditionally been Russia's strong side intellectually, and they enjoyed commensurate prestige over work of practical application. This bias, and the relative immunity of such fields from political interference, accounted for the attraction of the most creative and critical minds to the theoretical sciences, which consequently became the seedbed for some of the boldest expressions of dissent from the 1960s on. In Russia, as the emigré physicist Valentin Turchin pointed out, there was always a special pull of science for "a certain type of personality requiring the existence of a higher goal, . . . in other words, a religious type of person."[21]

Could the scientific-technical revolution have had a significant impact on political life in the USSR? Officially it was maintained that this movement would do nothing but enhance the building of communism. Many Western observers, on the other hand, argued that the requirements of technical innovation and information flow would compel the Soviet bureaucracy to loosen its centralist controls, and, as Erik Hoffmann put it, "to broaden and deepen specialist elite participation at all stages and levels of decision making."[22] It is the old question of changes in the mode of production—in this instance the high technology of the "postindustrial" era—generating pressures for change in the superstructure of economic and political organization. That meant putting more and more influence into the hands of the intelligentsia.

The political tension and cultural incompatibility between the Soviet bureaucracy and the intelligentsia, or at least its creative stratum, became dramatically evident in the currents of dissent that took form after the fall of Khrushchev and the end of the post-Stalin Thaw. The emigré dissident Andrei Amalrik calculated that of the more than seven hundred individuals who signed petitions of protest in 1968, only 6 percent were workers, the balance all being intellectuals or professionals.[23] Active dissidents tended to be youthful, and children of Stalin's purge victims were prominent among them. The only forms of articulate dissent that developed a broader popular basis were those of a religious or national-minority character (notably in the Baltic republics and among the Crimean Tatars).[24] In the broadest sense, dissent was a product of the unresolved contradictions between a changing society and a rigid political system, between the intelligentsia as an increasingly dominant class and the bureaucracy as a ruling class on the defensive. As in the nineteenth century, dissent arose from the class that was privileged and necessary to the state but at the same time driven to independent-mindedness by virtue of its training and tradition.

Again, as in the nineteenth century, the principal vehicle for dissent in the Brezhnev era was literature. Writers, endowed with unusual prestige compared with Western and particularly North American societies, again assumed a role as the nation's voice and conscience, insofar as they could bring their thoughts to the attention of the reading public. Literary works that could not be tailored to the party's requirements for official publication were disseminated privately in the celebrated form of samizdat—"self-publishing." Samizdat was usually accomplished by typing multiple carbon copies of a manuscript, which in turn could be copied and multiplied by friends, a little like the transmission of learning by monastic copyists in the Middle Ages. It was not very difficult to smuggle manuscripts abroad and allow them to be published, both in Russian and in foreign translation. This came to be known as *tamizdat*—"publishing over there." Samizdat and tamizdat materials were broadcast back by Western radio services and reached much wider audiences, despite Soviet efforts to jam the transmissions. Radio broadcasts in turn gave rise to *magnitizdat*—recording broadcasts with tape recorders (in Russian, *magnitofon*) and distributing them on tapes, a practice that quickly spread to officially disapproved forms of popular music. Bolder avenues of dissent included literary meetings, poetry readings, and actual political demonstrations. The latter invariably brought on police repression.

The Sinyavsky-Daniel case triggered a widening series of protests by intellectuals who saw it as a step toward the possible rehabilitation of Stalin. On Soviet Constitution Day, 5 December 1965, the first of many short-lived demonstrations took place in Pushkin Square in Moscow, when two hundred students from Sinyavsky's home institution, the Gorky Institute of World Literature, gathered to protest the arrests and to demand a public trial. The trial and conviction of Sinyavsky and Daniel prompted an unprecedented series of petitions signed by leading literary figures and scientists (including Andrei Sakharov in his first manifestation of political dissent), directed to the Twenty-third Party Congress. These actions may have helped avert the literal rehabilitation of Stalin, but the authorities did not hesitate to toughen the law against dissent by adding the infamous articles 190-1 and 190-3 to the criminal code, outlawing the dissemination of "political slander" and the holding of unauthorized demonstrations, respectively. This did not deter Alexander Ginzburg, already a victim of repression in the late 1950s for attempting to publish the first samizdat journal, from compiling and circulating an unofficial transcript of the Sinyavsky-Daniel trial. For this crime he was arrested in January 1967, along with the writer Yuri Galanskov, who had run afoul of the KGB for preparing the samizdat literary anthology *Phoenix-66*. Those arrests prompted another demonstration in Pushkin Square, organized by a group including the poet Vladimir Bukovsky (already a victim of two years' incarceration in a mental hospital) and the mathematician Aleksander Yesenin-Volpin, son of the noted 1920s poet Sergei Yesenin. The inevitable outcome was more arrests and trials and a deepening sense of agitation within wide circles of the intelligentsia.

At this point, Alexander Solzhenitsyn, whose own novels *The Cancer Ward* and *The First Circle* had been denied publication and forced into samizdat distribution, took the lead to protest the tightening curbs on the intelligentsia. Denied a chance to speak at the Fourth Writers' Congress in May 1967, Solzhenitsyn launched into a running battle of letters with the leadership of the Writers' Union, but to no avail. Bukovsky and the demonstrators of January 1967 were put on trial in August, and Bukovsky got three years for his uncompromising defiance. Then, in January 1968, the subjects of that protest, Ginzburg and Galanskov, were tried and convicted on the familiar charge of anti-Soviet slander.

These acts provoked even broader protests, distinguished by the participation of descendants of Old Bolsheviks—Pavel Litvinov, the physicist grandson of the foreign commissar, and Piotr Yakir, son of the purged Red Army general Iona Yakir—together with the dissident major general Piotr Grigorenko. Yakir and his friends warned in an open letter to the international Communist conference then being held in Budapest, "For several years ominous symptoms of a restoration of Stalinism have been evident in the life of our society. . . . We have no guarantees that the year 1937 will not come upon us again."[25] The *Chronicle of Current Events,* recording dissident activities and repressions, began to appear in samizdat in April 1968, just when Sakharov assumed a leading position in the dissident movement by distributing his essay "Progress, Coexistence, and Intellectual Freedom" reviewing the evils of Stalinism and calling for fundamental political reform.[26] None of these challenges deterred the authorities from stepping up their campaign of warnings, searches, and arrests of dissident intellectuals.

The confrontation between the regime and the dissidents was intensified by the Soviet intervention in Czechoslovakia in August 1968 that snuffed out a political evolution among the more Western-style Communists of Prague and Bratislava similar to the reforms that Soviet intellectuals were pressing for. Grigorenko and his friends immediately circulated a statement of protest, and on 25 August, four days after the invasion, a group led by Pavel Litvinov and Yuli Daniel's wife, Larissa Bogoraz, demonstrated in Red Square, only to be immediately beaten and arrested by the KGB. They were put on trial with dispatch, in October, and sentenced to terms of Siberian exile. Similar protests in Leningrad and other provincial centers were disposed of with corresponding harshness.

During the next two years, the regime's noose steadily tightened around the dissident intelligentsia. Notable acts of repression included the arrest of Grigorenko (for supporting the Crimean Tatars), the expulsion of Solzhenitsyn from the Writers' Union (for publication of *The Cancer Ward* in Italy), the removal of Tvardovsky from the editorship of *Novyi mir,* the arrest of Amalrik (for publishing *Will the Soviet Union Survive until 1984?*), and the brief commitment of Zhores Medvedev to a mental hospital (for publishing his exposé of Lysenkoism).[27] Nevertheless, the dissident movement continued to attract supporters and to assume a steadily more organized and programmatic form. In May 1969, the Initiative Group for the Defense of Human Rights in the USSR, including Yakir, tried to appeal to the United Nations about the treatment of Soviet dissidents. In March 1970, Sakharov, the historian Roy Medvedev, and the physicist Valentin Turchin issued a manifesto to the Soviet leadership calling for democratization of the system. In October of the same year Sakharov, together with the physicists Valery Chalidze and Andrei Tverdokhlebov, taking advantage of the law on the free association of authors, created the Committee for Human Rights in the USSR, described by Ludmilla Alexeyeva as "the first independent association [of dissidents] with parliamentary procedures and rules of membership."[28] The Democratic Movement was about to become a coherent vehicle for the aspirations of the Soviet intelligentsia.

Caught between this challenge and potential international embarrassment in the era of détente if they continued their earlier tactics, the Soviet authorities switched in 1973 to a new approach. This was to decapitate the dissident movement by allowing its more prominent members to emigrate abroad or even to deport them forcibly and deprive them of Soviet citizenship. The tactic was first employed against one of the earliest victims of neo-Stalinist repression, the poet Joseph Brodsky, released from prison and deported in 1972. During the next two years, a series of eminent dissidents was allowed or pressured to leave, including Chalidze, Sinyavsky, Litvinov, the balladeer Alexander Galich, and the cellist Mstislav Rostropovich. Zhores Medvedev was deprived of his citizenship while on a research visit to England in 1973. The most sensational application of the method of expulsion was the case of Solzhenitsyn, whose defiance—deliberate publication abroad of *August 1914* and his "Letter to the Soviet Leaders," which he wrote and distributed in the fall of 1973—had become utterly intolerable to the authorities. In March 1974 he was seized and placed on a plane for West Germany, to begin an even more famous career in exile.

Despite the authorities' attempt to eliminate the leadership of the Democratic Movement, it readily found new recruits, particularly as a result of the Helsinki Accords of August 1975 and the promises by all signatories including the USSR to respect basic human rights. In the spring of 1976, Sakharov and yet another physicist, Yuri Orlov, a corresponding member of the Academy of Sciences, founded the Moscow Helsinki Watch Group to try to hold the Soviet authorities to this commitment. Their step inspired a series of similar efforts in the union republics and among religious groups. Solzhenitsyn, using the royalties from his publications in the West, created the Russian Fund to Aid Political Prisoners, administered in Moscow by Alexander Ginzburg, and in January 1977 a Working Commission to Investigate the Use of Psychiatry for Political Purposes was announced. These steps represented the high point of organized, open dissidence in the Brezhnev era.

During the early months of 1977, on the pretext of an explosion in the Moscow Metro attributed to "terrorists," the regime began an intense crackdown on the Helsinki Watch movement. Orlov, Ginzburg, and Anatoli Shcharansky (already a leading advocate of Jewish emigration rights) were among those arrested. Defying the Belgrade conference of late 1977 on observance of the Helsinki Accords—"the first international meeting on a governmental level in which the Soviet Union was accused of human rights violations," in the words of Ludmilla Alexeyeva—the authorities followed through with trials and further arrests. Alexeyeva commented, "The dilemma facing the Soviet government had become quite obvious: Either it lost prestige in the West or lost control over its own citizens. The government preferred to sacrifice its prestige."[29]

By 1980, the human rights movement in the Soviet Union had been effectively suppressed, certainly as an organized phenomenon. Nevertheless, the regime had eased its methods, preferring foreign exile or mental hospital commitment to the traditional sanctions of trial and imprisonment. Some dissidents, including Bukovsky in 1976 and Ginzburg in 1980 (as well as Shcharansky in 1985) were actually traded for captured Soviet agents or imprisoned Western Communists. Other intellectual figures forced to emigrate during the final Brezhnev years included Amalrik, the novelist Vasili Aksionov, the satirist Vladimir Voinovich, and the sculptor Ernst Neizvestny. Finally, the device of internal exile to a closed city was applied to Sakharov. He was forcibly resettled in 1980 in the industrial center of Gorky, under constant surveillance by the KGB, to choke off his contacts with the Western press and deprive the dissident movement of his leadership.

In the early Brezhnev years, the common goals of intellectual freedom and survival against repression gave the dissident intelligentsia a strong sense of unity and cohesion. Later, particularly in the freer circumstances of foreign exile, sharp political differences appeared among them. Roughly three main tendencies emerged, symbolized respectively by Solzhenitsyn, Sakharov, and Roy Medvedev. On the right, Solzhenitsyn represented an appeal to traditional Russian culture and religion, with authoritarian and anti-Western overtones that quickly alienated most people in his country of ultimate refuge, the United

States. His philosophy was not far removed from that of the nineteenth-century Slavophiles. The center was represented by Sakharov, whose defense of democracy and human rights put him in the camp of Western liberalism, very much like the Westernizers of the mid-nineteenth century. Dissent on the left was represented by Roy Medvedev, accepting the socialist premises of the revolution and aspiring to work within the system to reform it—"socialism with a human face," in essence. Not unlike prerevolutionary days, the bitter polemics and struggles that broke out among the adherents of these diverse views destroyed any semblance of a united front against the Soviet regime.

The opposition was further disconcerted by the emergence of ultrarightist, Great-Russian chauvinist thinking, perhaps with some encouragement from inside the bureaucratic establishment. This current surfaced after 1985 in the organization Pamyat (Memory), ostensibly dedicated to the preservation of cultural and architectural monuments of the past but frankly expressive of a conspiratorial, ultranationalist, and anti-Semitic view of the world—in short, Russian fascism. As such, the Pamyat movement was analogous to the late-nineteenth-century "official" branch of Slavophilism represented by such figures as Fyodor Dostoevsky.

Under circumstances of censorship and police repression, the movement of intellectual dissent was never able to get its message to the mass of the population widely enough to win their sympathy. Nonintellectual Russians typically rejected the dissidents as unpatriotic complainers or even dismissed them all as Jews in disguise. Russia was experiencing an irreconcilable clash of cultures, as long as the bureaucracy continued to impose its values and to cultivate the innate authoritarianism and xenophobia of the less-educated masses. Meanwhile, the country was paying an inestimable price in the loss of creative talent, either through the brain drain of emigration and defection or the silencing and demoralization of the best-thinking people who remained at home. Sooner or later, it would prove impossible for the bureaucracy to sustain its archaic political culture and maintain Russia's international standing by any means other than armed might.

Could the bureaucratic culture not have perpetuated itself by continued selection of young people who shared the same outlook? Not without new purges and new recruitment from the most primitive and un-Westernized strata of Russian society, as Stalinism did in the 1930s. Absent such a new cataclysm, the bureaucracy drew its replacements more and more from the children of its own class, funneled through the educational pipeline; higher educational attainment among younger members of the political elite rose sharply. In consequence, the flavor of the intellectual culture could sweeten the sources of the political class. Mikhail Gorbachev was only the most famous representative of the younger and less hidebound echelons of the governing hierarchy. By the time Brezhnev died in November 1982, the elements of a powerful reform coalition were present, while the aging process among the leadership provided a unique opportunity to reset the country's direction.

The first decisive step in the direction of reform was the successful move by KGB chief Yuri Andropov to join the party Secretariat in May 1982, thereby positioning himself as a member of both the Politburo and the Secretariat to challenge Brezhnev's heir apparent, Konstantin Chernenko, for the party leadership as soon as Brezhnev himself left the scene. Though a member of the post-purge generation himself, entrusted with the supervision of the secret police and the antidissident campaign ever since 1967, Andropov made himself the personification of change over immobility. When Brezhnev died at the age of seventy-six, Andropov successfully orchestrated the cultural, generational, and institutional forces of reform to have himself nominated by the Politburo and confirmed by the Central Committee as the new general secretary.

Contrary to much Western speculation about his putative liberalism, Andropov was more the disciplinarian than the liberalizer, and the campaign against dissident intellectuals became even more severe during his year in office. Jews and unofficial peace groups were particularly victimized, and the famed director of the experimental Taganka Theater, Yuri Liubimov, went into voluntary exile in Italy. Chernenko, made ideological secretary, suggested even tighter controls in literature and the arts, despite his strictures against "formalism, dogmatism, and inertia" in party propaganda. Nevertheless, some of what was in store was suggested by Andropov's denunciation of the dogmatism and sterility of official economics and social science.

Andropov's death in February 1984 and his replacement by the equally elderly and infirm but decidedly conservative Chernenko came as a bitter disappointment to many Soviet intellectuals, who saw the chances for reform suddenly dashed. Chernenko's brief tenure of the general secretaryship did slow Andropov's reform momentum, but it quickly became apparent that Gorbachev and the reformers had only made a temporary accommodation with the Chernenko people. They succeeded in elevating their man to the de facto second secretaryship and putting him ahead of the candidate most feared by the liberalizers, the former Leningrad party secretary Grigory Romanov. When Chernenko's feeble leadership came to an end with his death in March 1985, Gorbachev was able to win a narrow endorsement in the Politburo over the representatives of Brezhnevian conservatism and point the country unequivocally on the road to reform.[30] The intelligentsia, and the culture it represented, had won its best chance since the 1920s to prevail in Russia's national life.

Most Russian regimes have regarded the intelligentsia more as a source of embarrassment than of support, however much its services may have been needed. Under Gorbachev, the relationship was reversed. To unfetter the modernization and competitiveness of their country from the bonds of Stalinist bureaucracy and Old Russian political habits, the new reformers turned to the intelligentsia not only as a human resource for national progress but as the key social force to sustain their political commitment to change the nation's ways.

Gorbachev's first year as general secretary was not particularly dramatic in the cultural sphere; his priority was consolidation of political power. He ousted Romanov and the other top neo-Stalinists from the leadership and achieved the highest rate of turnover in the Central Committee that had been seen in twenty-five years. By the spring of 1986, the reformers seemed firmly in control.

As far as the intelligentsia was concerned, the decisive turning point for Gorbachev came shortly after the Twenty-seventh Congress. Shaken by the Chernobyl nuclear power disaster and realizing the magnitude of opposition to his reform campaign that was still firmly rooted lower down in the party and governmental bureaucracy, he decided that he must make a political alliance with the intelligentsia. He worked out a deal, "a pact—tacit but nonetheless effective," in the words of the *L'unità* correspondent Giulietto Chiesa, to enlist its support and influence in the cause of reform in return for relaxation of political constraints on intellectual freedom.[31] Baring his concerns at a special gathering of writers in June 1986, in a speech that was widely reported though the official text remained unpublished,[32] Gorbachev lamented resistance to his economic reforms and put forth an extraordinary argument for a Soviet leader: "Restructuring is going very badly. We have no opposition. How then can we check up on ourselves? Only through criticism and self-criticism. The main thing is— through glasnost," that is, openness. "There cannot be a society without glasnost." Though he hastened to qualify this stance by warning, "Democratism without a framework is anarchy," he made his appeal to the intelligentsia crystal clear: "The Central Committee needs support. You cannot even imagine how much we need the support of such a force as the writers." In Roy Medvedev's mind, there was "a new atmosphere in the cultural life of the USSR," thanks to "the positive changes in the leading group in the CPSU."[33]

In May 1986, a veritable coup d'état took place at the congress of the Cinema Workers' Union when the delegates ousted the old secretary, Lev

Kulidzhanov, and installed the innovative director Yefrem Klimov. One member of the organization was reported to have shouted, "This is our Poland, our Czechoslovakia."[34] The move put the film union directly at odds with the State Committee on Cinematography under the conservative Filipp Yermash, who was soon removed.

The shakeup in the cinema was followed by a torrent of criticism at the Eighth Writers' Congress in June. Speakers complained of controls that crushed the creative spirit and called for the publication of long-banned books. Liberal, not-quite-dissident writers such as Yevtushenko and Voznesensky took the lead; declared Voznesensky, "Culture is under attack by spiritual emptiness."[35] In parallel with the film union, the writers' union secretary Georgi Markov was ousted in favor of Vladimir Karpov, editor of *Novyi mir,* once jailed under Stalin. Similar currents prevailed in the theater when the new Union of Theater Workers was formed in December 1986.

Along with these moves in the main cultural organizations, reformers were installed or encouraged in the editorial offices of a number of newspapers and journals. The weeklies *Moscow News* and *Ogonyok* emerged as regular and enthusiastic organs of reform, setting an example of the illumination of public problems by the press, that is, glasnost, almost in the Western style. *Novyi mir's* new editor was the novelist Sergei Zalygin, a nonparty member who up to a year or two previously could not even get his own work published. "The press will be the method for democratic control, not control from administration but control with the help of democratic institutions," said the noted journalist and theoretician Fyodor Burlatsky (by this time head of the philosophy section of the Central Committee's Institute of Social Science).[36] Preliminary censorship of books was officially suspended, except for military secrets. "Our people," said Voznesensky, "have the right to read everything and make their own judgments about everything."[37]

A key aide to Gorbachev in this new approach to the intelligentsia was Aleksandr Yakovlev, a former cultural functionary and diplomat made head of the Central Committee's Propaganda Department in 1985 and a full member of the Politburo in 1987. Yakovlev became even more explicit than Gorbachev in his promotion of glasnost and in his attacks on "dogmatism" and "authoritarian thinking elevated to a political, moral, and intellectual principle."[38] Other reformers installed in top ideological positions by 1986 included the new minister of culture, the new head of the Central Committee Cultural Department, the new director of the Institute of Marxism-Leninism, and the new editor of the party's theoretical biweekly *Kommunist,* Ivan Frolov (an expert in systems analysis, replacing the conservative-nationalist Richard Kosolapov).

At first Gorbachev drew the line at reopening painful questions of the Soviet past. "If we began to get involved in the past," he told the writers in his talk of June 1986, "we would kill off all our energy. . . . We will figure out the past. We will put everything in place. But right now we have directed all our energy forward."[39] Nevertheless, glasnost was taken by many writers, by economists, and—cautiously—by some historians as an invitation to look again at the unresolved issue of Stalinism. Plans were announced for the publication or performance of long-banned writers, films, and plays, even of Pasternak's *Doctor Zhivago.* Pasternak himself was posthumously readmitted to the Writers' Union in February 1987. Anatoly Rybakov's novel *Deti Arbata* (Children of the Arbat, serialized in *Druzhba narodov* in 1987) and Tenghiz Abuladze's film *Pokoyanie* (Repentance, released in Moscow in January 1987) directly or symbolically addressed the terror of the Stalin years, while Mikhail Shatrov's play *The Peace of Brest* (*Novyi mir,* April 1987) brought the Lenin years and Lenin's subsequently purged lieutenants—Trotsky, Bukharin, Zinoviev—back to life more or less objectively.

By early 1987, Gorbachev was evidently persuaded that the spotlight of glasnost could not be withheld from the dark corners of Soviet history. He told the Central Committee at the January 1987 plenum, "The roots of the present situation go back far into the past," and he acknowledged to a meeting of journalists shortly afterward, "There should be no forgotten names or blank spots in either history or literature. We must not push those who made the revolution into the shadows. . . . History must be seen as it is. Everything happened, there were mistakes—grave mistakes—but the country moved forward."[40] Historians voiced the need to reconsider the roles of Khrushchev and Brezhnev as well as Stalin, and rumors revived of the impending rehabilitation of Bukharin, whose economics of gradualism in the 1920s were quite compatible with Gorbachev's program of restructuring.

Gorbachev's turn toward the intelligentsia included receptiveness toward intellectual emigrés. Andrei Tarkovsky, director of the long-withheld historical film *Andrei Rublyov,* had gone to Italy in 1984 and there directed the highly patriotic *Nostalgia.* After his death in December 1986, he was hailed in the Soviet press, and *Nostalgia* was scheduled to be shown in Moscow. Yuri Liubimov of Taganka Theater fame and other performers who had defected, including Rostropovich and the dancer Mikhail Baryshnikov, declined invitations to return. The pianist Vladimir Horowitz of the old emigration did visit, to receive a hero's acclaim, and Marc Chagall's paintings were borrowed and exhibited though the artist had by then died.

The most spectacular step in this series of conciliatory moves was the release of Andrei Sakharov from his internal exile in Gorky in December 1986 and his return to an active presence in Moscow. A number of other imprisoned dissidents were released and allowed to emigrate in the early months of 1987, including Anatoly Koriagin, noted for leading protests against the political abuse of psychiatry. Dissidents both in the Soviet Union and abroad split in their estimate of all these gestures, some holding that Gorbachev had not really changed the system, others pointing out that he was now saying just what they had been arrested for. Continuing cases of the repression of religious and national-minority activists and the unofficial Trust Group gave grounds to support the skeptics.

The conservative opposition that Gorbachev repeatedly warned about materialized clearly on the cultural front in 1987 in response to all the startling innovations of the previous year. The leading spokesman for setting limits to glasnost and decontrol was the number-two man in the party, Yegor Ligachev, widely regarded as the rallying point for political and intellectual conservatism. Ligachev warned, "To concentrate on the negative alone is only part of the truth"; he urged a slowdown in the publication of previously banned works— "Sometimes the assessments given them are exaggerated"—and defended "state administration of the cultural sphere." Shortly afterward, he advised the editorial board of *Sovetskaya kultura* to insist on more "socialism" and to resist "democratic excesses."[41]

Conservative intellectuals, that is, those who represented party control, responded aggressively to Ligachev's initiative. Led by the nationalistic writer Yuri Bondarev, they secured a base in the Writers' Union of the Russian Republic, offsetting the liberal bent of the USSR Writers' Union. The new editor of *Kommunist,* Frolov, lost his post in May, and the editor of *Izvestia* warned the Journalists' Union in June of excessively loose interpretations of glasnost and the dangers in rejecting seventy years of history. He urged that critical comments be printed with the republication of any banned writers. It was in this counterclimate blowing in from the right that the ultranationalist society Pamyat, ostensibly devoted to the preservation of historic buildings, revealed itself as a chauvinistic and anti-Semitic political movement obsessed about Zionist-Masonic plots—in short, a grouping of fascist intellectuals.

Gorbachev and his intellectual supporters were obviously aware of the depth of resistance to reform. The social theorist Anatoly Butenko, a prominent spokesman for perestroika who had been one of the authors of Khrushchev's utopian program of 1961, recalled the fate of reform in those years: "The very same forces that prevented the complete implementation of the decisions of the Twentieth CPSU Congress, . . . and to all intents and purposes interrupted the process of the renewal of our life, do not want changes and are impeding them now, too."[42] Ironically, it was the neo-Stalinists who, in their effort to defend the principle of monolithic party control against the reformers, divided the party and created more pluralism than the Soviet Union had known since the 1920s.

After the battle lines were drawn up in 1986, Gorbachev harped repeatedly on the theme of making reform "irreversible," implying that short of such an attainment the reforms could indeed be reversed. As the playwright Shatrov declared at the theater congress in December 1986, "History is giving us one more chance. And it is our sacred duty not to let this chance slip by, to do everything that is in each person's power to make the process of democratization permanent."[43]

In the 1980s it was impossible to foretell the political fate of the Gorbachev leadership and its reform program. But there were circumstances that would not go away, social trends that demanded and sustained political change no matter what. Soviet society, like the entire world, was on the track of modernization and increasing complexity that made the intelligentsia, as the bearer of education and expertise, the decisive social element, whatever the institutional context in which it might have to operate. Three decades after Khrushchev's reform efforts, it had become increasingly difficult for Soviet society to function and develop without a free role for the intelligentsia. Life itself to that extent would make Gorbachev's restructuring irreversible.

There was a certain irony, familiar in Russian history, to the reform efforts of the Gorbachev era. The initiative for reform came from the state, and the limits of reform were set by the state. When misused, this ultimate power of the political authorities had been responsible for terror or for stagnation. To cure the ills of stagnation under totalitarian controls, Gorbachev simply launched a new effort to revivify society by political command.

One therefore had to view with some skepticism the aspirations of that leadership toward the "democratization" of the system. What might be the most significant consequence of the reform lay in what the leadership no doubt regarded as a mere instrument for national progress, namely, mobilization of the resources and enthusiasm of the intelligentsia. The intelligentsia might well have been expected to emerge from this critical transition period as an independent and irrepressible force to carry Russia truly into the ambit of modern civilization at last.

CHAPTER 30

Gorbachev's Opportunity

Zdeněk Mlynař, ideological secretary in the Prague Spring government of 1968 and Gorbachev's university roommate in the early 1950s, remarked as perestroika was getting under way that it would be politically risky for the cause of reform in the Soviet Union to reopen questions of the past.[1] Gorbachev started out by saying the same thing. Yet no genuine and durable reform of the Soviet system could have been accomplished without a fundamental reexamination of the relation of this system to the historical past that generated it, including its origins in the Revolution of 1917.

The Soviet regime came eventually to represent a very late stage in the typical life history of a revolution. Stalin's postrevolutionary synthesis of revolutionary rhetoric, traditional values, and totalitarian methods, his amalgam of socialism, nationalism, and bureaucracy, remained the basis of the Soviet political system to the end. But this long-established order was not the final phase in the revolutionary process in Russia. Certain historical parallels, notably in England in 1688 and in France in 1830, suggested that there was a potential for new and profound reform. The revolutionary experience is not complete until the nation has an opportunity to overthrow the postrevolutionary dictatorship (or the restored monarchy) and accomplish a moderate revolutionary revival recapturing the early principles of the revolution while excluding extremist fanaticism.

The logic of the revolutionary process indicated that a similar final step was due to take place sooner or later in Soviet Russia. In this case, the historical parallel called for throwing off the legacy of Stalinism and returning to the original hopes and enthusiasm of 1917, based on a democratic, multiparty, decentralized, participatory socialism. This was the ultrademocratic Russia of the early soviets, hailed even by Lenin in *State and Revolution,* but supplanted by one-party dictatorship after the hope of a government of all socialist parties was aborted by the Bolsheviks' violent seizure of power.

The possibility of a return to revolutionary beginnings in the Soviet Union was not just a matter of hypothetical historical reasoning. The real pressure for such a renovation was demonstrated time and again by attempts in Eastern Europe to reject the Stalinist system—in Poland and Hungary in 1956, in Czechoslovakia in 1968, and again in Poland in 1980. To a more limited degree, it figured in Yugoslavia after the early 1950s and in China under Deng Xiaoping in the 1980s.

For Russia itself, the first opportunity for a moderate revolutionary revival was the death of Stalin. The cultural Thaw and Khrushchev's de-Stalinization campaign were important steps toward actualizing this possibility. But Khrushchev failed to attack the Stalinist system of rule, confining his reforms to its excesses, and he did not develop an independent social base for reform, such as the English aristocracy provided in 1688 or the French bourgeoisie in 1830. The potential was there, in the form of the cultural and technical intelligentsias, but these elements had neither the independence nor the organization to influence the party or resist the police once their personal patron was unseated. Khrushchev left intact the postrevolutionary dictatorship, moderated and modernized to some extent, discredited in the outside world but unchanged in its essentials at home. In the 1980s, following the deaths of Brezhnev and his immediate successors and the accession to power of an altogether new generation, there was a historic opportunity once again to rid the country of its postrevolutionary burden and recover the genuine inspiration of 1917 and its socialism with a human face.

Was Gorbachev a leader with the intention or the ability to mobilize the available social forces and carry out the kind of reform that the logic of the revolution required? In his speeches calling for "radical restructuring" and glasnost, he made it plain that he was dedicated to fundamental change of some sort. "I would equate the word restructuring with the word revolution," he declared at Khabarovsk in July 1986.[2] His revolutionary steps ranged from permitting the election of liberal literary and film leaders to the release of Andrei Sakharov from internal exile. Mingling with workers at Krasnodar in September 1986, Gorbachev asserted, "If we now retreated from what we have begun, our people would be greatly disappointed. And that would affect everything. We can't allow this to happen."[3]

At first Gorbachev's ascendancy closely paralleled the era of Khrushchev. This time, the tensions between the reformist intelligentsia and the anachronistic party bureaucracy were even more pronounced. Judging by his extraordinary remarks to the writers in June 1986, Gorbachev was quite conscious of this. He called frankly upon the intelligentsia to help him offset the inertia of the "administrative layer—the apparatus of the ministries, the party apparatus—that does not want changes" and thereby clear the way for "restructuring" Soviet society. "Society is ripe for a sharp turn," he is reported to have said. "If we retreat, society will not agree to a return. We have to make the process irreversible. If not us, then who? If not now, when?" With Western Sovietologists in mind, he warned, "Our enemies . . . write about the apparatus that broke Khrushchev's neck, and about the apparatus that will break the neck of the new leadership."[4]

Ironically, the shift from Stalin's despotism to collective leadership made it more difficult for a reform-minded leader to command change from above. The mutual vulnerability of the general secretary and the representatives of the bureaucracy in the Politburo and the Central Committee was repeatedly illustrated, by the fall of Malenkov in 1955, then by Khrushchev's narrow escape in 1957 and his actual overthrow in 1964. Brezhnev never ventured to threaten the interests of the bureaucracy. To be sure, Gorbachev was able to use his new authority to accelerate the generational renovation of the bureaucracy begun by Andropov in 1982–83. Yet if the leader tried to move too far or too fast to change policy or personnel in the name of reform, and if the Politburo and Central Committee could coalesce in time, he could be removed and replaced. Second Secretary Ligachev, a protégé of Andropov who was ten years older than Gorbachev, offered early hints that he could be a rallying point for the conservatives if the time came.

Though politically the Russian historical legacy impeded reform, economically the same legacy made reform imperative. The Stalinist economic system was a premature imposition on a relatively backward society, where capitalism had not had the opportunity to develop the country's industrial potential fully. Even more serious, though not so widely appreciated, was the fact that capitalism had not yet accomplished the concentration and modernization of the country's petty-bourgeois economic sectors—agriculture, trade, and services—that might have made them ready for socialization. Abrupt nationalization in 1918, and its reaffirmation along with the collectivization of agriculture when Stalin ended the NEP in 1929, set these immature sectors back to an extent that they had not recovered from even by the 1980s. This error of premature socialization of precapitalist branches of the economy was sooner or later recognized and addressed in most Communist countries that were sufficiently independent of the Soviet Union (Yugoslavia, Poland, Hungary, China). By 1986, steps in the same direction were being hinted at in the Soviet Union itself.

While the Soviet economy in its preindustrial sectors suffered from revolutionary prematurity, in the industrial sector it suffered from the anachronistic Russian tradition of centralism, reinstituted in an extreme form in the Stalinist command economy. The cost of this in the inhibition of initiative and innovation was finally being recognized under Gorbachev, as economic growth stagnated and the technological gap vis-à-vis the West steadily widened. The well-known "Novosibirsk Report" of 1983 by Tatiana Zaslavskaya put the blame on "the lagging of the system of production relations, and hence of the mechanism of state management of the economy which is its reflection, behind the level of development of the productive forces." State management as practiced since the 1930s, Zaslavskaya observed, reflected "the predominance of administrative over economic methods, of centralization over decentralization."[5] Gorbachev warned (in his Khabarovsk speech of July 1986), "There will be no progress if we seek answers to new questions in the economy and in technology in the experience of the 1930s, the 1940s, the 1950s, or even of the 1960s and the 1970s." (He conspicuously left open the 1920s and the NEP for lessons in decentralization.) Here was the front line in the battle between the Gorbachevian modernizers and the Brezhnevian conservatives. The issue would not disappear, no matter what happened to the reformist leadership.

Hovering over all aspects of reform, political and economic, was the question of the relationship of the Soviet regime to its professed ideology and its actual history. As a postrevolutionary state still clinging to a revolutionary ideology and a revolutionary mythology for its legitimacy, the Soviet regime was compelled to control all channels of cultural and intellectual expression that might convey doubts about its legitimizing tie with the revolutionary past. This need, reinforced by Stalin's personal mania, was the basis for the whole system of stultifying dictation over all forms of artistic creation, historical investigation, and speculative thought. It was as though an entire nation were subjected to a pervasive historical neurosis, demanding repression or mythologizing of the regime's own record to fit the psychological needs of a defensive and anxious ruling elite. The price paid by the nation in lost creativity and in intellectual apathy was inestimable.

None of this was necessary. It was possible, as the Western European Left showed, to rethink one's ideological heritage and escape from the burden of historical and philosophical dogmatism. Referring to Gorbachev's "lesson of truth" pronounced at the Twenty-seventh Congress, Giuseppe Boffa commented, "We Italian Communists have been trying to tell this truth all these years."[6] The then secretary general Enrico Berlinguer of the Italian Communist Party had already gone further, in a celebrated pronouncement: "The propulsive force that had its origin in the October Revolution has become exhausted."[7]

Reform in Soviet Russia in the sense of a moderate revolutionary revival did not mean the repudiation of socialism. Socialism, in its essence as the overthrow of the power of private property in human relations, was the soul of the Russian Revolution, even though it may have appeared to many critics as a lost soul. What reform would require, as Mlynař pointed out, was a reconsideration of the bureaucratic, centralist, Russian-style socialism that had been maintained ever since Stalin's time as if it were the only conceivable expression of the ideal. Such a new approach was clearly Gorbachev's aim.

There was ample precedent in the history of the Communist movement for an antibureaucratic socialism—in the Worker's Opposition in Russia in 1921, in Yugoslavia in a limited way after 1950, in China in diverse ways both during and after the Cultural Revolution—not to mention the New Left of 1968 in Western Europe. The Spanish reformist Communist Santiago Carrillo suggested, "The progress of the socialist movement in the developed capitalist countries may help Soviet society and the Soviet Communists to go beyond that type of state . . . which . . . tends to place itself above its own society and above the societies of other countries, a type of state which tends toward coercion, . . . and to make progress in transforming it into a real working people's democracy."[8] In other words, the traditional Soviet notion that the first socialist country showed the way to all others had to be reversed.

As a practical matter, despite the exhortations of the European Left, fundamental reform based on a true return to revolutionary beginnings was perhaps a political impossibility in the Soviet Union, since it required just that reconsideration of the past that aroused more political resistance and thereby made the success of reform less likely. But there were underlying circumstances that had not yet had their full effect on the surface of Soviet reality—the pressures and needs of a modern society, the tension between the regime and its revolutionary origins, the impatience of a new generation of leadership. China in the 1980s illustrated how quickly and surprisingly a great nation in the Marxist-Leninist tradition might change under the pressure of such circumstances. To be sure, the more applicable precedents for reform offered by Eastern Europe had discouraging outcomes, thanks to Soviet intervention. But if any comparable reform were to be attempted within the Soviet Union itself, there was no outside force ready to intervene against it.

CHAPTER 31

Gorbachev and the Reversal of History

By the end of the 1980s, it had become obvious to all but the most obdurate skeptics that the reforms initiated in the Soviet Union under the leadership of Mikhail Gorbachev represented no mere tinkering with the Soviet system but an attempt at fundamentally redirecting what had manifestly become an obsolete political and economic structure. Whether the effort would succeed against the resistance of conservatives and amid conditions of economic crisis and nationality ferment was another matter, as was the question how and why Gorbachev managed to undertake such a radical reform to begin with.

Gorbachev clearly did not conceive his reform program all at once. Certainly its enunciation unfolded only step-by-step, and then in response to events and problems as they emerged. Initially, perestroika was indeed no more than tinkering, though it was based, as Gorbachev himself reported, on considerable discussion beforehand with intellectual critics of the old Brezhnev system.[1] For a time it was little more than a restatement of Andropov's program of discipline, incentives, and the acceleration of economic development within the framework of the old system.

Roughly a year after becoming general secretary, Gorbachev seems to have decided on a major new departure, centering on the concept of glasnost. There is plenty of evidence, some from Gorbachev himself, that he was encountering serious resistance in the party apparatus and in the central economic bureaucracy, opposing even the modest Andropovite reforms he was pursuing up to that time. Ironically, the relaxation of Stalin-type despotism made it harder for a reformist leader to command change from above; the behavior of the bureaucracy in the face of the Chernobyl nuclear disaster only confirmed this fact. Faced with such difficulties, Gorbachev turned to the intelligentsia as a social base for reform and liberated the press and the writers as instruments to prod reform along with the pressure of informed opinion. But he was still sensitive about the parallel between his own reform efforts and Khrushchev's, realizing by this time that he was involved in a fundamental shakeup of the whole Soviet system.

Glasnost unfortunately did not put an end to the political and economic difficulties standing in the way of Gorbachev's reform program. In economics, following the advice of liberals such as Abel Aganbegyan (director of the Institute of Mathematical Economics in Novosibirsk), Leonid Abalkin (director of the Institute of Economics in Moscow), and Nikolai Shmelyov (senior associate of the Institute of the USA and Canada in Moscow), he quickly concluded that incentives and exposés within the old structure were not enough. He would have to expand the meaning of perestroika to include an entirely new model of socialism, returning to the NEP for its inspiration. Central ministries and planning organs would be shrunk in favor of reliance on market relationships and an ever-widening sphere for individual and cooperative enterprise. This approach bore fruit, among other things, in the law on enterprises that took effect in January 1988. Moscow was soon awash with cooperative restaurants, offering Western-style service and Western-style prices. Agriculture would be radically reorganized by decentralizing the collectives and encouraging family and small-team work units on a contract basis, a reform that Gorbachev proceeded to implement vigorously. Industry, on a selected but cumulative basis, was directed to shift to the principles of "economic accounting" (*khozrashchot*) and self-financing.

Politically, glasnost and the expanded interpretation of perestroika met growing resistance, not only in the party apparatus and government bureaucracy but among the blue-collar working population as well. Even with the replacements he made after becoming general secretary, Gorbachev did not secure firm majorities in the Politburo and the Central Committee for his subsequent, more ambitious concept of reform. A new split appeared both in the Politburo and further down in the party, not between Brezhnevites and reformers, since the former had been discredited and cleaned out, but between reformers of the early, Andropovite variety and reformers of the bold Gorbachevian stripe. "A struggle of enormous intensity is being waged 'for' and 'against' . . . restructuring," asserted Tatiana Zaslavskaya early in 1987.[2] Even when Gorbachev elevated younger members of the party apparatus, they turned cautious when they confronted the prospect of radical change and a diminution in their own institutional power. Evidently a number of Politburo members and many lesser officials reserved judgment about reform and quietly dragged their feet or went along with Gorbachev without enthusiasm.

By 1987 a neoconservative wing in the party had rallied around Second Secretary Ligachev, with his strictures about socialist morality and the allegedly positive side of the Stalin era.[3] For almost a year, so it appeared, this faction was able to achieve an uneasy political equilibrium with the Gorbachevian reformers, beginning with the fall of Moscow party chief Boris Yeltsin in October 1987 and extending up to the Politburo shakeup of 30 September 1988. During this time, Gorbachev ventured very little further in the ideological realm, notably holding back from deepening his critique of Stalinism when he delivered his long historical speech on the occasion of the seventieth anniversary of the Bolshevik Revolution in November 1987. The high point of conservative pressure, evidently, was the so-called Andreyeva letter published in *Sovetskaya rossiya* in March 1988, calling into question any anti-Stalin campaign.[4] After some delay, the Gorbachevians responded in the form of a *Pravda* editorial denouncing the Andreyeva letter and those who inspired it for putting forth "a manifesto of antirestructuring forces."[5] But this did not allay the sense of conservative pressure.

In response to the antireform challenge, Gorbachev adopted a new strategy to broaden his power base. To advance his reform program, he had scheduled an All-Union Party Conference for June 1988, the first such midterm minicongress since 1941, but he was balked by the party apparatus in the matter of delegate selection, the republican and provincial officialdom preferring the time-tested method of slate rigging to assure conservative dominance of the meeting. His hand forced, Gorbachev made the momentous decision to break with the usual practice and go directly to the party rank and file to challenge the apparatchiki in genuine party elections, in order to avoid the fate of Khrushchev.[6] This touched off much acrimony, even to the point of public demonstrations when some local officials countermanded the results of party elections. But though he managed to get delegate seats for a few of the reformist intellectuals, independently of the bureaucratic responsibilities that had become the traditional prerequisite for selection, Gorbachev fell short of his goal.[7] A substantial majority of the conference delegates were products of the old system of manipulated selection on the basis of bureaucratic officeholding. The conference heard an extraordinary medley of independent voices, more so than any party gathering since the early 1920s, and Gorbachev got the resolutions he wanted on constitutional and economic reforms, but there was no progress on basic questions of power or the restaffing of the Central Committee that he had initially hoped for.

This setback was offset by Gorbachev's plan to shift substantial power and responsibility, both central and local, from the party as such to a strengthened presidency (soon to be occupied by him) and to the hierarchy of central and local soviets. There was much criticism of the new arrangements, among Soviet intellectuals (notably Andrei Sakharov) as well as outside commentators, on the ground that too much constitutional power was being vested in one person, despite the talk of democratization.[8] On the other hand, the shift gave the state a real political status that it had not had since the Russian Civil War. By making himself less dependent on the unreliable party apparatus, Gorbachev could better withstand subsequent challenges by the conservatives.

While pursuing reform and fighting off the conservative challenge, Gorbachev soft-pedaled all the familiar Marxist categories, starting with the proletariat, in favor of higher "humanist" values and "Socialist pluralism."[9] Gorbachev supporters were allowed to challenge the long-standing party monopoly in communications and intellectual life; scholars at the Institute of Marxism-Leninism claimed to have abjured their old role of ideological control and instead said they were merely exercising "initiative" in the context of a "normal intellectual life."[10] Anticipating the Eastern European drama of 1989, some of Gorbachev's people openly acknowledged the parallel with the Czechoslovakia of the Prague Spring. "Both reforms are based on the same principle," said the man who had been *Izvestiya* correspondent in Prague at the time of the Soviet intervention.[11] All this meant the end of Marxist-Leninist-Stalinist dogma, both as a system of doctrine and as a vehicle for imposing intellectual conformity.

One element of dogmatic thinking survived for a time, in the cult of Lenin. But now Lenin's image was itself modified, through the old technique of selective quotation, to play down the fanatical Lenin of the revolution and the civil war and to play up the pragmatic Lenin as he improvised during his first months of power and again as he expressed himself in his last, cautionary, even pessimistic writings while lying ill in 1922–23.[12] The Lenin of these short episodes was thus extrapolated as a sanitized picture of the whole man. Lenin would hardly recognize himself in this: He would find that the most fundamental premises of his thought, including the supremacy of (alleged) class values, the class criterion of ethics, the equation of the party and the proletarian mission, and the party's monopoly in all public political discussion, were all being abandoned.

In any case, by 1989 some Soviet political writers, seeking the roots of the nation's travails under Stalinism, had begun publicly to question Lenin's revolution and his responsibility for the dictatorship and terror that followed.[13] Gorbachev's second in command in the perestroika campaign, Aleksandr Yakovlev, delivered a remarkable address on the occasion of the bicentennial of the French Revolution, extolling democracy and the Rights of Man but warning against the kind of violent fanaticism represented by Robespierre and the Jacobins—and, by extension, the Bolsheviks: "It must be said that the idealization of terror made itself sharply apparent in the October Revolution. It is factually true that terror was necessitated by the counterrevolution. But there were also quite a few revolutionaries who fervently believed in violence—in its purifying power—and who drew directly from the experience of the Jacobins and saw in a repetition of 1793 something good, salvation for the country and the people. . . . A cruel price had to be paid for these mistakes, for the immorality of pseudo-revolutionary behavior."[14]

In foreign policy Gorbachev and his people called into question some of the most fundamental of Soviet ideological postulates, including the irreconcilable confrontation with capitalism, the class struggle dimension in international relations, and the mission of national liberation in the Third World.[15] "The backbone of the new way of thinking," Gorbachev wrote in 1987, "is the recognition of the priority of human values, or, to be more precise, of humankind's survival. . . . We deemed it no longer possible to retain . . . the definition of peaceful coexistence of states with different social systems as a 'specific form of class struggle.'"[16] Stalin's devious conduct of foreign affairs, along with his domestic crimes, finally began to be acknowledged for what it was—"hegemonistic great-power ambitions," in the words of one Soviet scholar.[17] The new thinking went so far as to recognize that Soviet hyperdefensiveness and even Soviet maintenance of conventional force superiority were actually counterproductive, contributing as they did to the hostility of foreign governments.[18] By 1989, the new thinking even extended to the repudiation of the "Brezhnev doctrine" in Eastern Europe and Soviet acceptance—even encouragement—of the extraordinary political chain reaction that toppled one Communist government after another in the former satellite countries. With the end of radio jamming, the relaxation of entry and exit controls on individuals—even emigrés—the solicitation of joint ventures with foreign business enterprises, and steps toward convertibility of the ruble, the Soviet Union moved a remarkable distance, if not all the way, toward behaving like a modern country.

Given the depth of the changes he introduced, it is little wonder that Gorbachev aroused misgivings and worse among the party professionals who had been trained throughout their careers to insist on discipline and conformity. Nevertheless, he appeared to have overcome the long standoff with the conservatives when he successfully brought off the palace coup of 30 September 1988, the "September Revolution," as some Soviet intellectuals called it. Reverting to the oldest methods of Muscovite conspiracy, Gorbachev carried out a preemptive strike against his adversaries, to cut their influence without actually trying to destroy them. He downgraded Ligachev by relegating him to the traditionally junior position within the Secretariat of responsibility for agriculture (Gorbachev's old job). Meanwhile, the search for a new, eclectic model of socialism was enunciated by the new ideological secretary, Vadim Medvedev: "In working out our socialist perspective, in formulating a contemporary conception of socialism, we cannot abstract ourselves from the experience of mankind as a whole, including even the nonsocialist part of the world. . . . In essence we are now in this country undertaking a historic attempt at creating a basically new system of power and administration."[19]

Following his constitutional changes in the summer and fall of 1988, Gorbachev prepared another step toward a power base independent of the party apparatus. By encouraging contested elections to the new Congress of People's Deputies and allowing free campaigning (insofar as he could impose these rules on reluctant provincial officials), Gorbachev threw open the door to a genuine, if imperfect, democratic process. For many Soviet citizens, this was the turning point when they suddenly began to feel free. (Gorbachev was sharply criticized for reserving one-third of the congress, 750 seats, for "social organizations," including 100 seats for the central party leadership plus token workers and peasants, but in fact this functional allocation actually widened the opportunity for leading intellectuals, writers, and scientists, including Andrei Sakharov and Roy Medvedev, to win places.) The results of the ballot on 26 March 1989 were astounding: dozens of radical critics and reformers elected, official candidates beaten in many places, some local bosses running on the old-style single-name ballot defeated by "none of the above" when more than 50 percent of the voters crossed their names off. One Soviet editor, elated by the outcome, opined, "Our future national holidays will be the 1st of May, the 7th of November, and the 26th of March."[20]

Subsequent developments confirmed the democratic momentum. In May and June, national television brought live broadcasts of the sessions of the People's Congress to the entire Soviet populace, treating them to a spectacle of political give-and-take such as Russia had never known except for the reform years around 1905. When the congress, pursuant to the newly amended constitution, chose a new Supreme Soviet from among its own members to do the actual legislating, there was a momentary letdown because the provincial conservatives holding the majority excluded many of the best-known reformers from the higher body. Nevertheless, the Supreme Soviet belied expectations and proceeded to function as a genuine parliament, rewriting and even defeating government legislative proposals and on occasion refusing confirmation to government nominees for the cabinet. There had been a profound shift in the nature and locus of power, extending even to the behavior of some Communist conservatives when they found themselves in a position of genuine legislative responsibility.

Largely overlooked in all this excitement were further steps Gorbachev took to wrest control of the now demoralized party machine away from the conservatives. In April 1989 he secured the resignations of the numerous "dead souls" on the Central Committee—members who had been removed from the bureaucratic positions that entitled them to membership—and promoted as many new people as the rules would permit. Then in September, he struck again at the Politburo level, removing the longtime Ukrainian boss Vladimir Shcherbitsky, the former KGB chief Viktor Chebrikov, and the chairman of the Party Control Commission, Mikhail Solomentsev, and promoting still more backers of reform. The chances of an organized conservative coup within the apparatus seemed to have been dissipated for good.

If Gorbachev's initially superficial reforms grew into a quest to fundamentally redirect Soviet society, how was such a turnabout possible within the doctrinaire and totalitarian framework of Soviet politics? Further, what were the implications of the Gorbachev "revolution" for overall understanding of the Soviet experience viewed as a continuous historical phenomenon?

If Gorbachev did indeed represent a fundamental change in the system, it follows that the totalitarian model of an immovable system of despotic power is inadequate. Historically, in every case, the totalitarian system had both a beginning and an end; it was never immutable, contrary to the celebrated doctrine formulated by Jeanne Kirkpatrick.[21] The collapse of Stalinist Communism in Eastern Europe, once the threat of Soviet intervention no longer backed it up, consigned this notion to the dustbin of academic history. Even before the dramatic autumn of 1989, examples abounded among Communist countries of the softening or decay of totalitarianism. Yugoslavia and Hungary by the 1980s could not be described as anything more severe than "authoritarian." In 1968, Czechoslovakia demonstrated the possibility of dismantling totalitarianism from within, and Poland in the Solidarity years of 1980–81 showed that totalitarianism could be overthrown from below by a sufficiently determined society. Even in the Soviet Union, when the time became ripe, totalitarianism could go the same way, without needing the shock of military defeat that ended Nazism in Germany and Fascism in Italy.

A recapitulation of Gorbachev's revisions of Stalinism and even Leninism demonstrates how far and how fast he moved toward dismantling the structure and the psychology of totalitarian control. In the spirit of a neo-NEP symbolized by the rehabilitation of Bukharin, Gorbachev and his advisers rejected the Stalin model of the centrally planned and bureaucratically administered economy, calling it, in the phrase coined by Zaslavskaya in her "Novosibirsk Report," the "braking mechanism."[22] Going further, they challenged the primal Leninist bias against petty-bourgeois enterprise. Gorbachev urged "democratization" and "mass participation" in industrial administration in terms that approached the semisyndicalist philosophy of the Workers' Opposition of 1920–21. He held out for the ideal of socialism, but he sought to redefine it in ways that would fundamentally change its nature.

In politics, Gorbachev called into question the most fundamental elements of the Soviet system, namely the role and structure of the Communist Party. He abandoned the ideals of "iron discipline" and "monolithic unity" that Lenin imposed during the civil war and in the fateful resolution against factions adopted by the Tenth Party Congress in 1921. He challenged the domination of the party by the apparatus that dated from the 1920s, with almost the same arguments that Trotsky used in protesting the emergence of machine politics under Stalin. He rejected direct administrative domination by the party apparatus over the civil government of the soviets that had prevailed since the civil war era and expressed arguments about the separation of powers that sound remarkably like the early left-wing opposition to Lenin's centralism. Nonparty organizations were now told that instead of serving as mere transmission belts of the party's will, they were genuinely to represent the interests of their constituencies and engage in pluralistic dialogue with the party.[23]

The elections of March 1989, if still restricted, were unparalleled in the Soviet Union since the election of the abortive Constituent Assembly a few weeks after the Bolsheviks took power in 1917. This concession implicitly opened the way toward the possible evolution of a pluralistic and de facto multiparty political system such as Communist Russia had never seen since the outbreak of civil war in the summer of 1918. Together with this fundamental political shift, Gorbachev surrendered the Communist Party's last word in cultural and intellectual life, imposed by Stalin in that crucial period of the early 1930s. Early in 1990, he prevailed upon the Central Committee to surrender the party's constitutionally protected monopoly of power, while he sought and won new governmental powers as president. These new arrangements, like glasnost, called into question not only the Stalinist domination of the apparatus over the party but also the Leninist principle of the hegemony of the Communist Party as a whole in the country's political life.

Many areas of policy evinced the same deep revisionism under Gorbachev. In foreign affairs, he moderated the confrontationist approach in Soviet Russia's relations with the outside world that had distinguished the country's behavior ever since the Bolshevik Revolution. At the risk of a major political explosion and Russian nationalist backlash, he tolerated a growing spirit of self-expression among the national minorities, calling a halt only where independence movements or hatreds between different minorities threatened to get out of hand. He spoke of a *Rechtstaat*—a state governed by the rule of law—and made promises to restrain the secret police and to respect the legal rights of individuals, to a degree not heard since the revolution.[24]

In accordance with his commitment to democratization and legality, Gorbachev had to allow the Soviet Union's long-suppressed national minorities, all originally conquered by the tsars, to voice their aspirations for autonomy and even independence. But nationalist sentiment was the Achilles' heel of the whole process of reform. Give the minorities democracy, and their number-one demand would be secession from the Union, which would inevitably threaten national security and provoke a reaction among Russian nationalists. Yet self-determination was a recognized right, as it had been, in the theoretical sense, even under Lenin.

To sum up Gorbachev's policies, it may be said that he took the country all the way back not only to the pre-Stalin era but to the earliest months of Lenin's rule, before the civil war, before the attempt to communize the entire economy, before the imposition of the Communist Party's total political monopoly. There was a short period then, from the October Revolution to the spring of 1918, before the wrenching and hardening experience of the civil war and War Communism, when the outlook of the new Soviet regime was substantially more cautious and more pluralistic than it became later, and when revolutionary politics were still highly decentralized and spontaneous. At the outset, Lenin had warned his followers, "Socialism is not created by decrees from above. Statist bureaucratic automatism is alien to its spirit."[25] The difference in the 1980s was that Gorbachev was orchestrating a return to the earliest forms of Soviet power from the top down in a politically stable system, without the fanaticism, revolutionary passion, and pure chaos that had destabilized the earliest version of the Soviet experiment.

Is there any explanation for the remarkable transformation of the Soviet political scene under Gorbachev other than the benevolent and practical judgment of the man in charge? Was there some logic inherent in the postrevolutionary dictatorship and its totalitarian manifestation that destined that trying phase of a country's experience to come to an end? The moderate revolutionary revival appears to be the natural resolution of the process.[26]

Can the concept of the moderate revolutionary revival be applied to Soviet Russia? The eras of reform under both Khrushchev and Gorbachev appear to qualify. In his condemnation of Stalin's crimes, his relaxation of the party's pseudo-revolutionary dictates in intellectual life, and his gestures toward egalitarianism, Khrushchev was moving in the direction of the moderate revolutionary revival. Unfortunately, he failed to question the economic institutions of totalitarianism established during the early Stalin years or the corresponding political institutions of apparatus rule formed earlier. As a result, the moderate revival under Khrushchev proved abortive. He did not develop an independent social base for reform apart from the party apparatus, and the apparatus remained committed in its own interest to the principles of the Stalinist dictatorship. To be sure, he had the natural support of the intelligentsia, but the intelligentsia remained physically at the mercy of the conservatives. The apparatus had little difficulty in subduing independent thinkers or driving them underground after the political terrain started to crumble under Khrushchev.

Upon the demise of the Brezhnev generation, and with the Khrushchev precedent in mind, another effort to bring about the moderate revolutionary revival was not only logical but predictable.[27] This is the real historical significance of Gorbachev's restructuring. In the perspective of the Russian Revolution and the country's long postrevolutionary travails, perestroika appeared as a fundamentally new step, opening a qualitatively new era in the history of the Soviet Union. Gorbachev called it a "revolution." In a sense this was true, although in the broader revolutionary scheme it was only the last phase of that long and onerous process.

Russia's moderate revolutionary revival under Gorbachev did not immediately become irreversible. As history shows, the moderate revival is a difficult time, when the relaxation of coercion liberates enemies of the compromise line both on the left and on the right. Gorbachev's unfolding campaign for democratization could still be aborted, as Khrushchev's reforms were, given the residual political power of the party apparatus. Soviet intellectuals were very sensitive to this danger.

Naturally, there were limits to Gorbachev's reconstruction of the Soviet system. He had neither the intention nor the capability to turn the Soviet

Union into one more capitalist country. For one thing, he hung on religiously to the concept of socialism while trying to invest the term with new content. His aim, as he constantly reiterated, was to overthrow the bureaucratic, centralist, Russian-style socialism of the Stalinist model and to recover both the humanist socialism that had initially inspired the revolution and the democratic legacy of earlier revolutions in the West.

Evaluating Gorbachev's Soviet Union and his model of socialism runs the familiar hazard of the two extremes. On the one hand, recognizing his progress toward the political values that most Westerners now share, it was easy to be carried too far by wishful thinking. On the other, some observers found it convenient to deny that any fundamental change had taken place or that it could endure; they thereby evaded the difficulty of rethinking old, originally well-founded but by this time outdated premises and stereotypes.

Enduring or not, Gorbachev's reforms posed a major new intellectual challenge to Western Sovietology. All the basic models—of the economy (the command system), of the political system (totalitarianism), of international behavior (Cold War bipolarity), of the ideological system (Marxist-Leninist orthodoxy)—were dissolving. These were models in which Western Sovietologists had invested entire careers. So they faced a challenge to received ways of thinking about the Soviet Union that was in a way analogous to the challenge experienced by Soviet conservatives when all their mental furniture went out of style.

Recognition of this need to rethink did not mean that all previous conceptions were meaningless and irrelevant. The Soviet Union as once understood became history, but it still existed as history. As such, the old Soviet picture remained just as relevant to the new processes of the present as any other feature of the Russian historical legacy. It was the point of departure for the changes initiated under Gorbachev as well as the basis for understanding the profound difficulties and uncertainties that lay ahead for Russia's new course. But the old model was still only history, a history with a beginning and an end.

CHAPTER 32

Soviet Federalism and the Breakup of the USSR

T he collapse of the Communist Party of the Soviet Union and the liquidation of the Union itself in 1991 are generally regarded both in the former Soviet republics and in the West as triumphs of democracy and national self-determination. These views are at best oversimplifications. The breakup of the Soviet Union was above all a failure of federalism. Soviet federalism had always been spurious, but the circumstances of the era of perestroika might have overwhelmed even the best-conceived federal experiment.

The great impediment to successful federalism in the Soviet Union was itself the original reason for the adoption of a nominally federal structure. This was the diverse ethnic makeup of the country, inherited from centuries of expansion and conquest by the Russian Empire. Whenever the Russian center was weakened by revolutionary events or democratic reforms—in 1905, in 1917, and again under perestroika—the automatic response of the minorities was to strive for independence. To them, democracy meant above all the opportunity to escape from Russian rule, while this prospect in turn raised doubts about democracy among the Russians if the outcome were to dismantle the empire and topple Russia from the ranks of the major world powers. The nationality question was always the Achilles' heel of democratic reform in the Russian Empire.

In contrast to the avowed centralism of the tsarist state, the Soviet regime attempted in its early years to come to terms with the multinational character of the country by adopting on paper a federal system of government. However, all of the administrative units of the Union, Russian and minority alike, were governed by the totally centralized dictatorship of the Communist Party, whose members running the union republics and other jurisdictions were appointed by and under the discipline of the party leadership in Moscow. Thus the federal structure of the USSR, enshrined in the Stalin Constitution of 1936, was an utter sham. It used to be remarked that newspapers were published in the Soviet Union in 140 different languages—but they all said the same thing.

Nevertheless, with the reforms of perestroika, the dummy federalism of the USSR came to life. The union republics and the lesser nationality units became the political framework through which the forces of minority separatism were expressed. Another policy to accommodate minority identity was to categorize every Soviet citizen according to nationality, independent of residence, and record this affiliation in the individual's internal passport. This ethnic concept of citizenship had potentially explosive consequences, like the federal structure of the union, once democratization released the expression of local identity.

One notion cultivated by the Communist leadership is still taken for granted as people look back at the Soviet era: that the Soviet Union was a genuine multinational state, distinct from its Russian component. In fact, the center has always been a Russian center, under the empire, under the Soviet system, and after. As far as the relations of power among the nationalities were concerned, the Soviet Union was only a refurbished form of the Russian Empire. To be sure, the autocrat from 1929 to 1953, Joseph Stalin, was not a Russian but a Georgian, though Lenin accused him of harboring the Great Russian chauvinism of Russified non-Russians. Stalin identified himself with the Russian majority, encouraged the revival of Russian nationalism from the 1930s on, promoted the Russification of the minorities, and viciously purged minority leaders—even Communists—accused of "bourgeois nationalism."

One cannot really speak of the "collapse" of the USSR. The Russian center remained intact. What happened in the last years was not a collapse but rather a struggle for power at the center and a weakening of the center's control over the non-Russian periphery. Both of these processes were evident in 1917 as well, and both were intertwined, then and again more recently.

Nowhere in Russian political experience was there any awareness of the fundamental principle of federalism: the distribution of different powers among the various levels of government (not to be confused with the separation of powers among the legislative, executive, and judicial authorities at any level). Whenever a lower jurisdiction could assert its independence against the higher, as in 1917 and again after 1989, it would try to assert unlimited "sovereignty," lay claim to all public property within its boundaries, and defy all outside authority. Among the union republics after 1989 this attitude led to the so-called war of laws, as republics acted to suspend the application to their territory of Union legislation that was not to their taste. Neither the Union government nor the republics had any sense of the limits on their own authority imposed by the sharing of jurisdiction with the other level.

The forces of long-suppressed minority nationalism and separatism released by political reform in the Soviet Union could well have overwhelmed any system of federalism. But there were weaknesses, moreover, in the structure of federalism that the Gorbachevian reformers inherited from their predecessors, weaknesses rooted in the origins of Soviet federalism as a system to accommodate the national minorities without compromising the power of the Russian center. The basis of the primary units, the union republics, was not a division into roughly equivalent territorial entities but ethnicity (as marked by language). This left the Russian Republic as one entity overwhelming all the others. Any system of representation in a central government would either give the Russians domination (if by population) or diminish them absurdly (if by republic), though until Gorbachev's reforms this quandary was not felt because the Supreme Soviet in Moscow was representative (one house by population, the other by nationality) only pro forma. Matters would have been quite different in 1991 if there had been no parallel government of the Russian Republic in Moscow and the Russian part of the country had been divided into regions— ten or twelve can readily be suggested—roughly equivalent in power and importance to the individual non-Russian republics. Then there could have been no question of dissolving the Union government, even if certain non-Russian republics ultimately decided to secede.

The surge of minority nationalism after the electoral reforms of 1989 quickly altered the terms of the federalism question and made it rather one of confederation at best. To be sure, the semantic distinction of federation and confederation is not that sharp in practice. But the demands posed by the non-Russian republics—separate currencies, separate military forces, independence from the legislative competence of the Union parliament—pushed the terms of the argument to the confederal extreme even before the August Coup.

This direction was clear in the Union Treaty finally drawn up in March 1991 and accepted in principle in the Novo-Ogarevo Agreement of the "nine plus one" (nine republics and the Union) in April.[1] The treaty—scheduled to be formally signed on 21 August but preempted when the coup was launched on the 20th—was intended to replace the coercive treaty of 1922 that created the USSR and to provide the basis for a new Union constitution. Its language leaned heavily to the rights of the republics, "sovereign states" that "possess full state power" and "retain the right to the independent resolution of all questions of their development." But in the assignment of powers to the Union and the republics the Union Treaty was nightmarishly vague. The draft specified the logical Union responsibilities—defense, state security, foreign policy, communications, the space program—but promised the republics a share in formulating policy for all these areas, while putting the bulk of governmental responsibilities for the economy and social policy in the hands of "the USSR . . . in conjunction with the republics." Then, as though to compensate, it declared, "Republic laws have supremacy on all questions, with the exception of those falling within the Union's jurisdiction." The new Constitutional Court was supposed to sort all this out if disputes arose.

The stakes in the struggle over federation or confederation were raised by the socialized character of the Soviet economy, where all industry and natural resources were state owned. If the republics were to gain preeminent powers, this would include ownership of the economic assets within their borders. There was no clear formula to determine what properties, if any, should remain the domain of the Union government. Yet the Soviet economy was actually highly integrated and centralized, a system that would be—and in fact was—grievously disrupted by the independence of the republics. Generally speaking, within any economic entity, planned or market, that operates as an undivided whole, it is unrealistic to speak of significant economic powers for lower levels of government. If, as the Soviet republics demanded, lower entities were to get real control over their respective economies, this would—and did—doom the functioning of the overall Soviet economy as a single unit.

Perhaps a distinctive line between federation and confederation is the right of a constituent entity to secede. To be sure, union republics had the right to secede under the Stalin Constitution, but anyone who took it seriously was purged. The issue was forced by the new anti-Communist Baltic governments that were elected democratically in 1990, and Gorbachev refused to face it squarely. He referred to a complex process of secession, subject to a Unionwide referendum, and made it clear that he would do anything within the terms of his democratized system—or even outside those terms—to prevent a republic from seceding. This attitude led him to order or condone military and economic action against separatists in Georgia in 1989 and in Lithuania in 1990 and again in early 1991. He responded to calls for "sovereignty" by alleging "fascistic tendencies," "superfragmentation and chaos," and "furious attempts to discredit the institutions of state power that embody the idea of a federal union state."[2] Alarm about the separatism that his own reforms had unleashed was undoubtedly a major factor in Gorbachev's shift toward the party conservatives in the winter of 1990–91.

At Novo-Ogarevo, in the course of his zigzag back toward reform, Gorbachev accepted language affirming the right of republics to secede or to become independent if they declined to sign the treaty.[3] Interestingly, the nine signatories at Novo-Ogarevo were the Slavic and Moslem republics where Communists and ex-Communists remained in command even after the August Coup; the six nonsigners were the non-Slavic, non-Moslem republics led (except for Moldova) by former anti-Communist dissidents. In any case, the prospect of the actual or virtual dissolution of the Union pursuant to the treaty was anathema to the Communist conservatives and appeared as a major item on the agenda of the August plotters against Gorbachev: "the confrontation between nationalities and the chaos and anarchy that are threatening the lives and security of the citizens of the Soviet Union and the sovereignty, territorial integrity, freedom and independence of our fatherland. . . . A mortal danger threatens our homeland, . . . the breakup of the state."[4] But even at the end, Gorbachev himself was unreconciled to the breakup of the Union. "I support the preservation of the union state and the integrity of this country," he said in his resignation statement on 25 December 1991. "Developments took a different course. The policy prevailed of dismembering this country and disuniting the state, which is something I cannot subscribe to."[5]

The survival of the Union, dubious enough between the pressures of minority separatism and the weakness of any conception of federalism, was further threatened after 1990 by the emergence of purely political considerations. These involved two elements, one institutional, the other personal. The institutional element was the existence of the huge Russian Republic, the main body of the Union with its capital in Moscow, like the capital of the Union as a whole. As long as the governments of the union republics, Russia included, were mere appendages of the Russian-dominated Communist Party, this division created no problem. But once Gorbachev implemented democratization in 1989, the potential existed for what Lenin called "dual power" in Moscow and an automatic struggle for power between the Union and Russian governments.

The potential institutional conflict quickly became a personal political contest, as the former Moscow party secretary Boris Yeltsin returned from the political wilderness to challenge his onetime leader Gorbachev. Yeltsin had been brought into the new Gorbachev leadership in 1985 to clean up the notoriously corrupt party organization in the city of Moscow, but in so doing he aroused the ire of party conservatives. In June 1987, in one of his many tactical retreats to appease the conservatives, Gorbachev allowed Yeltsin to be passed over for promotion to full member of the Politburo. This crucial event, overlooked in virtually all accounts of the Yeltsin-Gorbachev rivalry, accounts for Yeltsin's defiance of Gorbachev in the fall of 1987 and in turn Gorbachev's humiliation of his former lieutenant. Yeltsin repeatedly referred back to 1987 as the point when Gorbachev "began to go wrong" and "began . . . deceiving the people."[6] The record from that time on suggested a firm determination on Yeltsin's part to settle scores.

Yet in the spirit of his new democratization program Gorbachev had to leave Yeltsin free to speak out and to run for a seat in the new Congress of People's Deputies in March 1989, which he won triumphantly as a voice for accelerated reform. A year later, after the series of more fully democratic elections in the union republics, the radical reformers advanced Yeltsin as a candidate for the chairmanship of the newly democratized Supreme Soviet of the Russian Republic. Gorbachev campaigned vehemently against him but took no steps contrary to his own new constitution to stop his rival.

Once in command of the Russian Republic, Yeltsin worked assiduously to undermine Gorbachev's power as president of the Union. His approach was simple—to support the calls for "sovereignty" on the part of all the union republics, including his own, thereby curbing the authority of the Union government and enhancing the authority of his own alternative regime in Moscow. It did not matter that for Russia to be "sovereign" against a Russian-dominated Union was to be sovereign against itself, a patent absurdity. Russian "sovereignty" within the old structure of the Union could only mean Russian nonsovereignty over the other republics. The real question was which Russian government, under which Russian leader, would prevail. To win, Yeltsin was willing to pay the price, for the time being, of dissolving the authority of the Russian center exercised by Gorbachev's Union government. This process was under way well before the August Coup and directly underlay the final collapse of Union authority that followed the coup attempt.

After the failure of the August Coup, Yeltsin moved relentlessly to liquidate the Union government, while Gorbachev tried to sustain its ebbing life by reviving his project of a Union Treaty. The decisive undoing of this hope was the matter of taxation, where—still lacking the idea of a federal division of authority—revenues had been transferred to the republics, which were then supposed to share Union expenses, including the armed forces. Literally bankrupt, Gorbachev was helpless to resist Yeltsin's physical takeover of Union government ministries and assets, even the Kremlin itself. Finally came the Belovezhsk Agreement of 8 December between Russia, Ukraine, and Belorus to declare the Soviet Union dissolved. This was no less a coup d'état than the Communist coup of October 1917, technically preempting the rights of the nine other remaining members of the Union, though in fact none of them objected.

There is a curious parallel between the events of 1917 that brought the Communist regime into being and the events of 1991 that put an end to it. Kerensky's Provisional Government faced the Bolshevik-controlled Petrograd Soviet in circumstances of dual power, just as Gorbachev's Union government faced Yeltsin's Russian government and the radical reformers. Before the Bolsheviks ever acted, Kerensky had lost virtually all popular confidence as support drained away to the left and to the right—just as Gorbachev's support had drained away. There is even a parallel between the August Coup, crippling Gorbachev politically, and the abortive right-wing coup led by General Kornilov in August 1917, which was equally damaging to Kerensky. After the coup attempt, it was as easy for Yeltsin to step in as it had been for Lenin, when, as the latter said, he found power lying in the streets and picked it up.

Ironically, once Yeltsin had disposed of Gorbachev and the Union, he found himself face-to-face with the same urges and problems. Under the umbrella of the Commonwealth of Independent States he hoped to maintain some semblance of Russian influence over the former Union, with emphasis on the minimal features of a confederation—namely, the military, the currency, and foreign relations. He took it as a matter of course that the Russian government should inherit the position of the Soviet Union in international matters, including the embassies abroad, treaty obligations, and the UN Security Council seat. Yet he had gone so far in advancing the sovereignty of the republics against Gorbachev that there was no restraining them now, certainly not Ukraine with its assertion of complete economic independence and its claim on an independent share of the Commonwealth's armed forces. At the same time, Yeltsin was confronted within the Russian Federation with a series of separatist movements among the smaller minorities—notably the Tatars and the Chechens—analogous to those that had challenged Gorbachev in the Union at large. Toward these urges within the Russian Federation Yeltsin proved to be an even more adamant centralist than Gorbachev. His Federation Treaty between the Russian government and its subordinate minority units, the autonomous republics, ran into all the problems that Gorbachev's Union Treaty encountered.

Yeltsin's position after the breakup of the Union lends some credence to the notion that his embrace of sovereignty for the union republics was as much a matter of expediency as of principle. Nor did he consistently observe the principles of federalism in dealing with the Russian provinces under his rule, though in many cases they had also asserted powers of local self-government well before the coup. He responded immediately to the August Coup by dispatching his personal representatives to the Russian provinces to impose his authority over the local Communists who, ironically, hoped to use their "states' rights" to survive politically. Unfortunately, Yeltsin's methods remind the historian of the manner in which Joseph Stalin built his apparatus of personal power in the 1920s.

The circumstances of the Soviet Union in 1991 cried for a federal solution. Genuine federalism, made possible by the dismantling of the Communist Party dictatorship, would have given the minorities full scope for cultural self-expression. At the same time it could have avoided the divisive concept of citizenship based on ethnicity rather than territory, a principle that implied second-class citizenship for the subminorities present in every ethnic subdivision because of the historic mixing of nationalities. Federalism could have maintained the Unionwide economy without adding to the country's economic woes by placing barriers among the highly interdependent regions. It would have allowed institutions of democratic local administration to be fashioned more gradually and more constructively. It would have avoided the unnerving problems of dividing the Soviet armed forces while trying to maintain some form of responsible control over the nuclear weapons stockpile, and it would have preserved the Soviet Union, despite all its problems, as a more influential and less troublesome power on the international scene.

More statesmanship in all quarters might have made a difference. If Gorbachev had been more flexible toward the nationalities at an earlier point in perestroika, if Yeltsin had not chosen to use the Russian Republic as a weapon against Gorbachev, if some of the ex-Communist leaders in the other republics had not yielded to political pressure to outdo former dissident nationalists, the federal—or confederal—Union might have been preserved, at least with its essential powers in defense, money matters, and foreign relations. In the absence of these might-have-beens, the democratized Union was a lost cause, and the individual Soviet republics were left to cope with each other and with the outside world under very unpromising circumstances.

PART VII

After the Fall

Reflections on the Soviet Experience

CHAPTER 33

The Revolutionary Process and the Moderate Revolutionary Revival

T he startling series of events in Russia following the advent of Gorbachev and perestroika in 1985 generated a multitude of interpretations from every political direction. A new revolution, as Gorbachev himself maintained? A counterrevolution, as the few diehard Communists alleged? A "transition to democracy" on the Latin American model, as Western aid-givers hoped? Or a new "Time of Troubles" opening the way to a new authoritarianism and a new tsar, as pessimistic Russian liberals suggested? Russian politics after 1985 cannot be fully understood apart from the country's tortuous revolutionary experience going back to 1917. In turn, the Russian Revolution has to be viewed as one instance of a complex but recognizable phenomenon that has erupted in the history of many different countries.

The revolutionary process does not end with the postrevolutionary dictatorship or even with monarchical restoration. Typically, there comes a point—it was the Glorious Revolution of 1688 in Restoration England and the Revolution of 1830 in Restoration France—when postrevolutionary authoritarianism is thrown off. A similar purgation can be observed in countries where the revolution had come to grief in avowedly counterrevolutionary dictatorships. Seeking a new beginning at this point, the nation turns back to the principles of the earliest, liberal stage of its revolution, with emphasis on personal liberty and representative government. This final stage of the revolutionary process is the moderate revolutionary revival, when a country manages to start its revolution over again, so to speak, without the fanaticism and polarization that undermined the original attempt at reform and drove the process on to dictatorship and civil war.

The concept of the moderate revolutionary revival requires some kind of explanation in terms of the social forces underlying the revolutionary process and the political legacy that it bequeaths. Generally, every great revolution, as a developmental crisis, unleashes aspirations for social change that run ahead of what the given country's level of development or degree of modernization can sustain for long—hence the inevitability of retreat and consolidation, whether under revolutionary or counterrevolutionary auspices. But eventually social development again overtakes the political synthesis of postrevolutionary rule. Further, the eventual failure of the French experiment of 1830 suggests that if the moderate revival tries to turn the clock back too far—to 1789 instead of 1792 in the French case—its chances of success are diminished. This could be a lesson for post-Communist Russia.

In its early years, the process of revolution in Russia conformed closely to the Anglo-French model—a moderate phase represented first by the abortive revolution of 1905 and then by the February Revolution and the Provisional Government, and an extremist phase initiated by the October Revolution and pursued through the years of the civil war and War Communism. Thereafter, the actual course of events in Russia took an unusual turn. The survival of the one-party dictatorship and the centralist legacy of the War Communism period along with "the disintegration of societal life, . . . cynicism, dual morality, and loss of faith," to quote Aleksandr Yakovlev, created the opportunity for an aspiring postrevolutionary dictator.[1]

Joseph Stalin was the man to seize this opportunity, after Lenin made him general secretary of the party and then fell ill before he could correct his mistake. Building upon an apparatus of personal power within the party, Stalin achieved the functional analogue of Bonaparte's command of the revolutionary army. The party was the instrument that enabled him to bid successfully for the role of postrevolutionary dictator and to launch his "revolution from above."

Stalin naturally claimed full continuity with Lenin. In the early 1930s, he seemed in mood and method to be reviving the era of War Communism. Yet he subjected the country to a more oppressive and exploitative regime than anything it had suffered under tsarism, and with the aid of the bureaucratic hierarchy he amassed total power in his own hands. Thus, in the terms of the process model of revolution, Stalin brought the Soviet Union into the phase of postrevolutionary dictatorship, where an opportunistic egomaniac, mastering the main levers of power, proceeds to combine old autocratic methods of rule with revolutionary mythology and to declare war on the nation's alleged enemies. In

Stalin's case, up to World War II, they were internal foes—the bourgeois specialists, the "petty-bourgeois" peasants, former Communist rivals, and finally the men of his own political apparatus.

The USSR did not, of course, move on from the "Bonapartist" phase of postrevolutionary dictatorship to an outright monarchical restoration as England or France did. One can imagine something on this order if Adolf Hitler had waged political warfare in 1941 as astutely as he waged the Blitzkrieg militarily and had sponsored a counterrevolutionary government to get Russia out of the war. But even though a restoration did not materialize, assessment of the real character of Stalin's political and social system, including his reversal of most of the social policies and cultural standards stemming from the revolution and his introduction of nationalistic symbolism, could indeed support a description of the later years of Stalinism as the de facto equivalent of a monarchical restoration.

Naturally, the Russian Revolution differed from its predecessors in the details of each phase, thanks to the many accidents of leadership, timing, and circumstance. But there was a greater difference of a programmatic and ideological nature, a difference of basic social values, that distinguished the revolution in Russia from its "bourgeois" predecessors. The Russian Revolution was the first of its kind to be animated by the mission of transforming the economic order to realize the values of economic equality and community, in other words, socialism in its broadest sense.

Socialism was central to the self-righteous militancy of the Bolsheviks and to the compulsive self-justification of every succeeding form of Communist rule, whether in Russia or anywhere else. It was not lightly to be given up even when perestroika dawned in the 1980s: The limiting condition in Gorbachev's reformist mindset was the retention of some form of economic framework that he could continue to call socialist. "I have retained my loyalty and devotion to the socialist idea," he told a meeting of miners' representatives as late as April 1991.[2]

When Stalin broke with the NEP in 1928–29 in the course of disposing of his rivals within the party leadership, he committed the country to a particular new model of socialism, based on the totally nationalized or collectivized economy, centrally planned and bureaucratically administered. If this was "barracks socialism," it was barracks socialism complete with the hierarchy of military-style rank and privilege, and complemented with huge disciplinary battalions for the misfits. This was the end of the old revolutionary ideal and its honest believers.

Thanks to the durability of the Stalinist model of socialism and the intensity of propaganda equating it with the revolutionary goal, for much of the outside world the identification of socialism with Stalinism became axiomatic. This was true equally for adherents of the socialist ideal, for whom Stalinism was thereby prettified, and for enemies of socialism, for whom Stalinism was proof of its iniquity. The international Left was divided and confused, while up to World War II the international Right thrived on the Communist menace. Ongoing assumptions about the identity of the Stalinist model and the socialist ideal eventually caused the collapse of the one to carry the other down with it. "We ourselves," said Yakovlev, "did a great deal to deform the image and values of socialism."[3] It can well be said that historic identification with the Russian Revolution, the tragic burden of that tortuous experience, was the worst thing that could have happened to socialism.

From Stalin's time until the advent of perestroika, Soviet Russia seemed not to experience any further fundamental change. In effect, the revolutionary process was frozen at the stage of postrevolutionary dictatorship with restorationist trappings, thawed only slightly during Khrushchev's years of limited and erratic reform. Reaction under Brezhnev appeared to confirm the theory of irreducible totalitarianism. Yet consideration of the parallel processes of other revolutions should have raised the question, even before 1985, of whether the Russian Revolution, like the others, would eventually come to the stage of the moderate revolutionary revival. Just before Gorbachev came to power, this writer observed, "Today the revolutionary cycle in Russia is long overdue for a new turn, away from Stalinist conservatism and toward a revival of the revolution's early hopes for freedom and equality."[4] With more perspective, the era of perestroika did indeed fall into place as the concluding phase of the revolutionary process in Russia.[5]

The opportunity for change in Russia was the death of the postrevolutionary dictator—actually, of three old men in quick succession. Backed by a younger generation of administrators and determined to rouse the country out of its "era of stagnation," the eventual successor Gorbachev commenced a journey back in time to dismantle the postrevolutionary regime, piece by piece. He challenged the Stalinist centrally planned economic system, questioned the whole history of the Five-Year plans and collectivization, and tried to devise a sort of market socialism on the lines that had facilitated the country's economic recovery in the 1920s. Pushing further back, he questioned the primal Leninist bias against petty-bourgeois enterprise, especially in services and in agriculture, the nationalization of which has been universally inappropriate and counterproductive. He held out for the ideal of socialism and the sanctity of Lenin, but he allowed socialism to be redefined very loosely and extolled the very un-Leninist Lenin of the last, deathbed writings of 1923.

By 1987, Gorbachev found himself compelled by bureaucratic resistance to challenge the power of the Stalinist party apparatus. This led him to call into question the essence of Lenin's political system, the monolithic discipline of the Communist Party and its controls over all other institutions in Soviet society. To do battle with the apparatus conservatives, Gorbachev had to abandon the principle of unity that Lenin had imposed on the party with the 1921 ban on organized factions. Rejecting the party's direct domination over the civil government of the soviets and inviting nonparty organizations to engage in pluralistic dialogue with the party instead of serving as mere "transmission belts" of the party's will, he went against the power arrangements that had prevailed ever since the Russian Civil War.[6]

Other steps that Gorbachev took in 1989 and 1990 ran counter to the Bolshevik Revolution itself. Toleration of organized opposition groups in the 1989 elections and abdication of the Communist Party's constitutional leading role in 1990 carried Soviet politics all the way back to 1917 and the democratic election of the ill-fated Constituent Assembly, before the infant Soviet regime became a strictly one-party affair. Yakovlev condemned the Bolsheviks' "idealization of terror."[7] With these sentiments against revolutionary extremism, the Gorbachevian reformers had fully embraced the moderate revolutionary revival. Gorbachev told the Twenty-eighth Party Congress, "The Stalinist model of socialism is being replaced by a civic society of free people. . . . The atmosphere of ideological diktat has been replaced by free thinking, glasnost, and the openness of society to information."[8]

One obvious difficulty in applying the notion of the moderate revolutionary revival to the Gorbachev era is the great span of elapsed time under the postrevolutionary dictatorship. But this is not such a puzzle if we consider the Khrushchev years as an incomplete, irresolute, and eventually abortive attempt to bring about the moderate revolutionary revival thirty years earlier. Perhaps perestroika would have inspired more idealism and less cynicism if it had been successfully implemented in Khrushchev's time. Khrushchev's failure and the ensuing delay in fundamental reform can be explained partly as a failure of leadership, partly by the sheer immobility of the Stalinist bureaucratic system, and partly with reference to the deep roots that the Stalinist and neo-Stalinist regimes had been able to put down in the authoritarian soil of Russian political culture. Recognizing the inordinately long sway of postrevolutionary dictatorship in the Soviet Union, one can better appreciate the growing contradictions of modernizing society and rigid government that undermined the Brezhnev regime.

The moderate revolutionary revival does not immediately guarantee a stable outcome of freedom and democracy, nor does it determine exactly what mix of goals and values from the original moderate phase of the revolution will be recovered and preserved. England went through years of political infighting between crown and parliament—generating the first two-party system of pro-king Tories and pro-parliament Whigs—until parliamentary supremacy was firmly achieved in the first half of the eighteenth century. Meanwhile, periodic plots and uprisings of the absolutist Jacobites had to be fought off. France experienced a particularly chaotic sequel to its moderate revolutionary revival, when unresolved class conflict erupted in the Revolution of 1848, followed by a complete new revolutionary cycle taking the path under Louis Napoleon Bonaparte of a revolution of the Right, more in the direction of twentieth-century Germany and Spain. The end came only in the violence of the Paris Commune, before the moderate revolution was revived in the form of the Third Republic.

In Russia the course of the moderate revolutionary revival has not been any smoother. Gorbachev's experiment in reform, proceeding step-by-step to the introduction of semiconstitutional government in 1989, was fatally destabilized by economic crisis and ethnic separatism. The attempted coup of August 1991 was more serious than reactionary efforts in any other country's experience at the corresponding stage. Even so, there was no real prospect of restoring "Communism," that is, neo-Stalinism, after the shattering effect of the moderate revolutionary revival upon the old beliefs.

The August Putsch had the unexpected effect of displacing Russia's moderate revival back to an earlier revolutionary time. Gorbachev had addressed the bankruptcy of the postrevolutionary dictatorship gradually and had worked his way back to the turning point of October 1917 in terms of democracy and decentralized socialism. His successor, Boris Yeltsin, took his cue for more abrupt reforms not even from the turning point of February 1917 but from the semiconstitutional tsarist regime that followed the Revolution of 1905, repudiating all expressions of socialism and endorsing unfettered capitalism with a government of at best guided democracy.

This swing of Russia's moderate revolutionary revival back to such an early and relatively conservative reference point is related to the peculiarities of the long Stalinist epoch, still dressed up with ideological links to the original revolution. In many minds the only way to exorcise the successive traumas of

Leninism and Stalinism was to repudiate any institutions and policies even verbally associated with them, including any hint of socialism and even the simple Russian name of "soviet" for a local council. But none of this was likely to put an end to political perturbations and pendulum swings as Russia sought a normal, nonrevolutionary form of existence.

CHAPTER 34

The Communist Oppositions and Post-Stalinist Reform

Does the history of the Communist oppositions in the first dozen years of Soviet rule have any meaning today? Is the experience of those opposition movements of any value in reconciling democratic politics, social justice, and the realities of Russian life? Or has the story of the oppositions, since the collapse of the Soviet Union and Communist Party rule, become merely an antiquarian curiosity, irrelevant to the choices that Russia debates for its post-Communist future?

Encompassing all the waves of criticism in the Bolshevik/Communist Party that resisted decisions and policies of Lenin and of the leadership that succeeded him, the oppositions were history's castoffs. Nonetheless, their story is important in understanding the Soviet background of post-Communist Russia. It shows the way the Soviet system evolved in response to the circumstances in which it found itself, the alternatives that arose in its development, and the diverse personalities who helped shape its tortuous history.

The travails of the oppositions highlight the multistage revolutionary process that begot and shaped the Communist regime. Otherwise, the verbal continuity in Communist ideology could have obscured the profound divergence of theory and practice in the Soviet system. The historical existence of the oppositions challenges the ideological assumption that there was only one way properly to understand Lenin and Leninism, that is, Stalin's way, just as the existence of the Mensheviks challenges the assumption that there was only one way properly to understand Marx—namely, Lenin's way.

Seen close up, the oppositions may appear to be a series of hopeless protests by disillusioned idealists, always the losers in the ongoing struggle for leadership and power. Viewed in a longer time span, however, and in the comparative perspective of other revolutions, the oppositions come into focus as a natural phenomenon of the revolutionary process. In their tribulations they document the unfolding of that process as no official leadership statements ever did.

Movement from one revolutionary phase to another is driven by a combination of social and psychological forces over which revolutionary leaders try to preside while they are contending for power. But their ideas of what they are doing are usually dim, abstract, and wrong, as Engels observed about successful revolutionaries who "had no idea what they were doing."[1] It is just this inevitable discrepancy between aims and results that generates currents of protest within the revolutionary camp at every stage of the process and fuels the struggle for power.

Lenin was resisted at every turn by idealists of the left. They warned as early as April 1918 of "a deviation by a majority of the Communist Party and the soviet power directed by it into the channel of a petty-bourgeois policy of a new form. . . . The working class will cease to be the director, the exerciser of hegemony over the socialist revolution."[2] War Communism, with its terror and barracks socialism, brought out again the characteristic cleavage between utopian ideologues and pragmatic power seekers that reflected the incompatibility of theory and practice. The utopians in Russia were the Democratic Centralists and the Workers' Opposition, protesting the centralizing, bureaucratic, and antiegalitarian trends in the Communist dictatorship. "We are against the excessive extension of the concept of militarization, we are against the blind imitation of military models," declared the Democratic Centralists' leader Valerian Osinsky, as he defended the "collegial principle" and the role of "local organs which are responsible for all the particular spheres of work in the provinces."[3] Speaking for the Workers' Opposition, Alexandra Kollontai defended "workers' control" and denounced "one-man management" and the party leadership's "distrust toward the working class." She warned, "Bureaucracy is our enemy, our scourge, and the greatest danger for the future existence of the Communist Party itself."[4] These radical idealists were the equivalent of the "Enragés" and the Hébertists of the French Revolution, radical Jacobins based on the Paris workers, or of the Levellers back in the English Revolution. Though fruitless, opposition protests highlighted the rapid evolution of the Soviet regime in directions directly antithetical to the radical hopes of 1917.

The year 1921 has not always been recognized as the point of the Communist Thermidor, carried out as it was by the ruling extremists themselves, without interrupting the power of the revolutionary party or its ideological claims. It was as if Robespierre, foreseeing his possible overthrow in 1794, had called off the terror and the "Republic of Virtue" himself, or more exactly, as if the more adaptable Danton, like Lenin, had survived to make the pragmatic turn against Robespierre-Trotsky.

Reaction to the NEP was muted, in part because most Communists recognized that they had to retreat in order to keep power, and in part because Lenin clamped down on opposition through the ban on organized factions that he pushed through the Tenth Party Congress in March 1921. Thus Lenin accompanied the economic relaxation of the NEP-Thermidor with the political tightening that set up Stalin's later power in the party organization and thereby took the country another long step toward totalitarianism. Controversy resumed at the highest level upon Lenin's illness and death, and continued during the open struggle for power that those events triggered. Trotsky, at the center of debate until 1927, challenged what he regarded as an unrevolutionary, pro-peasant implementation of the NEP. At the same time, reversing the stance he took while in power under War Communism, he protested the bureaucratic and hierarchical development of the regime and the accompanying menace of Stalin's personal power. Thus the controversies of 1923–27 demonstrated the continued though constricted possibility of public debate among the leadership, and at the same time they dramatized the economic problems of the NEP and the divergence among Marxists on this score.

Was Trotsky the first Stalinist, as he has often been represented? This notion, discounting the notorious hatred between Stalin and Trotsky that ended only with the latter's exile and murder, derives from the image Trotsky established during the period of War Communism as the ultimate militarist and apologist for terror. But if Trotsky indeed were Stalin's predecessor, especially in his role under War Communism, then the Lenin of 1921 could not have been; and it would still be difficult to explain Trotsky's unyielding opposition to Stalin later on. The answer is that Trotsky changed, as did Lenin and Bukharin and most other Communist leaders, when the revolution moved through its successive phases, and when his own seat of power collapsed.[5] Lenin, before his death, came to regard the NEP as a long-term period of cultural modernization: "We can regard as achievements only what have become part and parcel of our culture, of our social life, our habits. . . . The most harmful thing here would be haste. . . . We . . . lack sufficient civilization to enable us to pass straight on to socialism."[6] One should not credit even Stalin with too much long-term consistency, as the official Stalinist history tried to do; as Bukharin said of Stalin, "He changes his theory according to whom he needs to get rid of."[7]

That remark came during the final stage in the history of the oppositions, the contest of 1928–29 between Stalin and the Right Opposition. As the main-stream party leadership, committed to the NEP, the rightists were the party of Thermidor, even though they bristled at the term. They did their best to adapt Marxism and proletarian dogma to the reality of a predominantly peas-ant country. Stalin, in contrast, was more interested in exploiting the economic difficulties of the NEP in order to enhance his personal power. In his sudden "left turn" of 1928, he borrowed and exaggerated the Trotskyist critique of the NEP (without acknowledgment) while consummating the trend to dictatorship within the party that the Trotskyists had vainly been resisting.

The record of the Right Opposition's resistance to Stalin's revolution from above and his violent implementation of the totalitarian state is of special signifi-cance for the historiography of the Soviet Union. Was Stalin essentially Lenin's continuator, or did he make a fundamental break with the Bolshevik tradition? Certainly no one can say that Stalinism was unrelated to Leninism; each rep-resented a successive phase of the same revolution, and Stalin had learned his political methods in Lenin's school of extremism. Nevertheless, even though Stalin capitalized on the organizational heritage of the Leninist party, he was improvising in the realm of economic policy as he felt out issues—the peasants and the grain supply, the role of experts, economic planning and the tempo of development—that he could use to outflank his opponents and brand them as antiparty deviators. It was only in the course of maneuvering against the Right Opposition that Stalin became committed to his distinctive programs of collectivization, crash industrialization, military-style commands instead of real planning, and antiexpert show trials.[8] Stephen Cohen has remarked that in 1927, "Stalinists were just beginning to grope towards positions of their own."[9] Michal Reiman agreed: "The Stalin of 1926 was not the Stalin of 1929, neither in the general nature of his policies . . . nor in the type of practical solutions he proposed."[10]

Under Stalin's new program of 1928–29, Thermidor with its relative relax-ation in economics and private life gave way to the postrevolutionary dictator-ship. Opposition to this development, after Bukharin's group was crushed in 1929, was fitful and shadowy, largely addressing the excesses of Stalin's policies more than his principles. A series of futile "platforms" criticizing Stalin's rash-ness were advanced by former Bukharinists—the platform of M. N. Riutin—and by apprehensive Stalinists—the platform of S. I. Syrtsov and V. V. Lomi-nadze—but these gestures served mainly to fuel Stalin's propaganda campaign against saboteurs. Moderates looked to Leningrad party secretary Sergei Kirov, thought to be Stalin's heir apparent, as a political alternative, but Kirov failed to lend himself to an anti-Stalin effort before he was assassinated in December 1934. Whatever the extent of resistance to his leadership, Stalin disposed of it by means of the unprecedented terror of 1935–38, directed in the first instance against the beaten survivors of the oppositions of the 1920s but rapidly extending into a war against the same officialdom who had supported him throughout his rise to power and the revolution from above.

There could not be any direct connection between Russia's rejection of the postrevolutionary regime between 1985 and 1991 and the original Communist opposition movements. Stalinist terror and the many decades of totalitarian discipline that followed had effectively extirpated that tradition except as a tale of villainy. Yet the historical record of criticism and alternatives that the oppositions had established, now cleansed of its Stalinist tarnish, furnished key guideposts that oriented and measured the progress of reform under perestroika.

Perestroika was a voyage back in historical time, as Gorbachev undertook to undo the legacies first of Stalin and then of Lenin. Where Khrushchev had only denounced Stalin's crimes against the Stalinists and had defended the dictator's record prior to 1934, Gorbachev repudiated the Stalin Revolution all the way back to its beginning in 1928, including forced collectivization, nationalization of small enterprise, and the "command-administrative" approach to managing the economy. Encouraged by advisors such as Abel Aganbegyan, Gorbachev embraced a philosophy similar to the Right Opposition and went back to the market socialism of the NEP for his policy model.[11] The official rehabilitation of Bukharin in 1988 was the logical culmination of these steps. As Gorbachev then turned to political reform, he called into question the basic principles of the Leninist party—top-down appointments, the ban on factions, the enforcement of an official Marxist orthodoxy, and finally the political monopoly of the Communist Party as a whole. This return to the past was accompanied by a spate of historical and documentary publications dealing with the oppositions, the first time since the 1920s that their true record was allowed to see the light of day.[12] It remained for Yeltsin to reject the October Revolution and the practice of even a tempered socialism, causing interest in Soviet history and the alternatives it presented to fall off accordingly. Trotsky, not quite attaining explicit rehabilitation under Gorbachev, faded again as one of the repudiated architects of Communism.

Do the oppositions now signify anything but a repository of old ideas, some perhaps applicable today, many not? Or did they represent a real historical alternative in their time? Were they doomed, or could they have prevailed in one form or another to divert Soviet Russia away from its fateful course toward totalitarianism?

The answer depends on which current of opposition one has in mind, and at which stage of the revolutionary process. Overall, a radically different alternative was unlikely: Lenin had pounded in too deeply the authoritarian habits of extremist dictatorship, and Stalin fit too well the role of the postrevolutionary dictator. But in matters of degree and detail, nothing in history is that fixed; alternative leadership with alternative policies could have made a significant difference in human terms.

After the first wave of oppositionists—the utopian decentralizers and communitarians of 1918–21—they had little or no chance. Their kind of movement has never been successful in any revolution, and the authoritarian reflexes of Russian political culture militated against them as well. The Left Opposition led by Trotsky in the 1920s was more realistic, but its vision of workers' democracy was warped by the single-party dogma, and it offered no practical way of accomplishing its program of rapid industrialization.

The most obvious candidate for a successful alternative to Stalinism was the program of the Right Opposition. Bukharin's gradualist and pro-peasant line would have been a realistic approach toward the country's future, if the accidents of leadership choices and political infighting had gone differently. Unfortunately, the Bukharinists were hobbled by their attachment to party discipline and ideological orthodoxy, principles inherited from Lenin and adroitly exploited by Stalin. If the Trotskyists' hopes for democracy and their fears about Stalin could have been joined with the Bukharinists' economic pragmatism, the opposition would have held a formidable position. In actuality, only one important figure in the opposition combined these views—Grigory Sokolnikov, the commissar of finance, and he remained isolated. Until too late, the Trotskyists and the Bukharinists were fatally divided by theoretical issues that in retrospect seem negotiable if not trivial. In the words of the German scholars Theodor Bergmann and Gert Schäfer, "The political tragedy lay in the fact that for too long the Left considered the theoretical controversy with Bukharin et al. more important than the erection of Stalin's despotism, and while the 'Rights' allied with Stalin the Left fought them, until it was too late."[13] Bukharin woke up abruptly in July 1928, when he told Kamenev, "The disagreements between us and Stalin are many times more serious than the disagreements which we used to have with you." But Trotsky was unyielding: "With Stalin against Bukharin?—Yes. With Bukharin against Stalin?—Never!"[14] The dream of a workers' commonwealth was fading. The Bukharinists accommodated themselves to this fact, while the Trotskyists went on trying to deny it.

There remained one other possibility, one that has never so far been raised in the literature. Stalin himself might conceivably have judged it more expedient to hew to the Right Opposition's gradualist position in economics (that is, the NEP line) while still perfecting his personal power in politics. If so, the particular form of Russia's postrevolutionary dictatorship could have been much less ruinous. Stalin could have avoided the cruelty and economic disruption accompanying collectivization, crash industrialization, and the purges. The country would have found itself in a far stronger position for war with Germany.[15] But in this event, Stalin would not have been Stalin, the demented personality who inflicted so much pointless pain on an already suffering country.

What if Trotsky, instead, had actually prevailed over Stalin?[16] The common answer, based again on the civil war picture of Trotsky, is that it would not have made any difference. This is implicitly to deny the role of personality in events, and it is hard to imagine two more different personalities than Trotsky and Stalin, the flamboyant intellectual and the crafty *praktik*. Trotsky could certainly have played the part of a postrevolutionary dictator, a Bonaparte, an ambition that his enemies repeatedly accused him of. But along with personality, the timing and circumstances of assuming the leadership have to be taken into account. Stalin fashioned a dictatorship over the party through behind-the-scenes maneuvering and machine politics while he was eliminating first the Left Opposition and then the Right. Trotsky's best shot at the leadership came sooner, in the early months of 1923 when Lenin tried unsuccessfully to get him to come out against Stalin. Had Trotsky taken that course instead of temporizing fatally for six months more in his nervousness over anti-Semitism, he might well have prevailed, but the party would not yet have been shackled by the disciplined unanimity and ideological obscurantism that Stalin subsequently forged. While Trotsky was strongly biased toward industrial development, there is little basis to suppose that he would have adopted Stalin's forcible collectivization, slapdash economic planning, antiexpert campaigns, or cultural know-nothingism. Neither Trotsky nor Bukharin would have pursued anything like Stalin's pseudo-revolutionary "third period" foreign policy and his connivance in the advent of Hitler, another product of his political maneuvering against the Bukharinists. In any case, as tough-minded historians like to remind us, history has no subjective mood. We can learn from it, be inspired by it, take warning from it, but we cannot change it.

The futility of the oppositions has its own special significance. For all their sense of principle and ideological zeal, the oppositionists were fighting against some of the most basic trends of modern society as well as Russia's special circumstances. While they saw their difficulties in terms of wrongheaded leadership in command of the Communist Party, their protests only underscored the forces that were inexorably working against them. These included not only the natural unfolding of the revolutionary process toward authoritarianism and compromise with the past but in addition the habits of arrogant command and sullen submissiveness embedded in centuries of Russian experience under a centralized despotism. The Left Opposition always aimed at direct democracy and group decision making, but it allowed itself to be locked into Lenin's one-party framework and the notion of democracy only for the working class, overlooking Rosa Luxemburg's warning, "Freedom only for the supporters of the government, only for the members of one party—however numerous they may be—is no freedom at all."[17] All of the opposition groups, no less than the leadership they criticized, were gripped by fear and suspicion of Russia's great peasant majority. They differed among themselves only on how to address the peasant threat, whether by concessions, containment, or attack; there was no question of admitting the rural population to equal political status. Once Lenin had suppressed the Ultra Left in 1921 in the name of monolithic unity and iron discipline, no one ventured to challenge these principles directly—though for some time the oppositions violated them in practice—and ultimately none of the oppositionists had any defense of principle against Stalin's Leninist logic.

The oppositions' nineteenth-century ideal of minimal authority and rank was confounded further by the twentieth-century trend toward a regime of officials and experts, corporate or governmental, required to manage society's affairs. From 1918 on, the Left Opposition in its various incarnations constantly lashed out at the employment of bourgeois specialists and at bureaucratic trends both in government and in the economy. Stalin exploited antiexpert feeling himself when he fought the Right Opposition and tightened his organizational grip, with a series of campaigns and show trials from 1928 on to blame managers and engineers for sabotaging his program. In the end, however, he only intensified the trend toward a bureaucratic and managerial society, his purges sufficing simply to restaff and terrorize the hierarchy of position and function, not to diminish it but to exclude any alternative.

No country can do without historical traditions to serve as reference points for its politics, above all in times of crisis. Even the Communists found their professed antecedents in Russia's pre-Marxist revolutionary tradition. Naturally, different political parties and movements will find different facets of their country's past to serve as their inspiration and legitimation. Indeed, it is often successive historical experiences that generate diverse parties and positions in the first place and give them much of their emotional momentum.

In Russia today the Communist and nationalist opposition has no difficulty finding its traditionalist legitimation by embracing almost the entire Russian past, tsarist as well as Stalinist. The Communists have practically submerged their Marxist identity in the bath of irredentist Russian nationalism, and the ease of this transmogrification underscores the real commitment that had inspired them for many decades. For democrats, the quest for a usable Russian past has been more difficult. Gorbachev and the reform Communists turned back to the economics of the NEP and the pretotalitarian politics of 1917–18— in other words, to the positions of various Communist oppositionists. The more radical reformers around Yeltsin, rejecting the entire Soviet record as well as the revolutionary tradition associated with it, could find very little in the Russian background to draw upon. Like the nineteenth-century intellectuals of the Westernizer persuasion, they turned to the West and to the Western ideas they felt most opposed to Russian reality; hence Russians' embrace of the socialist utopia in the nineteenth century and of the free-market utopia today. Oddly, no reformers have made reference to the Kerensky government of 1917 or the parties that supported it—after all, these were losers.

What lessons does the failure of the oppositions offer to Russia today? Nominally, Gorbachev and Yeltsin between them turned the country toward pre-Leninist, all-class democracy, though there was little tradition to draw upon. In practice, under Yeltsin, authoritarianism at the center and bossism in the provinces, coupled with general political apathy, delivered the country back into its old political habits. The great economic questions of the 1920s, of capital accumulation and industrialization, are no longer pertinent; instead, Stalinist superindustrialization and the hypertrophy of heavy industry left Russia with challenges of reconversion, updating, and efficiency that the oppositions never had to address. Planning and economic relationships are another matter: The history of the oppositions (especially of the right) underscores the variety in degrees of economic socialization that a country can choose and highlights the difference between the indicative planning and indirect controls of the NEP and the military commands and allocations that became synonymous with planning under Stalinism. The basic problem of workplace democracy versus bureaucratic administration, and the marginalizing of workers from decision making, central for the opposition of 1918–21, remains to be resolved. In the meantime, the nomenklatura as a class, targeted by the oppositions early on, still reigns in the middle strata of society, reformed only by new political coloration. Unfortunately, after the brief euphoria of 1991, both public opinion and the world of political thought in Russia appear to have succumbed to emotional exhaustion and rudderless apathy.

In this intellectually bleak scene, the tradition of the Communist oppositions, purged of its Leninist errors of party and class exclusiveness, might still have something to offer as a reference point. This record articulates the hope of implementing the democratic principle in the broadest sense of the word in all walks of life, including the world of work. Thanks to the vast economic and social transformation of the country accomplished under the Soviet regime, the notion of basing a democratic reform on the working class has acquired a measure of realism, if not of assurance. Presently the workers are the greatest unmobilized potential in Russian society, and a democratic left alternative might be a healthy competitor for their allegiance against the neofascist Right and quasi-fascist Communists. The peasantry, politically overestimated by all factions seventy years ago, is even weaker and more demoralized today. Its main political expression presently is the surviving collective farm bureaucracy and the neo-Communists. Here the Right Opposition's advocacy of genuine cooperatives would offer an alternative to the current prospects of either the collectives, agribusiness, or uneconomical parcelization, thus picking up where the NEP was broken off. Likewise, for the intelligentsia, the democratic left tradition would offer a positive vision of the future in place of the present value vacuum.

If Russia is to extricate itself from its current impasse and address the facts of modern social and economic life, it will have to extract more guidance from its late-nineteenth and early-twentieth-century experience and the ideas of both liberals and revolutionaries. The record of the oppositions has to come back in, along with the prerevolutionary constitutionalists and the local government movement of the *zemstva*, as a repository of ideas, hopes, and warnings about the centralization of power, about the relationship between the power elite and ordinary people, about the methods and costs of achieving a livable life. None of that record can be applied blindly, as fanatics and utopians are inclined to do. Protest thought both prerevolutionary and postrevolutionary has to be approached selectively, but it is Russia's only native resource for constructing a human vision of the future.

CHAPTER 35

Past and Present

Time marches on, and history marches with it. The past never stays in the same place.

Does an epochal and astonishing event therefore require the reconstruction of the entire history leading up to it? Not necessarily, if that history has been worked up in an open fashion receptive to all the possibilities, and not merely to demonstrate the inevitability of the previous arrangements in the manner of the "Whig interpretation of history." In the real world, to be sure, surprising changes can compel recognition of past potentialities that conventional conceptualizations may have neglected. But it is equally possible for such ex post facto reconsiderations to overdo the revision of previous history and the critique of the practitioners of that history.

Three ways come to mind in which the moving present generates new perceptions of the past. One is the new information that may be uncovered about bygone events, when old documents are discovered or rescued from custodial oblivion, governments' archival secrets are released, and personal memoirs and recollections become available. A second source of historical renewal is the new perspective conferred by more recent developments. History looks very different when one knows the outcome: Old events take on a new hue; winners become losers and losers become winners; obscure people, movements, countries come to center stage, and hitherto dominant features of history may seem to lose their importance. A third element in historical reconsideration is the quest to understand newly unfolding events. The new present demands that explanations be wrung out of a historical record that may have become stereotyped and conventionalized. At the extreme, the philosophy of postmodernism intrudes to contend that all history—like practically all knowledge—is a socially conditioned construct governed by the interests and needs of the present; so let revisionism roll.

No sharper instance has ever arisen of the forced reconsideration of history than the 1991 collapse of Communist rule in the Soviet Union and the breakup of the Russian Empire. The potential impact of these events on the understanding of Russian history was monumental in all three respects of historical revision. Oceans of documentary resources poured from once-secret repositories. The whole of the Soviet past came into a new light once its end point was known. And the debacle of 1991 put a new task to history, to support an explanation of that astounding event.

One leading representative of the simplest, straight-line view of the Soviet experience is Dmitri Volkogonov. A military intellectual in the Soviet Army who rose to become a colonel-general and chief of the military commissar system in the 1980s, Volkogonov turned to historical research and broke into international fame with his four-volume biography of Stalin published in 1990. He followed this work with biographies of Trotsky and Lenin and then his posthumously published history of the Soviet system as a whole, in the form of sketches of its seven leaders, Lenin, Stalin, Khrushchev, Brezhnev, Andropov, Chernenko, and finally Gorbachev.[1]

In the course of all this work, resting on his privileged access to the newly opened archives, Volkogonov had a conversion experience. "For many years I was an orthodox Marxist," he writes, "and it was only late in my life, after long and tortuous inner struggle, that I was able to free myself of the chimera of Bolshevik ideology."[2] But ideology, even in repudiation, remained for Volkogonov the key to understanding both the Soviet experiment and its collapse: "For seven decades . . . the Soviet Union followed the path mapped out by Lenin" under leaders who were "confined in the same Procrustean bed of Bolshevik tenets" and who "extolled the mass, the class, the collective," even though they represented rule by the "partocracy."[3] Following the collapse both of the Soviet Union and of his own apparently genuine faith, Volkogonov came to see the Soviet system as the unrelenting pursuit of a communist utopia, at least until the 1985 advent of Gorbachev, who gets his share of credit for loosening the old shackles even if he may have been trying to rescue the system. Volkogonov's kind of anti-ideology, of course, had been a familiar assumption in the West, particularly in nonexpert circles, long before the Soviet collapse. The test issue is the relation between Lenin's revolution and Stalin's later impact on the system. For Volkogonov, the answer was simple: "The system designed by Lenin was built by Stalin and the Party."[4]

Volkogonov could not have accomplished his studies without his use of long-secret archives. As Richard Pipes shows in his documentary collection, *The Unknown Lenin,* the archive material highlights the Soviet founder's hard-eyed cruelty.[5] It underscores Stalin's pathological indifference to the suffering his regime caused, and the petty sclerotic stupidity of Brezhnev and Chernenko. But the documentary revelations do not so far bring out anything of major significance that objective observers did not already know or surmise.

Long before the Soviet collapse and Volkogonov's road to Damascus through the archives, revelations about the Soviet past, above all in the work of Alexander Solzhenitsyn, had a seismic impact on French thinking about the Soviet Union. A nation long noted for its affection and apologies for the Soviets, especially among its intellectuals, was rudely shocked out of its illusions about applied Marxism Soviet-style. Rather late in the day, in *The Black Book of Communism,* a team of French commentators undertook a total reassessment of the Soviet phenomenon and its offshoots around the world.[6]

For the editor of the *Black Book,* Stéphane Courtois, and for Martin Malia, who introduced the English edition, as for Volkogonov, it all boils down to the utopian ideology of Leninism, driving the Communists to crimes worse than the Nazis as they sought to exterminate all who stood in the way of their agenda of class struggle. Personalities, culture, circumstances are not very important next to the malevolent force unleashed by a unique philosophy of revolution. This premise does not allow for significant differences among different regimes hewing to the banner of Marxism-Leninism or for evolution, for better or for worse, within them. Signally, it does not account for the near-cessation of criminal violence (as distinct from mere authoritarian repression) in the Soviet Union after the death of Stalin, and in China after the death of Mao Tse-tung.

A more nuanced view in the *Black Book* was Nicholas Werth's account of Soviet tyranny from 1917 to 1956. Ending his story for all practical purposes with Khrushchev's condemnation of Stalin, Werth implies that the power of a mad individual had more to do with the crimes of Communism than the official ideology, which at least pro forma continued in force for another three decades in Russia and still holds nominal sway in China.

In another summation of the Soviet record, Professor Manfred Hildermeier of Göttingen University asked, "How did Soviet Socialism come to grief?"[7] Socialist ideology, Russia's cultural impoverishment, and unsustainable international ambitions all share the blame. Thus, Hildermeier's answer to the running debate about the role of Marxist ideology versus factors of Russian tradition and the drive for personal power was to weave them all together. Socialist theory, he believed, defined the Soviet experience: It was "a quest for utopia," just as Volkogonov thought. Lenin's bequest to Stalinism is a matter Hildermeier did not try to resolve quite so simply. The question of responsibility, whether Stalin's or the environment he found himself in, was one of "the hen and the egg." Russian tradition exerted on Soviet society a continuity of statism and centralism on the one hand and of social irresponsibility on the other. Contrary to the ideal "socialist man," "people avoided their public and civic duties." Inevitably, theory and practice diverged, and Soviet socialism became "a living lie."[8]

Similarly surveying the Soviet record, Robert Service of the University of London emphasized the persistence of "administrative informality and disarray."[9] Though he allowed for leadership idiosyncrasies and for the force of Russian tradition and circumstances and gave a nod to ideology and its demise—"Communism is the young god that failed"—he dwelt on the improvisations by Communist leaders as they wrestled with the problems that previous improvisations of their own or their predecessors' making had caused. He did not visualize much of a Soviet grand design where none really governed. To take the test question of Stalin's relation to Lenin, Service split the difference: "Lenin's basic elements were maintained. . . . Certain other elements were greatly altered." Lenin's "centralized, ideocratic dictatorship" emerged in the smoke of civil war, when the Bolsheviks "dipped into their rag-bag of authoritarian concepts to work out measures to help them to survive in power." Stalin had no preconceived plan, other than "the framework of his prejudices and ambition," in the pursuit of "personal dictatorship" and "a mighty industrial state."[10]

　　Service's picture of chaos, improvisation, and contradictions in Soviet developments, paralleling the American school of Soviet social history, extends to the failure of Gorbachev and the demise of the Soviet regime. Given the contradictions within the Soviet system, Gorbachev's attempts at reform—themselves an unfolding series of improvisations without a guiding plan—fatally undermined the regime and accelerated its collapse. But improvisation and the pattern of reaction to self-created problems did not stop with the breakup of the Soviet Union and the advent of Boris Yeltsin. In this sense the unity in chaos of the Soviet phenomenon persists still.

To Ronald Suny of the University of Chicago, the title of his recent book notwithstanding, the Soviet phenomenon was not an "experiment" in the ideological sense but only "the rough modernization of a backward, agrarian society."[11]

However, ideology gave the Bolsheviks a "commitment to their own vision of history," which "made it impossible for them to contemplate giving up power," but it supplied "no a priori blueprint."[12]

In Suny's view, there was a fundamental break between Lenin's revolution and Stalin's. Stalin was the creator of totalitarianism; "Stalin's party elevated coercion in place of persuasion." The Stalinist system was "a perverse imitation of authentic social ownership, in which a ruling elite of party chieftains and bureaucratic managers ran the country"—a formulation close to Hildermeier's "living lie." But all of this could have been written a half century before. Disabused of the ideological interpretation, Suny was able to recognize the early end of Stalin's revolution from above in most social and cultural respects along the lines of Nicholas Timasheff's *Great Retreat* of 1946. The ultimate collapse was not inevitable, but, like all the great revolutionary changes in the course of Soviet history, the outcome of politics. It followed from "a program of liberalization . . . initiated from above" that "moved quickly out of the control of its initiators."[13]

The most concrete basis for revising history, naturally, lies in the archives, either the opening of hitherto classified collections or newly discovered materials. In the case of a totalitarian society like the Soviet Union, consumed as it was by a secrecy mania, the volume of documentary source material withheld from history is altogether staggering. It could take decades, now, for investigators to go through all the records that have become available, in part since Gorbachev's glasnost of the late 1980s and more so since the collapse of Communist Party rule in 1991.

Yet the impact of this tidal wave of historical revelation has been less than epochal. For one thing, layers of historical coverup have been peeled away, like Peer Gynt's onion, only one at a time, and the innermost kernel of official secrecy has not even yet been opened up. Under Khrushchev there was a surge in the accessibility of archival information that had come to be deemed nonsensitive because of its age or nonpolitical character. This fueled the explosion of Western research on Soviet social history and nourished the revisionist school of Sheila Fitzpatrick, Moshe Lewin, and many others, who found Soviet society less totalitarian than the theoretical model presumed. Under Gorbachev, the emphasis was to face more honestly the already known record in Soviet political history, especially the role of factional leaders such as Trotsky and Bukharin and policy debates within the Communist Party in the early Soviet years. Post-1991 archival revelations have shifted the focus all the more toward political history, with emphasis on the crimes and blunders of all the successive leaders of Soviet Communism. Writers who have most exploited these materials, like Volkogonov and Werth, make totalitarianism appear more severe, not less, as the revisionists had argued. But in broad outline, at least, all of this has been known for decades.

The organization of the Soviet archives on the basis of political sensitivity helps explain the selectivity in the opening of their contents. Broadest in scope was the Central State Archive of the October Revolution and Socialist Construction (TsGAOR), the main source for the Western research on Soviet social and economic history that burgeoned from the 1960s on. Far more restrictive if not totally closed was the Central Party Archive at the Institute of Marxism-Leninism (now the Russian Center for the Preservation and Study of Documents of Contemporary History) along with the military, security, and foreign relations archives. Separate from all these was the supersensitive Central Committee archive.

The new Russian Archival Service under Rudolf Pikhoya, an old friend of Yeltsin's, promised a sweeping declassification of historical materials in these archives, though the most sensitive materials (including most Politburo documents) had already been reserved by Gorbachev in a "presidential archive." This latter was inherited by Yeltsin and released only on a selective basis for political effect (for example, the documents proving Soviet responsibility for the Katyn massacre of Polish officers during World War II). Access to the presidential archive was Volkogonov's unique advantage. But ever since the political crisis of 1993, access to archives at all levels has been progressively tightened, and Pikhoya himself was eased out in 1996.

Meanwhile, very ambitious projects of reproduction and translation from the Soviet archives have been undertaken by various American publishers and institutions. As early as 1992 the Library of Congress organized an exhibit of over three hundred documents made available by the Russian authorities, sampling Soviet history from 1917 to 1991; the collection was ultimately published in 1997.[14] The Yale University Press launched its *Annals of Communism* documentary series in 1995, including a probing work on the calamitous 1930s, *The Road to Terror*.[15] Of equal interest for recent decades is the outburst of memoir publications in Russian, though only the highest-profile authors have been translated.[16]

The great irony of this plethora of inside secrets from the Soviet regime is that it has done little to alter knowledgeable outsiders' basic picture of the nature, development, and behavior of the Communist system. The details, to be sure, are fascinating, and that is what makes both Volkogonov and Werth, and even publications like *The Unknown Lenin* and *Revelations from the Soviet Archives*, compelling reading. To any Westerner not blinded by ideological commitment it was well known that Lenin was a single-minded fanatic; the documents only spell out how bloodthirsty he became under the pressure of the Russian Civil War. It was equally well known that Stalin was a murderous tyrant; the documents show in addition how deeply he immersed himself in the details of administering totalitarian power. In one area—foreign policy—the documentary revelations tip the balance in an old debate among outsiders, in this case away from the world revolution theory and toward the picture of what was at worse an aggressive security mania.[17] Yet the terms of Marxist-Leninist dogma continued to grip the Soviet leadership to the end. Whatever the degree of cynicism in their individual minds, observed Geoffrey Hosking, "even when writing to each other in private they used the same language and articulated the same thoughts as in their public utterances."[18]

The second way more recent events can modify understanding of past history is the new perspective that they provide, sometimes sharply altering historians' sense of what is important, natural, or problematical in the earlier record. One familiar example is the expansion in Western historical consciousness to take in the non-West. Another is the explosion of gender studies tracking the progress of women's movements. Sometimes startling occurrences—the French Revolution or the outbreak of World War I, for instance—may set down basic new benchmarks in overall perceptions of history and establish a new periodization from which the running present proceeds.

Soviet history is a notable instance where events wrote finis to a long segment of the past and thereby enabled it to be viewed and appraised as a whole. The regime's collapse in 1991 put many facets of the old order and its history into new relief—the social and economic weaknesses of the system, the quiet disaffection of the multitude, the self-consciousness of the national minorities, who made up half of the population of the empire. It showed both the burden and the impermanence of totalitarianism, if one may still venture to employ that embattled term.

Nevertheless, wide disagreement remains in interpretation of the now defined history of the Soviet system. What, indeed, was it that came to an end in 1991? Was it essentially the same animal that entered the world in 1917, or had it by the end turned into something factually if not verbally quite different? Was the Soviet system an essentially fixed entity or an evolving phenomenon that constantly changed its nature over the successive stages of its history? In the wake of the 1991 debacle, it has become the conventional wisdom to see the Soviet Union as "a seventy-year experiment that failed." Decades of efforts to understand the evolution of the Soviet system as the resultant of a complex interaction of factors both subjective and objective were reinforced by the revelations and revisions about the Soviet past allowed in Russia under Gorbachev. Since then, the new orthodoxy of the Marxist failure has taken hold among Western academics and publicists alike and threatens to marginalize the developmental approach to Soviet history. To this extent, new events have diminished rather than enhanced the understanding of a historical phenomenon.

This problematic has been politicized since the Soviet collapse even more than before. The new orthodoxy falls back on a much older one, to see the Soviet experience defined and governed, if not fully explained, by Marxist-Leninist ideology. Here is the anti-ideology often embraced by former true believers like Volkogonov, which rejects socialism even in its various nuances and denies any significant distinctions among socialism, Leninism, and Stalinism. At the same time, the concept of totalitarianism is identified with the whole Soviet past, without much appreciation of its development in a beginning, an apogee, and a step-by-step dissolution. Such ahistorical thinking has easily lent itself to political uses, serving as a rationale both for Russia's post-Communist experiment with the free-market economy and for Western encouragement of this course.

Russians, as Volkogonov illustrates, seem to be boxed in by the new simplicity more than scholars elsewhere, and understandably so, having been cramped by the old Soviet simplicity before. Stéphane Courtois in his prefatory essay to the *Black Book* accepted the same premise, a backlash from what he acknowledged to be the "self-deception" of the French Left.[19] However, the evils at various stages in the Soviet saga differed in kind as well as in degree. This point is a fundamental matter of accurate understanding that Western historiography has the responsibility of conveying back to its Russian counterpart as well as to the general public in the West.

One way or another, all writers on Russian history have to address the problem of Russia's national identity, the "Russian idea," in the phrase that Nikolai Berdiayev made a fundament of the Russian political lexicon. But definitions of the "Russian idea" range all over the map. Was the Soviet era an aberration in Russia's "normal" development toward modern statehood? Was Soviet identity something superimposed on Russian national identity? Can historians legitimately echo the Yeltsin government to hold that post-Communist Russia somehow recovered its "independence" from that extraterrestrial Soviet imposition, when actually the Soviet reincarnation of the Russian Empire was simply decolonized? It is far more appropriate, though intellectually more demanding, to view the Soviet experience, revolutionary and postrevolutionary,

as a phenomenon rooted in the Russian past and in the challenge of modernization. Showing that history matters, the answers to these issues had tremendous political implications for Yeltsin's Russia, including the dissolution of the
Soviet Union, the embrace of late tsarism as a political model (complete with
a "Duma"), and the abandonment of Soviet accomplishments ranging from
science and education to heavy industry.

The converse of new perspectives, where the evolving present casts the past in
a new light, is the reshuffling of the past to explain the most recent events. For
Russia, this means above all the collapse of Communist Party rule and the dissolution—read "decolonization"—of the Soviet Union.

All parties are now compelled to agree that the Soviet system was much
weaker than anyone imagined beforehand. The totalitarian school had to do the
most complete flip-flop, from its assurance that the system would yield to nothing but outside force to a conviction that internal weaknesses going all the way
back to 1917 assured its ultimate demise. Volkogonov was content to say that
the collapse of the system was inherent in the ideological origins of "Leninist
Bolshevism" and its doctrine of violent class struggle; the end was near when
"listless" leaders lost faith in themselves.[20] Thus his own break with the ideology serves as a paradigm for the regime's disintegration. Hildermeier located
the roots of the system's terminal weakness in Stalin's "political decision" to
launch his profligate Five-Year plans: "Stagnation was preprogrammed."[21]
Other authorities hold that had it not been for the loosening-up occasioned by
Gorbachev's reform-minded leadership, the system might have persisted for
decades more.

Less often remarked is the ability of the Soviet system to endure as long
as it did, given what the collapse and postcollapse revelations have shown of
its weaknesses. The miracle of victory in World War II is much more challenging to explain than the ultimate breakdown of the system: How could the
regime have braved the Nazi onslaught and rebounded to enjoy a half century
of superpower status, given the backwardness, poverty, and sheer incompe-
tent cruelty in Stalinist society that all the new documents underscore? There
were achievements, such as social security and cultural uplift, rewards to career climbers, and shakeups to keep everybody in line. There was a willingness
to take inordinate losses on the part of a regime that was already militarized
and saw victory as vindication of its rigidity, as Stalin claimed in his celebrated
"election" speech of February 1946.

Going beyond these issues is the problem of explaining why post-Communist reform in Russia failed to achieve either stable democracy or general

economic prosperity. That task is as difficult as accounting for the Communist collapse, the more so given the brevity of historical perspective on these recent events. Furthermore, interpretation of the most recent past is as politicized and controversial, among both Russians and outsiders, as are their assessments of the long Soviet experience. It is hard for the experts to agree even on defining *what* happened, let alone *why*.

In the last analysis, what changes have the events of 1991 compelled historians to make in their conceptions of the Soviet past? What revisions of outlook do the newly published studies and sources compel? Nothing of great substance, surprisingly. Despite all the new documentation, despite the closure on the Soviet era afforded by the events of 1991, the basic lines of interpretation and the debates among them have not been fundamentally altered.

There have been some marginal changes of emphasis. The new archival and memoir documentation gives the field a nudge back toward more traditional political history, focusing necessarily on the individual leaders who generated these materials. There is more stress on the weaknesses that the Soviet regime suffered from all along, especially inefficiencies in the economy and tensions involving the national minorities, who played a decisive role in the breakdown of the system. The totalitarian model, now left to historians to wrestle with, has to be modified historically to take account of the development and demise of Soviet Communism. We have to recognize the dialectic of modernization, posed by social historians such as Moshe Lewin, as regime and society interacted with each other. Finally, we should learn to temper the dogmatism that is likely to arise in the historical contemplation of events that are frightening, odious, and perplexing, even if there is still no consensus about individual and social determinants, about the unchanging essence and the evolving existence of the Soviet regime. The tragedy and the irony of that ultimately baffling chapter in human affairs still challenge all who venture into the field or who cannot pull themselves away from it.

CHAPTER 36

The Grand Surprise and Soviet Studies

When Communism collapsed in 1991, was the academic pursuit known as "Sovietology" invalidated because it failed to predict that epochal event? This proposition has come to be accepted even among people who used to practice that occult art themselves but have since been at pains to disown it. However, the question assumes too much. It has to be broken into a series of more specific queries in order to grasp the impact of 1991 on the study of Russian/Soviet affairs. What was "Sovietology"? What, in actuality, was "Communism," and what is meant by its "collapse"? Finally, was there a failure of prediction that was out of line with other surprises in human affairs?

Sovietology, of course, was never a science unto itself, let alone a monolithic academic cult, as some of its detractors seem to suggest. It was merely the specialized study of the Soviet Union from the standpoint of the familiar academic disciplines: history, economics, geography, occasionally sociology and anthropology, and above all political science. In common usage, the term *Sovietology* came to imply a much narrower approach, primarily in political science, focused on leadership politics and behavior. Herein lay the much-derided practice of Kremlinology, an art of interpolation developed by necessity out of the paucity of objective evidence (not unlike medieval history).

If Sovietology is defined as the study of contemporary Soviet leadership, the demise of the Communist regime left Sovietologists stranded, with "nothing left to do," in the words of Michael Cox.[1] But political scientists are certainly capable of leaving the old era to the historians and moving into the new one.

Recently they have taken up the subject of "transitology" to describe, compare, and analyze regimes undergoing "transitions to democracy."[2] Meanwhile, time moves on, and the subject matter of political science inexorably passes into history, but historians (including the many members of political science faculties who have done some of the best work in Soviet history) should be able to keep the old body of Sovietology very much alive.

An objection has arisen in the minds of some commentators who feel that encompassing Soviet material within the purview of the familiar disciplines implies a presumption that the Soviet Union as such was a "normal" subject of study, and hence not so different from the West. This suggests to the critics a certain moral denseness among Soviet specialists, if not actual softness on totalitarianism. Perhaps such criticism is a legacy of the Cold War and a parting shot at value-neutral social science.

Considering the political climate of hysterical anti-Communism in the United States in the 1950s, the growing field of Soviet studies remained on the whole remarkably objective in its approaches. This assertion may seem farfetched to younger practitioners in the field, raised on debates over Cold Warriors and the theory of totalitarianism. But as Robert F. Byrnes once noted, "Specialists in the Russian and East European fields were never subject to the pressures which afflicted those who studied the Far East, especially China, during the 1940s and 1950s."[3]

The much-criticized totalitarian model was not just an artifact of Cold War propaganda. First coined by Benito Mussolini in a positive sense, the term became familiar before World War II to bracket the Nazi and Communist dictatorships. Anti-Stalin Marxists from Trotsky to Rudolf Hilferding invoked totalitarianism to distinguish Stalinism from socialism.[4] Hannah Arendt popularized the concept in the early Cold War years and made it the basis for much nonspecialist polemicizing.[5] However, as developed by Carl Friedrich and Zbigniew Brzezinski, the concept did convey a reasonable working image of the Stalinist regime, even if it was weak on the origins and national peculiarities of the Communist system.[6] Other treatments, notably that of Merle Fainsod, took a more historical and developmental view of the singularities of Stalinist totalitariansim.[7]

Soviet studies did not feed the politicians' hysteria about Communist expansion but rather helped to defuse it with empirical knowledge of the system's past and current problems. Works in the vein of the Communist master plan for world domination were largely the product of nonspecialists and often of nonacademics. If there was any major intellectual split within Sovietology, it centered on interpretation of the role of Marxist-Leninist ideology, whether it still operated as a guide to action or only as a rationalization of power interests after the fact. But on the whole, to the later disgust of critics both on the right and on the left, Soviet studies tried to remain value free.

A new intellectual stage in Soviet studies was reached in the 1960s and 1970s, as the totalitarian model was called into question and the focus of scholarly interest shifted toward conditions and movements among the mass of the Soviet (usually Russian) people. This shift has sometimes been attributed to the political influence of the New Left or to the thawing of the Cold War in the era of détente. Actually, the alleged influence of the Cold War on scholarly opinion was exaggerated by the new cohort. Probably more relevant were changes of fashion in the mainstream disciplines, notably social history, combined with the new access to Soviet archives of low political sensitivity. In any case, Sovietology did not constitute a peculiar discipline, a unique method, or a single set of conclusions. Its critics notwithstanding, Sovietology was no different in principle from the mobilization of scholarly expertise for the study of any other exotic area of the globe.

The conventional wisdom is that Communism was a utopian experiment, based on the insidious theory of Marxism-Leninism, defying human nature, but cruelly foisted upon hapless populations until at length the Soviet Empire proved incapable of keeping up in the global competition for power. Ideological commitment to their elusive goal, it is said, drove the Communist leaders to erect the system of totalitarianism with all its horrors, paralleling (or perhaps copied by) the totalitarianisms of a rightist utopia in Central Europe. This is a thesis of the doctrinal genesis of totalitarianism, implying a sort of ideological determinism according to which evil results are due simply to evil ideas, independently of the historical circumstances. The resulting system, therefore, could not be altered in its essentials; it could only be overthrown from without, or—a possibility that no one expected—it could break down internally and be replaced by something altogether different. Gorbachev's perestroika, by this reasoning, was a futile attempt to salvage the Communist system without giving up its putative essence, whereas the Yeltsin regime, heir to the collapse, is presumed to have represented a wholly new departure.

This picture, for all its prevalence, does not withstand close scrutiny. The Soviet record from the revolution on manifested a profound transformation, proceeding through a series of markedly different stages and reflecting the traditions and conditions of the Russian scene as well as the ambitions, obsessions, and usually misbegotten choices by successive political leaders. Generally speaking, the more closely one looks into the details of any social system and its development, the less accurately do "models" such as totalitarianism fit the facts or reveal something that could not be observed directly. This is not to say that Soviet reality did not approach the totalitarian model, but the theory did not allow for either the complex development or the ultimate dissolution of the totalitarian state.

Another formula that needs to be reexamined is the so-called collapse of Communism. "Collapse" is a facile popular image of what was actually a complex, step-by-step, and still incomplete process of change in the society or societies of the Soviet Union. Moreover, it obscures the elements of continuity in the successor regimes and their problems.

The key to this experience of transition was a sequence of events at the political center, inherently unpredictable, that eviscerated the authority and legitimacy of the Communist Party dictatorship. Democratization and decentralization, set in motion by Gorbachev in 1988–89, quickly became irreversible. By the time of its Twenty-eighth Congress in 1990, more than a year before its debacle in the August Putsch, the party had become a hollow shell. In the last months of the Soviet Union governance was arguably less personalistic than it was to become later on in most of the successor states, including Russia. What came nearest to an abrupt collapse was the ideological rationale of official Marxism-Leninism, but this had long since turned into a mere liturgical façade, believed in by none but the few who now make up the unregenerate Communist splinter parties. (Brezhnev is reported to have told his brother that faith in the doctrine was only for the gullible masses.)[8] Russian nationalism and great-power pride was the real ideology of the Communists, and this mentality persists virtually unabated along much of the political spectrum in Russia.

The command economy and the principles of state socialism held on a little longer, while Gorbachev's attempts at reform and reinvigoration undermined the actual performance of the system. Yeltsin, as president of the Russian Republic in opposition to Gorbachev from mid-1990 on, espoused a more drastic break with the economic past and put it into effect following the dissolution of the Soviet Union. However, this economic change was not so much a "collapse" as it was the introduction of new principles from above by political command—an old story in Russia. Serious economic breakdown came not under Communism but under the regime that replaced it.

Combining both the accidents of political changeover and the deliberate actions of leaders were the crisis of the Soviet nationalities and the liquidation of the Union. To Yeltsin and his supporters, this was Russia's assertion of independence, along with the other republics, against an antinational Soviet dictatorship. This is absurd: The Soviet Union always was a revived version of the Russian Empire, and Russia was its core. It is more accurate to think of the breakup of the Union as sudden decolonization, driven by the minorities' assertion of autonomy as soon as Moscow began to democratize. Yeltsin's alternative Russian government in Moscow simply endorsed and accelerated this movement in order to strike at Gorbachev. De facto independence of the colonies and formal dissolution of the Russian Empire came easily once the August Coup had crippled the Union government. But within his Russian jurisdiction, Yeltsin showed no sympathy toward the separatist aspirations of lesser national minorities.

It is a metaphorical excess to term the events of 1991 a "revolution," even if this notion seems to preserve the purity of the totalitarian model, that is, a system that remained solid until abruptly overthrown. There was no sudden, violent breakdown in the nationwide structure of power comparable to 1917. All of the elements of the so-called collapse of Communism started gradually, defying the totalitarian model, and none have yet been completed, which defies the simplistic image of a transition to market democracy. Overall, Russia is still Russia, with its problems and obsessions rooted partly in the Communist past, partly in a political culture that is much older, and partly in the unique series of events that undid the Soviet system of government.

Analyzed into its elements, the so-called collapse of Communism was a large order for any effort at prediction. Exact forecasting of political events in an inherently uncertain world is beyond the claims of any social science, excepting only quasi-religious doctrines such as Marxism (which despite its pretensions could not even predict the Russian Revolution). Nevertheless, considering the specific elements that went into the transformation of the Soviet/Russian realm between 1985 and 1991, it is remarkable how much broad awareness had been developed by Sovietological research regarding the changes, stresses, and weaknesses that already marked the Soviet Union.

Signs of an impending crisis were perhaps clearest to Western economists. It was obvious to them that the methods of the command economy, no doubt effective as one alternative approach to extensive development, had become counterproductive when resource limits and foreign technological advantages forced the Soviets to shift to intensive development. A steady decline in the rate of economic growth between the 1960s and the 1980s made it impossible to reconcile the demands of consumers, investment, and the military, while the requirements of the information society collided with Russian habits of official secrecy, and the gray economy corrupted the whole of society. These problems, of course, were equally obvious to Soviet reformers, the people who, under Gorbachev, initiated the disruptive efforts to decentralize and marketize the economy that in turn set the stage for real economic crisis under Yeltsin.

Sovietologists and social historians were long aware of the truly dialectical contradiction between the social modernization promoted by the Soviet regime and the rigid and dysfunctional behavior of the regime itself. This is the typical recipe for revolution. An urbanized and educated populace with rising expectations pressed for material improvements and personal freedom, while the frustrations imposed by party controls undermined national morale. Soviet critics, up to the very top, themselves highlighted weaknesses in incentives and income fairness.

Soviet studies have been frequently faulted for neglecting the non-Russian minorities, yet in this area too an impending crisis had long been evident to specialists. Soviet propaganda about the "rapprochement" if not "merger" of nationalities was singularly unconvincing. Despite considerable ethnic mixing through internal migration and intermarriage, it was clear that the façade of unity was maintained only by the secret police, and that any degree of democratization at the center would be a signal to the forces of national autonomy on the periphery.[9]

Historians and political scientists saw signs of inevitable change in the Soviet political system even if its eventual depth took them by surprise. For one thing, analyses of generational differences in the Soviet leadership pointed to a major break when the cadre of Stalinist conservatives, growing old in office from the time of the purges of the 1930s, finally fell by the wayside. Political scientists noted the erosion of totalitarian discipline and ideological authority and the formation of interest group politics and enclaves of professional autonomy beneath the skin of party conformity. For this insight, incidentally, Sovietology was roundly denounced by some of the same defenders of the totalitarian model who subsequently faulted the alleged failures of Sovietological prediction.

Taken as a whole, the work of Western Slavists and Sovietologists in their various disciplines was remarkably accurate and insightful in defining the elements of the crisis that overtook the Soviet Union. Their judgments went as far as any social science scholarship could responsibly go without resorting to wild guesswork. What could not be accurately foreseen, in the nature of the matter, was how these elements of crisis would play out at the political level where decisions by leading personalities and the effects of chance events could be decisive. On this plane, contingencies and indeterminacies among alternative lines of development can never be ruled out. Above all, the August Putsch of 1991, widely anticipated and hardly surprising in its conservative intent, had totally unexpected consequences, first in its ignominious failure, and second in the fatal destabilization of the government that it had unsuccessfully tried to take over.

As reforms unfolded and crises sharpened in the USSR between 1985 and 1991, Western scholarship was closely attuned to the new developments. Again, economics—the most concrete of the social sciences—was most accurate and perspicacious about Soviet needs and shortcomings, more so than the Soviet leadership itself. Studies of culture and the media tracked Gorbachev's introduction of glasnost and had little difficulty anticipating its impact. In politics, and particularly in foreign policy matters, Sovietology fell behind events, reluctant as it was to take Gorbachev's "New Thinking" seriously enough soon enough. If the profession had a general fault, it was not lack of insight but excessive caution, perhaps reflecting the continuing influence of prominent exponents of the totalitarian model who insisted that the Communist system could never seriously change from within. Notions that democratization and accommodation with the West could really be under way under perestroika were widely dismissed as "Gorbymania."

In nationality matters, events bore out the reality of change under perestroika, as local nationalists seized the opportunities offered by loosening at the center, and Russian conservatives reacted against threats to the integrity of the empire. As two authorities on the minorities pointed out, "There is a nationalities component to every facet of Soviet politics. . . . In an era of reform, the nationalities problem presents Soviet leaders with their most serious challenge."[10] Gorbachev was caught in the middle and responded erratically, while Yeltsin's decision to play the nationality card against him was highly predictable if one considered the personal animosity between the two. Truly surprising, on the other hand, was Soviet tolerance of the overthrow of Communist rule in Eastern Europe. Here was a series of events that in some cases, above all in East Germany and in Czechoslovakia, really did amount to a "collapse." No doubt it was impressions of 1989 in the former Soviet bloc that lent the sense of "collapse" to events in the Soviet Union itself in 1991.

Notwithstanding its impressive record of achievement, Sovietology went into a state of shock after the political earthquakes of 1989 and 1991. Numerous high-profile commentators—some within the profession, more outside it—seized on these events to denounce the entire practice of Sovietology as worthless because it had "failed to predict" the unpredictable demise of

Communist rule. Many practitioners in the field, swamped by media amplification of the anti-Sovietological view, succumbed to the mood of professional breast-beating.

The actual crises of 1989 and 1991, governed as they were by personalities and contingencies, could not have been closely predicted from any model or precedent. Historians should be able to understand this truth better than those social scientists who try too hard to make events appear to be law-governed. What happened was just as surprising to all the political actors in the Soviet Union and Eastern Europe as it was to observers in the outside world. Unfortunately, shamed by its alleged failure to predict the Communist collapse, Sovietology—by now post-Sovietology—has in the main allowed itself to be seduced by the democratic and nationalist claims of the successor regimes, while putting its critical predictive powers on ice.

Since 1992, American Sovietology, or rather the hastily renamed field of "Russian, East European, and Eurasian studies," has been caught in a mood of pessimistic soul-searching. It has lost confidence in the merit of its analyses. It has lost the sense of a unifying context that had been provided by the geographical compass of Communist regimes. It has seen financial support for training, research, and publications begin to dry up; presumably we no longer need to "know our enemy." Practitioners of Soviet studies in the social sciences, losing their sense of relevance, have rejoined the mainstreams of their respective disciplines (usually theoretical, statistical, and parochially American), and they may fail to replicate their expertise on the Russian and East European area. All this at a time when the actual needs, opportunities, and available academic talent for study of the former Communist realm were never more compelling. The Slavist profession in the United States has been running on the oil left in the pipeline.

Confronted by such professionally disconcerting conditions, American post-Sovietology is in danger of embracing new simplicities that may render its analytical and predictive powers less effective than they actually were before perestroika. Political science manifests deceptively universalistic tendencies. History of the area is being carried away by the mainstream fashions of social history and gender studies at the expense of the political history of the Communist regimes now so interestingly documented by newly accessible archives. Economics, once the star discipline in Sovietology, has dismissed the planned economy as a synonym for Stalinism and has lapsed into simplistic mainstream assumptions that the post-Communist economies are almost "normal," or if not should be made so by shock therapy.[11]

Under the circumstances, does post-Sovietology have any future? It needs first of all to recognize the path it took to post-Soviet error. It was too skeptical of Gorbachev and too trusting of Yeltsin, too reserved about the possibility and progress of reform under Communist aegis, too uncritical about reform in its radical, post-Communist version. Like much of Sovietology in the old days, it read the successor regimes too literally: Gorbachev was still a Communist and therefore he could not really change; Yeltsin was an anti-Communist (notwithstanding his identical background) and therefore his every action had to be legitimate.

Second, post-Sovietology must emphasize that the Communist background is still relevant. To be sure, Communism has passed from the purview of the present-minded disciplines to the historical. Nevertheless, it still gives a unity of experience and circumstance to all the countries of the former Soviet bloc, however diverse their post-Communist lines of development may be.

Third, post-Sovietology should be chary of simplistic or rigid paradigms. This was the most obvious drawback in precollapse Sovietology, with its partiality to glib formulas such as totalitarianism or pat explanations such as Marxist ideology. Now new catchphrases have taken over—transitions to democracy, market economy, national self-determination—without enough critical reflection about their meaning and their relationship to actual events. Though Sovietology's effort to be value-neutral in the spirit of modern social science has been denigrated by ex–Cold Warriors, post-Sovietology needs to hew again to this standard, at least to the extent that it distinguishes between wish and reality.

Finally, area specialists in the various disciplines need to preserve their common identity so that they can continue to learn from each other as they have in the past. Someone needs to understand the singularities of the region as a whole, not to mention individual countries, as against the global generalities propounded by the traditional academic fields. Otherwise, expertise on the region will sink out of sight into the different disciplinary mainstreams, leaving afloat only the earliest pieces of Russian and East European studies—namely, a little language work and antiquarian history. This would be a sad conclusion to one of the most exciting facets of scholarly accomplishment in the last hundred years.

Notes

Introduction

This introduction is based on a paper commissioned by the Institute of Russian History of the Russian Academy of Sciences that appeared in Russian translation as "Revoliutsiya, obnovlenie, i paradoksy Rossii v XX veke" in their collective work, *Rossiya na rubezhe XXI veka* [Russia at the Threshold of the Twenty-first Century] (Moscow: Nauka, 2000). The English original was subsequently published as "Revolution, Modernization, and the Paradox of Twentieth-Century Russia," *Canadian Slavonic Papers*, Sept. 2000.

1. One of the earliest comparisons of the French and Russian revolutions was by Albert Mathiez, *Le bolchevisme et le jacobinisme* (Paris: Librarie du Parti Socialiste et de l'Humanité, 1920), 3–4.

2. V. I. Lenin, "Report on the Revolution of 1905" [9 [22] Jan. 1917; in Russian], in *Sochineniya* [Works], 2nd ed. (Moscow: State Press, 1929), 29:357.

3. See Nicholas S. Timasheff, *The Great Retreat: The Growth and Decline of Communism in Russia* (New York: Dutton, 1946); ch. 24 below.

4. See chs. 30 and 33 below.

5. Georgi Plekhanov, *On the Role of the Individual in History* [1898] (New York: International Publishers, 1929).

6. See Robert V. Daniels, *Red October: The Bolshevik Revolution of 1917* (New York: Scribners, 1967); ch. 8 below.

7. I originally developed this point in an unpublished paper, "Left and Right in the Extremist Phase of Revolution" (presented at the American Historical Association, Dec. 1969).

8. Cyril E. Black, *The Dynamics of Modernization: A Study in Comparative History* (New York: Harper & Row, 1966), 1, 7.

9. Nikolai Bukharin, "The Theory of The Imperialist State" [1916; in Russian], in *Revoliutsiya prava*, collection 1 (Moscow: Communist Academy, 1925), 30. See ch. 5 below.

10. See Max Weber, *Wirtschaft und Gesellschaft* (Tübingen: Mohr, 1922), pt. 3, ch. 6.

11. See ch. 12 below.

12. V. I. Lenin, "The Next Tasks of Soviet Power" [*Izvestiya,* 28 Apr. 1918; in Russian], in *Sochineniya,* 22:446.

13. See ch. 12 below.

14. Karl A. Wittfogel, *Oriental Despotism: A Comparative Study of Total Power* (New Haven: Yale University Press, 1957), 375–76.

15. See Abbott Gleason, *Totalitarianism: The Inner History of the Cold War* (New York: Oxford University Press, 1995).

16. Svetozar Stojanović, "Marxism and Democracy: The Ruling Class or the Dominant Class?" *Praxis International,* July 1981.

17. Vilfredo Pareto, *The Mind and Society,* vol. 3, *Theory of Derivations* (New York: Harcourt, Brace, 1935).

18. Karl Mannheim, *Ideology and Utopia: An Introduction to the Sociology of Knowledge* (1929; New York: International Library of Psychology, Philosophy, and Scientific Method, 1936).

19. Alfred G. Meyer, *Leninism* (Cambridge: Harvard University Press, 1957), 165.

20. V. I. Lenin, "Letters on Tactics" [Apr. 1917; in Russian], in *Sochineniya,* 20:102.

21. Joseph Stalin, "The October Revolution and the Tactics of the Russian Communists" [Oct. 1924], in *Problems of Leninism* (Moscow: Foreign Languages Publishing House, 1953), 121–30. See Robert V. Daniels, *The Conscience of the Revolution: Communist Opposition in Soviet Russia* (Cambridge: Harvard University Press, 1960), 250–52, 295–300.

22. Daniels, *The Conscience of the Revolution,* chs. 3–5. See ch. 34 below.

Chapter 1. Marx and the Movement of History

This chapter is based on my essay "Marxian Theories of Historical Dynamics," in Werner J. Cahnman and Alvin Boskoff, eds., *Sociology and History: Theory and Research* (Glencoe, Ill.: Free Press, 1964).

1. Karl Marx, *The Poverty of Philosophy* (New York: International Publishers, 1963).

2. George Lichtheim, *Marxism: An Historical and Critical Study* (New York: Frederick A. Praeger, 1961), 234–58; Maximilien Rubel, "The Present State of Marxological Studies" (seminar paper, Harvard University Russian Research Center, 24 Mar. 1961).

3. Karl Marx and Friedrich Engels, "The German Ideology," in Lewis S. Feuer, ed., *Marx and Engels: Basic Writings on Politics and Philosophy* (New York: Doubleday Anchor, 1959), 245–47.

4. Karl Marx, *A Contribution to the Critique of Political Economy* (New York: International Library, 1904), 11.

5. Karl Marx and Friedrich Engels, *Manifesto of the Communist Party* (New York: International Publishers, 1948), 9.

6. Friedrich Engels, *The Origin of the Family, Private Property, and the State* (Moscow: Foreign Languages Publishing House, 1954), 280.

7. Marx and Engels, "The German Ideology," 280.

8. Marx, *A Contribution to the Critique of Political Economy,* 13.

9. Ibid., 12.

10. Ibid.

11. Karl Marx, preface to first edition of vol. 1 [1867], *Capital: A Critique of Political Economy* (Chicago: Kerr, 1906; New York: Modern Library, n.d.), 13, 15.

12. Cf. ibid., 1:836.

13. Karl Marx, "Wage Labor and Capital" [1847], in Marx and Friedrich Engels, *Selected Works* (Moscow: Foreign Languages Publishing House, 1936), 1:96–98.

14. Marx, *Poverty of Philosophy*, 145.

15. Marx and Engels, *Manifesto*, 21.

16. Marx, *Capital*, 1:847.

17. Lichtheim, *Marxism*, 58.

18. Karl Marx to the editorial board of *Otechestvennye zapiski* [Nov. 1877], in *The Selected Correspondence of Marx and Engels, 1846–1895* (New York: International Publishers, 1942), 354.

19. Ibid., 353.

20. See Karl A. Wittfogel, *Oriental Despotism* (New Haven: Yale University Press, 1957) and "The Marxist View of Russian Society and Revolution," *World Politics*, July 1960, 487–508.

21. Marx and Engels, "The German Ideology," 247.

22. See particularly Marx, *Poverty of Philosophy*, 86–89, 100–102, 159 and *Capital*, 1:837.

23. See Alfred G. Meyer, *Marxism: The Unity of Theory and Practice* (Cambridge: Harvard University Press, 1953), 31–39.

24. Gustaf A. Wetter, *Dialectical Materialism: A Historical and Systematic Survey of Philosophy in the Soviet Union* (New York: Frederick A. Praeger, 1958), 130–36; Robert V. Daniels, *The Conscience of the Revolution: Communist Opposition in Soviet Russia* (Cambridge: Harvard University Press, 1960), 360–62.

25. Karl Marx, "Toward the Critique of Hegel's Philosophy of Right," in Feuer, *Marx and Engels*, 263.

26. Ibid., 265–66.

27. Karl Marx, *Economic and Philosophical Manuscripts of 1844* (Moscow: Foreign Languages Publishing House, 1944). See also Erich Fromm, *Marx's Concept of Man* (New York: Unger, 1961).

28. Marx, *Capital*, 1:291.

29. Marx and Engels, *Manifesto*, 30–31.

30. Quoted in Carl Landauer, *European Socialism: A History of Ideas and Movements from the Industrial Revolution to Hitler's Seizure of Power* (Berkeley: University of California Press, 1959), 1:133.

31. Karl Marx, *The Civil War in France* (1871; New York: International Publishers, 1940), 57.

32. Friedrich Engels, introduction to the 1894 edition of Marx's "Class Struggles in France, 1848 to 1850," in Marx and Engels, *Selected Works*, 1:123, 136.

33. Karl Marx, "Economic and Philosophical Manuscripts," in Fromm, *Marx's Concept of Man*, 125–27.

34. Karl Marx, "Critique of the Gotha Program," in *Selected Works* (Moscow: Marx-Engels-Lenin Institute, 1933), 2:566.

35. See V. I. Lenin, *The State and Revolution*, in *Selected Works* (Moscow: Foreign Languages Publishing House, 1952), vol. 1, bk. 2, pp. 294–300.

36. See ch. 12 below.

37. Karl Marx, "Theses on Feuerbach" (1845), in Feuer, *Marx and Engels,* 244.

38. Marx, *Poverty of Philosophy,* 94.

39. Friedrich Engels, *Herr Eugen Dühring's Revolution in Science (Anti-Dühring)* (Moscow: Foreign Languages Publishing House, 1954), 371.

40. Marx, *Capital,* 1:824.

41. Karl Marx, "The Eighteenth Brumaire of Louis Bonaparte," in *Selected Works,* 1:333–34. Cf. Marx's contemporary and co-Hegelian Lorenz von Stein and his three-volume *Geschichte der Sozialen Bewegung in Frankreich von 1789 bis auf unsere Tage* (Leipzig, 1850; new ed. with introduction by Gottfried Salomon, Munich: Drei Masken Verlag, 1921).

42. Friedrich Engels, 1891 introduction to Marx, *Civil War in France,* 20–21.

43. Nikolai Bukharin, "On the Theory of the Imperialist State," excerpts in Robert V. Daniels, *A Documentary History of Communisim* (New York: Random House, 1960), 1:85–86.

44. Sidney Hook, introduction to *From Hegel to Marx* (Ann Arbor: University of Michigan Press, 1962), 8–9.

45. Friedrich Engels to Joseph Bloch, 21–22 Sept. 1890, in *Correspondence,* 475–76; see ch. 2 below.

46. See, e.g., Karl Kautsky, *The Class Struggle* (1891; Chicago: Kerr, 1910).

47. See Eduard Bernstein, *Evolutionary Socialism: A Criticism and an Affirmation* (New York: Huebsch, 1909).

48. See, e.g., Rosa Luxemburg, *Reform or Revolution* (1899; New York: Three Arrows, 1937).

49. See George Plekhanov, *The Development of the Monist View of History* (1895; Moscow: Foreign Languages Publishing House, 1956) and *On the Role of the Individual in History* (1898; New York: International Publishers, 1940).

50. See ch. 3 below.

51. V. I. Lenin, "What Is to Be Done? [1902], in *Selected Works,* vol. 1, pt. 1, p. 287.

52. See V. I. Lenin, "Marxism and Insurrection" [26–27 Sept. (Old Style), 1917], in *Selected Works,* vol. 2, pt. 1, pp. 167, 173.

53. Herbert Butterfield, *History and Human Relations* (London: Collins, 1951), 79.

54. See Karl Mannheim, *Ideology and Utopia* (1929; New York: Harcourt, Brace & World, 1936).

Chapter 2. Fate and Will in the Marxian Vision

This chapter is based on my article "Fate and Will in the Marxian Philosophy of History," *Journal of the History of Ideas* 21:4 (1960).

1. Friedrich Engels to J. Bloch, 21 Sept. 1890, in *The Selected Correspondence of Karl Marx and Friedrich Engels* (New York: International Publishers, 1942), 475, 477.

2. See ibid.; Friedrich Engels to Conrad Schmidt, 27 Oct. 1890, in *Correspondence,* 475, 480–81.

3. V. I. Lenin, "What Is to Be Done?" [1902], in *Selected Works* (Moscow: Foreign Languages Publishing House, 1950), vol. 1, bk. 1, pp. 287, 339. See ch. 1 above.

4. Georgi Plekhanov, "The Working Class and the Social Democratic Intelligentsia" [*Iskra*, Aug. 1904; in Russian], quoted in Max Eastman, *Marxism: Is It Science?* (New York: Norton, 1940), 223.

5. Engels to Bloch, 21 Sept. 1890, 476.

6. Friedrich Engels, *Ludwig Feuerbach and the End of Classical German Philosophy* (Moscow: Foreign Languages Publishing House, 1950), 74.

7. George Plekhanov, *The Role of the Individual in History* (1898; New York: International Publishers, 1940), 41.

8. Friedrich Engels, *Anti-Dühring: Herr Eugen Dühring's Revolution in Science* (Moscow: Foreign Languages Publishing House, 1954), 392–93.

9. Ibid., 387.

Chapter 3. Lenin as a Russian Revolutionary

This chapter is based on my essay "Lenin and the Russian Revolutionary Tradition," in George Fischer, Martin Malia, and Hugh McLean, eds., *Russian Thought and Politics*, Harvard Slavic Studies, vol. 4 (The Hague: Mouton, 1957).

1. V. I. Lenin, "What Is to Be Done?" [1902], in *Selected Works* (Moscow: Foreign Languages Publishing House, 1950–51), vol. 1, pt. 1, pp. 243–44.

2. Joseph Stalin, "The October Revolution and the Tactics of the Russian Communists," in *Problems of Leninism* (Moscow: Foreign Languages Publishing House, 1940), 100.

3. V. I. Lenin, *Materialism and Empirio-Criticism* (New York: International Publishers, 1927), 338.

4. Karl Marx to Kugelman, 1 Oct. 1868, in *Letters to Dr. Kugelman* (New York: International Publishers, 1934), 77–78.

5. Cited in *Delo Petrashevtsev* (Moscow and Leningrad: Academy of Sciences, 1937–51), 1: 522. The reference is to Charles Fourier, the French utopian socialist.

6. Alexandre Herzen, *De l'autre rive* (Geneva, 1870), 72.

7. Lenin, "What Is To Be Done?" 233–34.

8. Pyotr Tkachev, "The Tasks of Revolutionary Propaganda in Russia" [in Russian] and Program of *Nabat* (the tocsin). See Michael Karpovich, "P. N. Tkachev: A Forerunner of Lenin," *Review of Politics* 6 (July 1944): 335–49.

9. V. I. Lenin to the Central Committee, Moscow Committee, Petrograd Committee, and the Bolshevik Members of the Petrograd and Moscow Soviets, in *Collected Works* (New York: International Publishers, 1927–30), vol. 21, pt. 2, p. 69; V. I. Lenin, "The Crisis Has Matured," in *Collected Works*, vol. 21, pt. 2, p. 278.

10. Vissarion Belinsky to V. P. Botkin, 8 Sept. 1841, in *Selected Philosophical Works* (Moscow: Foreign Languages Publishing House, 1948), 164.

11. V. I. Lenin, "One Step Forward, Two Steps Back" [May 1904], in *Selected Works*, vol. 1, pt. 1, pp. 644–45.

12. Pyotr Chaadaev, "Letters on the Philosophy of History" [in French], in *Sochineniya i pis'ma* (Moscow, 1913–14), 1:83.

13. Pyotr Chaadaev, "Apology of a Madman" [in French], in *Sochineniya i pis'ma*, 1:223–24.

14. Alexandre Herzen, *Lettres de France et d'Italie* (Geneva, 1871), 285.

15. Quoted in Thomas G. Masaryk, *The Spirit of Russia: Studies in History, Literature, and Philosophy* (London: G. Allen & Unwin/New York: Macmillan, 1919), 2:28.

16. Chaadaev, "Apology of a Madman," 231.

17. Herzen, *De l'autre rive*, 186.

18. Pyotr Lavrov, *Istoricheskie pis'ma*, 2nd ed. (St. Petersburg: Russkoe Bogatstvo, 1905), 139–42, 149–50, 152. *Rabotnik,* here rendered as "practitioner," connotes an active participant in the movement, or a full-time party functionary.

19. Nikolai Chernyshevsky, *Polnoe sobranie sochinenii* (St. Petersburg, 1905–6), 3:644–45. Italics supplied.

20. George Plekhanov, *The Role of the Individual in History* (New York: International Publishers, 1940).

21. Arthur Mendel, "N. K. Mikhailovsky and His Criticism of Russian Marxism," *American Slavic and East European Review* 14 (Oct. 1955): 339.

22. Joseph Stalin, "The Tasks of Business Executives" [1931], in *Problems of Leninism,* 359.

23. Rules drawn up by the Executive Committee of the Narodnaya Volya, quoted in Vera Figner, "Remembered Labor" [in Russian], in *Polnoe sobranie sochineni* (Moscow, 1928–29), 1:181–82, translated in Leopold Haimson, *The Russian Marxists and the Origins of Bolshevism* (Cambridge: Harvard University Press, 1955), 18.

24. Haimson, *Russian Marxists,* 102–3.

25. Herzen, *Lettres,* 285–88.

26. Mikhail Bakunin, "Letters on Patriotism" [in Russian], in *Izbrannye sochineniya* (Petrograd: Golos truda, 1919–22), 4:82.

27. P. F. Yudin, *The Prime Source of the Development of Soviet Society* (Moscow: Foreign Languages Publishing House, 1950), 21. For a discussion of the process of reinterpretation with respect to the role of the state, see ch. 5 below.

Chapter 4. The Bolsheviks and the Intelligentsia

This chapter is based on my article "Intellectuals and the Russian Revolution," *American Slavic and East European Review* 20 (Apr. 1961).

1. See David Footman, *Red Prelude: The Life of the Russian Terrorist Zhelyabov* (New Haven: Yale University Press, 1945), 244–57.

2. V. I. Lenin, "One Step Forward, Two Steps Back" [May 1904], in *Selected Works* (Moscow: Foreign Languages Publishing House, 1950–51), vol. 1, pt. 1, pp. 456, 481, 545, 609, 618–19.

3. V. I. Lenin, "Disruption of Unity under Cover of Outcries for Unity" [May 1914], in *Selected Works,* vol. 1, bk. 2, p. 256.

4. V. I. Lenin to the Central Committee [19 Oct. 1917], in *Collected Works* (New York: International Publishers, 1927), vol. 21, pt. 2, p. 136.

5. Stalin at the Fifteenth Party Congress, Dec. 1927, *Stenographic Report* (Moscow: Party Press, 1928), 74.

6. Robert A. Feldmesser, "The Persistence of Status Advantages in Soviet Russia," *American Journal of Sociology* 59 (July 1953): 19–27.

Chapter 5. Lenin's Vision

This chapter is based on my article "The State and Revolution: A Case Study in the Genesis and Transformation of Communist Ideology," *American Slavic and East European Review* 12 (Feb. 1953).

1. V. I. Lenin, *State and Revolution* (New York: International Publishers, 1932), 91–92.

2. Ibid., 28–29. Lenin is arguing for leadership by Marxists as against "opportunists" and asserts, "By educating a workers' party, Marxism educated the vanguard of the proletariat." The term *vanguard,* as well, though familiar in Communist jargon, rarely appears in *State and Revolution;* Lenin speaks simply of "the proletariat."

3. V. I. Lenin, "What Is to Be Done?" [1902], in *Collected Works* (New York: International Publishers, 1929), vol. 2, pt. 2, p. 208.

4. V. I. Lenin, "Letter to a Comrade on Our Organizational Tasks" [in Russian], in *Sochineniya,* 4th ed. (Moscow: State Press for Political Literature, 1946–50), 6:221.

5. *Ninth Congress of the Russian Communist Party (Bolsheviks): Minutes* [in Russian] (Moscow: Marx-Engels-Lenin Institute, 1934), 532.

6. *Tenth Congress of the RCP (B): Minutes* [in Russian] (Moscow: Marx-Engels-Lenin Institute, 1933), 128.

7. See Robert V. Daniels, *The Conscience of the Revolution: Communist Opposition in Soviet Russia* (Cambridge: Harvard University Press, 1960).

8. *Leninskii Sbornik* (Moscow: Lenin Institute, 1924), 2:284n7.

9. Ibid., 2:282–83.

10. Bukharin originally wrote this article in the middle of 1916 with the intention of publishing it in the semiperiodical *Sbornik Sotsial-Demokrata* edited by Lenin, but the article was rejected. It ultimately appeared in 1925 in *Revoliutsiya prava* (Moscow: Communist Academy), collection 1. In a note attached to the article at the time of publication (5n1), Bukharin advanced as the explanation for the original rejection the surmise that the editorial board "did not consider it possible to publish the article because it felt that there were developed here incorrect views about the state." In contrast to this, Lenin said in his letter to Kollontai of 17 Feb. 1917 (*Leninskii Sbornik,* 2:283) that it was simply the lack of funds that prevented the publication of the next number of the *Sbornik,* in which Bukharin's article was already scheduled to be included. This may indicate that Lenin was moving toward Bukharin's left-wing position faster than the latter thought.

11. *Revoliutsiya prava,* 1:21.

12. Ibid., 1:30.

13. Ibid., 1:26.

14. Ibid., 1:30.

15. Ibid., 1:31–32.

16. Lenin, *State and Revolution,* 96.

17. Anton Pannekoek, "Imperialism and the Tasks of the Proletariat," published in Russian translation in Lenin's journal *Kommunist,* no. 1–2 (Geneva, 1915): 75. Strangely enough, Pannekoek's ideas seem not to have come to Lenin's own attention until Bukharin took them up.

18. Anton Pannekoek, "Mass Action and Revolution" [in German], *Die Neue Zeit,* 12, 19, and 16 July 1912. This article directly influenced Lenin at the end of 1916, as the materials in *Leninskii Sbornik,* vol. 14, indicate.

19. See, e.g., R. N. Carew-Hunt, *The Theory and Practice of Communism: An Introduction* (New York: Macmillan, 1951), 64–65.

20. Bukharin, *Revoliutsiya prava,* 1:7.

21. Lenin, *State and Revolution,* 10–11.

22. Friedrich Engels, *The Origin of the Family, Private Property, and the State* (Chicago: Kerr, 1902), 206.

23. Ibid., 207.

24. Karl Marx, *The Eighteenth Brumaire of Louis Bonaparte* (New York: International Publishers, 1926), 130–31.

25. Karl Marx, *The Civil War in France* (Chicago: Kerr, n.d.), 42.

26. Ibid., 47.

27. Ibid., 42.

28. Ibid., 48.

29. Marx, *The Civil War in France* (New York: International Publishers, 1940), 20.

30. Ibid., 21.

31. Lenin, *State and Revolution,* 37.

32. Ibid., 52.

33. V. I. Lenin, "Will the Bolsheviks Retain State Power?" in *Collected Works* (New York: International Publishers, 1932), vol. 21, bk. 2, p. 33.

34. Lenin, *Sochineniya,* 3rd ed. (Moscow and Leningrad: State Press, 1935), 23:36.

Chapter 6. Russia and Revolution

This chapter is based on my article "Whatever Happened to the Russian Revolution?" *Commentary,* Nov. 1978.

1. J. Christopher Herold, ed., *The Mind of Napoleon: A Selection from His Written and Spoken Words* (New York: Columbia University Press, 1956), 64.

2. Friedrich Engels to Vera Zasulich, 23 Apr. 1885, in Karl Marx and Friedrich Engels, *Selected Correspondence, 1846–1895* (New York: International Publishers, 1942), 437–38.

3. Crane Brinton, *The Anatomy of Revolution* (1938; New York: Prentice-Hall, 1952); Lyford P. Edwards, *The Natural History of Revolution* (Chicago: University of Chicago Press, 1927).

4. See, e.g., Denis Brogan, *The Price of Revolution* (New York: Harper, 1951).

5. Joseph Stalin, Report on the Work of the Central Committee, to the Seventeenth Congress of the CPSU(B) [Jan. 1934], in *Problems of Leninism* (Moscow: Foreign Languages Publishing House, 1940), 634–35. See ch. 27 below.

6. Karl Marx, *A Contribution to the Critique of Political Economy* (New York: International Library, 1904), 13.

7. F. Engels, *The Peasant War in Germany* (New York: International Publishers, 1926), 135–36.

8. See chs. 1 above and 12 below.

9. See Sheila Fitzpatrick, *Education and Social Mobility in the Soviet Union, 1921–1934* (New York: Cambridge University Press, 1979).

10. Michal Reiman, "Spontaneity and Planning in the Plebeian Revolution," in Ralph Carter Elwood, ed., *Reconsiderations on the Russian Revolution* (Cambridge, Mass.: Slavica,

1976); "The October Revolution in the Context of Russian and Soviet History" [in Czech], in Michal Reiman, *Ruská revoluce* (Prague: Naše Vojsko, 1991), 276–81.

Chapter 7. Revolution from the Inside

This chapter is based on a paper presented at the international conference "Trotsky after Fifty Years," University of Aberdeen (Scotland), Aug. 1990, and published in Terry Brotherstone and Paul Dukes, eds., *The Trotsky Reappraisal* (Edinburgh: Edinburgh University Press, 1992).

1. Robert F. Lansing, *War Memoirs* (Indianapolis: Bobbs-Merrill, 1935), 337–38.

2. Crane Brinton, *The Anatomy of Revolution* (1938; New York: Prentice-Hall, 1952), 16–17.

3. A good example of this neglect is Karl Kautsky, *The Materialist Conception of History*, abr. ed. (New Haven: Yale University Press, 1988), where revolution is mentioned often but only in passing.

4. Karl Marx, *A Contribution to the Critique of Political Economy* (New York: International Library, 1904), 13.

5. V. I. Lenin, "Two Tactics of Social Democracy in the Democratic Revolution" [July 1905], in *Selected Works* (Moscow: Foreign Languages Publishing House, 1950–52), vol. 1, bk. 2, pp. 87, 107.

6. Published as "Results and Prospects" [in Russian], in Leon Trotsky, *Nasha revoliutsiya* (St. Petersburg, 1906); English translation in Trotsky, *Our Revolution* (New York: Holt, 1918). The more confusing term *permanent* was applied to the theory by later commentators, but it stuck, and Trotsky accepted it. See Baruch Knei-Paz, *The Social and Political Thought of Leon Trotsky* (Oxford: Oxford University Press, 1978), 152–53. On Trotsky's earlier steps in formulating the theory, see Michael Lowy, "The Theory of Permanent Revolution," in Francesca Gori, ed., *Pensiero e azione di Lev Trockij* (Florence: Olschki, 1982), 149–54.

7. See Z. A. B. Zeman and W. B. Scharlau, *The Merchant of Revolution: The Life of Alexander Helphand (Parvus), 1867–1924* (London: Oxford University Press, 1965), 66–68, 110–11.

8. Trotsky, *Our Revolution*, 92.

9. John Molyneux, *Leon Trotsky's Theory of Revolution* (New York: St. Martin's, 1981), 59.

10. Leon Trotsky, foreword to Ferdinand Lassalle's *Address to the Jury* [June 1905], quoted in "Results and Prospects," in Trotsky, *The Permanent Revolution and Results and Prospects* (London: New Park, 1962), 240. Cf. Lowy, "The Theory of Permanent Revolution," 1:154.

11. Leon Trotsky, "Two Faces: The Inner Forces of the Russian Revolution" [in Russian], *Novyi mir* (New York), 17 Mar. 1917, quoted in Knei-Paz, *Social and Political Thought*, 249. See also Leon Trotsky, *The History of the Russian Revolution* (Ann Arbor: University of Michigan Press, 1932, 1957), vol. 1, app. 2.

12. V. I. Lenin, "On the Tasks of the Proletariat in the Present Revolution" (the "April Theses") [7 [20] Apr. 1917], in *Selected Works*, vol. 2, bk. 1, p. 14. According to Heinz Schurer, "After February 1917 Lenin accepted the bold perspectives of the permanent revolution for Russia which would throw the lighted torch into the powder barrel of Western Europe" ("The Permanent Revolution: Leon Trotsky," in Leopold Labedz, ed., *Revisionism: Essays on the History of Marxist Ideas* [New York: Praeger, 1962], 75). Cf. Robert Wistrich, *Trotsky: Fate of a Revolutionary* (London: Robson, 1979), 79–80.

13. *Sixth Congress of the Russian Social-Democratic Party (Bolsheviks): Minutes* [Aug. 1917; in Russian] (Moscow: Marx-Engels-Lenin Institute, 1934), 101.

14. See Grigori Zinoviev and Lev Kamenev, Statement to the Principal Bolshevik Party Organizations [11 [24] Oct. 1917], in V. I. Lenin, *Collected Works* (New York: International Publishers, 1929), vol. 21, bk. 2, app., pp. 328–31.

15. Leon Trotsky, 1919 introduction to "Results and Prospects," in *The Permanent Revolution* (New York: Pioneer, 1931), 162–63.

16. Leon Trotsky, *From October to Brest-Litovsk* (New York: Socialist Publishing Society, 1919), 28.

17. Trotsky, 1919 introduction to "Results and Prospects," 185–87.

18. Leon Trotsky, *Uroki oktiabria* [1924], translated as *Lessons of October* (New York: Pioneer, 1937), 70–71.

19. Trotsky, 1919 introduction to "Results and Prospects," 163–64.

20. Leon Trotsky, *Terrorizm i kommunizm* [1920], translated as *Dictatorship vs. Democracy: A Reply to Karl Kautsky* (New York: Workers' Party of America, 1922), 54.

21. Leon Trotsky, Letter to the Bureau of Party History concerning the Falsification of the History of the October Revolution, the History of the Revolution, and the History of the Party [21 Oct. 1927], in *The Stalin School of Falsification* (New York: Pioneer, 1937), 29.

22. Brinton, *Anatomy of Revolution*, 228.

23. See Simon Wolin, "The Mensheviks under the NEP and in Emigration," in Leopold Haimson, ed., *The Mensheviks: From the Revolution of 1917 to the Second World War* (Chicago: University of Chicago Press, 1974), 248; Jay Bergman, "The Perils of Historical Analogy: Leon Trotsky on the French Revolution," *Journal of the History of Ideas*, Jan.–Apr. 1987, 82 and n40.

24. Karl Kautsky, *Terrorism and Communism: A Contribution to the Natural History of Revolution* (London: G. Allen & Unwin, 1920), 214–15.

25. Leon Trotsky, *Mezhdu imperializmom i revoliutsiei* [1922], translated as *Social Democracy and the Wars of Intervention in Russia, 1918–1921 (between Red and White)* (London: New Park, 1975), 83. See David S. Law, "Trockij and Thermidor," in Gori, *Lev Trockij*, 437.

26. Leon Trotsky, *The New Course* (New York: New International Publishers, 1943), 40.

27. First expressed by Trotsky, as far as can be determined, in a pamphlet of early 1923, "Mysli o partii" (Thoughts on the Party), in Leon Trotsky, *Zadachi XII s'ezda RKP* (Moscow: Ninth of January Press, 1923), app., pp. 54–55.

28. Trotsky, *The New Course*, 39–41.

29. See Robert V. Daniels, *The Conscience of the Revolution: Communist Opposition in Soviet Russia* (Cambridge: Harvard University Press, 1960), 248–52.

30. Leon Trotsky, "Theses on Revolution and Counterrevolution" [Nov. 1926; first published in English translation in *Fourth International*, Oct. 1941], in Isaac Deutscher, *The Age of Permanent Revolution: A Trotsky Anthology* (New York: Dell, 1964), 142.

31. The reference is to N. V. Ustrialov, an emigré Russian economist who had hailed the NEP as a return to capitalism.

32. Leon Trotsky, Speech to the Central Committee and Central Control Commission [June 1927], in *Stalin School of Falsification*, 143.

33. "The Real Situation in Russia and the Tasks of the Communist Party" [Opposition Platform of Sept. 1927], in Leon Trotsky, *The Real Situation in Russia* (New York: Harcourt, Brace, 1928), 187.

34. Leon Trotsky, "Class Relations in the Chinese Revolution" [3 Apr. 1927], *New International*, Mar. 1938, 89.

35. See Curtis Stokes, *The Evolution of Trotsky's Theory of Permanent Revolution* (Washington: University Press of America, 1982).

36. Pier Paolo Poggio, "The Historical Peculiarities of Russia in Trotsky's Analysis and Perspective" [in Italian], in Gori, *Lev Trockij*, 108.

37. Trotsky, *Permanent Revolution*; Les Evans and Russell Block, eds., *Leon Trotsky on China* (New York: Monad, 1976), 19.

38. Leon Trotsky, "The Defense of the Soviet Republic and the Opposition" [7 Sept. 1929; published in the *Militant*, 21 Dec. 1929 and 25 Jan. 1930], in *Writings of Leon Trotsky* (New York: Pathfinder, 1978), 1:280–84.

39. Ibid.,1:287.

40. Leon Trotsky, *Chto i kak proizoshlo* (Paris: De Nevarre, 1929) [What Happened and How, translated in *New York Times*, 1 Mar. 1929], in *Writings of Leon Trotsky*, 1:26.

41. Leon Trotsky, Letter to the Italian Left Communists [25 Sept. 1929], in *Writings of Leon Trotsky*, 1:323.

42. Leon Trotsky, "The Terror of Bureaucratic Self-Preservation" [2 Nov. 1935], in *Writings of Leon Trotsky*, 8:119.

43. Leon Trotsky, "The Workers' State and the Question of Thermidor and Bonapartism" [*New International*, July 1935], in *The Class Nature of the Soviet State* (London: New Park, 1968), 49.

44. Leon Trotsky, "On the Question of Thermidor and Bonapartism" [Nov. 1930], in *Writings of Leon Trotsky*, 2:71.

45. Leon Trotsky, *The Revolution Betrayed: What Is the Soviet Union and Where Is It Going?* (New York: Doubleday, Doran, 1937), 87–88.

46. Trotsky, "What Happened and How," *Writings of Leon Trotsky*, 1:51.

47. Trotsky, *The Revolution Betrayed*, 87.

48. Leon Trotsky, foreword to *Stalinskaya shkola fal'sifikatsii* [1932], in *Stalin School of Falsification*, xxxviii.

Chapter 8. The Bolshevik Gamble

This chapter is based in part on my paper "Communist Seizures of Power: Russia, 1917," presented at the American Historical Association, Dec. 1961; in part on my article "The Bolshevik Gamble," *Russian Review* 26:4 (1967); and in part on my essay "The Party History on the October Revolution," *Kritika*, Spr. 1968. The latter two items draw on my book *Red October: The Bolshevik Revolution of 1917* (New York: Scribner's, 1967).

1. C. W. Cassinelli, "Political Authority: Its Exercise and Possession," *Western Political Quarterly* 14:645 (1961).

2. Wladimir Woytinsky, *Stormy Passage* (New York: Vanguard, 1961), 358, 377.

3. Michael Florinsky, *Russia: A History and an Interpretation* (New York: Macmillan, 1953), 1475–76.

4. E.g., Alexander Kerensky, *Russia and History's Turning Point* (New York: Duell, Sloan & Pearce, 1965), esp. 432–33.

5. Alfred G. Meyer, *Leninism* (Cambridge: Harvard University Press, 1957), 180.

6. Z. A. B. Zeman, *Germany and the Revolution in Russia* (London: Oxford University Press, 1958).

7. N. N. Sukhanov, *The Russian Revolution, 1917* (London: Oxford University Press, 1955), 587.

8. John Reed, *Ten Days That Shook the World* (New York: Boni & Liveright, 1919), 56.

9. *Minutes of the Central Committee of the RSDWP (b), Aug. 1917–Feb. 1918* [in Russian] (Moscow: State Press for Political Literature, 1958), 118.

10. Leon Trotsky, *The History of the Russian Revolution* (New York: Simon & Schuster, 1932), 3:218.

11. In conferences of 1962 and 1963 on the history of the revolution, published as I. I. Mints et al., eds., *Lenin i oktiabr'skoe vooruzhennoe vosstanie v Petrograde* (Moscow: Nauka, 1964).

12. Sukhanov, *Russian Revolution,* 614, 620–21; Trotsky, *History,* 3:209.

13. G. N. Golikov, *Ocherki istorii Velikoi Oktiabr'skoi sotsialiticheskoi revoliutsii* (Moscow: State Press for Political Literature, 1959), 282–83.

14. Quoted in Trotsky, *History,* 3:212.

15. Cyril E. Black, *The Dynamics of Modernization: A Study in Comparative History* (New York: Harper & Row, 1966).

16. V. I. Lenin, "Advice of a Bystander" [in Russian], in *Sochineniya,* 3rd ed. (Moscow: Marx-Engels-Lenin Institute, 1928–37), 21:320.

Chapter 9. Left Communism in the Revolutionary Era

This chapter is based in part on my article "The Left Communists," *Problems of Communism* 16:6 (1967); and in part on my essay "The Communist Opposition: From Brest-Litovsk to the Tenth Party Congress," in Edward O. Acton, Vladimir Cherniaev, and William G. Rosenberg, eds., *Critical Companion to the Russian Revolution, 1914–1921* (London: Arnold, 1997). Both works drew on my book *The Conscience of the Revolution: Communist Opposition in Soviet Russia* (Cambridge: Harvard University Press, 1960).

1. Nikolai Bukharin, in *Seventh Congress of the Russian Communist Party (Bolsheviks): Stenographic Report* [in Russian] (Moscow: State Press, 1923), 33.

2. Karl Radek, "After Five Months" [in Russian], *Kommunist,* no. 1 (Apr. 1918): 3–4.

3. "Theses on the Current Situation" [in Russian], *Kommunist,* no. 1:9.

4. *The Program of the Russian Communist Party (of Bolsheviks)* [1919] (Moscow: Communist Library, 1920), in James H. Meisel and Edward S. Kozera, eds., *Materials for the Study of the Soviet System* (Ann Arbor: Wahr, 1920), 107–8.

5. See ch. 13 below.

6. Alexandra Kollontai, *The Workers' Opposition* (Chicago: IWW, 1921), 7.

7. See ch. 20 below.

Chapter 10. Russian Revolutionary Extremism

This chapter is based in part on the English original of my essay "The Civil War in Russia in the Light of the Comparative History of Revolution," published in Russian translation as "Grazhdanskaya voina v Rossii v svete sravnitel'noi istorii revoliutsii," in Ya. A. Poliakov and

Yu. I. Igritsky, eds., *Grazhdanskaya voina v Rossii: Perekrestok mnenii* [The Civil War in Russia: Intersection of Opinions] (Moscow: Nauka, 1994); and in part on an unpublished paper, "The Revolutionary Process, Russian Extremism, and the Postrevolutionary Dictatorship," prepared for the international conference "The Russian Revolutions of 1917," Elgersburg, Germany, Mar. 1997.

1. See ch. 3 above.

2. For data demonstrating this alignment, see Robert V. Daniels, *The Conscience of the Revolution: Communist Opposition in Soviet Russia* (Cambridge, Mass.: Harvard University Press, 1960), 16, 49–51.

3. See, e.g., Richard Pipes, ed., *The Unknown Lenin: From the Soviet Archive* (New Haven: Yale University Press, 1996).

4. See ch. 8 above.

5. See Lars T. Lih, *Bread and Authority in Russia, 1914–1921* (Berkeley: University of California Press, 1990).

6. This point is argued by Roy Medvedev in *The October Revolution* (New York: Columbia University Press, 1979).

7. Sheila Fitzpatrick, "The Civil War as a Formative Experience," in Abbott Gleason, Peter Kenez, and Richard Stites, eds., *Bolshevik Culture* (Bloomington: Indiana University Press, 1985), 74.

8. V. I. Lenin, Resolution "On the Syndicalist and Anarchist Deviation in Our Party" [Mar. 1921], in *Selected Works* (Moscow: Foreign Languages Publishing House, 1950–52), vol. 2, bk. 1, p. 503.

9. Robert C. Tucker, "Stalinism as Revolution from Above," in Tucker, ed., *Stalinism: Essays in Historical Interpretation* (New York: Norton, 1977), 91–93.

10. See Richard Stites, *Revolutionary Dreams: Utopian Vision and Experimental Life in the Russian Revolution* (New York and Oxford: Oxford University Press, 1989).

11. See Mark von Hagen, *Soldiers in the Proletarian Revolution: The Red Army and the Soviet Socialist State, 1917–1930* (Ithaca, N.Y.: Cornell University Press, 1990).

12. See Gabriele Gorzka, *A. Bogdanov und der russische Proletkult* (Frankfurt: Campus Verlag, 1980); Lynn Mally, *Culture of the Future: The Proletkult Movement in Revolutionary Russia* (Berkeley: University of California Press, 1990).

13. Zenovia A. Sochor, *Revolution and Culture: The Bogdanov-Lenin Controversy* (Ithaca, N.Y.: Cornell University Press, 1988), 212–17.

14. See ch. 7 above.

15. See T. Harry Rigby, *The Changing Soviet System: Mono-Organizational Socialism from Its Origins to Gorbachev's Restructuring* (Aldershot, Eng. and Brookfield, Vt.: Edward Elgar, 1990).

Chapter 11. The Militarization of Socialism in Russia

This chapter is based on my paper "The Militarization of Socialism in Russia, 1902–1946" (occasional paper no. 200, Kennan Institute for Advanced Russian Studies, Washington, D.C., 1985).

1. Emile Durkheim, *Socialism and Saint-Simon* (1928; London: Routledge & Kegan Paul, 1959), 19.

2. Cornelius Castoriadis, *Devant la guerre* (Paris: Fayard, 1981), 22.

3. Quoted in John Wheeler-Bennett, *The Nemesis of Power: The German Army in Politics* (New York: St. Martin's, 1954), 7.

4. V. I. Lenin, *What Is to Be Done?* [1902] (New York: International Publishers, 1926), 133, 166.

5. Friedrich Engels, 1895 introduction to Karl Marx, "The Class Struggles in France, 1848–1850," in Marx, *Selected Works* (New York: International Publishers, n.d.), 2:88.

6. See Karl Marx, *The Civil War in France* (Chicago: Kerr, n.d.). 47–48; ch. 5 above.

7. V. I. Lenin, "Two Tactics of Social Democracy in the Democratic Revolution" [July 1905], in *Selected Works* (Moscow: Foreign Languages Publishing House, 1950–52), vol. 1, bk. 2, p. 142.

8. V. I. Lenin, "The Lessons of the Moscow Uprising" [Sept. 1905], in *Selected Works*, vol. 1, bk. 2, p. 166.

9. V. I. Lenin, "The Situation and Tasks of the Socialist International" [Nov. 1914; in Russian], in *Sobranie sochinenii*, 2nd ed. (Moscow: Marx-Engels-Lenin Institute, 1928), 18:31, and "The War and Russian Social Democracy" [Nov. 1914], in *Selected Works*, vol. 1, bk. 2, p. 406.

10. *Leninskii Sbornik*, vol. 12 (Moscow: Marx-Engels-Lenin Institute, 1924–40).

11. A. S. Milovidov and V. G. Kozlov, *Filosoficheskoe nasledstvo V. I. Lenina i voprosy sovremennoi voiny* (Moscow: Voenizdat, 1972); U.S. Air Force translation, *Philosophical Heritage of V. I. Lenin and Problems of Contemporary War* (Washington, D. C.: GPO, n.d.), 2.

12. Leon Trotsky, "Marxism and Military Knowledge" [May 1922], in *Military Writings* (New York: Merit, 1969), 110–11.

13. V. I. Lenin to I. T. Smilga, 27 Sept. [10 Oct.] 1917, in *Collected Works* (New York: International Publishers, 1929), vol. 21, bk. 1, p. 265.

14. V. I. Lenin, "The Crisis Has Matured" [29 Sept. (12 Oct.) 1917], in *Collected Works*, vol. 21, bk. 1, pp. 227–28.

15. V. I. Lenin to the Central Committee, Moscow Committee, Petrograd Committee, and the Bolshevik members of the Petrograd and Moscow Soviets [3–7 (6–20) Oct. 1917], in *Collected Works*, vol. 21, bk. 2, p. 70, and Lenin to Bolshevik Comrades participating in the Regional Congress of the Soviets of the Northern Region [1 (14) Oct. 1917], in *Collected Works*, vol. 21, bk. 2, p. 100.

16. See Robert V. Daniels, *Red October: The Bolshevik Revolution of 1917* (New York: Scribner's, 1967); ch. 8 above.

17. See, e.g., Sheila Fitzpatrick, "The Civil War as a Formative Experience" (occasional paper no. 134, Kennan Institute for Advanced Russian Studies, Washington, D.C., 1981).

18. V. I. Lenin, "The Immediate Tasks of the Soviet Government" [Apr. 1918], in *Selected Works*, vol. 2, bk. 1, p. 476.

19. Ibid., p. 482.

20. Quoted in John Keep, "Lenin as Tactician," in Leonard Schapiro and Peter Reddaway, eds., *Lenin: The Man, the Theorist, the Leader* (London: PM, 1967), 146.

21. See Alec Nove, "Lenin as Economist," in Schapiro and Reddaway, *Lenin*, 203.

22. V. I. Lenin, Speech to the All-Russian Central Executive Committee [29 Apr. 1918; in Russian], in *Sobranie sochinenii*, 22:482.

23. V. I. Lenin, "On Left Childishness and the Petty-Bourgeois Quality" [May 1918; in Russian], in *Sobranie sochinenii,* 22:516.

24. Resolution of the Eighth Congress of the Russian Communist Party, "On the Organizational Question," in *Kommunisticheskaya Partiya Sovetskogo Soyuza v rezoliutsiyakh i resheniyakh s'ezdov, konferentsii i plenumov TsK* (Moscow: State Press for Political Literature, 1954), 1:444.

25. Leon Trotsky, *Terrorizm i kommunizm* (Moscow: State Press, 1920), translated as *Dictatorship vs. Democracy: A Reply to Karl Kautsky* (New York: Workers' Party of America, 1922), 54.

26. Ibid., 141–42.

27. Joseph Stalin, "The Foundations of Leninism" [Apr. 1924], in *Problems of Leninism* (Moscow: Foreign Languages Publishing House, 1940), 72–83.

28. Declaration by Nikolai Bukharin, Alexei Rykov, and Mikhail Tomsky, 9 Feb. 1929, as quoted in a Politburo resolution of the same date, *KPSS v rezoliutsiyakh,* 2:558.

29. Holland Hunter, "The Overambitious First Soviet Five-Year Plan," *Slavic Review* 32:2 (1973).

30. Branko Horvat, *The Political Economy of Socialism: A Marxist Social Theory* (Armonk, N.Y.: M. E. Sharpe, 1982), 46.

31. Dusko Doder, personal communication, 24 Apr. 1984.

32. Joseph Stalin, "Industrialization of the Country and the Right Deviation in the CPSU(B)" [Nov. 1928], in *Works* (Moscow: Foreign Languages Publishing House, 1949–54), 11:259.

33. Joseph Stalin, "The Tasks of Business Executives" [Feb. 1931], in *Problems of Leninism,* 365–66.

34. "For the Fatherland"[in Russian], *Pravda,* 9 June 1934. See ch. 20 below.

35. Joseph Stalin, Preelection speech [6 Feb. 1946], in *The Strategy and Tactics of World Communism,* sup. 1, U. S. House of Representatives doc. no. 619, 80th Cong., 2nd sess. (Washington, D.C.: GPO, 1948), 170, 177.

36. Joseph Stalin, Answer to *Pravda* correspondent, *Pravda,* 14 Mar. 1946.

37. *Marksizm-Leninizm o voine i armii* (Moscow: Military Press, 1968), 262.

38. Milovidov and Kozlov, *Filosoficheskoe nasledstvo,* 138.

39. In 1981, marshals, generals, and admirals held 40 seats out of a total of 545 in the Central Committee (including candidate members and the Central Auditing Commission), while representatives of the full-time party apparatus held 211, and central and republic officials of civil government held 179. See ch. 32 below.

40. Milovidov and Kozlov, *Filosoficheskoe nasledstvo,* 260.

41. *Marksizm-Leninizm o voine i armii,* 289.

Chapter 12. Bureaucratic Advance and Social Lag in the Revolution

This chapter is based on an essay that I prepared at the invitation of the *Jahrbuch für historische Kommunismusforschung* (Berlin: Akademie Verlag). It appeared in German translation in the 1997 number as "Bürokratischer Fortschritt und gesellschaftlicher Rückstand in der Russischen Revolution." The original English version was published in *Soviet and Post-Soviet Review* 25:1 (1998).

1. See Kiren Aziz Chaudhry, "The Myths of the Market and the Common History of Late Developers," *Politics and Society,* 21 Sept. 1993; Jon Mulberg, *Social Limits to Economic Theory* (London and New York: Routledge, 1995).

2. See Max Weber, *Wirtschaft und Gesellschaft* (Tübingen: Mohr, 1921), pt. 3, ch. 6; Gaetano Mosca, *The Ruling Class* (New York: McGraw-Hill, 1939); Adolf A. Berle and Gardiner C. Means, *The Modern Corporation and Private Property* (New York: Macmillan, 1933); C. Wright Mills, *The Power Elite* (New York: Oxford University Press, 1956); Daniel Bell, *The Coming of Post-industrial Society: A Venture in Social Forecasting* (New York: Basic, 1973), 14.

3. Milovan Djilas, *The New Class: An Analysis of the Communist System* (New York: Praeger, 1957).

4. See Michael Voslensky, *Nomenklatura: The Soviet Ruling Class* (Garden City, N.Y.: Doubleday, 1984).

5. Harold Perkin, *The Third Revolution: Professional Elites in the Modern World* (London and New York: Routledge, 1996).

6. A. Volsky [pseud.], *Umstvennyi rabochii* (Geneva, 1905); George Konrad and Ivan Szelenyi, *The Intellectuals on the Road to Class Power* (New York: Harcourt Brace Jovanovich, 1979).

7. Max Weber, *Economy and Society* (New York: Bedminster, 1968), 1:305.

8. Khristian Rakovsky, "Letter on the Causes of the Degeneration of the Party and Governmental Apparatus" [6 Aug. 1928; in Russian], *Biulleten' oppozitsii,* no. 6 (Oct. 1929): 15; Kh. Rakovsky, V. Kossior, N. Muralov, and V. Kasparova, "Appeal of the Bolshevik-Leninist Opposition to the Central Committee and the Central Control Commission of the All-Union Communist Party and to all Members of the Party" [in Russian], *Biulleten' oppozitsii,* nos. 17–18 (Nov.–Dec. 1930): 16.

9. Leon Trotsky, preface to *La révolution defigurée* [1929], and "Toward Capitalism or toward Socialism" [1930], in *Writings of Leon Trotsky* (New York: Pathfinder, 1975), 1:118, 2:207. See ch. 15 below.

10. Claude Lefort, *Eléments d'une critique de la bureaucratie* (Geneva: Droz, 1971), 357; Max Shachtman, *The Bureaucratic Revolution* (New York: Donald, 1962), 62. A number of these theories are reviewed in Donald C. Hodges, *The Bureaucratization of Socialism* (Amherst: University of Massachusetts Press, 1981), and in David Lane, *The End of Social Inequality? Class, Status, and Power under State Socialism* (London: George Allen & Unwin, 1982).

11. Bruno Rizzi, *La bureaucratisation du monde* (Paris: Hachette, 1939); James Burnham, *The Managerial Revolution* (New York: John Day, 1941).

12. Perkin, *The Third Revolution,* 123.

13. See Henri de Saint-Simon, "Considerations on Measures to Be Taken to End the Revolution," extracts in *Henri Saint-Simon: Selected Writings on Science, Industry, and Social Organization* (New York: Holmes & Meier, 1975), 211–13.

14. See Paul Dukes, introduction to Terry Brotherstone and Paul Dukes, eds., *The Trotsky Reappraisal* (Edinburgh: Edinburgh University Press, 1992), 4–6.

15. N. I. Bukharin, "Notes of an Economist" [in Russian], *Pravda,* 30 Sept. 1928. See Robert V. Daniels, *The Conscience of the Revolution: Communist Opposition in Soviet Russia* (Cambridge: Harvard University Press, 1960), 354–56.

16. N. I. Bukharin, "The Theory of Organized Mismanagement" [in Russian], *Pravda*, 30 June 1929, citing Hermann Bente, *Organisierte Unwirtschaftlichkeit: Die ökonomische Gestalt verbeamteter Wirtschaft und ihre Wandlung im Zeitalter des gesamtwirtschaftliche Kapitalismus* (Jena: Gustav Fischer, 1929).

17. See Albert Parry, *The New Class Divided: Science and Technology versus Communism* (New York: Macmillan, 1966).

18. Vilfredo Pareto, *The Mind and Society* (New York: Harcourt, Brace, 1935), 3:1423; Svetozar Stojanović, "Marxism and Democracy: The Ruling Class or the Dominant Class," *Praxis International* 1:2 (1981).

19. Max Weber, "Parliamentary Government" [1917; in German], in *Wirtschaft und Gesellschaft*, vol. 3, app. 2, pp. 1401–2. Cf. Bell, *The Coming of Post-industrial Society*, 93.

20. Mikhail Bakunin, *L'empire knouto-germanique et la révolution sociale* (1870; Leiden: Brill, 1981).

21. V. I. Lenin, "The Threatening Catastrophe and How to Fight It" [in Russian], in *Sochineniya*, 3rd ed. (Moscow: Marx-Engels-Lenin Institute, 1928–37), 21:157.

22. V. I. Lenin, "Will the Bolsheviks Retain State Power?" [in Russian], in *Sochineniya*, 21:261.

23. Published as "The Immediate Tasks of the Soviet Government: The International Position of the Soviet Government and the Fundamental Tasks of the Socialist Revolution" [Apr. 1918], in V. I. Lenin, *Selected Works* (Moscow: Foreign Languages Publishing House, 1950–52), vol. 2, bk. 1, pp. 448–88.

24. See E. H. Carr, *The Bolshevik Revolution* (London and New York: Macmillan, 1950–53), 2:85–87, 109–15, 394–96.

25. Lenin, "The Immediate Tasks of the Soviet Government," 450, 458–59.

26. Ibid., 482.

27. "Theses on the Current Situation" [in Russian], *Kommunist*, no. 1 (Apr. 1918): 7.

28. Rosa Luxemburg, *Leninism or Marxism* (1904; Glasgow: Anti-parliamentary Communist Federation, 1935), 15.

29. L. D. Trotsky, "Labor, Discipline, and Order" [speech to a Moscow City conference of the Russian Communist Party, 27 Mar. 1918; in Russian], in *Sochineniya* (Moscow: State Press, 1926), vol. 17, pt. 1, pp. 157–71.

30. Resolution of the Eighth Party Congress, "On the Military Question" [in Russian], in *KPSS v rezoliutsiyakh*, 7th ed. (Moscow: State Press for Political Literature, 1954), 1:432–33. See Mark von Hagen, *Soldiers in the Proletarian Dictatorship: The Red Army and the Soviet State, 1917–1930* (Ithaca, N.Y.: Cornell University Press, 1990).

31. Leon Trotsky, "Theses of the Central Committee of the Russian Communist Party on Labor" [in Russian], *Pravda*, 22 Jan. 1920; *Ninth Congress of the RCP(B): Minutes* [in Russian] (Moscow: Marx-Engels-Lenin Institute, 1934), 112.

32. V. I. Lenin, "On Cooperation" [in Russian], in *Sochineniya*, 27:397.

33. N. I. Bukharin, Speech at the Fourth Congress of the Communist International, 1922, requoted by him, *Pravda*, 12 Sept. 1928.

34. See, e.g., Hiroaki Kiromiya, *Stalin's Industrial Revolution: Politics and Workers, 1928–1932* (Cambridge: Cambridge University Press, 1988).

35. Moshe Lewin, *Russia-USSR-Russia: The Drive and Drift of a Superstate* (New York: New Press, 1995), 186.

36. Joseph Stalin, Report on the Work of the Central Committee, to the Seventeenth Congress of the CPSU(B) [Jan. 1934], in *Problems of Leninism* (Moscow: Foreign Languages Publishing House, 1953), 634.

37. See Karl Mannheim, *Ideology and Utopia: An Introduction to the Sociology of Knowledge* (1929; New York: Harcourt Brace, 1936).

38. Joseph Stalin, Report on the Work of the Central Committee, to the Eighteenth Congress of the CPSU(B) [Mar. 1939], in *Problems of Leninism*, 797–800.

39. Rudolf Hilferding, "State Capitalism or Totalitarian State Economy" [1940], *Modern Review*, June 1947, 270.

40. J. M. Keynes, "The End of Laissez-Faire," quoted in Edward S. Herman, *Corporate Control, Corporate Power* (Cambridge: Cambridge University Press, 1981), 9.

41. Bell, *The Coming of Post-industrial Society*, 112.

42. Perkin, *Third Revolution*, 145.

43. See Robert V. Daniels, "The Riddle of Russian Reform: Is Yeltsin a 'Bolshevik in Reverse'?" *Dissent* (Fall 1993): 492–93; N. I. Bukharin, *Oekonomik der Transformationsperiode* (Hamburg: Hoym, 1922), 55–56.

44. Albert Plutnik, "Comrade First Secretaries in the Role of Messrs. President" [in Russian], *Izvestiya*, 6 Dec. 1996.

45. Adam Przeworski, *Democracy and the Market: Political and Economic Reforms in Eastern Europe and Latin America* (Cambridge: Cambridge University Press, 1991), 101. See also Philippe C. Schmitter with Terry Lynn Karl, "The Conceptual Travels of Transitologists and Consolidologists: How Far to the East Should They Go?" *Slavic Review*, Spr. 1994.

Chapter 13. Socialist Alternatives in the Crisis of 1921

This chapter is based on a paper, "Socialist Alternatives in the Trade Union Controversy," presented at the international conference "Russia in the Twentieth Century," Moscow, USSR Academy of Sciences, Apr. 1990, and published in Russian translation in the proceedings of the conference, *Rossiya v XX veke: Istoriki mira sporyat* [Russia in the Twentieth Century: The World's Historians Debate] (Moscow: Nauka, 1994).

1. Thomas F. Remington, *Building Socialism in Bolshevik Russia: Ideology and Industrial Organization, 1917–1921* (Pittsburgh: University of Pittsburgh Press, 1984), 49.

2. See, e.g., Isaac Deutscher, *Stalin: A Political Biography* (New York and London: Oxford University Press, 1949), 222–23.

3. See Robert C. Williams, *The Other Bolsheviks: Lenin and his Critics, 1904–1914* (Bloomington: Indiana University Press, 1984), 85–93.

4. See, e.g., Lev Kritsman, *Geroicheskii period russkoi revoliutsii* (Moscow and Leningrad: State Press, 1926).

5. *Ninth Congress of the Russian Communist Party (Bolsheviks): Minutes* [in Russian] (Moscow: Marx-Engels-Lenin Institute, 1934), 100.

6. Leon Trotsky, *Terrorizm i kommunizm* (Moscow: State Press, 1920), translated as *Dictatorship vs. Democracy: A Reply to Karl Kautsky* (New York: Workers' Party of America, 1922), 143.

7. *Second All-Russian Congress of Trade Unions, Stenographic Report* [in Russian] (Moscow: Central Trade Union Press, 1919), 1:97; N. I. Bukharin, *Oekonomik der Transformationsperiode*

(Hamburg: Hoym, 1922), 86; Platform, "On the Tasks and Structure of the Trade Unions" [in Russian], in *Tenth Congress of the Russian Communist Party: Minutes* [in Russian] (Moscow: Marx-Engels-Lenin Institute, 1933), app. 16, p. 802.

8. Leon Trotsky, "The Trade Unions and Their Future Role" [in Russian], in *Tenth Party Congress*, app. 10, p. 786.

9. Program of the Russian Communist Party (of Bolsheviks) [in Russian], in *KPSS v rezoliutsiyakh i resheniyakh s'ezdov, konferentsii, i plenumov TsK*, 7th ed. (Moscow: State Political Press, 1954), 1:422.

10. *Vsesoyuznaya Kommunisticheskaya Partiya (bol'shevikov) v rezoliutsiyakh s'ezdov, konferentsii i plenumov TsK* (Moscow: Party Press, 1931), vol. 1, app., p. 813.

11. *Ninth Party Congress*, 564n32, 123–24.

12. Alexandra Kollontai, *The Workers' Opposition* (Chicago: IWW, 1921), 9.

13. *Ninth Party Congress*, 44.

14. Resolution of the Ninth Party Conference, "On the Next Tasks of Party Construction" [in Russian], in *KPSS v rezoliutsiyakh*, 1:507–12.

15. *Tenth Party Congress*, 371–72.

16. Resolution of the Tenth Party Congress, "On the Syndicalist and Anarchist Deviation in Our Party" [in Russian], in *KPSS v rezoliutsiyakh*, 1:531.

17. Lenin to the Organizations of the RCP(B) on the Question of the Agenda of the Party Congress [2 Mar. 1920; in Russian], in *Ninth Party Congress*, app. 2, p. 473.

18. Resolution of the Ninth Party Congress, "On the Question of the Trade Unions and Their Organization" [in Russian], in *KPSS v rezoliutsiyakh*, 1:493.

19. Leon Trotsky, *My Life: An Attempt at an Autobiography* (New York: Scribner's, 1930), 462.

20. *Tenth Party Congress*, 825n1.

21. V. I. Lenin, "On the Trade Unions, the Current Situation, and the Mistakes of Comrade Trotsky" [in Russian], in *Sochineniya*, 3rd ed. (Moscow: Marx-Engels-Lenin Institute, 1928–37), 26:67.

22. "The Role and Tasks of the Trade Unions": Draft for a decision of the Tenth Congress of the RCP, introduced by the Group of "Ten" [in Russian], *Tenth Party Congress*, app., pp. 663–74. The ten were Lenin, Zinoviev, Kamenev, Stalin, Tomsky, Mikhail Kalinin, Yan Rudzutak, A. L. Lozovsky, G. Y. Petrovsky, and F. A. Artem-Sergeyev.

23. *Tenth Party Congress*, 837n1.

24. Adopted as a resolution of the Eleventh Party Congress, "The Role and Tasks of the Trade Unions under the Conditions of the New Economic Policy" [in Russian], in *KPSS v rezoliutsiyakh*, 1:604.

25. Leon Trotsky, *Terrorism and Communism* (Ann Arbor: University of Michigan Press, 1961), 142.

26. Ibid., 169–70.

27. Nikolai Bukharin, "The Economics of the Transition Period," in *The Politics and Economics of the Transition Period*, ed. Kenneth V. Tarbusk (London: Routledge and Kegan Paul, 1979), 104–5, 142.

28. Ibid., 143.

29. Ibid., 144; Trotsky, *Terrorism and Communism*, 169.

30. Kollontai, *The Workers' Opposition*, 4, 15, 17.

31. See V. I. Lenin, "Two Tactics of Social Democracy in the Democratic Revolution" [July 1905], in *Selected Works* (Moscow: Foreign Languages Publishing House, 1950–52), vol. 1, bk. 2, pp. 86–90.

32. Joseph Stalin, "The Tasks of Business Executives" [speech delivered at the first All-Union Conference of Managers of Socialist Industry, 4 Feb. 1931], in *Problems of Leninism* (Moscow: Foreign Languages Publishing House, 1953), 458.

33. Milovan Djilas, *The Unperfect Society: Beyond the New Class* (New York: Harcourt, Brace & World, 1969), 220–23. Cf. Bogdan Denitch, *The Legitimation of a Revolution* (New Haven: Yale University Press, 1976), 152–53; Dennison Rusinow, *The Yugoslav Experiment, 1948–1974* (Berkeley and Los Angeles: University of California Press, 1977), 50–51.

34. See, e.g., G. I. Mirsky, *Tretii mir—Obshchestvo, vlast', armiya* (Moscow: Nauka, 1976).

35. Robert C. Tucker, "Stalinism as Revolution from Above," in Tucker, ed., *Stalinism: Essays in Historical Interpretation* (New York: Norton, 1976).

36. See Richard B. Day, *Leon Trotsky and the Politics of Economic Isolation* (Cambridge: Cambridge University Press, 1973), 182–85.

37. Trotsky, *My Life*, 463–64.

Chapter 14. The Left Opposition and the Evolution of the Communist Regime

This chapter is based on the English original of my essay "Die linke Opposition und die Entwicklung des Sowjetkommunismus," in Ulf Wolter, ed., *Sozialismusdebatte* (Berlin: Olle & Wolter, 1978).

1. Alexander Barmine, *One Who Survived* (New York: Putnam, 1945), 212.

2. See Robert V. Daniels, *The Conscience of the Revolution: Communist Opposition in Soviet Russia* (Cambridge: Harvard University Press, 1960), 183–86, 205–6; Leon Trotsky to all members of the Central Committee of the RCP [16 Apr. 1923], in Yu. Fel'shtinsky, ed., *Kommunisticheskaya oppozitsiya v SSSR, 1923–27* (Benson, Vt.: Chalidze, 1988), 2:53; Leon Trotsky, *Stalin: An Appraisal of the Man and His Influence* (New York: Harper, 1946), 362–63. In 1990 the Soviet historian Viktor Danilov brought to light Trotsky's speech to the party leadership in October 1923 in which he explained why he declined to serve as Lenin's chief deputy—out of fear that his "Jewish origin" would be seized upon by anti-Semitic enemies of the Soviet regime. V. P. Danilov, "We are Beginning to Get to Know Trotsky" [in Russian], *Eko* (Novosibirsk), no. 1 (1990): 57; Concluding remarks of Comrades Trotsky and Stalin at the joint session of the plenums of the Central Committee and the Central Control Commission together with representatives of ten proletarian party organizations [26 Oct. 1923], *Voprosy Istorii KPSS*, no. 5 (1990): 36.

3. See ch. 15 below.

4. In Fel'shtinsky, *Oppozitsiya*, I:83–88, English translation in E. H. Carr, *The Interregnum* (New York: Macmillan, 1954), 367–73.

5. Resolution of the Central Committee and the Central Control Commission, "On the Intraparty Situation" [25 Oct. 1923; in Russian], in *KPSS v rezoliutsiyakh I resheniyakh s'ezdov, konferentsii I plenumov TsK*, 7th ed. (Moscow: Gospolitizdat, 1954), 1:767–68.

6. According to Anton Antonov-Ovseyenko, son of Vladimir Antonov-Ovseyenko, Trotsky's supporter General N. I. Muralov, commandant of the Moscow Military District at the time, was ready to intervene. A. V. Antonov-Ovseyenko, "Trotsky as a Military Leader," paper presented at the International Trotsky Symposium, Wuppertal, Germany, Mar. 1990.

7. *Pravda*, 7 Dec. 1923.

8. Leon Trotsky, *The New Course* (New York: New International Publishers, 1943), 89–98.

9. Leon Trotsky, *The Lessons of October* (New York: Pioneer, 1937).

10. Joseph Stalin, Report to the Fifteenth Party Conference, "On the Opposition and on the Intraparty Situation" [in Russian], *Pravda*, 5 Nov. 1926. See Daniels, *Conscience of the Revolution*, 273–75.

11. Text in Fel'shtinsky, *Oppozitsiya*, 2:11–24.

12. See Leon Trotsky, "The Chinese Revolution and the Theses of Comrade Stalin" [7 May 1927], in *Problems of the Chinese Revolution* (New York: Pioneer, 1932).

13. See the "Declaration of the Fifteen" [27 June 1927], published as *Avant Thermidor: Révolution et contrerévolution dans la Russie des Soviets—Platforme de l'Opposition de Gauche dans le parti Bolchevique* (Lyons, 1928).

14. Published by Trotsky as *The Real Situation in Russia* (New York: Harcourt, Brace, 1928).

15. Richard Day, *Leon Trotsky and the Politics of Economic Isolation* (Cambridge: Cambridge University Press, 1973), 183.

16. Joseph Stalin, "The October Revolution and the Tactics of the Russian Communists," in *Problems of Leninism* (Moscow: Foreign Languages Publishing House, 1940), 86–117.

17. V. I. Lenin, "The United States of Europe Slogan" [Aug. 1915], in *Selected Works* (Moscow: Foreign Languages Publishing House, 1950–52), vol. 1, bk. 2, p. 416.

18. Lev Kamenev, Speech at the Fifteenth Party Conference, *Pravda*, 5 Nov. 1926.

19. See Thomas J. Blakeley, *Soviet Scholasticism* (Dordrecht: Reidel, 1951).

20. Alexander Erlich, *The Soviet Industrialization Controversy* (Cambridge, Mass.: Harvard University Press, 1960), 59.

21. Ye. A. Preobrazhensky, "Economic Equilibrium in the System of the USSR" [in Russian], *Vestnik Kommunisticheskogo Akademii*, no. 22 (1927): 70, quoted in Erlich, *Soviet Industrialization Controversy*, 59.

22. Lev Kamenev, Notes on conversation with Bukharin [11 July 1928, copy in Trotsky Archive, Harvard University, doc. T1897], extracts translated in Robert V. Daniels, ed., *A Documentary History of Communism* (New York: Random House, 1960), 1:308.

23. See chapter 19 below.

Chapter 15. Trotsky on Democracy and Bureaucracy

This chapter is based on a paper prepared for the International Trotsky Symposium, Wuppertal, Germany, Mar. 1990, that appeared in German translation in the proceedings of the symposium, Theodor Bergmann and Gert Schäfer, eds., *Leo Trotzki: Kritiker und Verteidiger der Sowjetgesellschaft* (Mainz: Decaton, 1993).

1. Leon Trotsky, *Nashi politicheskie zadachi* [Our Political Tasks] (Geneva: Russian Social Democratic Workers' Party, 1904), 54.

2. *Pravda,* 11 Dec. 1923; English version in Leon Trotsky, *The New Course,* ed. Max Shachtman, (New York: New International Publishers, 1943); republished in Russian, Lev Trotskii, "Novyi kurs," *Molodoi Kommunist,* no. 8 (1989).

3. Trotsky, *The New Course,* 154.

4. *Pravda,* 7 Dec. 1923. On the circumstances of the adoption of the resolution, see Robert V. Daniels, *The Conscience of the Revolution: Communist Opposition in Soviet Russia* (Cambridge, Mass.: Harvard University Press, 1960), 222–23. The resolution is sometimes attributed to the Central Committee.

5. Trotsky, *The New Course,* 89–98.

6. *Thirteenth Congress of the All-Union Communist Party (Bolsheviks): Stenographic Report* [in Russian] (Moscow: State Press for Political Literature, 1936), 158–59; Naomi Allen, ed., *Leon Trotsky: The Challenge of the Left Opposition* (New York: Pathfinder, 1975–81), 1:161–62.

7. Leon Trotsky, *Zadachi XII s'ezda RKP* [Speech at a conference of the Communist Party of the Ukraine, 5 Apr. 1923] (Moscow: Ninth of January Press, 1923), 24; "Tasks of the Twelfth Congress of the Russian Communist Party," in *Leon Trotsky Speaks* (New York: Pathfinder, 1972), 135.

8. Leon Trotsky, "Bureaucratism and Revolution (Outline of a Report That the Author Could Not Deliver)," first published in his pamphlet, *Novyi kurs* [1923], in Trotsky, *The New Course,* 45–46.

9. Cf. Karl Marx, *The Eighteenth Brumaire of Louis Bonaparte* (New York: International Publishers, 1926), 130–31, and *The Civil War in France* (Chicago: Kerr, n.d.), 42. See chs. 1 and 5 above.

10. Friedrich Engels, 1891 introduction to Marx, *The Civil War in France* (New York: International Publishers, 1940), 20.

11. Leon Trotsky, "Blok s Zinov'evym (k dnevniku)" [9 Dec. 1925], in Yu. Fel'shtinsky, ed., *Kommunisticheskaya Oppozitsiya v SSSR, 1923–27* (Benson, Vt.: Chalidze, 1988), 1:154, translated as "A 'Bloc' with Zinoviev (for Diary)," in Allen, *Leon Trotsky,* 1:386.

12. Leon Trotsky, "V Politburo" [To the Politburo; 6 June 1926], in Fel'shtinsky, *Oppozitsiya,* 1:235–38, translated as "Party Bureaucratism and Party Democracy," in Allen, *Leon Trotsky,* 2:68–72.

13. Trotsky, Speech to the Fifteenth Party Conference [1 Nov. 1926], *Pravda,* 6 Nov. 1926, in Allen, *Leon Trotsky,* 2:162.

14. "Proekt platformy bol'shevikov-lenintsev (oppozitsii) k XV S'ezdu VKP(b) (Krizis partii i puti ego preodoleniya)" [Sept. 1927], in Fel'shtinsky, *Oppozitsiya,* 4:139, 151, translated as "The Real Situation in Russia and the Tasks of the Communist Party," in Leon Trotsky, *The Real Situation in Russia* (New York: Harcourt, Brace, 1928), 95, 124.

15. Leon Trotsky, "At a New Stage" [in German], *Die Fahne des Kommunismus,* 21 and 28 Dec. 1927, in Allen, *Leon Trotsky,* 2:490–91.

16. Leon Trotsky, "Who Is Leading the Comintern Today?" [*Militant,* 15 Aug. and 30 Nov. 1928], in Allen, *Leon Trotsky,* 2:490–91.

17. Leon Trotsky, "Our Differences with the Democratic Centralists" [11 Nov. 1928; in French; *Contre le courant,* 6 May 1929], in Allen, *Leon Trotsky,* 3:294; "The Crisis in the Right-Center Bloc" [Nov. 1928; in French; *Contre le courant,* 22 Mar. 1929], in Allen, *Leon Trotsky,* 3:328.

18. Leon Trotsky, "Marxism and the Relation between Proletarian and Peasant Revolution" [Dec. 1928], Trotsky Archive, in Allen, *Leon Trotsky*, 3:347–51; "Philosophical Tendencies of Bureaucratism" [Dec. 1928], Trotsky Archive, in Allen, *Leon Trotsky*, 3:389–409.

19. Allen, *Leon Trotsky*, 3:391.

20. Khristian Rakovsky, "Letter on the Causes of the Degeneration of the Party and of the State Apparatus" [6 Aug. 1928; in Russian], *Biulleten' oppozitsii*, no. 6 (Oct. 1929): 15.

21. Kh. Rakovsky, V. Kossior, N. Muralov, and V. Kasparova, "Appeal of the Bolshevik-Leninist Opposition to the CC and the CCC of the AUCP(B), and to All Members of the AUCP(B)" [Apr. 1930; in Russian], *Biulleten' oppozitsii*, nos. 17–18 (Nov.–Dec. 1930): 16.

22. Cf. Bruno Rizzi, *La bureaucratisation du monde* (Paris: Hachette, 1939); James Burnham, *The Managerial Revolution* (New York: John Day, 1941); Milovan Djilas, *The New Class: An Analysis of the Communist System* (New York: Praeger, 1957); Rudolf Bahro, *Die Alternative: Zur Kritik des real existierenden Sozialismus* (Cologne: Europäische Verlagsanstalt, 1977); Michael Voslensky, *Nomenklatura: The Soviet Ruling Class* (Garden City, N.Y.: Doubleday, 1984).

23. Rakovsky et al., "Appeal," 16.

24. Kh. Rakovsky, V. Kossior, and M. Okudzhava, Theses of Aug. 1929, *Biulleten' oppozitsii*, no. 7 (Nov.–Dec. 1929): 9.

25. Leon Trotsky, *Chto i kak proizoshlo?* (Paris: De Nevarre, 1929) [translated in *New York Times*, 1 Mar. 1929, as "Trotsky Reveals Origins of His Fall"] in *Writings of Leon Trotsky* (New York: Pathfinder, 1975), 1:47, 50.

26. Leon Trotsky, preface to *La révolution défigurée* (Paris: Reider, 1929), in *Writings of Leon Trotsky*, 1:118.

27. Leon Trotsky, "K kapitalizmu ili k sotsializmu," *Biulleten' oppozitsii*, no. 11 (May 1930): 9, translated as "Toward Capitalism or Socialism?" in *Writings of Leon Trotsky*, 2:207.

28. Leon Trotsky, "K XVImu s'ezdu VKP(b)," *Biulleten' oppozitsii*, nos. 12–13 (June–July 1930): 5, translated as "Toward the Sixteenth Congress of the CPSU," in *Writings of Leon Trotsky*, 2:261. Oddly enough, in commenting on the 1930 statement by Rakovsky and his associates, which among other things explains the bureaucracy as a new class, Trotsky overlooked the point altogether. Trotsky, "Introduction to the Rakovsky Declaration" [22 Oct. 1930, *Militant*, 15 Jan. 1931], in *Writings of Leon Trotsky*, 3:49–50.

29. Leon Trotsky, "Chto dal'she? (K kampanii protiv pravykh)" [*Biulleten' oppozitsii*, no. 17 (Nov. 1930): 23, translated as "What Next in the Campaign against the Russian Right Wing?" *Militant*, 1 Jan. 1931], in *Writings of Leon Trotsky*, 3:63–65.

30. Leon Trotsky, Declaration of the Bolshevik-Leninist Delegation at the Conference of Left Socialist and Communist Organizations [Paris, 17 Aug. 1933], *Militant*, 23 Sep. 1933, in *Writings of Leon Trotsky*, 4:42.

31. Leon Trotsky, *The Soviet Union and the Fourth International* (New York: Pioneer Publishers, 1934), in *Writings of Leon Trotsky*, 6:104.

32. Ibid., 6:112–13.

33. Leon Trotsky, Declaration at the Conference of Left Socialist and Communist Organizations, in *Writings of Leon Trotsky*, 6:43.

34. Trotsky, *The Soviet Union and the Fourth International*, 6:104.

35. Leon Trotsky, *The Revolution Betrayed: What Is the Soviet Union and Where Is It Going?* (Garden City, N.Y.: Doubleday, Doran, 1937). Cf. Richard B. Day, "Democratic

Control and the Dignity of Politics—An Analysis of *The Revolution Betrayed*," *Comparative Economic Studies* 29:3 (1987).

36. Trotsky, *The Revolution Betrayed*, 47.

37. Ibid., 149, 255.

38. Ibid., 278, 279.

39. Ibid., 287.

40. Ibid., 266, 267.

41. Ibid., 270.

42. Leon Trotsky, Statement to the Preliminary Commission of Inquiry, John Dewey, Chairman, in *The Case of Leon Trotsky: Report of Hearings on the Charges Made against Him in the Moscow Trials* (New York: Harper, 1937), 440–41.

43. Leon Trotsky, "The USSR and War," in *In Defense of Marxism* (New York: Pioneer, 1942), 9.

44. Baruch Knei-Paz, *The Social and Political Thought of Leon Trotsky* (Oxford: Oxford University Press, 1978), 426.

45. See, e.g., Trotsky Archive, doc. T2992, in Fel'shtinsky, *Oppozitsiya*, 4:52–67; Trotsky, Speech to the Joint Plenum of the CC and the CCC [6 Aug. 1927], in Allen, *Leon Trotsky*, 2:270–90.

46. Trotsky, "Party Bureaucratism and Party Democracy," 2:69.

47. "Proekt platformy," Fel'shtinsky, *Oppozitsiya*, 4:174; *The Real Situation in Russia*, 194.

Chapter 16. The Left Opposition as an Alternative to Stalinism

This chapter is based on a paper of the same title prepared for a Soviet-American conference on "Political Alternatives in the NEP," Moscow, USSR Academy of Sciences, Oct. 1989. It appeared in the *Slavic Review* 50:2 (1991).

1. Robert V. Daniels, *The Conscience of the Revolution: Communist Opposition in Soviet Russia* (Cambridge, Mass.: Harvard University Press, 1960), 50–51, referring to the biographies of revolutionary leaders in *Entsiklopedicheskii Slovar'* (Moscow and Petrograd: Granat, 1925–28), appendices to vols. 41–43.

2. Viacheslav Molotov, Speech at the Central Committee School for District Party Workers [2 Oct. 1926], *Pravda*, 5 Oct. 1926.

3. See Sheila Fitzpatrick, "The Bolsheviks' Dilemma: Class, Culture, and Politics in the Early Soviet Years," *Slavic Review* 47 (Winter 1988): 599–613.

4. Leon Trotsky, "Theses on Industry" [6 Mar. 1923; in Russian], in Yu. Fel'shtinsky, ed. *Kommunisticheskaya oppozitsiya v SSSR, 1923–27* (Benson, Vt.: Chalidze, 1988), 1:35.

5. Declaration of the Thirteen [July 1926; in Russian], Trotsky Archive, doc. T880a, in Fel'shtinsky, *Oppozitsiya*, 2:13.

6. Trotsky, "Theses on Industry," 1:35–36, 39.

7. Leon Trotsky, "Our Differences" [Nov. 1924; in Russian], Trotsky Archive, Harvard University, doc. T2969, English translation in Naomi Allen, ed., *Leon Trotsky: The Challenge of the Left Opposition (1923–1925)* (New York: Pathfinder, 1975), 301.

8. Evgeny Preobrazhensky, *Novaya ekonomika*, 2nd ed. (Moscow: Communist Academy, 1926), 92–94.

9. *Pravda*, 28 Dec. 1924.

10. *Fourteenth Congress of the All-Union Communist Party (Bolsheviks): Stenographic Report* [in Russian] (Moscow: Party Press, 1926), 230–32.

11. Preobrazhensky, *Novaya ekonomika*, 99.

12. Leon Trotsky, Statement to the Politburo [6 June 1926]; Trotsky, Theses for the Fifteenth Party Conference [19 Sept. 1926]; Trotsky et al., Declaration on the Speech of Comrade Molotov on the Insurrectionism of the Opposition [4 Aug. 1927]; all in Fel'shtinsky, *Oppozitsiya*, vols. 1 and 2; Trotsky, Speech to the Presidium of the ECCI [27–28 Sept. 1927], Trotsky Archive, doc. T3094.

13. Leon Trotsky, Speech to the Central Committee [23 Oct. 1927], in Trotsky, *The Real Situation in Russia* (New York: Harcourt, Brace, 1928), 7.

14. Nikolai Bukharin, Report to the Leningrad Party Organization [28 July 1926], *Pravda*, 3 Aug. 1926.

15. Joseph Stalin, Concluding remarks at the Seventh Plenum of the ECCI, *Pravda*, 19 Dec. 1926; Political Report of the Central Committee, Fifteenth Congress of the All-Union Communist Party (of Bolsheviks): Stenographic Report [in Russian] (Moscow: State Press, 1928), 75.

16. Bukharin, Report to the Leningrad Party Organization, *Pravda*, 3 Aug. 1926.

17. One Soviet specialist on the subject suggested in private conversation in Apr. 1990, "Stalin ne byl paranoik, a bandit" (Stalin was not a paranoid but a bandit).

18. Richard B. Day, *Leon Trotsky and the Politics of Economic Isolation* (Cambridge: Cambridge University Press, 1973), 182–85.

19. Ibid., 186.

20. Evgeny Preobrazhensky, Statement "To All Comrades regarding the Opposition" [Apr. 1929, in Russian], Trotsky Archive.

Chapter 17. Foundations of Stalinism

This chapter originally appeared as "The Legacy of Stalinism," in the Italian annual *Socialismo/Storia*, no. 1, "Ripensare il 1956" (Rome: Lerici, 1987).

1. See Eric Voegelin, *From Enlightenment to Revolution* (Durham, N.C.: Duke University Press, 1975).

2. See J. L. Talmon, *The Origins of Totalitarian Democracy* (London: Secker & Warburg, 1952).

3. See ch. 10 above.

4. V. I. Lenin, "On the Question of the Nationalities or of 'Autonomization'" [30–31 Dec. 1922; in Russian], in *Pis'mo s'ezdu* (Moscow: State Press for Political Literature, 1956), 22.

5. Platform of Nikolai Bukharin, Aleksei Rykov, and Mikhail Tomsky, presented to the Politburo [9 Feb. 1929], quoted in Joseph Stalin, "The Right Deviation in the AUCP(B)" [Apr. 1929; in Russian], in *Sochineniya* (Moscow: Marx-Engels-Lenin Institute, 1946–53), 12:3–4.

6. Carl J. Friedrich and Zbigniew K. Brzezinski, *Totalitarian Dictatorship and Autocracy* (Cambridge, Mass.: Harvard University Press, 1956).

7. See Erich Fromm, *Escape from Freedom* (New York: Farrar & Rinehart, 1941); T. W. Adorno et al., *The Authoritarian Personality* (New York: Harper, 1950).

8. See, e.g., Branko Horvat, *The Political Economy of Socialism: A Marxist Social Theory* (Armonk, N.Y.: M. E. Sharpe, 1982); Rudolf Hilferding, "State Capitalism or Totalitarian State Economy," *Modern Review,* June 1947.

Chapter 18. Stalinism as Postrevolutionary Dictatorship

This chapter is based on the English original of my paper "Lo Stalinismo come dittatura postrivoluzionaria," Gramsci Institute and University of Urbino conference on "The Age of Stalinism," in Aldo Natoli and Silvio Pons, eds., *L'età dello Stalinismo* (Rome: Riuniti, 1991).

1. Quoted in *New York Times,* 13 Mar. 1989.
2. Max Weber, *Wirtschaft und Gesellschaft* (Tübingen: Mohr, 1976), 1:157. See also H. H. Gerth and C. Wright Mills, eds., *From Max Weber: Essays in Sociology* (New York: Oxford University Press, 1958), 54.
3. See ch. 22 below.
4. See ch. 20 below.
5. See, e.g., Robert C. Tucker, "Stalinism as a Revolution from Above," in Tucker, ed., *Stalinism: Essays in Historical Interpretation* (New York: Norton, 1977).
6. The First Five-Year Plan was formally adopted by the Congress of Soviets in May 1929, but backdated to Oct. 1928 to include the annual plan for 1928–29 already in effect under the so-called control figures. When Stalin declared the Five-Year Plan fulfilled in four years at the end of 1932, it had officially been in effect for only three years and eight months—an example of the ascendancy of irrational propaganda purposes over rational economic calculations.
7. See Sheila Fitzpatrick, ed., *Cultural Revolution in Russia, 1928–31* (Bloomington: Indiana University Press, 1978), esp. 1.
8. See James R. Millar, "Mass Collectivization and the Contribution of Agriculture to the First Five-Plan," *Slavic Review* 33 (Dec. 1974); Holland Hunter, "Soviet Agriculture with and without Collectivization," *Slavic Review* 47 (Summer 1988).
9. Joseph Stalin, Report on the Work of the Central Committee, to the Seventeenth Congress of the CPSU (B), in *Problems of Leninism* (Moscow: Foreign Languages Publishing House, 1953), 635.
10. See, e.g., Vera Dunham, *In Stalin's Time: Middle-Class Values in Soviet Fiction* (Cambridge: Cambridge University Press, 1976); Roy A. Medvedev, *Let History Judge: The Origins and Consequences of Stalinism,* rev. ed. (New York: Columbia University Press, 1989), 686–88.
11. See ch. 27 below.
12. See chs. 30 and 33 below.
13. Anatoly Butenko, personal communication, Moscow, Sept. 1988.

Chapter 19. From Distributive Socialism to Production Socialism

This chapter is based on my article "Toward a Definition of Soviet Socialism," *New Politics* 1:4 (1962).

1. See Karl Marx to the editor of *Otechestvennye Zapiski* [1879], in Karl Marx and Friedrich Engels, *Selected Correspondence, 1846–1895* (New York: International Publishers,

1942), 352–55; Marx and Engels, preface to the Russian edition of *The Communist Manifesto* [1882], quoted in *Selected Correspondence*, 355; Engels to N. F. Danielson, 24 Feb. 1893, in *Selected Correspondence*, 508–10.

2. See Adam Ulam, *The Unfinished Revolution* (New York: Random House, 1960), 6–10.

3. See Alexander Erlich, *The Soviet Industrialization Debate* (Cambridge, Mass.: Harvard University Press, 1960).

4. See Alfred G. Meyer, "USSR Incorporated," *Slavic Review* 20:3 (1961).

5. See, e.g., *The Doctrine of Saint-Simon: An Exposition, First Year, 1828–1829* (Boston: Beacon, 1958), esp. introduction by Georg G. Iggers.

6. See ch. 12 above.

Chapter 20. Stalin's Cultural Counterrevolution

This chapter is based on my article "Soviet Thought in the 1930s: An Interpretive Sketch," *Indiana Slavic Studies* 1 (1956).

1. There are noteworthy exceptions. See Nicholas S. Timasheff, *The Great Retreat: The Growth and Decline of Communism in Russia* (New York: Dutton, 1946); Harold J. Berman, *Justice in Russia* (Cambridge, Mass.: Harvard University Press, 1950); Raymond A. Bauer, *The New Man in Soviet Psychology* (Cambridge, Mass.: Harvard University Press, 1952); Klaus Mehnert, *Stalin vs. Marx* (London: Allen & Unwin, 1952).

2. For suggestions relevant to the psychological functions of Soviet social policy, see Bauer, *The New Man;* T. W. Adorno et al., *The Authoritarian Personality* (New York: Harper, 1950); Erich Fromm, *Escape from Freedom* (New York: Farrar & Rinehart, 1941); Wilhelm Reich, *The Mass Psychology of Fascism* (New York: Orgone Institute Press, 1946).

3. Quoted in Harriet Borland, *Soviet Literary Theory and Practice during the First Five-Year Plan, 1928—1932* (New York: King's Crown, 1950), 13.

4. Ibid., 14. For a general discussion of the arts in the twenties and early thirties, see Max Eastman, *Artists in Uniform* (New York: Knopf, 1934).

5. John C. Fiske, "Dostoevsky and the Soviet Critics, 1947–1948," *American Slavic and East European Review* 9:1 (1950), 45.

6. Quoted in Borland, *Literary Theory*, 33–34.

7. See Gleb Struve, *Soviet Russian Literature, 1917–50* (Norman: University of Oklahoma Press, 1951), 172.

8. Kurt London, *The Seven Soviet Arts* (New Haven: Yale University Press, 1938), 61.

9. Ibid.

10. Struve, *Soviet Russian Literature*, 242.

11. See Maxim Gorky, Speech to the Soviet Writers' Congress [1934], in *Problems of Soviet Literature* (New York: International Publishers, [1935]), 65.

12. *Literaturnaya gazeta*, 23 Mar. 1946.

13. Paul Aron, "The Impact of the First Five-Year Plan on Soviet Historiography" (unpublished seminar paper, Russian Research Center, Harvard University, 1950); E. Maksimovich, "Historical Science in the USSR and Marxism-Leninism" [in Russian], *Sovremennyia zapiski* (Paris) 32 (1936).

14. Joseph Stalin, "Some Questions concerning the History of Bolshevism" [a letter to the editors of *Proletarskaya revoliutsiya*], in *Problems of Leninism* (Moscow: Foreign Languages Publishing House, 1953), 484, 494.

15. *Izvestiya*, 16 May 1934, translated in *Slavonic and East European Review*, July 1934, 204–5.

16. Text of the decree in *Istorik marksist*, no. 1 (1936): 3–5.

17. M. Kammari, "The Theoretical Roots of the Erroneous Views of M. N. Pokrovsky in History" [in Russian], *Pod znamenem marksizma*, no. 4 (1936): 7.

18. P. Miliukov, "The Greatness and Downfall of M. N. Pokrovsky" [in Russian], *Sovremennyia zapiski* (1937): 384. Shestakov's book appeared in English as *A Short History of the USSR* (Moscow: Co-operative Publishing House of Foreign Workers in the USSR, 1938).

19. Joseph Stalin, Political Report of the Central Committee to the Seventeenth Congress of the CPSU (B), in *Problems of Leninism*, 644.

20. See Berman, *Justice,* 35–37.

21. See Harold J. Berman and Donald H. Hunt, "Criminal Law and Psychiatry: The Soviet Solution," *Stanford Law Review* 12:6 (1950): 635.

22. Berman, *Justice,* 30–33.

23. Ibid., 43–50.

24. Ibid., 47; Berman and Hunt, "Criminal Law," 635.

25. See ch. 5 above.

26. Joseph Stalin, "Foundations of Leninism" [1924], in *Problems of Leninism,* 105–6.

27. Joseph Stalin, Political Report of the Central Committee to the Sixteenth Party Congress, in *Leninism* (New York: International Publishers, 1933), 2:402.

28. Stalin, Report to the Seventeenth Congress, 631.

29. See Joseph Stalin, "On the Draft Constitution of the USSR" [report delivered at the Extraordinary Eighth Congress of Soviets of the USSR, 25 Nov. 1936], in *Problems of Leninism*, 683.

30. See *History of the CPSU (B): Short Course* (New York: International Publishers, 1939), 346–48.

31. Ibid., 793–94.

32. Joseph Stalin, Concluding Remarks at the Fifteenth Party Conference, *International Press Correspondence*, 25 Nov. 1926, 1350.

33. M. J. Shore, *Soviet Education* (New York: Philosophical Library, 1947), 189.

34. Ibid., 138–41; V. I. Lenin, "Pages from a Diary" [Jan. 1923], in *Selected Works* (Moscow: Foreign Languages Publishing House, 1952), vol. 2, bk. 2, pp. 709–14.

35. Shore, *Soviet Education,* 144.

36. Ibid., 155.

37. Bauer, *New Man,* 43.

38. Shore, *Soviet Education,* 156–61.

39. Ibid., 172–74, 191–92; Timasheff, *Great Retreat,* 213–14; Bauer, *New Man,* 45.

40. Bauer, *New Man,* 94–96.

41. Timasheff, *Great Retreat,* 214–18.

42. Bauer, *New Man,* 124; Shore, *Soviet Education,* 176–79.

43. Shore, *Soviet Education,* 193–95.

44. Timasheff, *Great Retreat,* 195.

45. For the texts of laws and for much interesting Soviet commentary, see Rudolph Schlesinger, ed., *Changing Attitudes in Soviet Russia: The Family in the USSR* (London: Routledge & Kegan Paul, 1949). This is a collection of source materials that vividly documents the shifts in official social policies.

46. *Pravda*, 28 May 1936, cited in Schlesinger, *Changing Attitudes*, 252.

47. S. Vol'fson, "Socialism and the Family" [in Russian], *Pod znamenem marksizma*, no. 6 (1936): 64.

48. *Sotsialisticheskaya zakonnost'*, no. 2 (1939), cited in Timasheff, *Great Retreat*, 198.

49. *Komsomolskaya pravda*, 4 June 1935, cited in Timasheff, *Great Retreat*, 202.

50. Leon Trotsky, *The Revolution Betrayed* (New York: Doubleday Doran, 1937), 151–52.

51. Timasheff, *Great Retreat*, 317–18.

52. Ibid., 317.

53. Schlesinger, *Changing Attitudes*, 22; Alex Inkeles, "Family and Church in the Postwar USSR," *Annals of the American Academy of Political and Social Science*, May 1949, 38.

54. See Timasheff, *Great Retreat*, 228–29.

55. Nicholas S. Timasheff, *Religion in Soviet Russia* (London: Sheed & Ward, 1943), 65.

56. See Barrington Moore, *Soviet Politics: The Dilemma of Power* (Cambridge, Mass.: Harvard University Press, 1950), 183.

57. Joseph Stalin, "New Conditions, New Tasks in Economic Construction" [speech delivered at a conference of business executives, 23 June 1931], in *Problems of Leninism*, 464.

58. Moore, *Soviet Politics*, 185, 445n99.

59. Joseph Stalin, "Address to the Graduates from the Red Army Academies" [4 May 1935], in *Problems of Leninism*, 662; Moore, *Soviet Politics*, 238–39.

60. See Rudolph Schlesinger, *The Spirit of Post-war Russia* (London: Dobson, 1947), 123–24, for an apologist's admissions.

61. See Joseph Stalin, "New Conditions, New Tasks," in *Problems of Leninism*, 471–76.

62. See Schlesinger, *Spirit*, 40.

63. Joseph Stalin, "On the Draft Constitution," in *Problems of Leninism*, 683–86.

64. Schlesinger, *Spirit*, 40.

65. Merle Fainsod, *How Russia Is Ruled* (Cambridge, Mass.: Harvard University Press, 1953), 226, 246.

66. G. F. Malenkov, Report to the Eighteenth Party Conference, "On the Tasks of Party Organizations in the Field of Industry and Transportation" [in Russian], *Pravda*, 16 Feb. 1941.

67. Alex Inkeles, "Social Stratification and Mobility in the Soviet Union," *American Sociological Review* 15:4 (1950): 477.

68. Shore, *Soviet Education*, 193–95.

69. See Merle Fainsod, "The Komsomols: A Study of Youth under Dictatorship," *American Political Science Review* 45:1 (1951).

70. See F. Beck [pseud.] and W. Godin [pseud.], *Russian Purge and the Extraction of Confession* (New York: Viking, 1951).

71. Ibid.; cf. Henry Dicks, "Observations on Contemporary Russian Behavior," *Human Relations* 5:2 (1952): 130–31.

Chapter 21. Stalinism and Russian Political Culture

This chapter is based on my commentary "Russian Political Culture and the Postrevolutionary Impasse," *Russian Review* 16:2 (1987).

1. See Edward Keenan, "Muscovite Political Folkways," *Russian Review* 15:2 (1986).

2. Edward Tyler, *Primitive Culture* [1871], quoted in Robert C. Tucker, "Culture, Political Culture, and Communist Society," *Political Science Quarterly* 88:2 (1973): 173.

3. See Lucian W. Pye and Sidney Verba, eds., *Political Culture and Political Development* (Princeton: Princeton University Press, 1965); Gabriel A. Almond and Sidney Verba, *The Civic Culture: Political Attitudes and Democracy in Five Nations, an Analytical Study* (Boston: Little, Brown, 1965).

4. See A. H. Brown, *Soviet Politics and Political Science* (London: Macmillan, 1974); Archie Brown and Jack Gray, eds., *Political Culture and Political Change in Communist States* (New York: Holmes & Meier, 1977); Stephen White, *Political Culture and Soviet Politics* (New York: St. Martin's, 1979).

5. The two conceptions of political culture are contrasted by Tucker, "Culture,"176–77, and by Mary McAuley in "Political Culture and Communist Politics: One Step Forward, Two Steps Back," in Archie Brown, ed., *Political Culture and Communist Studies* (London: Macmillan, 1984), 14.

6. Ralph Linton, *The Cultural Background of Personality* (New York: Appleton-Century, 1945), 38; Clyde Kluckhohn and William H. Kelly, "The Concept of Culture," in Kluckhohn, *Culture and Behavior: Collected Essays* (Glencoe, Ill.: Free Press, 1962), 62–63.

7. Vilfredo Pareto, *The Mind and Society,* vols. 2 and 3 (New York: Hancourt, Brace, 1935).

8. Keenan, "Folkways," 116.

9. See Archie Brown, introduction, and Stephen White, "The USSR: Patterns of Autocracy and Industrialism," in Brown and Gray, *Political Culture,* 14–15, 35–38; Gabriel Almond, "Communism and Political Culture Theory," *Comparative Politics* 15:2 (1983): 131.

10. See, e.g., Frederick Barghoorn, "Soviet Russia: Orthodoxy and Adaptiveness," in Pye and Verba, *Political Culture.*

11. Lev Kopelev, "A Lie Is Conquered Only by Truth," in Roy Medvedev, ed., *Samizdat Register* (London) 1:227 (1977): 237, quoted in McAuley, "Political Culture," 32–33.

12. Keenan, "Folkways," 169.

13. See, e.g., Phyllis P. Kohler, ed., *Custine's Eternal Russia: A New Edition of Journey for Our Time* (Miami: University of Miami Center for Advanced International Studies, 1976).

14. Stephen White, "The USSR: Patterns of Autocracy and Industrialism," in Brown and Gray, *Political Culture,* 25.

15. Keenan, "Folkways," 135–38, 141–42.

16. Yuri Glazov, *The Russian Mind since Stalin's Death* (Dordrecht: Reidel/Kluwer, 1985), 222.

17. Keenan, "Folkways," 125–31.

18. Piero Ostellino, *In che cosa credono i russi?* (Milan: Longanesi, 1982), 17.

19. Keenan, "Folkways," 119.

20. Ibid., 127–28.

21. Ibid., 118.

22. See Gyula Jozsa, "Political Seilschaften in the USSR," in T. H. Rigby and Bohdan Harasymiw, eds., *Leadership Selection and Patron-Client Relations in the USSR and Yugoslavia* (London: Allen & Unwin, 1983).

23. See "Conflict and Authority" [discussion with Carl Linden, T. H. Rigby, and Robert Conquest], *Problems of Communism* 12:5 (1963), continued as "How Strong Is Khrushchev?" 12:6 (1963); H. Gordon Skilling and Franklyn Griffiths, eds., *Interest Groups in Soviet Politics* (Princeton: Princeton University Press, 1970); ch. 26 below.

24. Keenan, "Folkways," 145.

25. Ibid., 133–34. See below, ch. 27; Robert V. Daniels, "Evolution of Leadership Selection in the Central Committee, 1917–1927," in Walter M. Pintner and Don K. Rowney, eds., *Russian Officialdom: The Bureaucratization of Russian Society from the Seventeenth to the Twentieth Century* (Chapel Hill: University of North Carolina Press, 1980); Graeme Gill, "Institutionalization and Revolution: Rules and the Soviet Political System," *Soviet Studies* 26:2 (1985).

26. Keenan, "Folkways," 145.

27. Alain Besançon, "Soviet Present and Russian Past," *Encounter* 50:3 (1978), 89.

28. Edward Allworth, "Ambiguities in Russian Group Identity and Leadership of the RSFSR," in Allworth, ed., *Ethnic Russia in the USSR* (New York: Pergamon, 1980), 34.

29. For a more recent example, see "Yuri Lyubimov, Director in Exile," *Washington Post*, 10 Mar. 1985.

30. Karl Federn, *Zur Psychologie der Revolution: Die vaterlose Gesellschaft* (Leipzig and Vienna: Anzengruber, 1919).

31. Alberto Ronchey, in *Corriere della sera*, 12 Mar. 1985.

32. Michal Reiman, "Spontaneity and Planning in the Plebian Revolution," in R. Carter Elwood, ed., *Reconsiderations on the Russian Revolution* (Cambridge, Mass.: Slavica, 1976).

33. Theodore Shanin, personal communication, 1985. See Robert V. Daniels, *The Conscience of the Revolution: Communist Opposition in Soviet Russia* (Cambridge, Mass.: Harvard University Press, 1960), 304–311; Sheila Fitzpatrick, "Stalin and the Making of the New Soviet Elite, 1928–1939," *Slavic Review* 38:3 (1979).

34. Jack Gray, "Conclusions," in Brown and Gray, *Political Culture*, 260.

Chapter 22. Stalinist Ideology as False Consciousness

This chapter is based on my paper of the same title prepared for the Feltrinelli Colloquium, Cortona, Italy, Apr. 1989, and first published in the proceedings of the colloquium, Marcello Flores and Francesca Gori, eds., *Il mito dell'URSS: La cultura occidentale e l'Unione Sovietica* (Milan: Franco Angeli, 1990).

1. Giuseppe Boffa, *Storia dell'Unione Sovietica* (Milan: Mondadori, 1976), 1:613. The "Short Course" was published in English as *History of the Communist Party of the Soviet Union (Bolsheviks): Short Course* (New York: International Publishers, 1939).

2. Resolution of the Second All-Union Conference of Marxist-Leninist Scientific Research Institutions, Apr. 1929, "On Contemporary Problems of the Philosophy of Marxism-Leninism" [in Russian], *Pod znamenem marksizma*, no. 5 (1929): 7–8.

3. Joseph Stalin, "Some Questions concerning the History of Bolshevism," in *Problems of Leninism* (Moscow: Foreign Languages Publishing House, 1953), 483–84.

4. See Vilfredo Pareto, *The Mind and Society* (New York: Harcourt, Brace, 1935), 3:1421–32.

5. Anton Pannekoek, in *De Arbeidersraden* (Amsterdam: Van Gennep De Vlam, 1946), and Bruno Rizzi, in *La bureaucratisation du monde* (Paris: Hachette, 1939), were among the first writers to advance this argument. A more recent version is Michael Voslensky, *Nomenklatura: The Soviet Ruling Class* (Garden City, N.Y.: Doubleday, 1984), 112–18.

6. See ch. 4 above.

7. Svetozar Stojanović, "Marxism and Democracy: The Ruling Class or the Dominant Class?" *Praxis International* 6:2 (1981); Antonio Gramsci, "Notes on Italian History," in *Selections from the Prison Notebooks of Antonio Gramsci,* ed. Quentin Hoare and G. N. Smith (New York: International Publishers, 1971), 104–5. Pareto anticipated the distinction when he wrote of "governing elites and non-governing elites." *The Mind and Society,* 3:1423.

8. Karl Mannheim, *Ideology and Utopia: An Introduction to the Sociology of Knowledge* (Bonn, 1929; New York: Harcourt, Brace, 1936), 70–71.

9. Ibid., 71–72.

10. See George Lichtheim, *The Concept of Ideology and Other Essays* (New York: Random House, 1967), 15.

11. Karl Marx and Friedrich Engels, *The German Ideology* (New York: International Publishers, 1947), 39–41.

12. Friedrich Engels to Franz Mehring, 14 July 1893, in Karl Marx and Friedrich Engels, *Selected Correspondence, 1846–1895* (New York: International Publishers, 1942), 511–12. Cf. Melvin Rader, *Marx's Interpretation of History* (New York: Oxford University Press, 1979), 42.

13. Georgi Plekhanov, *The Materialist Conception of History* (New York: International Publishers, 1940), 34.

14. Eduard Bernstein, *Evolutionary Socialism* (1904; New York: Schocken, 1961), 205.

15. Aleksandr Bogdanov, *Empiriomonizm* (St. Petersburg: Dorovatovsky & Charushnikov, 1905), 1:40–41. Cf. Zenovia Sochor, *Revolution and Culture: The Bogdanov-Lenin Controversy* (Ithaca, N.Y.: Cornell University Press, 1988), 68–72.

16. See Massimo L. Salvadori, *Karl Kautsky and the Socialist Revolution, 1880–1938* (London: New Left, 1979), esp. 261.

17. Otto Bauer, *Kapitalismus und Sozialismus nach dem Weltkrieg* (Vienna, 1921), 154, quoted in Christine Buci-Glucksman, "L'Austro-marxisme," in Lily Marcou, ed., *L'Urss vue de gauche* (Paris: Presses Universitaires de France, 1982), 90.

18. Salvadori, *Karl Kautsky,* 288–92; Karl Kautsky, *Der Bolschewismus in der Sackgasse* (Berlin: Dietz, 1930), 65–69, and "The Prospects for Socialism in Soviet Russia" [in German], *Die Gesellschaft* 8:2 (1931): 437–38.

19. See Tom Bottomore, "Class Structure and Social Consciousness," in Istvan Meszaros, ed., *Aspects of History and Class Consciousness* (London: Routledge & Kegan Paul, 1971), 52.

20. Morris Watnick, "Georg Lukács: An Intellectual Biography," *Soviet Survey,* July–Sept. 1958, 63.

21. Antonio Gramsci, "Problems of Philosophy and History," in *Prison Notebooks,* 376.

22. Antonio Gramsci, "Some Problems in the Study of the Philosophy of Praxis," in *Prison Notebooks,* 406–7.

23. Leon Trotsky, *The Revolution Betrayed: What Is the Soviet Union and Where Is It Going?* (New York: Doubleday, Doran, 1937), 238, 244–45, 255.

24. Rizzi, *Bureaucratisation*, 29–35.

25. James Burnham, *The Managerial Revolution* (New York: John Day, 1941), 65, 185.

26. Milovan Djilas, *The New Class: An Analysis of the Communist System* (New York: Praeger, 1957), 47, 124.

27. George Konrad and Ivan Szelenyi, *The Intellectuals on the Road to Class Power* (New York: Harcourt Brace Jovanovich, 1979), 14.

28. Veljko Korać, "Socialism in Underdeveloped Countries," *Praxis*, nos. 2–3 (1964): 301.

29. Najdan Pašić, "The Essence and Meaning of the Struggle of the Yugoslav Communists against Stalinism" [in Serbo-Croatian], *Socijalizam* (Belgrade) 12:5 (1969): 634.

30. Svetozar Stojanović, *Izmedju ideala i stvarnosti* (Belgrade: Prosveta, 1969), 13.

31. Stojanović, "Marxism and Democracy," 106.

32. Branko Horvat, *The Political Economy of Socialism: A Marxist Social Theory* (Armonk, N.Y.: M. E. Sharpe, 1982), 28–29, 43–46.

33. Zagorka Golubović, *Staljinizam i Socijalizam* (Belgrade: Philosophical Society of Serbia, 1982), 283.

34. Boffa, *Storia dell'Unione Sovietica*, 2: 595.

35. Giuseppe Boffa, *Il fenomeno Stalin nella storia del XX secolo: Le interpretazioni dello Stalinismo* (Rome-Bari: Laterza, 1982), 259–60.

36. Roy Medvedev, *Let History Judge: The Origins and Consequences of Stalinism* (New York: Knopf, 1971), 362, 363, 375, 418.

37. Roy Medvedev, *On Soviet Dissent: Interviews with Piero Ostellino* (New York: Columbia University Press, 1980), 88, 146.

38. *Neva* (Leningrad), no. 7 (July 1988); Zbigniew Safjan, quoted in *New York Times*, 15 July 1988.

39. Mannheim, *Ideology and Utopia*, 55–56.

40. Martin Seliger, *Ideology and Politics* (New York: Free Press, 1976), 14.

41. See Paul Ricoeur, *Lectures on Ideology and Utopia* (New York: Columbia University Press, 1986), esp. 119–20, 254–58.

42. Rudolf Bahro, *The Alternative in Eastern Europe* (New York: Schocken, 1978), 247.

43. Georg Lukács, "Reflections on the Cult of Stalin," in *Marxism and Human Liberation: Essays on History, Culture, and Revolution by Georg Lukács*, ed. E. San Juan (New York: Dell, 1973), 66–69.

44. Tatiana Zaslavskaya, "Viewpoint: Perestroika as a Social Revolution" [*Izvestiya*, 24 Dec. 1988], translated in *Current Digest of the Soviet Press*, 18 Jan. 1989, 2–3.

Chapter 23. Was Stalin Really a Communist?

This chapter is based on my article of the same title in *Soviet and Post-Soviet Review* 20:2–3 (1995).

1. Aleksandr Tsipko, "The Roots of Stalinism" [in Russian], *Nauka I zhizn'*, no. 11 (1988).

2. George F. Kennan, *Russia and the West under Lenin and Stalin* (Boston: Little, Brown, 1961), 254.

3. Lev Kamenev, Notes on conversation with Bukharin [11 July 1928, copy in Trotsky Archive, Harvard University, doc. T1897], extracts translated in Robert V. Daniels,

A Documentary History of Communism in Russia, 3rd ed. (Hanover, N.H.: University Press of New England, 1993), 164; Georg Lukács, "Reflections on the Cult of Stalin," in *Marxism and Human Liberation: Essays on History, Culture, and Revolution by Georg Lukács,* ed. E. San Juan (New York: Dell, 1973), 66.

Chapter 24. Khrushchev and the Party Apparatus

This chapter is based in part on my article "The Soviet Succession: Lenin and Stalin," *Russian Review,* July 1953; in part on my essay "Khrushchev and Gorbachev—Similarity and Difference," in Theodore Taranovsky, ed., *Reform in Modern Russian History: Progress or Cycle?* (Washington and Cambridge: Woodrow Wilson Center Press and Cambridge University Press, 1995, from a conference at the Kennan Institute for Advanced Russian Studies, May 1990); and in part on the hitherto unpublished text of a paper I presented at a meeting of the Mid-West Slavic Conference, Columbus, Ohio, Mar. 1966, "Khrushchev and the Party Secretaries" (deriving from a complete tabulation of appointments and removals of republic and provincial party secretaries from 1953 to 1961).

1. See ch. 32 below.
2. Robert Conquest, *Power and Policy in the USSR: The Study of Soviet Dynastics* (London: Macmillan, 1961), 390–92.

Chapter 25. Khrushchev and the Intelligentsia

This chapter is based on my paper "The Critical Intelligentsia and the Failure of Reform," prepared for the international conference of the Feltrinelli Foundation and the Gramsci Institute, Florence, Oct. 1986, and published in the conference proceedings, Francesca Gori, ed., *Il XX Congresso del Pcus* (Milan: Franco Angeli, 1988).

1. Edward Keenan, "Muscovite Political Folkways," *Russian Review* 15:2 (1986). See chapter 21 above.
2. Alexander Herzen, "The Russian People and Socialism: An Open Letter to Jules Michelet," in *From the Other Shore* (London: Weidenfeld & Nicolson, 1956), 199, 203.
3. Valery Chalidze, "Andrei Sakharov and the Russian Intelligentsia" [speech to the Sakharov Symposium of the American Physical Society, 26 Jan. 1981], in Edward D. Lozansky, ed., *Andrei Sakharov and Peace* (New York: Avon, 1985), 308–9.
4. Vladimir Shlapentokh, *Soviet Public Opinion and Ideology: Mythology and Pragmatism in Interaction* (New York: Praeger, 1986), 45.
5. Boris Shragin, *The Challenge of the Spirit* (New York: Knopf, 1978), 153.
6. Kathryn Feuer, "Russia's Young Intellectuals," *Encounter* 8:2 (1957), 10.
7. *Pravda,* 19 Apr. 1987.
8. L. I. Brezhnev, Report of the CPSU Central Committee to the Twenty-Sixth Congress of the CPSU, *Pravda,* 24 Feb. 1981.
9. Feuer, "Russian's Young Intellectuals," 11.
10. Alexander Solzhenitsyn, *The Oak and the Calf: Sketches of Literary Life in the Soviet Union* (New York: Harper & Row, 1980), 10.

11. Svetozar Stojanović, "Marxism and Democracy: The Ruling Class or the Dominant Class?" *Praxis International* 1:2 (1981).

12. *Ogonyok*, 11 July 1987.

13. Isabelle Esmein, "Chronological View of Relations between the Intellectuals and the Party in the USSR before and after the Fall of M. Khrushchev" [in French], *Cahiers du monde russe et soviétique* 6 (Oct.–Dec. 1965): 561.

14. Ilya Ehrenburg, *The Thaw* (Chicago: Regnery, 1955).

15. Leo Gruliow, ed., *Current Soviet Policies* (New York: Praeger, 1953), 115.

16. Robert Conquest, *Power and Policy in the USSR: The Study of Soviet Dynastics* (London: Macmillan, 1961), 248.

17. George Gibian, *Interval of Freedom: Soviet Literature during the Thaw* (Minneapolis: University of Minnesota Press, 1960), 9.

18. Ibid., 11–12.

19. Lev Kamenev, Notes on conversation with Bukharin [11 July 1928, copy in Trotsky Archive, Harvard University, doc. T1897], extracts translated in Robert V. Daniels, ed., *A Documentary History of Communism in Russia*, 3rd ed. (Hanover, N.H.: University Press of New England, 1993), 164.

20. *Current Soviet Policies* 2 (1957): 61.

21. Ibid., 86.

22. Ibid., 118.

23. See Edith R. Frankel, *Novy Mir: A Case Study in the Politics of Literature, 1952–58* (Cambridge: Cambridge University Press, 1981), 78.

24. Solzhenitsyn, *The Oak and the Calf*, 9.

25. B. A. Nazarov and O. V. Gridneva, "On the Problem of the Lag in Drama and Theater" [*Voprosy filosofii*, no. 5 (1956)], translated in *Current Digest of the Soviet Press*, 19 Dec. 1956, 3–4, 6–8.

26. Gibian, *Interval of Freedom*, 13–15; Vladimir Dudintsev, *Not by Bread Alone* (New York: Dutton, 1957).

27. *Pravda*, 2 Feb. 1959, translated in *Current Soviet Policies* 3:133–34.

28. *Pravda*, 24 May 1959, translated in *Current Digest of the Soviet Press*, 24 June 1957; Ronald Hingley, "The Soviet Writers Congress," *Soviet Survey*, July–Sept. 1959, 14–16.

29. Peter Benno, "The Political Aspect," in Max Hayward and Edward J. Crowley, eds., *Soviet Literature in the Sixties* (London: Methuen, 1965), 181.

30. *Literaturnaya gazeta*, 19 Sept. 1961, translated in *Current Digest of the Soviet Press*, 4 Oct. 1961, 18.

31. Abraham Rothberg, *The Heirs of Stalin: Dissidence and the Soviet Regime, 1953–1970* (Ithaca, N.Y.: Cornell University Press, 1972), 56–57, 394–95.

32. *Ogonyok*, 9 Feb. 1987.

33. See chs. 6 above and 28 below.

34. Recounted by a Western diplomat to Michel Tatu. *Power in the Kremlin from Khrushchev to Kosygin* (New York: Viking, 1969), 306.

35. Priscilla Johnson, *Khrushchev and the Arts: The Politics of Soviet Culture, 1962–1964* (Cambridge, Mass.: MIT Press, 1965), 7–9. The purported transcript of Khrushchev's remarks first appeared in *Encounter* 28:4 (1963), 102–3. Johnson, seconded by Rothberg (*Heirs*

of Stalin, 62, 396n3), suspected that the Manezh affair was either a conservative provocation or a stage-managed maneuver by Khrushchev himself.

36. *Pravda,* 10 Mar. 1963, translated in *Current Digest of the Soviet Press,* 10 Apr. 1963, 10.

37. Solzhenitsin, *The Oak and the Calf,* 70–72.

Chapter 26. The Fall of Khrushchev and the Advent of Participatory Bureaucracy

This chapter is drawn in part from a lecture delivered in a 1968 Carleton University series and published as "Soviet Politics since Khrushchev," in John W. Strong, ed, *The Soviet Union under Brezhnev and Kosygin* (New York: Van Nostrand Reinhold, 1971); and in part from my paper "Participatory Bureaucracy and the Soviet Political System," presented at a symposium of the Washington chapter of the American Association for the Advancement of Slavic Studies, Apr. 1971, and published in the proceedings of the symposium, Norton T. Dodge, ed., *Analysis of the 24th Party Congress and 9th Five-Year Plan* (Mechanicsville, Md.: Cremona Foundation, 1971).

1. Carl Linden, *Khrushchev and the Soviet Leadership* (Baltimore, Md.: Johns Hopkins University Press, 1966).

2. See, e.g., Victor A. Thompson, *Modern Organization: A General Theory* (New York: Knopf, 1961).

3. John Kenneth Galbraith, *The New Industrial State* (New York: Harcourt, Brace, 1967).

Chapter 27. The Central Committee as a Bureaucratic Elite

This chapter is based on my essay "Office Holding and Elite Status: The Central Committee of the CPSU," in Paul Cocks, Robert V. Daniels, and Nancy Whittier Heer, eds., *The Dynamics of Soviet Politics* (Cambridge, Mass.: Harvard University Press, 1976).

1. See Michael P. Gehlen and Michael McBride, "The Soviet Central Committee: An Elite Analysis," *American Political Science Review* 62 (1968): 1232–41; Robert H. Donaldson and Derek J. Waller, "The 1956 Central Committees of the Chinese and Soviet Communist Parties: A Comparative Analysis of Elite Composition and Change" (paper presented at the American Political Science Association, Los Angeles, Sept. 1970).

2. See, e.g., Robert H. Donaldson, "The 1971 Soviet Central Committee: An Assessment of the New Elite," *World Politics* 14 (Apr. 1972); Frederick Fleron, "Representation of Career Types in Soviet Political Leadership," and Michael P. Gehlen, "The Soviet Apparatchiki,"in R. Barry Farrell, ed., *Political Leadership in Eastern Europe and the Soviet Union* (Chicago: Aldine, 1970); Vincent E. McHale and Joseph H. Mastro, "The Central Committee of the CPSU: Analysis of Composition and Long-Term Trends" (paper presented at the American Political Science Association, Los Angeles, Sept. 1970).

3. See Frederick Fleron, "Towards a Reconceptualization of Political Change in the Soviet Union," in Fleron, ed., *Communist Studies and the Social Sciences* (Chicago: Rand McNally, 1969), 235; Robert Conquest, *Power and Policy in the USSR: The Study of Soviet*

Dynasties (London: Macmillan, 1961), 35; Donaldson and Waller, "Central Committees," 2; Zbigniew Brzezinski and Samuel P. Huntington, "Cincinnatus and the Apparatchik," *World Politics* 6 (Oct. 1963).

4. A major exception is the analyses prepared for Radio Liberty by Christian Deuvel and his associates. See, e.g., "Who Has the 'Right' to Election to the Leading Organs of the Party at the 24th Congress of the CPSU?" *Radio Liberty Research*, 25 Feb. 1971. ("The right to a seat in the central organs is given by definite offices.") Another exception is Darrell P. Hammer, *USSR: The Politics of Oligarchy* (Hinsdale, Ill.: Holt, Rinehart & Winston, 1974), 190. ("Members of the Central Committee . . . in current practice . . . are chosen on the basis of the positions they hold.")

5. See ch. 26 above. Evidence of these rules of promotion and demotion was developed in Peter D. Coburn, "The Central Committee of the Communist Party of the Soviet Union: Patterns and Politics, 1952 to 1971" (master's thesis, University of Vermont, 1975), 25–30.

6. Contrary to McHale and Mastro, "Central Committee," 5, it was not election to the Central Committee that conferred elite status but appointment to the Central Committee–level job with its assurance of subsequent election to the Central Committee.

7. There is good reason to believe that the same principles of job-slot composition and status representation operated down through the entire system of party committees at the republic, provincial, and local levels. See Hammer, *USSR*, 154.

8. The status of Moscow, deducible from Central Committee ranking practices, is indicative of both the fine sense of status involved in Central Committee membership and the analytical value of the status concept. As of 1971, the first secretary of Moscow City (V. V. Grishin) was a member of the Politburo; the first secretary of the province (V. I. Konotop) was a mere Central Committee member, as was the second secretary of the city (L. I. Grekov). The second secretary of the province (V. S. Paputin) was merely a candidate member. The third and fourth secretaries of the city, R. F. Demetieva (incidentally representing women) and V. M. Yagodkin, were candidate members; the third secretary of the province had no Central Committee status at all. It follows that the party administration of the city could not be subordinate to that of the province but in fact had an independent and higher status. In Leningrad, by contrast, though its representation was consistent with its status as the second-most important center in the country, the assignment of seats made it clear that the city was secondary to the province (first and second secretaries of the province on the Central Committee but only the first secretary of the city; second secretary of the city merely on the Central Auditing Commission). It may be further noted that Leningrad Province, subsuming the city, had more status (two full Central Committee memberships) than Moscow Province excluding the capital city (only one full membership).

Chapter 28. The Generational Revolution

This chapter is based on my essay "Political Processes and Generational Change," in Archie Brown, ed., *Political Leadership in the Soviet Union* (London: Macmillan, 1989), used with permission of Palgrave Macmillan.

1. See T. H. Rigby, "The Soviet Political Executive, 1917–1986," and John H. Miller, "Putting Clients in Place: The Role of Patronage in Cooption into the Soviet Leadership," in Brown, *Political Leadership*. See also ch. 26 above.

2. See Stephen White, *Political Culture and Soviet Politics* (New York: St. Martin's, 1979), esp. chs. 2 and 3; also Stephen White, "The USSR: Patterns of Autocracy and Industrialism," in Archie Brown and Jack Gray, eds., *Political Culture and Political Change in Communist States* (New York: Holmes & Meier, 1977). See also ch. 21 above.

3. The generational phenomenon is described in Seweryn Bialer, *Stalin's Successors: Leadership, Stability, and Change in the Soviet Union* (Cambridge: Cambridge University Press, 1980), 59–61, 86–89. Jerry Hough, *Soviet Leadership in Transition* (Washington, D.C.: Brookings Institution Press, 1980), 37–60, distinguishes four "generations," or more accurately subgenerations, in the postwar Soviet leadership, based on their differing experiences of the purges and the war—the "Brezhnev generation," born in 1900–9, who benefited most from the purges; the slower-moving but better-educated cohort of 1910–18; the wartime group born in 1919–25, whose educations again fell short; and the postwar generation, born after 1925, a true elite educationally, and moreover less scarred by Stalinism. The "postpurge" generation described here is primarily Hough's first group and secondarily the second.

4. See T. H. Rigby, "Was Stalin a Disloyal Patron?" *Soviet Studies* 37:3 (1986).

5. This calculation assumes that the nine one-time members whose birth year is unknown were distributed equally above and below the median. If they were preponderantly younger, the median would have been forty-eight. Practically all ages of full members in subsequent cohorts are known. The time of year is ignored in computing median ages. Median ages are used in this analysis in preference to mean ages as a more meaningful reflection of the balance of older and younger individuals.

6. Sheila Fitzpatrick, "Stalin and the Making of the New Elite, 1928–1939," *Slavic Review* 38:3 (1979): 377–402.

7. Edward Keenan, "Muscovite Political Folkways," *Russian Review* 45:2 (1986), 167–69.

8. See ch. 27 above.

9. Risto Bajalski, Moscow correspondent of *Politika* (Belgrade), personal communication, Sept. 1988.

10. A more extensive statement of this proposition is John H. Kress, "Representation of Positions on the CPSU Politburo," *Slavic Review* 39:2 (1980): 218–38.

11. See ch. 26 above.

12. Bialer, in *Stalin's Successors* (122–23), notes the surprising frequency of youthful (fortyish) first secretaries of provinces.

13. Keenan, "Folkways," 170.

14. See Miller, "Putting Clients in Place."

15. See Archie Brown, "Andropov: Discipline *and* Reform?" *Problems of Communism*, Jan.–Feb. 1983.

16. Seweryn Bialer, "The Political System," in Robert F. Byrnes, ed., *After Brezhnev: Sources of Soviet Conduct in the 1980s* (Bloomington: Indiana University Press, 1983), 23.

Chapter 29. Reform and the Intelligentsia

This chapter is based on the English original of my article "Il potere e l'intellighentsia," *Transizione* (Bologna), Oct. 1988.

1. *Pravda*, 30 Mar. 1966.

2. *Ogonyok,* 9 Feb. 1987.

3. Deming Brown, *Soviet Russian Literature since Stalin* (Cambridge: Cambridge University Press, 1978), 18–19.

4. Mikhail Suslov, Speech to the All-Union Academy of Sciences [17 Mar. 1976], quoted in John Turkevich, "How Science Policy Is Formed," *Survey* 26:6 (1977–78), 115.

5. Cyril R. Black, "New Soviet Thinking," *New York Times,* 24 Nov. 1978.

6. *Pravda,* 17 July 1955, quoted in Julian M. Cooper, "The Scientific and Technical Revolution in Soviet Theory," in Frederick J. Fleron, ed., *Technology and Communist Culture: The Socio-Cultural Impact of Technology under Socialism* (New York: Praeger, 1977), 153.

7. Alexander Vucinich, *Empire of Knowledge: The Academy of Sciences of the USSR, 1917–1970* (Berkeley: University of California Press, 1984), 359, 361.

8. Eugene Zaleski et al., *Science Policy in the USSR* (Paris: OECD, 1960), 571.

9. Jerry F. Hough and Merle Fainsod, *How the Soviet Union Is Governed* (Cambridge, Mass.: Harvard University Press, 1979), 286.

10. Zaleski et al., *Science Policy,* 561.

11. Zhores A. Medvedev, *Soviet Science* (New York: Norton, 1978), 67.

12. V. G. Afanasiev, *The Scientific and Technological Revolution: Its Impact on Management and Education* (Moscow: Progress Publishers, 1975), 294.

13. Vucinich, *Empire of Knowledge,* 294.

14. Afanasiev, *Scientific and Technological Revolution,* 295.

15. Medvedev, *Soviet Science,* 196–98.

16. Afanasiev, *Scientific and Technological Revolution,* 295–97.

17. Robert W. Campbell, *Soviet Scientific and Technological Education* (McLean, Va.: Science Applications International, 1985), 31.

18. Cited in Mark Popovsky, *Manipulated Science: The Crisis of Science and Scientists in the Soviet Union* (New York: Doubleday, 1979), 142–43.

19. Campbell, *Soviet Scientific and Technical Education,* 29, 46.

20. Interview with T. I. Zaslavskaya, *Argumenty i fakty,* 28 Mar.–3 Apr. 1987, 5.

21. Valentin Turchin, "Scientists among Soviet Dissidents," *Survey* 22:12 (1978), 87.

22. Erik Hoffmann, "Technology, Values, and Political Power in the Soviet Union: Do Computers Matter?" in Fleron, *Technology and Communist Culture,* 399.

23. Andrei Amalrik, *Will the Soviet Union Survive until 1984?* (New York: Harper & Row, 1970), 15.

24. See Ludmilla Alexeyeva, *Soviet Dissent: Contemporary Movements for National, Religious, and Human Rights* (Middletown, Conn.: Wesleyan University Press, 1985), 293–94.

25. Quoted in Abraham Rothberg, *The Heirs of Stalin: Dissidence and the Soviet Regime, 1953–1970* (Ithaca, N.Y.: Cornell University Press, 1972), 211.

26. Andrei Sakharov, *Progress, Coexistence, and Intellectual Freedom* (New York: Norton, 1968).

27. Zhores A. Medvedev, *The Rise and Fall of T. D. Lysenko* (New York: Columbia University Press, 1969).

28. Alexeyeva, *Soviet Dissent,* 293–94.

29. Ibid., 344–45.

30. Rumors of a five-to-four Politburo decision were supported in an article by the playwright Mikhail Shatrov, *Ogonyok,* 26 Jan. 1986.

31. Roy Medvedev and Giulietto Chiesa, *L'Urss che cambia* (Rome: Riuniti, 1987), 266.

32. Notes of Gorbachev's speech circulated in samizdat. See "Beseda chlenov SP SSSR s M. S. Gorbachevym," *Arkhiv samizdata* (Radio Liberty), no. 5785. A partial summary appeared in *Pravda,* 21 June 1986. Excerpts are translated in Robert V. Daniels, ed., *A Documentary History of Communism in Russia,* 3rd ed. (Hanover, N.H.: University Press of New England, 1993), 339–41.

33. Roy Medvedev, "The Second, Contested Thaw" [in Italian], *Rinascita* (Rome), 8 Nov. 1986, 6.

34. *Newsweek,* 9 June 1986.

35. *Literaturnaya gazeta,* 2 July 1986.

36. In a press conference at the Reykjavik summit meeting. *Radio Liberty Research,* no. 396/86, 4.

37. *Literaturnaya gazeta,* 25 Feb. 1987.

38. A. N. Yakovlev, Speech at a meeting of intelligentsia in Dushanbe, *Pravda,* 10 Apr. 1987.

39. *Archiv samizdata,* no. 5785, 5.

40. *Pravda,* 17 Jan. and 14 Feb. 1987.

41. *Pravda,* 5 Mar. 1987; *Sovetskaya kultura,* 7 July 1987.

42. Interview with Anatoly Butenko, *Moskovskaya pravda,* 7 May 1987.

43. *Pravda,* 7 Dec. 1986.

Chapter 30. Gorbachev's Opportunity

This chapter is based on the English original of my article "Il risveglio del rivoluzionario russo," *Rinascita* (Rome), 14 Feb. 1987, reprinted in Zdeněk Mlynář et al., *Il progetto Gorbaciov* (Rome: Rinascita, 1987).

1. Zdeněk Mlynář, "The Crossroads of Political Reform" [in Italian], *Rinascita,* 8 Nov. 1986.

2. M. S. Gorbachev, Speech at a conference of the Khabarovsk Territory party organization, 31 July 1986, *Pravda,* 2 Aug. 1986.

3. M. S. Gorbachev, Talk with citizens in Krasnodar [18 Sept. 1986], *Pravda,* 19 Sept. 1986.

4. "Conversation of Members of the Writers' Union of the USSR with M. S. Gorbachev" [in Russian], *Arkhiv samizdata,* no. 7585, 1, 6.

5. Tatiana Zaslavskaya, "The Novosibirsk Report," *Survey* 38:1 (1984), 88–89.

6. *L'unità,* 8 Mar. 1986.

7. Enrico Berlinguer, Statement on Italian television, 15 Dec. 1981.

8. Santiago Carrillo, *Eurocommunism and the State* (Westport, Conn.: Lawrence Hill, 1978), 172.

Chapter 31. Gorbachev and the Reversal of History

This chapter is based on a paper I prepared for the Olin Foundation Critical Issues Series at the Russian Research Center, Harvard University, Oct. 1988. Versions of it were published in *Global Economic Policy* 2:1 (1990); in Josef C. Brada and Michael P. Claudon, eds., *Reforming the Ruble: Monetary Aspects of Perestroika* (New York: NYU Press, 1990); and in *History Teacher*, May 1990.

1. Mikhail Gorbachev, Speech to a meeting of scientists and cultural figures, *Pravda*, 8 Jan. 1989.

2. Academician T. Zaslavskaya, "Questions of Theory: Restructuring and Sociology" [in Russian], *Pravda*, 6 Feb. 1987. Translations from Russian sources in this chapter are generally from *Current Digest of the Soviet Press*.

3. See Philip Taubman, "Envoys See Signs of Kremlin Rifts," *New York Times*, 23 Dec. 1987; Robert G. Kaiser, "Red Intrigue: How Gorbachev Outfoxed His Kremlin Rivals," *Washington Post*, 12 June 1988; Yegor K. Ligachev, Speech at the 19th CPSU Conference [1 July 1988], *Pravda*, 2 July 1988.

4. Nina Andreyeva, "I Cannot Forgo Principles" [in Russian], *Sovetskaya Rossiya*, 13 Mar. 1988.

5. "The Principles of Restructuring: The Revolutionary Nature of the New Thinking" [in Russian], *Pravda*, 5 Apr. 1988.

6. Gorbachev hinted at this shift as early as the January 1987 Plenum of the Central Committee. See his speech "On Restructuring and the Party's Personnel Policy" [in Russian], *Pravda*, 28 Jan. 1987. Cf. Philip Taubman, "Gorbachev, Citing Party's Failures, Demands Changes," *New York Times*, 30 Jan. 1987.

7. See *Radio Liberty Research*, RL238/88 (5 June 1988), RL237/88 (8 June 1988), and RL242/88 (10 June 1988).

8. See Andrei Sakharov, Press conference in Boston [7 Nov. 1988], *New York Times*, 8 Nov. 1988.

9. M. S. Gorbachev, Speech to leaders in the media and the creative unions [10 July 1987], *Pravda*, 15 July 1987. Cf. *Radio Liberty Research*, RL280/87 (16 July 1987).

10. Staff of the Institute of Marxism-Leninism, personal communication, Sept. 1988.

11. V. Krivosheyev, "August, 1968," *Moscow News*, 28 Aug. 1988.

12. See, e.g., "Reading Lenin: More Democracy" [in Russian], *Pravda*, 22 Apr. 1988; see also Bill Keller, "Kremlin Reinterprets and Re-emphasizes the Legacy of Lenin," *New York Times*, 10 May 1987.

13. See, most dramatically, the series by Aleksandr Tsipko, "The Roots of Stalinism" [in Russian], *Nauka i zhizn*, Nov. and Dec., 1988, Jan. and Feb. 1989; Yu. Olshevich, "Bridge to the 21st Century" [in Russian], *Pravda*, 12 Oct. 1989.

14. A. N. Yakovlev, "The Great French Revolution and the Present Day" [in Russian], *Sovetskaya kultura*, 15 July 1989, 3.

15. See, e.g., interview with V. I. Dashichev, "The Paths That Are Chosen for Us" [in Russian], *Komsomolskaya pravda*, 19 June 1988.

16. Mikhail Gorbachev, *Perestroika: New Thinking for Our Country and the World* (New York: Harper &Row, 1987), 146–47.

17. Vyacheslav I. Dashichev, "The Search for New East-West Relations" [in Russian], *Literaturnaya gazeta*, 18 May 1988.

18. See, e.g., Stanislav Kondrashev, "Conventional Forces" [in Russian], *Izvestiya*, 2 Apr. 1988.

19. Vadim Medvedev, "The Contemporary Conception of Socialism" [in Russian], *Pravda*, 5 Oct. 1988.

20. Len Karpinsky, personal communication, Apr. 1989.

21. Jeanne Kirkpatrick, "Dictatorships and Double Standards," *Commentary* 68:5 (1979).

22. Tatiana Zaslavskaya, "The Novosibirsk Report," *Survey* 27 (Spr. 1984), 99, 106.

23. See M. S. Gorbachev, Report to the Nineteenth Party Conference [28 June 1988], *Pravda*, 29 June 1988.

24. Ibid.

25. V. I. Lenin, "Answer to a Question of the Left SRs" [Central Executive Committee, 4 Nov. 1917; in Russian], in *Sochineniya*, 3rd ed. (Moscow: Marx-Engels-Lenin Institute, 1928–37), 22:45.

26. See ch. 30 above and ch. 32 below.

27. See Robert V. Daniels, *Russia—The Roots of Confrontation* (Cambridge, Mass.: Harvard University Press, 1985), 363–65.

Chapter 32. Soviet Federalism and the Breakup of the USSR

This chapter was originally prepared for the Hofstra University conference on government structures in the United States and the states of the former USSR, Apr. 1992, and published in the proceedings of the conference, James E. Hickey Jr. and Alexej Ugrinsky, eds., *Government Structures in the U.S.A. and the Sovereign States of the Former U.S.S.R.: Power Allocation among Central, Regional, and Local Governments* (Westport, Conn.: Greenwood, 1996). Copyright © 1996 by Hofstra University. Reproduced with permission of Greenwood Publishing Group, Inc., Westport, Conn.

1. See Draft Treaty of the Union of Sovereign Republics [in Russian], *Pravda* and *Izvestiya*, 9 Mar. 1991.

2. M. S. Gorbachev, Report to the Supreme Soviet, 16 Nov. 1990.

3. *Izvestiya*, 25 Apr. 1991.

4. Appeal to the Soviet People by the State Committee on the State of Emergency in the USSR [in Russian], *Pravda* and *Izvestiya*, 20 Aug. 1991.

5. Text in *New York Times*, 26 Dec. 1991.

6. *Newsweek*, 30 Dec. 1991, 21; John Morrison, *Boris Yeltsin: From Bolshevik to Democrat* (New York: Dutton, 1991), 290.

Chapter 33. The Revolutionary Process and the Moderate Revolutionary Revival

This chapter is based on my article "The Revolutionary Process, the Moderate Revolutionary Revival, and Post-Communist Russia," in Martine Godet, ed., *De Russie et d'ailleurs: Feux croisés sur l'histoire* (Paris: Institut d'Études Slaves, 1995). Copyright © Institut d'Études Slaves, Paris, 1995.

1. Alexander N. Yakovlev, "The Great French Revolution and the Present Day" [in Russian], *Sovetskaya kultura*, 15 July 1989.

2. M. S. Gorbachev, Speech at a meeting with representatives of the country's miners [3 Apr. 1991], *Pravda* and *Izvestiya*, 6 Apr. 1991.

3. Yakovlev, "The Great French Revolution."

4. Robert V. Daniels, *Russia—The Roots of Confrontation* (Cambridge, Mass.: Harvard University Press, 1985), 363.

5. See ch. 30 above.

6. See M. S. Gorbachev, Report to the Nineteenth Party Conference [28 June 1988], *Pravda*, 29 June 1988.

7. Yakovlev, "The Great French Revolution."

8. M. S. Gorbachev, Political report of the CPSU Central Committee to the 28th CPSU Congress [3 July 1990], *Pravda*, 4 July 1990.

Chapter 34. The Communist Oppositions and Post-Stalinist Reform

This chapter is based on the English original of my contribution "Die kommunistiche Opposition und der revolutionäre Prozess in post-kommunistische Persprecktive," in Wladislaw Hedeler, Mario Kessler, and Gert Schäfer, eds., *Ausblicke auf das vergangene Jahrhundert: Die Politik der internationale Arbeiterbewegung von 1900 bis 2000* (Hamburg: VSA-Verlag, 1996).

1. See ch. 6 above.

2. "Theses on the Present Moment" [4 Apr. 1918, in Russian], *Kommunist*, no. 1 (Apr. 1918), thesis 9.

3. V. V. Osinsky, Minority Report on Building the Economy, Ninth Congress of the Russian Communist Party: Protocols [in Russian] (Moscow: Party Press, 1934), 123.

4. Alexandra Kollontai, *The Workers' Opposition* (Chicago: IWW, 1921), 32–33.

5. See ch. 19 above.

6. V. I. Lenin, "Better Fewer, but Better" [Mar. 1923], in *Selected Works* (Moscow: Foreign Languages Publishing House, 1950–52), vol. 2, bk. 2, pp. 735, 751.

7. Lev Kamenev, Notes on conversation with Bukharin [11 July 1928, copy in Trotsky Archive, Harvard University, doc. T1897], extracts translated in Robert V. Daniels, ed., *A Documentary History of Communism in Russia*, 3rd ed. (Hanover, N.H.: University Press of New England, 1993), 164.

8. Robert V. Daniels, *The Conscience of the Revolution: Communist Opposition in Soviet Russia* (Cambridge, Mass.: Harvard University Press, 1960), 348–60, 495n32.

9. Stephen F. Cohen, *Bukharin and the Bolshevik Revolution: A Political Biography, 1888–1938* (New York: Knopf, 1971), 267.

10. Michal Reiman, *The Birth of Stalinism: The USSR on the Eve of the "Second Revolution"* (Bloomington: Indiana University Press, 1987), 119.

11. See Abel Aganbegyan, *The Economic Challenge of Perestroika* (Bloomington: Indiana University Press, 1987), 119.

12. See, e.g., "From the Party Archives: Intraparty Controversies of the 1920s. The Controversy of 1923" [in Russian], *Izvestiya TsK*, no. 5–7 (1990); M. M. Gorinov, "Alternatives and Crises in the Period of the NEP: On the Questions of the Social-Economic Problems of the Intraparty struggle in the 1920s" [in Russian], *Voprosy istorii KPSS*, no. 1 (1990); G.A. Bordiugov and V. A. Kozlov, *Istoriya i kon'yunktura: Sub'yektivnye zametki ob istorii sovetskogo obshchestva* (Moscow: Press for Political Literature, 1992).

13. Theodor Bergmann and Gert Schäfer, "Trotsky and Bukharin" [in German], in Bergmann and Schäfer, eds., *Leo Trotzki: Kritiker und Verteidiger der Sowjetgesellschaft* (Mainz: Decaton Verlag, 1993), 253.

14. Kamenev, Notes; Isaac Deutscher, *The Prophet Unarmed: Trotsky, 1921–1929* (London and New York: Oxford University Press, 1959), 315.

15. See Holland Hunter, "The Overambitious First Soviet Five-Year Plan," *Slavic Review*, June 1973; Holland Hunter and Janusz M. Szyrmer, "Testing Early Soviet Economic Alternatives," *Slavic Review*, Summer 1991.

16. At least one present-day Russian historian has considered this possibility seriously. Vadim Rogovin, *Byla li al'ternativa? "Trotskizm": Vzglyad cherez gody* (Moscow: Terra, 1992).

17. Rosa Luxemburg, *The Russian Revolution* (1918; New York: Workers Age, 1940), 44.

Chapter 35. Past and Present

This chapter is drawn in part from my commentary "Does the Present Change the Past?" *Journal of Modern History* 70 (June 1998); and in part from my review essay "The Soviet Union in Post-Soviet Perspective," *Journal of Modern History* 74 (June 2002). Copyright © 1998/2002 by The University of Chicago. All rights reserved.

1. Dmitri Volkogonov, *Autopsy for an Empire: The Seven Leaders Who Built the Soviet Regime* (New York: Free Press, 1998).

2. Ibid., xxvi.

3. Ibid.

4. Ibid., 84.

5. Richard Pipes, *The Unknown Lenin: From the Soviet Archive* (New Haven: Yale University Press, 1996).

6. Stéphane Courtois et al., *The Black Book of Communism: Crimes, Terror, Repression* (Cambridge, Mass.: Harvard University Press, 1999).

7. Manfred Hildermeier, *Geschichte der Sowjetunion, 1917–1991: Entstehung und Niedergang des ersten sozialistischen Staates* (Munich: C. H. Beck, 1998).

8. Ibid., 1081, 1088.

9. Robert Service, *A History of Twentieth-Century Russia* (Cambridge, Mass.: Harvard University Press, 1997), xxv.

10. Ibid., 167, 99, 171, 189.

11. Ronald Gregor Suny, *The Soviet Experiment: Russia, the USSR, and the Successor States* (New York and Oxford: Oxford University Press, 1998), 505.

12. Ibid., 57, 231, xv, 484.

13. Ibid., 231, xv, 484; cf. Nicholas S. Timasheff, *The Great Retreat: The Growth and Decline of Communism in Russia* (New York: Dutton, 1946).

14. Diane Koenker and Ronald Bachman, eds., *Revelations from the Russian Archives: Documents in English Translation* (Washington, D.C.: Library of Congress, 1997).

15. J. Arch Getty and Oleg Naumov, eds., *The Road to Terror: Stalin and the Self-Destruction of the Bolsheviks, 1932–1939* (New Haven: Yale University Press, 2000). See also Oleg Khlevnyuk et al., eds., *Stalinskoe politbiuro v 1930s: Sobranie dokumentov* [Stalin's Politburo in the 1930s: A Collection of Documents] (Moscow: AIRD, 1995).

16. Notably *Molotov Remembers: Conversations with Felix Chuev* (New York: Ivan R. Dee, 1993).

17. This is brought out, among others, by Vladimir Zubok and Constantine Pleshchev, *Inside the Kremlin's Cold War: From Stalin to Khrushchev* (Cambridge, Mass.:

Harvard University Press, 1996) and by Vojtech Mastny, *The Cold War and Soviet Insecurity: The Stalin Years* (New York: Oxford University Press, 1996).

18. Geoffrey Hosking, *Times Literary Supplement*, 28 Jan. 2000.

19. Courtois et al., *The Black Book of Communism*, 30.

20. Volkogonov, *Autopsy*, xxiv–xxv, 531.

21. Hildermeier, *Geschichte*, 425, 428.

Chapter 36. The Grand Surprise and Soviet Studies

This chapter is based on my essay "Soviet Society and American Soviet Studies: A Study in Success?" in Michael Cox, ed., *Rethinking the Soviet Collapse: Sovietology, the Death of Communism, and the New Russia* (London and New York: Pinter, 1998).

1. Michael Cox, "The End of the USSR and the Collapse of Soviet Studies," *Coexistence* 31:1 (1995): 1.

2. Philippe C. Schmitter with Jerry Lynn Karl, "The Conceptual Travels of Transitologists and Consolidologists: How Far to the East Should They Attempt to Go?" *Slavic Review* 53:1 (1994): 173.

3. Robert F. Byrnes, "USA: Work at the Universities," *Survey*, no. 50 (Jan. 1964): 62.

4. See Rudolf Hilferding, "State Capitalism or Totalitarian State Economy"[(1940], *Modern Review*, June 1947.

5. Hannah Arendt, *The Origins of Totalitarianism* (New York: Harcourt, Brace, 1951).

6. Carl J. Friedrich and Zbigniew Brzezinski, *Totalitarian Government and Autocracy* (Cambridge, Mass.: Harvard University Press, 1956).

7. Merle Fainsod, *How Russia Is Ruled* (Cambridge, Mass.: Harvard University Press, 1953).

8. Luba Brezhneva, *The World I Left Behind: Pieces of a Past* (New York: Random House, 1995), 162.

9. See Robert V. Daniels, *Russia—The Roots of Confrontation* (Cambridge, Mass.: Harvard University Press, 1985), 365; Alexander Motyl, *Will the Non-Russians Rebel? State, Ethnicity, and Stability in the USSR* (Ithaca, N.Y.: Cornell University Press, 1987).

10. Lubomyr Hajda and Mark Beissinger, eds., *The Nationalities Factor in Soviet Politics and Society* (Boulder, Colo.: Westview, 1990), 305.

11. See James R. Millar, "Rethinking Soviet Economic Studies," Ford Foundation Workshop Series—Rethinking Soviet Studies (Kennan Institute for Advanced Russian Studies, Washington, D.C., 23 Oct. 1992).

Index